FOUNDATIONS OF GROUP COUNSELING

David Capuzzi
Walden University

Mark D. Stauffer
Walden University

Pearson

330 Hudson Street, NY, NY 10013

Director and Publisher: Kevin M. Davis
Portfolio Manager: Rebecca Fox-Gieg
Content Producer: Pamela D. Bennett
Portfolio Management Assistant: Casey Coriell
Executive Field Marketing Manager: Krista Clark
Executive Product Marketing Manager: Christopher Barry
Procurement Specialist: Deidra Smith
Cover Designer: Melissa Welch, Studio Montage
Cover Photo: Matteo Colombo/Moment/Getty Images
Full-Service Project Manager: Sudip Sinha, iEnergizer Aptara®, Ltd.
Editorial Production and Composition: iEnergizer Aptara®, Ltd.
Printer/Binder: LSC Crawfordsville
Cover Printer: Phoenix Color
Text Font: 10/12 Palatino LT Pro

Library of Congress Control Number: 2018931036

1   18

ISBN 10:   0-13-484480-7
ISBN 13: 978-0-13-484480-0

PREFACE

Group work transforms lives! Upon examination of empirically-based research, client self-reports, and descriptions by seasoned group leaders, the beginning graduate student soon realizes counseling groups are indispensable in practice. The therapeutic elements of a positive group experience are well documented. These "curative factors" have been described as acceptance, altruism, universalization, belonging, security, instillation of hope, increased awareness of emotional dynamics, interpersonal learning, and many other descriptors. The role of professional counselors in educational, corporate, mental health, private practice, and rehabilitation settings calls for knowledge, experience, and competence in facilitating groups. Therefore, the aspiring group leader must develop the knowledge and competencies necessary to provide powerful, growth-enhancing opportunities for clients involved in group counseling. These responsibilities often seem overwhelming and intimidating to the beginning practitioner.

Group work is demanding and requires that the professional counselor both obtain skills and learn about theory and research to competently facilitate groups. Readers who are interested in specializing and being proficient in group work will find the information in this text essential to successful group work practice.

ORGANIZATION AND FEATURES OF THIS TEXTBOOK

This introductory group counseling text is unique in its content and organization:

- Multiple experts have contributed chapter content that provides their unique perspectives on their respective group work specializations.
- The text is divided into two parts: (1) Foundations for Group Work and (2) Useful Approaches and Best Practices. The eight chapters in Part I provide the reader with essential information on theory, basic skills, ethics, evaluation, and diversity in group work. The nine chapters in Part II were conceptualized with the needs of the practitioner in mind, with a robust emphasis on how to do the "work," so to speak, since we know that competent facilitation means understanding how practice is informed by theory and research.
- The content of this text goes beyond that usually addressed in introductory group work texts. The chapters are not devoted entirely to the adaption or application of theories of individual counseling to the group work setting. Instead of focusing one chapter after another on the application of individual counseling theory to group work, the editors have emphasized other important content areas. Specifically, we have included content-specific chapters on the following topics:

  ○ Creative approaches to group work (Chapter 9)
  ○ Group work with challenging formats and member behaviors (Chapter 10)
  ○ Groups with children (Chapter 11)
  ○ Groups with adolescents (Chapter 12)
  ○ Groups with older adults (Chapter 15)
  ○ Groups and addictions (Chapter 16)

- Chapter 8 on the specialty groups identified by the Association for Specialists in Group Work (ASGW)—work/task, psychoeducational, counseling, and psychotherapy—complements and extends the information included in the chapters focused on professional issues related to group work.
- Coverage is included on current, vital topics: ethical/legal considerations in group work (Chapter 5), diversity issues in group work (Chapter 6), and efficacy and evaluation of group work (Chapter 7).
- The text includes informational sidebars to encourage reader contemplation.
- The text includes many case studies and technique descriptions to help the reader identify with and make applications to current or future clients.
- Instructors will have access to an Instructor's Manual with Test Bank and Power-Point slides via Pearson's online Instructor's Resource Center. These provide invaluable resources and teaching tools to support mastery of content for each of the 17 chapters.

The editors have attempted to give readers a broad perspective on group work as they begin to learn and practice. The book provides a comprehensive overview of major issues connected with group work, as well as insight and practical guidelines for group work in general. We know that one book cannot cover all the factors involved in preparing a person to be a group work specialist. With few exceptions, each chapter contains a combination of research, theory, and practice information pertinent to the role of the group work specialist. We hope our text will be well received and seen as one that provides a balance between the needed knowledge base and the skills and techniques that translate theory and research into practice. We look forward to input from our readership.

ACKNOWLEDGMENTS

We would like to thank the contributing authors who so generously gave their time, expertise, and experience to the development of this textbook for the beginning group work specialist. We would also like to thank our families who provided the support to make our writing and editing efforts possible. Our thanks are also directed to the editors and staff of Pearson for their encouragement, understanding, and editing. Without the collaboration and interest of all those whose efforts are reflected in these pages, this edition could not have become a reality. Finally, we would like to honor Doug Gross, who contributed to the of development this book. We valued his contributions and viewed him as an exemplary role model and personable colleague.

MEET THE EDITORS

David Capuzzi, PhD, NCC, LPC, is a counselor educator and member of the core faculty in mental health counseling at Walden University and professor emeritus at Portland State University. Previously, he served as an affiliate professor in the Department of Counselor Education, Counseling Psychology, and Rehabilitation Services at Pennsylvania State University and scholar in residence in counselor education at Johns Hopkins University. He is past president of the American Counseling Association (ACA), formerly the American Association for Counseling and Development, and past chair of both the ACA Foundation and the ACA Insurance Trust.

From 1980 to 1984, Dr. Capuzzi was editor of *The School Counselor*. He has authored several textbook chapters and monographs on the topic of preventing adolescent suicide and is coeditor and author with Dr. Larry Golden of *Helping Families Help Children: Family Interventions with School Related Problems* (1986) and *Preventing Adolescent Suicide* (1988). He coauthored and edited with Douglas R. Gross *Youth at Risk: A Prevention Resource for Counselors, Teachers, and Parents* (1989, 1996, 2000, 2004, 2008, and 2014); *Introduction to the Counseling Profession* (1991, 1997, 2001, 2005, 2009, and 2013); *Introduction to Group Work* (1992, 1998, 2002, 2006, and 2010); and *Counseling and Psychotherapy: Theories and Interventions* (1995, 1999, 2003, 2007, and 2011). His other texts are *Approaches to Group Work: A Handbook for Practitioners* (2003), *Suicide Across the Life Span* (2006), and *Sexuality Issues in Counseling*, the last coauthored and edited with Larry Burlew. He has authored or coauthored articles in several ACA-related journals.

A frequent speaker and keynoter at professional conferences and institutes, Dr. Capuzzi has also consulted with a variety of school districts and community agencies interested in initiating prevention and intervention strategies for adolescents at risk for suicide. He has facilitated the development of suicide prevention, crisis management, and postvention programs in communities throughout the United States; provides training on the topics of youth at risk and grief and loss; and serves as an invited adjunct faculty member at other universities as time permits.

An ACA fellow, he is the first recipient of ACA's Kitty Cole Human Rights Award and a recipient of the Leona Tyler Award in Oregon. In 2010, he received ACA's Gilbert and Kathleen Wrenn Award for a Humanitarian and Caring Person. In 2011, he was named a distinguished alumni of the College of Education at Florida State University, and in 2016 he received the Locke/Paisley Mentorship award from the Association for Counselor Education and Supervision.

Mark D. Stauffer, PhD, NCC, is a core faculty member in the clinical mental health counseling program at Walden University. He specialized in couples, marriage, and family counseling at Portland State University and in counselor education and Supervision at Oregon State University. He has worked in the Portland area in Oregon at crisis centers and other nonprofit organizations working with individuals, couples, families, and groups, often with homeless and at-risk populations.

Dr. Stauffer has worked with groups and groupwork in the realm of mental health, counseling, counselor education, and supervision, at the associate, bachelor, master, and doctoral levels of higher education. Dr. Stauffer was a Chi Sigma Iota

International Leaders in Counselor Education fellow and was also awarded the Emerging Leaders Training Grant by the American Counseling Association. Dr. Stauffer has served as co-chair of the American Counseling Association International Committee and serves as president of the Association for Humanistic Counseling during 2018–2019.

In addition to this textbook on group counseling with Dr. Capuzzi, Dr. Stauffer has coedited several other textbooks in the counseling field, *Counseling and Psychotherapy: Theories and Interventions* (2017); *Career Counseling: Foundations, Perspectives, and Applications* (2006, 2012); *Foundations of Addictions Counseling* (2008, 2012, 2016); *Foundations of Couples, Marriage and Family Counseling* (2015); and *Human Growth and Development Across the Life Span: Applications for Counselors* (2016).

MEET THE CONTRIBUTORS

Cynthia A. Briggs, PhD, completed her BS in psychology at Guilford College, her MAEd in community counseling at Wake Forest University, and her PhD in counseling at Oregon State University. Her experience as a group counselor ranges from addiction counseling in intensive outpatient programs (IOP) to expressive arts groups to general mental health counseling groups. She is coauthor of the text "Women, Girls and Addiction: Celebrating the Feminine in Counseling Treatment and Recovery." She is also the creator of a community-based oral history project capturing the lived experiences of World War II, Korean War, and Vietnam War veterans. She is completing her certificate in documentary arts at Duke University.

David U. Burkholder, PhD, LPC, ACS, received his doctorate in counselor education from Kent State University. He is currently associate professor and program director of the Department of Professional Counseling at Monmouth University in West Long Branch, New Jersey. Dr. Burkholder is a licensed professional counselor in New Jersey and has a clinical specialization in mental health counseling with children and adolescents, with clinical experience working in both school systems and agencies. His areas of research interest include ethics, values, and spirituality, with a specific concentration in applied ethics. Dr. Burkholder's most current research and publications address how educators and students navigate conflicts between personal and professional values.

Jessica R. Burkholder, PhD, LPC, NCC, ACS, is an assistant professor of professional counseling at Monmouth University in West Long Branch, New Jersey. She received a PhD in counselor education and supervision from Kent State University.

Dr. Burkholder's research interests focus on the ethical development and multicultural training of counselors. Clinically, she has specialized in the treatment of adolescent sexual behavior problems, trauma, and mood and anxiety disorders in children and adolescents. She is a licensed professional counselor in New Jersey.

Jonathan W. Carrier, PhD, is the department chair of the Albany County Campus and a psychology instructor at Laramie County Community College in Cheyenne and Laramie, Wyoming. Jonathan has been teaching psychology courses for the past 11 years and was a rehabilitation and mental health counselor for 4 years before that. In addition to his roles as a department chair and college educator, Jonathan also spends time writing scholarly articles, writing book chapters, and giving presentations in the fields of counseling, psychology, and adult education. His published work focuses on suicide assessment, counseling theory, group work, classroom management skills, and best practices in adult education.

Tamara E. Davis, EdD, is a professor in the counseling program at Marymount University in Arlington, Virginia. Prior to her move to Marymount, Dr. Davis was an elementary and high school counselor (who led many group-counseling sessions) for nine years in Manassas, Virginia. Her professional positions have included serving as past president of the Virginia Association for Counselor Education and Supervision and of the Virginia School Counselor Association. She was named the 2007 Counselor Educator of the Year by the American School Counselor Association (ASCA), and she served as counselor educator vice president for ASCA from 2010 to 2013. Dr. Davis has presented over a hundred workshops locally, regionally, and nationally on several topics in school counseling, including developing resilience and positive thinking in students. Her publications include *Exploring School Counseling: Professional Practices & Perspectives* (2015) and articles in school counseling, as well as book chapters on a variety of topics in counseling. She teaches courses at Marymount in both the school and mental health counseling graduate programs and serves as the coordinator for the Northern Virginia School Counseling Leadership Team. She resides in Manassas, Virginia, with her husband, Ken (a PE teacher), and their Siberian Husky, Phoenix.

Janice DeLucia, PhD, is currently an associate professor and school counseling program director in the Department of Counseling, School, and Educational Psychology at the University of Buffalo, SUNY. She has been active in the field of group counseling for over 30 years, including serving as president and executive director of the Association for Specialists in Group Work and as the secretary for Division 49: Group Psychology and Psychotherapy, of the American Psychological Association. She has received the honor of fellow in ASGW, Division 49 of APA, and the American Counseling Association. She has published eight books and more than 50 book chapters and refereed journal articles, most focusing on groups, school counseling, and multicultural issues.

Thelma Duffey, PhD, served as the 2015–2016 president of the ACA. She is a professor and department chair in the Department of Counseling at the University of Texas at San Antonio and owner of a multidisciplinary private practice. Dr. Duffey was the founding president of the Association for Creativity in Counseling (ACC), a division within the ACA, and she served two terms on the ACA Governing Council. Dr. Duffey is a past president of the Texas Association for Counselor Education and Supervision (TACES), and she served on the executive board of the Southern Association for Counselor Education and Supervision (SACES). Dr. Duffey is the editor for the *Journal of Creativity in Mental Health* (JCMH) and guest coeditor for the *Journal of Counseling and Development's* (JCD's) special issue on counseling men and special section on relational-cultural theory (RCT). She is a licensed professional counselor and a licensed marriage and family therapist in Texas. Dr. Duffey's published books include *Creative Interventions in Grief and Loss Therapy: When the Music Stops, a Dream Dies* and two coedited books, *Child and Adolescent Counseling Case Studies: Developmental, Systemic, Multicultural, and Relational Contexts* and *A Counselor's Guide to Working with Men*. She also has over 60 publications in the areas of creativity, innovations in grief and loss counseling, relational competencies (relational-cultural theory), and addictions.

Cass Dykeman, PhD, received his master's in counseling from the University of Washington and his doctorate in counseling from the University of Virginia. Prior to his work in higher education, he worked as both an elementary school and high school counselor in Seattle. As a counselor educator, Dr. Dykeman has worked at Eastern Washington University (1993–1997) and Oregon State University (1997–present). At the university level, he has served in the following roles: school counseling program lead, PhD program lead, counseling academic unit lead, associate dean for research, and department chair. Dr. Dykeman has published two books and is in the double-digits in peer-reviewed articles and book chapters. In addition, he has received over $1.2 million in federally sponsored external funding. He also has served in the following roles: president of the Washington Association for Counselor Education and Supervision, president of the Western Association for Counselor Education and Supervision, member of the *Journal for Counseling and Development* editorial board, and member of CACREP's on-site accreditation team.

Jeannie Falkner, PhD, received her master of science in social work (MSSW) and doctorate in counselor education from the University of Mississippi. She currently serves as core faculty for the clinical mental health counseling program at Walden University. Dr. Falkner has been an educator for both social work and counseling programs for 18 years and is a licensed certified social worker (LCSW) and an approved LCSW clinical supervisor. Dr. Falkner is a member of the American Counseling Association, the Association of Counselor Educators and Supervisors, and the Association for Specialists for Group Work. She routinely presents research at the state and national level and is published in multiple professional counseling textbooks. Dr. Falkner continues to engage in her private practice, which spans over 30 years of counseling individuals, couples, children, and groups. Dr. Falkner's research interests include supervision and remediation with supervisees who present with unresolved trauma, best practices in training group counselors, counselor wellness and self-care, and financial wellness.

Delini Marina Fernando, PhD, LPC-S, recently joined the Department of Educational Psychology at the University of Oklahoma after being a counselor educator for 10 years at the University of North Texas. She has worked as a counselor and supervisor in Texas and Oklahoma. Her publications include book chapters and articles focused on group work and clinical supervision, with a more recent focus on international group work and disaster counseling. She regularly presents at learned society conferences at the state, regional, national, and international levels. She primarily teaches group work, family and couples counseling, and counselor supervision. She continues to serve on the editorial boards of the *Journal for Specialists in Group Work* and *Counseling and Values.*

Linda H. Foster, PhD, is a core faculty member in the clinical mental program. She received her undergraduate degree from Samford University, master's and education specialist degrees in community counseling from the University of Alabama in Birmingham, and a PhD in counselor education at Mississippi State University in 2003. Dr. Foster worked as a licensed professional counselor for over 10 years at the elementary, middle, and high school levels and has been a counselor educator since 2007. She has served on local, state, national, and international counseling boards and editorial boards. Dr. Foster's research interests include professional identity of counselors, counselor education faculty dynamics, and the use of single-subject research methods by counselors. Dr. Foster has presented various topics at the state, national, and international levels and has published numerous articles in peer-reviewed journals, as well as several book chapters.

Shane Haberstroh, EdD, is associate professor and chair of the doctoral program at the Department of Counseling at the University of Texas at San Antonio. He is currently the governing council representative for the Association for Creativity in Counseling and the governing council liaison for the Research and Knowledge Committee of ACA. Dr. Haberstroh serves as the associate editor for the *Journal of Creativity in Mental Health.* He is also the coeditor of *Case Studies in Child and Adolescent Counseling.* He has published over 30 articles and book chapters primarily focused on developmental relational counseling, online counseling, creativity in counseling, and addiction treatment and recovery.

Melinda Haley, PhD, received her master's in counselor education at Portland State University (Oregon) and her doctorate in counseling psychology from New Mexico State University (Las Cruces) and was an assistant professor at the University of Texas, El Paso, in the counseling and guidance program for 5 years. Dr. Haley currently works as a core faculty member in the counselor education and supervision doctoral program at Walden University. She has written numerous book chapters and journal articles on diverse topics related to counseling. She has extensive applied experience working with adults, adolescents, children, inmates, domestic violence offenders, and culturally diverse populations in the areas of assessment, diagnosis, treatment planning, crisis management, and intervention. Dr. Haley's research interests include multicultural issues in teaching and counseling, personality development over the lifespan, personality disorders, the psychology of criminal and serial offenders, bias and racism and social justice issues, and trauma and post-traumatic stress disorder, particularly as it relates to combat and terrorist acts.

Stephanie F. Hall, PhD, LPC, NCC, ACS, is associate professor and chair of the Department of Professional Counseling at Monmouth University in West Long Branch, New Jersey. She received a bachelor of arts degree in psychology from the University of Kentucky, master of arts degree in counseling from Louisiana Tech University, and PhD in counselor education from the University of New Orleans. Her areas of interest and research are varied and include multicultural counseling, gender issues in counseling, mentoring, counselor supervision and training, and ethics in counseling. Her teaching experiences include grief counseling, counseling techniques, family counseling, counseling diverse populations, career counseling, counseling practicum and internship, and counseling supervision and consultation. She is licensed as a professional counselor in New Jersey and works part time in private practice.

Debra A. Harley, PhD, CRC, LPC, is a provost's distinguished service professor in the Department of Early Childhood, Special Education, and Rehabilitation Counseling at the University of Kentucky. She completed her doctoral degree at Southern Illinois University at Carbondale. She has published *Contemporary Mental Health Issues Among African Americans* and *Handbook of LGBT Elders: An Interdisciplinary Approach to Principles, Practices, and Policies.* She is past editor of the *Journal of Applied Rehabilitation Counseling* and the *Journal of Rehabilitation Administration.* Her research foci include substance abuse, cultural diversity, and gender issues.

Barbara J. Herlihy, PhD, LPC, NCC, is a professor emeritus at University of New Orleans and a board-approved counselor and counselor supervisor in Louisiana and Texas. She has also served on the faculty at University of Wisconsin-Whitewater, University of Houston-Clear Lake, and Loyola University of New Orleans. Dr. Herlihy's research and teaching interests include ethical issues in counseling, social justice and advocacy, feminist therapy, and the internationalization of counseling. Her most recent books are *Ethical, Legal, and Professional Issues in Counseling* (5th ed., 2016, with T. P. Remley), the *ACA Ethical Standards Casebook* (7th ed., 2015, with G. Corey), and *Boundary Issues in Counseling* (3rd ed., 2015, with G. Corey). She is also the author or coauthor of more than 80 journal articles and book chapters. In 2017–2018, Dr. Herlihy has served as the senior co-chair of the ACA Ethics Committee, president of Chi Sigma Iota International, and chair of the Ethics Roundtable of the International Association for Counselling. She is a frequent presenter of seminars and workshops on ethics across the United States and internationally.

Mita M. Johnson, EdD, NCC, LPC, LMFT, ACS, LAC, MAC, SAP, AAMFT-Approved Clinical Supervisor, is a core faculty member in Walden University's School of Counseling. Dr. Johnson maintains a private practice in which she provides clinical supervision and consultation and sees clients. She is past president of the Colorado Association of Addiction Professionals and the current ethics chair and treasurer for NAADAC, the National Association for Addiction Professionals (NAADAC). She speaks and trains regionally, nationally, and internationally on topics specific to substance-use disorders, counseling, ethics, supervision, and treatment. She was appointed by the governor of Colorado to two committees working on behavioral health integration, is a consultant to the state regulatory agency, and is a consultant and committee member for public and private organizations. Her passion is empowering students, supervisees, and clinicians to be effective and confident helpers. She loves studying anything to do with drugs of addiction, neuroscience, and the amazing human brain.

Byung Jin Kim, MS, is a doctoral student in rehabilitation counseling at the University of Kentucky. He received his master's degree in counseling psychology from the Handong Global University, South Korea. He joined several research projects at the University of Kentucky and Handong Global University. His clinical experiences include school counseling and addiction counseling; his research interests include substance abuse, Internet addiction, treatment intervention, group counseling, therapeutic community, cultural diversity, and program evaluation.

Martina Moore, PhD, is a faculty member at John Carroll University in the Counseling and Mental Health Department. Her specialty is substance-use disorders. Dr. Moore is the owner of Moore Counseling & Mediation Services, Inc. (MCMS). MCMS is an outpatient alcohol- and substance-abuse treatment facility with seven locations throughout northeastern Ohio. Dr. Moore holds a PhD from Walden University in counseling education and supervision. She is a licensed professional counselor in Ohio. She is also a licensed independent chemical dependency counselor/clinical supervisor. Her research interest is focused on building self-efficacy, motivational interviewing, and family systems. She served as president for the Association of Humanistic Counseling in 2017 and 2018.

Jane E. Atieno Okech, PhD, is a professor of counselor education in the College of Education and Social Services at the University of Vermont. She received her master's in counseling psychology from the United States International University (Africa) and doctorate in counselor education and counseling from Idaho State University. Dr. Okech and her collaborators have been recognized multiple times for excellence in group-counseling publications by the Association for Specialists in Group Work, recently with the 2015 Outstanding Article Award and the 2017 Outstanding Article Award. Her areas of specialization are group counseling, multicultural counseling competencies, clinical supervision practices, and qualitative research.

Jonathan J. Orr, PhD, is a clinical assistant professor and program coordinator for the clinical mental health counseling program in the Department of Counseling and Psychological Services at Georgia State University. He earned his PhD in counselor education from the University of New Orleans in 2005, and his counseling and research interests include group dynamics, social justice, supervision, multicultural counseling, counseling theory development, and professional counselor identity. He has authored or coauthored several journal articles and book chapters and conducted workshops and presentations at the local, state, regional, and national levels. Dr. Orr is a nationally certified counselor (NCC), an approved clinical supervisor (ACS), and a licensed professional counselor (LPC) in Georgia. He served as president of the Association for Specialists in Group Work in 2014–2015 and continues to be an active leader in that association. In addition to his service to ASGW, Dr. Orr is a recognized leader within Chi Sigma Iota, the American Counseling Association, and the Association for Counselor Education and Supervision.

Deborah J. Rubel, PhD, is an associate professor of counseling in the College of Education at Oregon State University. She received her master's in mental health counseling and doctorate in counselor education from Idaho State University and is an Association for Specialists in Group Work fellow. Her areas of specialization are group work, multicultural/social justice counseling, and qualitative research methodology.

Ann Vernon, PhD, is professor emerita at the University of Northern Iowa, where she served as professor and coordinator of the school and mental health counseling programs for many years. She is the author of more than 20 books, as well as numerous chapters and journal articles, primarily related to counseling children and adolescents and applications of REBT. Dr. Vernon is the president of the Albert Ellis Institute, currently conducts RE and CBT training programs in various parts of the world, and teaches in the counseling program at the University of Oradea, Romania.

BRIEF CONTENTS

CONTENTS

Chapter 17 Group Work: Gay, Lesbian, Bisexual, and Transgender Clients 321

Stephanie F. Hall, Jessica R. Burkholder, and David U. Burkholder

1

An Overview of Group Work

David Capuzzi and Mark D. Stauffer

We spend a considerable amount of time in groups, whether at home, at work, at school, at social gatherings, at religious centers, or at civic, professional, or political meetings. There are many ways in which groups can be defined (Johnson & Johnson, 2017; Ohrt, 2014), but all involve interpersonal interactions. Counselors have become increasingly aware that many of the problems that bring clients to counseling are interpersonally based (Corey, Corey, & Corey, in press; Johnson & Johnson, 2017) and that, for many clients, group counseling or therapy may be ideal because of the interpersonal learning opportunities that groups provide.

Like other institutions and training activities, group counseling reflects both the culture and the history of the moment as influenced by national, regional, and local concerns (Gladding, 2015; Klein, 1985). Humans are born social beings, with incredible neurobiological pathways for learning with and from others. Before the recent era and for thousands of years, it was in groups that oral history, natural history, and religious and spiritual lessons were conveyed through story, song, and chant (Reyes-García et al., 2016). Outside of learning from direct observation of the world, face-to-face groups transmitted most everything a person knew and believed about being a human, being part of a culture, and being part of this world throughout human history.

It is only in the last hundred years—or maybe even the last few decades—that this has changed markedly. A schism between our ancestral hardwiring and our digitized technological way of life now can be seen. Granted, technologies have created new opportunities for groups to meet and connect, yet many deeply need "quality time" and face-to-face time. The replacement of consistent social contact with friends and co-workers by smartphones and programs such as Skype, Adobe Connect, and other communication networks will create a much greater need for interpersonal communication on a person-to-person basis (Trotzer, 2013).

This is a great era for group work and group counseling because the possibilities have expanded and the need for such services may be even greater. Groups will provide an antidote to isolation, and increasing numbers of counselors, therapists, and other human development specialists will be called upon to serve as group facilitators.

THE HISTORY OF GROUP WORK

Group work has a long and eventful history (Barlow, Burlingame, & Fuhriman, 2000) that includes milestones and changes along the way. Ahead, we will trace it from its beginnings to contemporary group work.

The Beginning

Although there is evidence of the therapeutic use of groups in both England and the United States prior to the 1900s (Gladding, 2015), more formal group counseling can be traced back to the first decade of the 20th century (Berg, Landreth, & Fall, 2006; Gazda, 1985). In 1905, Joseph Hersey Pratt, a physician, applied the "class" method to provide assistance to patients with tuberculosis in Boston, Massachusetts (Hage & Romano, 2010). A few years later, in 1909 Cody Marsh began to offer psychiatric inpatients what could be called *inspirational group lectures* (Scheidlinger, 1994). Marsh soon became known for his motto: "By the crowd they have been broken; by the crowd they shall be healed."

During the 1920s, Edward Lazell, a psychiatrist, used a similar lecture method when working with severely disturbed inpatients suffering from schizophrenic and manic-depressive psychoses. In later years, Lazell applied this didactic approach to out-patients, relying upon concepts from Jungian psychology (Hage & Romano, 2010; Scheidlinger, 1994).

As noted by Rudolf Dreikurs (1932), Alfred Adler used collective therapy with families and children in his child guidance clinics in Vienna in the 1920s. Dreikurs brought these methods with him to America. His work with groups complemented that of early American group pioneers such as Jesse B. Davis (Berg et al., 2006), who used public school classrooms in Michigan as forums for vocational guidance, and the followers of Frank Parsons, who worked with vocationally undecided individuals in small groups via the Vocational Bureau of Boston (Gladding, 2015). By the middle of the 1920s, Trigant Burrow, one of the founders of the American Psychoanalytic Association (Kline, 2003), had begun conducting groups for his patients, members of his patients' families, and mental health professionals (Scheidlinger, 1994). This method, termed *group analysis*, replaced Sigmund Freud's emphasis on the individual intrapsychic themes with a new focus on interactive themes.

From 1908 to 1925, Jacob L. Moreno, known as the founder of psychodrama, used group action techniques in Vienna. Following his arrival in the United States, Moreno continued developing his psychodramatic techniques; his ideas influenced later American Gestalt, existential, and encounter group movements (Gladding, 2015; Scheidlinger, 1994).

The 1930s

In the 1930s, several psychoanalytic clinicians began to apply Freudian principles to group work in hospitals (Scheidlinger, 1994). One of these individuals, Louis Wender, facilitated small groups in a private hospital and differentiated his approach from those of Pratt, Lazell, and Marsh by emphasizing family transference manifestation. Paul Schilder, a colleague of Louis Wender and a research professor of psychiatry at New York University School of Medicine, also helped legitimize the growing interest in group modalities (Berg et al., 2006).

Among the first to apply group work to children was Loretta Bender, who pioneered children's cathartic expression in groups by using puppets. She was followed by Betty Gabriel, the first American to bring adolescents to the group experience (Scheidlinger, 1994). S. R. Slavson, a contemporary of both Bender and Gabriel and founder of the American Group Psychotherapy Association, also pioneered the use of groups for children (Slavson & Schiffer, 1975). His groups, which he called *activity therapy groups*, each consisted of about eight children of the same sex and similar ages. He used handicrafts, games, and food to foster interactions, and the groups were conducted in the context of a nondirective climate. Counselors and therapists of the day welcomed Slavson's approach because they had difficulty engaging children in one-to-one "talking" sessions. Variations of activity group therapy directed at more seriously disturbed youth were soon introduced.

This early emphasis on group work with children provided the basis for the use of psychoeducational groups with children in elementary schools. In recent years, elementary school counselors have seen children in groups centering on issues of divorce, substance abuse, enhancement of self-esteem, conflict resolution, and other concerns (Greenberg, 2003; Hage & Romano, 2010).

The 1930s also bore witness to the inception of Alcoholics Anonymous (AA), which provides self-help support group experiences to help alcoholics maintain sobriety. AA groups currently are chartered in most U.S. communities.

The 1940s

During World War II, military psychiatrists saw large numbers of American military personnel who were "psychiatric casualties" of the war experience (Scheidlinger, 1994). Out of sheer necessity, many of these psychiatrists adopted group methods. Indeed, many of the subsequent leaders of the American group work movement gained their experience in military hospitals. These American army psychiatrists included Samuel Hadden, Harris Pick, Irving Berger, and Donald Shaskan.

America's chief of military psychiatry during the war, William C. Menninger, believed that the practice of group work at the time constituted a major contribution of military psychiatry to civilian psychiatry. During the World War II era, Great Britain also contributed to the emerging interest in the use of groups. Joshua Bierer, S. H. Foulkes, Wilfred R. Bion, and Thomas Main all provided leadership (Scheidlinger, 1994).

Another influential promoter of group work during the 1940s was Kurt Lewin, who emphasized field theory and the interaction between individuals and their environments (Gladding, 2015; Johnson & Johnson, 2017). Much of his work was based on the ideas of *Gestalt psychology*, which emphasizes the relationship of the part to the whole. Lewin was influential in establishing a workshop on intergroup relations in New Britain, Connecticut, in 1946 (Gladding, 2015). Later, with the help of Ron Lippitt, Lee Bradford, and Ken Benne, he founded the National Training Laboratories in Bethel, Maine (now called *NTL Institute for Applied Behavioral Science*; Schmuck & Schmuck, 1997). The laboratories directed research on groups at improving personal learning and organizational processes.

An important derivation of the work of these individuals was the training group, or *T-group* (Bradford, Gibb, & Benne, 1964). Participants in T-groups learn to understand themselves and others better and to develop collaboration skills. The T-groups popularized in later decades emphasized individual and personal growth goals, understanding of interpersonal relations, and the application of group dynamics to social change.

Two important group organizations were established in the 1940s: the American Society of Group Psychotherapy and Psychodrama (ASGPP), established by J. L. Moreno, and the American Group Psychotherapy Association (AGPA), founded by Samuel R. Slavson.

These same men established two important journals: *Group Psychotherapy* and *International Journal of Group Psychotherapy*, respectively. Both journals were characterized by the philosophies of their founders (Gladding, 2015).

The 1950s

One of the first references to group work with the elderly population appeared in 1950 with the work of J. J. Geller (1950). Early efforts in this area consisted of groups in residences for older adults. Reports on this work were often anecdotal in nature and most often appeared in social work and nursing journals (Scheidlinger, 1994). The reports described groups for well-functioning elderly people, for widows and widowers, for retirees, and for people with physical and emotional disabilities. These reports also pointed out the positive response of older adults to group experiences aimed at anxiety and pain reduction and social skills training. As time has passed, more journals have published research and practice articles for professionals who are interested in group work with elderly people (the topic of Chapter 15).

The 1950s also were characterized by the application of group procedures to family counseling (Gladding, 1997). Rudolph Dreikurs, John Bell, Nathan Ackerman, Gregory Bateson, and Virginia Satir are just a few of the notables who addressed group work with families (Berg et al., 2006). Most practitioners who are licensed as marriage and family therapists are familiar with the growing body of literature addressing aspects of group work with families.

The 1960s and 1970s

The 1960s were a time of great social upheaval and questioning. There were riots on university campuses and in cities as civil rights groups struggled to raise the consciousness of the nation after years of unfair discrimination and prejudice. Charismatic leaders such as John F. Kennedy and Martin Luther King, Jr., became the idolized champions and international symbols of a people's determination to change a society and to promote social responsibility. The nation united in grief-stricken disbelief as its heroes were martyred, and determination to counter the human rights violations of the decades escalated.

As the 1960s ended, the encounter group movement, emphasizing personal consciousness and closer connection with others, reached its zenith. It gradually waned in the 1970s (Kline, 2003), and events such as the first presidential resignation in the history of the United States in the aftermath of the Watergate scandal, the Charles Manson murders, the group killings at the Munich Olympics, and the rise of fanatic cults caused people throughout the country to question the extent to which permissiveness and "human potential" should be allowed to develop (Janis, 1972; Rowe & Winborn, 1973).

Federal legislation that created a national network of community mental health centers in the 1960s was an important influence on group work. In their attempts to fill newly created positions intended to provide counseling and mental health services to the less affluent members of communities, administrators often resorted to less than advisable solutions (Scheidlinger, 1994). They frequently assigned counselors and therapists, whose education and supervised practice were limited to one-to-one counseling and psychotherapy, to facilitate groups. When poorly run groups proved to be ineffective, and sometimes even harmful, a frantic search began for counselors and therapists trained in group work.

In addition to the group work conducted at community mental health centers, the youth revolt kindled by the Vietnam War gave rise to many nontraditional group models that flourished outside the auspices of the mental health profession. Among the most publicized of these groups were the *encounter* and *transcendental meditation* groups (Berg et al., 2006). Because they functioned without adequate pregroup screening, these commercial undertakings often attracted disturbed and emotionally vulnerable participants. Many participants were harmed by membership in these groups. However, a protest by qualified mental health professionals resulted in eliminating the most serious abuses by individuals who organized these community programs.

Journalists of the era sensationalized the use and misuse of group approaches. Nevertheless, many developments in the use of groups did occur. Most notably, Fritz Perls's applications of Gestalt theory in groups at the Esalen Institute in California, Eric Berne's application of transactional analysis to groups, William C. Schutz's contributions that stressed aspects of nonverbal communication in groups, Jack Gibb's study of competitive versus cooperative behavior in groups, Irvin Yalom's work on curative factors in groups, and Carl Rogers's encounter group philosophy all provided important insights and methods for group counselors and therapists (Berg et al., 2006).

As the 1970s continued, counselor education, counseling psychology, psychology, and social work departments on university campuses instituted more coursework and supervised experiences in aspects of group work. The Association for Specialists in Group Work (ASGW) was chartered in 1973 (Forester-Miller, 1998), and by 1974 it had become a division of the American Counseling Association (ACA; known then as the American Personnel and Guidance Association). ASGW publishes *The Journal for Specialists in Group Work,* which provides group work specialists with information on research, practice, and supervision related to group work. Similar developments also took place during the 1970s in the context of other large professional groups, such as the American Psychological Association (APA) and the National Association of Social Workers (NASW).

The 1980s

Interest in group work and in working with specialized populations grew during the 1980s. Groups sprang up for alcoholics, adult children of alcoholics, incest victims, adults molested as children, overweight people, unassertive individuals, and victims of violent crimes. There were groups for elderly people, individuals dealing with death and other losses, people with eating disorders, smokers, and victims of the Holocaust (Shapiro & Bernadett-Shapiro, 1985). This increasing specialization brought with it a need for higher standards for the preparation of group leaders, as evidenced by the development of ethical standards for group work specialists (ASGW, 1989) and the inclusion of specific group work specialist preparation guidelines for graduate-level university educators in the standards of the Council for the Accreditation of Counseling and Related Educational Programs (CACREP; CACREP, 1994).

The 1990s

The escalating interest in group work and in working with special populations that became so evident in the 1980s continued into the last decade of the century. The 1983 ASGW *Standards for the Training of Group Counselors* were revised, and a new set of standards was adopted in 1991 (ASGW, 1991).

The 1991 standards built on the 1983 standards, which emphasized the knowledge, skills, and supervised experience necessary for the preparation of group workers. The updated standards broadened the conception of group work, clarified the difference between core competencies and specialization requirements, defined the four prominent varieties of group work, and eliminated the distinctions made previously among different kinds of supervised field experience. In addition, in its 1994 revision of accreditation standards, CACREP reemphasized the importance of group work by identifying principles of group dynamics, group leadership styles, theories of group counseling, group counseling methods, approaches used for other types of group work, and ethical considerations as essential curricular elements for all counselor education programs (CACREP, 1994, 2001, 2016).

THE 21ST CENTURY

As ethical codes and standards continued to develop into fullness, so too did the profession's guidelines for best practices, training standards, and professional competencies. ASGW revised its *Standards for the Training of Group Counselors* in 2000 and created *Best Practices Guidelines* (2007; see both in full at www.asgw.org). Importantly, the American Counseling Association (ACA) continues to endorse various counseling competencies. As of 2017, ACA has endorsed competencies in the following areas: advocacy; counseling lesbian, gay, bisexual, queer, intersex, questioning, and asexual (LGBQIQA) individuals; animal-assisted therapy; spiritual and religious issues; counseling the multiracial population; multicultural and social justice; and multicultural career counseling (see www.counseling.org/knowledge-center/competencies). Each of these either directly addresses some part of group work or impacts the use of group work.

The use of groups has expanded to virtually all settings connected with counseling and therapy, as well as to schools, hospitals, and corporate environments. Group programs for individuals with chronic diseases (e.g., cancer, heart disease, AIDS), for people suffering from eating disorders, and for people involved in the recovery process connected with substance abuse, sexual abuse, and other traumas are just beginning to

SIDEBAR 1.1

Publications Addressing Group Counseling and Group Work

Examine several issues of the journals published by the ASGW, the ASGPP, and the AGPA. What are your observations about the kinds of articles (research, theory, or practice) that characterize each publication?

capture the attention of the general public. In conjunction with the escalating number of older adults and dropping fertility rates in many countries, the use of group approaches is bound to expand as the percentage of elderly adults rise (Duyan, Şahin-Kara, Camur Duyan, Özdemir, & Megahead, 2016). Regardless of the current legislative fluctuations related to the U.S. healthcare system, interest in group work will continue to grow, and the qualified group work specialist will be in high demand as cost containment via managed care will be a continuing reality.

All indications point to interest in group counseling and other forms of group work continuing to grow as time passes. Increasing numbers of platforms for groups of people (e.g., videoconferencing, Facebook) will likely emerge. In 2015, *The Journal for Specialists in Group Work* dedicated a volume to international issues in group work, which reflected a movement toward internationalizing group work in a global and multicultural manner. Bemak and Chung (2015) suggested that group workers from Western industrialized nations must address their lack of understanding of collectivist cultural contexts, political countertransference, mental health imperialism and colonialism, and international group work voyeurism to be part of this movement appropriately, especially as climate change, migration, and bicultural identity shape the future of group work. They also pointed to the need for group work associations and group workers to redefine ethics and boundaries in an international way, to partner with traditional healers, to establish appropriate training methods for international group work, and for group workers to take on the role of "learner" rather than "teacher," thus making them competent from a cultural perspective and from a social justice standpoint.

GOALS FOR GROUPS

In the early or *definitive* stage of a group, each member must develop a clear understanding of the goals of the group experience (Chen & Rybak, 2004; Trotzer, 2013). In fact, being clear about the purpose of a group is one of the most important responsibilities of the group facilitator (Jacobs, Masson, & Harvill, 2009; Johnson & Johnson, 2017). Counselors help group members to attend to processes useful to effective group performance because doing so influences how groups collectively interpret feedback, regulate behavior, and feel efficacious as a group (Winton & Kane, 2016). Members who have not developed some ownership of the reasons they are participating in the group may not make constructive use of the group experience. Group goals can be addressed in several ways: as (a) general goals for groups, (b) goals for specialized groups, (c) goals based on theoretical perspectives, and/or (d) goals developed by individual members.

General Goals for Groups

Although many group work leaders believe that the goals for each counseling group should be established by the members and leaders of those groups, group work leaders have proposed some general group goals through the years (George & Dustin, 1988). Early in group work's history, J. Frank (1957) proposed a general statement defining group goals as helping members to release their feelings constructively, strengthen self-esteem, face and resolve problems, improve their skills in recognizing and resolving interpersonal and intrapersonal conflicts, and fortify their ability to consolidate and maintain therapeutic gains.

In another example, Carroll and Wiggins (1997) identified the general goals of helping the group member to become a better listener, develop sensitivity and acceptance of others, increase self-awareness and develop a sense of identity, feel a sense of belongingness and overcome feelings of isolation, learn to trust others and self, recognize and state areas of belief and values without fear of repression, and transfer what is learned in the group to the outside by accepting responsibility for solving his or her own problems. Consider how Carroll and Wiggins's goals make sense for gay, lesbian, bisexual, transgendered, queer, and questioning (GLBTQQ) groups: Group counseling helps reduce feelings of isolation due to stigma, provides a sense of universality and acceptance, and provides a place to process repressed experiences and important identities through affirmative group connections (Horne, Levitt, Reeves, & Wheeler, 2013). In addition, Carroll and Wiggins (1997) proposed the following process goals as helpful to group members: help members stay in the here and now, prevent storytelling related to the there and then, help members confront others with care and respect, learn to give nonevaluative feedback, and learn to risk by speaking in the first person.

Because goals for group work vary by culture, and goals are viewed differently based on a person's worldview, counselors need to understand the cultural and learning needs of members as they consider general group work goals (Ibrahim, 2015). In addition to reflecting cultural considerations, modifications to goals may reflect the group leader's style and philosophy and the type of group. For example, a group of adult survivors of childhood molestation would modify the process goals proposed by Carroll and Wiggins (1997) so that members could disclose there-and-then information relative to their own experiences as victims of sexual abuse because they may not have been able to verbalize their thoughts and feelings in the past.

Goals for Specialized Groups

Specialized groups often have specific goals based on the issues of individual members of the groups. The goals for a weight management therapy group, for example, might be for members to identify specific reasons that food has become such an important part of their everyday life; to discuss nutrition, exercise, and motivation; to provide understanding and support for one another's efforts; and to learn to avoid using food to manage stress. The goals for a group of incest survivors might be for members to talk about their incidents of sexual abuse; to learn that other members have similar feelings of hurt, shame, and anger; to develop trust; and to identify ways in which their earlier experiences affect their current friendships and relationships with significant others.

Goals for a men's group might include discussion of gender role expectations, relationships with fathers, transitions, overworking, navigating a new culture as an immigrant, or how to enhance self-esteem. Regardless of the specific purpose for which multiple individuals meet as a group, goals must be discussed thoroughly and understood by every group member.

Goals Based on Theoretical Perspectives

As authors such as Gibson and Mitchell (1995) and Corey (2017) have noted, the theoretical orientation of the group leader can have a primary influence on group goals. The psychoanalytic, Adlerian, psychodramatic, existential, person-centered, Gestalt, transactional analysis, behavior therapy, rational emotive behavior therapy, and reality therapy conceptual frames of reference all provide perspectives for the establishment of group goals, as illustrated in the following examples.

The Adlerian group leader may focus on establishing a working relationship in which the leader and the members are equal; aiding the members in exploring the personal goals, beliefs, feelings, and motives that are determining factors in the development of their lifestyles; helping members to enhance their involvement with others and to extend their social interest as it applies to self and others; assisting members in considering alternative lifestyles; and helping them in strengthening their commitment to change.

The Gestalt group leader may focus on allowing members to find their own way in life and accept the responsibility that goes with it by aiding members in accepting all aspects of themselves and encouraging them to share hidden and self-disguised aspects of self, assisting members in recognizing the blocks/barriers that impede their growth, and helping members recognize the splintered parts of self and work toward integrating those parts.

The person-centered group leader may focus on establishing a facilitative climate within the group, characterized by congruence, unconditional positive regard, and empathic understanding; providing an environment in which all group members perceive the constructs of safety and mutual trust; supporting members in finding their own way in life and accepting the responsibility that goes with it; refraining from giving advice and direction; and allowing members to positively activate their organismic valuing process.

Chapter 4 of this book provides a more comprehensive overview of theoretical perspectives and goal setting as related to group counseling.

Goals Developed by Individual Members

Group participants often need assistance to personalize their reasons for wanting to be part of a group (Johnson & Johnson, 2017). Often, their goals must be refined and clarified. The goal of "wanting to get in touch with feelings," for example, might relate to feelings of loss, anger, or guilt. A member who says she is "having trouble with assertiveness" might be talking about the workplace, the home, or the responsibilities of parenting. Another member, who says he is "having trouble with depression," could be experiencing difficult circumstances or having a chemically based, genetically linked, endogenous problem. The group leader must help individual members continuously

Identify as many conferences or workshops as you can that are scheduled for the next few months on the topic of group work. Prepare a description of costs, locations, dates, focus of content sessions, and so forth, and share the information with the rest of the class. Investigate the possibility of working with some of your peers to submit a program proposal for one of the conferences you have identified. Ask your professor to mentor you as you develop the proposal and serve as the content session sponsor and convener.

analyze their reasons for participating in a group to ensure that they state and realize their personalized goals (Jacobs et al., 2009).

TYPES OF GROUPS

Many textbooks for introduction to counseling courses begin the discussion of group work by attempting to make distinctions between group therapy, group counseling, and group guidance.

Group therapy typically is described as longer term, more remedially and therapeutically focused, and more likely to be facilitated by someone with doctoral-level preparation and a more "clinical" orientation. *Group counseling* usually is differentiated from group therapy by its focus on conscious problems, by not being aimed at major personality changes, by an orientation toward short-term issues, and by being less concerned with treating more severe psychological and behavioral disorders. *Group guidance* describes a classroom group in a K–12 setting in which the leader presents information or conducts mental health education. In contrast to group therapy and group counseling, which generally involve no more than 8 to 10 participants, a group guidance experience could involve 20 to 40 participants, lessening the opportunities for individual participation and facilitator observation and intervention.

For the purposes of this chapter, ASGW's definitions of the four group work specialties—task/work groups, guidance/psychoeducational groups, counseling groups, and psychotherapy groups—are presented as a point of departure for classifying groups. Readers are referred to Chapter 8 in this book for a thorough discussion of the four group work specialties.

Other Models for Group Work

Various other distinctions are made among types of groups (Gibson & Mitchell, 1995; Jacobs et al., 2009). For example, *T-groups* help members develop self-awareness and sensitivity to others through the verbalization of feelings. *Encounter groups*, initiated by Carl Rogers, became known as *personal growth groups* because of their emphasis upon the individual development of each of their members (Gladding, 2015). Both T-groups and encounter groups are sometimes called *sensitivity groups*.

In J. L. Moreno's *psychodrama* groups, participants stage a production in which they sometimes play themselves and sometimes play the alter egos of others. By acting out their issues and concerns and "processing" the experience afterward, members progress to higher levels of self-awareness and begin to exert more control over their emotions and behaviors (Aichinger & Holl, 2017).

Marathon groups, introduced in the 1960s by George Bach and Fred Stoller, are intense experiences lasting 24 hours, 48 hours, or even longer, and they require that group members stay together for the duration of the experience. Because fatigue and intensity are built into the marathon, participants' defenses break down, truthfulness and openness increase, and personal growth can take place in a different way than in groups conducted once a week for an hour and a half. (Provisions usually are made for participants to receive individual or small-group follow-up counseling after they participate in a marathon group.)

Adventure-based counseling (ABC) groups integrate group counseling with experiential education in an outdoor environment (Bowen, Neill, & Crisp, 2016). As an example, counselors leading *wilderness adventure therapy* (WAT) groups might take clients backpacking with a team in a wilderness area for a few days to a week, and for some programs even longer, working at the prevention and intervention levels. These groups often are holistically focused in nature and employ an eclectic combination of mental and physical health activities and leisure, as well as real-life obstacles geared to increase self-efficacy and empowerment (Bowen et al., 2016).

Jacobs et al., (2009) facilitate *impact therapy groups* based on the use of impact therapy. In their approach, the leader is primarily responsible for making sure that individuals get the best help possible as they work on issues. They describe their approach as active, multisensory, and theory driven. The leader does whatever is needed and helpful and, at times, conducts therapy with an individual member of the group while others watch and listen and periodically share.

Self-help groups are utilized widely as adjunct support for individual or group counseling or therapy conducted by professionally prepared, licensed counselors and therapists (Corey, 2017; Kottler, 2001). As Gladding (2015) noted, self-help groups take at least two forms: (a) those that are organized by an established professional helping organization (e.g., Alcoholics Anonymous) and (b) those that emerge spontaneously. Members of these groups share something in common, and the groups can be psychoeducational, therapeutic, or task focused. Self-help groups can be powerful catalysts in helping people take charge of their lives. Some of these groups lack the advantage of professional leaders but often compensate through the contributions of committed and experienced lay leaders.

Closed and Open Groups

Closed and open groups are subcategories of most groups. A *closed group* is characterized by a membership that remains together until the group terminates. In an *open group*, new members are added during the life cycle of the group.

Both the closed group and open group models have advantages and disadvantages. Open groups permit members to resolve problems and issues in their own timeframe and then leave the group. New members may enter the groups as openings occur. Although new members coming in at various times may be viewed as adding stimulation to the group, the group may go through a process of regression, with accompanying fluctuations in cohesion and trust, when a new member is added.

SIDEBAR 1.3
ASGW and Specialty Groups

Study the ASGW definitions of specialty types of group work as described in this chapter. Identify courses, internships, and supervisors that might be available on your campus or in the local community to provide you with the knowledge and skills base to facilitate each type of group. Share your findings with the rest of the class.

By contrast, closed groups offer stability of membership and facilitate cohesion and trust. Because not all members of a group progress at the same rate, however, some group members lose the advantage of being able to work hard and terminate their membership in a manner consistent with their own ability to learn, resolve intrapersonal or interpersonal issues, and obtain closure based on an appropriate resolution (Gruner, 1984). The closed format also can impact virtual group formats by only allowing those in the group to join, for example, an ongoing synchronous virtual meeting or asynchronous discussion forum monitored by the counselor (Lemma & Fonagy, 2013).

COMPOSITION OF GROUPS

The composition of a group has an influence on how the group functions (Corey, 2017; Yalom, 1985). Groups can be based on gender, age, issues facing members of the group, psychological maturity, and numerous other variables (Trotzer, 2013). There are two general approaches to combining members of a group: the heterogeneous approach and the homogeneous approach.

The *heterogeneous* or *mixed-gender* group addresses fundamental assumptions for creating groups composed of both men and women. The heterogeneous group is a microcosm of society, self-defeating behavior can be identified and confronted more easily in a group approximating the composition of society, the group focus is on the present rather than on the past, reality testing can and does occur, and the heterosexual group situation generates anxiety that produces change. A *homogeneous group* consists entirely of members of a given population or members who share a specific need, concern, or situation; for example, a women's recovering group (WRG) for substance use disorders is homogenous in two ways (Greenfield et al., 2014). The cohesiveness theory underlies this approach to group composition and supports the idea that similarity of members can lead to a great deal of cohesion, openness, and exploration of issues (Perrone & Sedlacek, 2000).

THERAPEUTIC FACTORS IN GROUPS

Therapeutic factors in groups have been extensively researched and discussed for many years (Chen & Rybak, 2004; Kennair, Mellor, & Brann, 2016; Ohrt, Ener, Porter, & Young, 2014; Schechtman & Perl-Dekel, 2000). A *therapeutic factor* in a group is "an element occurring in group therapy that contributes to improvement in a patient's condition and is a function of the actions of a group therapist, the patient, or fellow group members" (Bloch, 1986, p. 679). This definition is important (Kline, 2003) because it

---

SIDEBAR 1.4
Therapeutic Factors in Groups

Invite several group practitioners from the local community to make a panel presentation to your class on the topic of therapeutic factors in groups. Ask them to discuss how they structure the groups they facilitate to ensure that the experience is therapeutic for group members. If the panelists conduct groups for specific populations of clients, ask them also to describe the education and supervision needed to competently facilitate such groups.

---

helps distinguish between therapeutic factors and necessary conditions for change in a group, as well as group interventions or techniques. Examples of conditions for change include the presence of a group leader and group members who are willing to listen and provide feedback. An example of a Gestalt intervention or technique that a group leader might employ is "making the rounds." Conditions and interventions or techniques increase the impact of therapeutic factors in groups.

Corsini and Rosenberg (1955) published the first major work that presented a unifying paradigm of factors that group leaders considered therapeutic from a variety of theoretical perspectives (see George & Dustin, 1988). After clustering statements reflecting therapeutic factors, they formed the following nine-category classification system:

1. *Acceptance:* a sense of belonging
2. *Altruism:* a sense of being helpful to others
3. *Universalization:* the realization that one is not unique in one's problems
4. *Intellectualization:* the process of acquiring knowledge about oneself
5. *Reality testing:* recognizing the reality of issues such as defenses and family conflicts
6. *Transference:* a strong attachment to either the therapist or comembers
7. *Interaction:* relating within the group that brings benefits
8. *Spectator therapy:* gaining from observing and imitating fellow members
9. *Ventilation:* the release of feelings and expression of previously repressed ideas

In what is now considered a landmark classification of *curative factors*, Yalom (1970, 1975, 1985, 1995) proposed a list of 11 therapeutic elements based on research that he and his colleagues conducted:

1. *Instillation of hope:* receiving reassurance that the group experience will be constructive and helpful
2. *Universality:* developing an awareness that what seems to be a unique problem may be like the experience of another member of the group
3. *Imparting of information:* learning about mental health and mental illness via group discussion
4. *Altruism:* sharing with others and being willing to reach out
5. *The corrective recapitulation of the primary family group:* reliving family-of-origin conflicts and resolving them through the group
6. *Development of socializing techniques:* learning social skills
7. *Imitative behavior:* imitating positive behaviors modeled by other group members
8. *Interpersonal learning:* developing new insights and correcting past interpretations
9. *Group cohesiveness:* developing bonds of trust, support, and caring

10. *Catharsis:* sharing feelings and experiences
11. *Existential factors:* accepting responsibility for one's life, including decisions, meaning making, and spiritual dimensions

These listings represent only a few of the many possibilities for viewing the therapeutic elements of a positive group experience.

PERSONAL CHARACTERISTICS OF EFFECTIVE GROUP LEADERS

Many professionals in the field have described the personal traits and characteristics of effective group leaders (e.g., Berg et al., 2006; Choate & Manton, 2014; Corey, 2017; Counselman, 2017; Dinkmeyer & Muro, 1979; Kottler, 1983).

We believe the group leader must possess certain characteristics to be effective. As Kottler (2001) noted, who you are is as important to your success as a group facilitator or leader as what you know and do in the process of working with group members. Others who have presented their views on this topic include Arbuckle (1975), Carkhuff and Berenson (1977), Jourard (1971), Truax and Carkhuff (1967), and Yalom (1975). In the following subsections, we will summarize Corey's views on the personal characteristics of effective group leaders as a starting point for the beginning group work specialist. This point of view is congruent with ours and is similar to discussions presented by Gladding (2015) and others.

Presence

The group leader must have the capacity to be emotionally present as group members share their experiences. Leaders who are in touch with their own life experiences and associated emotions are better able to communicate empathy and understanding because they can relate to similar circumstances or emotions. Group leaders must not lose perspective by being overly focused on their own reactions; rather, they must allow themselves to be connected with the experience of group members in such a way that they can communicate compassion and concern and still facilitate constructive personal growth.

Personal Power

Personal power is derived from a sense of self-confidence and realization of the group leader's influence on a group. Personal power channeled in a way that enhances the ability of each group member to identify and build upon his or her strengths, overcome problems, and cope more effectively with stressors is both essential and curative. Leaders who have the most power are accepting of their own strengths and weaknesses and do not expend energy attempting to prevent others from seeing them as they are.

Courage

Group leaders must be courageous. They take risks when they express their reactions to aspects of group process, confront members, share life experiences, act on a combination of intuition and observation, and direct group movement and discussion. These risks are the same risks that group members are expected to take. In this regard, the leader's role modeling can help make a group more productive and better able to communicate and bond.

Self-Awareness

Serving in any kind of a counseling role is difficult without highly developed self-awareness. In facilitating a group, personal needs, defenses, apprehensions, relationship conflicts, and unresolved issues of any kind come into play. These can enhance or detract from one's ability to lead the group, depending upon the group leader's level of awareness and the extent to which these factors make the leader's role more difficult. Many counselor education departments require that graduate students obtain personal counseling outside the department to resolve "unfinished business" so that personal issues do not impede their ability to serve constructively in a counseling role.

Belief in Group Process

Group leaders must be positive about the healing capacity of groups and must believe in the benefits of the group experience. If they are unsure, tentative, or unenthusiastic about the healing capacity of the group experience, group members will develop the same tenor. Although the outcome of a group experience does not depend totally on its leader, the leader does convey messages, both verbally and nonverbally, that impact the overall benefit of the experience.

Inventiveness

Group leaders who are spontaneous in their approach to a group often catalyze better communication, insight, and personal growth than those who rely on structured interventions and techniques. Creative leaders usually accept those who are different from themselves and are flexible about approaching members and groups in ways that seem congruent with a specific group. In addition, a certain amount of creativity and spontaneity is necessary to deal with the unexpected. In a group situation, the leader is presented continuously with comments, problems, and reactions that cannot be anticipated before a given session.

Stamina and Energy

Unlike an individual counseling session, during which the counselor listens to and interacts with one client, the group experience requires the leader to track, remember, and diagnose several clients simultaneously. This set of circumstances requires more alertness, observation, responsiveness, proactivity, and energy. Therefore, a group leader should not overschedule groups. Many leaders prefer the cofacilitation model, in which the cofacilitator or coleader assumes part of the responsibility for group process and observation.

Goodwill and Caring

Group leaders must place the welfare of group members first. They ensure that members are achieving the goals that have been established for the group experience. Caring about those in a group is also vital to successful outcomes. If a group leader has difficulty in this regard, he or she must evaluate what is blocking this capacity and what steps he or she can take to ensure that member needs will be met.

Openness

Group leaders must be open with and about themselves, open to experiences and lifestyles that are different from their own, and open to how the group is affecting them. Openness does not mean that the leader should reveal every aspect of his or her personal life. Rather, it can mean being open enough to give members an understanding of who he or she is as a person. The leader's willingness to be open promotes a corresponding spirit of openness and willingness to communicate among group members.

Awareness of the Leader's Own Culture and the Culture of Group Members

In today's globally connected and diverse society, group leaders must be aware of diversity issues and cross-cultural competency in group work. They must understand that just as their cultures influence their worldviews and decision making, the same is true of the culture of each member of a given group. Cultural diversity encompasses more than ethnic influences; it also encompasses age, gender, sexual orientation, disability, and numerous other factors. Effective group leaders are sensitive to aspects of diversity and respect the differences that individual members bring to the group.

Nondefensiveness in Coping with Attacks

Members of a group often test their leaders by being critical or confrontational with them. These attacks can occur if the leader has made a mistake or has been insensitive. They also can occur if a member is jealous, wishes to control, or is projecting feelings about someone else onto the leader. Regardless of the reason, the leader must remain nondefensive and explore the reasons for the member's behavior. To do this, the leader must have a strong sense of ego integrity and confidence. Becoming angry or refusing to explore reasons for the attack models behavior that can interfere with openness, trust, and positive outcomes.

Sense of Humor

Humor can be crucial to a group's success. Laughter can help release tension and help members retain perspective on their problems. So long as humor does not become a roadblock to performing the therapeutic work that must be accomplished, it can be a tremendous asset to a group.

Personal Dedication and Commitment

To be effective, the group leader must be dedicated to the value of the group process and be committed to continuing to develop his or her leadership skills. If the group leader believes that group membership can empower and benefit participants, his or her enthusiasm and energy will be sensed by participants and contribute to some of the therapeutic elements of group work discussed earlier in this chapter.

Willingness to Model

Group members learn how to respond to others in the group and how to communicate their own thoughts and feelings by watching the facilitator. The facilitators who are

---

SIDEBAR 1.5
Personal Characteristics of Group Facilitators

The discussion of personal characteristics of effective group leaders in this chapter can seem overwhelming to the beginning group work specialist. Prepare a group presentation for the class summarizing these characteristics and the kind of supervision that a group leader might need to learn to function effec- tively with groups. After giving the presentation, ask members of the class to share what they would be comfortable sharing about their own strengths and weaknesses with respect to the recommended charac- teristics and the kind of supervision that probably would be needed.

---

best at creating a safe and therapeutic "holding environment" for members to perform their "work" also are likely to be exceptional role models for participants in their groups. Willingness to be authentic, spontaneous, and immediate in facilitating a group means being comfortable in knowing that members will imitate their communication style increasingly as the group progresses.

Willingness to Seek New Experiences

The best group facilitators make a personal commitment to lifelong learning about themselves and others. A facilitator would have difficulty relating to the issues that par- ticipants bring to the group if he or she did not strive continuously to learn more about his or her own way of being and relating in the world and about the contemporary struggles of clients who live in an ever-changing culture and set of life circumstances. Group workers must remain engaged with the world around them by seeking new experiences, new people, and differing cultures and by striving to attain ever-increasing levels of self-understanding and insight. This may require additional education, travel, introspection, personal counseling, supervision, and taking advantage of myriad other precipitants to expand the facilitators' worldview of themselves and others.

MYTHS CONNECTED WITH GROUP WORK

Counselors who are group leaders are usually enthusiastic about the benefits for clients who participate in a small group. A group experience facilitated competently can engender personal growth (Capuzzi & Gross, 2017) that affects clients well into the future. Like other forms of therapeutic assistance (e.g., individual or family therapy), however, group work can be for better or for worse (Carkhuff, 1969). Many group lead- ers adhere to a belief system that can be challenged by empirical facts. The following myths connected with group work are given quite a bit of attention here, with the hope that group leaders will not base their practices on any belief system that is not sup- ported by research (Anderson, 1985; Capuzzi & Gross, 2017; Kottler & Brown, 2000).

Myth 1: Everyone Benefits from Group Experience

Groups do provide benefits. Research on the psychosocial outcomes of groups demon- strates that groups are a powerful modality for learning, the results of which can be used outside of the group experience itself (Gazda & Peters, 1975; Parloff & Dies, 1978). At times, however, membership in a group can be detrimental. For example, one real concern among adolescent groups is *social contagion*, via which, for example, an adolescent might be negatively influenced by the self-injury behaviors of peers (Richardson, Surmitis, & Hyldahl, 2012).

There are two important principles to consider about how clients can be harmed by the group experience:

1. Group members with unrealistic expectations have the greatest potential to be hurt by the experience.
2. These expectations seem to be reinforced by leaders who coerce the group members to meet them.

To prevent harm, members' expectations for the group must be realistic, and the leader must maintain a reasonable perspective.

Myth 2: Groups Can Be Composed to Ensure Success

Unfortunately, there is no guarantee that groups will be successful if you compose them via the pregroup screening; however, selection protocols and preparing group members can reduce risks. Earlier findings suggested that behavioral characteristics should be selected on a heterogeneous basis (Bertcher & Maple, 1979) and that groups should be composed so that each member is compatible with at least one other member (Stava & Bednar, 1979). This composition seems to prevent the evolution of neglected isolates or scapegoats in a group. It gains additional importance when considering the essence of group process in terms of benefit to members and effective outcomes (helping others, a feeling of belonging, interpersonal learning, instillation of hope, etc.; Butler & Fuhriman, 1980; Long & Cope, 1980; Yalom, 1975), which cannot be achieved when members feel isolated. Group members should be selected if their needs and goals are compatible with the group design (ASGW, 2007).

Group composition research does suggest that members of groups that are well-prepared by the group leaders (a) experience greater levels of cohesion, hopefulness, and self-disclosure; (b) are not as likely to prematurely drop; and (c) attend more sessions (Jensen et al., 2012). Counselors also can use assessment tools such as the *Group Therapy Questionnaire* (GTQ) and the *Group Readiness Questionnaire* (GRQ); these self-report measures help counselors sort through important client variables (Jensen et al., 2012).

Myth 3: The Group Revolves Around the Leader's Charisma

Although leaders do influence groups tremendously, two general findings in the research on groups should be noted (Ashkenas & Tandon, 1979): (a) The group, independent of the leader, has an impact on outcomes, and (b) the most effective group leaders are those who help the group develop so that members are primary sources of help to one another (Schechtman & Toren, 2009).

According to Anderson (1985), research on leadership styles has identified four leader functions that facilitate the group's functioning:

1. *Providing:* This is the provider role of relationship and climate setting through such skills as support, affection, praise, protection, warmth, acceptance, genuineness, and concern.

2. *Processing:* This is the processor role of illuminating the meaning of the process through such skills as explaining, clarifying, interpreting, and providing a cognitive framework for change, or translating feelings and experiences into ideas.
3. *Catalyzing:* This is the catalyst role of stimulating interaction and emotional expression through such skills as reaching for feelings, challenging, confronting, and suggesting, using program activities such as structured experiences.
4. *Directing:* This is the director role through such skills as setting limits, roles, norms, and goals; managing time; pacing; stopping; interceding; and suggesting procedures.

Providing and processing seem to have a linear relationship to outcomes: The higher the providing (or caring) and the higher the processing (or clarifying), the higher the positive outcomes. Catalyzing and directing have a curvilinear relationship to outcomes. Too much or too little catalyzing or directing results in lower positive outcomes (Lieberman, Yalom, & Miles, 1973).

Myth 4: Leaders Can Direct Groups Through Structured Exercises or Experiences

Structured exercises create early cohesion (Lieberman et al., 1973), helping to bring about the early expression of positive and negative feelings. At the same time, they restrict members from dealing with group themes such as affection, closeness, distance, trust, mistrust, genuineness, and lack of genuineness. All these areas form the basis for group process and should not be hampered by too much structure. The best principle around which to plan and use structured exercises to get groups started and to keep them going can be stated as follows: "Overplan and underuse."

Myth 5: Therapeutic Change in Groups Comes About Through Here-and-Now Experiences

Much of the research on groups indicates that corrective emotional experiences in the here and now of the group increase the intensity of the members' experience (Levine, 1971; Lieberman et al., 1973; Snortum & Myers, 1971; Zimpfer, 1967). The intensity of emotional experiences, however, does not seem to be related to outcomes. Higher level outcomes are achieved by group members who develop insight or cognitive understanding of emotional experiences in the group and can transfer that understanding into their lives outside the group. The Gestaltists' influence on groups in the 1960s and 1970s (Perls, 1969) suggested that group members should "lose their minds and come to their senses" and stay with the here and now. Research, however, suggests that members should "*use* their mind *and* their senses" and focus on the there and then, as well as the here and now.

Myth 6: The Greatest Member Learning in Groups Is Derived from Self-Disclosure and Feedback

Most of the learning of members in a group is assumed to come from self-disclosure in exchange for feedback. To a large extent, this statement is a myth. Self-disclosure and feedback per se make little difference in outcome (Anchor, 1979; Bean & Houston, 1978). Rather, the *use* of self-disclosure and feedback is what seems to make the difference (Martin & Jacobs, 1980). Self-disclosure and feedback seem to be useful only when deeply personal sharing is understood and appreciated and the feedback is accurate (Berzon, Pious, & Farson, 1963; Frank & Ascher, 1951). The actual benefit of self-disclosure and feedback relates to how these processes generate empathy among group members. *Empathy*, or the ability to understand and share the feelings of another, is what catalyzes personal growth and understanding in the context of a group.

Myth 7: A Leader Does Not Have to Understand Group Process and Group Dynamics

All groups are characterized by a natural evolution and unfolding of processes and dynamics (Fonagy, Campbell, & Bateman, 2017; Schechtman & Toren, 2009). Anderson (1979) labeled these processes and dynamics as *trust, autonomy, closeness, interdependence,* and *termination* (TACIT). Tuckman (1965) suggested the more dramatic terminology of *forming, storming, norming, performing,* and *adjourning.*

In Chapter 2, we suggest four stages in the evolution of a group: the definitive stage, the personal involvement stage, the group involvement stage, and the enhancement and closure stage. Two reviews covering more than 200 studies of group dynamics and group processes (Cohen & Smith, 1976; Lacoursiere, 1980) revealed remarkably similar patterns (despite differences in the terms chosen as descriptors) in the evolution of group processes. To enhance benefits from group participation competently, group leaders must understand group processes and dynamics (Finlay, Abernethy, & Garrels, 2016; Li, Kivlighan, & Gold, 2015; Ohrt et al., 2014).

Myth 8: Changes in Group Participants Are Not Maintained

Groups can be powerful! Members can maintain changes for as long as 6 months to a year after a group has disbanded, even when the group met for only 3 or 4 months (Lieberman et al., 1973). The positive effects of having participated in a group can be subtle but pervasive. For example, graduate students at Portland State University who took part in a 10-week off-campus personal growth group focusing on art therapy reported that skills they learned in the group, such as the need for creativity in their lives, relaxation techniques, insight into personal family dynamics, and ways of working with daily stress, continued to be relevant and useful a year later.

Myth 9: A Group Is a Place to Get Emotionally High

Although feeling good after a group session can be a positive outcome, it is not the main reason for being in a group (Corey, 2017). Some group members have periods of depression after their group has disbanded because they don't find daily the kind of support they received from members of the group. Group members should be prepared for this possibility and assisted in their ability to obtain support, when appropriate, from those around them.

SIDEBAR 1.6

Analyzing a Positive Group Experience

Analyze positive experiences you have had as a member of a group. What did the facilitator of the group do that made the experience "therapeutic" and avoided buying into myths? Could you learn to create a similar atmosphere for members of a group you were conducting? What do you see as the biggest challenge for you personally in this regard? What might be needed to meet this challenge?

Myth 10: A Group's Purpose Is to Make Members Close to Every Other Member

Although genuine feelings of intimacy and cohesiveness develop in effective groups, intimacy is a by-product, not the central purpose of the group. Intimacy develops as individual members risk self-disclosure and problem solving, and other group members reach out in constructive ways (Corey, 2017).

Myth 11: Group Participation Results in Brainwashing

Professional groups do not indoctrinate members with a philosophy of life or a set of rules about how each member "should be." If this does occur in a group, it is truly a breach of professional ethics and an abuse of the group. Group participation should encourage members to look within themselves for answers and to become as self-directed as possible.

Myth 12: To Benefit from a Group, a Member Must Be Dysfunctional

Group counseling is as appropriate for individuals who are functioning relatively well and who want to enhance their capabilities as it is for those who are having difficulty with certain aspects of their lives. Groups are not just for dysfunctional people (Corey, 2017).

Summary

Group counseling has its roots in the early 1900s, when it was applied in medical settings and with children, adults, and families. The first "laboratory" group, or T-group, emerged in 1947, and groups later branched out to universities and other settings. Interest in group work has increased dramatically over time, illustrated by the recent flood of self-help groups led by either professionals or lay people.

Goals for groups include facilitating the release of feelings, strengthening members' self-esteem, helping members face and resolve their problems, helping members learn how to recognize and solve interpersonal and intrapersonal conflicts, and facilitating members' maintenance of their therapeutic gains. Group goals can be addressed in several ways: as (a) general goals for groups, (b) goals for specialized groups, (c) goals based on theoretical perspectives, and (d) goals developed by individual members.

Distinctions can be made between group therapy (more likely to be longer term and have a therapeutic emphasis), group counseling (which has a focus on conscious problems and an orientation toward short-term issues), and group guidance (in which the leader presents

information or conducts mental health education for a larger group). Specialized types of
group experiences include sensitivity groups,
psychodrama groups, marathon groups, and
task groups, among others. Based on ASGW's
definitions, groups can be classified into four
primary categories: task/work groups, guid-
ance/psychoeducational groups, counseling
groups, and psychotherapy groups. All these
types of groups can be either heterogeneous
(mixed gender) or homogeneous (same gender)
and can be closed (members stay together until
the group is terminated) or open (new members
are added as others leave).

Therapeutic factors in a group include
acceptance, altruism, universalization, intellectualization, reality testing, transference,
interaction, spectator therapy, and ventilation.
Translated into leader qualities, these factors
entail presence, personal power, courage, self-
awareness, belief in group process, inventiveness, stamina and energy, goodwill and caring,
openness, becoming aware of the leader's own
culture and the culture of group members,
nondefensiveness in coping with attacks,
sense of humor, and personal dedication and
commitment.

Numerous myths commonly associated
with group work, by group leaders and others,
can detract from group effectiveness. These mis-
conceptions include the following: Everyone
benefits from group experience, groups always
have advantageous outcomes, the group
revolves around the leader's charisma, group
members should be limited to discussion of
here-and-now experiences, and dysfunctional
people are the only ones who can benefit from
groups.

2

Group Work: Stages and Issues

Mark D. Stauffer and David Capuzzi

As Ari left the group counseling class that evening, he was emotionally and cognitively overwhelmed by the implications of counseling groups. He would start his practicum within two terms and would be practicing as a professional counselor shortly after. He knew that any position would require both group and individual counseling with diverse clientele on a range of issues. He felt comfortable with his individual skills but remained concerned about his ability to work with groups. As he reflected that evening, Ari verbalized the concern that plagued him: "How will I become confident and competent as a group leader?"

The concerns felt and sometimes expressed by students, like Ari, are common and have been part of the learning curve since the inception of group counseling. First, social anxiety and related phobias (e.g., public speaking) are some of the most commonly shared forms of anxiety (Cheng, Craske, & Niles, 2017; Phillips Sheesley, Pfeffer, & Barish, 2016). Performing as a leader tugs at any socially related performance anxiety a novice leader already faces. Second, novice leaders may be unprepared in attitude, knowledge, and skills for the various group development stages and types of groups covered later in this book (i.e., psychoeducational, task-work, counseling, psychotherapeutic; Springer, 2016). Third, group counseling and group development both involve anxiety due to the psychological complexity and intensity for both group leaders and group members (Springer, 2016). Addressing group complexity, Ward (1985) stated:

> Group work is challenging and complex because groups are complex because each group member has complex thoughts, feelings, and behaviors. The complexity is magnified many times because most group members who have psychological exploration, growth, and change as their goals interact with one another and with the group leaders in intricate patterns. In addition, if members have an opportunity to interact over a period of time, the group develops a set of overt and covert guidelines or group norms that help regulate individual behavior and interactions between and among members. (p. 59)

The challenge and complexity of group work have been further substantiated in the literature by Berg, Landreth, and Fall (2013); Corey (2015); Gladding (2015); Jacobs, Schimmel, Masson, and Harvill (2015); Kline (2003); and Trotzer (2006). Although addressing different facets of group work, these authors arrived at similar conclusions related to issues of challenge and complexity. They highlighted areas such as group membership; leadership styles; group methods; issues surrounding confidentiality, resistance, silence, conflict, termination, and follow-up; and stages and transitions inherent in the group experience. Add to these the complexity of each individual involved, and it is easy to see why group work generates anxiety for the leader and members and sets forth a challenge for both.

Adding to this challenge are the complexities of the individuals involved, and often groups are designed around special themes and populations, as identified in several chapters toward the end of this text. Theme- and population-specific groups often carry special directives related to membership, leadership, methods, processes, dynamics, multicultural issues, ethics, theme-specific expertise, and stages and transitions. Current group texts and journals are replete with research on themes and special populations, covering topics such as borderline personality disorder groups (Antonsen et al., 2017), groups dealing with recovery from addiction (Lyons, 2016), complicated grief groups (Sierra Hernandez, Piper, Ogrodniczuk, Joyce, & Weideman, 2016), groups for compulsive overeating (Schwartz, Nickow, Arseneau, & Gisslow, 2015), wilderness therapy groups for adolescents (Bowen, Neill, & Crisp, 2016), groups for adult survivors of childhood abuse (Lowe, Willan, Kelley, Hartwell, & Canuti, 2017), groups for women of color (Short & Williams, 2014), international groups from various cultures and nationalities (Bemak & Chung, 2015), and groups for families (Bradshaw et al., 2015). With the abundance of specialized groups and their diverse directives, many group workers have questioned whether group work can even be approached from a generic perspective or whether all groups should be viewed in terms of their specialized members and purpose. The answer to this question is not readily available; it depends on the group leader's philosophical and theoretical viewpoint.

In this chapter, we explore just one aspect of the complex process of group counseling or therapy: the stages and transitions through which groups move from initiation through termination. The information presented herein, we believe, has applications across both generic and specialized approaches to group work. We begin by discussing both early and current conceptualizations of stage development and then present our own view of this developmental process, based on our extensive literature review and experience in working with groups. Member and leader behaviors are discussed for each stage. We conclude with recommendations for how group leaders can use this knowledge of stage development to enhance member growth and leader effectiveness.

STAGES AND TRANSITIONS

The distinct stages that groups move through as they pass from pregroup to termination are difficult to describe in definitive terms. The nature of the group, its membership, its leadership style, and the open or closed nature of the group all influence the developmental process. In terms of stages of development, a closed group, which maintains the same membership through its lifetime, is more easily described than is an open group, in which members come and go. The addition of new members as old members leave complicates the developmental process. Because of the variables affecting group development, any developmental scheme must be based on experience more than on hard-and-fast rules governing a group's development.

Further, group stages are not discrete or neatly separated, and according to Berg et al., (2013), they "grow from observation and clinical experience rather than hard data" (p. 96). In discussing this lack of discreteness, George and Dustin (1988) stated:

> The stages described do not occur in discrete and neatly separated points in the life of a real group. There is considerable overlap between the stages, as groups move from one stage to the other in a somewhat jerky, hesitant manner. As a result, there may be some movement toward the next stage and then regression to the previous stage. (p. 102)

Despite these caveats, authors have been in apparent agreement about a generalized pattern of stages and transitions in groups (Berg et al., 2013; Corey, 2015; Gladding, 2015; Tuckman & Jensen, 1977; Yalom & Leszcz, 2005). The stages and transitions identified within this pattern are outlined in Table 2.1. Before we discuss these stages, however, we will present the following background information.

Early Conceptualizations

Much has been written about the stages through which groups progress from inception to closure. In the 1940s and 1950s, Bales (1950), Miles (1953), and Thelen and Dickerman (1949) conceptualized stages of groups based on the problem-solving behaviors exhibited in task groups. These early developmental schemas emphasized tasks the group was expected to accomplish, such as becoming organized, sharing ideas and opinions, and reaching solutions through suggestions. From this task orientation, early researchers examined specific member roles in groups. Researchers then began to translate group maintenance behaviors (member behaviors utilized to either promote or impede the group's progress) into interactional behaviors, which added a dimension to the early emphasis on task behaviors. Subsequent approaches to stage development in small groups combined task and member behaviors into descriptions of group process over time.

An example of how task and member behaviors have been combined is found in the work of Bennis and Shepard (1956). Integrating the work of Bales (1950, 1953) with their own concepts, these authors developed a conceptualization of group movement based on their observations while teaching group dynamics to graduate students. They proposed that groups generally move through six developmental phases:

1. Dependence–flight
2. Counterdependence–fight
3. Resolution–catharsis
4. Enchantment–flight
5. Disenchantment–fight
6. Consensual validation

This conceptualization indicates that groups begin in a somewhat dependent state and that they grow as group members strive to move toward interdependent functioning.

TABLE 2.1 Stages of Group Development

	Stage 1	Stage 2	Stage 3	Stage 4	Stage 5	Stage 6
Tuckman (1965)	Forming	Storming	Norming	Performing	Adjourning	
Yalom & Leszcz (2005)	Orientation	Conflict		Cohesiveness		
Gladding (2015)	Forming Orientation	Transition Storming/Norming		Work	Mourning/ Termination	
Corey (2015)	Forming	Exploration/Transitions Orientation		Working	Consolidation/ Termination	Evaluation/ Follow-up
Trotzer (2006)	Security	Acceptance	Responsibility	Working	Closing	

Expanding on the work of Bennis and Shepard (1956), Reid (1965) discussed the developmental stages of groups in terms of an *authority cycle*. He viewed the growth and development of the group in direct relationship to the leader's authority. Groups move from dependence on an established leader through counterindependence and counterdependence until they establish interdependence with the original authority leader. A crisis within the group may cause it to fall back to dependence on the established leader and begin the circular developmental pattern again. Like Bennis and Shepard, Reid stressed that growth occurs in groups as the members move from degrees of dependence to degrees of interdependence.

Other researchers (Bion, 1961; Gazda, 1971; Gibb, 1964; Kaplan & Roman, 1963; Mills, 1964; Ohlsen, 1970; Schutz, 1958) aided in the early development of stage theories applied to the group process. Each described the various stages through which groups progress. Their descriptions cover the content of each of the stages and the behaviors that individual group members display at each stage.

Current Conceptualizations

The authors listed in Table 2.1 expanded on early theories, viewing the movement of groups from origination to termination from a stage/transition perspective. Although the authors differed in the terminology they used to describe each stage and the number of stages they delineated, a pattern emerged that emphasizes the importance of

- pregroup planning (*formation*),
- member inclusion (*orientation, security*),
- member interaction (*storming, transition, conflict, acceptance*),
- member/group cohesion (*norming, conflict, responsibility, cohesiveness*),
- member and group goal achievement (*performing, cohesion, working*), and
- member and group parting (*adjourning, mourning, termination, closing, consolidation, follow-up/evaluation*).

Within this pattern, there is a degree of consistency in the member behaviors characteristic of each of the stages, as discussed ahead.

SIDEBAR 2.1

Stage 1 Behaviors and Examples of Related Underlying Questions

- Orienting self to the environment: "What is my role in this group?"
- Testing the environment: "What happens if I or someone in the group stands out, doesn't speak, no-shows, demonstrates anger, or challenges someone?"
- Identifying boundaries and building relationships: "What can and cannot be shared here?"
- Coming together and developing commitment: "How can we support each other?"
- Seeking acceptance: "Can I be myself here?"
- Searching for structure and meaning from the group experience: "How do we best spend our time together?"

- Defining goals, exploring expectations, and establishing a group culture: "What is our purpose and way of being together?"
- Learning group functioning and defining power: "How does this group work, and who is in charge of what?"
- Dealing with anxiety, suspicion, resistance, and group tension: "How do I deal with tension, mistrust, and conflict within the group?"
- Establishing trust and exploring safety issues: "How long will it take to feel safe to do the level of work of our group?"

STAGE 1   Labeled by terms such as *forming, orientation,* and *security,* Stage 1 incorporates both the preparatory work that must take place prior to group formation and inclusion of members in the group process. Corey (2015) stressed the importance of the formation phase by calling it *pregroup issues* and making this stage separate from orientation. In this phase he included functions such as group planning, group structure, member recruitment and screening, and leader and member preparation. The other authors in Table 2.1 discuss these same issues but combine them with orientation.

Key behaviors emerge that typify each stage of group development. From another view, these behaviors also signal critical underlying questions members and the group are trying to resolve (see Sidebar 2.1). Whether these behaviors are viewed from an individual's perspective or from the group's perspective, Stage 1 in group development is a period of *definition* for the individual members and the group. Individuals are defining where—and perhaps *if*—they fit in the group, what role they will take in the group, degrees of acceptance and approval within the group, and expectations for themselves and for others related to the group process.

If the group can be viewed as an entity unto itself, separate from its individual parts, other elements of definition appear. This entity called *the group* is seeking to define its structure and meaning, functions, goals, and boundaries. Through such definition, the group attempts to build a networking system that connects its individual parts—its members. The extent of success in this endeavor often rests in the strength of the constructed network and the skill of the group leader in helping members build this network.

In addition to being a period of definition, Stage 1 is characterized by *anxiety.* The amount of anxiety seems to be related to perceptions of risk, threat, power, impact, member behaviors, leader behaviors, and expectations, either perceived or real. To some degree, even positively viewed emotions such as excitement connect with anxiousness. Anxiety is present to some extent in the beginning stages of most groups. As a reader, reflect on your memories of Stage 1 for different types of groups you have been involved in: What were some of your thoughts, behaviors, emotions, and interpersonal connections? What thoughts, behaviors, and emotions were going on for others in your group?

Another characteristic is *dependence*. Aspects of dependence seem to be much more pronounced during this initial stage than in subsequent stages, possibly due to factors such as the unknown elements of the new group members' need to test, seek, and explore to find their place in the group and the challenge involved in attempting to reach a definition of self in relationship to the group.

STAGE 2   Labeled by such terms as *storming, transition, conflict, acceptance, orientation,* and *exploration,* Stage 2 is characterized by active personal involvement as group members begin to test their positions and power in the group, as well as the behavioral parameters of the group and its members. Anxiety, tension, fear, and defensiveness related to control and power may be most prevalent at this point in the group lifespan. Members may think, behave, and communicate in passive, aggressive, passive-aggressive, and assertive ways as a group looks to find social order and how they fit into it. *Assertive* means being oneself and pursuing self-actualization while honoring others' processes to do the same. A great resource for the layperson and counselor alike is Randy Patterson's (2000) *The Assertiveness Workbook.*

Group leaders intervene in various ways depending on group member composition to achieve whole group cohesion. Group leaders will use the skills of *blocking* or *cutting off* (see Sidebar 2.2) and *linking* (see Sidebar 2.3) to help a group toward therapeutically useful cohesion. Polarization may occur as members attempt to find their places. *Polarization* occurs when a group splits into subgroups of members centered on salient aspects and attributes (e.g., race/ethnicity, life experience, values).

Beyond action and reaction, behaviors in Stage 1 (Sidebar 2.1) also demonstrate interactions on the part of individual members as they attempt to establish themselves within the group structure. Group development theory suggests that action, reaction, and interaction are all natural phenomena that arise when we bring together new people. Also, questions naturally arise about the self in relation to the group and about the nature of the group itself. Questions arise about commitment to the group process and earnest participation. The presence of struggle, conflict, and confrontation attest to the need of individual group members to move from the safety of passive involvement to the more risk-oriented position of active involvement. How else can meaningful work be accomplished?

SIDEBAR 2.2
Blocking or Cutting Off

A leader will need to block antigroup behavior and cut off member sharing at times to further the progress of the group. Blocking is not adversarial but requires being directive. A group leader may say "Before we move on to your subject, Meredith, I think Jorge was trying to add something." Or "I notice that you are speaking for Shaniqua. I would like the group to hear her words on this. In group counseling, it is important that people speak for themselves and that we get used to asking for their perspective, even when we think we know what others think, feel, or might share." In general, when blocking or cutting off, do so with an unassuming, light tone, without built-up energy, so that the receiver sees it as a behavior request and not an ill message about rapport and esteem.

SIDEBAR 2.3

Linking

Group leaders connect or *link* members so that they can build rapport with each other and to make explicit the importance of expressing shared experiences, questions, impressions, thoughts, and emotions with one another. Often this linking occurs by noticing and making explicit to the group nonverbal communications that are shared or affirming another's sharing. For example, "I noticed that several of you were nodding your head, affirming what Paula shared about heartache and moving on. Please share with Paula and the group what was going on for you as she was speaking." In addition, leaders verbalize the similarities of content, emotion, and meaning that they have tracked to connect. For example, a leader may tie together several members while directing the focus: "Erica, Ali, and Martine, although each of you had different types and experiences of loss, I sensed in your voices a 'rawness' or vulnerability during this last period of sharing. What goes on for you when you hear each other sharing about loss?"

STAGE 3   Terms applied to Stage 3 include *norming, conflict, responsibility,* and *transition.* Yalom and Leszcz (2005) noted that conflict is part of both Stages 2 and 3, but the conflict associated with Stage 3 is a more productive interaction, out of which group cohesion develops. This stage often is viewed as a transitional period during which greater degrees of commitment and productive interaction take place within the group. Some key behaviors begin to emerge at this stage: cohesiveness, intimacy, belonging, solidarity, standardization of group processes, role adoption, group skill development, compromise, trust, action exploration, and problem exploration.

Activities in Stage 3 involve blending and merging. In this move from independence to more interdependence, individuality is not lost; instead, it becomes enmeshed in the group. That is, Stage 3 encompasses behaviors and activities that are more group specific than member specific. Whereas in Stage 2 individual members strive for greater self-involvement through testing, checking, and confrontation, in Stage 3 members put group purposes, processes, and membership ahead of maximizing their own development.

STAGES 4, 5, AND 6   Stages 4, 5, and 6 are combined here because of their overlapping nature. Words used to describe these stages include *performing, adjourning, termination, cohesiveness, work, mourning, closing, consolidation,* and *follow-up/evaluation.* Stages 4 and 5 can be considered work intensive, as group members direct much of their effort to developing new behaviors and perspectives, resolving personal issues, and enhancing self and the group.

If this process is successful, termination and/or closure of the group is the expected outcome. With the exception of Corey (2015), the authors in Table 2.1 implied or discussed process evaluation and planning for follow-up as part of Stage 4 or Stage 5. Corey identified these important group tasks as a separate stage, which he labeled Stage 6. He referred to this process as *postgroup issues,* giving it the same weight as he did Stage 1's pregroup issues. Discussing the importance of follow-up/evaluation, Corey (2008) stated, "Just as the formation of a group and the leader's preparatory activities greatly affect the group's progress through its various stages, the work of the leader once the group has come to an end is also highly important" (p. 111).

With group members drawing on the growth and development that have taken place during the previous stages, the final segment is best viewed in terms of self and group enhancement, closure, and evaluation and follow-up. Enhancement is seen in greater involvement and development as they apply to the group and to the individual. Group development is furthered by deeper exploration of problems, action orientation, solidarity, integration, and problem resolution. Personal development is seen when work on honesty, spontaneity, intimacy, feelings of belonging, inclusion, and integration come to fruition.

As the group approaches culmination, the cyclical nature of group development (Capuzzi & Gross, 2006, 2009) becomes obvious. As individuals begin to see closure as a reality, loss anxiety and dependence evolve, evidenced by questions such as these: Will I be able to take what I have learned and apply it outside the group? Will I be able to function without the group?

The anxiety and dependence inherent in these questions are characteristic of Stage 1 behaviors, and the leader must have the skill to turn this anxiety and dependence into positive attributes as members leave the group. In discussing the closure process, Berg et al., (2013) made the following observations:

> A certain ambiguity of feelings can be anticipated that approximates the grieving process. Leave taking will produce denial and withdrawal in some and elation in others. Overriding these natural feelings of loss and anticipation should be a general optimism and a sense of completion. The group leader needs to take special care in dealing fully with feelings of anxiety associated with leaving the group. (p. 105)

COMPOSITE CONCEPTUALIZATIONS

Based on the preceding information and calling on our own collective experience, we developed our own view of the developmental stages of groups. As described in the following sections, we divide the developmental process into four stages: definitive stage, personal involvement stage, group involvement stage, and enhancement and closure stage.

Definitive Stage

The *definitive stage* contains two definitive aspects. The first, which we label *formative/developmental*, addresses all the foundational steps that must be taken prior to the first meeting of the group. These steps include but are not limited to

- developing a rationale for the group,
- making decisions regarding the theoretical format to be used in conducting the group,
- determining group logistics such as time, place, number of meetings, and open versus closed format,
- delineating operating guidelines (ground rules; see Sidebar 2.4),
- recruiting members,
- screening members, and
- selecting/identifying the group leader(s).

After successfully completing these foundational steps, the second component of the definitive stage, which we call *member inclusion*, begins. Provided with the group's rationale, logistics, and operating guidelines and an opportunity to react

SIDEBAR 2.4
Ground Rules of the Group

Ground rules depend on the group's type, size, topic, and other variables. Group rules can be created by the leader or by the group members with additional rules added by the group leader. Sometimes ground rules will be given to members prior to group or discussed to some degree at a pregroup screening session. When groups are carried out by teleconference or videoconference, ground rules are added to meet the needs of the technology; for example, teleconference members may be asked to mute their lines when not speaking and to start sharing by stating their names so that members know who the speaker is (Chou, Promes, Souza, Topp, & O'Sullivan, 2012). The most common and essential ground rules for members are to attend and be on time; keep confidential what is shared in group; be engaged, responsible, and share; and be honest and honor differences.

to the group's structural format, members begin to define for themselves the purpose of the group, their commitment to it, their potential involvement, and how much they are willing to share of themselves. Member questions such as the following—in addition to those in Sidebar 2.1—are characteristic of this component of the definitive stage:

- Will this type of group help me?
- Can I fit into this type of group?
- Can I trust the leader?
- Can I trust the other members?
- Where will I find support?
- Will I be hurt by others knowing about me?
- How much of myself am I willing to share?

Dealing with these questions and the lack of immediate answers, members in the definitive stage show increased anxiety, excitement, and nervousness. Certain uncomfortable emotions will be heightened during this stage of the group. Group leaders help members increase awareness and ownership of emotional experiences and how to process this information on interpersonal and intrapersonal levels. The dialogue during this stage tends to be self-protective and of a "small talk," social nature as the members test the waters of group involvement. To help group members deal effectively with the definitive stage, the group leader must possess skill in dealing with such issues as trust, support, safety, self-disclosure, and confidentiality.

As noted, individuals define, demonstrate, and experiment with their own role definitions; test the temperament, personality, and behaviors of other group members; and arrive at conclusions about how personally involved they are willing to become during this stage of group development. An individual's movement through this stage can be enhanced or impeded by the group's makeup (age, gender, number, values, attitudes, socioeconomic status, etc.), the leader's style (active, passive, autocratic, democratic), the group's setting (formal, informal, comfortable, relaxed), the personal dynamics the individual brings to the group (shy, aggressive, verbal, nonverbal), and the individual's perceptions of trust and acceptance from other group members and from the group leader. Leaders use the skills of

SIDEBAR 2.5
Drawing Out

Drawing out occurs when a group leader wants a member to express and share more in a group. Leaders sometimes do this directly, with curiosity, and without a condescending tone: "Jaime, I am curious what your thoughts are on the topic." At other times we might draw out several quiet members to equalize voice: "I am wondering what those who have not yet shared on this topic are thinking and feeling about it." Nonverbal eye communication may be another subtle way to prompt someone to share. Using rounds and breaking the group into dyads are other useful ways to help members share and express (Jacobs et al., 2015).

drawing out to engage members and use *linking* to help bond members and increase trust (see Sidebar 2.5).

The definitive stage is crucial in group development: It can determine for the individual—and therefore for the group—future involvement, commitment, and success or failure in the long run. If appropriate foundational steps have been taken in establishing the group, the following member and leader behaviors are descriptive of the definitive stage.

Member behaviors for the definitive stage:

- Members evaluate the leader in terms of skill, ability, and capacity to trust.
- Members evaluate other members in terms of commitment, safety, and confidentiality.
- Members evaluate themselves in terms of taking risks, sharing themselves with others, and being willing to participate fully.
- Members search for meaning and structure within the group.
- Members search for approval from members and from the leader.
- Members define themselves in relationship to other members and to the leader.
- Members define the group experience in terms of their other life experiences.

Leader behaviors for the definitive stage:

- The leader attempts to foster inclusion of all group members.
- The leader explains the rules and regulations that will operate within the group.
- The leader attempts to draw rules and regulations from the members that will aid their participation in the group.
- The leader explains the structure, timelines, and leader behaviors that members can expect within the group.
- The leader attempts to model the behaviors expected of group members.
- The leader attempts to deal effectively with the various emotions within the group.
- The leader discusses issues of confidentiality, behavior, and goals and expectations for the group.
- The leader attempts to draw from the members their goals and expectations for the group.
- The leader attempts to provide an environment that facilitates growth.

Personal Involvement Stage

Once individuals have drawn conclusions about their commitment and role in the group, they move into the *personal involvement stage* of group development, a period of member-to-member interactions, including sharing personal information and engaging in confrontation and power struggles. The stage also is characterized by the individual's growing identity as a group member. Statements such as "I am," "I need," and "I care" are characteristic of this stage of group involvement. Through their speech and behaviors, group members demonstrate the extent to which they are willing to share personally and confirm the commitment they made during the definitive stage.

The personal involvement stage is one of action, reaction, and interaction. This stage is manifested by both fight and flight as members strive to carve their place within the group. The process often involves heated member-to-member interactions followed by retreat to regroup and battle again. The battles that ensue enhance members' place within the group and aid in firmly establishing the group as an entity in its own right. A question often emerges for new counselors: What does it mean that group members are engaging in conflict? How the group counselor frames conflict and the development of a conflict helps group leaders create an environment for a strong, growth-oriented group (see Sidebar 2.6).

The personal involvement stage offers the individual an opportunity to try out various behaviors, affirm or deny perceptions of self and others, receive feedback in the form of words or behaviors, and begin the difficult process of self-evaluation. Individual involvement in this stage is crucial to the eventual outcome of the group. The following member and leader behaviors are descriptive of the personal involvement stage.

Member behaviors for the personal involvement stage:

- Members openly challenge other members and the leader as they strive to find their places in the group.
- Members test their personal power within the group in attempts at manipulation and control.

SIDEBAR 2.6
Working with Conflict and Ruptures

Ideally, group leaders will process those conflicts that will result in greater group cohesion and member growth and self-awareness when resolved. Leaders will also block harmful member behaviors and educate members on unhelpful or antigroup behaviors (see Chapters 4 and 10). Adept group leaders have a consistent pattern of using the counseling skill of challenging and confronting so that members are accustomed to such interventions by the leaders. This is also true for providing support; there should be a balance. Challenging and confrontation occur with positive regard to reduce unnecessary and lasting ruptures. Leaders welcome those confrontations and ruptures that lead to greater levels of intimacy when repaired. In their everyday lives, many clients do not receive feedback from others, nor do they have relationships in which ruptures (a) occur and (b) are then repaired. Providing members with an opportunity to have conflict and express emotion and yet come to resolution allows for new ways of being that can be transferred. If appropriate, consider processing with the group the effects of having ruptures and repairs for member and group growth (Safran & Muran, 2000).

- Members struggle as they try to find safety and comfort in sharing themselves with others.
- Members resist integrating the feedback they receive, because the suggested changes are perceived as being too painful to implement.
- Members join with other selected members in attempting to build safety and security.
- Members increase their commitment to themselves and to the group, its goals, and its purposes.
- Members become more willing to share themselves with others and take a more active role in the group process.
- Members expand their ability to share feelings, ideas, and needs as they relate to the group process.

Leader behaviors for the personal involvement stage:

- The leader demonstrates awareness of the emotional makeup of the group and encourages affective expression.
- The leader participates in the struggle, confrontation, and conflict that are part of this stage.
- The leader communicates to the members the appropriateness of their member-to-member reactions and interactions.
- The leader allows members to move through this stage at their own pace, knowing the dangers of rushing them.
- The leader provides an environment that is conducive to greater comfort and safety.
- The leader encourages members to explore new ways of behaving within the group.
- The leader acknowledges his or her own struggles as the group moves to deeper levels of interaction.
- The leader emphasizes the importance of all members of the group, aiding in the transition from definition to involvement.
- The leader helps the group adjust when there is a member who unexpectedly leaves the group, especially if this occurred after a challenging period in the group.

Group Involvement Stage

At the *group involvement stage,* group members now have trust in the leadership, other members, and group cohesiveness; aggression resulting from insecurity and fears of intimacy and trust decrease. The newfound working mode is further emboldened by the group's trust that the group has experience and knows how to resolve conflicts. Cooperation and cohesiveness gradually replace conflict and confrontation as members who are now more confident in their role in the group direct more of their attention to what is best for the group and all its members. Conflicts related to self-growth now can arise, but there is trust in the membership to work through them. With heightened solidarity, group members desire the well-being of others and thus are more willing to compromise and work for a greater good.

With the information they gained about themselves in the personal involvement stage, group members move into the group involvement stage, characterized by self-evaluation and self-assessment of behavior, attitudes, values, and methods used in relating to others, and also characterized by members channeling their energies to better meet group goals and purposes. The group has a sense of *we.* Appreciation for each other and for group leaders emerges, along with dedication to grow and help others grow.

During this stage, the member and the group become somewhat more synonymous. This stage reveals increasing clarification of roles, intimacy, exploration of problems, group solidarity, compromise, conflict resolution, and risk taking.

As trust increases in the group, members are now more willing to have uncomfortable emotions for the sake of intimacy and personal growth, and they are more willing to support others. For example, members might share their own reactions and vulnerabilities to a traumatic experience after another member has become transparent about and self-disclosed his or her own traumatic reaction and vulnerability. With the help of group leaders, members begin to empathize and demonstrate compassion and active listening for others. In this stage, at their best, members can "get real" with each other's blind spots, "games," and areas of hurt, while at the same time, demonstrating compassion and care for the rawness of each other's wounds and protected places.

The group's purposes and goals are merging with the individual purposes and goals of its members. Individual agendas are replaced by group agendas, and members identify more with the group. Members bond as they join forces to enhance the group and in turn enhance their individual selves in relation to the group. References to *insiders* and *outsiders* differentiate the group and others in the members' lives outside the group. Members become protective of other group members and of the group itself.

The group and its membership take on special significance unique to those who are part of the process. The melding of member and group purposes and goals is necessary for the group's ongoing success. The following member and leader behaviors are descriptive of the group involvement stage.

Member behaviors for the group involvement stage:

- Members develop confidence in themselves and their ability to relate effectively in the group environment.
- Members develop better helping skills and apply these to working with other group members and to themselves.
- Members devote increasing energy to helping the group meet its purposes and goals.
- Members direct more attention to cooperation and cohesiveness and less to conflict and confrontation.
- Members display a perspective more characterized by belonging and inclusion than by nonbelonging and exclusion.
- Members operate more in a problem exploration/solution mode than in a problem developmental mode.
- Members provide support for other members and the group.
- Members demonstrate more solidarity in their view of group members and the group.

Leader behaviors for the group involvement stage:

- The leader encourages and facilitates the development of individual strengths within the group.
- The leader encourages members in their development of group identity and solidarity.
- The leader provides more opportunity for members to serve in leadership roles within the group.
- The leader gives positive direction as the members move from individual to group-directed purposes and goals.

- The leader demonstrates, in words and through his or her behaviors, the benefits to be derived from individuals working cooperatively.
- The leader demonstrates, in words and through his or her behaviors, the benefits to be derived for individual members and for the group from reinforcement of positive change.
- The leader becomes more involved as a participant, sharing in the changing dynamics of the group.
- The leader functions more in a helping capacity than in a leader capacity to enhance the development of individual members and the group.

Enhancement and Closure Stage

The final stage in a group's life, the *enhancement and closure stage*, is often described as the most exhilarating but also the saddest aspect of group work. The exhilaration stems from a combination of members' evaluation of the group process and individual and group progress, individual and group reinforcement of changes in individual members, and a commitment to continue self-analysis and growth. Members share what they believe have been significant growth experiences during the group tenure, and they receive feedback—generally positive—from other group members and the leader.

Members are encouraged to review the process of the group and to measure changes within themselves resulting from the group experience. At this stage of group development, members' statements tend to be along the following lines: "I was . . . , now I am"; "I felt . . . , now I feel"; "I didn't . . . , now I do"; "I couldn't . . . , now I can." The following member and leader behaviors are descriptive of the enhancement and closure stage.

Member behaviors for the enhancement and closure stage:

- Members evaluate the amount of progress they have made during the life of the group.
- Members evaluate the extent to which the group accomplished its purposes and goals.
- Members share their perceptions of the strengths and weaknesses of other members and the leader.
- Members share their concerns about what will happen after the group ends.
- Members attempt to evaluate the group experience in terms of their other life experiences.
- Members try to build contacts with group members and the leader that will continue after closure.
- Members start to handle the loss that group closure will bring.
- Members consider alternative actions to take the place of what the group provided.

Leader behaviors for the enhancement and closure stage:

- The leader assists group members in evaluating their growth and development during the group's tenure.
- The leader aids group members in resolving any issues that remain.
- The leader facilitates closure early in this last stage by initiating certain activities, such as structured ways of saying good-bye.
- The leader makes sure that each member in the group receives appropriate feedback.

- The leader offers his or her view of the dynamics of the group and its members.
- The leader reviews individual members' strengths and weaknesses from his or her perspective.
- The leader encourages the emotional venting that is necessary in the closure process.
- The leader encourages each member to discuss what he or she plans to do after the group ends.
- The leader explains and encourages members to take advantage of proposed follow-up procedures that will be scheduled at specified times in the future.

The movement of a group from initiation to termination varies. Groups and their individual members differ in this movement for myriad reasons. No single conceptualization offers all the answers or addresses all the issues inherent in this developmental process of groups. The various conceptualizations do provide guidelines and directions for working with groups, however. According to Hershenson, Power, and Waldo (1996):

> The group as a whole can be seen as passing though different periods in its life, similar to the way individuals pass through periods in their lives. When a group first forms it is in childhood, then moves into adolescence, followed by young adulthood, then adulthood, and then maturity as it is about to disband. (p. 211)

OTHER IMPORTANT LEADER BEHAVIORS AND GROUP WORK SKILLS

Some leader behaviors and skills are first learned in the context of individual and couples counseling. Most of the active listening skills, for example, are used in group counseling but take on a different capacity. As another example, rather than summarizing at the beginning, when stuck and needing focus, or at the end of an individual session, group leaders will summarize group themes and when the group has shared. How might reflection of feeling, probing, use of eyes, use of voice, use of person, changes in the group context, immediacy, empathy, or advocacy be used differently in a group context and in different types of groups? Ahead are a few additional leader behaviors and skills of importance.

Managing the Focus of a Group

The group leader will manage the focus of a group for therapeutic outcomes. Sometimes the therapist will shift the focus between topics or shift from focusing on a topic to one person's experience, shift from a shallow to a more in-depth focus on a topic, or shift from a less personal sharing of outside stories to a more personal, here-and-now level of sharing. A group might shift the focus from a topic to the salient emotional experiences of the group, for example, by saying "This topic has brought up sadness, shame, and anger. Are there other emotions you're noticing?" Sometimes group members will want to shift focus to a different person, topic, or depth and the leader will want to hold the focus. A counselor might hold a hand out in a "stop" signal to nonverbally suggest to one member to wait when another client needs to be heard or needs silence. The counselor might say "Before we move on, I want to hear from those who haven't shared about this topic." The counselor often will let the group know early on when creating the group that he or she might do this occasionally to keep the focus in one area and that it is not meant to be rude, as it might otherwise be taken (Jacobs et al., 2015).

Managing Resistance

Resistance occurs as group members settle into the reality of the group demands, goals, risks, and group member differences; natural barriers may form and require contemplation, processing, and normalization of member reactions. Resistance can be a message to the leader that something else needs to be attended to. Rather than trying to avoid or go around a point of resistance, often it is most effective for group leaders to make that point of resistance the point of group process and content. "I can see that it is hard to open up when members may not know each other well. Intimacy does come with time and trust. I am wondering what your experiences are with developing trust in a group? What did you and others need?"

It is important to notice and manage group resistance. Resistance is not conceptualized as a negative client event but as a communication that something else may need to be attended to first, before addressing other therapeutic goals. Rather than seeing a point of resistance as in the way of the group, see resistance as the doorway to the most vital point of the group process.

Making Rounds

Rounds are an intervention or exercise in which each person shares in the group on a chosen topic. Rounds often can be set up to include *no cross talk*, meaning that a member shares without others in the group responding to what they have shared. Consider how removing cross talk as a rule in rounds might allow for both equality of sharing and group time management. Rounds can occur by having members share one after another in a clockwise fashion around the circle, or they can take place in "popcorn" style, meaning that sharing happens at will and "pops" around the circle without prescription. If handled in a sequential order, often leaders allow members who are not ready to pass and speak later. Examples of ways to structure making the rounds include the following:

- Share introductory information (who are you, what brought you here, where are you from, why) for members to bond.
- Use scaling rounds (on a scale of 1–10) to explore changes in emotion or perception.
- Focus on metaphors, themes, and symbols important to member identities.
- Begin with "check-ins" or close with closure statements.
- Share a capturing word or simple phrase to describe one's current state.
- Probe for essential themes.
- Cap a more significant discussion with a final takeaway or comment.

Intratherapeutic Self-Disclosures

These are self-disclosures about how the counselor is feeling and thinking about the group, group members, and group process in the here and now of the session, rather than the there-and-then disclosures of the leader's personal lived experiences outside of the session: "*My sense* is that the group has worked hard today. *I'm touched* by your sharing today. *I imagine others* feel the same. . . . *I would like* to conclude with a brief, no cross talk, capping comment round" (Henretty, Currier, Berman, & Levitt, 2014).

Modeling Through Coleadership of Group

Often groups are run by coleaders, sometimes with one as the primary leader and the other as the secondary or assistant leader. Relationship modeling by the coleaders can be a wonderful method to impart important group behaviors. For example, by demonstrating mutuality while also being open to each other's ideas and feedback, by encouraging and supporting each other, and by honoring cultural differences through openness and curiosity about lived experience, privilege, and bias.

Summary

The concerns expressed at the beginning of this chapter by the hypothetical student Ari are legitimate. The process of group work is both complex and challenging, and the information that has been written about this process at times results in more questions than definitive answers. Novice and experienced group leaders alike strive to increase their level of comfort in leading groups. The following recommendations for group leaders summarize the information covered in this chapter:

1. Knowledge of group stages and transitions provides useful information about typical member behaviors and the developmental process of groups as they move from initiation to termination.

2. Knowledge of group stages and transitions offers the following directives:

   a. During the early stages of group development, the leader must address the anxiety and dependence of group members. One way to do this is to establish operating procedures and structures that will alleviate some of this anxiety and dependence.

   b. During the middle stages of group development, the leader should facilitate empowerment of group members as they work on personal and group issues. These are the working or productive stages of the group and the stages that foster both individual and group development.

   c. During the final stages, the leader must be aware of the dichotomy of exhilaration and sadness the group members feel. Allowing members to discuss and handle both ends of this emotional continuum will facilitate positive closure.

3. Knowledge of group stages and transitions allows the leader to plan and structure the group to better meet the needs of its members.

4. Knowledge of group stages and transitions enables the leader to instruct and orient the members regarding their experiences when moving from initiation to termination of the group.

5. Knowledge of group stages and transitions helps the leader to better judge the types of individuals who would benefit most from the group experience and, accordingly, enhance the group outcome.

6. Knowledge of group stages and transitions enables the leader to better understand the cyclical nature of groups and be better prepared to deal with forward and backward movement within the group and with the behaviors and emotional reactions that can be expected throughout the group's life.

7. Knowledge of group stages and transitions allows the leader to integrate his or her experiences in a group with information from past and current research. He or she then can restructure or reconceptualize the group process to the best advantage of all.

8. Knowledge of group stages and transitions allows the leader to measure or evaluate the developmental processes within his or her groups by comparing them with what others in the field have reported.

9. Knowledge of group stages and transitions allows the leader to become comfortable with the overall process of group work by understanding certain dynamics that are generally predictable.

10. Knowledge of group stages and transitions offers the leader the freedom to work within the known parameters of the group process and to create and develop his or her own conceptualizations within the process.

3 Group Counseling: Elements of Effective Leadership

David Capuzzi and Mark D. Stauffer

Many factors contribute to the outcomes of group counseling (Bemak & Chung, 2015; DeLucia-Waack & Donigian, 2004; Li, Kivlighan, & Gold, 2015). Studies have focused on the relationship between group counseling outcomes and the counselor's personality (Rast, Hogg, & Giessner, 2016), the counselor's experience (Li et al., 2015), group membership (Case & Maner, 2014), the leader's directiveness (Dai & DeMeuse, 2013), the counselor's self-disclosure (Corey, 2017; Dies, 1973), and counselor–group interaction (Young, 2013). In interesting analyses of the bases of influence in groups, Richard and Patricia Schmuck (1997) and David and Frank Johnson (2017) concluded that group outcomes are influenced by the following aspects of the power of the group leader:

1. *Expert power:* the extent of expertise and knowledge that group members attribute to the leader. Members see the leader as having expertise that will assist them in achieving their goal, and group members do what the leader suggests because of respecting and liking the leader and wanting to be liked.
2. *Referent power:* the extent to which group members identify with and feel close to the group leader. In general, the more members like the leader, the more they will identify with him or her, and the more they want to be like the leader.
3. *Legitimate power:* the power attributed to the leader by group members because the "leader" is in the position of facilitating the group. Usually, members believe they have a duty to follow a leader whom they perceive as having legitimate power, and often this kind of leadership influence can reduce conflict or confusion in a group.
4. *Reward power:* the extent to which group members view the leader as having the ability to reward them by providing reinforcement and attention during group sessions. The more the leader is viewed as being able to dispense the reward and the less the members believe they can receive the reward from someone else, the greater will be the leader's power.
5. *Coercive power:* the extent to which the group leader is seen as having the ability to move the group in a certain direction by levying negative consequences, removing positive consequences, or even "punishing" group members. Coercive power often causes group members to avoid the leader and to dislike the leader.
6. *Informational power:* the amount of information the leader has about the members of the group or resources that will be useful to members as they work toward

a goal. The leader's power is based upon his or her ability to demonstrate knowledge and is similar to expert power (see #1).

7. *Connection power:* the number of close relationships the leader has developed with other professionals outside the group that may prove helpful to members of the group.

Because the leader of a group can influence the outcome of a group counseling experience in multiple ways, elements of effective leadership are important to consider for anyone interested in leading or coleading a group.

LEADERSHIP STYLES

Leadership style relates to the way something is said or done (Johnson & Johnson, 2017). Leadership style can be contrasted with the "substance" related to the leader's words and behaviors. The leader's style carries as many messages as the leader's words and actions and either adds to or detracts from the credibility and legitimacy of what the leader is saying or doing.

Lewin's Classic Three Leadership Styles

Discussing elements of effective leadership is not possible without understanding the contributions of Kurt Lewin and his colleagues. In the late 1930s, Lewin studied the influences of different leadership styles or patterns on groups and group members. He observed small groups of 10- and 11-year-old children who met for a period of weeks under the leadership of adults who behaved in one of three ways: democratically, autocratically, or in a laissez-faire manner (Johnson & Johnson, 2017). The impact of these leadership styles on the group members was dramatic and definite. A great deal of scapegoating, for example, occurred in groups led by autocratic leaders. Further, when some of the autocratic groups terminated, the children destroyed the items they had been making. Lewin's studies made it clear that the leader's style can greatly influence the outcomes for group members (Tidikis, 2015). His identification of authoritarian, democratic, and laissez-faire leadership styles provided group leaders with a point of departure for understanding this element of group leadership (Lewin, 1944). A more recent study on dyad groups suggested that autocratic styles of leadership solved problems faster, but the solutions were less correct (Tidikis, 2015).

AUTHORITARIAN STYLE   *Authoritarian* group leaders assume a position as the "expert" and direct the movement of a group. They interpret, give advice, explain individual and group behavior, and generally control most facets of group process. Professionals with strong psychoanalytic, medical, or teaching backgrounds may prefer this style of leadership. In general, the authoritarian leader does little self-disclosing.

Authoritarian leaders wield a great deal of power and usually are quite safe from being personally vulnerable (Berg, Landreth, & Fall, 2013; Gladding, 2015). In directing and controlling the group, they typically create a structure that protects them from self-disclosing or being confronted by group members. This type of leader is sometimes referred to as a *Theory X leader* (Gladding, 2015) and is often quite effective with psychoeducational and task groups.

DEMOCRATIC STYLE   *Democratic* group leaders are more group- and person-centered in the way they interact with group members (Berg et al., 2013). They place more emphasis on the responsibility of each participant to create a meaningful individual and group experience (Kline, 2003). Implicit is their trust in the ability of members and the phenomenon of the group experience. Professionals who subscribe to a Rogerian frame of reference (Dai & DeMeuse, 2013) or who align themselves with humanistic or phenomenological viewpoints are more likely than others to adopt a democratic leadership style. They are more accessible and self-disclosing than authoritarian leaders. This type of leader is sometimes called a *Theory Y leader* (Gladding, 2015).

LAISSEZ-FAIRE STYLE   In contrast to authoritarian and democratic leaders, group leaders who adhere to the *laissez-faire* style do not provide structure or direction to a group. Group members are expected to take responsibility for making the group experience beneficial. Some group leaders (usually inexperienced) select this style in an attempt to be "nondirective" (a misnomer itself), as a way to avoid decision making and enhance their liability, or because they believe a completely unstructured group works best (Gladding, 2015). Some evidence shows that many laissez-faire groups accomplish little during the life of the group. A *laissez-faire* leader is sometimes called a *Theory Z leader*.

The case against the laissez-faire style suggests that leadership isn't just about "being" in a role but relies also on "doing." Platow, Haslam, Reicher, and Steffens (2015) defined leadership as "the process of influencing others in a manner that enhances their contributions to the realization of group goals" (p. 20). Successful outcomes may increase to the extent that the group leader is both active and supportive in her or his role.

In discussing the authoritarian, democratic, and laissez-faire styles of leadership, Posthuma (1999) emphasizes that the leader's style has an impact on the behavior of the members of the group. As Platow and colleagues (2015) noted, "the absence of followers indicates the clear absence of leadership," clarifying that leadership is the result of complex group processes (p. 20). Members in groups with authoritarian leaders tend to be compliant, unenthusiastic, and somewhat resentful of the leader. They may take little initiative, resist responsibility, and fail to be collaborative. Members of groups led by democratic leaders usually are enthusiastic about the group, motivated, collaborative, connected to each other, and interested in taking responsibility and initiative. Members of groups who have a leader with a laissez-faire style usually are confused and frustrated because of a lack of direction on the leader's part, not very productive, much less collaborative, and less able to take responsibility because of a perceived lack of purpose for the group. Leadership may require a balanced leadership approach in relation to control, structure, and direction. For example, members of parent-education groups often do not want leaders to be directive and teaching oriented, but at the same time they want to have a leader create opportunities for interaction and participation (Frykedal & Rosander, 2015).

Leader-Directed and Group-Directed Styles

Another way to conceptualize leadership styles is based on the extent to which the group is leader centered or group centered (Jacobs, Masson & Harvill, 2016; Schuh, Zhang, & Tian, 2013). In a leader-centered group, the leader is the center of focus, and he or she determines what will most benefit group members. In this kind of group, the leader may emphasize a predetermined theme, a sequence of structured exercises, or a format for each group session and likely will direct interaction quite assertively at times. Group members are expected to cooperate with the leader and to deal with personal issues as they fit into the leader's agenda. By contrast, a more group-centered style encourages members to establish the agenda for the group and to more freely discuss personal concerns, issues, and plans. Each of these styles can facilitate the growth of group members, depending upon the group's purpose, the expectations and personalities of group members, and the leader's ability to apply techniques and interventions in a comfortable, congruent, and sensitive manner.

Interpersonal and Intrapersonal Styles

In 1978, Shapiro described two leadership styles: interpersonal and intrapersonal. Leaders with an *interpersonal* style (Corey, 2017; Gladding, 2015) emphasize the importance of understanding and processing interactions among group members and relationships that develop within a group as group sessions progress. Interest centers on the nature, quality, and dynamics of the interactions among members and *what* is occurring in the here and now of the group.

Leaders with an *intrapersonal* orientation are likely to explore *why* group members have certain responses by focusing on individual members and the conflicts, concerns, and dynamics within those members. This style is directed more toward the past, and it facilitates insight and resolution of internal conflicts. At times, leaders with an intrapersonal orientation engage in individual counseling or therapy in the context of the group experience.

Charismatic Leadership Style

Grabo and van Vugt (2016) described charismatic leadership as a dynamic process of leadership and followership whereby "leaders signal their ability to benefit the group by increasing the perceived likelihood that cooperation will succeed. . . . and serve as a focal point for aligning and synchronizing prosocial orientations in followers, suppressing sensitivity to cooperative risks, and enhancing the salience of perceived cooperative rewards" (p. 399).

Group members tend to admire and respect the group leader, particularly in the early stages of a group (Rutan & Rice, 1981). Group leaders may derive some of their power from a combination of traits that are particularly appealing to group members, such as being personable, having an appealing appearance, and having good verbal ability. Group leaders with charisma may inspire group members, who may at times become almost devoted to them (Johnson & Johnson, 2017; Schmuck & Schmuck, 1997).

Group leaders whom members perceive as charismatic may have an advantage during the early stages of a group in terms of their ability to facilitate the work occurring at that time. If group members view the leader as an ego ideal, however, they may become dependent upon his or her leadership and initiatives. Some charismatic leaders begin to enjoy the admiration of group members to such an extent that they fail to encourage the autonomy of the participants (Rutan & Rice, 1981). Group leaders, it must be stressed, should work to develop the skills they need to promote the personal growth of group members and to guide the group from the beginning to the middle and later stages of the group's life.

Textbooks used by counselor education, counseling psychology, psychology, and social work programs present numerous discussions of different leadership styles that prepare professionals for group work. One of the most integrative of these discussions appears in the Johnson and Johnson (2017) text referenced earlier in this chapter. We recommend that you use the discussion in conjunction with this chapter to begin evaluating and developing your own leadership style.

THE IMPORTANCE OF LEADERSHIP STYLE

Leadership styles do make a difference in how groups function, as shown by Lewin's pioneering study mentioned earlier in this chapter. After reviewing numerous studies, Stogdill (1974) reached the following conclusions:

1. Person-centered styles of leadership are not always related to group productivity.
2. Socially distant, directive, and structured leadership styles that tend to promote role differentiation and clear member expectations are related consistently to group productivity.
3. Person-centered styles of leadership that provide for member involvement in decision making and show concern for the welfare of members are related consistently to group cohesiveness.
4. Among task-focused leadership styles, only the structuring of member expectations is related consistently to group cohesiveness.
5. All person-centered leadership styles seem to be related to high levels of member satisfaction.
6. Only the structuring of member expectations is related positively to member satisfaction in task-focused leadership styles.

The single aspect of leadership style that contributes positively to group productivity, cohesiveness, and satisfaction is for the leader to initiate structure by being clear about her role as a leader and what she expects from members (Johnson & Johnson, 2017). The most effective group leaders are those who show concern for the well-being and disclosures of members and structure member role responsibilities. The importance of taking the time to establish goals during the definitive stage of a group, as discussed in Chapter 2, cannot be overstated.

DEVELOPING YOUR OWN LEADERSHIP STYLE

You should place considerable emphasis on analyzing and developing your own style of leadership in groups. Corey (2017) suggests that this will be influenced by whether you lead long-term or short-term groups, as well as by the theory base you use as the conceptual frame of reference for your work with groups (Chapter 4 covers theoretical systems and their applications to groups). In addition, before you are in the position of providing leadership, you should acquire an understanding of your own inherent qualities, characteristics, and inclinations as a group facilitator (Arnold, Connelly, Walsh, & Martin Ginis, 2015; Trotzer, 2006). However, you will have to go far beyond assessing your personal qualities before leading a group. In addition to gaining self-awareness and an understanding of how personality traits and personal qualities can enhance or detract from what you as the leader contribute to a group experience, you must master a set of core knowledge and skill competencies in the process of developing a personalized leadership style.

In 2000, the Association for Specialists in Group Work, a division of the American Counseling Association, published a revised version of its training standards, entitled *Professional Standards for Training of Group Workers.* (These standards were mentioned in Chapter 1 in conjunction with the discussion of group types.) These standards specify knowledge and skill competencies, as well as education and supervision requirements. Some examples of the specified *knowledge competencies* include an understanding of the basic principles of group dynamics, an awareness of the specific ethical issues unique to group work, an understanding of the specific process components in the typical stages of a group's development, and comprehension of the therapeutic factors inherent in a group experience.

Examples of specified *skill competencies* include the ability to explain and clarify the purpose of a given group, the ability to encourage the participation of group members, the ability to open and close sessions effectively, and the ability to help group members integrate and apply what they have learned in the group.

Depending upon whether the group leader wants to be prepared at a beginning (generalist) or an advanced (specialist) level, *education* requirements range from a minimum of two group work courses to a wide range of related coursework in areas such as organizational development, sociology, community psychology, and consultation. *Supervision* requirements involve group observation, coleading, and leading expectations, ranging from 30 to 55 clock hours (minimum) depending on the type of group work under study.

Professionals who are interested in becoming competent group leaders must develop a leadership style that integrates their personal qualities with a myriad of knowledge and skill competencies engendered through master's or doctoral coursework and must meet requirements for group observation and supervised practice. In many ways, developing a leadership style is an integrative, sequential, and creative endeavor resulting in the group leader's ability to transmit knowledge and skill competencies in a unique, individualized way, linked and integrated with a variety of personal characteristics to encourage emotional, cognitive, and behavioral changes on behalf of each member of a group.

PREGROUP LEADERSHIP SKILLS

Before conducting groups, leaders must know how to screen potential members. This screening is followed by organizing the group program.

Conducting Pregroup Screening

Group leaders must develop expertise in screening potential group members (Brown, 2014; Corey, 2017; Remley & Herlihy, 2016). As noted in the *Best Practices Guidelines for Group Work* (Association for Specialists in Group Work, 2007), leaders must screen prospective members of a group to select individuals whose needs and goals are congruent with the group goals. Members should be appropriate for the group they are selected for, meaning that those selected will not be detrimental to the group nor be jeopardized by the group experience. All groups are not appropriate for all who may be interested in participating, and we believe that pregroup screening should always be conducted.

Screening may be accomplished through individual interviews, group interviews of potential group members, an interview as part of team staffing, or reviewing questionnaires completed by prospective members. Jacobs et al. (2016) suggest that prospective group members be asked questions such as "Why do you want to be in the group?", "What are your expectations of the group?", "Have you ever been in a group before? If so, what was your experience like?", "What do you want to talk about in the group?", "Is there anyone you do not want to be in group with?", "How do you think you can contribute and participate in the group?", and "What questions do you have about the group or the leader?"

Pregroup screening must provide prospective members with information about expectations for participation in the group, goals, payment methods and fee schedules, termination and referral procedures, client rights, and so on. The group leader also must inquire about prospective members' current and past experience with counseling and provide clients with a written disclosure statement of his or her qualifications and the nature of the services to be provided. (See *Code of Ethics and Standards of Practice* from the American Counseling Association [2014], which addresses screening procedures.)

George Gazda (1989) made some interesting screening recommendations that also serve to establish ground rules for prospective group members. He suggested providing group candidates with the following guidelines as part of the screening:

1. Before you attend the first group session, you should establish personal goals. You will be able to refine and clarify these goals as the group progresses.
2. Whenever you contribute during a group session, you should be as honest and straightforward about yourself as possible. Success and lack of success with respect to aspects of your behavior may be important for you to discuss.
3. Listen carefully when other members of the group are contributing, and try to communicate nonjudgmental understanding and caring.
4. Do not discuss any information about other group members outside the group.
5. Attend all sessions, and arrive on time.
6. Respect your counselor's right to suggest that you terminate participation in the group if the counselor believes it is best for you and best for the group.
7. Respect the rule that no one group member can control the group and that group decisions are made by consensus.
8. Let the group counselor know if someone in your group poses a barrier to your open participation as a member of the group due to a prior relationship.
9. If you request an individual meeting with your group counselor, recognize that you may be asked to share the content of the discussion with the full group.
10. Be aware of the amount and schedule of fees for membership in the group prior to committing to group participation.

Selection of group members through pregroup screening also grants potential members the opportunity to assess their readiness for, and interest in, being a group member (Gladding, 2015). Group leaders who have not conducted a group previously should conduct pregroup screening under the supervision of an experienced group work specialist.

Organizing for Groups

Several elements must be considered in organizing a group or group program. These considerations include, among others, publicizing the group, attending to the physical setting, setting the length and frequency of group meetings, and determining the size of the group.

Publicizing the Group

Letting potential group members know about their potential to participate in a group can be accomplished in several ways (Gladding, 2015). If the group leader lets colleagues know about the plan to initiate the group or group program, her or his colleagues could help publicize the group and possibly refer clients for the pregroup screening and orientation. Although this approach has the advantage of personalizing the announcement and referral, it does leave the group leader and the success of the group or group program dependent on the time and opportunities that colleagues have to contribute to publicizing it. At times, the group leader already has clients—perhaps clients who have been engaged in individual counseling—who stand to benefit from membership in a group. Suggesting the possibility of group participation (if participation would be appropriate and pertinent to the client's reasons for engaging in counseling) is one way in which groups sometimes are formed. This approach has the advantage of being personalized, but it may have the disadvantage of reaching few potential members.

Sometimes counselors place advertisements about upcoming groups in community newspapers, post flyers, or distribute brochures about the groups they conduct. This method has the advantage of reaching more individuals who might be interested, but it may not be comprehensive enough to answer the questions of those who might like to participate. In addition, it is important to consider the ethical aspects of advertising, as addressed in the *Code of Ethics and Standards of Practice* published by the American Counseling Association (2014).

Selecting the Physical Setting

Group sessions may be conducted in a variety of settings, so long as the room used allows privacy and relative freedom from distraction for participants (Trotzer, 2006; Yalom, 1985). Some leaders seat participants around a circular table. Others prefer to place chairs in a circle so that members' nonverbal or body language responses are observed more readily. No matter what type of seating arrangement is selected, the room must be comfortable for the group. A group of eight members and a group leader in a room large enough to seat 30 or 40 people can be just as inappropriate and unconducive to the development of cohesiveness as a room that is too small to readily accommodate chairs for nine people. If group sessions are to be observed or videotaped, group members must give permission ahead of time and must have the opportunity to ask questions about and discuss the purposes of observation and taping procedures.

Deciding Length and Frequency of Meetings

The agency or the setting may dictate the duration and frequency of group sessions, but the group leader also must consider the purpose of the group when determining scheduling (Corey, 2017; Jacobs et al., 2016). Some groups require longer time periods and more frequent scheduling than others. Typical groups require 1-hour sessions to provide for a warm-up period and for the participation of each person in the group.

Sessions scheduled for more than 2 hours, unless they are designed specifically as part of a marathon group, tend to become nonproductive and fatiguing for all concerned. Groups conducted in educational settings, such as high schools and middle schools, may be limited by necessity to a 40- or 50-minute time period based on the school's standard class schedule. Ideally, groups should meet once or twice a week to promote continuity in the group experience.

Determining Size of the Group

Yalom (1985) suggested that the ideal size of a counseling/therapy group is 7 or 8 members, with 5 to 10 members constituting an acceptable range. He noted that a minimum number is required for a group to function and interact as a group; a group of fewer than 5 members often results in a sequence of individual therapy or counseling sessions within the group context. As the size of the group diminishes, many of the advantages of a group—particularly the opportunity to receive validation and feedback from a microcosm of society—are lost.

OTHER ASPECTS OF ORGANIZATION

The following are several additional possibilities for group leaders to consider in conjunction with groups they lead or colead (Yalom, 1985):

1. Weekly, written summaries, describing some aspects of the group experience during a given week, could be mailed to group members, providing reinforcement and continuity.

SIDEBAR 3.2
Organizing for Groups

This chapter makes several suggestions for how to organize the group you are planning to conduct. Develop an outline of your plan for the type of group you will be conducting. Look at some of the other chapters in this text for some initial ideas of how you might structure each of your sessions, and include a session-by-session outline in your plan. Share your outline and ask for feedback.

2. In addition to a disclosure statement from the counselor, written material describing the ground rules, purposes, expectations, and so on of the group could be distributed. Beyond providing important information, material of this nature reinforces group participants. Providing this written material after the first session may be particularly helpful because anxious members may not have been able to totally integrate information about what a group experience would be like.

3. Group members might be afforded an opportunity to see a movie or a videotape presenting information about group participation, like the information described in the previous list item.

4. Group members could be provided the option of watching videos of their own group after each session. This would give members a chance to evaluate their participation and to obtain additional feedback from other group members. As noted earlier, group members must have provided written permission before filming.

5. Group members could be offered pregroup training sessions during which they would be taught skills for self-disclosure, expressing feelings, staying in the here and now, and so forth. Obviously, this suggestion depends upon the time and resources available to the group leader and group participants and may work better in the context of inpatient rather than outpatient situations.

RECOGNIZING MEMBERSHIP ROLES

When a group is formed and begins to meet, all the members have just one role—that of group member (Vander Kolk, 1985). As time passes, however, roles are differentiated as members interact and become more comfortable about being themselves in the group. Most groups are characterized by a combination of roles (Corey, 2017; Gladding, 2015; Posthuma, 1999; Trotzer, 2006). This combination results in a dynamic interaction among members that energizes or deenergizes the group in some way. For example, a group composed of several task-oriented members might identify objectives for the group experience and monitor interactions to ensure movement and progress during each session. Another group might consist of several task-oriented members and several process-oriented members who value spontaneous interaction and disclosure. This group might find itself in conflict from time to time if task-oriented members feel time is being spent unproductively and process-oriented members think they are not always able to complete interactions or express deep feelings without others pressuring them to refocus on the original objectives established for the session.

The group leader must recognize the types of roles that group members are taking and institute appropriate interventions to maintain balanced interaction and movement through the definitive, personal involvement, group involvement, and enhancement and closure stages of a group (described in Chapter 2). One way of conceptualizing membership roles in groups is to view roles as facilitative, vitalizing and maintenance, or antigroup (blocking) in nature.

Facilitative Roles

Facilitative roles serve to keep the group on task and to clarify aspects of communication. Members who behave in facilitative ways contribute to the group constructively and increase the likelihood of participation and cooperation. Examples of member behaviors that can be facilitative are those that precipitate ideas and encourage the group to follow up, seek clarification of what someone said, organize the agenda of the group, keep the group focused, or provide information.

Vitalizing and Maintenance Roles

Vitalizing and maintenance roles help develop social–emotional bonds among members of a group and usually contribute to cohesiveness and feelings of connectedness. Group members who fill vitalizing and maintenance roles usually are sensitive to the affective components of a group and respond in ways that either escalate or reduce tensions related to affective aspects of intra- and interpersonal communication. These roles might take the form of encouraging positive feelings, mediating conflict, making and describing observations about the group, or making sure all members have opportunity to participate.

Antigroup (Blocking) Roles

Individual needs of group members (Vander Kolk, 1985) often inhibit a group's progress. Group leaders must recognize these *antigroup roles* and learn to recognize and diffuse problematic behaviors in individuals so that the entire group does not become unproductive. Members who are aggressive, attempt to limit discussion, constantly seek recognition, derail conversation by switching the topic, unnecessarily rescue other members, use humor to interrupt member disclosure, or disapprove of another member's behavior can often block progress and create tension.

SIDEBAR 3.3
Leadership Styles and Membership Roles

If you are participating in a small group in conjunction with the course you are taking on group counseling, keep a log and make entries in the log after each small-group session. How would you describe the leadership style of the facilitator of your group? How would you describe the role you are playing as a member of the group? Is the style of the group leader one that would be natural for you? If not, how do you think your style will differ? Are you comfortable with your role in the group? If not, what would you like to change?

FACILITATING THE GROUP STAGES

Understanding the developmental stages of groups helps the group leader anticipate apprehensions, needs, and fears of members of a group that has just been convened (Capuzzi & Gross, 2013b). Understanding how to facilitate the definitive, personal involvement, group involvement, and enhancement and closure stages should prove helpful to the beginning group worker.

Facilitating the Definitive Stage

As discussed in Chapter 2, in the definitive stage of the group's developmental process, group members define for themselves and for each other the purpose of the group, the quality of their commitment to it, and their involvement level. Members have questions about trust, support, safety, self-disclosure, confidentiality, and many other aspects of group participation. During the initial sessions, the group leader must be sensitive to members' questions and uncertainties and be able to model behavior that encourages constructive communication and gradual movement toward achieving individual and group goals. Several group specialists (Corey, 2017; Gladding, 2015; Jacobs et al., 2016) have discussed the importance of mastering special skills unique to group work. Among the leader's skills vital to the definitive stage of a group are the following:

1. *Active listening:* paying attention to and paraphrasing the verbal and nonverbal aspects of communication in a way that lets members know they have been listened to and have not been evaluated
2. *Supporting:* providing reinforcement and encouragement to members to create trust, acceptance, and an atmosphere in which self-disclosure can occur when appropriate
3. *Empathizing:* communicating understanding to members by being able to assume their frames of reference
4. *Goal setting:* assisting in planning by helping members define concrete and meaningful goals
5. *Facilitating:* opening communication between and among group members so that each member contributes in some way to the group and begins to feel some involvement with others and with the group
6. *Protecting:* preventing members from taking unnecessary psychological risks in the group
7. *Modeling:* teaching members the elements of constructive communication by demonstrating desired behavior in conjunction with each interaction with group members

Certain practical tasks also must be accomplished. Establishing ground rules, for example, is something the group leader usually does during the first and, if necessary, subsequent sessions, even if some aspects have been addressed in pregroup screening. Examples of ground rules that may be established include attendance at all meetings, no advice giving, no physical violence, no smoking during meetings, no sexual relationships with other members of the group, and no arriving late. The leader should explain all the ground rules (Brown, 2014) and the rationale behind each one. As the group continues to meet, members may add ground rules so long as none of these rules endangers the well-being of group members. The following ground rules have been used often by the authors of this text:

1. Respect and accept one another at all times. (This does not mean you need to agree with each other at all times).
2. Remain silent while another group member is talking.
3. Be present and participate constructively.
4. Pass at a particular time, if you need to do so.
5. Let other members know, very briefly, the reason you need to pass.
6. Support decision making by consensus.
7. Communicate with "I" rather than "you" messages.
8. Do not discuss anything that takes place during a group session outside the session with other group members or with your significant other. If, for some reason, you do not adhere to this ground rule, describe the nature of the interchange at the beginning of the next group session.
9. Do everything possible to create a safe, nonjudgmental environment.
10. Avoid giving advice.

Finally, confidentiality (Remley & Herlihy, 2016) is another aspect of group participation that should be discussed during the definitive stage. The group leader must stress the importance of confidentiality and possible violations (e.g., talking about the disclosures of group members outside the group or telling individuals outside the group the identity of those participating in the group). During the definitive stage of a group, members' uncertainties about what the group experience may be like are often related to their individual fears and apprehensions. Group leaders can anticipate some of the following misgivings and should help members address any that might interfere with participation (Corey, Corey, & Corey, 2014):

- Concern about being accepted by other members of the group
- Uncertainty about whether other group members will accept honesty or whether their contributions must be carefully framed so that others won't be upset
- Questions about how communication in the group will be different from communication outside the group
- Apprehension about being judged by other group members
- Wondering about similarities to other group members
- Concern about pressure to participate
- Uncertainty about whether to take risks
- Apprehension about appearing to be inept
- Confusion about how much to self-disclose
- Fear about being hurt by other members of the group
- Fear of being attacked by the group
- Wondering about becoming dependent on the group experience
- Apprehension about facing new insights about oneself
- Uncertainty about changing and whether significant others will accept these changes
- Concern about being asked to do something that would be uncomfortable

In addition to establishing ground rules, discussing confidentiality, and addressing individual members' apprehensions, the leader may wish to provide structural elements, such as leader and member introductions, exercises to be completed in dyads or triads followed by sharing in the full group, guided fantasies followed by discussion of the experience, sentence-completion exercises, and written questionnaires with subsequent discussion. Structural elements such as these can promote involvement and productivity. The amount of structure necessary to catalyze group interaction will always depend on pregroup screening, the purpose of the group, the age and functionality of group members, and the leader's style. As a rule, we recommend that the leader provide and use structure when needed, but not depend on group exercises to the extent that members are unable to express their concerns, desires, and issues. Finally, the leader should think about how he or she will close the group sessions in a way that provides time for reflection, summarization, and integration. We recommend setting aside at least 5 to 10 minutes at the end of each session for this purpose so that group members do not feel frustrated by a lack of closure or what might be perceived as an abrupt ending. This might be an ideal time to suggest introspection, behavioral rehearsal, or other homework, if applicable.

Facilitating the Personal Involvement Stage

The personal involvement stage of a group is best thought of as one of member-to-member interactions, the sharing of personal information, confrontation with other members of the group, power struggles, and the individual's growing identity as a member of the group. This stage of action, reaction, and interaction requires the group leader to demonstrate awareness of the emotional makeup of the group and the intra- and interpersonal struggles that are part of this stage of a group. In addition to the skills discussed for the definitive stage, the following skills are required of the leader during this challenging stage of group life:

1. *Clarifying:* helping members sort conflicting feelings and thoughts to arrive at a better understanding of what is being expressed
2. *Questioning:* asking questions to gain additional information or to promote members' self-exploration and description of feelings and thoughts
3. *Interpreting:* providing tentative explanations for feelings, thoughts, and behaviors that challenge members to explore their motivations and reactions in more depth
4. *Reflecting feelings:* letting members know they are being understood in a way that goes beyond the content of their communication
5. *Confronting:* challenging members to become aware of discrepancies between words and actions or current and previous self-disclosures
6. *Initiating:* being proactive to bring about new directions in individual sharing or interpersonal communication
7. *Giving feedback:* offering an external view of how a member appears to another by describing concrete and honest reactions in a constructive way
8. *Self-disclosing:* describing here-and-now reactions to events in the group
9. *Blocking:* preventing counterproductive behavior from one or more group members

During the personal involvement stage of any group, some practical considerations must be dealt with. As self-disclosure becomes more open and interactions among members become more straightforward and more focused on the here and now, some group members may become threatened and remain silent to avoid taking risks. When this happens, the group leader should use his or her skills to acknowledge the way those members may be feeling and encourage them to participate without demanding more participation than they are able to contribute at the time. The longer members remain silent, the more difficulty they may have entering dialogue and interacting spontaneously. Also, silent members often engender suspicion and criticism from other group members who begin to wonder why the silent members are not involved in the group.

Silence is not the only reaction from members who become threatened by the dynamics of the personal involvement stage. Benjamin (1981); Corey (2017); Corey, Corey, and Corey (2014); Sack (1985); and Yalom (1985) offered these additional possibilities the group leader should recognize:

1. *Intellectualization:* Members who are feeling threatened by the openness of communication may focus completely on their thoughts to avoid making connections with either their own or others' emotions. A cognitive pattern of communication should signal the leader that these members may not be comfortable with their feelings.

2. *Questioning:* Questions from members can direct the discussion toward why something was said or has happened rather than focus it on how members are feeling and what they are experiencing now. Members often ask questions to avoid dealing with their true feelings.

3. *Advice giving:* Offering advice rarely helps another group member resolve personal issues or solve problems independently, but it does provide a means for the advice giver to avoid struggling with internal issues, empathizing, and adopting the internal frame of reference of other group members.

4. *Band-Aiding:* Band-Aiding is the misuse of support to alleviate painful feelings. Group members who Band-Aid prevent themselves and others from fully expressing their emotions.

5. *Dependency:* Dependent group members invite advice giving and Band-Aiding by presenting themselves as helpless and stuck. This, too, prevents complete and accurate self-disclosure from those who feel threatened by aspects of group interaction.

6. *Behaviors related to struggles for control:* During this stage of group development, struggles for control are common. Some of the behaviors that might surface are competition and rivalry, jockeying for position, jealousies, affronts to leadership, and arguing about the division of responsibility and decision making. The leader must be able to recognize these issues and help members talk about them.

7. *Conflict and anger:* Conflict and anger are other common responses to feeling threatened. When conflict and anger are recognized, expressed, and discussed, cohesion in a group usually increases. Participants learn that it is safe to openly disagree and express intense feelings. Further, group members learn that bonds and relationships are strong enough to withstand honest levels of communication.

8. *Confrontation:* Confrontation in a group is not helpful when the emphasis is on criticizing others, providing negative feedback and then withdrawing, or assaulting others' integrity or inherent personality traits. If, however, confrontation is presented in a caring and helpful way, it can catalyze change. For responsible confrontation, group leaders should provide members with guidelines such as the following:

   • Know why you are confronting.
   • Avoid dramatic statements about how another member appears to be.

SIDEBAR 3.4
Group Stages

Reread the descriptions of the stages—definitive, personal involvement, group involvement, and enhancement and closure—in Chapter 2. If you are currently in a group, in what stage of the developmental process is your group? What observations about yourself and other group members have led you to identify this stage as characteristic of your small group at this time? What skills has the leader of your group employed to assist members at this stage?

- Include descriptions of both observable behaviors and the impact they have on you.
- Imagine being the recipient of what you are saying to another member.
- Provide the recipient of a confrontational statement with time to integrate and reflect. Do not expect an immediate change in behavior.
- Think about whether you would be willing to consider what you are expecting another group member to consider.

9. *Challenges to the group leader:* Although a leader may feel uncomfortable when a member challenges his or her leadership, the leader must recognize that confrontation often is a member's first significant step toward realizing his or her independence and trust in the group. The way the leader responds to a challenge from a group member can have a powerful effect on the member's willingness to trust and to take risks. Leaders can be excellent role models if they respond to challenges nondefensively and ask members to talk about the thoughts and feelings behind these challenges.

One or more members may verbally attack the group leader. Attacks usually are the result of the leader modeling some inappropriate behavior or a member feeling threatened by the energy or interactions in the group. During the session, the leader must work through the criticism by encouraging those who have negative feelings toward him or her to describe those feelings. A give-and-take discussion may lead to acceptable resolution of the difficulty. If a leader does not provide opportunities for members to describe and resolve their feelings, the feelings may escalate to a point at which group sessions become counterproductive.

Facilitating the Group Involvement Stage

As explained in Chapter 2, the group involvement stage is characterized by much self-evaluation and self-assessment of behavior, attitudes, values, and methods in relating to others and by members' channeling their energies toward meeting the group's goals and purposes. During this stage, the terms *members* and *group* become somewhat more synonymous. The group, with its purposes and goals, is merging with members' individual purposes and goals. Individual agendas are replaced by group agendas, and the members identify more with the group.

Facilitating this stage of the group's life requires the leader to use all the skills needed during the definitive stage and, from time to time, some of the skills important to positive resolution of the personal involvement stage. Additional skills that may be needed include the following:

1. *Linking:* stressing the importance of interpersonal communication within the group by connecting what one member is feeling or doing to what another member is feeling or doing
2. *Providing group identity:* encouraging members in their development of a group identity
3. *Suggesting direction:* providing suggestions as the members progress from individual- to group-directed purposes and goals
4. *Sharing leadership:* encouraging members to assume leadership responsibility within the group when appropriate
5. *Participating in the group:* involving oneself as a member of the group and sharing leadership as opportunities arise
6. *Reinforcing cooperation:* demonstrating, on verbal and nonverbal levels, the benefits of cooperative participation

During this stage, practical considerations for constructive leadership relate to the higher level of self-disclosure and intimacy that members have developed. In one situation that often arises, a member gains sudden insights as another member self-discloses and solves problems. Because members now are readily able to put aside personal agendas and listen and empathize as others in the group share during this stage, they may become aware of incidents in their own lives (e.g., interactions designed to prevent intimacy from occurring) that are emotionally laden.

At times, these memories may be extremely difficult to express and then integrate into a new perspective or set of behaviors. During these circumstances, the leader must provide the safety and support needed to guide resulting disclosure and group response and interaction. Insights about previously denied experiences can be powerful and difficult for an individual to handle.

During the group involvement stage, the group may be immersed in risk taking, and self-disclosure may progress more rapidly than is necessary or appropriate for the participant or the full group. The leader may have to slow the rate and intensity of self-disclosure to safeguard members from unnecessary psychological risks. Because of the cohesive atmosphere that has developed during this stage, other members may reinforce a participant's self-disclosure or offer suggestions that the leader might have to ward off to avoid escalating the risk.

Group efforts to help a member with a problem sometimes become detrimental during this stage. Unlike advice giving and Band-Aiding in the personal involvement stage, these efforts are not meant to direct the group away from discussing emotional or painful issues. Instead, they derive from the strong feelings of closeness that have developed, and they follow intense discussion and thorough exploration. The problem arises when a participant receives so many suggestions for resolving a problem that he or she begins to feel confused and at a loss to deal with the many options presented. The group leader must intervene so that an option or two can be considered carefully and then either adopted or discarded. Alternately, the leader, more appropriately, might encourage participants to discuss a specific problem or area in future sessions after they have identified their own solutions.

During the group involvement stage, group members begin discussing their desire to establish outside of group the same kind of cooperation, cohesiveness, and communication patterns they enjoy during the group sessions. The leader should encourage discussion, helping members to understand that they should not expect the same level of cooperation and the same level of self-disclosure in all groups. Still, they should not assume that nothing can improve in established outside circles. Members also may express how much they look forward to group sessions and how much they dislike the idea of their group terminating at some future time. This latter sentiment, which may begin to be expressed as the group moves toward the enhancement and closure stage, must be addressed.

Facilitating the Enhancement and Closure Stage

This final stage in group development is often described simultaneously as the most exhilarating and the saddest aspect of group work. The exhilaration stems from evaluation and reevaluation as members are encouraged to review the group process and to measure changes from the time they entered the group to this point just before closure and termination. The sadness centers on leaving an environment that has provided safety, security, and support and leaving individuals who have offered encouragement, friendship, and positive feedback related to a member's growth potential.

Facilitation of this stage requires the leader to draw upon the following skills in addition to any of those used during previous stages:

1. *Evaluating:* assessing both individual and group process during the group's tenure
2. *Resolving issues:* assisting individual members and the group to achieve closure on remaining issues
3. *Reviewing progress:* helping group members obtain an overview of the progress and changes that have taken place since the group was initiated
4. *Identifying strengths and weaknesses:* encouraging members to pinpoint the strengths they have developed in the group, as well as the weaknesses they have acknowledged and begun to overcome, so that they can apply this learning outside the group after it terminates
5. *Terminating:* preparing group members to finalize the group's history, assimilate the experience, and separate from the group as sessions come to an end
6. *Referring:* recommending possibilities for individual or group counseling after the group ends

Practical considerations for the group leader are numerous. Corey (2017), Corey, Corey, and Corey (2014), George and Dustin (1988), Gladding (2015), Jacobs et al. (2016), Ohlsen, Horne, and Lawe (1988), Vander Kolk (1985), and others have discussed aspects of effective leadership associated with closure and termination. The following are some suggestions the leader can draw upon for facilitating closure and termination, although this is by no means an exhaustive list of possibilities:

1. *Reminders:* Make sure that members are aware of the approaching termination date to enable them to achieve the essential review and closure. This suggestion applies to groups that have a predetermined closure date established by the members themselves or by a set of external circumstances.
2. *Capping:* During the last few sessions of a group, do not encourage members to initiate discussions of intensely emotional material or to facilitate powerful emotional

interchange in the full group. *Capping* means easing members and the group out of affective expression and into intellectual consideration of progress, change, and strengths because time is running out for processing new emotional material.

3. *Logs:* If members have been keeping written logs chronicling the group experience, suggest that they share particularly meaningful segments as the group reaches its conclusion. This can be an excellent vehicle for evaluation, review, and feedback.

4. *Unfinished business:* Ask group members to share and work on resolving any unfinished business (whether individual or group focused). Allow enough time for members to adequately achieve resolution.

5. *Homework:* Suggest that each group member identify, discuss, and commit to some homework to be completed after the group ends. This may help group members integrate learning and develop perspectives for the future.

6. *Making the rounds:* Offer members the opportunity to look at each person in the group and provide some final feedback (or to hand each person some written feedback). This can provide the basis for one or more sessions aimed at easing the emotions that sometimes are associated with the end of a positive group experience. To allow feedback to be discussed and processed adequately, the leader should allow more than one group session for this activity.

7. *Saying good-bye:* Allow each member to express his or her unique personality and perspective in saying good-bye when a group is ending. Suggest that members frame this good-bye as it relates to the entire group, to each participant, or both.

8. *Future planning:* Discuss how group members can approach the future in a proactive way. This helps participants integrate new learning and plan to meet future needs. Members need plenty of time to think about how they will function in the absence of support from the group.

9. *Referrals:* Make arrangements for members who need further counseling, whether group or individual. Discuss the possibilities during a specifically scheduled group session. Members may decide to share with the group their decision for follow-up counseling.

10. *Questionnaires:* If desired, use questionnaires to assess the strengths and weaknesses of a specific group. If these questionnaires are filled out before the group ends, share excerpts with the group, with advance permission of the members.

11. *Follow-up interviews:* Ease the apprehension often associated with the end of a group by offering the opportunity for individual follow-up sessions. Members can utilize the follow-up meeting to discuss postgroup progress, difficulties, or issues and to obtain the support they need to continue in productive ways.

12. *Group reunions:* Organize a group reunion. The reunion might be in the form of a group session, a potluck dinner or picnic, or group attendance at a lecture, for example. The purpose of the reunion is to give members a chance to reconnect, share, and provide support and encouragement.

DEALING WITH DIFFICULT MEMBERS

Counselors sometimes face some difficult group members—members who attempt to control or take over the group in some way. Typical patterns—presented by Berg et al. (2013), Brown (2014), Carroll, Bates, and Johnson (1997), Chen and Rybak (2004), Corey (2017), Dyer and Vriend (1973), Jacobs et al. (2016), Kline (2003),

Kottler (1994b), Milgram and Rubin (1992), and Trotzer (2006)—are given here, with suggestions for how the group leader might respond. The 18 examples that follow concretize the use of the skills discussed for facilitating the four stages of a group.

Group Member Speaks for Everyone

A group member typically says something like "We think we should . . .," "This is how we all feel," or "We were wondering why. . . ." Often, this happens when a member does not feel comfortable making statements such as "I think we should . . ." or "I'm wondering why . . ." or when a group member is attempting to garner support for a point of view. The difficulty of allowing the "we" syndrome to operate in a group is that it inhibits members from expressing their individual feelings and thoughts. The group leader might give *feedback* ("You mentioned 'we' a number of times. Are you speaking for yourself or for everyone?") or engage in *linking* ("What do each of you think about the statement that was just made?").

Group Member Speaks for Another Member in the Group

Examples of one group member speaking for another include "I think I know what he means" and "She's not really saying how she feels; I can explain it for her." One member speaking for another often connotes a judgment about the ability of the other member to communicate or a judgment that the other member is about to disclose uncomfortable information. Regardless of the motivation behind the statement, the group member who permits another group member to do the talking for him or her must assess the reason for doing so and whether the same communication patterns happen outside the group. The "talker" must evaluate his or her inclination to make decisions for or to rescue others.

Appropriate leader skills here include *questioning* ("Did Jim state your feelings more clearly than you can?" or "How does it feel to have someone rescue you?") and making *interpretive statements* ("Did you think June needed your help?" or "Do you find it difficult to hold back when you think you know what someone else is going to say?").

Group Member Behaves in an "Entitled" Manner

The entitled group member is someone who attempts, in a variety of ways, to keep the focus of the group on himself or herself. This member may monopolize the conversation, tell stories that are related only tangentially to the topic under discussion, arrive late or miss sessions and then expect everyone to accommodate him or her by using most of the time to bring him or her up to date, or be needy and demanding of attention a great deal of the time. If such a member can control the proceedings of the group, then he or she can demonstrate a sense of power. Such a client must be taught the capacity for empathy and attentiveness to the needs of others, and groups can be ideal for teaching those skills.

Possible leader interventions include *modeling* ("I realize that what you are saying is important to you; perhaps we can provide you with more time after others have had an opportunity to participate in today's session") and giving *feedback* ("Have you noticed how much time you have taken today and how restless some other group members appear to be?"). Another option is to cue a group member to do the work ("John, you seem to be getting progressively restless as Bonnie has been speaking; tell her how you feel.").

Group Member Remains Silent

As noted, silent group members can create difficulties for groups. A group member's silence can have many different sources. Sometimes a member is silent because he or she cannot find the words to describe a subjective experience. Other times silence occurs because the member is observing and taking things in. If a group member lacks self-confidence and generally avoids taking the initiative in conversations, he or she may be behaving in his or her normal pattern and does not intend to be resistant or difficult. At times, however, a group may have a member who is not committed to participation and uses the silence as a means of manipulation.

In any case, when a group member *remains* silent, the possibility increases that this member eventually will be confronted, or even attacked, by other group members. Group members may begin to imagine that the silent member does not approve, has definite opinions that ought to be shared, or simply does not care about others in the group. Group leaders may have to *empathize* ("I get the feeling that it's difficult for you to speak up in a group.") or *facilitate* ("Jim, is there anything you can add to the discussion at this time?"). Although the leader may use *questioning* ("I'm wondering what you're thinking and feeling right now?") and *blocking* ("I don't think it's a good idea for you to remain so silent; others may wonder why you don't participate.") to elicit participation, these methods may engender even more resistance. Working with the silent group member can be difficult.

Group Member Identifies a Scapegoat

Scapegoating is a common and difficult problem for the group leader. Often, the person who is scapegoated is the target of the displaced anger of another member of the group. Something in his or her behavior has elicited the attack. Although leaders sometimes encourage group members to give feedback to the scapegoat so that this member can better understand why others are upset with his or her behavior, they must be cautious so that the scapegoat is not attacked unnecessarily.

Leaders who are not experienced group work specialists often allow the attention to remain on the scapegoat because of the interaction and participation occurring in the group. Even if the feedback is accurate, the leader is responsible for seeing that the rights of the scapegoated member are not being violated.

At times, a silent member may be inclined to support the scapegoat but may need the help of the leader to vocalize a minority point of view. To reach a constructive resolution, the leader also might ask the group members to imagine how they would feel if they were in the place of the scapegoat.

Group Member Challenges the Leader's Authority

Because this topic is so important to the group leader, it merits additional attention in this chapter. Group members who challenge the leader's competence sometimes do so in a nonaggressive way, suggesting how the leader might be more effective. At the other end of the continuum of member behavior is the angry, hostile member who overtly attacks the leader's competency and expertise. Members usually view the leader as a source of authority, so the leader should set norms and establish leadership during the first few sessions to stave off such challenges, at least until the group has met two or three times.

When coping with a challenger, the most important things for a group leader to do are to stay calm and to avoid responding defensively. A response such as "I'm glad you're able to express those feelings. Can you tell me more about what led up to this?" implies that the leader is willing to listen to the challenger, is not going to withdraw from the confrontation, and is not going to abdicate the leadership role. Once some interchange takes place, the conflict may be seen as a misunderstanding and may be resolved in a way that makes the group even more cohesive and able to function constructively. In any event, the behavior the leader *models* for the group when facing a challenge is crucial to the group's future productivity and comfort levels.

Group Member Focuses on Persons, Conditions, or Events Outside the Group

Many times, group counseling sessions turn into gripe sessions. Group members tend to enjoy complaining about a colleague, a friend, or a partner if they are allowed to reinforce one another. The difficulty of this type of interaction is that it might erroneously substantiate that others are at fault and that group members do not have to take responsibility for those aspects of their behavior contributing to their complaints.

The group leader might use skills such as *initiating* ("You keep talking about your wife as the cause of your unhappiness. Isn't it more important to ask yourself what contributions you can make to improve your relationship?") or *clarifying* ("Does complaining about others really mean you think you would be happier if they could change?") when faced with this challenge.

Group Member Seeks the Approval of the Leader or a Group Member before or after Speaking

Some group members nonverbally seek acceptance by nodding, glancing, or smiling at the leader or another group member. These members may be intimidated by authority figures or by personal strength or may have low self-esteem, causing them to seek sources of support and acceptance outside themselves. When a group member glances at the leader for approval when speaking, one tactic is for the leader to look at another member, forcing the speaker to change the direction of his or her delivery. Another is to give *feedback* ("You always look at me as you speak, almost as if you're asking permission.").

Group Member Says, "I Don't Want to Hurt Her Feelings, so I Won't Say What I'd Like to Say"

Especially in the early stages of a group, this sentiment is common. Sometimes a member believes another member is too fragile for feedback. At other times, the member is revealing apprehension about being liked by other group members. The group leader should explore reasons for the reticence to offer feedback. In doing so, the leader may reinforce cooperation, asking the member to check with the person to whom feedback may be directed to validate his or her fears.

Group Member Suggests His or Her Problems Are Someone Else's Fault

This example may seem to overlap with group members who focus on persons, conditions, or events outside the group, but it presents a different problem than a group gripe session. When a group member periodically attributes difficulties and unhappiness to another person, the leader might use *blocking* ("Who is really the only person who can be in charge of you?" or "How can other people determine your mood so much of the time?"). We are not suggesting a stance that would be perceived as lacking empathy and acceptance, but the leader should facilitate members taking responsibility for themselves.

Group Member Suggests "I've Always Been That Way"

This suggestion indicates irrational thinking and lack of motivation to change. Believing that the past determines all of one's future can limit one's future growth. The group leader must help members such as this to identify irrational thoughts that cause them to be ineffective in specific areas and learn that they are not doomed to repeat the mistakes of the past. *Interpreting* ("You're suggesting that your past has such a hold over you that you never will be any different") and *questioning* ("Do you think everyone has certain parts of their life over which they have no control?") are possible responses to stimulate the examination of faulty thinking and assumptions.

Group Member Engages in Cross Talk

Cross talking occurs when group members engage in simultaneous parallel conversations, disrupting the flow of the group and making it difficult for other members to interact. Sometimes this occurs because some members of the group are not comfortable with a given topic or not really committed to the purpose of the group. The group leader should address cross talking as soon as it occurs by using the skill of *immediacy* and saying something like "I am having difficulty tracking what is being said right now because two conversations are occurring simultaneously. Is anyone else having the same experience?" or "Can you say a little about why you are talking at the same time your colleague is trying to express herself?"

Group Member Intellectualizes

Intellectualizing is sometimes an indication of resistance or apprehension on the part of a member of the group. This could occur because the focus of the conversation is one that is threatening or uncomfortable and the member does not know what to say or does not want to share personal information relating to the discussion that is occurring. It may seem easier to depersonalize the discussion by addressing it on a theoretical level devoid of any indication of current thoughts, feelings, behaviors, or problems. Doing so can disrupt other members of the group or make members feel awkward about what has been shared. The leader may need to say something like "I notice that you seem to be uncomfortable with what the group is discussing and are avoiding disclosing your feelings. Can you say a little about that?" or "I have the impression that the topic under discussion right now is making you uneasy. Could you talk a little about the observation I've described?"

Group Member Uses Humor to Sidetrack the Discussion

The member who can get the group laughing helps relieve tension and lessens the intensity, pain, and discomfort that accompany the process of addressing issues. At times, the use of humor can provide an appropriate interlude or respite needed by group members and can help the group, or a member of the group, to refocus and continue exploring an issue or problem. At other times, humor can interfere with the therapeutic process and group dynamics and, if left unaddressed, can interfere with progress the group has made. The group leader must assess whether a member's use of humor is appropriate or keeps getting in the way of here-and-now discussion. The group leader may need to say something like "I'm noticing that, whenever our discussions become intense and feeling laden, you divert the group with your use of humor. Have you noticed a similar pattern, and could you say a little about what this may mean for you?"

Group Member Suggests "I'll Wait, and It Will Change"

Frequently, group members are willing to discuss their self-defeating behavior during a group session but are not willing to try to change outside the group. At times, they take the position that if they postpone action, problems will correct themselves. A competent group leader will use *initiating* to help members develop strategies for doing something about their problems outside the group and will assign *homework* as a means of tracking or checking with members to evaluate their progress.

Group Member Shows Discrepant Behavior

When discrepancies appear in a member's behavior, the group leader must intervene. Discrepancies may arise between what a member is currently saying and what he or she said earlier, in a lack of congruence between what a member is saying and what he or she is doing in the group, in a difference between how a member sees himself or herself and how others in the group see him or her, or in a difference between how a member reports feelings and how his or her nonverbal cues communicate what is going on inside. The statements a leader uses to identify discrepancies may be *confrontational* in nature because the leader usually needs to describe the discrepancies so that the group member can begin to identify, evaluate, and change aspects of the behavior.

Group Member Bores the Group by Rambling

Sometimes members use talking as a way of seeking approval, and it may become "overtalk." In response, the leader might ask other members to give *feedback* to the "intellectualizer" to let him or her know how the rambling affects them. If this behavior is not addressed, other members may become angry and hostile toward the offender and toward the leader.

Group Member Cries

Sometimes group leaders, especially those who are just beginning to lead groups, see the member who cries as "difficult." Maybe the perceived difficulty is related more to the discomfort of the group leader and to his or her uncertainty about how to respond than it is to this behavior on the part of the group member. When a member of the group cries, it could be because the member is attempting to convey feelings that are painful and anxiety laden. Or a member might cry because what another member is sharing is similar to his or her own unresolved feelings or issues.

The leader must decide whether to focus on the crying member. The leader should ask the member if he or she would like to "process" the emotions and thoughts behind the tears or let some time pass before doing so. An important consideration on the leader's part relates to the amount of time left in the group session. If time is short, the leader may have to acknowledge the member's pain and, if the member wants to share, structure the sharing so that the member deals with only one aspect of his or her feelings, with the understanding that there will be time during the next session to continue.

The following are the most important guidelines for the leader:

1. Acknowledge the tears.
2. Ask for permission to work with the member and give him or her some time to regain composure, if that is what the member seems to need.
3. Avoid exploring too many areas and making the member feel vulnerable if there is not sufficient time to attain closure near the end of the session.

SIDEBAR 3.5
Difficult Group Members

Reread the discussion on Dealing with Difficult Members and pick the three member behaviors you think would be the most troublesome for you to handle. Think about what would make these member behaviors difficult for you. How can you improve your ability to respond to the member behaviors you have identified? What assistance might you need from your personal counselor, your supervisor, or both?

Summary

The group leader's style, personality, experience, and skills have many ramifications for group experiences and outcomes. The three classic leadership styles that Lewin identified—authoritarian, democratic, and laissez-faire—may relate somewhat to the group's purpose and its composition. In another conceptualization, groups can be viewed as leader centered or group centered. A third way of looking at leadership style is to characterize it as interpersonal or intrapersonal. Group members tend to admire leaders who have charisma, though this carries the danger of the leader's relying too much on this characteristic and failing to facilitate the autonomy of group members. Leaders are encouraged to develop their own unique styles through self-awareness, an understanding of their own personal traits and qualities, and the acquisition of specific skills common to all group needs.

In planning for a group experience, leaders should conduct pregroup screening, which may be done through interviews or completion of questionnaires, to select members whose needs and goals are compatible with those of the intended group and who will not be detrimental to other group members or themselves. During pregroup screening, potential members should receive full information about all aspects of the group and what to expect.

When organizing meetings for a group, the leader has to consider the physical setting, the length and frequency of meetings, and the size of the group (within a recommended range of 5 to 10 members). Other organizational aspects may include weekly summaries, written material, movies or videotapes, and pregroup training sessions.

Among the various roles that members assume within a group are maintenance, blocking, and facilitative roles, as well as subroles of each category. The leader must be able to recognize these roles and intervene appropriately. The leader also must apply a repertoire of skills in leading each of the stages in a group's development. In a group's life, the leader likely will encounter difficult members and behaviors, which he or she must counteract to ensure that the group progresses as intended from beginning to termination.

CHAPTER

4

Group Work: Theories and Applications

Jeannie Falkner, David Capuzzi, and Mark D. Stauffer

The group procedures class was just beginning, and Dr. Patel asked if anyone had questions about the material the students read prior to class. Alisha, a first-year student, raised her hand and said she was confused about the information dealing with theory applied to groups. When Dr. Patel asked Alisha to be more specific in her question, Alisha said that when she had taken the counseling theory class last semester, she had understood that the various counseling theories had been developed to work with the individual, and that the research done in developing these theories was all completed on individual cases. Her confusion resulted from the author of the assigned material seeming to simply transfer these theoretical concepts from the individual to the group.

Alisha's question was "How do I transfer these individual concepts into a group of eight or ten members?" Dr. Patel's response—"Carefully"—brought laughter from the class. He continued, however, by stating that Alisha had a good question—one that continues to concern even the most experienced group leaders. This scenario probably has taken place, in one form or another, in every group class.

Confusion about how to transfer individual counseling theory to groups plagues students, as well as professionals who operate in the broad arena of group counseling or therapy. Authors such as Capuzzi and Stauffer (2016), Corey (2016), Gladding (2015), and Yalom (2005) all have addressed these difficulties and caution the counselor about making the transition from individual to group counseling. These difficulties should not be interpreted to mean that transferability is impossible, however. On the contrary, current practice indicates that most theoretical/ therapeutic systems have been applied, with varying degrees of success, across both individual and group counseling.

Many of the factors that dictate the selection of one or more theoretical/therapeutic systems in the individual realm also apply in the group domain (Capuzzi & Stauffer, 2016; Yalom, 2005). The selection of a theoretical system is often based on the counselor's philosophical position and his or her beliefs about the nature of the individual as it relates to development and change. The counselor's preferred theory can also reflect his or her education, work background, style of leadership, and cultural identity. At this juncture in your development as a group leader, you should familiarize yourself with the most prominent theories and notice which one or ones seem to be most appealing to you, as well as which ones best fit your style and your desired practice setting. Regardless of the reasons for selecting any theoretical system, those who choose to work with groups should do so with a basis in theory. Theory provides a foundation for understanding what could be happening with group members and the group. Theory also provides a cognitive roadmap for selecting appropriate interventions for members to meet their goals.

In this chapter, you will explore selected theoretical/therapeutic systems and their application to groups. This discussion is followed by an integration of the theoretical concepts, leader behaviors, group stages and process, and strategies for change. Let's get started!

THEORETICAL SYSTEMS

Although all the major theoretical/therapeutic systems have been adapted for the group modality, we have limited our discussion to six systems that are widely accepted in the group setting and have applicability and adaptability for developing short-term group models. The six systems are Adlerian, psychodrama, Gestalt, cognitive behavioral, transactional analysis, and solution-focused therapy. We will present the basic concepts of each theory, followed by expected leader behaviors, group processes, and techniques drawn from each concept that are applicable to group counseling. You may want to make some brief notes as you review each theory and how you might see yourself applying the theory to a group you might lead.

Adlerian Theory

Adlerian psychology is both an individual and a social psychology. Adler assumed the individual to be purposeful and goal directed and not destined by heredity, environmental stress, or early sexual impressions. Instead, through their creative power and self-determination, individuals are believed to be able to achieve a deeper understanding and "perception of self through the development of physical, intellectual, social, occupational, emotional, and spiritual capacities" (Pomeroy & Clark, 2015, p. 25). According to Dufrene, Henderson, and Eckart (2016), Adlerian psychology is a social psychology interested in a person's beliefs and perceptions and how one's self-perception interconnects with and impacts others. Adlerian theory is one of the few theories interested in reciprocal

---

SIDEBAR 4.1
Theories that Appeal to You

As you continue to develop your professional identity, consider your life experiences, working background, cultural identity, and what you have learned about your style of leadership in Chapter 3. As you reflect on your leadership style, consider what you believe about how problems arise and the nature of change. Some theories focus on the role of the past, some on problem solving and finding solutions, some are based on encouragement, and some on rational and logical thinking and problem solving. With these factors in mind, make some notes about each theory applied to group work and which ones most appeal to you.

processes in the home, school, and workplace. Hamm, Carlson, and Erguner-Tekinalp (2016) further suggest that social interest and the emphasis on community comprise possibly the most distinctive and valuable concept in Adlerian psychology. The social perception involves individuals' attitudes in dealing with the social world and includes concern and striving for a better world for all. Based on this social interest, individuals strive to master three main tasks as they move through life: their relationships with society, work, and love. Most counselors find this social system perspective fits nicely with the wellness paradigm in counseling. As an Adlerian group leader, with these fundamental assumptions in mind, you would listen carefully as your group members

- strive from a perceived negative (inferiority) to a hoped-for positive (superiority) position in life,
- strive in the direction of a unique goal or ideal self,
- strive to belong in one's social world,
- strive to understand one's spiritual nature, and
- strive to better comprehend the "I" and "me" aspects of self.

None of these motivating forces stands alone. They are interrelated, and movement in one area impacts movement in another. In other words, the individual's sense of self is in context to his or her perceived social context.

THE FAMILY AND SOCIAL CONTEXT   The Adlerian group counselor works to understand each group member's family-of-origin influences in areas in which they are frustrated in achieving their goals. Adler (1938) believed that problems were derived from childhood experience of thwarted acceptance within the family structure. Feelings of inferiority were thought to be common in children because of the dependent, small, and socially inferior position they hold in the family and in society. Several factors influence this early narrative and may impede the individual's development toward a more genuine way of being; these would be areas for the group leader to explore. These factors include

1. fictional goals (unconscious assumptions regarding what must be done to develop worth as an individual, such as striving for superiority),
2. birth order (the individual's chronological and psychological position within the family), and
3. the family constellation/atmosphere (variables related to personality, relationships, developmental issues, structural factors, attitudes, and values within the family).

This early family representation serves as the child's schema for life. This pattern is the reference point for the individual's attitudes, behaviors, and view of self, others, and community. The pattern or *style of life* is goal oriented and characterized by positive growth and development or characterized by maladjustment. If individuals base their style of life on faulty self-assumptions, they may find they are unable to achieve self-confidence, gratifying relationships, and satisfying work and may often lack connectedness to community. The key to understanding group members rests in conceptualizing their perceptions and interpretations of self in context, which translate into member goals. Thus, group members bring to the group "non-conscious, embodied, implicit memories of how relationships work based on early relational experience, trauma, and other social learning from families, school, work, culture, etc." (Adler, 2013, p. 150). Group counseling provides a social milieu in which these unconscious patterns may come to life in the here and now for examination and possible reorientation. The Adlerian group leader provides insight and encouragement to the group members for each to create a more authentic self-concept and to work toward more fulfilling life goals.

CONCEPTS TRANSLATED INTO LEADER BEHAVIORS   Based on Adlerian concepts, the group leader must be able to

- establish a working relationship in which the leader and members are collaborative,
- serve as models for group members,
- communicate to the members feelings of mutual trust and respect,
- aid the members in exploring the personal goals, beliefs, feelings, and motives that are determining factors in the development of the members' style of life,
- assist the members in gaining insight into their fictitious goals and their self-defeating behaviors,
- aid members in accepting themselves with the assets and the liabilities that make up the self,
- help members accept responsibility for their freedom and personal effectiveness,
- aid members in considering alternative lifestyles and assist them in strengthening their commitment to change,
- help members enhance their involvement with others and extend their social interest as this applies to self and others,
- assist members in developing a sense of belonging and a sense of community because their self-meaning is tied closely to their social purpose, and
- aid members in exploring alternative behaviors and gaining new insights and empower them to put these behaviors and insights into action.

GROUP STAGES AND TECHNIQUES   According to Hamm et al. (2016) and Sonstegard and Bitter (2004), the Adlerian approach to working with groups can be described in four stages, each with a purpose and task. As with all group work, stages may not always occur but may emerge simultaneously with the growth and development of the group. The four stages are as follows:

- *Stage 1, engagement and connection:* The counselor and group members must create a trusting relationship providing warmth, empathy, and acceptance.
- *Stage 2, assessment:* Members of the group are encouraged to speak about their early family experiences to reveal their overall style of life patterns. The Adlerian group counselor assists the group members to discover *fictional goals*, which are roadblocks to enhanced self-worth and a sense of belonging.
- *Stage 3, insight and interpretation:* Members are encouraged to examine their erroneous self-assumptions and develop new ways of making meaning of their current situation. The group leader may use Socratic questioning to promote creative future visions with enhanced confidence and self-worth.
- *Stage 4, reorientation:* The group counselor will encourage the members to engage in authentic actions that support new insights and connection to self, others, and society in ways that increase a sense of belonging.

In each of these stages, certain techniques enhance group members' growth and development. These techniques are not limited to only one stage, however. Their use throughout the group process is highly effective in bringing forth positive group interaction. The following is a summary of techniques that may aid the Adlerian group leader in enhancing growth and development within the group:

- Model appropriate social skills and show interest to demonstrate acceptance.
- Create contracts to demonstrate the equality of the leader–member relationship.
- Use active listening skills (e.g., restatement, reflection, summarization).
- Employ visual imagery to help members clarify and put into concrete terms some of the absurdities of their thinking and behavior.
- Elicit early recollections to aid members in identifying emotional patterns and feelings and discovering the basis for negatives carried from childhood into adulthood.
- Make use of paradoxical intention by having members attempt to increase debilitating thoughts and behaviors.
- Use confrontation in a constructive fashion, pointing out discrepancies between what group members say and their actions.
- Assess members' current functioning in work and social relationships.
- Assess members' goals and how they translate into individual lifestyles.
- Observe members' interactions, which may be descriptive of their feelings regarding the self and their development of social skills.
- Observe members' nonverbal behaviors, and do not hesitate to interpret from these observations.

In summary, Adlerian group counseling is both individual and social psychology focused on a person's beliefs and self-perceptions. The Adlerian group leader's goal is to guide group members to value themselves. Encouragement and insight are utilized to transform group members from feelings of inferiority to feelings of self-confidence with active engagement in a supportive community.

Psychodrama

Created and developed by Jacob L. Moreno in the 1920s and 1930s, *psychodrama* is an action-oriented and spontaneous approach that emerged from Moreno's work in the theater.

SIDEBAR 4.2
Adlerian Counseling Techniques

Clearly, the list in this section is not an exhaustive list of techniques associated with Adlerian counseling. Both Bitter and Main (2011) and Dufrene et al. (2016) identified additional techniques that have applications in Adlerian groups, including the following:

- The question
- Catching oneself

- Lifestyle assessment
- Methods of encouragement
- Paradoxical intention
- Acting as if

If Adler's theory of counseling applied to group work appeals to you, we encourage you to learn more at http://www.AlfredAdler.org.

The precursor of psychodrama was the Theater of Spontaneity, which Moreno created in Vienna in 1921 to entertain a variety of audiences. Moreno encouraged his young actors to develop improvisational presentations on current issues of the day. This spontaneous acting proved to be cathartic for the actors and audiences alike. In 1925, Moreno moved to New York, where he began to use this extemporaneous drama technique to work with groups of patients in hospitals. Moreno, along with his wife, Zerka, continued to develop, practice, and teach psychodrama until his death in 1974 (Moreno, 1987).

The foundation of psychodrama rests in role theory and the relationships that individuals have with others, their views of others, and the psychological distance between individuals based on both their relationships and their viewpoints. In other words, the group counselor uses theatrical staging techniques to help group members discover restrictive roles, which may be the source of challenging relationships in their lives. Psychodrama can be conceptualized as a process of externalizing the internalized process of a group member that otherwise may be difficult to express in words. This approach requires a group member (called the *protagonist*) to spontaneously act out his or her problems(s) with the assistance of the group leader (called the *director*) and other members of the group (called *auxiliaries*, or *the audience*).

Let's look at how this concept might play out in the group encounter. The protagonist, with the assistance of the group leader as the director, identifies the situation and/or relationship of concern, creates the scenario to be acted out, and selects other group members to play roles in the scenario. A member might be selected to play the protagonist's double, another his son, and another his wife. The auxiliaries playing the identified family members may give spontaneous voice to the role or be coached by the director and the protagonist. Once the scenario has been established, the group leader (director) facilitates the psychodrama, much like a director might do during a scene rehearsal for a movie production, thus bringing the protagonist's relationships to life in the here and now. In this example, the father (the protagonist whose role as father is to be explored) hears his double (the member speaking as if he was the father) spontaneously saying, "I'm scared to let you make your own decisions, son, because you have made so many serious mistakes. I don't want to lose you." The protagonist looks at his double with tears in his eyes as he slowly takes in this new perspective.

Cathartic moments such as this one are created to amplify feelings, increase insight, and provide group members opportunities for creating new behaviors. When the encounter is completed, the group provides feedback for the protagonist as group members reflect on their experience in the psychodrama encounter. Support for the protagonist is provided as he processes his new self-awareness and searches for options in a modified role as father that incorporates new, more productive behaviors.

CONCEPTS TRANSLATED INTO LEADER BEHAVIORS   Based on psychodrama concepts, the group leader must be able to

- establish a working relationship within the group, based upon equality,
- establish a group atmosphere that is accepting and tolerant of change,
- establish a format within the group that allows group members to identify and work on significant issues in their lives,
- spontaneously create direct encounters, which elicit responses that provide a degree of "newness" for a past situation,

- encourage group members to risk aspects of self in playing out the psychodrama,
- provide protection for group members from abuse that may arise from playing out the psychodrama,
- utilize his or her creativity as a model for members of the group and encourage group members in their own creative development,
- utilize his or her knowledge and skill in directing all aspects of the psychodramatic enactment,
- cultivate the ability to actively direct an ongoing emotional drama that could entail, but should not be limited to, actor movement, role switching, role creation, and drama reconstruction,
- be prepared to cast various group members effectively in roles that will enhance the ongoing psychodrama process,
- effectively weave members of the audience into roles as auxiliaries or alter egos for the protagonist,
- determine which of the myriad techniques available within psychodrama are best suited to which types of presenting problems, relationships, and concerns, and
- aid all participants in desensitizing the emotional impact of the psychodrama enactment during closure.

GROUP STAGES AND TECHNIQUES   Psychodrama, like all group counseling, progresses through predictable stages, with each stage allotted certain tasks. The first stage in a psychodrama is called the *warm-up.* Its purpose is to make sure that the group leader is ready to lead the group and that the group members (protagonist, auxiliaries, audience) are ready to be led. According to Blatner (2007), the warm-up may be done either verbally or through structured activities. Once the group leader determines the group is ready, the group moves to the *action* phase.

Action involves the actual psychodrama played out for the group, as you saw in the previous example. The group leader as director aids in setting the scene, assists the other members (auxiliaries) with their roles, encourages role change within the acting-out phase of the scenario, helps the protagonist to expand his or her emotional response pattern, and encourages the protagonist to work through the situation by trying out alternative attitudes, behaviors, and emotional responses. In other words, this might be compared to the working stage of group process.

The third and last stage, *sharing*, allows for group feedback and reflection for the protagonist. The group (audience and auxiliaries) is encouraged to provide the protagonist with personal, supportive, and constructive affective feedback. As you saw in the earlier example, emphasis initially is on the emotional aspects of the enactment. In this stage, the emphasis may be directed to a more cognitive assimilation of the experience. The goal is to encourage the protagonist with ways to act differently in the future if similar situations arise (Chung, 2013).

Although advanced training is needed to conduct a psychodrama, many of Moreno's techniques (see, e.g., Moreno, 1987) have been expanded and incorporated into a variety of counseling settings. Role theory and role play are now widely used in counseling and educational settings (Crane & Baggerly, 2014). Techniques such as the *empty-chair* technique in Gestalt originated from the *auxiliary chair* technique in psychodrama. Many contemporary expressive therapies that rely on creativity and spontaneity, such as play therapy for children, art therapy, and music/movement therapy, have their roots in psychodrama theory, methods, and techniques.

Special techniques identified by Corey (2016) and Haley, Golden, and Nate (2016) that have application in psychodrama groups include, but are not limited to, the following:

- Monodrama
- Role reversal
- The double and multiple double
- The mirror technique
- The magic shop
- The soliloquy technique
- Family sculpting

For more information on psychodrama and these specific techniques, visit http://www.asgpp.org/index.php.

Gestalt Theory

Gestalt counseling or therapy is rooted in *Gestalt psychology*, a school of perception that originated in Europe before World War I. Gestalt psychology began with the study of the perceptual field as a whole. Using the body of knowledge collected in this academic field, Fritz and Laura Perls translated the perceptual approach to psychology into Gestalt therapy, which moved it from the primarily academic realm into the arena of counseling.

Gestalt counseling is both existential and phenomenological. The individual is considered fully responsible for determining the essence of his or her being and reality. Beyond accepting responsibility for the problems created by their decisions, individuals must accept the responsibility of dealing effectively with these problems. Gestalt is also phenomenological as the subjective life experience is thought to give a person meaning and purpose.

An important concept for the Gestalt counselor is the principle of *holism*: the individual's interdependent combination of *body* and *spirit* and his or her relationship to the environment. The individual continually strives to achieve balance or equilibrium. According to Polster and Polster (1973), this striving for balance provides the individual with a sense of order. When the individual perceives a need, a state of disequilibrium is created and order is temporarily lost as the perceived need demands the individual's focus. Through the individual's *aggressive capacity* or *drive*, he or she can interact with the environment and find what is needed for growth and change. When that need is met, balance and order are once again attained until a new need emerges.

These same three aspects (body, spirit, and aggressive capacity) play a role in the development of dysfunctional behavior. Instead of using these aspects for growth, the individual uses them to protect him- or herself against real or imagined threats and in so doing develops defense structures that prevent positive growth and change. Some of these defensive behaviors include *introjection*, *projection*, *retroflection*, *deflection*, and *dichotomies*, which then become barriers to the individual's authentic growth and development.

The major goal of counseling is to help individuals attain a greater awareness of these artificial boundaries (defenses) and become more aware of their potential, which, in turn, will allow individuals to exercise their potential in positive growth and change (Yontef & Jacobs, 2014). According to Haley et al. (2016), intervention strategies are *experiments* that emerge from the cooperative relationship between the client and the counselor. The experiments are procedures aimed at discovery and are conducted with a here and now that deals with present functioning. By dealing with behaviors in the here and now, through sensing, feeling, and experiencing any restrictions (defenses), the individual can move through the impasse and reformulate his or her awareness for more productive results. According to Haley et al. (2016) and Yontef and Jacobs (2014), the purpose of experiments is to bring into focus that which remains on the periphery of awareness, identify those defenses prohibiting knowing, shed light on what is needed, and empower the individual to take charge of the process.

To enhance their effectiveness in aiding clients in this experimental process, counselors may adhere to some of the major principles of Gestalt (Gladding, 2015):

- Focus on the present rather than the past.
- Experience what is real, not imagined.
- Notice where energy may be blocked.
- Listen carefully to language that inhibits potential, such as "can't" or "should."
- Be open to both the unpleasant and the pleasant experience.
- Be authentic. Claim who you are.

CONCEPTS TRANSLATED INTO LEADER BEHAVIORS Gestalt therapy, as originally practiced by Perls (1969), would be considered overly confrontational by current counseling practices. However, according to Frew (2013) and Yontef and Jacobs (2014), the role of the Gestalt counselor is changing based on a softening or changing emphasis among Gestalt practitioners. Approaches that emphasize support, acceptance, compassion, and kindness with less emphasis on direct confrontation are more accepted. Based on these past and contemporary trends, the Gestalt group leader must be able to

- establish an environment in which leader and members share equally in the process of change,
- establish an environment that is supportive, compassionate, accepting, and challenging,
- allow members to find their own way in life and accept the responsibility that goes with this,
- focus members on their experiences in the present moment (the here and now),
- recognize the blocks and boundaries that impede members' growth and be willing to bring them to the members' attention,
- aid members in accepting all aspects of themselves and encourage their sharing of hidden and self-disguised aspects of self,
- assist members in understanding, accepting, and dealing with the concept that they are responsible for their existence,
- confront members with their defensive structures and their unwillingness to take responsibility for self,
- aid members, through exercises, in addressing the unfinished business in their lives,

- help members try out new forms of behavior, to open themselves to the full spectrum of their being, and
- help members recognize the splintered parts of the self and work toward integrating these parts.

GROUP STAGES AND TECHNIQUES   Perls (1969) never claimed to conduct group therapy; he emphasized one-on-one work in a group setting, much like his training workshops for professionals. Although Gestalt group counseling allows for creativity, spontaneity, and inventiveness (much like psychodrama), it is not necessarily based on a set of techniques that can be quantified. The first stage of any group must be to create an atmosphere of safety. For group members to engage in the experiments suggested by the group leader or to be willing to risk the here-and-now experience, the group leader must educate the members about expectations and goals for the group and the group members. Preparing the members for risk taking within a supportive atmosphere is imperative.

The second or transitional stage of the group might include a series of experiments that challenge members to shed defenses and be in the present. Naranjo (1993/ 2007) described the goal as "taking the responsibility for our present actions and omissions" and said that "the way toward organismic self-regulation is letting go of the armor of conditioned personality this very moment" (p. 131). The leader is actively involved with members of the group and, for example, may direct exaggerations of the members' "defenses" to intensify the feelings associated with the behaviors. The use of confrontational skills to startle or shock members into greater awareness of their self-defeating behaviors is not unexpected. Counselors who are not trained in Gestalt therapy may be uncomfortable in this process because, unlike in other theories, feelings such as embarrassment, remorse, and anxiety are not considered authentic but are seen as the result of attitudes that diffuse, deny, or resist reality (Naranjo, 2007).

As mentioned in this section, most counselors will adopt more accepting experiments aimed at the same goals of authenticity. Many special techniques, such as the empty chair, have been incorporated into associated theoretical orientations. Some of these special techniques (experiments) identified by Corey (2016), Gladding (2015), and Haley et al. (2016) as having application in a Gestalt group include, but are not limited to, floating hot seat, dialoging with self and others, playing the projection, letting the little child talk, dream work, the empty-chair or two-chair strategy, unfinished business, and fantasy approaches.

For more specific information on Gestalt therapy strategies and techniques, visit http://newyorkgestalt.org.

SIDEBAR 4.3
Theories and Leadership Goals

Select one of the three theories applied to group work covered so far (Adlerian, psychodrama, or Gestalt). Imagine you are the group leader. Describe the goal(s) of the group in terms of expected outcome (changes) for the members. Note what you will focus on in each stage of the group process. Name two or three techniques you might select that are synonymous with your chosen theoretical orientation. Compare this description to your response in Sidebar 4.1.

Transactional Analysis

Unlike many counseling theories that were developed for individuals and adapted for group work, transactional analysis (TA), discussed here, and psychodrama, discussed previously, were designed specifically for groups. TA is based on ideas and concepts developed by Eric Berne (1961, 1964) and "was a bold step in linking the intrapsychic and interpersonal." (Eusden & Pierini, 2015, p. 128). Eusden and Pierini note that Berne's work has evolved and that many contemporary writers have taken transactional analysis "into the relational and intersubjective realms of psychotherapy" (p. 219). One school resulting from such evolution of TA is Bob and Mary Goulding's redecision therapy (Goulding & Goulding, 1979; Joines, 2010), which combines strategies from Gestalt, psychodrama, and cognitive behavioral therapy into a strengths approach that empowers group members to enhance self-awareness, change early-script decisions, and move toward a goal-directed future.

Like Adler and Moreno, Berne thought the experience of the child in the family system was the source of the individual's challenges. According to TA, the three ego states—Parent, Adult, and Child—form early in life, and each carries with it a script or pattern for how a person is to behave, think, and feel. The developing individual takes in messages—verbal and nonverbal—delivered by the environment and by significant people within that environment, processes those messages, and develops from them a set of scripts that form the framework for the individual's behavior (Joines, 2016). Individuals are not passive in this process; they may adjust to the environmental pressures with compliance, rebellion, or some combination of adaptive responses. Although these adaptations in behavior and cognition serve a purpose in the current relational environment, the early decisions may become barriers to relationships and opportunities in later life (Eusden & Pierini, 2015; Joines, 2016).

The important key concepts that are the foundation and cognitive roadmap used in both TA and redecision are as follows:

- Ego states
- Strokes
- Injunctions
- Decisions
- Script formation
- Life positions

The first key concept of TA is that of ego states. A theory contends that the ego states (Parent, Adult, and Child) are the foundation for personality. Berne (1961) defined an *ego state* as "a consistent pattern of feeling and experience directly related to a corresponding consistent pattern of behavior" (p. 13). From these ego states, individuals build the cognitive, affective, and behavioral dynamics that direct their lives. Ego states can be observed and identified phenomenologically through behavior. The *Parent ego state* consists of both a nurturing and a critical component. It functions to provide caring, rules, regulation. The *Adult ego state* is the reality-oriented and logical part of the person. It receives and processes information and does its best to make the best decisions possible. The *Child ego state* consists of an *adapted child* and the *natural child* and is considered to contain powerful affective memories. As development proceeds, these ego states, although separate and distinct, interplay with one another and, based upon internalized scripts, form the basis of behavior.

The second key concept of TA, *strokes*, is defined as units of positive or negative attention that stimulate the individual and serve as a motivational force for human interaction. This attention may be positive or negative. Strokes may stem from both internal and external sources, and if strokes are not readily available, the individual may devise *games* and *rackets* (transactions that allow the individual to gain needed strokes) to provide this motivational force.

The next three concepts—injunctions, decisions, and script formation—are most easily understood in combination. *Injunctions* are parental messages that children receive at an early age. These messages are generally prescriptive in terms of ways of being: "Don't be, don't feel, don't love, don't trust." Upon hearing and processing these messages, the child makes *decisions* in response to the parental demands. Based on these decisions, the child *forms a script* for living his or her life. If the messages are reinforced and repeated, the foundation for this early scripting becomes a lifelong pattern.

The last of the major concepts, *life positions* represent the resolution of the three-part process of injunctions, decisions, and script formation. Life positions form the framework within which individuals structure and operate the behavioral, cognitive, and affective domains of their lives.

CONCEPTS TRANSLATED INTO LEADER BEHAVIORS   Based on TA concepts, the TA group leader must be able to

- develop a therapeutic contract with the group members that emphasizes equality and identifies the goals to which the leader and members mutually agree,
- analyze at least four elements in group members' communications: (1) structures, (2) transactions, (3) games, and (4) scripts,
- enhance group members' awareness of their scripts that result from early decisions and their power and ability to change these scripts,
- provide permission, protection, and power for members as they examine old patterns and create new, more authentic ways of living,
- reinforce the redecisions that group members make during the group process and encourage them to act upon these redecisions, and
- enhance group members' autonomy to reduce dependence on the leader or on other group members.

GROUP STAGES AND TECHNIQUES   Berne (1966) differentiated "group treatment" from "group process" (p. 315); group treatment focuses on contract fulfillment within the group setting, whereas group process is interpersonal and relational with attention directed toward group dynamics and less toward the individual. This resulted in the TA group sometimes feeling impersonal with the leader's attention focused on the resolution of the individual member's concern to the detriment of the interpersonal process of the group. More recently, Joines (2016) has suggested a combination of TA group work that provides a strategy for brief effective individual change with group-as-a-whole strategies that allow the group to provide a corrective experience in a social microcosm beyond the individual's new scripting. Building on Berne's (1961) four stages of *imago* (Latin for *image*) adjustment, the TA group leader may view the individual's development as parallel to Tuckman's (1965) developmental stages (forming, storming, norming, performing), with the following four stages:

- *Stage 1*, the provisional imago, when the individual expectation and fantasy of the group emerges early in the group formation
- *Stage 2*, the adapted imago, when the individual begins to see the group for who and what it is
- *Stage 3*, the operative imago, as the individual begins to compete for need fulfillment
- *Stage 4*, the secondary adjustment imago, during which the individual accepts a realistic assessment and acceptance of self and group

This combination of leader attention to the individual development in conjunction with group development may prove to add depth and richness to earlier models of TA group work.

In summary, transactional analysis is a humanistic approach based on the philosophy that individuals are inherently okay and have the potential and the desire to move toward a positive, growth-oriented position. This potential, however, is sometimes stifled because of early adaptations and decisions that require a reorientation for individuals to move toward their growth potential. To do so, individuals must become aware of their current scripting and how it impacts their way of being. An important element is the solidification of the member's personal power and ability to change the scripts and to create for her- or himself a more positive and productive way of living.

Special techniques that have application in TA-oriented group work have been identified by Capuzzi and Stauffer (2016), Eusden and Pierini (2015), and Joines (2010). These techniques include, but are not limited to, the following:

- Analysis of rituals and pastimes
- Life-script analysis
- Game analysis
- Redecision contracting
- Therapeutic contracting
- Closing escape hatches

SIDEBAR 4.4

What Might a Redecision Group Look Like?

Let's look at an example of a redecision group session. Whereas in psychodrama the group might participate in the reenactment, in redecision only the group leader and the individual will engage as the group observes the work. As the group leader listens to a group member at risk of losing his job due to being late repeatedly on major projects, she or he may hypothesize that there is an internal conflict between ego stages. An experiential exercise might have the individual's internal Parent (what he imagines his father would say) discuss work and responsibility. The Parent voice might say "Always finish what you start and be on time!" As the group member replies from a childlike position, he may find himself responding "You can't make me!" This internal struggle is often hidden from the conscious awareness of the individual until the scene is replayed during the group session. As the group member becomes aware of the impasse, options for new behaviors become available to him.

If learning more about TA and redecision therapy is of interest to you, you may want to visit http://www.seinstitute.com/redecision-therapy.

Cognitive Behavioral Therapy

Most counselors integrate some form of cognitive behavioral therapy (CBT) into their counseling practice today. According to Powers and Kalodner (2016), there is no single CBT theory but, rather, many associated theories that share mutual assumptions. Basic to all CBT is the fundamental work of Beck (1976), which first stressed the influential role of cognition in behavior and is considered by many to be the first CBT-oriented theory.

The underlying principle of all CBT is that thoughts (cognitions) lead to behaviors. Individuals are thought to hold a mixture of conditioned beliefs that have been learned and are assumed to be categorically true (Sauer-Zavala et al., 2017). The counselor is in a position of authority to challenge the client's conditioned belief processes and initiate interventions that may be directive and often psychoeducational in nature. Miller and Rollnick (2009) posit that "the expertise of CBT provider[s] is based on their knowledge of and technical skill in applying principles of learning" (p. 134). Thus, the CBT group leader will be commissioned to identify and challenge such erroneous thinking. To do so, group leaders use a behavioral assessment to gather detailed information about the problem. Behavioral assessments are specific and generally do not include a more descriptive evaluation of the client's overall personality. Cognitive behavioral assessments may include worksheets to help the counselor understand the nature of the problem. The client's life situation, altered thinking about the problematic situation, and feelings elicited by the thought process and resulting behaviors are carefully tracked. After gathering information from the behavioral assessment, the group leader will challenge the client to recognize maladaptive patterns of thinking. When new patterns of thinking are shaped and the undesired behavior is changed or eliminated, the problem is considered resolved.

More recently, counselors have gravitated to an approach that is more collaborative and less directive in challenging cognitions. Federici, Rowa, and Antony (2010) noted that counselors using more traditional CBT frameworks sometimes "encounter ambivalence, poor homework compliance, and premature treatment dropout" (p. 11). This led to a new paradigm, which is considered the third wave of CBT. The inclusion of empirically based practices such as mindfulness-based stress reduction (MBSR), mindfulness-based cognitive therapy (MBCT), and acceptance and commitment therapy (ACT) have expanded the role of CBT beyond its early limitations. This latest generation of CBT has incorporated a holistic perspective and acceptance of client thoughts with a new emphasis on exploring the meaning behind the client thought processes (Sauer-Zavala et al., 2017). Acceptance-based behavioral therapies adopt a present-focused awareness of the client's inner processes without judgement. A desired outcome is cognitive diffusion, which empowers the client to review his or her own thought process and act as the authority of his or her own experience. Cultivating mindfulness, reducing internal dissonance, and increasing psychological flexibility all are factors thought to promote behavioral change (Arch, Wolitzky-Taylor, Eifert, & Craske, 2012). As the growth of CBT continues to evolve, new techniques and strategies will likely be integrated into the expanding category of cognitive behavioral strategies in group work.

CONCEPTS TRANSLATED INTO LEADER BEHAVIORS   Based on CBT concepts, the CBT leader will

- develop a group climate that is genuine, instructional, didactic, and accepting,
- create behavioral assessments to identify problematic behaviors,

- instruct group members about the nature of faulty thinking and the relationship between cognition and behavior,
- confront faulty thinking related to problem behaviors and instruct group members to do so as well, and
- help group members identify specific measurable goals to address maladaptive behavior.

If incorporating MBSR, MBCT, or ACT components of CBT, the leader may also encourage self-acceptance and nonjudgmental exploration of thoughts and teach mindfulness-based stress-reduction techniques.

GROUP STAGES AND TECHNIQUES   Traditional CBT brief counseling groups are ideal for psychoeducation group counseling in which a curriculum and planned exercises are used to educate and instruct group members. Group members can learn to identify and change the thinking that directs the undesired behavior and ultimately modify the behavior (Nielsen, 2015).

During the initial stage, the leader will be directive and instruct group members in CBT concepts. Behavioral assessments may be initiated to further identify problems presented to the group for change. Once the leader has established a level of group trust and a commitment to the work appears solidified, the leader may employ behavioral rehearsals, cognitive restructuring exercises, and didactic problem-solving procedures (Corey, 2016). The group members provide social support and a forum for social learning. The final stage involves anchoring the learning though practice sessions, behavioral role rehearsals, and careful measurement of the progress.

Special techniques which are used in, but not unique to, CBT include the following:

- Behavioral assessment
- Homework assignments
- Thought records
- Core belief worksheets
- Coping cards
- Behavioral rehearsal
- Coaching

Solution-Focused Therapy

Solution-focused therapy (SFT), also referred to as *solution-focused brief therapy* (SFBT), was developed as a strengths-based model through the work of Steve de Shazer and Insoo

---

SIDEBAR 4.5

Planning an Adolescent Group Using CBT

Assume you are asked to design a group for adolescents struggling with self-esteem and at risk of academic failure. Your population will be high school students between the ages of 13 and 15 who are referred by the school counselor to the community mental health center where you are a student intern. Your supervisor asks you to design a CBT group for this population. Review the basic concepts of CBT presented in this chapter and briefly outline your plan for the group.

Kim Berg at the Brief Family Therapy Center in Milwaukee, Wisconsin (de Shazer, 1985; de Shazer et al., 2007). SFT is adaptable for individual, couples, and groups in a variety of settings and with diverse populations (Suitt, Franklin, & Kim, 2016).

SFT is founded on distinct principles very different from those underlying approaches such as interpersonal, psychodynamic, and cognitive behavioral models, which assume a problem must be thoroughly understood and examined prior to seeking a solution (Kim & Franklin, 2015; Proudlock & Wellman, 2011). SFT is future focused, with emphasis on client strengths rather than client problems. Although the SFT counselor will listen carefully in the beginning to client descriptions of the problem, the strategy is to quickly guide the client to identifying past successes, however small, rather than focusing on the manifestation of the problem.

Throughout the group, the leader will utilize techniques that highlight and reinforce client strengths (West-Olatunji & Rush-Ossenbeck, 2016). Identifying exceptions in the group member's experience—times when the identified problem was either less problematic or nonexistent—encourages the member to search for specific strategies that may again be called into action. In keeping with a brief therapy approach, leaders may utilize scaling questions to measure change and progress with a focus on continued movement toward effective solutions (Schmit, Schmit, & Lenz, 2016).

A limitation that has been noted is that client feelings may be overlooked in favor of finding and/or creating new ways of responding in future efforts to solve problems. For example, an SFT counselor may convert emotional references into "contextual and behavioral descriptions," which guide the client toward a future vision of when the feeling experience will be more pleasant (Kim & Franklin, 2015, p. 29). However, recent findings from positive psychology tend to support such a facilitation of positive emotions as an effective pathway for lasting behavioral change (Lipchik, Derks, LaCourt, & Nunnally, 2012).

CONCEPTS TRANSLATED INTO LEADER BEHAVIORS   Based on solution-focused concepts, the group leader will

- develop an open and collaborative working relationship within the group,
- foster an atmosphere that is positive, respectful, and hopeful,
- establish a format that is present oriented,
- focus on what is working, not on problems,
- help members take small steps toward clear, concise, and realistic goals,
- keep the group on task for solutions/possibilities,
- co-construct workable solutions with group members,
- encourage visualization of a future in which the problem is solved,
- harness the group members to facilitate the work, and
- take a "not-knowing" position.

GROUP STAGES AND TECHNIQUES   Because SFT is a brief model, the group may be limited to as few as three to five sessions (Proudlock & Wellman, 2011). The SFT group leader assumes that all clients have some knowledge of what would make their life better and that there have been times when all members were problem free (exceptions). Initially, the leader will hear the group member's description of her or his problem, listen for current resources (and exceptions), and begin to direct the members to articulate goals for change. Group members are encouraged to cofacilitate

SIDEBAR 4.6
More Theories and Leadership Goals

Select one of the next three theories applied to group work that you have now reviewed (transactional analysis, CBT, or solution focused). Again, imagine you are the group leader. Describe the goal(s) of the group in terms of expected outcome (changes) for the members.

Note what you will focus on in each stage of the group process. Name two or three techniques you might select that are synonymous with your chosen theoretical orientation. Compare this description to your response in Sidebar 4.1.

the group process through support for and encouragement of member strengths. Leaders quickly shift focus from problems to solutions. Questions that elicit contextual and behavioral details about when the problem may be resolved begin to foster hope and identify transitional tasks for solutions. For example, a leader may ask a member "What will you be thinking and/or doing when you are no longer angry with your partner?"

Leaders promote weekly accomplishments by asking members what the member did differently since the last group meeting. This positive reinforcement supports change and empowers members to take small steps between group sessions toward a solution. Group leaders may suggest the use of daydreams or fantasies or may ask the *miracle question* to help formulate member goals and identify ways of changing behavior, changing the perspective of the problem, or finding resources to create solutions (O'Hanlon & Weiner-Davis, 2003). Genuine complements from the leader are used to highlight progress and provide suggestions for what to strengthen. This feedback opens the door for suggestions in the form of homework assignments that harness potential creativity and experimentation with new solutions by group members. The SFT counselor is consistently working toward termination and may have the group use scaling to operationalize its progress at the end of each session. A final step of hope and empowerment is the belief that each group member can and will continue to build and use discovered strengths and build new competencies after the termination of the group.

Special techniques identified by de Shazer (1985), de Shazer et al. (2007), Lipchik et al. (2012), and West-Olatunji and Rush-Ossenbeck (2016) that have a unique application in SFT include, but are not limited to, the following:

- Exceptions
- Solution talk
- The miracle question
- Compliments
- Scaling questions to measure progress

INTEGRATING THE THEORETICAL APPROACHES

The six theories presented in this chapter offer the group leader options for working with groups. At first glance, each of these approaches seems to represent a unique underpinning for group process, but in fact the six approaches have many elements in common, which enhances the possibility for integrating these theories and applying them to the ongoing group process. The following subsections address this integrative theme by discussing the therapeutic relationship, the leader role, group member responsibilities, the group process, and expected group outcome.

The Therapeutic Relationship

A working relationship between the leader and the members is basic to all six theoretical approaches. Each approach includes a need for trust, safety, mutual respect, and leader competence, and five of the six approaches present a need for equality in leader–member interactions. As in most group work, the therapeutic relationship is the foundational building block on which all other aspects of group dynamics rest. Each approach underlines the importance of taking time to build this foundational structure and to ensure that group members understand the nature and limitations of this relationship. It is from this counselor–client–group relationship that trust and group cohesion emerge to create a safe environment for change.

The Leader Role

In all six theoretical positions, the leader's role is an active one. Action-oriented descriptors such as *develop, instruct, analyze, establish, enhance, provide, reinforce, demonstrate, aid, confront, communicate, direct,* and *observe* instruct the leader to take an active role in his or her interaction with the group. Each leader will operate from his or her theoretical orientation, which informs the leader how problems emerge and how changes occur and identifies those strategies and techniques that promote human growth and development. A knowledgeable and competent group leader is necessary in all six theoretical approaches and seems to be a key element for a successful outcome in all six approaches.

Group Member Responsibilities

In all the theoretical perspectives, group members also play an active role. To maximize group success, members must be responsible; committed to change; willing to risk; willing to try out new behaviors; willing to share themselves with others; able to deal with affect, cognitions, and behaviors; willing to do the hard work that change demands; willing to express creativity through role play; and open to new information, insights, and awareness. Screening for group members who can meet these responsibilities is imperative for the success of the group.

In addition, all the theoretical perspectives stress that if change is to occur, members must assume major responsibility for this change. Each approach has the same underlying message about the role of members: If you desire change, you must be willing to take major responsibility for that change and be willing to take the necessary action to make that change possible.

Group Process and Strategies

The area that seems to have the most variability across the six theoretical approaches is the group process, which encompasses the various actions that take place within groups. For example, for the Adlerian group counselor, giving and receiving feedback and providing encouragement are proposed as ongoing means of facilitating group interaction and member growth. Alternatively, the Gestalt group leader might take a more experiential approach, providing structured activities such as the empty-chair technique to heighten the awareness of a problematic relationship and allow the group to offer feedback on a here-and-now, cathartic group member experience. Similarly, the TA or redecision group leader may guide a member to an earlier memory and invite the member to discover the inhibiting early decision. Group members would be encouraged to provide supportive feedback to each other.

In psychodrama, giving and receiving feedback centers on a group member's staged scenario. Group members may be invited to take part in the individual member's scene and thus become active participants in the experience. An example of this type of group process might be a family "sculpture" in which group members are directed by the leader to play each family member and provide feedback from that family role, as you saw in the example provided in the psychodrama discussion.

From a solution-focused perspective, the group process might include future-oriented, creative, reciprocal communication in which group members are encouraged to focus on strengths. Members are thus empowered to build on those strengths and create a vision of a satisfying and fulfilled lifestyle within a supportive community. The cognitive behavioral group counselor might assign homework and elicit a report on the member's discovery of cognitive distortions that are inhibiting the member's move toward new behaviors. Group members are encouraged to identify and change the thinking that directs the undesired behavior and ultimately to modify the behavior. Overall, though each group process may look unique, all six approaches provide a process to expand the affective, cognitive, and behavioral realms of the group members and the potential for positive growth.

Expected Group Outcomes

The greatest similarity across the theoretical approaches is in intended group outcomes. Common to all six approaches are concepts including increasing awareness, changing dysfunctional behaviors, enhancing self-concept, fostering insight, accepting responsibility, and increasing trust in self and others. Regardless of theoretical approach, the desired outcomes all center on change. Each group works for positive change: change in the way group members *feel* about themselves and their world, change in the way group members *think* about themselves and their world, and change in the way group members *behave* as a result of changes in the way they feel and think. Although the words used to describe this change vary from theory to theory, the end result is to have group members live more productive and satisfying lives.

SIDEBAR 4.7

Reflections on Becoming a Group Leader

You have completed your review of the six theories applied to group counseling. Now write a brief reflection of your thoughts and feelings about being a group leader. Which theory most resonates with you now? Has this changed since your response in Sidebar 4.1? How will you plan to continue learning about applying theory to group counseling?

Summary

Recall the question expressed at the beginning of this chapter by the hypothetical student, Alisha: "How do I transfer individual concepts into a group of eight or ten members?" This challenge is a legitimate concern for experienced and novice group leaders alike. Group approaches are derived largely from theories and therapies developed for individuals. Because group counseling must be based in theory, group leaders must become knowledgeable about the major theories and learn how to integrate and apply them within the group modality. As a developing group leader, you should become familiar with the various theoretical approaches, experiment with different techniques, and strive to find one theory or a combination of similar theories that works best for you and your groups. Your approach ideally will reflect your personal philosophy, your personal style, and your training in group process and dynamics. We trust that the discussion of the six theories highlighted in this chapter—Adlerian, psychodrama, Gestalt, transactional analysis, cognitive behavioral, and solution focused—will aid you as you discover your favored theoretical orientation and become a skilled and competent group leader.

5 Group Work: Ethical/Legal Considerations

Delini M. Fernando and Barbara J. Herlihy

Ethical values are integral to the practice of group work (Association for Specialists in Group Work, 2000). This chapter will focus on the ethical responsibilities of group workers and related legal issues that must be considered when conducting groups.

Group counselors have a dual responsibility to protect the welfare of each individual group member and to ensure that the group functions in a way that benefits everyone involved. All the major ethical issues that pertain to individual counseling apply to group work as well. However, these issues can be more complex in group work because of the significant differences between the two modalities. In addition, some ethical issues unique to group work, such as screening of potential group participants and outside-of-group socializing among members, must be considered.

Several features of group work distinguish it from individual counseling, and each of these features has ethical implications:

- Group members disclose personal information to the counselor and to other group participants. This changes the nature of confidentiality and affects how the counselor deals with privacy issues.
- The dynamics of therapeutic change are different in group counseling. In individual counseling, the mechanism that fosters growth and change is the relationship between the counselor and client, along with the interventions utilized. By contrast, the effectiveness of group work results as much from interactions among the members, including feedback and mutual support among members, as it does from the interventions of the group leader (Welfel, 2016). Thus, the leader has an ethical obligation to screen and select participants who are compatible and can assist each other in meeting their goals.
- Counselors have less control over events that occur during and between group sessions than they have in individual counseling situations (Remley & Herlihy, 2016; Welfel, 2016). Group members can respond to each other in some unpredictable ways that the group leader may not be able to anticipate. In addition, if some members of the group interact with each other between sessions, this can have a profound impact on the group's functioning. These factors may make it more difficult for counselors to uphold their ethical duty to protect clients from harm.

- In an individual counseling relationship, the client has the right to terminate the counseling relationship at any time. Likewise, group participants have the freedom to exit the group at any time, but when group members drop out of an ongoing group, it can have significant effects on other participants and on the functioning of the group as a whole. Thus, group counselors must manage conflicts between the rights of individual group members and the rights of the entire group.
- Research has demonstrated that group counseling is a powerful intervention. Some writers (e.g., Kottler, 1994a; Yalom & Leszcz, 2005) have argued that this creates a potential for greater good or greater harm than may be present in individual counseling. Because such powerful forces are generated in groups, leaders have a complex set of responsibilities.

This chapter is organized into three main sections. The first presents a brief overview of ethical codes and other guidelines for group practitioners. The second addresses pregroup issues, examining the ethical considerations that go into preparing to lead a group. Foremost among these issues is the competence of the group leader. Counselors who are thinking about forming and leading a group need to have adequate training, experience, and qualifications, as well as multicultural and diversity competence. Counselors also must understand how to avoid malpractice, which is a legal consequence of lacking competence. Planning carefully, recruiting members, performing pregroup screening, and ensuring the informed consent of members also are important steps that must be completed prior to the formation of a group.

The third section focuses on ethical and legal issues that arise during the life of a group. These issues include dealing with confidentiality and privileged communication, establishing and maintaining boundaries, minimizing risks, dealing with diversity, handling premature withdrawals from the group, and ending a group in an ethically appropriate manner.

ETHICAL GUIDELINES FOR GROUP WORKERS

All counselors, including group counselors, should be familiar with and adhere to the American Counseling Association (ACA) *Code of Ethics* (2014). The Association for Specialists in Group Work (ASGW) has adopted the ACA code as its sole code of ethics. The ASGW has published two key documents about ethics in group work:

1. *Best Practice Guidelines, 2007 Revisions* (ASGW, 2008), intended to clarify how the ACA code can be applied to group work
2. *Principles for Diversity-Competent Group Workers* (1999), the purpose of which is to help counselors understand how issues of diversity affect all aspects of group work

These ASGW documents are aspirational—that is, there is no mechanism for enforcing them. Adherence to the ACA *Code of Ethics* is mandatory for all ACA members, including members of ASGW (Cottone & Tarvydas, 2007).

Counselors who are engaged in group work should be completely familiar with the contents of the ACA code and both sets of ASGW guidelines. We also recommend that group workers who conduct psychotherapeutic groups familiarize themselves with the ethical guidelines of the American Group Psychotherapy Association and National Registry of Certified Group Psychotherapists (2002). These guidelines can be accessed online.

PREGROUP ISSUES

In the pregroup stage, the competence of the group leader is crucial for planning and recruiting members. To avoid malpractice lawsuits, thorough training in group counseling is essential.

Determining Competence and Avoiding Malpractice

Researchers have expressed concern over the casual attitude that some mental health professionals take toward their preparedness to conduct groups. Counselors should not assume that they are qualified automatically to lead all, or even most, types of groups just because they have earned a master's degree or have considerable experience in counseling individuals (Corey, Corey, & Corey, 2017; Welfel, 2016). Different types of groups require different leader competencies. For instance, a counselor may be well qualified to facilitate a reminiscence group for elderly residents of a nursing home but not at all prepared to lead adolescent groups in a school environment. Or a counselor might be competent to conduct a personal growth group for college students but might be practicing beyond the boundaries of competence by trying to lead process groups in an inpatient setting for clients diagnosed with chronic schizophrenia. Thus, if you are thinking about forming and conducting a group, the first question you should ask yourself is whether you have the competencies you need to lead the group effectively.

Developing competence begins with training. The ASGW's publication *Professional Standards for the Training of Group Workers* (2000) describes the knowledge and skill objectives that comprise the core competencies in general group work in eight areas:

1. Coursework and experience
2. Knowledge and skills
3. Assessment
4. Planning
5. Implementing interventions
6. Leadership
7. Evaluation
8. Ethics

The standards also specify advanced competencies that are required to lead specialized task and work groups, psychoeducational groups, counseling groups, and psychotherapy groups.

If you are enrolled in or have graduated from a counselor education program accredited by the Council for the Accreditation of Counseling and Related Educational Programs (CACREP), you can be assured that your training has met the ASGW standards for content and clinical instruction. Although most graduate counseling programs are not CACREP accredited (Remley & Herlihy, 2016), many nonaccredited programs meet or even exceed the ASGW standards. We recommend that, whatever the accreditation status of your graduate program, you review the ASGW (2000) training standards as part of your planning process to assess your preparedness to lead a group.

You must be aware that achieving professional competence in group work is not a one-time event. Professional growth is a continuous, ongoing, developmental process (ASGW, 2008). Therefore, maintaining and increasing your competence as a group worker is a lifelong task. You will need to work to remain current and continue to work to increase your knowledge and skills in group work by keeping up with your professional reading and seeking continuing education, supervision, and consultation. Joining a peer-supervision group can be an excellent way to increase your knowledge and raise your awareness of even minor misjudgments as a group counselor (Gladding, 2016).

Diversity Considerations

Group counselors must understand how issues of diversity affect all aspects of group work. The ASGW publication *Principles for Diversity-Competent Group Workers* (ASGW, 1999) provides a thorough description of attitudinal, knowledge, and skills competencies in three domains: self-awareness, awareness of group members' worldviews, and intervention strategies. As a beginning point, you should be aware of how your own cultural background and multiple cultural identities, attitudes, values, and beliefs influence the way you conceptualize and conduct groups.

As you work with diverse group members, you will need to be alert to issues of oppression, bias and prejudice, power and privilege, and discrimination, both within the workings of the group and in the sociopolitical contexts of members' lives. You must be careful not to impose your values on group members or proceed as if all members of your group share your worldview or cultural assumptions. This awareness is particularly important because so many value-laden issues—such as sexuality, religion, divorce, and family of origin—are brought into groups (Remley & Herlihy, 2016).

To be a diversity-competent group worker, you must possess relevant knowledge and skills, as well as awareness of self and others. Being able to send and receive both verbal and nonverbal messages accurately and to utilize a variety of methods of group facilitation are among the key skills. Knowledge of both the characteristics of different cultural groups and within-group differences is essential. It is essential that you understand the barriers that can prevent members of marginalized groups from participating fully in various types of groups and know how to employ institutional intervention skills on behalf of group members. Having the skills to advocate working toward removal of barriers or obstacles to client access, growth, and development is an ethical

---

SIDEBAR 5.1

Self-Awareness: Group Workers' Need for Being Alert to Issues of Oppression, Bias, Prejudice, Power, Privilege, and Discrimination

So often, group workers are unaware of how issues of oppression, bias, prejudice, power, privilege, and discrimination affect group members or play out in groups. To be a diversity-competent group worker, awareness of self and others is equally as important and relevant as knowledge and skills.

We encourage group leaders to self-reflect on how each of the issues listed previously has affected them personally. As group leaders, it is imperative that we engage in self-reflective exercises and/or peer or coleader discussions around these issues. Ongoing self-reflection and self-monitoring of our biases and prejudices, no matter how slight or varied they may be, can help us be more aware of how these value-laden issues may play out in group sessions among members and/or between member and leader. Being more familiar with how these issues affect group members also makes it easier for group leaders to initiate or intervene when difficult topics such as oppression and prejudice arise and makes it easier to accurately receive and send both verbal and nonverbal messages when necessary.

SIDEBAR 5.2
Case Study: Tom's Involvement in Group

Tom is 38 years old and works as a salesman. He suffers from low self-esteem because of his unattractiveness, lack of education, and poor social skills. He finds himself obsessively worrying about how his peer group members view his comments and mannerisms in group. Tom is mostly quiet in group and often says that he does not have much to say but enjoys listening to his peer members. The group members come from different backgrounds and education levels, and some also appear to be in positions of power and privilege. He often thinks the group leader prefers other members to him, and he often thinks about quitting group. How can you help Tom be more comfortable in group and feel more like a member? How can Tom be given opportunities to share his experiences and bring them to the here and now? How can difficult topics of discrimination, prejudice, power, and privilege be introduced in a safe and non-threatening environment in this group?

---

mandate (ACA, 2014, Standard A.7.a.). The ASGW *Diversity Principles* (ASGW, 1999) provide a more complete understanding of the specific competencies you need to have to become a diversity-competent group leader.

Legal Considerations

Our society expects professionals to be competent and enforces these expectations through the courts and licensing boards (Remley & Herlihy, 2016). If a client is harmed by an incompetent counselor, the client can bring a malpractice lawsuit against the counselor.

   Although few malpractice suits are filed against counselors (Remley & Herlihy, 2016) and court cases involving group counseling are relatively rare (Paradise and Kirby, 1990), group counselors may be at risk for two reasons: (a) clients are vulnerable to harm from both the leader and other participants and (b) the powerful nature of the group experience could exacerbate any negative outcomes. Possibly the greatest area of risk for group counselors is in working with group members who pose a danger to self

---

SIDEBAR 5.3
Case Study: Using Group Interventions to Help Arnold

Arnold has struggled with generalized anxiety disorder and sexual addiction for many years. His high levels of anxiety have fueled his obsession with pornography. He works in a construction company. After 8 years of marriage, his wife divorced him, so the men he works with are his major source of support. He continues to drink with them after work and shares jokes and information about specific online porn sites. He has made comments to a few group members about socializing outside of the group. Arnold discloses in group that he feels very bad about himself and the ways his addiction has hurt his marriage, children, and other family members. You are the group leader in Arnold's recovery program. He made a porn joke in group, which you first ignored because you did not feel competent enough to intervene. His repeated comments about porn and sexuality are beginning to irritate other group members, and they make you feel uncomfortable. What personal challenges do you face in working with Arnold in the group given that you have a family member who you know is addicted to porn? How would you intervene in group if it happened again? How would you address the problem of subgrouping and socializing outside of group?

(may be suicidal) or others (are prone to violent behavior) because of the increased possibility that someone could be harmed.

Malpractice suits by participants in a group try to prove negligence on the part of the leader. To establish negligence, the group member must demonstrate that she or he was harmed or injured by group participation and that the leader's mistake was what caused the harm. The services the leader provided are measured against the prevailing *standard of care*, defined as the quality of care that other, similarly trained professionals would have provided in this situation (Welfel, 2016).

If a participant is injured and sues, the plaintiff will likely try to show that the leader failed to uphold his or her obligation to "protect clients from physical or psychological trauma" (ACA, 2014, Standard A.9.b.). Group leaders in these cases might have to demonstrate several points in their defense, including that they could not have reasonably foreseen the harm, that they were adequately trained to lead the group in question, that they provided the plaintiff with fully informed consent regarding the risks, and that they took professionally appropriate precautions against harm or injury. Certainly, the leader would need an attorney to assist in her or his defense. To ensure affordable access to an attorney, obtaining professional liability insurance is imperative before conducting any kind of group work.

Planning the Group and Recruiting Members

Thorough planning is essential to the success of a group. As you plan for a group, you will want to consider several questions, including the following:

- What are the goals and purposes of this group? What is the role of the group members in determining or influencing the group's goals?
- What are the needs of the community? Does this group intend to meet those needs?
- What type of group (task or work, psychoeducational, counseling, psychotherapeutic) is best suited to achieving the group's goals?
- What techniques and leadership style are most appropriate for this group?
- Will I need a coleader? If so, what would be the coleader's roles and responsibilities?
- What resources do I need to have available for this group to function successfully (e.g., funding, space, privacy, marketing and recruiting members, collaborative arrangements with community agencies and organizations)?
- How will the members be screened?
- How will I evaluate the group's success?

In considering these questions, you might conclude that a successful group takes time, effort, and adequate knowledge in the planning phase.

Once planning for a group is complete, leaders must move to the next step, which is to advertise and recruit members. As Corey (2016) noted, the manner in which the group is announced and advertised will strongly influence who will be attracted to joining the group. Therefore, you will want to give potential members enough information to make clear the group's goals and purposes. You may want to ask other professionals to refer clients whom they think might be good participants for the group.

When recruiting for groups in school settings, you must exercise special caution. If you ask teachers to recommend students for possible inclusion in groups for children of divorce, children of alcoholics (COA), children who have suffered abuse, or in groups with similar themes, you might be labeling the students and violating their privacy. Ritchie and Huss (2000) recommend that counselors avoid naming their groups in this way and that counselors invite children to come at their own discretion to discuss their interest in participating.

Screening Potential Members

Screening of potential group members involves deciding both whom to exclude and whom to include. Because not all people can benefit from a group experience and some can even be harmed by participating (Yalom & Leszcz, 2005), these individuals must be identified during screening and directed to individual counseling or other sources of assistance.

The literature suggests that individuals who generally are not good candidates for group counseling include those who are likely to monopolize group time or dominate the group, have aggressive or hostile interpersonal styles, are suicidal or in severe crisis, are actively psychotic, or have been diagnosed with paranoid, narcissistic, or antisocial personality disorders. Others who are likely to inhibit the development of group cohesion are self-centered people who would be prone to use the group as an audience, as well as those lacking in ego strength who might display fragmented, acting-out, or bizarre behavior (Corey, 2016). Individuals who are addicted to drugs or alcohol also are poor candidates for most types of groups (Yalom & Leszcz, 2005). Criteria for inclusion usually depend on the purpose of the group. As a general guideline, however, groups are most useful for individuals whose problems or concerns are interpersonal in nature and who appreciate the commitment they will be making when they join a group (Yalom & Leszcz, 2005).

Ideally, potential members are screened in an individual, face-to-face interview. This allows for initiating a therapeutic relationship and provides the leader with an opportunity to explore the prospective member's expectations and concerns about group participation, presenting issue(s), personal background, commitment to change, and suitability for participation in the group (Goodrich & Luke, 2015).

Unfortunately, it is not always possible or feasible to conduct individual screening interviews. Alternative procedures might be to interview prospective members in small groups or individually by phone or Skype, or to have them complete a written questionnaire. After all prospective members have been screened, the leader's task is to select the prospective members whose goals seem to be compatible with the purpose of the group, who will not impede the group process, whose well-being will not be jeopardized by the group experience (ACA, 2014, Standard A.9.a.), and who seem likely to be compatible with each other.

Securing Informed Consent

Informed consent is based on the principle that clients have the right to know what they are getting into before they enter counseling (Remley & Herlihy, 2016). Informed consent is especially important in group work because group counseling involves risks and responsibilities beyond those typically involved in individual counseling (Welfel, 2016). To gain the fully informed consent of group members, the leader will need to provide them with a considerable amount of information and work to ensure that they understand all the risks and responsibilities of participation.

Securing informed consent is both a pregroup task and an issue that must be revisited during the first session. Here we will focus on the information that group participants have a right to receive *before* they join a group. The leader can relate this information to prospective members during the screening interview or at a pregroup meeting.

Potential group members usually find it helpful to have information in written form so they can take it home and review it. As part of this written information, the leader must provide prospective members with a professional disclosure statement. *Best Practice Guidelines* (ASGW, 2008) declares that a statement should include information on confidentiality and its limits and exceptions (which we will discuss in more detail in the next section) and on the nature, purposes, and goals of the group. The document should describe the roles and responsibilities of the group's members and leader(s) and the services the group can provide. In addition, the statement must include the leader's qualifications to lead the specific group (e.g., degrees earned, licenses, certifications, professional affiliations, address of licensing/credentialing body, and relevant experience). A brief but clear description of the leader's theoretical orientation expressed in lay language also can be included.

Prospective members need certain practical information so they can make an informed decision regarding participation. The leader should explain the group's format, procedures, and ground rules. Prospective members will want to know the duration of the group (weeks or months), how frequently it will meet, how long each session will last, and cancellation policies. Certainly, they will need to know about any fees involved and what arrangements they can make for payment. If insurance will be billed, potential participants should know what information will be disclosed to third-party payers (ACA, 2014, Standard B.3.d.).

Best Practices Guidelines (ASGW, 2008) specifies that certain policies should be discussed as part of the informed consent process, including policies regarding (a) entering and exiting the group, (b) substance use, (c) documentation of the group, (d) disclosure of information to others, (e) implications of out-of-group contact or involvement among members, (f) how consultation between group leader(s) and group members will happen, and (g) potential impacts of group participation. If there will be a coleader, the leader will want to explain the coleader's role and qualifications.

Some topics are best approached as matters for discussion rather than as information to be disseminated. Members may want or need help in developing their personal goals for participating in the group (Corey, 2016), and the leader should be prepared to assist them in this endeavor. The leader may want to discuss with participants ways in which the group process may be congruent or at odds with their cultural beliefs and values. Leaders should discuss the possible impact, in terms of both potential risks and benefits, of participating in the group. Some of the risks that should be explained include the possibilities of scapegoating, undue group pressure or coercion, inappropriate confrontation, or physical harm (ASGW, 2008; Corey et al., 2017).

Finally, prospective members should be offered the opportunity to ask questions and explore any concerns they may have. Although these discussions might be time-consuming, research has shown that pregroup preparation of members tends to facilitate positive outcomes in group counseling (Goodrich & Luke, 2015).

SPECIALIZED GROUPS

When working with specialized groups, such as child and adolescent groups or mandated clients and involuntary groups, there are additional issues of ethics and legality pertaining to informed consent. Although it is imperative to secure informed consent at the beginning of a group, group counselors may find it essential to revisit several aspects of consent throughout the life of the group.

Child and Adolescent Groups

When a group will be composed of minors, informed consent must be gained in a different way. Legally, the rights of children belong to their parents (Remley & Herlihy, 2016) and must be exercised through their parents. From a *legal perspective*, then, parents or guardians are the ones who must give their informed consent for their children to participate in the group. From an *ethical perspective*, children and adolescents have the same rights as adults to receive information about a group in which they may be participating. During the screening interview or pregroup meeting, you will want to provide children and adolescents with this information, in language they can understand. Remley and Herlihy (2016) have offered a model consent form that can be signed by parents or guardians indicating their permission for the child to participate. It is good practice to have the child sign the consent form, too, giving his or her assent to participation.

Mandated Clients and Involuntary Groups

Group counselors sometimes perceive mandated clients as "troublesome" because these clients typically attend the group against their will, with heightened defenses, and with limited motivation to change. Informed consent can be a problem with this population. Ethical guidelines usually require that group members feel they have the freedom to withdraw their consent to participate at any time, without prejudice or penalty. However, because withdrawal would place clients in a seriously compromised legal position, possibly leading to jail, their freedom to withdraw consent is abridged when counseling is court ordered.

The best way to deal with this reality is to present this information in a nonconfrontational but clear manner, making sure that potential group members are aware of the possible consequences of choosing not to participate (DeJong and Berg, 2001). It is important to let them know that they do have a choice. They need to feel that, at least in some areas, they do have choices.

GROUP PROCESS ISSUES

Group leaders and members are concerned about confidential information that is shared in groups. Leaders not only have to keep the confidences of group members but also must make sure that members keep the confidences of other members.

Confidentiality and Privileged Communication

One of the key conditions for effective group work is *confidentiality* (Corey et al., 2017). Confidentiality builds trust within the group members and develops cohesion among the members as they move through the stages of group development. Group members must have a sense of safety when disclosing personal issues that are sensitive in nature. Thus, the trust and belief that this information will not be disclosed outside the group is the first building block in developing safety and trust in group work.

Group leaders need to spend adequate time discussing and stressing the importance of confidentiality to all members so that members have a clear understanding of what is meant by *confidentiality* (Lasky & Riva, 2006). By using clinical examples to illustrate intentional and unintentional violations of confidentiality, group leaders can help members fully grasp the various parameters of confidentiality (Lasky & Riva, 2006). These conversations need to begin at the screening stage and continue throughout the group process until termination. Although the group leader is responsible for protecting members' confidentiality, leaders are cautioned to refrain from offering guarantees of confidentiality. The leader's commitment to confidentiality is individual and independent of the group. Leaders can ensure confidentiality on their own part but cannot guarantee the behavior of the group members (ASGW, 2008). Leaders cannot promise that "leaks of confidentiality" will not occur, but they can utilize their skills to empower the members to take ownership of their group's effectiveness by upholding confidentiality and honoring the trust they are building throughout the group process.

Leaders have an ethical responsibility to make members aware of the difficulties involved in enforcing and ensuring confidentiality in a group setting. The ACA (2014) *Code of Ethics* requires counselors to "clearly explain the importance and parameters of confidentiality for the specific group" (Standard B.4.a.). Groups need to create norms for confidentiality that are agreeable to all members (Barlow, 2013), and leaders should provide examples of how confidentiality can be broken even unintentionally or inadvertently. They also should ensure that members clearly understand the potential consequences of intentionally breaching confidentiality (ASGW, 2008). Because leaders cannot prevent breaches of confidentiality after the group ends, they must address this reality with the group (Gladding, 2016).

Another issue with risk of breach in confidentiality can occur when members of a group engage in social media. Group counselors should address the issue of online behaviors that do not jeopardize the privacy of other members. Refraining from posting pictures, comments about members or leaders, or disclosing members' confidential information can help in safeguarding the privacy and trust of members and the group as a whole. Online groups are susceptible to blurred boundaries and to inaccurate or unidentified group types (Barlow, 2013). In such groups, there is lack of clarity about leader roles, unsecured sites, and little access to emergency management.

Despite a leader's best efforts, confidentiality leaks sometimes do occur. If a breach of confidentiality does occur, the first step on the leader's part is to reflect on and assess his or her work in modeling and protecting the confidentiality of the group. Leaders can self-reflect by asking themselves the following questions:

- Have I defined confidentiality clearly, or was I vague in my definition?
- Did I stress the importance of confidentiality in a way that my group members can understand?
- Did I facilitate the group in such a way that the members can take ownership of the effectiveness of their group?
- Was I clear that confidentiality cannot be guaranteed?
- How do I help the group move forward?

The second step in handling a confidentiality leak is to bring up the situation in the group for the members to process and collectively develop a resolution. Because group leaders can model inappropriate breaches of confidentiality in subtle ways, they should be aware of and maintain confidentiality in all informal conversations with members outside the group. Discussions regarding an absent member should be deferred until that member returns to the group. Coleaders also should be mindful of confidentiality during their conversations when they meet to process and plan group sessions.

Group leaders sometimes want to make audiotapes or video recordings of group sessions for educational or professional purposes. When this is done, group members must have a clear understanding as to the purpose and use of the recordings and must sign a written informed consent stating that they agree to and understand the intended use of the recording. Members have the right to deny consent or withdraw consent at any time. If a group has any members who do not wish to be recorded on video, the leader could ask them if they would be comfortable with being positioned outside the view of the camera but still participating in the group because their input in the group process is valued. This compromise might suffice to allow recording on video without the member feeling uncooperative.

Legal Considerations

The legal counterpart to confidentiality is *privileged communication*. Privileged communication laws protect clients from having their confidential communications with their counselors disclosed in a court of law without their permission. Except for the relatively rare trials involving counselors that take place in federal courts, a state statute must exist for communications between counselors and their clients to be privileged. Although some type of counselor–client privilege existed in 44 of 45 states that licensed counselors in 2000 (Glosoff, Herlihy, & Spence, 2000), the extent to which privilege applies in group counseling varies widely from state to state (Welfel, 2016).

In some states, the privileged communication statutes are worded in such a way that courts could conclude that because a client shared information in the presence of third parties (group members), the information was not truly intended to be confidential (Knapp & VandeCreek, 2003). When such decisions have been appealed, state courts usually have held that statements made in front of third parties are not privileged (Swenson, 1997).

As you can see, many complexities are involved in privileged communication as it applies to group counseling. You will need to research the law in your state and keep current with any legislative developments. As part of the informed consent process with group members, leaders must explain to each participant that there is no privilege for other group members who will hear what that participant says. Thus, other members could be compelled to testify in a lawsuit. So that participants are not unduly alarmed, the leader should inform them that the probability of this happening is extremely low (Welfel, 2016).

Child and Adolescent Groups

Safeguarding confidentiality in group counseling with children and adolescents is more difficult than it is with adults (Gladding, 2016; Koocher, 2003). When counseling children individually or in a group, two questions that arise constantly are "Who is my client?"

and "Who owns the right to confidentiality?" Legally, group leaders working with children may have to disclose some information to parents if the parents insist (Corey et al., 2017). Ethically, however, children and adolescents have a right to privacy and confidentiality just as adults do (Remley & Herlihy, 2016). The mandated breaches of confidentiality intended to protect children from harm, or from harming others, constitute a clear exception (Koocher, 2003).

Group leaders should be aware of the local and state laws regarding confidentiality with minors because state laws vary regarding this population. Respecting parents' rights while establishing and maintaining the trust of minor clients is a delicate balance. To reduce the likelihood that parents will ask what their child has discussed in a group, group leaders are wise to discuss with parents in advance the importance and purpose of confidentiality (Corey et al., 2017). A key to working with children and adolescents is to raise the issue of confidentiality limits early and directly, in a manner that fosters the therapeutic alliance (Koocher, 2003).

Maintaining Privacy of Records

The group counselor's obligation to protect clients' privacy and confidentiality extends to the records the counselor keeps. In our experience, many counselors who are diligent about keeping clinical case notes on their work with individual clients are rather lax in documenting their work with groups. However, this task is important, as special considerations apply to keeping records of group counseling sessions because of the need to respect the confidentiality rights of the individual members.

It is good practice for leaders to make process notes soon after each group session has ended while the memory is still fresh. These notes are valuable in helping leaders perform their work effectively. Leaders may want to use notes to keep track of the group's progress through the developmental stages, record any issues requiring special attention, document the leader's observations about group dynamics such as the development of trust or cohesion, and describe interventions used and the leader's assessment of their effects. Leaders must be careful, though, that the group session notes do not refer to individual group members by name or other identifying information. If the records were ever subpoenaed by an attorney representing a group member and those records were to become public, the leader would be violating the confidentiality rights of the other group members named in the records.

Counselors have a responsibility to write separate case notes for group sessions for each member of the group (Cottone & Tarvydas, 2007). These individual files should not contain any information about other group members, particularly in situations in which the client is being seen for both individual and group counseling. If any participants in the group are concurrently participating in individual counseling with another mental health professional, the group leader should establish clear guidelines about sharing information with the other counselor. Leaders should consult with the participant's individual counselor only with the participant's permission. Clients have a right to view any or all of their records.

In many institutional settings, clients are concurrently seen in individual counseling, group counseling, occupational or expressive therapy groups, and by a psychiatrist if they are taking psychotropic medications. Whenever treatment teams are involved in client care, the clients must be informed of the team's existence and composition, information being shared (including records), and the purposes of sharing the information (ACA, 2014, Standard B.3.b). Group counselors also need to be familiar with the provisions of the Health Insurance Portability and Accountability Act (HIPAA), which went into effect in 2003 and has a direct impact on counselor records and informed consent practices.

Mandated Clients and Involuntary Groups

Members of mandatory groups must be informed that their confidentiality cannot be assured because the group leader usually is required to report to a third party. For this reason, mandated clients should be required to sign a waiver of their privacy rights before they enter a group (Remley & Herlihy, 2016). Leaders who work with involuntary groups must keep in mind that the members deserve a full understanding of the group leader's role and obligations to fulfill any reporting requirements of the court or referring state agency (Adams, 1998).

MANAGING BOUNDARIES

Ethical and legal issues related to the boundaries of the therapeutic relationship have been hotly debated by helping professionals: over 1,500 books, articles, and other scholarly works have been generated on the topic over the past 25 years (Pope & Keith-Spiegel, 2008). What constitutes appropriate boundaries has been questioned ever since the time of Freud, who emphasized the importance of neutrality, yet analyzed his own daughter. In short, there is no single correct answer about where therapeutic boundaries should be drawn. Boundaries exist along a continuum from very fluid to overly rigid (Marshall, 2000).

Most of what has been written about boundaries relates to counselor behaviors in individual counseling relationships (Marshall, 2000). Boundaries are created with an understanding that counseling is a professional relationship with parameters and certain limits that might not apply to a personal relationship. Clients are in a vulnerable position in the therapeutic relationship; therefore, boundaries serve to protect the structure of the therapeutic relationship (Remley & Herlihy, 2016).

The term *boundary* is closely related to other terms such as *dual relationship* or *multiple relationship*. In a dual relationship, a group leader takes on more than one role simultaneously or sequentially (Herlihy & Corey, 2014) with a member or members. Dual relationships can involve combining the role of counselor with another professional relationship, such as teacher, minister, supervisor, employer, or business partner (Smith & Smith, 2001), or combining the leader's role as counselor with a personal relationship, such as friend, relative, or, in the worst case, lover. Because the terms *dual relationship* and *multiple relationship* have caused both confusion and controversy, they are no longer used in most ethical guidelines.

The ASGW's *Best Practice Guidelines, 2007 Revisions* (ASGW, 2008), addresses boundary issues only minimally, in the statement that group workers "clearly define and maintain ethical, professional, and social relationship boundaries with group members as appropriate to their role in the organization and the type of group being offered" (Standard B.3.c.). The ACA's *Code of Ethics* (ACA, 2014) addresses boundary issues more extensively. The standards recognize the fact that not all dual relationships are problematic, nor are they always avoidable. Standard A.6.e advises counselors to avoid nonprofessional relationships with clients, except when the interaction is potentially beneficial to the client. The standard that follows gives examples of potentially beneficial interactions and provides safeguards to prevent harm or exploitation.

Avoiding dual relationships can be difficult if not impossible in some circumstances. Considering the adage of six degrees of separation, depending on the community in which you live, there may be only two degrees of separation between you as the group leader and the members of your group. This situation is more prevalent in rural and isolated communities. In other situations, dual relationships may be avoidable and counselors must use their professional judgment in making decisions such as whether to admit an acquaintance into one of their groups. Counselors should consider whether the specific relationship could impair professional judgment or increase the risk of harm to clients. Counselors should not attempt to make these judgments without seeking consultation or supervision. When you are faced with these kinds of choices, you may find that you are too close to the issue to decide what is just and fair in the situation. If you and your consultant or supervisor determine that there is a risk of harm, exploitation, or clouded judgment, you should decline to enter the dual relationship or rectify an existing problem, if possible, by way of a referral.

The one type of dual relationship that is absolutely prohibited is a sexual and/or romantic relationship with a current client (including counseling group members). This prohibition is consistent across codes of ethics in all major helping professions. That is not to say you are being unethical if you find yourself feeling attracted to a group member or if you find an individual in your group to be sexually appealing. If you take steps to actualize your sexual fantasy, however, you have committed an ethical violation.

Although sexual dual relationships are the most obvious boundary issue, group leaders also must be cognizant of issues associated with nonsexual relationships and boundaries. These include bartering, social relationships with clients (in person or virtual) or their friends or family members, social relationships between members, and self-disclosure.

Bartering

When a potential group participant cannot afford to pay the fee to participate, the leader may be tempted to enter an agreement to receive goods or services in lieu of payment for services. The intent behind such an arrangement might be altruistic, but there are reasons to be cautious.

Two types of bartering arrangements may be especially problematic for group leaders: exchange of services and exchange of goods. In an *exchange of services*, a group participant would provide a service in which he or she has particular expertise, such as plumbing or carpentry. For example, imagine you are forming a new group for adolescents, and the parent of one of the potential members can't afford the fee. The parent happens to be a plumber. Your office needs plumbing repairs, so you barter with the parent to fix your plumbing in exchange for group counseling for her son, which might seem to be a fair trade.

The problem with this arrangement is that the value of services—both those provided by the parent and those provided by the group leader—is subjective. What if you are not satisfied with the plumbing repairs? What if the parent does not think the group was helpful for her son? What if other, paying parents find out that this group member is receiving services based on a bartering arrangement? The very subjective nature of perceptions about fairness and value or quality of work could compromise the thera-peutic relationship and create an awkward circumstance that could deter development of the group.

Bartering for *goods in exchange for counseling services* presents the same problems with perceptions of fairness, value, and quality. However, bartering is an acceptable (and sometimes the only) method of payment in some communities. The ACA's *Code of Ethics* (ACA, 2014) standard on bartering acknowledges that there are cultural factors involved in bartering, cautioning counselors to barter only when this is an accepted practice among professionals in the community, when the client requests it, and when the relationship is not exploitive or harmful to the client. Again, if you are faced with a decision about whether to barter, you would do well to seek supervision or consult with professional colleagues because your needs or desires for the potential services or goods could bias your judgment. In addition, you should document any bartering arrangements you have made with group members (ACA, 2014, Standard A.10.e).

Social Relationships with Clients

In general, group leaders are discouraged from developing friendships with group members and from admitting current friends into their groups (Herlihy & Corey, 2014). A group member who is also a friend could be reticent to fully engage in the group out of fear of jeopardizing the relationship with the leader. Or the opposite could occur: The member who has a "special relationship" with the leader might feel privileged and play out his or her role as the "favorite" during the group sessions. This could easily give rise to feelings of resentment and anger in the other group members who do not have the privilege of friendship with the leader.

Group leaders should be aware that occasionally some members will attempt to insinuate themselves into the role of the leader's "special friend." When leaders find themselves in this situation, they must be careful not to relax their boundaries. Some group members, particularly those who have experienced prior violations of their boundaries or who find themselves unable to accept limits, can be expected to test the boundaries of their relationship with the leader (Haug, 1999). These clients need to feel safe to discuss or even act out their conflicts, and they need to be assured that the group leader will remain committed to appropriate professional boundaries.

Former Clients as Group Members

Sometimes a group leader's prior relationship with a potential group member will be pro-fessional rather than personal. For example, you might want to form a group of people who have been your clients in individual counseling. You might see this as a useful pro-gression in that the group setting will allow clients to continue to make therapeutic gains while minimizing their expenses. Problems can arise, however, if your group is composed of some members who had been in individual counseling with you and some who had not. The group members who had all your attention when they were seeing you for individual counseling could easily feel resentful about having to share you with the other members. The members who did not know you before they joined the group might feel jealous of the group members who already have built a relationship with you. These reactions would have to be processed in the group, and this discussion could be therapeutically useful.

To summarize, admitting a friend of the group leader to a group is quite a different matter than admitting a former client to the group. With a former client, the relationship was professional and had inherent boundaries. By contrast, the relationship with a friend with whom the leader has shared personal experiences is not a professional relationship. In this case, the shifting of roles from a personal relationship to a professional relationship could create many difficulties for the group leader, for the friend who becomes a group member, and possibly for other members of the group (Herlihy & Corey, 2014).

Socializing Among Members

Group leaders have taken varying positions on the question of whether socializing among group members facilitates or hinders the group process (Remley & Herlihy, 2016). This issue is complicated because the leader has limited control over interactions that occur among the members outside of the group. This situation parallels the issue of confidentiality limits in that the leader cannot offer guarantees that a member will not socialize or converse about group outside of group. Some group leaders set ground rules at the outset to prohibit or discourage members from socializing outside of group time. Group members must understand that the purpose of group is not to make friends (Herlihy & Corey, 2014) but, instead, to normalize and validate each other's experiences and learn adaptive interpersonal skills that will transfer to outside relationships.

Notwithstanding any rules that might be established, socializing can and will occur between and among members outside of group time. If this becomes evident due to cliques developing within the group, the leader is responsible for raising the issue for the entire group to process.

It should be noted that socializing among members is not always discouraged. For example, substance abuse groups and support groups may actually encourage members to socialize outside of group time. Members of substance abuse groups typically cling to other members of their group to maintain their sobriety as they develop a new community.

Self-Disclosure

Self-disclosure can be a powerful intervention, and group leaders must recognize its limits. Hanna, Hanna, and Keys (1999) have suggested that group leaders avoid self-disclosing around issues or incidents that they have not resolved internally. If leaders use the groups to obtain their own therapy, members will be confused as to the specific

---

SIDEBAR 5.4

Self-Awareness: How Much Do I Self-Disclose?

A group leader's self-disclosure can be a powerful intervention if handled appropriately and within limits. Self-disclosing is used as an intervention to benefit a member, members, or member issue. However, if leaders self-disclose because of wanting attention to their problem or as a way of receiving their own therapy, members can become confused as to the specific role of the leader. How comfortable are you with self-disclosure? How would you monitor what to self-disclose and to what extent? What specific details would you include/exclude?

SIDEBAR 5.5
Case Study: Self-Disclosure in Group

You have planned to open a group for divorced individuals, both men and women. Your group is now advertised, and potential members are being interviewed and screened. You have gone through a bitter divorce experience yourself many years ago, including attending a divorce group. You have internally resolved many things related to your divorce and now feel that you are in a better place to help other individuals who have had similar experiences. Janet and John, two of your former long-term clients, contact you and want to join the group because they are both in different stages of the divorce process. While they were in individual counseling with you, you had mentioned to them (separately) that you were in the process of going through a divorce. They are the only two potential group members who know this information about you. Would you bring up the topic with them separately and, if so, why? Do you think this information needs to be shared by all the group members? Would this be a topic of self-disclosure or discussion with the other group members? If so, how would you go about discussing this?

---

roles of the leaders. The leader must keep in mind that the main purpose of the leader is to facilitate the growth of others, not to work through the leader's own personal issues or problems. The leader should consider joining a group in which he or she does not have the responsibility of leadership if it becomes apparent that a specific issue or theme that arose in the group has tapped into his or her own unfinished business (Herlihy & Corey, 2014).

Group leaders must develop guidelines to help them determine appropriate disclosures. A leader's self-disclosure can be beneficial to a group when it is used to let members know that the leader can identify with and is personally affected by their struggles (Herlihy & Corey, 2014) and when it does not shift the focus away from the members' issues.

ADOLESCENT GROUPS

Group leaders must be acutely aware of boundary issues when working with adolescents. Hanna et al. (1999) caution counselors against underestimating the sexual intensity of many defiant adolescents. Sexuality rages particularly in many adolescent boys. It follows that female counselors should be aware that hugs and touching can be highly

---

SIDEBAR 5.6
Self-Awareness: Barriers to Working with Individuals from Different Cultural Backgrounds

There are many different types of group counselors who work in a variety of different settings, including inpatient and outpatient groups, recovery groups, groups in school settings, task groups, support groups, and psychotherapy groups. You are a school counselor who is asked by the lead counselor to begin a group for middle school students struggling with gender and sexual identity issues. How might you go about preparing yourself to lead this specific group, given that you attend a church that is not very accepting of different kinds of lifestyles or the LGBTQ communities? What are your personal barriers or challenges? What can you personally do to overcome them? What stands in the way of bringing up difficult topics such as gender and sexual identity in this adolescent group?

erotic to many boys even when the counselor does not intend any eroticism. Likewise, male counselors may have to deal with adolescent girls who dress provocatively, seeking approval and validation of their own sexual identities. This behavior should not be ignored but must be handled with extreme sensitivity (Bernstein, 1996).

Legal Considerations

In cases in which clients have sued a counselor with whom they have had a sexual relationship, the client has an excellent chance of winning the lawsuit (Remley & Herlihy, 2016). Boland-Prom (2009) found that most frequent violations transpired in the areas of dual relationships, licensing problems, basic-practice elements, criminal actions, and not meeting care standards. As you can see, developing a sexual relationship with a client who is a group member is extremely risky in a legal sense, in addition to being wrong from an ethical and moral perspective.

Legal consequences for most nonsexual dual relationships are much less clear than they are for sexual relationships. Gutheil and Gabbard (1993) distinguished between *boundary violations*, which cause harm to clients, and *boundary crossings*, which can be beneficial to clients. A boundary crossing is a departure from customary practice to benefit a particular client at a particular time. Most group leaders, like most counselors who provide individual counseling services, probably cross boundaries occasionally. You might, for instance, lend a group member cab fare if the member discovered after a group meeting that he had left his wallet at home. You do not want to be too rigid in maintaining your boundaries, but you should be careful not to let boundary crossings become routine. If a judge or jury could perceive a pattern of blurring your professional boundaries over time, this might persuade her or him that you have not been practicing in accordance with professional standards (Herlihy & Corey, 2014; Remley & Herlihy, 2016).

Minimizing Risks

Because groups can be powerful catalysts for change, they involve some risk. The ACA's *Code of Ethics* (ACA, 2014) requires counselors to take "precautions to protect clients from physical or psychological trauma" in group settings (Standard A.9.b). This standard reflects both the concern that group participants might be harmed and the leader's responsibility to take preventive measures.

The leader's job is not to try to *eliminate* risks; taking risks is essential to meaningful growth and change. Rather, the leader's responsibility is to *minimize* the inevitable psychological risks inherent in group work (Corey, 2016). To accomplish this, the leader's task is twofold:

1. Leaders must ensure that the group members are aware of the potential risks. This element of informed consent must be addressed before the group begins, as well as throughout the life of the group as needed.
2. Leaders must have skills that enable them to manage problems effectively as they arise.

Perhaps the most important discussion a group leader must have with members is to ensure that they understand that they may make some changes in their lives due to participating in the group and that, even though these changes may be healthy, other people in their lives might react with resistance or hostility. Thus, there is the risk of putting a strain on relationships. Group members must understand the possibility that their participation in the group could disrupt their lives, and they must be willing to accept that risk.

The leader's discussion with members or potential members should address some of the group dynamics that could make the group feel unsafe to a member or members. These factors include scapegoating, confrontation, undue pressure or coercion, and, in some groups, the possibility of physical injury resulting from exercises or activities that involve physical contact (Remley & Herlihy, 2016):

- *Scapegoating.* Occasionally a group will seem to "gang up on," or scapegoat, one member and blame that person for difficulties within the group. This person then becomes the "odd person out" toward whom the members' frustrations are channeled. If the leader does not intervene skillfully to deal with this phenomenon, the participant who is the target of the scapegoating may withdraw into silence or quit the group altogether.
- *Confrontation.* Although confrontation is a valuable tool in group work, it is easily misused. Leaders first must be comfortable with offering and being the recipient of confrontation. They also need to know how to model constructive feedback and appropriate confrontation within the group. Group members who have not learned how to confront others constructively might misuse the technique. Thus, the leader must be able to intervene when members' confrontations are inappropriate or abrasive.
- *Undue pressure and coercion.* Group members have the right to be respected within the group and not be subjected to coercion or undue pressure. Leaders may want to coax or gently pressure members to challenge them in taking necessary risks to become more involved and invested in the group (Corey, 2016), but this can be tricky. At times, they may feel pressure to speak up, to relate something personal, to be honest with the group, or to verbalize their reactions to events occurring in the group. Gentle pressure in these directions can be beneficial to individual members and the group, but it is not appropriate to pressure a member into doing what the group wants or the group thinks is right when that member truly does not talk about those wants or desires.

  When a participant is being pressured to change in a direction that the participant has not chosen, the leader should intervene (Remley & Herlihy, 2016). Leaders may have to remind the group at times that it is okay for members to "pass" or abstain from certain activities or exercises, or to see things differently than others do. Leaders should keep in mind, too, that members who bend to the social pressure of their peers to change their behavior might attribute some change they make to external influences rather than to themselves. Leaders must remain sensitive to the individual rights of group members and intervene when these rights are being compromised.
- *Possibility of physical injury.* Although the odds are remote that a group member might be physically harmed by another group member, the possibility should not be ignored. Some groups present a greater potential for inappropriate acting-out behaviors than do other groups. Examples of groups that carry a greater risk are anger-management groups for perpetrators of domestic abuse, therapeutic groups

for veterans diagnosed with post-traumatic stress disorder (PTSD), and groups for violent offenders in a prison setting. The leader is responsible for ensuring the safety of group members and for carefully monitoring any members who have known potential for harming others.

On a related topic, leaders should keep in mind that individuals can feel violated by physical touching even when no offense was intended. If leaders plan to conduct an activity or an exercise that involves physical contact or touching, they should explain this in the disclosure statement and again before implementing the exercise. Leaders should avoid touching group members in a way that might be considered sexual, offensive, or intrusive and should be aware of cultural differences in how members perceive touching.

Special cautions apply when working with groups whose members are close peers or workplace associates. Although leaders can monitor group sessions for problems developing, such as estranged work relationships, embarrassment, or loss of prestige, they cannot control what happens when the members leave the safety of the group sessions. Thus, leaders should encourage members to be accountable for their actions in their life outside the group, as well as within the group.

Skill as a leader is the crucial element for keeping risks within acceptable bounds. It is incumbent on leaders to know their members' limits and respect their requests. Having an invitational style and being skilled at giving feedback that describes (rather than judges) and tentatively suggests (rather than interprets) will do much to help members feel safe to take risks (Corey, 2016). To minimize risk, some writers (e.g., Corey, Corey, Corey, & Callanan, 2015; Cottone & Tarvydas, 2007) have suggested having a contract that specifies the responsibilities of the leader and the members. However, even in the absence of a contract, competent and good leaders intervene at critical moments to protect members and to prevent potential harm.

During the duration of a group's life, the needs of a specific member may seem to conflict with the needs of the group (as a whole). In these instances, if the individual member is at risk of being traumatized or harmed, the leader's job is to protect the individual (Cottone & Tarvydas, 2007). At the same time, the leader cannot abdicate responsibility for the group. This is a delicate balance that requires leaders to carefully exercise professional judgment.

A final element of risk addressed here relates to the leader's own values and biases. Leaders might be inclined to give more attention to a member they find likeable or attractive, or to project their own unfinished business onto a member whose concerns trigger countertransference reactions in them. Thus, leaders must self-monitor throughout the group process.

Leaders should not try to hide their values, as this may do more harm than good in certain situations (Gladding, 2016). Rather, leaders will want to be honest and at the same time work to understand and respect the roles of family and community, religion and spirituality, and ethnicity and culture in the lives of the group members (Remley & Herlihy, 2016).

PRACTICING WITH SENSITIVITY TO DIVERSITY

Group counselors historically have not paid substantive or systemic attention to working across ethnically and culturally diverse boundaries and have based their work on predominantly European–American models of counseling (Bemak & Chung, 2004a).

The ASGW first formally incorporated multicultural competencies into its *Best Practice Guidelines* in 1999. The guidelines state that group workers are expected to know, understand, and apply the ACA's *Code of Ethics*, the ASGW diversity competencies, and the ACA's *Multicultural Counseling Competencies and Standards* (Arredondo et al., 1996), among other regulatory documents that influence the practice of group work (ASGW, 2008, A.1,). Diversity is addressed throughout the ASGW (2008) guidelines as follows:

- "Group Workers actively assess their knowledge and skills related to the specific group(s) offered. Group Workers assess their values, beliefs and theoretical orientation and how these impact upon the group, particularly when working with a diverse and multicultural population" (Standard A.3.a).
- "Group Workers assess community needs, agency or organization resources, sponsoring organization mission, staff competency, attitudes regarding group work, professional training levels of potential group leaders regarding group work; client attitudes regarding group work, and multicultural and diversity considerations" (Standard A.3.b).
- "Group Workers apply and modify knowledge, skills and techniques appropriate to group type and stage, and to the unique needs of various cultural and ethnic groups" (Standard B.3.a).
- "Group Workers practice with broad sensitivity to client differences including but not limited to ethnic, gender, religious, sexual, psychological maturity, economic class, family history, physical characteristics or limitations, and geographic location. Group Workers continuously seek information regarding the cultural issues of the diverse population with whom they are working both by interaction with participants and from using outside resources" (Standard B.8).

These general guidelines, along with the more detailed and specific guidance given by the ASGW's *Principles for Diversity-Competent Group Workers* (ASGW, 1999), provide a blueprint for assessing multicultural competence as a group leader. Inherent in multicultural group work is fostering acceptance, respect, and tolerance for diversity within and among members (Bemak & Chung, 2004). Practicing with sensitivity to diversity may be as simple as adjusting the group's pace for cultural reasons to include members whose worldview may require a slower pace, or selecting an intervention that is drawn from another culture, such as the Cherokee inner/outer circle (Garrett, 2001).

Group leaders should be intentional in their approach to addressing diversity issues. They should address multicultural issues before beginning a group and should collaborate with community resources on recruitment and appropriate locations for persons of color. Leaders should also consider beyond racial and ethnic identity as there are many variations within broad racial categories that need to be considered (Delgado-Romero, Barfield, Fairley, & Martinez, 2005). Culturally competent leaders should be aware of social policy, know the characteristics of and resources in the areas in which their group members live, and be aware of overt and covert discriminatory practices at social and community levels. They also need to foresee possible conflicts between ethnic and therapeutic values (Shechtman, Hiradin, & Zina, 2003).

Cultural awareness includes the leader accepting his or her possible limitations in facilitating a group experience with members from diverse backgrounds. Accepting these limitations might mean that the leader would ask another professional who is a member of a specified cultural group to cofacilitate the group experience.

Some guidelines drawn from various sources (Corey, 2016; Corey et al., 2017; Remley & Herlihy, 2016) are as follows:

- In designing groups and in orienting members to the group process, be aware of the implications of cultural diversity.
- Take time to reflect on your personal identity, especially as it influences your professional work.
- Think about your needs and behavior styles and the impact these might have on your group participants.
- Assess the group's goodness of fit with community needs.
- Develop the purpose and goals for the group in collaboration with the constituency for which the group is intended.
- Identify techniques and a leadership style appropriate to the type of group for which intervention is planned and the culture in which it is to be implemented.
- Consider the impact of adverse social, environmental, and political factors in designing interventions.
- Be alert to issues of oppression, sexism, racism, ableism, and other forms of discrimination as you work with diverse group members.
- Acquire the knowledge and skills you need to effectively work with the diverse members of your group. If you lack some of the needed background, seek consultation, supervision, and further education and training.

HANDLING PREMATURE WITHDRAWALS FROM THE GROUP

Whenever group participation is voluntary, members have the freedom to exit the group at any time. This can be problematic because all group members are affected when one participant decides to drop out of the group.

As a foundation, leaders must have clear policies regarding expectations for members' attendance, commitment to remain in the group for a specified number of sessions, leaving a session if unhappy with what is going on in the group, and handling an intended departure from the group before the group ends. These policies should be discussed both in the screening interview and during the group's first session (Corey, 2016).

Even though leaders may be clear about their expectations and members may be sincere in their intentions to live up to these expectations, an individual sometimes will want to drop out of the group. If this happens, the trust and cohesion of the group likely will be jeopardized. For this reason, the leader may be tempted to try to dissuade the individual from exiting the group. If the group is counterproductive for an individual or if the group is not meeting that individual's needs, however, that member certainly has the right to leave.

There is no consensus regarding just how to handle such a situation (Remley & Herlihy, 2016). In general, it is recommended that the individual who is considering withdrawing be encouraged to bring up the matter for discussion in the group (Corey, 2016; Cottone & Tarvydas, 2007) or to at least inform the other members about the decision to exit (Welfel, 2016). The outcome of that discussion might be that the member decides to stay after all. Welfel noted that one aspect of what makes a group beneficial is its power to help clients work through difficult emotions and honor their commitments to others.

A potential problem with this approach, however, is that the individual might feel pressured to stay by the other group members. Statements such as "The group just won't be the same without you" or "Your input is always so insightful" could cause the member who is thinking about leaving to feel guilty for wanting to leave. Leaders must be careful not to have a "hidden agenda"—a desire that the person will be persuaded to stay so the group will not be disrupted—as that could affect how they handle the discussion. Careful self-monitoring by leaders is crucial here.

This approach could have an advantage, though, in that even if the individual decides to withdraw from the group, both the individual and the other group members are less likely to be left with "unfinished business." The individual can achieve a sense of closure by expressing what has made him or her feel uncomfortable or threatened, and the remaining group members won't be left wondering whether they somehow "caused" the person to depart.

This is a difficult situation for the leader. Ideally, the member who is contemplating dropping out of the group will be willing to talk with the group, or at least with the leader. If the individual still chooses to withdraw, that person should be allowed to leave without being subjected to pressure to remain. One strategy that has been suggested to avoid the problem is to have a trial period, after which members can formally leave the group if they so choose (Cottone & Tarvydas, 2007).

TERMINATING AND FOLLOWING UP

Although terminating a group usually is not considered an ethical issue, leaders do have certain ethical responsibilities to fulfill in bringing a group to closure. During the termination phase of a group, three essential leader tasks are to help the participants

1. make meaning of the experience,
2. transfer in-group learnings to their everyday lives, and
3. access further resources if needed.

As the group prepares to end, the leader's work can be challenging. The leader must deal simultaneously with the difficult emotions that accompany saying good-bye, wrap up any unfinished business, help members personalize what they have learned from the experience, and provide members with suggestions for applying these learnings in their lives after the group ends. ASGW's *Best Practice Guidelines* (ASGW, 2008) reminds counselors of the importance of assisting members to generate meaning from the group experience (Standard B.5).

After the group ends, leaders have two additional responsibilities: evaluation and follow-up. ASGW's *Best Practice Guidelines* (ASGW, 2008) emphasizes the need for evaluation at the conclusion of the group and for follow-up contact with members (Standards B.7, C.3). Evaluation is a necessary part of the process of increasing one's competence as a group leader, and the leader must assess the group and use the assessment results to help plan, revise, and improve groups to be conducted in the future.

Leaders have an ethical obligation to make themselves available for follow-up contact with group members as needed (ASGW, 2008, Standard C.3.b). Corey (2016) recommends that leaders hold individual follow-up interviews if feasible. Even though these interviews can be brief, they might prove valuable in determining how well the members integrated and transferred their learnings. In addition, the interviews provide an opportunity to discuss referral for further counseling or development—an issue that is best handled on an individual basis.

Summary

Myriad ethical responsibilities affect every aspect of group leaders' work, from the planning stage of a group through termination and follow-up. Helpful written guidelines include the ACA's *Code of Ethics* (ACA, 2014) and three publications of the ASGW: *Best Practice Guidelines* (2008), *Principles for Diversity-Competent Group Workers* (1999), and *Professional Standards for the Training of Group Workers* (2000). Although these guidelines are helpful, they cannot substitute for sound, clinical judgment.

The planning phase of a group begins with determining if you have the competencies needed to lead the group in question. Lack of competence can lead to malpractice lawsuits. Other pregroup tasks include addressing an array of planning issues, recruiting and screening potential members, and securing informed consent for prospective members to participate in the group. Groups for children and adolescents and groups for mandated clients have special considerations.

Ethical and legal issues accompanying the life of a group include explaining confidentiality and privileged communication, maintaining privacy of records, managing boundaries, minimizing risks, practicing with sensitivity to diversity, dealing with premature withdrawals, and handling termination and follow-up. Again, groups of minors and mandated clients raise unique ethical and legal considerations.

Taken together, these ethical and legal issues paint a picture of the complexities and ambiguities involved in conducting group work. Ethics committees, licensing boards, and courts of law do not expect leaders to be perfect or flawless in their practice of group work. Rather, the expectation is to exercise due diligence—by staying current in your knowledge, keeping careful documentation, seeking consultation and supervision as needed, and using sound professional judgment.

6 Diversity and Multicultural Group Counseling

Deborah J. Rubel and Jane E. Atieno Okech

It can be said that all group counseling issues are related to diversity. The primary question to be answered during group counseling is "How can we work together in a way that benefits us all?" (Kline, 2003, p. 7). While the primary concern of individual counseling is the functioning of the individual, the emphasis in group counseling is facilitating a balance between the needs of the group and the needs of individual members. This mirrors the challenge of living in a pluralistic society, where too often the needs of some members are devalued or ignored. Diversity and multicultural issues are a primary concern for group counselors due to changing demographics and the prioritization of culturally competent counseling (Bemak & Chi-Ying Chung, 2004; Okech & Rubel, 2007). This chapter covers key concepts of diversity and multicultural counseling and then explores their implications for group counseling.

UNDERSTANDING THE CONCEPTS OF DIVERSITY AND MULTICULTURALISM

According to U.S. Census Bureau projected estimates, racial and ethnic minority numbers will make up more than 50% of the population by the year 2044; by 2060, nearly 20% of the population will be foreign-born (Colby & Ortman, 2015). The 2012 Census Bureau projections revealed that approximately 20% of the population is identified as having a disability, and updated projections in 2015 revealed that individuals that are 65 years and older will account for 20% of the population by 2030. In addition, although the U.S. Census does not address sexual orientation, many estimates indicate that people who identify as gay, lesbian, or bisexual account for between 2.3% (Ward, Dahlhamer, Galinsky, & Joestl, 2014) and 3.5% of the population (Gates, 2011). These estimates, coupled with the reality that most of the aforementioned groups still do not have status and power equivalent to dominant groups in this society (Sue & Sue, 2003), suggest that adapting to an increasingly diverse and multicultural population is a major issue facing society.

Social and cultural diversity has the potential to enrich society but also may result in misunderstanding, conflict, and oppression (Bell, 2007). Although society increasingly values diversity and the promotion of social and economic equality, this exemplar has not been achieved (Sue & Sue, 2003). These inequalities are difficult to discuss because of the strong emotions they generate and because of the many terms and concepts that are used to describe diversity and its effects on individuals, groups, and social processes (DeLucia-Waack & Donigian, 2004).

When discussing group and individual differences, two terms that often are used interchangeably are *diversity* and *multiculturalism*. Smith and Kehe (2004) defined *diversity* as "aspects of difference among individual and groups" (p. 329). Bell (2007) suggested that a useful framework when exploring diversity is social identity group membership, which is generally categorized in terms of race, ethnicity, gender, sexual orientation, socioeconomic status, disability, age, and religion (Bell, 2007; Green & Stiers, 2002). The term *multicultural* is used most often in relation to differences based on culture, ethnicity, and race (Helms & Cook, 1999). Smith and Kehe (2004) defined *race* as a categorization of individuals based on skin color and other physical attributes; historical, geographic origin; and the perceptions of the dominant group. In comparison, they defined *ethnicity* as identification with a group based on culture, nationalism, citizenship, or the interactions of race, religion, and sociopolitical history.

When exploring the impact of diversity upon group counseling, the three elements that form an essential framework for understanding are (a) culture and its implications for individuals, (b) the impact of diversity upon individual identity development, and (c) the impact of diversity upon relationships between social identity groups. These three elements relate to and interact with each other and must be understood to fully grasp how diversity impacts group counseling.

Diversity implies, but is not limited to, differences in culture. Smith and Kehe (2004) defined *culture* as the "characteristic values, behaviors, products, and worldviews of a group of people with a distinct sociohistorical context" (p. 329). Cultural differences are often represented as members of a given cultural group eating different foods, having different customs, and speaking different languages (Anderson, 2002). Subtler, but critical, dimensions of cultural difference may include differences in parenting beliefs, family structure, social hierarchy, gender role expectations, use of verbal and nonverbal communication, relationship to time and space, help-seeking behavior, and other variables (Matsukawa, 2001). These differences shape individual and group life and affect relationships among groups or individuals of different cultures. Although surmountable, these differences can be the basis for misunderstanding, mistrust, conflict, and stereotypes that lead to prejudice, discrimination, and systemic oppression (Bell, 2007).

Diversity also affects individual identity formation. Tatum (2000) stated, "The concept of identity is a complex one, shaped by individual characteristics, family dynamics, historical factors, and social and political contexts" (p. 9). Sue and Sue (2003) described similar dimensions. They indicated that the *individual level* of identity is shaped by an individual's unique genetic variation and nonshared experiences, whereas the *group level* of identity is shaped by social identity group membership and interaction. The *universal level* of identity is characterized by shared human experiences, such as self-awareness, birth, death, and love. Although counseling traditionally has focused on the individual and universal aspects of identity, the group level of identity is central in the discussion of diversity and its impact on group counseling.

MODELS OF IDENTITY DEVELOPMENT

Throughout life, identity is shaped by reflections from a person's social context, consisting of family; institutions such as schools, churches, and legal systems; and the broader cultural environments of communities, regions, and nations (Harro, 2000).

Within these contexts, each individual characteristic or group membership is valued differentially. People internalize these valuations to some extent as identity, and this affects how they view themselves, members of their identity group, and those in other groups (Helms & Cook, 1999). This is further complicated by the reality that social identity is multilayered or intersectional. Hardiman, Jackson, and Griffin (2007) suggested that people experience a blend of social identities, resulting in complex views of themselves and the world.

In an attempt to simplify the complexities of identity development, theorists have created identity-development models. A key assumption behind these models is that individuals have varying degrees of awareness and acceptance of their social identities. The predominant identity-development models describe minority individuals' characteristics as they come to terms with their own cultural or racial group membership, the dominant group culture, and the relationship between the groups. Examples of these models are Atkinson, Morten, and Sue's racial/cultural identity development (R/CID) model (Sue & Sue, 2003) and the people of color racial identity model (Helms, 1995). These models share a progression from a status of dominant culture acceptance, to minority culture acceptance, and then to a more complex state of minority culture acceptance that allows for connection to and valuing of aspects of other cultures, including the dominant culture.

In contrast, Helms's White racial identity model (Helms, 1995) is an example of a dominant-group-identity model, which assumes that healthy identity development for dominant groups' individuals involves becoming aware of their privileged status in society and the effect of that status upon other cultural groups. Helms's model consists of six stages, moving from the first stage, *contact,* in which the White individual is unaware of racism and is content with the racial status quo, to the sixth stage, *autonomy,* which finds the White individual having formed a positive, White, nonracist identity, valuing diversity and taking an active stance toward relinquishing White privilege.

One way to understand diversity and its effect on relationships among social identity groups is through the *oppression model* (Bell, 2007). This model highlights how, within each identity group category, specific identities have more power than others in the context of any given society. The collection of social identities with more power constitutes what is known as the *dominant* or *agent group.* In the context of the present-day United States, agent groups include White; heterosexual; male; Christian; physically, emotionally, and intellectually "abled"; high-income; and young or middle-aged adults (Bell, 2007; Green & Stiers, 2002). *Target groups* have less power. In the present-day United States, target groups include, but are not limited to, people of color; gay, lesbian, or bisexual individuals; female or transgendered individuals; those with physical, emotional, or intellectual disabilities; people of low socioecomonic status; the elderly; and the very young (Bell, 2007; Green & Stiers, 2002).

SIDEBAR 6.1
Self-Awareness: The Intersection of Your Identities

Review the seven categories of social identity presented by Bell (2007). Reflect upon your own array of social identities, then consider whether you fit into the agent or target group for each of these identities. What is the overall balance of agent and target identities? Do you at times experience an intersection of some of your identities? How do these identities affect how you experience the world? Within your family? At school? With clients?

Oppression is a condition that occurs when agent groups systematically devalue the values, beliefs, and experiences of target groups. Although this devaluation is the product of many social and psychological processes, its dynamics can be understood by examining the concepts of stereotypes, prejudice, discrimination, and privilege. *Stereotypes* are negative generalizations about social identity groups and group members. Stereotypes encourage people to attend selectively to negative group attributes and form simplistic views that deny the complex reality of group identity. Many prejudices are based upon stereotypes. *Prejudices* are judgments of social identity groups or group members made without adequate information or contact (Smith & Kehe, 2004). Prejudice serves the needs of a cultural group by solidifying its identity in contrast to another group and by justifying their unequal treatment (Blumenfeld & Raymond, 2000). *Discrimination* is behavior by the individuals or institutions of one social identity group that has differential and harmful effects on members of other social identity groups. Whereas *individual* and *institutional discrimination* result from the actions of individuals and institutions, respectively, *structural discrimination* results from seemingly neutral policies, procedures, and practices that result in unintentional discrimination. *Privilege*, a concept related to structural discrimination, is defined as unearned access to resources that are readily available to members of some social identity groups (Smith & Kehe, 2004). Those who lack privilege can easily identify it, whereas those with privilege may struggle to do so because they do not have to understand target groups to function and may be oblivious to the experience of target group members.

Having less power profoundly affects how individuals of oppressed groups view themselves, life, and agent groups. Prolonged exposure to oppressive environments may result in *internalized oppression* or internalization of negative cultural messages (Harro, 2000). Being relegated to a position of less power by those with privilege may compound the painful experience of being discriminated against. The result is that the relationship between agent and target groups can be marked by mistrust and anger.

MULTICULTURAL COUNSELING

Early permutations of counseling were based on the experiences of White European or Euro-American males (Sue & Sue, 2003). According to Jackson (1995), clinical psychology literature did not include multicultural themes until the 1950s, and it wasn't until the 1960s that significant attention began to be directed to the inadequacy of traditional counseling methods for minority populations defined by race or ethnicity, particularly African-Americans. The 1970s brought a broader focus that included other racial/ethnic groups, as well as women and people with disabilities. Issues impacting sexual minorities did not become a core focus of the helping professions until the 1990s, which marked the true prioritization of diversity issues in the counseling profession (Jackson, 1995).

Despite this progress, the process of evaluating and renovating a profession is slow work, and the profession still has a long way to go toward serving diverse groups equally (Sue & Sue, 2003). Some of the chief concerns about counseling that does not fully consider the client's cultural identity include incongruent expectations of the counseling process, the counselor not understanding the impact of social forces upon the client, interpretation of cultural differences as pathology, lack of access to counseling for diverse groups, and the use of culturally biased assessments (Neukrug, 1998). Furthermore, counselors who are "culturally encapsulated," or expect diverse clients to share their cultural standards, will not be effective in helping a client form relevant goals, will not fully recognize the significance of the client's story, will use interventions and techniques that may be ineffective, or will alienate or harm the client (Neukrug, 1998). Awareness of these deficiencies resulted in the emergence of multicultural counseling, which Sue and Sue (2003) defined as

> both a helping role and process that uses modalities and defines goals consistent with the life experiences and cultural values of clients, recognizes client identities to include individual, group, and universal dimensions, advocates the use of universal and culture-specific strategies and roles in the healing process, and balances the importance of individualism and collectivism in the assessment, diagnosis, and treatment of client and client systems. (p. 16)

MULTICULTURAL AND SOCIAL JUSTICE COMPETENCIES AND OBJECTIVES

In an effort to provide a conceptual framework that will assist counselors in better serving diverse clients, the American Counseling Association (ACA) has endorsed the *Multicultural and Social Justice Counseling Competencies* (MSJCC; Ratts, Singh, Nassar-McMillan, Butler, & McCullough, 2015). The MSJCC "offers counselors a framework to implement multicultural and social justice competencies into counseling theories, practices, and research" (p. 3). The MSJCC describes four domains critical to the development of multicultural and social justice competence:

1. Awareness of own assumptions, values, and biases
2. Understanding the worldview of the client
3. Investing in the counseling relationship
4. Developing culturally appropriate counseling and advocacy-intervention strategies and techniques

The MSJCC further outlined essential aspirational counselor beliefs and attitudes, knowledge, skills, and actions in the first three domains. The emphasis in this model of multicultural and social justice competency is on counselors' actively seeking understanding of themselves, their clients, and their clients' environments, and combining these understandings to provide counseling interventions and services that fully respect, embrace, and utilize the client's unique life experiences. In addition, the model highlights the "intersection in identities and the dynamics of power, privilege, and oppression that influence the counseling relationship" (Ratts et al., 2015, p. 3).

Counselor Self-Awareness

Counselors themselves are cultural beings, members of multiple social identity groups, and, as such, have identities, values, beliefs, social norms, and ways of communicating that are based on these contexts. Counselors' views of themselves and others are based on these social contexts, too. Without adequate awareness of the stereotypes, biases, privileges, marginalized status, and culturally based reactions that are part of life as cultural beings, counselors unknowingly view culturally different clients' lives, issues, goals, and interactions within the counseling relationship from their own perspectives, which may be inaccurate, nonfunctional, and harmful to clients (Ratts et al., 2015).

SIDEBAR 6.2

Self-Awareness: Exploring Your Biases and Stereotypes

Take out a sheet of paper and something to write with. Pick a social-identity category from Bell's (2007) list of seven, then pick a specific identity from that group that is different from your identity. Without self-censoring, list as many thoughts or ideas about people from that identity group as you can in 5 minutes. When the 5-minute period is over, read what you have written. Discern which ideas are based on actual knowledge and experiences. What are the origins of the other ideas? Which would you say are biases or stereotypes? How do you feel as you read these?

Awareness of the Client's Worldview

Worldview is a concept related to racial/cultural identity, but is more inclusive and can be seen as people's view of themselves in relationship to the world (Sue & Sue, 2003). In comparison to *cultural identification*, which can be seen as individuals' sense of belonging to a group, *worldview* is the sum total of their conceptions of the world that guide their meaning making, decisions, and behavior. To understand a client's worldview is to fully understand his or her individual, social, and universal context. This context may consist of dimensions of family, social identity, history, language, and biological, ecological, or environmental factors (Smith & Kehe, 2004). Worldview also is impacted by the dimensions of locus of control, locus of responsibility, and collectivistic/individualistic views of self-concept (Matsukawa, 2001; Sue & Sue, 2003). Although knowledge of clients' culture is important, specific knowledge of the client's privilege or marginalized status is necessary for an accurate understanding (Ratts et al., 2015).

Counseling Relationship

The counseling relationship is impacted by the privileged or marginalized status of the counselor and client (Ratts et al., 2015). The degree to which the privileged or marginalized status of the counselor impacts the therapeutic relationship is influenced by the extent of the counselor's awareness of her or his own and the client's worldview, attitudes, beliefs, and privileged or marginalized status, and should remain by the counselor's knowledge of the impact of these factors on the client's presenting concerns. Counselors who understand the intersection between their identities and those of their clients and who are willing to broach and engage in conversation about clients' identities and worldviews and their impact on clients' presenting concerns are more likely to develop an effective relationship with their clients. To develop a meaningful relationship with the client requires an understanding of the client's worldview and a full understanding of her or his individual, social, and universal context, including experiences associated with the client's privileged or marginalized status (Ratts et al., 2015).

Counseling and Advocacy Skills

Culturally appropriate group-counseling interventions consider several factors related to culture and social justice. In addition to ensuring that a client's marginalized or privileged status is understood, the client's worldview, values, and beliefs need to be respected (Ratts et al., 2015). Group-intervention skills should therefore reflect an acknowledgment of client social norms and their incorporation to the extent possible in the group. In addition, culturally skilled group counselors attend to differences in communication style. These differences may include a person's (a) culturally influenced sense of personal space, (b) use of facial expressions, posture, gestures, and eye contact, and (c) use of verbal loudness, pauses, silence, speech rate, and inflection to express different meanings (Sue & Sue, 2003). Group counselors should consider that communication style may be *low-context*, relying largely on the verbal content, or *high-context*, relying less on verbal content and more on shared understanding, nonverbal language, and paralanguage to convey the full meaning of the message (Hall, 1989; Okech, Pimpleton, Vannata, & Champe, 2015; Singh, Merchant, Skudrzyk, & Ingene, 2012a). Culturally appropriate group counseling interventions may also incorporate indigenous or culturally based healing practices if necessary (Sue & Sue, 2003) but only when the group leader possesses the knowledge and skill to incorporate them respectfully. When necessary, group counselors should "intervene with, and on behalf of, clients at the intrapersonal, interpersonal, institutional, community, public policy, and international/global level" (Ratts et al., 2015, p. 11).

DIVERSITY ISSUES IN MULTICULTURAL GROUP COUNSELING

Bemak and Chi-Ying Chung (2004) stated, "Historically, group counseling has not paid sustentative or systematic attention to counseling across ethnically and culturally diverse boundaries" (p. 31). Although group counseling is commonly assumed to promote collective values more than individual counseling does, current systems of group counseling continue to express White, Euro-American therapeutic values, such as emotional expressiveness, self-disclosure, and open expression and resolution of conflict.

Realization that group counseling has not met its potential for benefiting diverse members has resulted in increased attention to these issues both in practice and in training over the last 10 years (Anderson, 2007; Okech & Rubel, 2007; Okech et al., 2015; Okech, Pimpleton-Gray, Vannata, & Champe, 2016). A result of this focus has been the development of the Association for Specialists in Group Work's (ASGW's) *Multicultural and Social Justice Competence Principles for Group Workers* (MSJCP; Singh et al., 2012a), which revised and replaced an earlier version of the same document, the *Principles for Diversity-Competent Group Workers* (Association for Specialists in Group Work, 1998). Unlike the ACA's MSJCC, these diversity and social justice principles are specifically focused on the dynamics of groups and how social–cultural factors manifest in group member interactions, as well as group leader dynamics.

The diversity and multicultural issues of group counseling and individual counseling are distinct from one another. Although many of the same concerns of multicultural individual counseling also apply to group counseling, the multilevel nature of group counseling results in key differences between the theory and the practice of individual counseling and group counseling (Okech & Rubel, 2007). Some of the key concepts of group counseling that must be examined for their applicability to diverse populations include the group as a social microcosm, the therapeutic factors, group cohesion, group development, pregroup planning, and specific skills used during group facilitation.

Groups as a Social Microcosm

A key concept that differentiates group counseling from individual counseling is the idea of groups as a social microcosm in which the dynamics of groups mirror the dynamics of the outside social environment (Yalom & Leszcz, 2005). With respect to diversity in group counseling, this means the potential reenactment of oppression (Green & Stiers, 2002). Although this may offer an opportunity to discuss, learn, and heal from oppression during groups, it may also propagate and reinforce oppression (Brooks, Gordon, & Meadow, 1998). Without adequate, competent leadership that addresses oppressive dynamics early in the group process, the latter is more likely to occur (Green & Stiers, 2002).

According to Helms and Cook (1999), three main diversity themes occur in the dynamics of groups. First, power is distributed within the group according to each person's social role in the group. This means that group leaders and group members of privileged status will tend to have more influence in the group. Second, power may be distributed according to the numerical representation of social-identity groups within the group. Third, members of agent social-identity groups generally have more power than target or marginalized members. These themes present themselves in different ways depending on the leader's social identity, the diversity in coleadership relationships, and the social-identity composition of the group. Recognizing these dynamics is essential in preparing for multicultural group counseling and for preventing harm from occurring to members. Examples of these dynamics include the following:

1. Without specific intent otherwise, privileged or marginalized group leaders who have cultural biases, prejudices, or blind spots will tend to perpetuate these attitudes in the group because the leader generally is the most powerful person in the process (Kline, 2003).
2. Agent/privileged group members may dominate group interaction. Group norms and process will conform to agent standards, and topics will be those of relevance to agent group members (Han & Vasquez, 2000).
3. Members with nonvisible target identities, who hide their identity in many social settings, may hide this identity as well in groups. Although they may do this for safety reasons, the experience parallels the sense of invisibility and powerlessness that the member may have in society at large.
4. Members with target identities/marginalized status may be unwilling to discuss their feelings or experiences associated with their status. This dynamic may be related to feeling unsafe or ashamed (Helms & Cook, 1999).
5. When target/marginalized members share their feelings and experiences honestly, agent group members who are uncomfortable with their status may deny, minimize, or openly challenge the reality of such feelings and experiences (Griffin & Ouellet, 2007).
6. Agent/privileged members may scapegoat target members for resisting dominant group norms or for expressing oppression-related anger, mistrust, or pain. Group leaders may compound this damaging dynamic by labeling a target member too quickly as resistant or problematic (Sue & Sue, 2003).
7. Members with target/marginalized identities may be pressured into roles representative of their identity group or pressured to act as educators of agent group leaders or members. These roles absolve agent group members and leaders of

---

SIDEBAR 6.3
Case Study: Why Is Chris So Quiet in Group?

Devin is leading a counseling group for people dealing with the breakup of a significant relationship. The group is composed of five women, four of whom identify as White and one as African-American. The ages of the group members are 22, 29, 38, 41, and 67. Chris, who is 67, has been almost silent in the group and has shared only minimally when directly asked. Devin knows that Chris's silence may be part of her personality but wants to consider if social and cultural diversity might be playing a role. How might the concept of groups as a social microcosm be applied to understanding this situation? What role might Chris's age play in her silence? What about her race? What are some other ways social and cultural diversity might be involved?

---

responsibility for oppressive dynamics in the group and depersonalize target members. Each of these dynamics results in diminishing the target group member's experience, and this may affect the entire group process. These dynamics are more likely to occur if the group leader is unable to recognize when they are occurring or if the leader is unable to steer the group toward more effective ways of interacting.

Therapeutic Factors

One of the most accepted and well-researched concepts in group counseling (Dierick & Lietaer, 2008; Helms & Cook, 1999), *therapeutic factors* are elements of group experience from which group members derive benefit. Yalom and Leszcz (2005) have published the most accepted list of therapeutic factors based on research, which includes instillation of hope, universality, imparting information, altruism, corrective recapitulation of the primary family group, development of socializing techniques, imitative behavior, interpersonal learning, group cohesiveness, catharsis, and existential factors.

Helms and Cook (1999) have described Yalom's therapeutic factors as a fruitful starting point for exploring diversity-sensitive group intervention, recognizing that his work provides the framework for much of the group counseling conducted today. Helms and Cook indicated that without attention to diversity issues and the differential effects on group members, the therapeutic factors might be counterproductive for some group members. The following discussion summarizes and builds upon their critiques.

INSTILLATION OF HOPE   Diverse group members should be exposed to people who are similar in background, either in the group or through supplementary material, who have overcome similar challenges and been helped by participating in groups. Group leaders must openly acknowledge the differential limitations to success that society places on some group members, particularly those of marginalized status.

UNIVERSALITY   Although sharing issues and experiences at the universal level may be helpful, diverse group members may benefit from sharing with others who in addition have similar backgrounds and experiences. Group leaders must be prepared to connect diverse group members who have similar cultural experiences or experiences of marginalization while also pointing out universal themes that may unite the group.

IMPARTING INFORMATION   Diverse group members may benefit greatly from receiving information about differing cultural interpretations of behavior, along with information about the group process. Group leaders may have to facilitate information exchanges when members have different communication norms. Leaders also must ensure that didactic group material is relevant to the experiences of diverse group members.

ALTRUISM   Diverse group members may experience validation of their worth as they provide support, advice, and feedback to others. To ensure this, group leaders must be aware that the contributions of diverse group members may be discounted, and the leaders may have to assist group members in seeing the value of all contributions.

CORRECTIVE RECAPITULATION OF THE PRIMARY FAMILY GROUP   Although family issues may play a part in any group member's distress, societal dynamics may be even more relevant for diverse group members. Group leaders must be aware of different societal dynamics and exercise caution before interpreting group members' issues as deficits in family relationships or structure.

DEVELOPMENT OF SOCIALIZING TECHNIQUES   Definitions of basic social skills are culturally determined. Diverse group members may benefit from learning how to switch cultural styles when necessary. Group leaders must be familiar with a variety of culturally appropriate behaviors and should assist members in determining which are most useful in multicultural contexts. Group leaders should also ensure that all group members, not just diverse members, share the expectation of flexibility.

IMITATIVE BEHAVIOR   Diverse group members may imitate the behavior of group leaders or, in mixed groups, dominant group members. This may be beneficial if the behavior is antioppressive and useful to the diverse member. Diverse coleadership relationships that model effective cross-cultural respect and communication may be particularly effective in this case. Imitative behavior will not be beneficial if the group leader demonstrates biased behavior or allows racist, sexist, or other oppressive behavior to continue unchecked.

INTERPERSONAL LEARNING   Interpersonal learning can provide value to agent and target group members by uncovering the impact of cultural differences in behavior through the feedback process and allowing them to experience cross-cultural connections that were not possible before. Engaging in honest feedback in a diverse group, however, can be anxiety provoking and frustrating. Group leaders must be comfortable with conflict and provide adequate support, structure, and encouragement to group members as they communicate with each other. Leaders also must be cognizant that self-disclosure of personal reactions may be culturally inappropriate for some group members.

CATHARSIS   Expression of strong emotions may be helpful to some diverse group members. Different cultures view the expression of strong emotions, or *catharsis*, in varying ways, and group leaders should be aware of these differences, should allow for different modes of expression, and should ensure that the emotional expressions of diverse group members have a reasonable chance of being understood and accepted by other group members.

EXISTENTIAL FACTORS Most diverse group members will relate to universal experiences such as connection and death, but the existential givens of freedom and responsibility may not be relevant to group members who have experienced chronic oppression and marginalization. In fact, oppression and related powerlessness may deserve status as an existential condition. Group leaders should not assume that all group members experience existential factors equally.

GROUP COHESION The final therapeutic factor, group cohesion, is one of the most critical to the group process (Yalom & Leszcz, 2005) but also is considered difficult to achieve in diverse groups (Brinson & Lee, 1997). Thus, the following is a more in-depth discussion of group cohesion and the related element of trust.

Importance of Group Cohesion and Trust

Group cohesion, which is defined as group members' attraction to the group and other members, is essential for the development of a therapeutic group environment (Yalom & Leszcz, 2005). Without group cohesion, group members will not be willing to take the necessary risks to participate in the group and to continue to participate when interaction becomes anxiety provoking or frustrating.

Although trust between group facilitators and group members and among group members is necessary for developing cohesion, diverse group members may have difficulty developing trust, especially with dominant-culture group leaders and members (Brinson & Lee, 1997). When diversity issues affect group members' ability to trust each other or the group leader, communication and understanding are impeded and group cohesion is affected adversely, and then the group's overall functioning toward its goals suffers. As a cautionary note, it is necessary to distinguish between mistrust that is rooted in societal dynamics and suspicions that are rooted in mental disorders (Fenster & Fenster, 1998; Sue & Sue, 2003).

Fenster and Fenster (1998) used the term *good enough basic trust* to describe a condition in which diverse group members feel safe enough to engage in the group process, and they offered several suggestions to the group leader for establishing this level of trust in mixed-identity groups:

1. The group leader should be aware of the standard group-counseling practices for developing a safe environment.
2. The group leader must show an eagerness to learn about other cultures, as well as basic knowledge about cultural differences.
3. The leader must model acceptance and respect for diverse identities and experiences.
4. The leader must communicate that the group culture is one in which cultural stereotypes, prejudices, discrimination, and oppressive dynamics will be identified, discussed, and challenged.
5. The leader also must adequately manage the anxiety level of the group during discussion of diversity-related issues.

In addition, Sue and Sue (2003) discussed factors that influence the perception of dominant-group counselors as trustworthy, and these factors may be relevant to developing trust and cohesion in diverse groups. First, Sue and Sue place the responsibility of developing trust on the people in power in the relationship, which in a group is usually the leader and any group members in powerful roles. Sue and Sue also indicated

SIDEBAR 6.4

Case Study: Helping a Socially and Culturally Diverse Group Build Trust

In the middle school environment, Brett is leading a counseling group for young teens coping with stress. He identifies as a White, cis-gender male, heterosexual, and in his mid-40s. The school he works in and the group he will be leading are predominantly Latinx, though he knows at least two of the eight students will be White. He is aware that he will have both male and female students in his group and a variety of immigration statuses. He hopes to build trust in the group so that students will share more deeply about the things that cause them stress. What are some suggestions you might give Brett?

that diverse clients may test dominant-culture counselors for sincerity and openness and indicated that responses that would be perceived as trustworthy include honesty, sincerity, genuineness, and possibly some self-disclosing.

Group Development Stages

Group development theories describe stages, transitions, and issues common to all groups. Group counselors who understand group development can better understand the needs of the group and group members during the transitional phases and can gauge the progress of their groups by monitoring the group's development. From the many group development theories, Gross and Capuzzi (2002) created a composite incorporating the main commonalities of many theories. They conceptualized the group development process as having four stages:

1. The definitive stage
2. The personal involvement stage
3. The group involvement stage
4. The enhancement and closure stage

During the definitive stage, leaders set up the group, and members evaluate the group for fit, acceptance, and belonging and begin to make sense of the group's process and structure. During the personal involvement stage, members begin to develop enough trust to engage each other, the group, and the leader in more challenging ways. To enter the group involvement stage, members must have worked through their basic differences and conflicts. During this phase, group members begin to work together toward achieving group and personal goals. Finally, in the enhancement and closure stage, group members consolidate the meaning of their group experiences, plan for life after group, and process the loss of the group.

Groups that are diverse in composition may not develop past the early stages without specific attention to differences in culture and issues of diversity (Fenster & Fenster, 1998). Diversity affects each phase of group development, and group leaders should adjust their leadership accordingly (Brinson & Lee, 1997).

DIVERSITY CONCERNS DURING THE DEFINITIVE STAGE   Appropriate group composition is essential for diverse groups to progress through the definitive stage and develop the trust necessary to move to more challenging issues. In addition to other group screening criteria, potential group members should be evaluated for social identity and levels of identity development and be placed in groups the purpose and composition of which will allow them to meet their objectives (Anderson, 2002).

During the early definitive group phase, diverse group members may experience anxiety because of unfamiliarity with group counseling and mistrust of the helping system (Brinson & Lee, 1997). This entry anxiety can be addressed in pregroup interviews by outlining the group's goals, objectives, and process to reduce ambiguity and provide an opportunity for processing anxieties and questions. These issues may be revisited several times during the early definitive phase (Brooks et al., 1998).

Nearly all group members experience some anxiety during the definitive stage, and establishing ground rules and connection between members can lend a sense of safety. A diverse group should acknowledge cultural differences in how members self-disclose and express feelings, and respecting self-determined levels of participation is important. During this formative phase, diverse group members should be encouraged to tell their stories at their own pace, using, if necessary, their primary language or alternative modes of communication.

Throughout this phase, group leaders should check for understanding between group members and encourage members to acknowledge and support each participant's experience (Brinson & Lee, 1997). Culturally appropriate structured activities may ease the diverse group through this early phase, though such activities should not be overused as they may decrease spontaneity and keep the group at a superficial level (Merta, 1995).

DIVERSITY CONCERNS DURING THE PERSONAL INVOLVEMENT STAGE Groups that have developed sufficient trust can move into the personal involvement stage. Because of increased trust, group members may begin to express deeper differences (Kline, 2003). Interactions during this phase are characteristically more challenging, and conflict may arise. Helms and Cook (1999) stated, "Once implicit racial or cultural issues occurring with a group are made explicit, it is likely that related conflicts will also move to the forefront of the group" (p. 242).

In diverse groups, challenge and conflict may center on uncovered power relationships, bias, and feelings related to social identity (Camacho, 2001). Strong leadership is essential during this phase to encourage diverse group members to deal with their differences, maintain a level of safety in the group, set limits on inappropriate or culturally insensitive expressions of anger, guide group members through conflict resolution or management, and help the group make sense of the process (Camacho, 2001; Yalom & Leszcz, 2005).

In addition, group leaders should be aware that many cultural groups view conflict differently (Okech et al., 2016). Group leaders should be flexible about how conflict is expressed and resolved within the group and be prepared to suggest and negotiate alternative means of resolution. Successful negotiation of culturally based conflict will increase levels of trust within the group.

DIVERSITY CONCERNS DURING THE GROUP INVOLVEMENT STAGE Successful negotiation of the challenging personal involvement stage will result in the diverse group moving to the group involvement stage. Brinson and Lee (1997) described this stage as one of cohesiveness and productivity in which group members can explore significant personal issues in depth and work actively toward the group's goals and objectives. Focusing on these goals, leaders of diverse groups should continue to encourage group members to explore the impact of diversity and culture on personal problem formation, problem resolution, and resiliency.

Some view the social-identity development of both target and agent group members as a worthy goal for diverse group experiences (Sue & Sue, 2003). Revisiting diversity themes and issues in the group may be necessary because group development is not a linear process and groups cycle back through phases as new issues come up; trust must be rebuilt after addressing challenging issues (Kline, 2003).

DIVERSITY CONCERNS DURING THE ENHANCEMENT AND CLOSURE STAGE   As groups meet their objectives and begin to draw to a close, they enter the enhancement and closure stage. For all groups, this time is essential for acknowledging member gains in the group, solidifying application of these gains to the outside environment, and bringing the group experience into meaningful perspective. For members of marginalized groups, the goal of transferring new behaviors to their everyday lives may be counterproductive—or even dangerous. Group leaders should be aware of the receptiveness of the local community to diversity and should encourage group members to weigh the consequences of trying out new ideas and behaviors in environments that may be less than receptive.

Impact of Diversity on Group Leaders' Actions

Just as diversity affects the dynamics, development, and impact of groups, it affects group leaders' actions. Based on the preceding discussion, the recommendations in this section are made for the group leader regarding pregroup planning and the group-leadership process. (Resources for group counseling with specific multicultural populations are provided in the following section.)

PREGROUP PLANNING   Planning is the first step toward conducting any successful group (Kline, 2003), and planning is doubly important for diverse groups. In particular, leaders of diverse groups have to make careful decisions regarding group purposes and goals, group composition and screening, and group duration and settings.

GROUP PURPOSES AND GOALS   Clear purposes and goals are particularly important for diverse groups because they provide the foundation upon which further structure and planning of the group must occur, and they must be evaluated for compatibility with group members' worldviews (DeLucia-Waack & Donigian, 2004). Goals that are clearly understood and accepted by group members may provide a basis for uniting leaders and group members as they take on the challenge of navigating through their differences (Hogan-Garcia, 2003).

The counseling profession typically values individual achievement, emotional independence, and individual responsibility, and these are the values encouraged through traditional group counseling (Matsukawa, 2001). These values, however, may be inconsistent with the values of some diverse group members. Group leaders should be aware of their own orientation toward these values and remain vigilant in evaluating whether diverse group members will benefit from goals based on these values. In addition, two common goals mentioned in multicultural counseling literature are (a) to promote social-identity development and (b) to develop *bicultural competence*, or the ability to function in multiple cultural contexts (Han & Vasquez, 2000). Group counselors should consider these as potential outcome goals for diverse groups.

GROUP COMPOSITION AND SCREENING   Leaders' choices regarding the composition of their groups impact group functioning (Yalom & Leszcz, 2005). In addition to concerns that apply to all groups, a key question for leaders of diverse groups is whether the composition should be homogeneous or heterogeneous (Han & Vasquez, 2000). *Homogeneous groups* are composed of group members who share similar characteristics within dimensions such as issues (e.g., depression) or sociodemographic identity (e.g., people with disabilities), or combinations of both. By contrast, *heterogeneous groups* have a more varied composition with respect to these dimensions.

Han and Vasquez (2000) summarized the potential benefits of homogeneous groups as earlier cohesion, more support, less conflict, better attendance, and faster symptom relief. Gazda, Ginter, and Horne (2001) summarized the potential drawbacks of homogeneous groups as lack of dissent or independent thinking, lack of risk taking, and resistance to leader-suggested changes. Conversely, heterogeneous groups are believed to develop cohesiveness more gradually, have a higher probability of conflict, and have higher rates of early termination (Gazda et al., 2001). Group heterogeneity, however, is believed to contribute to greater potential for interpersonal learning through varied feedback, potentially beneficial levels of change-producing anxiety, and a more realistic environment for reality testing (Yalom & Leszcz, 2005).

Leaders' decisions about the composition of their groups should be based on the purpose and structure of the group and the social-identity characteristics of potential group members. Homogeneous groups may be best suited for short-term groups that require quick cohesion. Leaders should consider homogeneous composition for groups the purpose of which is to support or develop stronger social identity for target-group populations (Han & Vasquez, 2000). Heterogeneous group composition may be appropriate for groups the purposes of which are to develop cross-cultural communication or assertiveness skills and to develop deeper levels of self-understanding and change.

When composing a group, the level of identity development of agent (marginalized) and target (privileged) group members should be considered. For instance, target group members who are in the resistance phase may be limited in their openness to giving and receiving support or seeking connection with agent group members and as such may benefit more from homogeneous groups. Target group members who are in stages in which they devalue their social identity may benefit more from homogeneous groups in which they will receive support for and validation of that identity (Brinson & Lee, 1997). Heterogeneous groups may be less suited for group members for whom the presence of agent group members will prevent their experiencing a sense of safety and trust. In general, agent group members might benefit more from heterogeneous group composition than target members will (Brown & Mistry, 1994). Nevertheless, target group members who are moving from resistance phases to redefinition phases may benefit greatly from cross-cultural contact.

These important decisions regarding group composition highlight the importance of group leaders' use of adequate screening procedures. Adequate screening is part of the ethical practice that protects group members from harm and aids in determining group compositions that will increase the chances for beneficial group experiences.

Although screening may be minimal for some groups, such as content-oriented psycho-educational groups, and not used at all for others, such as task groups, typical screening procedures for process-oriented psychoeducational groups, counseling groups, and therapy groups may involve personal or group interviews to collect data on presenting concerns, psychosocial history, and past treatment.

Traditional psychosocial intakes, assessments, and diagnosis have been critiqued for ignoring sociocultural dimensions (Anderson, 2002). As such, screening also should involve gathering information about the client's self-identification, cultural background, experiences of oppression, and comfort with other social-identity groups. Gathering this information will assist in determining diverse individuals' suitability for group counseling and the best group composition for their needs.

PREGROUP ORIENTATION   Pregroup orientation may be a critical factor in the success of diverse groups (Han & Vasquez, 2000). The screening interview presents an ideal opportunity to begin pregroup orientation. Pregroup preparation involves providing potential group members with information regarding the group's policies, goals, and processes. Although diverse group members may come into the group with many assumptions about group counseling based on their cultures and experiences in society, the potential negative impact of these assumptions can be minimized by providing information and processing anxieties and concerns. For instance, orientation coupled with a clearly communicated commitment from the leader to respect the diverse group members' experiences, feelings, values, and beliefs can alleviate anxieties about being mainstreamed and/or stereotyped (Han & Vasquez, 2000).

TIME CONSIDERATIONS AND SETTINGS   The natural ebb and flow of relationships and learning rarely match the hectic schedules of professional environments. In diverse groups, however, ample time is needed to build trust, negotiate bicultural group norms, and facilitate understanding between differing group members. Although structure may be important, the temptation to crowd group sessions with topics and content should be resisted. Instead, sessions should be planned and paced so there is adequate time to process communication challenges and strong emotions. Planning for more sessions than is customary or making sessions longer may be necessary, and leaders may have to justify these departures based on their diversity-related goals.

The group setting may be significant to the experience of diverse members. Diverse members who are unaccustomed to, or mistrustful of, traditional mental health settings might benefit from having the group located in a safe, familiar setting. If this is not possible, attempts should be made to make the environment safe and comfortable. This includes considering the arrangement of the room and the social norms of the different members.

Although all needs may not be met, in diverse groups it is important to acknowledge and process the limitations of the setting. Economic factors, too, may affect diverse individuals' access to groups. As such, groups that may benefit underserved populations should be marketed, priced, and located so they are accessible to members of these populations.

PROCESS GOALS AND SKILLS   Much of what the group leader does in a group is to encourage facilitative norms or process goals. The process goals of counseling groups are generally emotional expressiveness, self-disclosure, open communication, a here-and-now focus, egalitarian participation, democratic process, personal responsibility, and open expression and resolution of conflict (Kline, 2003). In diverse groups, process goals may have to be adjusted to "recognize cultural and sociopolitical differences in group members' socialization while simultaneously uniting group members" (Helms & Cook, 1999, p. 226). This may require that the group leader evaluate the overarching purpose of process goals and find other ways to meet them. For example, leaders who value open communication may facilitate connection between group members by having the members talk directly to each other about their feelings and experiences. If a culturally diverse group member cannot adapt comfortably to this norm, the leader and group members may want to explore alternative means of facilitating connection, such as storytelling, artwork, or rituals.

Process goals are related directly to the skills that group leaders use during sessions. Just as process goals are utilized to advance outcome goals, skills are used to promote process goals. When working with diverse groups, group leaders have three choices regarding the skills they can use (Helms & Cook, 1999; Sue & Sue, 2003):

1. They can use the *generic group skills* that most group counselors are taught, or skills associated with specific theoretical orientations.
2. They can *adapt specific skills* to be more culturally compatible.
3. They can investigate using *helping skills from other cultures.*

Working with diverse groups does not mean throwing out customary group skills, but skills must be evaluated for use with culturally different clients. Skills that violate cultural norms may have to be adapted or not used at all. Also, using the customary group-counseling skills with diverse groups will be much more useful if the group members are well-oriented to the group-counseling processes. In any case, when using traditional group skills, leaders must be alert to any adverse reactions in diverse group members.

Adapting customary group skills to work with diverse groups can range from using the skills as is but providing context to members about the purpose of the skill or intervention, to incorporating cultural variations. Diverse group members may become comfortable with a customary intervention if they have enough information about its purpose. Providing context also can be useful if group members decide to brainstorm or suggest alternatives that may work better for themselves and the group.

Another alternative is the use of indigenous or culturally based interventions. This may be most helpful in homogeneous groups in which members share a culture and have similar levels of identity development. Heterogeneous groups in which members have expressed openness to experimenting with different cultural activities or forms of communicating also may benefit. Extra care should be taken if the chosen interventions are considered sacred so that important rituals are not trivialized or abused. Research and consultation with culturally knowledgeable community leaders may be necessary to increase the credibility of group leaders (Sue & Sue, 2003).

Group facilitators who want to deal with diversity issues openly and competently in their groups must be prepared to deal with conflict between group members (Camacho, 2001; Okech et al., 2016; Yalom & Leszcz, 2005). Dealing with conflict effectively in a group—particularly a group with diverse membership—begins with preparing group members before the group begins. Members who anticipate and accept conflict as part of the process will be more apt to participate in resolving the conflict (Kline, 2003).

SIDEBAR 6.5

Self-Awareness: Conflict in Cross-Cultural Groups—How Comfortable Are You?

Conflict is inevitable in groups and can be particularly uncomfortable in cross-cultural groups. Watch the video *The Color of Fear* (Lee et al., 1994), paying particular attention to the scenes in which group members express differences. As you watch, take notes about your emotional reactions and thoughts. Try not to censor yourself. Afterward, read your notes and reflect on any patterns you see in your reactions.

Group members also should be provided with a tentative framework outlining how the leader will help to resolve conflict. An example of such a framework is Hogan-Garcia's (2003) conflict recovery process. Frameworks such as this one prepare members for the process and lower their anxiety during conflict (Han & Vasquez, 2000). Because group members whose cultures are more collectivistic may view conflict as a breach of the group and may wish to resolve such conflicts in a less confrontational manner, negotiating a process that works for most group members is important (Camacho, 2001).

To maintain a sense of safety during conflict in diverse groups, leaders must maintain their role as leader, be vigilant about setting limits on aggression and blaming, be aware of their own cultural triggers, and maintain a strong boundary between their own issues and the issues of the group (Okech et al., 2016). Group leaders also may want to remind the group of the existing purposes, process, and goals so that members can focus on commonalities beyond the conflict, adhere to communication guidelines (such as being nonjudgmental or not interrupting), and remain motivated when conflict becomes frustrating (Camacho, 2001).

MULTIPLE PERSPECTIVES ABOUT CULTURE-SPECIFIC GROUP COUNSELING

The previous section provided general guidelines and suggestions for group counseling with diverse members. In addition, the literature provides a broad spectrum of information and suggestions for providing group counseling to diverse racial, ethnic, and cultural groups. As cautioned earlier in this chapter, this information should not be used without evaluation for its fit with particular groups and individual group members. However, these resources can add richness and detail to group counselors' understanding of how culturally different group members may experience life and membership in a group, as well as potential techniques and ways of helping.

Chi-Ying Chung (2004) provides a comprehensive starting point for understanding the implications of Asian cultures on group counseling. Pack-Brown, Whittington-Clark, and Parker (1998) provide an example of a richly described approach to counseling African-American women. Torres-Rivera, Wilbur, Roberts-Wilbur, and Phan (1999) describe a psychoeducation group for Latino clients that highlights potential issues and directions for those leading groups with Latino clients. Finally, DeLucia-Waack and Donigian (2004) provide a comprehensive list of books, chapters, journal articles, and videos that may be helpful in planning groups for diverse clients. Group counselors working with diverse members should read the culture-specific group-counseling literature to gain a broad perspective of and strive to synthesize it with their real-life experiences.

SIDEBAR 6.6

Case Study: Advocacy as a Part of Group Counseling

Erica is leading a counseling group for refugees adjusting to their new lives. She is running the group pro bono for a nonprofit that is assisting with all aspects of the refugees' transition. During the first few groups, she notes that several group members have brought up issues with the temporary housing provided by the nonprofit, stating that it is not sanitary or private and that this is causing stress for the group members and their families. Some members also haltingly share that they feel pressured to take jobs for very low pay through a relative of the housing manager. What should Erica consider as she decides what her role should be with these issues?

ADVOCACY AS PART OF GROUP COUNSELING

Increasingly, group counselors are encouraged to include advocacy in their work, particularly with clients who have experienced oppression or environmental barriers to their success (Ratts et al., 2015; Singh et al., 2012a). *Advocacy* has been described as "those purposive efforts to change specific existing or proposed politics or practices on behalf of or with a specific client or group of clients" (Ezell, 2001, p. 23), with the goals of empowering of clients and changing the environment to better meet client needs. The ASGW's MSJCP emphasizes the importance of understanding how oppression affects groups and group members and of knowing how to intervene to address inequalities resulting from biases, prejudices, oppression, and discriminatory practices (Singh et al., 2012a).

Rubel and Pepperell (2010) explored the implications of advocacy conducted within the context of group work. They indicated that the complex environment of groups, characterized by a web of relationships among members and between leader and members, affects advocacy in several ways, including the following: (a) advocacy interventions must not be detrimental to other group members and the group-as-a-whole, (b) advocacy interventions should take into account group members' increased vulnerability due to the heightened potential for psychological harm and threats to confidentiality in groups, (c) advocacy interventions may be required to address inequalities in the group process, and (d) advocacy interventions, including empowerment, should be included in the planning of groups for optimal group functioning and advocacy effectiveness.

Summary

Diversity and multiculturalism are increasingly important in society. Models of social-group-identity development provide a way to understand how people ascribe the defining characteristics of their social-identity groups. Identity is multifaceted and may reflect memberships in many social groups. Identifying with these groups affects a person's self-concept and relationships with others.

Awareness that diverse populations have not received adequate counseling treatment has resulted in a focus on four essential areas for counselor multicultural and social justice competence: counselor self-awareness, awareness of clients' worldviews, the counseling relationship, and counseling and advocacy interventions.

Group counseling has been similarly scrutinized. Social and cultural diversity can affect group members' experience of therapeutic factors and how groups develop. Lack of attention to social and cultural differences or poor leadership may result in propagation of harmful societal dynamics during group counseling. Developing trust and cohesion is crucial to diverse groups meeting their goals. Careful preparation is necessary, and group leaders should consider the social identity of group members, along with other psychosocial factors, when making decisions about group goals, composition, structure, and process.

Customary group interventions should be introduced carefully to groups with social and cultural diversity as these interventions may not be appropriate for all members. Leaders may have to adapt interventions to be compatible with cultural norms or may have to incorporate culturally based interventions.

7 Efficacy and Evaluation of Group Work

Cass Dykeman

In professional training, the curriculum usually is determined by an accreditation agency. In counselor preparation, the main accreditation agency is the Council for the Accreditation of Counseling and Related Educational Programs (CACREP). In CACREP's accreditation manual (CACREP, 2016), eight curricular areas are designated as core training for any counselor. Of most relevance to readers of this textbook is the Group Counseling and Group Work core curricular area (Standard 2.F.6). The other counselor-preparation accreditation agency is the Council on Rehabilitation Education (CORE), which accredits rehabilitation-counseling programs. Like CACREP, CORE mandates group-counseling training (CORE, 2014).

Students in counseling programs often raise the question of whether group counseling or therapy courses should be required. If there is no scientific evidence that group counseling or therapy works, then this book and the group-counseling courses required of counseling students seem to be nothing more than hoops to jump through that some scholastic bureaucracy imposes on them. Moreover, if counselors cannot show the administrators at their school or agency evidence that group work is effective, that work will soon be dismissed.

This chapter will help readers develop their own sense of group work efficacy research and program evaluation. The chapter will unfold in five distinct sections. First, definitions of group counseling, efficacy, and evaluation will be provided. In the second, third, and fourth sections, research on topics related to group work efficacy will be addressed. The chapter concludes with a discussion of how counselors can evaluate their own group work.

DEFINITIONS

The key terms in this chapter are *group work*, *efficacy*, and *evaluation*. Without a clear understanding of these terms, the rest of this chapter will be meaningless.

Group Work

In this chapter, we will operate within the Association for Specialists in Group Work's (ASGW's) definition of group work. ASGW defines *group work* as "the application of knowledge and skill in group facilitation to assist an interdependent collection of people to reach their mutual goals which may be intrapersonal, interpersonal, or work-related" (Wilson, Rapin, & Haley-Banez, 2000a, pp. 2–3). The four forms of group work are task groups, group psychoeducation, group counseling, and group psychotherapy.

Efficacy

In the human-services professions, *efficacy* refers to "the degree to which desired goals or projected outcomes are achieved" (Barker, 1995, p. 116). A sample group-counseling efficacy question one could ask is "To what extent does cognitive group counseling impact people with bulimia?" Such a question, however, would be difficult to answer because each of the two key terms in the question (*cognitive group counseling* and *bulimia*) can mean many things. Does the term *bulimic* refer to people with nonpurging bulimia or to those with purging bulimia? When possible, consideration will be given to more fine-grained efficacy questions. In the example of bulimia, then, the question could be "To what extent does challenging shape and weight distortions in a small-group counseling setting decrease the number of eating binges per week in nonpurging bulimic individuals?"

Evaluation

In the human-services professions, *evaluation* refers to a systematic effort to determine the success of a specific program without regard to the production of generalizable knowledge (Arora et al., 2017). A sample evaluation question would be "At the Jane Doe Counseling Center in Eugene, Oregon, to what extent does the weekly bulimia group help clients lower their purging behavior?"

GROUP COUNSELING EFFICACY

In this section, we will address four topics of group counseling efficacy: professional issues, effective counselor practices, specific populations, and critical issues.

Professional Issues in Group Counseling

At first glance, efficacy questions such as the one posed at the end of the previous section may seem to be more the domain of researchers than clinicians. However, efficacy questions are critical to counselors in the trenches. Specifically, efficacy questions play an important role in ethics, professionalism, and economics.

ETHICS   There are two prime ethical considerations for all counselors, including those engaged in group work. These ethical considerations are nonmaleficence and beneficence.

One of the oldest ethical dictates in health care is "Above all, do no harm." This dictate captures the spirit of the moral principle of nonmaleficence. Later in this chapter, what is known about group counseling "casualties" is reviewed with the goal of teaching group counselors how to prevent such casualties.

The ethical principle of beneficence carries the imperative that counselors engage in activities that will benefit the client. Thus, counselors must seek out efficacious interventions and avoid or discard interventions that are found to be inefficacious. For instance, several rational–emotive therapy psychoeducational programs have been developed for school counselors' use in the classroom. However, as will be discussed

---

SIDEBAR 7.1

Case Study: Benefits and Problems from the Client Perspective

Read pages 9 to 11 in Wanlass, Moreno, and Thomson's (2005) "Group Therapy for Eating Disorders: A Retrospective Case Study," which appeared in *The Journal for Specialists in Group Work*. The article is available full-text online for free at http://digitalcommons.calpoly.edu/psycd_fac/60.

In all forms of counseling, it is important for researchers and evaluators to attend to client perspectives. After reading the three assigned pages of the case study, name two things you drew from the clients' voices about benefits and problems that can occur during group counseling.

---

later in this chapter, researchers have not found these interventions to be efficacious. Although no evidence suggests that these large-group interventions harm children, they do waste instructional time that could be spent on more fruitful activities.

PROFESSIONALISM   One behavior that separates a professional from a layperson in any activity is that the professional bases his or her actions upon scientific knowledge rather than on personal preference or whim. The specific term for this professional behavior is *informed practice*. Indeed, the psychologist's code of conduct demands that a clinician's work reflect the pragmatic application of scientific knowledge based upon research (American Psychological Association, 2017a). Thus, it is incumbent upon the group counselor to seek out and use such knowledge.

ECONOMICS   Spiraling expenses have prompted business and government alike to impose cost-control mechanisms upon the healthcare system (McConnell et al., 2017). The generic term for these mechanisms is *managed care*. The advent of managed healthcare will force group counselors to demonstrate the cost-effectiveness of their group methods (Roback, 2000). Thus, efficacy issues are becoming paramount in the practice settings that professional counselors inhabit. We have moved into an environment in which efficacy issues are no longer the sole concern of university-based researchers.

EFFECTIVE COUNSELOR PRACTICES IN GROUP COUNSELING

The components of effective group counseling have been defined by ASGW, which has developed specific knowledge and skill competencies for counselors. Many of these competencies direct students to discover what is efficacious in group-counselor practice and apply it (Wilson et al., 2000a). The general group-counseling literature will be reviewed here, followed by a discussion of the counseling practices that have been found to be especially effective. The research will be considered in terms of specific factors, nonspecific factors, and group-counseling modes.

Specific Factors and Outcomes

The term *specific factors*, as used here, refers to a counselor's acts that are unique to a particular theory of counseling. An example is the use of cognitive-distortion refutation to combat body-imagery problems. Specific factors that are commonly employed in group counseling include applying structure and providing alternatives and instruction.

USING STRUCTURE   In an analysis of the research literature, Gazda, Horne, and Ginter (2000) found a definite trend toward the use of structured group strategies, which stands in opposition to the traditional unstructured group approach. Structured groups developed as a result of the influence of behavioral counseling and skills training. Rohde and Stockton (1994) reviewed the 40-year controversy over the role and efficacy of structure in therapeutic groups. Early group-counseling theorists recommended that group leaders avoid influencing the natural development of group culture. Later, however, group-counseling researchers found that the lack of structure created the undesired client phenomena of cognitive distortion, interpersonal fear, subjective distress, and premature termination.

Applying structure to groups has been found to be beneficial, but counselors should exercise caution in this regard. All types of structure are not beneficial to all groups. For example, although the application of self-disclosure contracts can increase attraction to a group, it can decrease the members' "mutual liking" (Ribner, 1974). Of note is that the positive impact of structure may be related to clients' ability to engage in risk taking (Evensen & Bednar, 1978). Specifically, higher levels of structure tend to be associated with more negative evaluations of counseling by low risk takers. Also, high levels of structure may result in lower levels of group cohesion (Lee & Bednar, 1977). The practitioner is encouraged to match the techniques utilized with the personalities of the group members.

PROVIDING ALTERNATIVES AND INSTRUCTION.   The power of instruction in group counseling lies in the counselor's ability to be clear with clients about the tasks and goals of counseling. The power of providing alternatives to clients is that it often prevents client reactance (Brehm, 1966). The judicious application of instruction and the judicious provision of alternatives have been identified as causal factors of client behavior change with certain populations.

Flowers (1979) discovered that trained group counselors produced more improvement in their clients than did student counselors because they gave less advice and offered more alternatives and instruction in their feedback to group members. Also, student counselors who used alternatives and instruction produced more improvement in their clients than those who did not. The student counselors, however, used these interventions less frequently and produced less client improvement overall. Of interest, group clients often viewed alternatives and instruction as superior therapeutically, but the group counselors often did not, to the detriment of their clients. Flowers's study showed that counselors who are not trained specifically to avoid giving advice may be inclined to do so.

Nonspecific Factors and Outcomes

Nonspecific factors of counseling are change-producing elements in counseling, regardless of theoretical orientation. Gelso and Carter (1994) identified a number of nonspecific factors they believed to be operating in all counseling. The most studied of these factors is working alliance. Other nonspecific factors mentioned in the group-counseling literature include curative factors, group development, and leadership.

WORKING ALLIANCE   Substantial empirical evidence indicates that a *working alliance* (also called a *working relationship*) is an important component in all counseling. In fact, working-alliance scores are the best-known predictor of counseling outcomes

(Horvath, 2000). Bordin (1994) defined the working alliance as having three equal and interacting components: (a) goal (collaboration on the goals of counseling), (b) task (collaboration on the tasks of counseling), and (c) bond (mutual affective bonding).

Group process stimulates the unfolding of the working alliance in all clients (Glatzer, 1978). In group counseling, both client–therapist and client–group (as a whole) working alliances have been found to be predictive of outcome (Compare, Tasca, Lo Coco, & Kivlighan, 2016).

Curative Factors.   Although working-alliance theory has had an enormous impact on individual-counseling research, its impact on group-counseling research has been limited. Most of the literature on the nonspecific factors in group counseling has focused on Yalom's (1985) curative factor theory, which postulated that the following 11 curative factors operate in group counseling: instillation of hope, universality, imparting information, altruism, corrective recapitulation of the primary family group, development of socializing techniques, imitative behaviors, interpersonal learning, group cohesiveness, catharsis, and existential factors. Barry and Panel (1999) contains online open and full-text descriptions of these factors. Butler and Fuhriman (1983) reviewed 10 years of research on Yalom's curative factors. In the studies they reviewed, clients were asked to rank the 11 factors with regard to their curative value. Butler and Fuhriman's research supported Yalom's idea of a triad of highly curative factors consisting of (a) self-understanding, (b) catharsis, and (c) interpersonal interaction (input).

More than 10 years later, Shaughnessy and Kivlighan (1995) suggested that the analyses in these early studies were not sufficiently complex. Instead of ranking the clients' views of the 11 factors, Shaughnessy and Kivlighan utilized cluster analysis and described three clusters of client responders: (a) broad-spectrum responders, (b) self-reflective responders, or (c) other-directed responders. The broad-spectrum responders, the largest cluster, endorsed all 11 curative factors evenly. The next largest cluster, the self-reflective responders, valued a specific curative factor triad most highly. Based on the results of their analysis, Shaughnessy and Kivlighan recommended that group counselors include a broad range of curative factors in their group counseling, rather than concentrate on a few factors that appeal to a minority of clients.

GROUP DEVELOPMENT   Fundamental to the assessment of group progress and outcome is understanding the stages of group development (Zimpfer, 1984). Most research on group development has been based upon Tuckman's (1965) five-stage theory, in which he identified the five stages as forming, storming, norming, performing, and adjourning. Maples (1988) refined Tuckman's work through 5 years of data collection, and from an analysis of her data she developed a 20-substage model designed in the shape of a star. At each stage, or point of the star, Maples offered definitions that can be used in practice to better evaluate clinical progress.

LEADERSHIP   Group leadership research fills the counseling literature as group leadership involves the interaction of so many features of group counseling that it defies any simple definition (Stockton & Morran, 1982). Furthermore, confusion continues to surround leadership functions and their relationship to the therapeutic gains that group members make (Conyne, Harvill, Morganett, Morran, & Hulse-Killacky, 1990). Regardless of the counselor's technique, however, when the counselor's attitudes are acceptable to the client, the client is more likely to report positive therapeutic outcomes (Beutler, Jobe, & Elkins, 1974).

SIDEBAR 7.2

Case Study: Interpersonal Psychotherapy Group (IPT-G)

MacKenzie and Grabovac (2001) presented a series of case studies in an article entitled "Interpersonal Psychotherapy Group (IPT-G) for Depression" that appeared in *The Journal of Psychotherapy Practice and Research*. Read the Group Management Issues section (p. 48) and the case study of Member #6 (p. 49). The article is available full-text online for free at https://www.ncbi.nlm.nih.gov/pmc/articles/PMC3330631. After reading these two pages, check which aspects of the IPT-G noted in the article (p. 48) you see yourself incorporating in your own group work. Use the following table to note your results.

#	Text	Use
1	Prolonged discussion of symptoms is discouraged after the full review of symptoms in session two.	
2	The group environment is used to promote and explore behavioral and affective responses to interpersonal relationships.	
3	Negative relational themes between members are addressed with a problem-solving approach rather than through the use of psychodynamic interpretations.	
4	Past relationship patterns, including those in the family of origin, are used to develop an understanding of current patterns.	
5	The main focus is on modifying key relationships and socialization patterns in current circumstances.	
6	A major challenge in adapting IPT for the group format is to ensure a continuing focus on interpersonal phenomena.	
7	The structure of the first four sessions ensures that all members are aware not only of the issues they must address but also the other members' issues.	
8	The focus is primarily oriented to current external relationships or situations.	
9	Tensions in the group are addressed at an early point in a problem-solving fashion. Extended exploration of process meaning is not pursued.	
10	Apply changes to present outside circumstances, using the group as a reflecting arena to report on these efforts and the personal issues that are raised.	

In addition to counselor attitude, the literature has pointed to three important nonspecific leadership factors: (a) sense of hope, (b) group leadership style, and (c) personal characteristics.

Effective leaders were found to project a sense of hope to their clients, manifested in behaviors such as acknowledging the client's resources and potential to change, conveying a clear and strong belief in the effectiveness of group counseling, and communicating a sense of confidence or personal power (Couch & Childers, 1987). Although the literature indicates that hope is a curative factor in group counseling, it is devoid of strategies for its use.

Abramowitz, Roback, Abramowitz, and Jackson (1974) found another leadership factor of effective leaders: matching counselor leadership style with client personality promotes positive group-counseling outcomes. They described client personality based on Rotter's (1966) research on internal and external locus of control. Clients described as having an internally oriented locus of control believe that life events are the result of initiative. By contrast, clients who believe that luck or powerful forces determine life outcomes are described as having an externally oriented locus of control. Abramowitz et al. (1974) found that nondirective techniques were more effective than directive techniques with internally oriented clients. The reverse was true for clients with an external orientation.

Certain personal characteristics also may distinguish effective from ineffective group leaders (Combs, Avila, & Purkey, 1978). The literature indicates that effective leaders are more positive than less effective leaders, and effective leaders hold more positive perceptions of clients. Also, effective group counselors display emotionally supportive behaviors (e.g., care, listening, and flexibility) more often than ineffective counselors during group interactions (Stockton, Morran, & Velboff, 1987).

Group Counseling Modes and Outcome

The group-counseling literature is replete with reviews of outcome research for different types of groups. These reviews can be digested more easily when the types of groups are categorized into four modes: task/work (TASK), psychoeducational (EDUC), counseling (COUN), and psychotherapy (THRP). These are the modes officially recognized by the ASGW (Wilson et al., 2000a).

TASK/WORK MODE   The TASK classification includes task forces, committees, planning groups, and study circles, all of which are directed at identifying and completing specific goals. Because this is not a therapeutic mode, individuals other than professional counselors usually lead these groups. At times, however, counselors work in a consultant role with these groups. Given the nontherapeutic nature of TASK groups, the literature on these groups will not be reviewed in this chapter.

PSYCHOEDUCATIONAL MODE   The purpose of EDUC groups is to prevent psychological maladjustment (Wilson et al., 2000a). Although EDUC interventions originally were developed for educational settings, the use of EDUC groups has expanded beyond schools and students. EDUC interventions currently are used to educate all types of clients about potential threats (e.g., AIDS), developmental life events (e.g., the empty nest), and life skills (e.g., assertiveness).

COUNSELING MODE   COUN interventions focus on interpersonal growth and problem solving (Wilson et al., 2000a). Examples of COUN interventions are T-groups, sensitivity groups, and encounter groups. The emphasis in COUN groups is on promoting growth and resolving normative life crises. As such, COUN groups typically do not address remediation of pathology. The American School Counselor Association's (2014a) position statement on group counseling states that this treatment modality is "an integral part of a comprehensive guidance and counseling program" (p. 1).

PSYCHOTHERAPY MODE   THRP groups are designed to address personal and interpersonal problems of living, remediate perceptual and cognitive distortions or repetitive patterns of dysfunctional behavior, and promote personal and interpersonal growth and development in individuals with severe and/or chronic maladjustment (Wilson et al., 2000a).

Budman, Demby, Feldstein, and Gold (1984) provide an excellent example of research on a THRP intervention, in which their psychodynamically oriented group approach was found to be effective in treating clients with severe characterological problems.

GROUP COUNSELING EFFICACY WITH SPECIFIC CLIENT POPULATIONS

Regardless of the mode, group-counseling outcomes with specific client populations fall along a single continuum. The main points on this continuum are effective interventions, ineffective interventions, and harmful interventions. Scientific knowledge is relayed on what works, what does not work, and what has been found harmful for specific client populations.

The literature indicates that group counseling is effective with a wide variety of concerns and diagnoses. In terms of client concerns, group work has produced positive outcomes for the following:

- Anxiety
- Childhood aggression
- Divorce
- Encopresis
- Fibromyalgia
- Gambling
- Grief
- Internet overuse
- Loneliness
- Sex abuse trauma
- Sexual dysfunctions

For individuals diagnosed with mental disorders, group counseling improves quality of life and reduces symptoms associated with the following:

- Addictive disorders
- Bipolar disorders
- Depression
- Eating disorders

SIDEBAR 7.3
Self-Awareness: Intervention Continuum

Group work interventions can fall on a continuum from effective to harmful. Think of the last group (task, psychoeducational, counseling, or psychotherapy) you were part of as a member. Where would you place this group experience on the continuum shown here? Why? Also think of the last group (task, psychoeducational, counseling, or psychotherapy) in which you served as a facilitator. Where would you place this group experience on the continuum? Why?

EFFECTIVE   INEFFECTIVE   HARMFUL

- Obsessive–compulsive disorders
- Personality disorders
- Post-traumatic stress disorder
- Schizophrenia
- Social anxiety disorder

Now that we have looked at efficacy in specific areas, let's turn to the relationship between group-counseling efficacy and several critical issues.

CRITICAL ISSUES IN GROUP COUNSELING EFFICACY

Group counseling is a complex therapeutic activity. In this section, we will look at five critical issues that impact group counseling efficacy: (a) multicultural understanding, (b) harmful interventions, (c) minimizing group-counseling casualties, (d) counselor actions, and (e) casualty prevention.

MULTICULTURAL UNDERSTANDING   Diversity is a critical factor in determining the outcomes of group counseling. Methods for addressing culture, identity, and socialization will influence our discussion of group-counseling efficacy. In one study of working women, for example, career self-efficacy and vocational exploration increased only when the group counseling specifically addressed female-socialization issues (Sullivan & Mahalik, 2000). In other studies, culturally focused group interventions have led to positive results with youth from the following groups: Native American, Hawaiian, Latinx, LGBTQ, Black, and Asian. For example, Craig, Austin, and McInroy (2014) studied the impact of a school-based counseling group to support multiethnic sexual minority youth resiliency. The program, entitled ASSET, was delivered in a format of 8 to 10 weekly sessions that averaged 45 minutes. The groups operated with 6 to 12 participants. Positive pretest/posttest outcomes were found with two of the three outcome variables (i.e., self-esteem and proactive coping). If you are interested in learning more about this group-counseling intervention, you can find it detailed in Craig (2013).

Unfortunately, studies such as Craig et al. (2014) are rare in the literature. Empirical studies on group efficacy must consider the entire spectrum of people served. We recommend that counselors continue to inform themselves about cultural boundedness in group counseling (Sayin et al., 2008). The ASGW document on multicultural competencies provides helpful guidance on issues to consider when researching or evaluating group work with diverse populations (Singh, Merchant, Skudrzyk, & Ingene, 2012c).

HARMFUL INTERVENTIONS   As discussed thus far, group counseling offers the professional counselor a powerful tool to apply to many mental and physical health issues. However, any potent therapeutic tool also contains the potential to harm clients (Hadley & Strupp, 1976). Therefore, the potency of group counseling can produce casualties. By *casualty*, here we mean a client whose lasting deterioration of psychological functioning is directly attributable to a counseling intervention (Crown, 1983).

Bergin (1963) introduced the idea into the research literature that counseling can produce both negative and positive results for clients. Concerning the production of negative results, Bergin (1966) suggested that counselors should be more cautious about and critical of their practices—careful to eliminate ineffective or harmful therapeutic techniques. Later, Bergin and his colleagues examined the research literature on

SIDEBAR 7.4
Multicultural Case Study: Jorlan

Read Case Study 2, "Jorlan," in the ASGW's *Multicultural and Social Justice Competence Principles for Group Workers* (Singh et al., 2012c). This case study is available full-text for free at www.asgw.org.

Then, rate yourself on the awareness competencies contained in the Jorlan case study, using the following form.

Which awareness competency did you rate as the lowest for yourself? What is one thing you can do to improve yourself in this awareness competency?

I.	Awareness of Self and Group Members: As group workers move towards multicultural and social justice advocacy competence they will...	Awareness Competencies Self Rating
		Low High
2	Demonstrate movement towards being increasingly aware of and sensitive to the multiple dimensions of the multicultural and multi-layered identities of group members.	1 2 3 4 5 6 7
3	Demonstrate an awareness of different connecting and communicating styles. Group workers recognize different communication styles related to the various nuances of one's cultural worldviews. They are aware of how myths, stereotypes, and assumptions learned by living in a society that bases one's cultural identity on excluding and devaluing others, impacts group dynamics.	1 2 3 4 5 6 7
5	Recognize obstacles that group members encounter based on lack of opportunities and systems of oppression (e.g., sexism, classism, heterosexism) and gain awareness of how to integrate an advocacy focus into group learning to address these barriers.	1 2 3 4 5 6 7

(*Source:* ASGW's *Multicultural and Social Justice Competence Principles for Group Workers* [Singh et al., 2012c], www.asgw.org.)

negative effects and reported that the general casualty rate in counseling was somewhere between 9% and 11% (Lambert, Shapiro, & Bergin, 1986).

Group-counseling researchers have not ignored the ongoing debate over casualty rates in the general counseling literature. They first directed their attention to personal-growth-group interventions (e.g., T-groups, encounter groups, and marathon groups). The reported casualty rates for the interventions varied widely (Kaplan, 1982). Careful studies on these group interventions, however, found that casualty rates were no higher than the casualty rate for general counseling (Lambert et al., 1986).

Therapist selection of intervention can lead to group-counseling causalities. For example, Davies, Burlingame, Johnson, Gleave, and Barlow (2008) found that for members who reported that the group was high in conflict, the group-climate feedback intervention had a negative effect on outcome.

Client variables can also lead to group-counseling causalities. Smokowski, Rose, and Bacallao (2001) found in their study that "individuals who became group casualties were (a) particularly vulnerable or sensitive due to their 'pileup' of life course problems, and (b) lacking in supportive social relationships inside and outside of the group" (pp. 247–248). Smokowski et al. emphasized that to prevent casualties, counselors must establish group norms that are "inclusive and sensitive to diverse personality configurations, learning styles, and emotive orientations" (p. 248).

MINIMIZING GROUP-COUNSELING CASUALTIES   Although group counseling does not seem to be any more dangerous than other counseling interventions, it still does produce casualties. Thus, in light of the ethical imperative of nonmaleficence, professional counselors must learn how to minimize group-counseling casualties, which result from two sources: poor pregroup screening and misguided counselor actions. We will discuss these issues next, as well as casualty prevention.

Professional counselors cannot conduct proper pregroup screening without knowledge of group-counseling contraindications. *Contraindication* refers to a client's symptom, condition, or circumstance that warns against taking some course of action (Barker, 1995). Fortunately, group-counseling researchers have catalogued a number of contraindications for COUN and THRP interventions. In reference to the COUN and THRP modalities, Toseland and Siporin (1986) detailed three types of contraindications: practical barriers, specific treatment needs, and client-personality functioning. To aid practitioners in screening clients for COUN and THRP group-counseling interventions, we will examine these three areas in greater detail. First, Toseland and Siporin (1986) listed the following practical barriers to prescribing group counseling:

- Lack of clients with similar issues
- Clients' resistance to a group-counseling prescription
- Scheduling problems
- Lack of qualified counselors
- Lack of agency or school support

In terms of clients' treatment needs, some clients, such as those in crisis and those with a high potential for suicide, need more immediate one-on-one attention than group counseling can provide (Gazda et al., 2000). Also, some clients may have an authentic need for a private therapeutic setting in which to discuss a highly sensitive issue or critical decision (Toseland & Siporin, 1986).

Many personality factors can contraindicate an assignment to group counseling. In their study of group-counseling outcomes, Budman, Demby, and Randall (1980) encountered one treatment casualty—a client who had scored high on scales measuring interpersonal sensitivity, paranoid thinking, and psychotic thinking. Similarly, other researchers have commented that strong contraindicators for group counseling include extreme interpersonal sensitivity, paranoid thinking, and psychoticism.

Researchers also have consistently indicated that low motivation for change is a strong contraindicator for group counseling (Crown, 1983). Consequently, professional counselors should take care to assess this obvious but often forgotten client characteristic. See Gusella, Butler, Nichols, and Bird (2003) for an excellent discussion of the measurement of this variable for group counseling.

Delsignore, Carraro, Mathier, Znoj, and Schnyder (2008) examined whether therapy-related control beliefs predicted long-term (i.e., posttreatment) outcomes in group counseling. They found that group-counseling clients who had a high expectation that clinical improvement depended on therapist competence had the worst long-term outcomes. Delsignore et al. theorized that clients who hold these expectations are extrinsically motivated and thus regress after treatment due to a lack of external contingencies (e.g., group feedback, counselor support). They advised counselors to screen clients for such maladaptive expectations and address these expectations prior to treatment.

Another obvious client characteristic that group counselors often forget to assess is the client's tolerance for anxiety and frustration. Low tolerance puts a client at risk of becoming a casualty of group counseling. With reference to this tolerance, Horwitz (1976) commented:

> A group often tends to induce frustration due to competition among members for its time and attention. A common wish is to become the favorite "child." Although support is also an important dimension of the group experience, it may be overshadowed by anxiety in the opening phases of group membership. Patients who deal with heightened tension by engaging in self-destructive actions, who tend to take flight in reaction to anxiety, are best excluded from a group. (p. 506)

One specific type of anxiety that has been mentioned as a contraindicator is acute fear of self-disclosure (Gazda, 1986).

Personality issues that contraindicate group-counseling placement include borderline personality disorder and psychopathy. Also, the presence of severe schizophrenia contraindicates group counseling placement. Marked emotional lability is an additional contraindicator.

Finally, two contraindications specific to children and adolescents should be considered. First, Sugar (1993) advised that encounter and marathon group interventions are contraindicated for these populations as these group interventions can present material that is too intense for nascent egos. Second, Baider and De Nour (1989) cautioned that adolescent cancer patients have to be medically stable before they begin any group counseling. They exerted this caution because of their finding that group counseling can strip away denial defense mechanisms that cancer patients who are medically unstable need so they can function adaptively and with hope.

The contraindications for group counseling are as follows:

- Acute self-disclosure fears
- Borderline personality disorder
- Extreme interpersonal sensitivity
- Low anxiety tolerance
- Low frustration tolerance
- Low motivation for change
- Marked emotional lability
- Paranoia
- Psychopathy
- Psychotic thinking
- Schizophrenia
- Severe depression
- Severe impulse-control problems
- Unstable medical condition

Also, it has been found that reviewing case studies can make counseling facts "come alive." Therefore, we recommend that you examine the rich descriptions of group-counseling casualties by Billow (2016), Brandes (1977), Budman et al. (1980), and Kaplan (1982).

Two caveats about our research review on contraindications should be considered. First, this discussion pertains solely to the COUN and THRP modalities. The research literature gives no indication of whether the contraindications would hold true for EDUC interventions. For example, it is known that a COUN group would be contraindicated for a client with extreme fear of self-disclosure. The same client, however, might find an EDUC group helpful (Gazda et al., 2000). Indeed, an EDUC group experience might set the stage for an effective COUN intervention or might be in itself a sufficient intervention. Second, growing evidence indicates that homogeneous EDUC interventions are effective with clients who have borderline personality disorder or schizophrenia (*homogeneous* here denotes groups in which all clients share the same diagnosis; *heterogeneous* refers to groups containing clients with a mixture of diagnoses). Also, in general, treating clients with schizophrenia or borderline personality disorder in homogeneous group settings is gaining in popularity. Given unanswered and conflicting information about contraindicators, what is a counselor to do? It is believed that the current best practice when screening for group counseling is to consider, but not slavishly apply, the contraindicators listed previously. It cannot be emphasized enough that counselors best serve clients through a case-by-case application of contraindicators.

COUNSELOR ACTIONS   Although the research on client contraindicators for group counseling is somewhat muddled, the research on counselor actions and group-counseling casualties is crystal clear. Counselors' behaviors are a primary source of group-counseling casualties (Hadley & Strupp, 1976; Kaplan, 1982). Hadley and Strupp (1976) discussed two sources of counselor behaviors that can lead to counseling casualties: training/skills deficits and a counselor's noxious personality traits.

Deficits in the counselor's skill or knowledge can lead to client casualties in multiple ways. For example, counselors who are unaware of client contraindicators for group counseling will put clients in ill-advised therapeutic situations. Also, counselors may choose to work with client populations or employ counseling techniques for which they have had little training. Counselors also may have the proper skills but apply those skills rigidly regardless of the clinical situation (Crown, 1983).

For example, a psychoanalytically oriented counselor may make an accurate transference interpretation for a client during a session. Despite skillful application of this technique, the intervention will fall flat if the client does not have the needed observing ego to use the insight contained in the interpretation. To speak metaphorically, when all that a counselor has in his or her professional toolbox is a hammer, the whole world becomes just a collection of nails. Builders of good counseling experiences possess and use a variety of tools in their work.

Personality traits can be a key factor as well. Hadley and Strupp (1976) detailed the following 12 personality traits that can generate counseling casualties: coldness, obsessiveness, excessive need to make people change, excessive unconscious hostility, seductiveness, lack of interest or warmth (neglect), pessimism, absence of genuineness, sadism, narcissism, greed, and dearth of self-scrutiny. Combinations of these traits can lead to destructive behaviors by leaders. In their classic examination of group casualties in which they identified five group-counseling-leadership styles, Lieberman, Yalom,

SIDEBAR 7.5
Self-Awareness: Johari Window and Casualty-Genic Traits

Most counseling students are familiar with Luft and Ingham's (1961) Johari window. In this self-awareness exercise, we want to assist you to push the vertical center of your Johari window to the right. Hadley and Strupp (1976) detailed 12 personality traits that can generate counseling casualties, listed in the following table. In the column labeled "See in Self," rank the frequency with which each trait manifests itself in your interactions with others. In the column labeled "Others Report Seeing in You," place a checkmark if others have told you that they see this trait in you.

Now, look at the completed table. In the "Self" column, what three traits did you rank as occurring with the highest frequency? Are these traits checked in the "Others" column? Given the information present in this table, is there a personality trait that speaks to you as needing some work? What is the first step you want to take to address this trait?

Personality Trait	See in Self		Others Report Seeing in You
	Low	High	
Coldness	1 2 3 4 5 6 7		
Obsessiveness	1 2 3 4 5 6 7		
Excessive need to make people change	1 2 3 4 5 6 7		
Excessive unconscious hostility	1 2 3 4 5 6 7		
Seductiveness	1 2 3 4 5 6 7		
Lack of interest or warmth (neglect)	1 2 3 4 5 6 7		
Pessimism	1 2 3 4 5 6 7		
Absence of genuineness	1 2 3 4 5 6 7		
Sadism	1 2 3 4 5 6 7		
Narcissism	1 2 3 4 5 6 7		
Greed	1 2 3 4 5 6 7		
Dearth of self-scrutiny	1 2 3 4 5 6 7		

(*Source:* Hadley and Strupp, 1976.)

and Miles (1973) found that one leadership style produced almost half of the casualties, including the most severe ones. They called this style *aggressive stimulator*. It is characterized by high stimulus input, intrusiveness, confrontation, challenging but demonstrating, and high positive caring (Lieberman et al., 1973). According to Hartley, Roback, and Abramowitz (1976), the critical causal factor of group-counseling casualties relates to leadership characteristics.

Counselor use of known effective intervention with the wrong population can also produce negative group-counseling outcomes. Take, for example, the intervention of a counselor providing process feedback to a group. In one study on this topic, counselor feedback on group climate had a significant negative effect on outcome for group members who reported that the group was high in conflict (Davies et al., 2008).

Counselor inattention to ongoing group process can lead to premature termination in the group treatment of borderline personality disorder. Hummelen, Wilberg, and Karterud (2007) found that counselor inattention to the strong negative emotions that a client may experience in group counseling can lead to dropout.

CASUALTY PREVENTION   How can group counselors prevent themselves from producing casualties? Taking a group-counseling class is a start because it helps counselors to build their skills. Roback (2000) emphasized that counselors who practice group work "need to be specifically trained to prevent or reduce nonconstructive confrontation and to identify patients being harmed by it" (p. 120). As for personality traits, access to quality supervision is the key to recognizing and remediating noxious personality traits. In fact, quality supervision is so important that CACREP standards mandate 1 hour per week of individual supervision for all practicum and internship students. Also, both CACREP and CORE set strict faculty-to-student ratios (1:5) for practicum and internship supervision classes (CACREP, 2016; CORE, 2014).

GROUP COUNSELING EVALUATION

The ASGW professional standards require group counselors to possess skills in evaluation (Wilson et al., 2000a). In addition, private, state, and federal funding sources typically require proof of effectiveness. In this section, we will highlight one approach to evaluation that can be easily carried out in the field settings in which counselors work. This approach is known as *nonconcurrent multiple baseline design* (Watson & Workman, 1981). Before walking through an example, let's cover a little nomenclature. The term *multiple baseline* refers to use of three or more groups undergoing a Phase A and Phase B. *Phase A* is a period of successive assessment points with no group-counseling intervention (i.e., the baseline). *Phase B* is a period of successive group-counseling intervention sessions where an assessment point occurs at the end of each intervention. Typically, the minimum number of assessment points in each phase is three. Control is obtained by varying the length of Phase A. The term *nonconcurrent* denotes that each group runs nonconcurrently with the other groups.

Now, for example, imagine that you want to show your administration that the group intervention you are conducting at your agency lowers nonsuicidal self-injury (NSSI) among adolescents. This group intervention is designed to meet twice a week on Tuesdays and Thursdays for 2 weeks. The dependent variable is the number of NSSI behaviors per day on the day prior to the one for which an assessment is planned (recorded by a smartphone app). Also, imagine that your agency does not have the capacity to run more than one NSSI group at a time. With the aforenoted parameters in mind, let's look at the steps of this evaluation. First, randomly assign a different Phase A length (3-, 5-, or 7-day baselines) to each group. Second, conduct the Phase A assessments and Phase B interventions and assessments for each group. Running just one group at a time, the whole process should take a little over 3 months (Sidebar 7.6 details when assessments and interventions should occur). Third, input the data for each time point for each participant in Excel. Finally, use the percentage of nonoverlap of all Phase A/Phase B data pairs (i.e., nonoverlap of all pairs, NAP) to analyze the effectiveness of the intervention. Parker and Vannest (2009) contains excellent guidance on how to use NAP, and there is a simple online program available for free to calculate this percentage (Vannest, Parker, Gonen, & Adiguzel, 2016).

SIDEBAR 7.6
Case Study: Multiple Baseline Design

			Phase A	Phase B							
Day	Tues	Thur	Tues	Tues	Tues	Thur	Tues	Tues	Tues	Thur	Tues
Week	1	1	2	2	3	3	4	4	5	5	6
Time	1	2	3	4	5	6	7	8	9	10	11
Group 2*	Asm	Asm	Asm	I&A	I&A	I&A	I&A				
Group 1**	Asm		Asm	Asm	Asm	I&A	I&A	I&A	I&A		
Group 3***	Asm			Asm	Asm	Asm	Asm	I&A	I&A	I&A	I&A

*Group randomly assigned to three-point baseline (i.e., Phase A) length.
**Group randomly assigned to five-point baseline (i.e., Phase A) length.
***Group randomly assigned to seven-point (i.e., Phase A) baseline length.

Think about a group you want to run in the future, then answer the following questions:

1. What would you do for the intervention (i.e., independent variable)?
2. What would you use to assess your desired outcome (i.e., dependent variable)?
3. How many times per week would you conduct assessments and/or interventions?

Remember to record this information in the provided table.

Summary

A common experience of nascent professionals in any field is their enthusiasm to apply their newly learned skills. These skills can be used to heal pain and promote peak performance. Like any powerful tool, however, group-counseling skills can cause harm as well as good. Thus, we defined efficacy first, followed by a discussion of how it is measured. Then, we covered the influence of specific and nonspecific factors on group counseling outcomes. Finally, we discussed the efficacy of group counseling with specific client populations.

All group counselors face many situations in which they are unsure of what to do to help their clients. Time and human complexity inevitably outstrip even the best counselor-preparation training. In confusing clinical circumstances, the counseling research literature can serve as an invaluable resource.

8

The Four Types of Groups: Work/Task, Psychoeducational, Counseling, and Psychotherapy Groups

Melinda Haley and Jonathan W. Carrier

Group work encompasses many types of groups intended to accomplish a variety of purposes. In this chapter, we will discuss four specialized types of groups identified by the Association for Specialists in Group Work (ASGW): task/work, psychoeducational, counseling, and psychotherapy groups (Corey, Corey, Callanan, & Russell, 2014). Although each type of group shares common features, each is specialized to achieve different goals and thus requires different skills of the group leader(s). In this chapter, we will describe the most important and unique features of each type of group that counselors commonly lead, and we will include a discussion of effective leadership strategies within each group type.

TASK/WORK GROUPS

The ASGW defined the specialization of *task groups* (commonly referred to as *task/work groups*) as applying principles and processes of group dynamics to improve the practice and accomplishment of identified work goals (Conyne, 2014). Task/work groups differ from other groups, such as psychoeducational, counseling, and psychotherapy groups, primarily in their emphasis on completion of some group goal that is not specific to an individual's education, growth, or development (Grow, Flache, & Wittek, 2015). Instead, task/work groups focus on meeting performance goals or the completion of a task. This difference includes a production agenda instead of a personal change agenda. Therefore, task/work groups have *externalized outcomes* rather than internalized outcomes. The externalized product of a task/work group is often the reason for membership, whether the product is a report, recommendation, performance, event, or project (Cohen, 2011; Grow et al., 2015). The range of outcomes for task/work groups is as wide and as diverse as the membership, the settings, and the purposes for which this type of group meets. How group members go about completing the group's tasks is equally varied (Benchmark Institute, 2010).

Another aspect of the task/work group that sets it apart from other specializations in group work is that it often has a sudden end (Shepherd, Patzelt, Williams, & Warnecke, 2014). Once a given task is complete, the group tends to terminate quickly (Gladding, 2011). This is an important consideration in forming the group and for the life of the group itself. Unlike other groups (e.g., counseling groups), in which members invest personally, and rely upon emerging relationships within the group to accomplish personal outcomes, members of task/work groups may see little relevance in attending to any interpersonal relationships in the group. In addition, these task/work groups are often "run" by untrained individuals who may see little relevance in attending to interpersonal relationships within the group (Nielsen, 2013).

Task/work groups, especially the "meeting" subtype, are often led by lay-volunteers, who are people with little if any training in group leadership (Benchmark Institute, 2010; Dykeman & Appleton, 2006). These lay leaders can easily lead people to conclude "What's the big deal? Running a group . . . leading this meeting . . . facilitating this committee . . . can't be too challenging." Many such groups are poorly organized and managed, which can lead to group member frustration and be detrimental to the goals of the group (Benchmark Institute, 2010). The rich literature on task/work groups bears witness to the contrary: Leading a successful task group is often a complex job (Gladding, 2011; Nielsen, 2013) and one well-suited to professional counselors with formal training in group dynamics.

There are also other occasions when the opposite dynamic is evidenced, such as when task group members hold impressive credentials (e.g., doctor, lawyer, CEO, teacher, or professor) and therefore might appear to other group members to hold more power in the group. These individuals may be viewed as experts related to the task, even when in fact they may not be (Goodman, Alexander, Chizhik, Chizhik, & Eidelman, 2010.) These individuals might be viewed by others as more competent and may unduly influence the dynamic of the group and thus the outcome of completion of the task.

Collaboration (working together) is not always easy. People can recall productive meetings and groups, as well as groups in which little was accomplished and which seemed like a waste of time (Crichton & Templeton, 2013). Further, what is considered a successful group experience by some participants may be perceived by others as ineffective (Crichton & Templeton, 2013; Shepherd et al., 2014). We espouse the belief that skilled leadership, such as that commonly exemplified by professional counselors, is a key to the success of task/work groups. Expertise in leading task/work groups can and should be developed through education and training before the leadership of a task group is undertaken (Benchmark Institute, 2010; Gladding, 2011).

The concept of *task* can be either ongoing or finite. For example, a board of directors of a company has the *ongoing* task of governing or overseeing the company's financial well-being: how productive and competitive the company is in the marketplace,

---

SIDEBAR 8.1

Choosing a Task Group Leader

The dean of the education department at a community college has directed five English instructors to form a task group. The stated purpose of the group is to identify courses within the English department that have a low student success rate and create strategies to increase student success in these courses. None of the five English instructors have experience or training in leading or facilitating a task group. What are some steps the dean could take to increase the effectiveness of this task group?

what it invests in, how it distributes profits, and the like. This task is ongoing, long term, and may outlast the terms of the members. Boards of directors typically are appointed or elected for a term (Walther, 2015).

Other task/work groups—such as a community response group rallying to a cause, a hiring committee, or volunteers for a single night's community outreach effort—illustrate the *finite* form of a task/work group. These groups consist of a group of people who gather together with a common purpose and endpoint. The task/work group addresses a specific issue, and the group dissolves once the goal is attained (Benchmark Institute, 2010).

Crichton and Templeton (2013) espoused that certain criteria are necessary for the successful completion of tasks within collaborative groups. These are (a) the collaborative environment of the group, (b) the resources that are at the disposal of the group for it to achieve its goals, (c) investment from the group members, (d) investment in the mutual purpose of the group to complete the task, (e) facilitative and honest communication and respect and trust among group members, (f) group members' ability to process information and navigate interpersonal dynamics, (g) how the group is structured, (h) the ability of the group to set clear goals, (i) sharing the workload equally across all of its members, and (j) group members' prior experiences related to the task.

Furthermore, the Benchmark Institute (2010) has defined factors that create a successful task/work group experience. These factors include (a) the productivity of the group, (b) how satisfied the members are with the experience, and (c) how well the group develops over time. Ultimately, whether a task/work group is effective is based on the size of the group, the purpose of the group and what its end goals are, and how well group members work together (Benchmark Institute, 2010).

Models of Task/Work Groups

In this section, we will briefly review three models for conceptualizing task/work groups. Due to space constraints, we cannot provide a detailed outline of each model. Therefore, readers are encouraged to seek out additional information on these and other models of task/work group leadership not mentioned here.

The *task group performance* model (Conyne, 2014; Conyne, Rapin, & Rand, 1997) focuses on the critical choices that leaders make in selecting interventions that promote successful task/work groups. The second model, the *balancing process and content model*, emphasizes the balance between process and content (Hulse-Killacky, Killacky, & Donigian, 2001). The third model, *the integrative model*, helps group leaders evaluate the group's productivity based on factors related to environment, group activity, and group productivity (Tziner & Chernyak-Hai, 2012).

TASK GROUP PERFORMANCE MODEL   The task group performance model, which was conceived by Conyne et al. (1997), is grounded in two principles: (a) the *open system*, in which specific attention is paid to the unique context in which the task/work group is to function, and (b) a *performance-based framework*, in which a task group's final outcome is the completion of a task or of a product (Conyne, 2014; Conyne et al., 1997). Group leaders using this model choose interventions at critical moments within their groups' development during periods of time when more than one choice is available.

Each choice then has the potential to lead the group down a different developmental pathway, hence potentially influencing the success of the group.

Conyne et al. (1997) and Cohen and Smith (1976) stated that the leaders make these choices from among the complex interactions of three components: (a) the *type* of leader intervention (i.e., problem solving, or group process), (b) the *level* of leader intervention (i.e., individual, interpersonal, group, or organizational), and (c) the *function* of leader intervention (i.e., caring, meaning, motivation, or managing).

Each intervention the task/work group leader selects will influence how the task group will proceed. The leader's selection is based upon what he or she believes will produce the best pathway for the group's success (Cohen & Smith, 1976; Conyne et al., 1997). Therefore, the task group performance model attends to the specific context of the group, clarity of the performance demands, and the choices that leaders make in selecting interventions.

BALANCING PROCESS AND CONTENT MODEL   Hulse-Killacky et al. (2001) and Hulse-Killacky, Kraus, and Schumacher (1999) developed the balancing process and content model for conceptualizing meetings within a specialized form of task/work groups. These authors, as well as others, espoused that the balance of process and content is vital to the success of the group (Breshears & Volker, 2013).

How a task is tackled by a group is considered *process*, and the actual goal of the group is the *content* (Breshears & Volker, 2013; Hulse-Killacky et al., 2001). Process and content are intertwined and interdependent upon each other (Benchmark Institute, 2010). This codependency is complex (Breshears & Volker, 2013). Group leaders must effectively balance these two processes to maximize group success (Breshears & Volker, 2013). For example, if the group places too much attention on content related to the task, the group can then undercut the attention that is placed on group member interactions and dynamics, which could lead to the group being less successful in the completion of its task. Conversely, too much attention to process, especially process that is not effectively and clearly linked to content, could hinder the group's ability to address important task and purpose issues (Breshears & Volker, 2013; Hulse-Killacky et al., 2001).

Obtaining balance is accomplished by careful attention to the dynamics (what goes on) during the warm-up, action, and closure phases of the task/work group (Hulse-Killacky et al., 1999, 2001). The balancing process and content model has three phases: the *warm-up phase*, the *action phase*, and the *closure phase*.

The *warm-up phase* is attended to during the formation of the group itself, as well as in the early moments of each group session or meeting. Hulse-Killacky et al. (2001) emphasized that the warm-up phase addresses three questions—two with a process focus and one focused on content: "Who am I? Who am I with you? What do we have to do?" (p. 31). In the warm-up phase, time is dedicated to learning who members are, to purposefully establishing rapport among members, and to creating a direction toward the group's goal (Benchmark Institute, 2010).

The *action phase* can be characterized as the work stage of the task/work group. It is characterized by these focus questions: "Who are we together? What do we have to do to accomplish our goals?" (Hulse-Killacky et al., 2001, p. 61). The answers to these questions are vital to the group's success (Benchmark Institute, 2010). Although the task to which members are committed may be concrete, the ways in which members can reach the goal seem unlimited (Breshears & Volker, 2013).

The *closure phase* is dedicated to bringing the group members' experience to an end. Hulse-Killacky et al. (2001) identified four themes of the closure phase:

1. Reviewing goal accomplishment
2. Preparing for future activities
3. Reviewing the impact of group relationships on goal accomplishment
4. Expressing appreciation

There can be considerable variance regarding the ending of a work/task group that is contingent upon the task, the successful completion of the task, and the needs of the larger entity that formed the task/work group (e.g., university or corporation; Shepherd et al., 2014). Abrupt terminations can have an emotional impact on task/work group members or an adverse effect on key stakeholders (Shepherd et al., 2014). In effect, closure counters the tendency for task/work groups to finish their tasks and disband abruptly (Hulse-Killacky et al., 2001).

INTEGRATIVE MODEL   Tziner and Chernyak-Hai (2012) proposed an integrative model for task/work group leadership in order to help leaders balance changes in a group's environment and connect those changes to the group's internal functioning and thus their output via three processes: (a) internal group structural change, (b) redefining the group's goals, and (c) exploring and changing the group's perceptions of the task. These processes are viewed via (a) the group's situational factors, (b) the group's interpersonal interactions, and (c) individual group member characteristics.

This model helps group leaders recognize and facilitate the group while distinguishing that groups are both a system and a dynamic entity, upon which internal or external forces can act to facilitate or debilitate the group process. Group leaders need to be able to manage these forces as conditions and situations change (Tziner & Chernyak-Hai, 2012). Tziner and Chernyak-Hai (2012) conceptualized that these various forces could impact group performance, which at times would require a change to the structure of the group, a redefinition of the group's goals, or a change in the group's perception of what would be required to meet the goals or the tasks of the group. For example, an external obstacle encountered during task performance might call for an internal structural change to solve the issue. Such an internal structural change might require an evaluation of what each group member is contributing to the group, an evaluation of the interpersonal dynamics of group members, or a need to capitalize on certain strengths of some group members to address a threat related to ability or motivation of a given group member (Tziner & Chernyak-Hai, 2012).

Leadership Skills for Effective Task Groups

As recommended by the ASGW (ASGW, 2000), skills for effective task/work group leadership are developed through practice, experience, and knowledge of the professional competencies and standards of the ASGW. Like the training of group work specialists covered elsewhere in this text, the task/work group leader will benefit enormously by observing, modeling, coleading, and leading task/work groups under supervision (ASGW, 2000).

The following skills are outlined by the ASGW (2000) as expectations of skills and behaviors for leaders of task/work groups: (a) focus and maintain attention on task and

SIDEBAR 8.2
Setting and Mobilizing Goals for Experiential Learning Task Group

A high school counselor has been tasked with helping the school's teachers expand the experiential learning opportunities for juniors and seniors with businesses and agencies in the local community. The school counselor is to lead a task group composed of high school teachers, local business owners, and agency administrators to explore ways that students can learn to apply classroom knowledge in workplace settings. The task group is large and is composed of high school teachers representing a variety of subjects, as well as business owners and agency leaders from multiple areas of business and social service. How might the school counselor obtain goal clarity in this task/work group and mobilize energies toward a common goal for such a wide array of interests?

work issues, (b) obtain goal clarity in a task/work group, (c) prompt discussion of and consensus on how the agreed-upon goals will best be achieved, (d) select a task/work group model appropriate to the age and clientele of the group leader's specialty area(s) (e.g., school counseling), (e) mobilize energies toward a common goal in task/work groups, (f) implement group decision-making methods in task/work groups, (g) manage conflict in task/work groups, (h) blend the predominant task focus with appropriate attention to human relations factors in task/work groups, and (i) sense and use larger organizational and political dynamics in task/work groups (ASGW, 2000).

When Conflicts Arise in Task/Work Groups

Conflict, although seemingly paradoxical, is important in task/work groups (Cohen, 2011). Conflicts and the effort to work effectively through them are catalysts for sound decision making, establish trust among members, and can unify often-divergent points of view about the group process (Boyle, Hanlon, & Russo, 2012).

The topic of dealing effectively with challenging group members and conflicts in groups is addressed thoroughly in the literature, particularly for counseling and psychotherapy groups (Anwar, 2016; Yalom & Leszcz, 2005). From this literature, much can be inferred for the leadership of task/work groups. Leaders who intervene successfully with difficult members and group conflicts enhance the quality of the group experience and create more pleasant and productive working conditions (Cohen, 2011).

The unique functions that task/work groups are often called upon to fulfill raise several challenges. The group typically has a time-limited lifespan: The group forms, performs, and disbands (Gladding, 2011; Shepherd et al., 2014). Because productivity of the membership in a task/work group is often externally driven, participants may easily underestimate or overlook the importance of how the group functions in its effort to reach its goal (Boyle et al., 2012). Although the eventual aim is to achieve some specific product, the group as a whole might not care about how the members interact to attain that goal or accomplish the group's purpose (Anwar, 2016).

Leaders should promote interdependence between members, enhance productivity of the task, and manage group and task conflicts (Boyle et al., 2012). When the behaviors of individuals create conflict among members, productivity can suffer (Boyle et al., 2012). The leader's role in selecting members, which is vital in counseling and psychotherapy groups, is often not feasible for task/work groups. Leaders often have no say regarding who volunteers for any group project (Anwar, 2016).

PSYCHOEDUCATIONAL GROUPS

Psychoeducational groups (often referred to as *psychoeducational/guidance groups*) are structured therapeutic groups that emphasize learning more about a problem or issue and/or developing new life skills for prevention, growth, or remediation (Burnes & Hovanesian, 2017). As directive and short-term counseling interventions have gained favor over open-ended, long-term approaches, psychoeducational groups have become increasingly popular (Burnes & Hovanesian, 2017). Although practitioners originally developed these groups for use in educational settings, those time-limited groups that focus on learning and experiential avenues for change are proving useful in a variety of clinical and community settings (Tatham, Athanasia, Dodd, & Waller, 2016).

In 2000, the ASGW revised and adapted its standards for training group workers. The guidance/psychoeducational group differs from the other group specializations in that leaders of groups of this type focus on helping clients grow through knowledge and skill building (Cheng, Hasche, Huang, & Su, 2015). Compared to other group types, such as counseling or psychotherapy groups, psychoeducational groups are more structured, issue specific, and leader directed. In addition to emphasizing education and skills training, these groups may stress self-awareness and self-empowerment (Burnes & Hovanesian, 2017). Although members may compare stories, share anecdotes, or offer suggestions about specific issues, the emphasis is not on deep self-disclosure or member interactions as might be the case in a counseling or psychotherapy group (Corey, Corey, & Corey, 2014). A fundamental task of the psychoeducational group leader is to keep the group focused on established group goals while effectively balancing content and process (Burnes & Hovanesian, 2017). These groups focus on current life situations, and group processes are related to the central group theme.

Psychoeducational groups require a structured group design, the dissemination of relevant new material, meaningful experiential activities, and opportunities for members to process their experience and learning (Burnes & Hovanesian, 2017). Examples of psychoeducational groups include school-counseling groups that address students' responsible sexual behavior, information regarding substance use, strategies for making healthy life choices, or the development of conflict-resolution skills. These groups are led by a school counselor (Brouzos, Vassilopoulos, & Baourda, 2015; Burnes & Hovanesian, 2017). Likewise, psychoeducational groups offered by career or university counselors might address stress management, wellness, diversity awareness, anger management, and career readiness (Cheng et al., 2015). Other examples of psychoeducational groups include those that emphasize healthy lifestyle choices for seniors, present effective parenting strategies for parents of adolescents, or provide information and education related to eating disorders via agency counselors (Tatham et al., 2016).

Psychoeducational groups are ideally suited to the current emphasis on short-term treatment modalities (Brouzos et al., 2015). A well-planned and executed psychoeducational group combines some of the therapeutic aspects of traditional group counseling with the goal-directed emphasis of psychoeducation (Cheng et al., 2015). Common goals for participants in psychoeducational groups include learning new information, developing new or increased skills, finding more effective ways of communicating or relating, increasing self-management abilities, and developing personal insights (Brouzos et al., 2015).

Psychoeducational group work is firmly rooted in the history of the counseling profession (Corey, M. S., et al., 2014). From the early part of the 20th century, the guidance movement emphasized teaching clients to make better choices, while working with populations that needed direction and support (Corey, G., et al., 2014). A physician, Joseph Pratt, often is credited with beginning the group movement in the early 1900s (Northeastern Society for Group Psychotherapy Foundation [NSGPF], 2015). Pratt offered psychoeducational groups to tuberculosis patients, which included a presentation of didactic material followed by patients' telling their own stories and processing the information (NSGPF, 2015). At the turn of the century, schools began to offer vocational and moral guidance in group settings (Baker, 2011). Although school guidance groups were often directive in nature and offered little opportunity for reflective discussion, they established the importance of education in group settings.

Psychoeducational groups are becoming uniquely independent therapeutic entities that do more than simply supplement individual counseling (Burnes & Hovanesian, 2017)—and they are therapeutic without being "therapy." These groups stress learning but may incorporate emotional, behavioral, cultural, and spiritual elements of change, depending upon the group's purpose and structure (Brouzos et al., 2015; Burnes & Hovanesian, 2017). A psychoeducational approach to group work is consistent with the wellness model of counseling, focusing on prevention, personal responsibility, and empowerment, and it can be used in a wide array of settings, including in elementary, middle, and high schools, colleges and universities, and clinical practice (Brouzos et al., 2015; Burnes & Hovanesian, 2017).

Common Types of Psychoeducational Groups

Psychoeducational groups can be classified by their primary purpose: education, skills training, or self-understanding/self-knowledge.

1. *Education groups* have as a primary purpose the learning of new material through lecture, discussion, observation, or participation (Burnes & Hovanesian, 2017). The emphasis is primarily cognitive, with the leader acting as a teacher, disseminating new information as ideas, concepts, or facts.
2. *Skills-training groups* have a strong experiential component. Participants are challenged to practice new skills in the group setting while the leader models the desired skills and structures the experiences to emphasize mastery. Feedback is included as a component of the training (Tchanturia, Doris, & Fleming, 2014).
3. *Self-understanding/self-knowledge groups* may resemble counseling groups, but they differ by deemphasizing self-disclosure, working through resistances, or exploring past relationships. The understanding and knowledge gained are expected to reassure the members, to give them feedback on the impact of their behavior on others, or to build self-confidence (Burnes & Hovanesian, 2017).

Although categorizing groups by primary purpose is helpful, most psychoeducational groups contain elements of all the above groups. In addition, these groups often provide support to members, through interactions both with the leader and with one another (Burnes & Hovanesian, 2017). Hage and Romano (2010) emphasized other related purposes of psychoeducational groups—specifically, prevention, examination of personal beliefs and attitudes, and integration of information with life experiences.

Effective psychoeducational groups differ from simple informational workshops in that groups are tailored to meet the needs of the members, both in design and as an evolving entity (Burnes & Hovanesian, 2017). Rather than a one-size-fits-all presentation, psychoeducational groups are specific to a given population at a given time. Although they are structured in nature, effective groups are designed to allow for flexibility (Burnes & Hovanesian, 2017).

Basic Characteristics of Psychoeducational Groups

Psychoeducational groups can range in size from 5 to 50 or more members (Delgadillo et al., 2016). To aid in processing exercises or fostering discussions, larger groups may have to be broken into subgroups. The length and duration of groups can vary widely, depending upon the group design and composition (Belmont, 2016; Colbert & Erickson-Klein, 2015). The time allotted to each session often depends upon the group's composition. For example, children often benefit from shorter sessions that meet more frequently (Haen & Aronson, 2016). In general, weekly group sessions last from 1 to 2 hours (Belmont, 2016; Colbert & Erickson-Klein, 2015). The number of sessions often depends upon the scope of the group, institutional parameters, or other external time constraints. Most psychoeducational groups meet for between 4 and 12 sessions. Groups emphasizing skill development or self-knowledge and support may benefit from more sessions than groups with a primarily educational focus (Belmont, 2016; Colbert & Erickson-Klein, 2015).

Incorporating Learning Principles into Psychoeducational Groups

The most important component of psychoeducational groups is *learning* (Burnes & Hovanesian, 2017). Counselors who lead these groups should understand some of the important principles of learning so they can plan activities, develop attainable goals and objectives, and tailor the group to meet the needs of the participants (Kit & Teo, 2012). In designing learning activities for the group, general characteristics of the members should be kept in mind. Age, developmental level, education, and cultural factors all influence preferred learning modalities (Burnes & Hovanesian, 2017). Varying teaching strategies is also advisable, as some members may be primarily auditory in their learning, whereas others might absorb information visually or kinesthetically (Cohen, 2011).

Ability to learn is also affected by *motivation* (Zhuang, Feng, & Liao, 2017). This is a complex concept affected by many factors, but essentially group members are most motivated to learn and participate when the group offers something of value to them (Önemli & Yöndem, 2012). In counseling or psychotherapy groups, the attractiveness of the group to its members is often described as *cohesion*, an essential component of group process that develops over time (Anwar, 2016). Conversely, in a psychoeducational group, interactions among members are directed and purpose specific (Belmont, 2016; Colbert & Erickson-Klein, 2015). In general, interpersonal communication within the group is a method of learning, rather than a group goal (Burnes & Hovanesian, 2017). It falls upon the leader to manage content and process in a manner that attracts and motivates group members (Burnes & Hovanesian, 2017).

Another factor affecting learning is *anxiety* (Paolini, Harris, & Griffin, 2015). Members who are anxious or nervous about participating in the group are often too

---

SIDEBAR 8.3

Reflecting on Psychoeducational Group Experience Can Make You a Better Psychoeducational Group Leader

Consider your experience participating in psychoedu-cational groups. Some of these groups were undoubt-edly more interesting to you than others. Thinking back to these experiences, what group leadership style engaged you the most? Did you benefit more from hands-on experiences in these groups and par-ticipatory learning, or did you prefer to sit back and listen to the information presented by an expert group leader? Were there groups in which other group members were highly engaged but you were not? Reflecting on these experiences may help you to lead psychoeducational groups that are engaging, reach all learning styles, and meet the needs of all your group members.

---

focused on their own internal dialogues to gain maximally from the experience (Gholamreza, Aziz, & Maryam, 2016). All group work involves taking risks and self-disclosing, and members may feel vulnerable, especially in groups that tackle sensi-tive topics or work on overcoming real or perceived personal deficits (Gladding, 2011). Effective group leaders address and normalize anxiety from the beginning and incorporate strategies for offering encouragement and support to members (Jacobs, Schimmel, Masson, & Harvill, 2016). Effective group leaders also understand intra-group differences and attend to the cultural diversity and intersectionality of group members (Burnes, 2014).

The strategies or approaches described in the following subsections are recom-mended to incorporate learning principles into psychoeducational group work.

DEVELOP GOALS AND OBJECTIVES THAT ARE SPECIFIC, REALISTIC, CLEARLY ARTICULATED, AND APPROPRIATELY CHALLENGING   (See Bridbord, DeLucia-Waack, Jones, & Gerrity, 2004; Brown, 2011.) Leaders should consider the impact of the group intervention on mem-bers' lives and evaluate their own expectations of how participants will change or grow following the group's completion (Burnes & Hovanesian, 2017). Although goals may be broad, objectives should articulate specific learning or behavioral changes. For example, if the goal of a group is to help women increase their self-esteem, objectives might include reframing criticism, countering negative self-talk, engaging in daily self-affirmations, and identifying self-denigrating behaviors (Kit & Teo, 2012). This is accompanied by work aimed at replacing these behaviors with positive activities (Cheng et al., 2015).

CONSIDER THE DEVELOPMENTAL LEVEL OF GROUP MEMBERS   (See Burnes & Hovanesian, 2017.) With children, it is important to choose learning activities that approximate their reading or processing levels (Haen & Aronson, 2016). Adolescents may greet activities geared toward grade-school children with disdain (Haen & Aronson, 2016). Likewise, educational factors including reading level and appropriate content must be considered in learning activities for adults (Cheng et al., 2015).

INCORPORATE CULTURALLY MEANINGFUL LEARNING ACTIVITIES   (See Burnes & Hovanesian, 2017.) As with all counseling interventions, group leaders must develop an understanding of, and communicate respect for, diversity and cultural differences.

Learning materials should be culturally appropriate (Cheng et al., 2015). Counselors are urged to consult when working with diverse cultures, especially with cultures outside their own (Proctor & Simpson, 2016). When a group is culturally homogeneous, culture-specific learning activities can be incorporated into the group design (Cheng et al., 2015). For example, an anger-management group serving a primarily Hispanic male population should address cultural issues such as gender-role socialization, and learning examples should incorporate Hispanic individuals, families, and customs as revealed by group members (Villalba, Gonzalez, Hines, & Borders, 2014). Group leaders must be familiar with, and abide by, the Principles for Diversity Competence endorsed by the ASGW because all group work contains some multicultural aspects that must be attended to for optimally effective group experiences (Burnes & Hovanesian, 2017).

VARY METHODS OF INSTRUCTION TO ACCOMMODATE DIFFERENT LEARNING STYLES
(See Burnes & Hovanesian, 2017.) In general, leaders should keep in mind that few members will attentively absorb more than 15 minutes of content lecture and that members who learn primarily through visual or kinesthetic pathways may be limited in the amount of information they can hear and process at one time. Visual strategies, such as incorporating video or other visual images, are often helpful as auxiliary teaching methods. Activities involving movement help kinesthetic learners master new material (Huang, Liu, Shadiev, Shen, & Hwang, 2015).

INCORPORATE ACTIVE AND/OR DISCOVERY TEACHING METHODS   Hands-on activities and activities that allow members to reach conclusions during the group session are likely to create more lasting impressions. Directed learning exercises that promote active participation and interaction are powerful teaching tools. Educational games often are applicable to group settings and may provide an effective balance between content and process (Maarif, 2016).

TIE CONTENT TO RELEVANT EXAMPLES OR STORIES   The best teachers are often described as the best storytellers. In relating didactic material, real-life examples are often helpful. Depending on the purpose and structure of the group, some leaders use self-disclosure (Song, Kim, & Luo, 2016). In this way, the leader serves as a model for the participants and gains credibility as someone who understands their challenges. This teaching technique is most common in groups that incorporate support and psychoeducation, such as a group on parenting skills led by a counselor who is also a parent.

WHEN TEACHING BEHAVIORAL SKILLS, BREAK THE OVERALL TASK INTO SMALL STAGES OR COMPONENT PARTS   Behavioral skills should be taught systematically, from the simple to the more complex. The following strategies are useful for teaching behavioral skills: (a) *instruction* (teach, using oral instruction and providing rationale), (b) *modeling* (show, by demonstrating the skill via videotape, leader, or another member), (c) *role-play* (practice, in which the group member is encouraged to imitate and use the skill), (d) *feedback* (reinforce, through leader encouragement and coaching), and (e) *homework* (apply, by asking students to perform the newly acquired skill outside the group; Fazal, 2015).

GIVE OPPORTUNITIES FOR FEEDBACK   Although it is critical to develop a structured plan for a psychoeducational group, an effective leader will solicit formal and informal feedback throughout the group and make changes when necessary (Burnes & Hovanesian, 2017).

Planning and Implementing a Psychoeducational Group

To be meaningful and effective, psychoeducational groups must be well crafted, with a predetermined plan and clearly articulated goals and objectives (Brouzos et al., 2015). One method to structure the group has two processes for development. The first process is called the *conceptual phase* and has three steps: (a) statement of purpose, (b) establishing goals, and (c) setting objectives. The second process is called the *operational phase* and also has three steps: (a) selecting content, (b) designing experiential activities, and (c) evaluating effectiveness (Brown, 2011). In this model, group design begins with a broad conceptual idea and moves toward specific content and exercises. In structuring the group, each step is derived from the preceding step.

STEP 1: STATEMENT OF PURPOSE   A *statement of purpose* is an explicit statement of the reason for a group's existence. Ideas about psychoeducational groups often evolve from clinical practice, as counselors notice similarities in clients' problems or recognize that many clients could benefit from learning certain skills. Ideas for groups also may arise from community needs, such as a public outcry for more anger-management groups, groups for male batterers, or groups that meet the developmental needs of LGBTQ students (Burnes & Hovanesian, 2017). School counselors often find that several students share a need for addressing a certain issue and would benefit from a structured group approach. A college counselor may find that many students could benefit from a group on how to develop time-management skills (Burnes & Hovanesian, 2017).

At the conceptual level, the leader must determine the theoretical perspective of the group. Some groups work best from an insight-oriented perspective, and others are more behavioral in nature (Brown, 2011). The group may be conceptualized as primarily educational or skills based, primarily focused on self-awareness, or some combination of these. In addition, the leader must become familiar with the topic and investigate which theoretical approaches have been most effective (Brown, 2011).

STEP 2: ESTABLISHING GOALS   Goals indicate how a participant may change due to group involvement (Burnes & Hovanesian, 2017). The leader must specify the type of change expected from the members, and the goals must be consistent with the theoretical approach selected in the statement of purpose. Goals are often expressed as specific areas of mastery so that success can be evaluated and measured (Corey, M. S., et al., 2014). For example, a group for which the statement of purpose is to help college students gain time-management skills may establish several group goals, such as (a) learning to structure daily activities, (b) developing strategies to combat procrastination, and (c) prioritizing responsibilities. The goals of the group should be reasonable and attainable, given the characteristics of the members and the timeframe (Corey, M. S., et al., 2014). In addition, the goals should be culturally appropriate for the target population (Burnes & Hovanesian, 2017).

STEP 3: SETTING OBJECTIVES   *Goals* can be described as the compass setting the direction for the group and *objectives* as providing the road map for how to get there (Brown, 2011). Objectives specify, generally in behavioral terms, the steps needed to reach each group goal (Corey, G., et al., 2014). Each goal involves multiple objectives, the completion of which signals successful mastery of the goal. Group members who complete the objectives will gain insight into how they use their time and be more capable of realistically structuring the day's activities (Brown, 2011).

STEP 4: SELECTING CONTENT   Group content may be organized into three categories—didactic, experiential, and process (Brown, 2011)—described as follows:

1. *Didactic material* is often presented first, incorporating teaching strategies that are mindful of members' developmental level and attention span (Keck School of Medicine of USC, 2016).
2. *Experiential learning* allows the material to be understood on a personal level. Experiential activities should be chosen to reinforce didactic content in a way that is consistent with the group's theoretical orientation (Clark, 2015).
3. The goal of the *process* component is to help members connect the didactic and experiential components of the group (Brown, 2011). Participants may have to clarify the conclusions they derived from the experience or examine questions that arose from the experience. Members who can link their experiences with didactic material will be more likely to generalize their learning to a broader life context (Brown, 2011). Processing may include discussing what happened in the activity; participants' reactions to the activity; what thoughts, feelings, and insights were generated; and how these insights can be applied outside the group (Corey, M. S., et al., 2014).

STEP 5: DESIGNING ACTIVITIES   To be effective, group activities must be tailored to address group goals and objectives. When choosing activities, the primary theoretical orientation of the group should be considered (Burnes & Hovanesian, 2017). As examples: Groups with the goal of behavioral change might include exercises such as role-play and relaxation techniques, groups emphasizing cognitive change might use activities on identifying and changing self-talk, and groups with goals reflecting insight and greater self-understanding might employ activities that link affective, cognitive, and/or behavioral domains. Activities should be designed to be brief and simple to implement and should require active participation (Belmont, 2016).

STEP 6: EVALUATING EFFECTIVENESS   Psychoeducational groups address specific concerns through education, skill building, and member processing. Leaders should evaluate the effectiveness of their intervention through a combination of process and outcome methods (Burnes & Hovanesian, 2017). The *process evaluation* involves soliciting and incorporating feedback during each session and incorporating changes when necessary (Chapman et al., 2012). Many leaders incorporate process evaluation informally, and some solicit written feedback following each session (Brown, 2011; Corey, M. S., et al., 2014).

Leaders also should conduct an *outcome evaluation* of the group (Chapman et al., 2012). Two ways to evaluate the success of the group are to (a) measure goal attainment

SIDEBAR 8.4
The Importance of Group Outcome Evaluation

A counselor at a university has been facilitating the same psychoeducational group on study skills every semester for the past decade. The counselor built the objectives and curriculum for the group based on the published best practices for group work on university student study skills that were current at the time. Lately, the counselor has noticed that group enrollment has been dwindling, and several students have reported that their study skills have not improved significantly after participating in the group. What steps might the counselor take to reevaluate the group's goals and curriculum and ultimately test the effectiveness of the group to improve the study skills of her students?

and to (b) assess members' satisfaction with the group experience. Measuring *goal attainment* involves giving the members a pretest before the group experience, followed by a posttest after group has ended (Chapman et al., 2012). For example, if the group targeted test anxiety, the participants' responses to questions such as "When I see the questions on the test, my mind goes blank" should improve on average after completion of the group. In the other method of outcome assessment, *member satisfaction*, participants report their subjective reaction to the group (Pender, 2009). They may evaluate the leader's style, content of the group, and group activities. Although group satisfaction itself is not sufficient to create change, it is a facilitative condition for nurturing change, and this feedback is helpful to the group leader (Pender, 2009).

COUNSELING AND PSYCHOTHERAPY GROUPS

Although there has been some disagreement over the exact point of origin, it is widely held that the end of World War II and the subsequent influx of "psychiatric casualties" led to the widespread group practices we see today (NSGPF, 2015). Much of this debate has been definitional in nature. Earlier groups, such as Pratt's 1905 *class method* for treatment of individuals with tuberculosis (intended to save time in teaching patients hygiene practices) was found to have a psychotherapeutic effect, although this was not its initial purpose (NSGPF, 2015; Pratt, 1907, 1945).

Other early practitioners, such as E. W. Lazell and L. C. Marsh, also provided what many would consider to be group counseling and group psychotherapeutic intervention. Lazell's group procedures consisted mainly of lectures, whereas Marsh utilized group discussions, music, art, and dance in his efforts to aid individuals residing in mental hospitals (American Mental Health Foundation [AMHF], 2017). It was Marsh who uttered the famous statement "By the crowd they have been broken; by the crowd they shall be healed" (Malat & Leszcz, 2015, p. 1923). Other noted contributors to the development of group counseling and psychotherapy include Bion, Eziel, Foulkes, Whitaker, Lieberman, Lewin, and Yalom (AMHF, 2017; NSGPF, 2015).

Group counseling and group psychotherapy have been discussed as interventions meant to lessen psychological distress, reduce maladaptive behavior, or encourage adaptive behavior through counseling, structured or unstructured interaction, a training program, or a predetermined treatment plan (Burlingame et al., 2015).

Group counseling and psychotherapy can be used in almost every setting, with most categories of mental illness or "normal" problems of adjustment, and with a wide range of age groups, which sets these group modalities further apart from other, more limited forms of group therapy (Burlingame et al., 2015).

Similarities and Differences Between Counseling and Psychotherapy Groups

There are more similarities than differences between what can be defined as a *counseling group* and what can be defined as a *psychotherapy group*. For example, in a psychotherapy group, a match must be made between the counselor, group members, theory base, developmental level of the group, and the issue at hand. The case can clearly be made that such considerations are equally as important in counseling groups. Two similarities between counseling and psychotherapy groups are the considerations of transference and change, and one difference is diagnostic foundation (American Psychological Association [APA], 2017b).

TRANSFERENCE   A similarity between counseling groups and psychotherapy groups is the issue of transference. *Transference* is the client's carrying forth expectations, impressions, and feelings from a past person to the therapist (Turri, 2015). Although transference can occur in almost any situation, it is very likely to happen within both the process of counseling and psychotherapy, and especially within the group experience (Cornell, 2013). It is important to note that transference may also occur among group members (Resnik, 2015).

CHANGE   An additional similarity between counseling groups and psychotherapy groups is the goal of change. The aim of both counseling and psychotherapy groups is to influence change in the group members (American Group Psychotherapy Association [AGPA], 2007b). Both psychotherapy and counseling can be viewed as methods for understanding why, what, and how a person responds to life's challenges (APA, 2017b). The ultimate goal is to change the "why" and "what" because these things often have not been adaptive.

The focus of both counseling and psychotherapy is on changing or refining ingrained personality traits, behavioral patterns, or cognitive miscues that are disabling the client or group member from functioning effectively in the world (AGPA, 2007a; Capuzzi & Gross, 2013a). Therefore, the aim is not to educate the client, as it would be in a guidance/psychoeducational group, or to develop teamwork or group skills in completing a project, as would be the case in a task/work group. The goal of counseling and psychotherapy groups is to achieve actual change in basic personality structure and clients' ways of living and behaving in their world (Corey, G., et al., 2014).

DIAGNOSTIC FOUNDATION   Perhaps the only difference between counseling groups and psychotherapy groups is the diagnostic makeup of group members. Many theorists have noted that psychotherapy, in its purest form, requires a diagnostic basis for the foundation of the group (Corey, G., et al., 2014). For example, a *homogeneous* psychotherapeutic group experience (e.g., a group in which group members share a common diagnosed characteristic) might have as a goal changes in the behavior or cognitions of group members in a group formed of members who are experiencing a diagnosed anxiety disorder, an eating disorder, or an adjustment disorder (Corey, M. S., et al., 2014). This psychotherapeutic group would not deal with issues relating to transitional events, with issues relating to specific life problems, or with "normal" problems of adjustment. Instead, psychotherapy groups seek to remediate *diagnosed* personality, emotional, behavioral, or interpersonal maladjustments (Capuzzi & Gross, 2013a; Corey, M. S., et al., 2014).

Regardless of the difference between counseling groups and psychotherapy groups on the issue of diagnostic foundation, the strictest sense of the definition of both counseling and psychotherapy is that the culmination of therapy should affect or produce growth within the client (Corey, G., et al., 2014). For our purposes, both counseling groups and psychotherapy groups bring about change for individuals who seek to remediate diagnostic conditions and symptoms. Psychotherapy has been designed as a "change process designed to provide symptom relief, personality change, and prevention of future symptomatic episodes and to increase the quality of life, including the promotion of adaptive functioning in work and relationships, [and] the ability to make healthy and satisfying life choices" (Vasquez, 2007, p. 878). Thus, we will use the terms *counseling groups* and *psychotherapy groups* interchangeably for the remainder of this section (Corey, M. S., et al., 2014).

Leadership Variables of Effective Counseling and Psychotherapy Groups

Many factors interact to determine the outcome of a group experience (APA, 2017b). These factors often are explicitly under the group leader's control or direction (AGPA, 2007b). Some of the variables are obvious and are covered by the ASGW in the knowledge, skill, and core competencies (ASGW, 2000). However, some considerations when evaluating whether a group experience will be effective may not be so obvious. These include the personal characteristics of the group leader; others relate to the counselor's belief in the group process, the therapeutic environment the counselor provides, and how the counselor uses his or her knowledge of theory and group process.

PERSONAL CHARACTERISTICS   One could say that a psychotherapeutic group is only as good as its leader. Using the analogy of a painting to describe the group therapeutic process, the leader is the framework upon which the group canvas is laid. While the members themselves do the painting and artwork, the leader provides the structure and boundaries that contain the experience. Without the framework the leader provides, the therapeutic process cannot be fulfilled (Kivlighan & Kivlighan, 2016).

Effective group leaders have specific personal characteristics that further the group process (Cohen, 2011). The group counselor's personality and behaviors can have a profound impact upon the group experience (Wu & Wang, 2015). This can be especially true in the early stages of the group, as members tend to rally around the leader, who becomes an interpersonal anchor around which the group can coalesce and establish a sense of group cohesion (Anwar, 2016). Extensive lists have been published on this topic, and the factors we find most relevant are described in the following subsections.

Willingness to Confront Oneself.   Willingness to confront oneself entails asking hard questions: Who am I as a person? As the group leader? Effective leaders are aware of all the facets of their personality, values, and beliefs, and they use their interpersonal style to enhance the group process. Once psychotherapists have achieved this knowledge of self, they display courage in exploring their own weaknesses (Corey, G., et al., 2014). This includes having the courage to face mistakes, admit to fears, act upon hunches or hypotheses, feel genuine emotion, be able to examine their own lives and values, and model positive behaviors (Corey, M. S., et al., 2014).

Authenticity.   Successful group leaders are genuine with group members and do not hide behind the cloak of professionalism, stereotyped images of what they think a counselor is or should be, or the *psychotherapist* title. Rather, they accept the same risks and vulnerabilities as other group members (Capuzzi & Gross, 2013a; Wright, 2014). This also means they can be emotionally present with group members. Group leaders cannot be truly empathetic unless they are in touch both with their own emotions and the emotions of other group members (Wright, 2014).

Self-Care.   If one takes to heart the adage that a client is bound by the limits of his or her counselor, the group counselor's own mental health is imperative (Conyne, 2014). Because group needs come first, good leaders know how to take care of their own mental health requirements without imposing upon the group to provide the context for doing so. Leaders of groups, or any psychotherapeutic counselors, should seek personal counseling when needed. Leaders also should not be afraid to get professional support, supervision, or evaluation when indicated (Conyne, 2014).

Self-Awareness.   Along with good mental health, effective leaders are self-aware. Effective counselors have an identity; they know who they are, what they can become, what they want out of life, and what is essential (Corey, 2016). This also means knowing their own power and how to use it for the benefit of the group. The leader must show confidence in himself or herself as an effectual human being and show his or her authentic self to group members (Corey, 2016).

Interpersonal Style.   Leaders, too, must be aware of their interpersonal style of relating (Corey, 2016). Does the leader need to be the center of attention? Does the leader need always to feel accepted? Does the leader need to be the authority? Is the leader uncomfortable in confrontational situations? The group leader must be aware of

---

SIDEBAR 8.5
Self-Care Among Group Counselors

A community mental health counselor has been leading a counseling group focused on anxiety treatment for sexual assault survivors for the past 8 weeks. Although the group has been functioning extremely well, lately the counselor has noticed that she has had a poor attention span during the group and has lost track of what her clients were saying or responding to several times in recent group sessions. The counselor also has had difficulty falling and remaining asleep throughout the night and has experienced several nightmares involving sexual assault in recent days. Imagine that you are this counselor's supervisor and that she has shared these concerns with you. From a self-care perspective, what might you encourage the counselor to do moving forward?

his or her true self, including personal biases, preferences, and prejudices, so as not to project these onto group members or let them influence the group process (Capuzzi & Gross, 2013a). The counselor must be comfortable with himself or herself and have self-respect, affirmative self-beliefs, and projected positive self-worth.

Faith and Enthusiasm.   One of the most important individual traits that directly influence the group outcome is the level of personal faith and enthusiasm the group leader brings to the group process. If the group leader does not believe in the group process, group members likely will not either, and the opportunity for therapeutic benefit may be lost (Brown, 2011). Group leaders who do not genuinely believe in the value of psychotherapeutic work and who engage in it only for power or money are behaving unethically (Corey, G., et al., 2014).

Group psychotherapy works to a certain extent because the group leader and the group members alike believe in the group's power to effect change (Ruzek et al., 2016). The faith of the group transcends from the faith of the leader. Along with this faith in group process, an effective leader expresses faith in the group members' ability to achieve their goals and effect change and believes strongly that the group is the best vehicle to effect that change (Capuzzi & Gross, 2013a).

THE THERAPEUTIC ENVIRONMENT   Another leadership variable that contributes to the success or failure of any group experience is the ability to create an environment in which the psychotherapeutic process can take place (Hoffman, 2013). Obviously, if the atmosphere is hostile and uncomfortable, psychotherapeutic work is impeded because the essential elements of trust and safety are missing (Rutan, Stone, & Shay, 2014). It is the leader's role to provide the climate, or arena, in which members can safely explore their feelings, thoughts, and behavior patterns; arrive at solutions to their problems; and achieve personal growth (Corey, M. S., et al., 2014). In the absence of this atmosphere, psychotherapeutic, self-curative activities will not take place (Corey, 2016).

Ensuring a Safe Environment.   The leader ensures a safe environment by providing structure, boundaries, and group interactive guidelines (Gladding, 2011). There is a fine line between respecting individual autonomy and establishing overall safety of the group (Rutan et al., 2014). The counselor can provide safety by modeling congruent behavior, demonstrating personal boundaries and effective modes of confrontation, and being honest and authentic (Gladding, 2011). Because group members initially "follow the leader," it is imperative that the counselor model positive behavior (Capuzzi & Gross, 2013a).

Setting Rules and Norms.   If the counselor leading the group will prescribe any group rules, prohibitions, or restrictions, he or she must be exceedingly clear about these at the beginning of the group process (Cohen, 2011). Effective group leaders keep rules to a minimum and empower the group by letting the members develop their own rules and norms. Although group members should be encouraged to develop their own rules, it is the leader's role to make sure that these rules and norms will not hinder the therapeutic process (Cohen, 2011).

Setting Goals.   Effective group leaders encourage members to set group and individual goals, and to make sure that these goals are actually set, to avoid aimless wandering without purpose or direction (Corey, M. S., et al., 2014). The group psychotherapist must ensure that these goals are realistic and obtainable. Once the goals are in place, the group leader must keep the group focused (Foxx, Baker, & Gerler, 2017). The leader can help group members structure goals and expectations to provide optimum benefit and maximum use of peer support and individual learning (Gladding, 2011).

An Atmosphere of Respect.   The leader should provide an atmosphere in which each group member can feel important, respected, worthwhile, and that he or she is a contributing member of the group (Coco, Gullo, Fratello, Giordano, & Kivlighan, 2016; Gladding, 2011). In that way, the group leader helps to mold and develop individual and group esteem and integrity (Corey, 2016). The leader does this by setting clear boundaries regarding relational issues.

Positive Interchange.   The group leader must be ready to confront any member who is attacking or abusing another, including possible termination of the offending member (Coco et al., 2016; Jacobs et al., 2016). The competence of the group leader is the best defense against member-to-member abuse and exploitation. This is a weighty responsibility, and the group leader must be able to deal with this issue effectively to ensure the viability of the group process (Wright, 2014). As part of this responsibility, the leader must be able to discern when a member is being destructive to the group process and when he or she is being resistant, uncooperative, or defensive, the latter of which signals psychotherapeutic intervention, not dismissal from the group (Jacobs et al., 2016).

The psychotherapist leading the group must go beyond intervening in conflicts to promote positive interchange among group members (Gladding, 2011). An effective leader understands that members move at differing paces. Again, the leader should model behavior and interactional techniques that will encourage group members to talk with one another in a nonhostile, noncoercive way (Kottler & Shepard, 2014).

INTEGRATION OF TECHNICAL KNOWLEDGE AND THEORIES   Personal characteristics and a positive therapeutic environment are two requisites for an effective group (Hoffman, 2013; Kivlighan & Kivlighan, 2016). An additional leadership variable relates to how the group leader integrates technical knowledge and theories learned in training (Watson & Bedard, 2006).

Use of Knowledge.   It is not just *what* the psychotherapeutic group leader knows but *how* he or she uses that knowledge that is important (Jacobs et al., 2016). It is not enough to know which theories apply to groups. The leader must understand which theories work best for which populations and with which therapeutic issues, and it is just as important to know in which populations or issues those theories would be contraindicated (Jacobs et al., 2016).

Application of Theories.   An effective leader of a psychotherapeutic group applies theory and modality to the group and not vice versa (Vasquez, 2007). It is also essential that the group leader interject his or her personal style in whatever theory he or she uses (Cohen, 2011). The wooden application of theory straight out of a textbook is unlikely to be effective and probably will be perceived as stilted and phony.

SIDEBAR 8.6

Selecting Members for a Psychotherapy Group

Imagine that you are a psychotherapist working at an inpatient treatment center for young women and men suffering from eating disorders. The treatment center has, at any given time, newly admitted clients who must be placed on supportive nursing care immediately to increase weight, clients in the beginning stages of recovery who receive individual cognitive behavioral therapy, and recovering clients who participate in psychotherapy groups before they are released from the center. Considering that placing clients with eating disorders into group psychotherapy too early can lead to competition for weight loss and poor group dynamics, how might you determine psychotherapy group membership to encourage a fully functional and successful group experience for your clients?

The successful psychotherapy group leader is flexible and considers each group unique. This type of leader will mold his or her role to the needs of the group (Billow, 2017).

To attain the best possible group membership, the leader must understand group dynamics. The interpersonal qualities of each member, as well as those of the leader, are the determinants of how far the group can grow (Billow, 2017). Each member's limitations and growth potential must be carefully determined and weighed to provide the best possible group composition for therapeutic gain (Coco et al., 2016). For example, researchers have found that similarities among group members are conducive to interpersonal attraction and mutual support, whereas differences among group members are conducive to confrontation and change. Therefore, when selecting group members, the leader should have a working knowledge of what he or she wants to accomplish.

INTERVENTIONS   The leader must have a thorough understanding of what occurs in each stage of group development and which interventions are prudent for each stage. Interventions should be timed in a stage-specific context (Jacobs et al., 2016). For example, using an anxiety-provoking exercise during the group-cohesion stage would be detrimental to the group process. Effective leaders further understand what the likely outcomes of their interventions will be and know what interventions will facilitate group goals (Gladding, 2011; Jacobs et al., 2016).

A FACILITATIVE STYLE   One other leadership variable that must be considered is leadership style (Nielsen, 2013). The leader's style affects how a group is composed, how it proceeds, and whether the psychotherapist leading the group is viewed as a *technical expert* or as a *model-setting participant*. These two approaches are very different, and group leaders should understand the applications for each approach.

Technical Expert Style.   In the role of *technical expert*, a leader imparts knowledge of the psychological process, asks probing questions, and uses specific therapeutic techniques such as guided imagery, hypnotherapy, making the rounds, psychodrama, sculpting, and bibliotherapy (Conyne, 2014; Jacobs et al., 2016). This approach is directive. An image that comes to mind with this approach is the group leader as conductor of an orchestra and the group members playing the instruments and parts. The group makes the music, and the leader directs the score.

Model-Setting Participant Style.   In the *model-setting participant style*, the leader is a part of the group, but his or her role is to help the group process information, and he or she is responsive to members. This style is less directive and more contingent on group needs. The model-setting participant assists group members as they work through their issues and helps members deal with each other honestly, authentically, and with respect. This type of group leader also helps members reach their full growth potential (Rutan et al., 2014; Wright, 2014). The leader's ability to serve as a role model for members aids considerably in facilitating insight and interpersonal learning.

Summary

In this chapter, we provided an overview of the similarities, differences, and practices of different types of counseling groups: task/work, psychoeducational, counseling, and psychotherapy. Each type of group has its own distinctions and purpose. Today, much of society is adopting a group orientation in task and work groups. Concepts of consensus, collaboration, and teamwork are finding their way into business, politics, and social circles (Benchmark Institute, 2010; Tziner & Chernyak-Hai, 2012). Successful task/work groups do not spring forth without considerable effort. The effectiveness of task/work groups is grounded firmly in group dynamics, "the interactions fostered through the relationships of members and leaders in connection with the complexities of the task involved" (Gladding, 2011, p. 24–25).

Members of these groups collaborate on meaningful tasks and goals, engage in new learning, and access technical and human resources as necessary to accomplish the task (Boyle et al., 2012; Cohen, 2011). Members and leaders of task/work groups must invest in the accomplishment of their agreed-upon goal. The outcome of a successful task/work group is greater than the product or performance it produces. It is also an outcome of people working together toward a common goal.

Psychoeducational groups are structured groups that emphasize learning or developing skills for prevention, growth, or remediation (Burnes & Hovanesian, 2017). Psychoeducational groups are becoming increasingly popular as both primary and supplemental interventions in a variety of settings (Brouzos

et al., 2015). Effective psychoeducational groups are highly organized and time limited, and they integrate principles of learning with traditional group-intervention strategies (Brown, 2011). Compared to counseling groups and other types of group work, psychoeducational groups are highly cognitive, involve fewer sessions, include more members, do not emphasize catharsis or deep personal disclosure, have predefined goals for members, incorporate specific activities with desired outcomes, and limit group content to predetermined topics (Brouzos et al., 2015).

Leaders of psychoeducational groups must be knowledgeable and skilled regarding group leadership and teaching strategies (Brouzos et al., 2015; Burnes & Hovanesian, 2017). At their most effective, these groups integrate the best elements of counseling and teaching and provide effective and powerful interventions for many clinical and adjustment issues (Burnes & Hovanesian, 2017). Researchers have provided copious empirical evidence that these groups are effective in treating a variety of issues, including eating disorders, substance abuse, and depression (Brouzos et al., 2015; Burnes & Hovanesian, 2017). Clients who benefit from psychoeducational groups find their emphasis on knowledge and skill building to be empowering, either as a primary source of help or as an adjunct to individual or other counseling interventions (Brown, 2011). These groups are popular in primary, secondary, and postsecondary education settings, in which they often provide an important component of comprehensive guidance programs (Brouzos et al., 2015).

Mental health professionals historically have used the terms *group therapy, group counseling,* and *group psychotherapy* interchangeably. This has led to confusion as to exactly what group counseling and group psychotherapy entail. The only noted difference between counseling groups and psychotherapy groups is that psychotherapy groups require a diagnostic basis for the foundation of the group and counseling groups do not (APA, 2017b); Corey, M. S., et al., 2014; Malat & Leszcz, 2015). In both counseling groups and psychotherapy groups— but not as likely to be present in other groups, such as guidance/psychoeducational or task/work groups—you will encounter transference and the requirement of actual change in group members (Corey, M. S., et al., 2014; Cornell, 2013; Turri, 2015).

The process of a psychotherapeutic group can be largely impacted by its group leader. Noted personal characteristics of effective group leaders include self-awareness, willingness to engage in self-confrontation, authenticity, self-care, and faith in group process. The role of an effective group leader also involves creating a suitable environment that will facilitate members' growth and change. Effective group environments are safe, include suitable rules and norms, engender an atmosphere of respect, and allow for confrontation (Coco et al., 2016; Cohen, 2011; Gladding, 2011).

9

Creative Approaches to Group Work

Thelma Duffey and Shane Haberstroh

People join groups for many reasons. Some people seek group experiences to work on identified issues or to reach out to others with similar difficulties (Gladding, 2008; Yalom & Leszcz, 2005). Others may be referred to group sessions or attend them as part of treatment or educational programs (Celinska, 2015). Clients may attend various kinds of groups across a range of purposes, formats, lengths, and intensities (Corey, Corey, & Corey, 2014). As counselors plan to lead various types of groups, they consider how to balance the group content with the underlying systemic processes inherent in groups. For example, psycho-educational groups focus on educational activities and provide growth-promoting information (DeLucia-Waack, 2006; Hall, 2006; Lefley, 2009), and they may include experiential-learning activities and process commentary. However, their purpose differs from counseling and psychotherapy groups, which tend to focus less on content and more on interpersonal processes (Aasheim & Niemann, 2006). Although the format and focus of groups differ, certain factors tend to facilitate group functioning (Yalom & Leszcz, 2005).

Groups tend to function well when facilitators use their power respectfully, carefully plan the group experience, communicate clearly, empathize, and lead with an understanding of group theory and process (Corey et al., 2014). Knowledge of specific therapeutic factors (Yalom & Leszcz, 2005), common group stages (Tuckman & Jensen, 2010), systems theory (Agazarian, 2012), interpersonal relationships, and human development inform group leaders' strategies and interventions. Creativity is one such core human developmental process that group leaders can harness to promote hope, enliven the learning process, and bring greater closeness within the group. Creative interventions and the creative process can bond small groups, unite communities, and provide a forum for members to develop social skills (Averett, Crowe, & Hall, 2015). Although clients may not intentionally join a group to develop their creativity, groups do provide an optimal forum for clients to think in novel ways about their experiences, find new resources, and experience connection with others.

CREATIVITY, GROUP STAGES, AND THERAPEUTIC FACTORS

Most group practitioners and scholars contend that groups move through predictable stages (Corey, 2012b; Tuckman & Jensen, 2010). During each group stage, leaders expect common dynamics and plan their creative interventions accordingly. Typically, effective groups progress from reliance on structure and direction from the leader to more egalitarian and mutual interactions (Jacobs, Masson, Harvill, & Schimmel, 2012; Kottler, 1994). Correspondingly, as a group progresses through its lifecycle, leaders infuse their creativity and creative interventions intentionally. As leaders attend to the developmental aspects of their group, they also focus on nurturing the therapeutic factors that emerge from productive groupwork (McLaughlin, 2013).

Forming, Cohesion, and Universality

Creativity in counseling groups can deepen therapeutic factors and enhance group cohesion (Whitten & Burt, 2015; Yalom & Leszcz, 2005). In the forming stage of a group, leaders focus on interventions that contribute to group cohesion and encourage the expression of universality (Tuckman & Jensen, 2010). Many icebreaker activities lend themselves to connecting members through humor, personal sharing, and spontaneity (Jacobs et al., 2012). In the beginning stages of a group, it is important that members feel safe and begin to learn the norms guiding communication in groups. Creative icebreakers invite clients to shift perspectives and see themselves in a new light while becoming increasingly authentic with others. For example, instead of opening the group by asking members to discuss a litany of reasons for joining the group, a counselor could ask members to share information about a song, movie, or poem that best represents their current situation (Duffey, 2005). This small change in an introduction exercise invites clients to disclose but also to describe their experiences in an unexpected way (Haberstroh, 2005).

Beginning a group with a focus on creativity through art, music, literature, or movement invites members to engage and share their creativity. DeLucia-Waack (2006) noted that using music in introductory groups helps reduce anxiety and can bond members around common themes expressed in song. These kinds of activities promote universality (Gladding, 2012), can inspire hope, and can help the group develop cohesiveness (Tuckman & Jensen, 2010; Yalom & Leszcz, 2005). These elements set the stage for an effective group process and serve as a foundation for when the group faces challenges later.

Storming, Open Communication, and Reconnection

As groups move into the storming stage, issues related to power, personal differences, group structure, and direction emerge (Johnson, 2013). Clearly, navigating this stage requires counselors to think innovatively, quickly, and with compassion and honesty (Tuckman & Jensen, 2010). The goals for navigating the storming stage include facilitating conversations in which group members (a) hear each other with authenticity, (b) express empathy, and (c) move toward a narrative of reconnection (Duffey, Haberstroh, & Trepal, 2016).

To successfully navigate the storming stage, counselors engage the group in honest and compassionate conversations and seek to spark new ways to perceive their stuck points. For example, Burns (2008) described the use of fictional stories in counseling. This is one approach counselors can use during the storming stage. Themes from poems, short stories, and lyrics can give words and expression to emotions that group members may be feeling (Duffey, 2005) but may hesitate to express. Literature can provide a productive outlet to begin discussing difficult topics because meaningful lyrics or phrases can provide the words to open a difficult dialogue.

Norming and Working Stages: Deepening Ties and Learning

When a group successfully works through its process of storming, members may begin to develop a more realistic sense of unity. They know that the group can handle tough conversations (McLaughlin, 2013). As members feel more connected to the group and more willing to take risks with each other, creative interventions can serve as powerful tools for personal and shared growth. In the working stage of the group, members learn about themselves and their impact on others and find new ways to apply this awareness to their lives (McLaughlin, 2013). Many creative interventions can tap into unexpressed feelings, provide a medium to communicate complex situations and reactions, and deepen bonds among members as they experience growing awareness and cathartic moments together.

Depending on the theoretical focus of a group, working-stage creative interventions can facilitate cathartic moments, bring about deepened insight, provide impactful learning experiences, and draw members closer together. We provide examples of working-stage activities later in this chapter. The working stage is a time when creativity can make a lasting impact and prepare people to apply their experiences in group to their lives. This is especially important as groups begin the process of terminating.

Termination, Meaning, and Disconnection

As members begin to end their time together, the focus of the group centers on reminiscing, saying goodbye, exploring existential issues, and preparing for the future beyond the group experience (Duffey, Haberstroh, & Trepal, 2009). This is a time well-suited to involve creativity as members face these issues in the group and their lives (Headley, Kautzman-East, Pusateri, & Kress, 2015). Times of reminiscence inspire creativity. Van Tilburg, Sedikides, & Wildschut (2015) found that when participants connected with nostalgic memories, they scored higher on measures of creative thinking. As group members reflect on their group experience and apply the lessons learned in group to their lives, creative-thinking skills can help them integrate their learning in meaningful ways. The end of a group can feel bittersweet, and when a group has worked together well, members often experience many benefits. These benefits include feeling less isolated, gaining knowledge about themselves, learning new skills, and exploring new ways to act in the world. The development of a client's creative capacities can translate into other areas of life and offer clients tangible benefits for future change. Creativity can be a powerful force in people's lives, and group leaders embrace creativity as a process that is grounded in theory, grows through relationships, and supersedes the mere use of activities.

CREATIVITY IN GROUPS: RELATIONAL CULTURAL THEORY

Relational cultural theory (RCT) is a progressive theory that promotes connection and relationship over autonomy and independence with respect to how human beings grow and develop (Jordan, 2010). According to RCT, opportunities for growth occur in relationship with others, and forming growth-fostering relationships is a primary and essential goal of all counseling. Forming relationships that genuinely work well—that promote the well-being of all parties involved—is an important, albeit challenging, process. RCT details the process of connection, disconnection, and reconnection, and it purports that authenticity and mutual empathy support growth in relationships. Although RCT acknowledges that all relationships undergo times of disconnection, it identifies the healing power of reconnection and its role in relational resiliency–that is, people become more resilient in relationship with others and as they navigate disconnecting experiences and isolating periods of time. RCT also cautions, however, that when people are not able to navigate the reconnection process and hide important aspects of themselves from others in order to attempt to stay in connection, they can experience what RCT refers to as *condemned isolation*. According to RCT, condemned isolation is one of the more painful experiences that a person can encounter.

Group members desiring connection in their lives can learn important relational skills using an RCT framework. Given that groups thrive in connection and through creative expression, identifying ways for group members to connect with one another and access their creativity can be salient group-process goals. In this chapter, we offer a number of creative applications for group practice and suggest that group facilitators consider and apply RCT constructs, such as (a) creating a place in which group members can relate to one another authentically, (b) promoting mutual empathy, which differs from one-way empathy, as a virtue, (c) identifying strategies of disconnection or those behaviors that interfere with relationship growth, and (d) creating opportunities for group members to increase their relational competencies through their work together. RCT is the foundation that explains the relational components for *creativity in counseling* (Duffey et al., 2016), a novel theoretical approach.

CREATIVITY IN COUNSELING: A THEORETICAL MODEL

Creativity in counseling (CIC) is a theoretical model that incorporates the use of creativity within a relational framework (Duffey et al., 2016). "CIC is defined as a shared counseling process involving growth-promoting shifts that occur from an intentional focus on the therapeutic relationship and an inherent human creative capacity to affect change" (Duffey et al., 2016, p. 448). All group counseling has an expressed or implied goal of promoting change, growth, and healing. Further, group-counseling experiences offer myriad opportunities for group members to connect with their creative resources while developing relational skills and deepening connections with themselves and others. Ahead, we offer several group activities, grounded in CIC and framed using an RCT lens.

We offer the guidelines ahead for the following group activities:

1. The facilitator addresses any housekeeping issues, such as bathroom location and other important information.
2. Like most group processes, group facilitators engaging in creative activities inform the members about expectations for confidentiality. They also provide any guidelines relevant to the groups they are facilitating.
3. The facilitator introduces him- or herself and invites participants to share their names and one quality point of information each they would like the group to know about them.
4. Toward the end of the session, group members are invited to reflect on the experience and their shared process.

You are considering the inclusion of creative interventions in your upcoming group. As you plan for the first session, what kind of activities will you include? Given that CIC "is defined as a shared counseling process involving growth-promoting shifts that occur from an intentional focus on the therapeutic relationship and the inherent human creative capacity to affect change" (Duffey et al., 2016, p. 528), how will you emphasize the relational aspects of group work and creativity?

APPLICATIONS OF CREATIVITY IN COUNSELING GROUPS

A review of articles focused on group counseling and creativity in counseling in the *Journal of Creativity in Mental Health* (JCMH; Gladding, 2008) revealed over 80 articles highlighting research and practice in this area. Topics in the *JCMH* spanned the wide variety of groups and populations that counselors encounter (Burns, 2008; Desmond, Kindsvatter, Stahl, & Smith, 2015; Duffey & Haberstroh, 2012; Ziff, Pierce, Johanson, & King, 2012). As leaders implement creative interventions, they conceptualize the many factors at play in group sessions. Members come to group with varying levels of relational competence, communication skills, life experiences, and motivation for growth. It is important for counselors to implement creative group interventions based on an operational framework that explains interrelationships among people, personal growth directions, and approaches to assess issues. In our work with groups, we understand the dynamics of interpersonal connection, help people access their creativity, provide a framework for feedback, and conceptualize growth using developmental relational counseling (Duffey & Haberstroh, 2012, 2014, 2016).

Developmental Relational Counseling in Groups

Developmental relational counseling (DRC) is an integrated theoretical model founded on RCT principles, and it integrates tenets from cognitive therapies, narrative therapy, and the enneagram personality typology (Duffey & Haberstroh, 2012). DRC (see Figure 9.1) provides a road map that illustrates the nature of a person's disconnection in group settings by focusing on personal and relational awareness, members' use of power, and unique relational styles (Duffey & Haberstroh, 2012; Jordan, 2010). The DRC approach recognizes that people live within varied social contexts, function differently with different people, and face tribulations and issues throughout their lives. Counselors who lead groups based on DRC principles attend to how clients understand themselves in relation to others.

Based on your counseling theory, how could you use creative interventions to help clients grow and change? What are the ethical implications for using multimedia approaches in counseling?

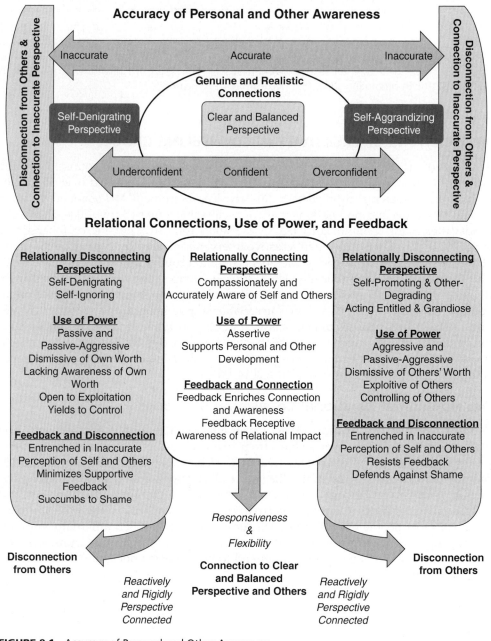

FIGURE 9.1   Accuracy of Personal and Other Awareness

(*Source:* Duffey & Haberstroh, 2012.)

SELF-DENIGRATING, AGGRANDIZING, AND CLEAR AND BALANCED PERSPECTIVES
Operating from a DRC framework, a group leader listens for members' tendencies to self-denigrate or self-aggrandize. From the narrative tradition, we named these tendencies *perspectives*—lenses that people use to understand themselves and others. Counselors conceptualize people according to their views of themselves and other people. Depending on the issue, circumstances, or situation, group members may see themselves in an aggrandized way, a denigrated manner, or with a clear and balanced view. These perspectives are relational because when a person views her- or himself in a self-denigrating way, she or he may aggrandize others, and those interacting from self-aggrandizing perspectives can perceive others as less than worthy. Group leaders assess whether members use power in controlling, dismissive, or exploitive (Duffey, Haberstroh, & Trepal, 2009) ways.

RELATIONAL STYLES AND CONNECTIONS   Grounded in the enneagram personality typology, group members' relational styles (see Table 9.1), in concert with their adopted perspectives, further define their relational connections and disconnections. For example, if a member approaches group from a self-aggrandized perspective and tends to be information focused in his relational style, he may challenge the leader, seek to diminish the leader's knowledge and authority, and overintellectualize the experience.

TABLE 9.1 Relational Styles, Connections, and Perspectives

Relational Focus	Connected to Self-Denigrating Perspective	Connected to Clear, Balanced, and Compassionate Perspective	Connected to Self-Aggrandizing Perspective
Rules	Embarrassment around being perceived or exposed as wrong or making a mistake	Factual, objective, and humane	Punitive, defensive, and critical
Service	Feeling victimized	Giving and appreciative	Demanding, entitled, and patronizing
Status	Shame and worthlessness around status	Efficient and successful	Opportunistic and inflated sense of self
Individuality	Ashamed and self-conscious of self-perceived flaws	Creative and accessible	Judgmental and superior
Knowledge	Worthlessness around competence	Open minded, alert, perceptive	Callous, cynical, and intellectually arrogant
Strategy	Paranoid and fearful	Cooperative and trusting	Berating, belligerent, and withholding
Obligation	Brief shame and despair	Grateful and considerate	Greedy, self-righteous, and inconsiderate
Power	Hidden vulnerability and hurt	Courageous, confident, and generous	Abusive, domineering, and vengeful
Agreement	Lacking self-awareness and self-trust	Fulfilled, connected, and receptive	Dismissive, self-absorbed, and unconcerned

---

SIDEBAR 9.3

Self-Awareness: Your Relational Style in Groups

===

Take a moment to reflect on how you relate in group settings. Do you intellectualize, like to help others, or seek ways to gain control and power? Do you look for allegiance, or do you find yourself mediating difficulties? Maybe you want to experience more fun in group? Do you consider yourself a romantic at heart? Do you strive for success in all settings? These are some questions to ask yourself as you attend group sessions as a member and as you begin to lead groups. The enneagram personality typology is a resource to help you understand your relational styles and motivations.

The leader's goal would then be to approach the member from a clear and balanced perspective, hear his concerns, provide feedback aimed at tempering the member's aggrandizement, learn about his impact on others, and hopefully experience connection in his vulnerability. Integrating DRC and CIC, group leaders focus on how members relate to each other and use creativity to increase awareness and deepen relationships.

Art, Music, and the Written Word in Groups

Many counselors employ creative arts in groups (Whitten & Burt, 2015; Ziff, Ivers, & Shaw, 2016). Relatedly, expressive-arts therapists work from their respective theoretical bases, ethical standards, and credentialing practices (e.g., art therapy, music therapy, poetry therapy). Counselors, guided by their training theoretical orientation and ethical standards, use creative interventions in group work to achieve counseling goals. Ziff et al. (2012) outlined art-based approaches and specific interventions and materials to focus on sensory, affective, and symbolic themes clients bring to counseling. For example, they listed materials like clay, watercolors, finger paints, and pastels as ones that encourage relaxation and assist members with expressing their feelings (Ziff et al., 2012). Musical interventions, counseling using poetry and the written word, and movement-based approaches all have the power to tell stories in ways that transcend words alone. *A Musical Chronology and the Emerging Life Song* (Duffey, 2005) is one approach that uses music as a medium for storytelling and goal setting.

A Musical Chronology and the Emerging Life Song

A Musical Chronology and the Emerging Life Song (Duffey, 2005) is a counseling intervention used with individuals, couples, families, and groups. This intervention is based on an integrative theoretical foundation, including narrative therapy, RCT, and cognitive theories. When used in a group-process setting, participants can use music that reflects their life experiences. Given the process orientation of group work, members of a group can use music and the musical chronology to (a) share their respective stories, (b) connect with one another in the process, and (c) explore meaningful aspects of life, while (d) discovering new opportunities for resiliency and growth. As part of this process, group members are well positioned to deepen self-empathy and compassion, two qualities that often support personal growth and productive relationships. They also have opportunities to deepen their compassion toward members of the group and others in their larger worlds.

A musical chronology can help group members find words for the sometimes complicated feelings, and complex situations, that bring them to the group experience. Often, people attend group to heal from challenging experiences or to find and give support to others. Sometimes, people attend group to learn new ways of connecting with people they love and those around them. By connecting with their memories and feelings via a resource as powerful as music, group members have an opportunity to safely and courageously revisit life experiences that may appear overwhelming or isolating when experienced alone. Further, when the music is part of a person's story, it can feel very personal, and its familiarity has the potential to share with others what words alone may not. Given that music stimulates the part of the brain associated with empathy (Duffey & Haberstroh, 2013), music can facilitate the understanding for self and others that is a frequent goal of many process groups.

Group facilitators can use the musical chronology with (a) older adults participating in a reminiscence group (Duffey, Somody, & Clifford, 2006/2007; Somody, 2010), (b) members recovering from substance-use disorders, (c) adolescents involved in a process group, (d) group members experiencing grief and loss, and (d) members of an educational cohort culminating their time together. Utilizing music in group process (Duffey, 2015, 2016, 2017) can be especially beneficial to group members with an interest in music because it can provide a universal language to express their collective ideas. Finally, music is cited as a valuable therapeutic tool because listening to songs can evoke memories and facilitate meaning making (Cady, Harris, & Knappenberger, 2008).

THE CHRONOLOGY PROCESS   The musical chronology group can be structured with four to six members when the overall time allotted to the group experience is limited. This allows each group member to thoughtfully share music and make meaning of his or her process. However, group sizes can vary, and they often do. The musical chronology group begins with the group facilitator elaborating on the focus and rationale for the musical chronology group process. Members are invited to share questions or concerns related to the process, and the facilitator responds with as much clarity as possible. Participants are then asked to briefly discuss the role of music in their life experiences. The following steps specifically outline suggested aspects of a musical chronology group process.

STEP ONE: GUIDED IMAGERY   The facilitator begins a guided-imagery process by inviting group members to close their eyes, take a deep breath, and join together in the experience of separately and privately reminiscing on their life journeys. The guided imagery may begin as follows:

"Imagine you are driving in your car, and you are traveling down a beautiful road through one of the most beautiful landscapes you have ever seen. As you drive down the road, you turn on the radio to a station playing songs from every decade throughout your life. As you listen to the songs, beginning with today's date, what memorable music comes to your mind? Allow yourself to connect with the experiences that you associate with these memories. Gently allow yourself to acknowledge your thoughts and feelings and the memories that come to mind as you move on to the next decade. For example, the radio is playing music from the decade of 2000. . . ."

The facilitator continues the guided imagery until all members of the group are afforded an opportunity to recall the decades relevant to them. For younger members whose memories are not connected with earlier decades, the facilitator can ask that they stay with their individual experiences until they are guided further in their process. When all members have completed their processes, the facilitator gently closes the guided-imagery session with a statement such as the following:

"When you are ready, please gently open your eyes, and know that this group is a sacred and safe place for you to be with your experience. Now, I ask that you individually write down any songs that you recall from this guided-imagery experience. This is only the beginning of your chronology process. You will have an opportunity to add to your own chronology over the six weeks that we are together."

STEP TWO: SHARING STORIES AND MAKING MEANING   The facilitator states the following regarding the musical chronology as a whole: "The music that you identify throughout the group process is here to help you share your story and make meaning of those areas that are most relevant."

STEP THREE: SONG FOR THE PRESENT   Participants will select a song that begins their story and share it with the group; this is their *song for the present* (Duffey, 2005). The group will listen to excerpts of each member's song while the members share their stories. In subsequent sessions, they will select three to four songs that will continue to give context to their stories and support members in further grasping their experiences.

STEP FOUR: SONG FOR THE FUTURE   During the last session, group members will collectively share and process their *songs for the future* (Duffey, 2005). These songs are often reflective of the group members' original counseling goals.

Musical Chronology of a Group Class Experience

As a presenter at a master therapist series with soon-to-graduate masters counseling students, I (Duffey) used *A Musical Chronology and the Emerging Life Song* as an activity for group members to (a) connect with one another, (b) reflect on their shared experiences as a group, (c) make meaning of their time together, and (d) commemorate their time together by collectively participating in a group musical chronology. As part of their activity, the participants were given the following instructions:

"Cohorts such as yours, and communities and groups of various kinds, can use creative interventions like music to come together in times of crisis or celebration. Graduate students have many experiences, many of them very meaningful. Today, we are going to use your music to celebrate your accomplishments and commemorate your time together. I ask that you take a few minutes to privately reminisce about your time in the program. Jot down three songs that remind you of your experience as a graduate student. There is no need for the lyrics to match the feelings. Rather, it is more important that the songs connect with the memories that you recall. Now, recognizing that each of your individually selected songs relates to the larger group experience, let's share the songs you feel comfortable sharing to create a collective chronology. What music from your selection could this group identify as particularly relevant to your shared time together? This chronology tells the story of your cohort. Next, every chronology concludes with a song or songs that express some hopes for the future—so now, what songs might you identify that reflect your collective hopes for your individual futures and your future as a group?"

SIDEBAR 9.4
Case Study: Creativity in Beginning Groups

You begin your first group with a creative icebreaker and ask people to identify a song that represents their current situation. Jason shares with the group that music is like math to him and that he finds that his analytical skills are superior to those of most people he knows. As people share in the opening group, Jason sits back in his chair and begins to offer analytic commentary on each person's song. Members of the group seem uncomfortable and feel put off by Jason's behavior. This is your first group, and you are trying to balance a welcoming and inviting atmosphere with feedback. You're frustrated that you need to intervene so early in the group. How would you respond to Jason? How could you use DRC to conceptualize Jason's interactions?

The cohort members engaged in the process enthusiastically selected songs such as "With a Little Help from My Friends" (Lennon & McCartney, 1967) and "Stressed Out" (Joseph, 2015) as metaphors for their shared cohort experiences. As a group, the members reminisced on the pleasures and pains of their training experiences. They shared laughter, memories, and appreciation for their achievements. Finally, they each contributed songs to illustrate their collective hopes and expectations for the future. The group settled on the songs "We Are Family" (Edwards & Rodgers, 1979) and "Celebration" (Bell et al., 1980) as their future songs. One member selected "Miss You" (Jagger & Richards, 1978), which appeared to accurately reflect the group's expectations about how they would feel upon graduating. A Musical Chronology and the Emerging Life Song can be applied in small- or large-group settings and can be used as a termination ritual for cohorts and groups upon graduation. This structure can also be used with process groups involving people of all ages and with diverse group-counseling goals.

RECOVERY VISION BOARD   People in recovery from substance-use disorder (SUD) often participate in groups. In fact, groups are often the cornerstones of much SUD treatment. According to the Substance Abuse and Mental Health Services Administration (SAMHSA, 2016b), people can participate in group-counseling experiences to receive social support as they pursue recovery. Envisioning the future is an important aspect of instilling hope. There are a number of ways in which people can identify their dreams for the future, such as creating recovery vision boards. When conducted as a group activity, this has an opportunity to capture a full range of hopes and desires and to inspire those who may be shut down to possibilities. When created in a safe, inclusive, and affirming environment, recovery vision boards can present new options and future dreams for people in recovery. The following are guidelines and instructions for a recovery vision board intervention:

1. The group facilitator places several large pieces of butcher paper on the wall and makes magazines, markers, and other art supplies available to the participants.
2. The group facilitator engages participants in a collaborative and respectful conversation about their outlook and goals for recovery. The time allotted will vary with the needs and structure of the overall group.

3. The group facilitator asks participants to use magazine images or create artistic images to depict their representations of what recovery can look like.
4. Participants work together to decide where to place materials on the butcher paper.
5. Group members then collectively discuss the vast opportunities and possibilities that come with healing and recovery. Participants who cannot grasp the healing images are invited to join in the hopes of the larger group. The facilitator structures these discussions in ways that honor group members who have doubts while continuing to direct the discussion toward hope and positivity.

Compassion for self and others is an important aspect of recovery from substance-use disorder and other life challenges. Groups that focus on fostering compassion can assist group members in developing a vocabulary and compassionate repertoire. It is often said that one cannot easily give others what one does not possess. This can, at times, be the case with the expression of compassion. Developing skills for self-compassion, which is not the same as self-pity, is an important therapeutic goal.

SELF-COMPASSION   According to Neff (2012), *self-compassion* involves "self-kindness, a sense of common humanity, and mindfulness" (p. 856). More specifically, self-compassion is the practice of self-empathy, the release of judgment and criticism, and the ability to honor our humanness. For some people, the ability to offer compassion to ourselves often does not come as easily as our efforts to comfort others. Other people have a more difficult time seeing others' pain and relate to others from a self-focused perspective, lacking compassion. Still, at the core of many people's experiences of healing is a need for genuine self-compassion and compassion for others. Group experiences can be ideal forums for group members to increase these capacities. Ahead, we provide a rationale for compassion development and activities that can be used within group settings to foster deepened compassion.

Compassion, much like empathy, involves one person understanding the experience of another. Compassion, however, takes the situation one step further. It motivates people to move beyond empathy and to take steps toward action. This action is generally motivated by a person's desire to help. Although the virtues of compassion are obvious, the consequences of lack of compassion are particularly striking. Lacking compassion for others can result in harmful behaviors or, at best, negligence for and indifference to one's impact on others. Being injured by others who are unaware of or indifferent to their impact is not a unique or isolated experience. Sadly, it is often the kind of experience that can lead some group members to seek healing and restorative counseling and group services.

Group activities that promote compassion for self and for others can be especially powerful. Given that a lack of self-compassion may be part of a person's thoughtless or hurtful behavior toward others and that interpersonal issues and concerns are sometimes processed in groups, activities that promote self-compassion can be especially salient in group experiences. An activity sometimes referred to as a *loving-kindness meditation* (Metta Institute, 2011) can be used by facilitators to begin their discussions on compassion. Many groups focusing on compassion building can begin their process with a collective loving-kindness meditation.

The following are recommended elements of a loving-kindness meditation: Invite the group members to think about a person with whom they feel safe in the world.

If one of the group members cannot identify such a person, he or she can imagine a safe place in which he or she feels secure. Ask the group to connect with the experience of sharing space with the person or place that brings them comfort. Then, ask them to recognize the humanness of the person they bring to mind and consider their desire for that person's comfort and safety. Finally, ask them to imagine that the person who they identify is enveloped in love, security, and comfort. Have them relish the tranquility of their loved one and the peace that he or she feels in that moment. Now, ask them to imagine that they, too, are enveloped in peace and tranquility. Ask them to take in the grace and generosity that life can bring and to appreciate the opportunity of today and the hope for tomorrow (Duffey, 2015, 2016, 2017).

Compassion is a quality that can bring dignity to our memories and a sense of appreciation for our experiences. Our memories are fuel for the stories we carry and the histories we share. Group members have an opportunity to connect with their memories, stories, and histories by creating a memory box. When memory boxes are created within a group context, group members have an added opportunity to create in connection and to connect their stories with the universal stories shared within the sacred space of group.

MEMORY BOXES   *Memory boxes* are a physical representation of a collection of memories that allow people to reflect on and celebrate important life events or significant relationships (Young & Garrard, 2015). During the process of creating a memory box, people place objects into the box to stimulate the memories, feelings, and meaning behind a particular artifact (Young & Garrard, 2015). This often allows the person creating the box to more deeply appreciate and further process the experience. Memory boxes have been used with individuals mourning the loss of a loved one (Young & Garrard, 2016) and people experiencing Alzheimer's disease (Wegerer, 2014). In addition, constructing a memory box served as a source of reminiscence for an entire community of older persons in long-term care (Royal College of Nursing, 2010). Memory boxes can be created within a group setting to allow individual members to memorialize a particular event or to process a collective experience. In either case, group members can follow a format similar to the following:

1. Prior to the initial group meeting, the facilitator verifies that members are interested in participating in an activity that requires them to gather items related to a significant life experience or relationship.
2. The facilitator then explains the rationale behind the use of memory boxes and the necessary items they will need to bring to the next group, including:
   a. A box or container to be decorated
   b. An object or objects of reminiscence or significance to place in the box (this can include photos, artifacts, emails, music, etc.)
   c. Art supplies or other materials to decorate their respective boxes
3. At the beginning of the meeting in which the group creates a memory box, the facilitator asks group members to make note of any significant feelings or thoughts they have during the process.
4. At the end of the group meeting, members who are interested in sharing their experiences are reminded that they can do so in a safe, respectful environment.

Creative Adaptations of Experiential, Psychodramatic, and Gestalt Approaches

Jacobs and Schimmel (2013) incorporate a wide range of props and materials to illustrate counseling theory in action with clients. Counselors can use everyday materials as metaphors that reflect life situations, personal awareness, and counseling goals. The timing of experiential work is important, and counselors plan interventions that encourage increased vulnerability and risk taking during the working stage. Experiential work can be powerful, and it is important that clients report feeling connected and safe in group. In training and counseling groups, I (Haberstroh) have incorporated props that represent life themes related to group topics (Haberstroh, 2005). The following are steps a leader outlines for the use of props in groups:

1. The group leader places a set of keys in the middle of the group.
2. The leader shares that the keys represent an applicable group topic (e.g., hope, relapse, happiness, confidence, peace).
3. The leader asks the members to move toward the keys or away from the keys to represent how close they are to the identified theme. For example, if the keys represent relapse and members feel they may be close to relapse, they would stand closer to the keys.
4. Leaders can then ask members to consider steps they would take in the direction of wellness and then move to their new position in the room.
5. The members and leader spend time discussing their assessment of their situation, the process of moving, and how they illustrated change in this activity.

Depending on the topic chosen for this activity, members will need time to debrief and share about their experience. As with all creative interventions in groups, leaders allow ample group time for postintervention processing. Leaders can implement more intensive interventions that draw from and integrate psychodynamic, Gestalt, and other experiential models. For example, I (Haberstroh) led addiction-process groups for many years. In these groups, I structured interventions that integrated concepts from psychodrama (Karatas, 2014), Gestalt work (Frew, 2016), and narrative therapy (White & Epston, 1990). Consider the following scenario:

Janine is just over 90 days sober and has been attending an intensive outpatient program for the past 60 days. Every Tuesday night, she and her small group meet for an hour and a half, and she has grown very close to the other members. Her group has shared struggles, unexpected connections and similarities, breakthroughs, and losses. The group will be terminating in 5 weeks, and Janine feels apprehensive. Last week, she shared with the group that she experienced persistent and troubling thoughts and urges to relapse. Each day on her way home from work, she passes her favorite bar, the place where she would turn off each evening for happy hours that often turned into all-night benders. She feels frustrated and ashamed. These thoughts feel frightening and exciting. They seem foreign because they would upend her current life and recovery. They feel all too familiar because she knows the smell of her favorite bar intimately. She remembers how the smell of smoke and murmur of the other patrons soothed her troubles. She feels truly conflicted. She knows what is at stake. Every night, Janine comes home to two empty bedrooms. Her children were removed from the home after she was arrested for a DUI. There's a hollow feeling in the house; a perpetual sadness and loss seems to echo throughout her home. Her supervised weekly visitations with her two daughters at a McDonald's, break her heart, especially as she watches her daughters leave. Despite these feelings, the call of her old life is seductive and persistent.

Given Janine's connection to the group and her desire for awareness and expression, experiential work can help her share her feelings, gain clarity about her ambivalence, and develop tailored relapse-prevention strategies.

The group setting is an optimal format in which to employ psychodramatic work. It is an approach that can help group members gain awareness into their lives and motivations. Founded by Jacob Moreno (Schermer, 2015), psychodrama plays out conversations, tensions, and dynamics often unexpressed. A *psychodrama* is a structured intervention that highlights the drama between a protagonist (usually the client) and an antagonist. Along with these roles, psychodramas include auxiliary egos and an audience. The auxiliary egos are roles that represent different aspects of a person's experience. In groups, other members can volunteer to play the various roles. In the scenario described earlier, Janine wanted to explore her feelings and ambivalence and gain insight from the group's feedback. After explaining the basic tenets of a psychodrama, we planned the intervention for the following week. We implemented the following steps in a creative adaptation of a psychodrama in addiction treatment (Haberstroh, 2005):

1. Begin with a group check-in and summarize last week's session and psychodrama intervention.
2. Ask Janine to identify two group members to play the roles of her auxiliary egos. These will be people who provide recovery support and messages to her during the psychodrama experience.
3. Invite a member to play the role of the addictive voice. An active member who knows Janine's situation well and who also exhibits strong recovery should play this role. The person who plays this role will need time to debrief.
4. The leader takes the role of the director.
5. The leader asks the group to reconfigure from a circle to a format in which Janine faces her addictive voice, with her supportive auxiliary egos to her sides.
6. The director asks Janine and her addictive voice to begin a conversation, as follows, as if they were in the car on the way home from work:

Addictive Voice:	Exit 512. Two miles ahead . . .
Janine:	I'm tired. I just want to get home.
Addictive Voice:	To what? Really?
Janine:	Home. Boring, lonely home.
Addictive Voice:	Come on. No one will know if we drop by. Just stop in and say hi. You see Rick and Mick's car there every day. You know this won't last. Next exit.
Janine:	It's so hard.
Auxiliary Ego:	You have friends who love you.

Director:	[Whispering to Janine:] Look at your addiction. Tell it "You took everything from me. You're a liar."
Janine:	You took my girls! [She begins to sob.] I've got nothing now! And you want to take it all again! God, I hate you! I hate me! [Janine continues to sob. She feels profound sadness, fear, and awareness of the power and persistence of her addiction.]
Addictive Voice:	I can take all this pain away . . . you know, you know.

At this point, the director stopped the conversation and processed the psychodrama with the members. Janine realized that reengaging in her addiction would bring back an all-too-familiar pain, moments of drunken arrogance, and shame-filled moments of sobriety. She faced a stark reminder about the seriousness of her addiction, while also experiencing the care, identification, and support of her peers. The leader also spent time debriefing with the person who played the addictive voice. To transition this member back to his role as a peer, the leader asked Janine where she would like to place the chair where the addictive voice sat. She said, "Behind me, in the corner, but where I can see it so I don't forget." To focus on recovery strategies, the group leader invited Janine to imagine herself five years sober. When she saw a clear vision of her future self, she moved to a new chair in the group and faced the empty chair where she had just sat. The leader asked, " From this future perspective, what would you say to yourself as you struggle on your drives home?" She thinks for a moment, "You know in your heart where drinking leads, and where it will lead. When you drink you lose it all. All of it. And when you work your program, you live again. I'm here to tell you the girls are home. No more supervised visits or CPS workers. It's not perfect. It's not easy. But, I finally feel something like freedom. It gets better."

Creative and experiential activities in groups can move members to new awareness and create novel avenues for self-expression and relating with others. Counselors carefully time interventions and ground creative interventions in theory, allowing members to participate voluntarily in the process.

SIDEBAR 9.5
Case Study: Creativity in the Storming Stage

Your group seems to have stalled in the storming stage. People are hesitant to talk, topics remain at the surface level, and two members seem to dominate most conversations. You decide you want to liven things up in the group and request that Tammy work on a psychodrama related to her issues with being assertive at work. She seems hesitant and unsure. You tell her you would like her to move forward anyway.

You set the activity for the next week. In your supervision session, you share this plan with your supervisor, who seems surprised and concerned. You're not sure why. She gives you feedback related to not coercing members to engage in experiential work before they're ready and not implementing working-stage activities while a group is storming. What are your thoughts about the timing of this activity and supervisory feedback?

SIDEBAR 9.6
Case Study: Creativity in Termination

You have led a group process experience in which the group members have expressed feeling inspired, connected, and sad to see the group conclude. Recognizing that "good-byes" can be as important as "hellos," you want this group's "good-bye" to be meaningful and relevant. What are some creative ways that group members can commemorate their time together through a closing ritual, and what therapeutic factors would you consider to help group members terminate from their time together through these activities?

Summary

Group counseling experiences have the potential to impact the growth and healing of their individual members in profound ways. When facilitators and group members are connected to their creativity, this impact can be particularly rewarding. As a model applied to group process, creativity in counseling (CIC) can inspire recovery, resiliency, and connectedness. In this setting, hope can be contagious. Isolation can be replaced with connection. Self-judgment can be transformed into self-compassion. Moreover, resentments and hurts can give way to peace and forgiveness. Indeed, shared creativity can open hearts, clarify minds, and bring needed perspective. When the group leader's creativity creates a setting of flexibility, wonder, and possibility, and group members connect with their innate gift of creativity within a relationally safe and productive setting, group counseling experiences can be truly transformative.

10 Facilitating Groups with Challenging Member Behaviors

Jonathan J. Orr

It is not at all unusual for group facilitators to request supervision or consultation due to the behavior of a group member, and often such a member is referred to as being *difficult*. In practice, however, a member whose behavior is perceived as difficult by one group facilitator may not be perceived as difficult by another group facilitator. After discussion of the typical ways a group member may be perceived by the facilitator to be troublesome, the process of reframing is used to describe the behavior as *challenging* and thus to enable the facilitator to act in ways that constructively address the disruptive behavior. The process of reframing, identifying group members who are challenging, three steps that can be used to diagnose challenging group members, and three steps that can be used to respond to challenging group members are presented for consideration in this chapter. The chapter concludes with an exercise described in Sidebar 10.5 to review and apply the concepts and suggestions presented in the chapter so that they can be integrated more easily into the skill set of the group facilitator.

DEFINING DIFFICULT GROUP MEMBERS

The task of creating a distinct definition for difficult group members is itself a considerable challenge. The myriad variables that contribute to group member behavior can lead to difficulty both individually and in combination. Isolating those contributions and responding to them effectively is a primary task for group leaders across settings and types of group. For the purposes of this chapter, a difficult member will be defined as a member whose contributions and/or participation in group negatively impact the expected process of a group. A difficult group member's negative behavior may be directed toward the leader, other members, or the group as a whole and has the overall effect of disrupting the purpose and derailing the process of group dynamics. Having a general definition for difficult group members helps characterize what is happening in the group; however, clearly identifying what is difficult presents additional challenges. Difficulty in group counseling is a relative construct reliant on the perceiver as much as on the direct actor. Stated plainly, members perceived as difficult by some group facilitators may be characterized completely differently by others based on their interpretations of group purpose, leader characteristics, group process, and so on. The potential discrepancies among those individual perspectives can render discussion of difficult member behavior perplexing, especially when considering the diverse identities of group members. Thus, the first difficulty encountered is characterizing how to address these members and their behaviors in groups, and it requires discussion of the first intervention: reframing.

REFRAMING DIFFICULT GROUP MEMBERS

The initial definition of a difficult group member was helpful to begin this chapter; however, as is often the case in group counseling, the dynamic of the discussion has evolved and become refined to the point that a more flexible characterization is required to fully capture the nature of members who disrupt group process. In a parallel manner, disruptive group members also defy singular characterization in their impact on a group. Most often, their disruption in group is not isolated to one contribution or characteristic; rather, it is ongoing and changing based on a variety of conditions (Gans, 2010).

Reframing is a process of redefining or differently characterizing an action, belief, experience, or emotion that results in a more positive alternative. Reframing is utilized extensively in cognitive therapy and is a basic skill taught to most beginning counselors (Beck, 2011; Ivey, Ivey & Zalaquett, 2013). In the case of a disruptive group member, reframing is most useful for the group facilitator, as opposed to a skill to teach group members. Reframing empowers the group facilitator to act in the group and to address the disruption caused by members. For example, reframing a disruptive group member as *challenging* rather than *difficult* provides for many options to meet the challenge posed by the group member. Furthermore, reframing a member as *challenging* can also encourage leaders' reflection on the ways in which they are being challenged by the member. Simply labeling members as *difficult* suggests that members' behaviors are linked to their character rather than the transient state that they occupy in the group. Applying the practice of reframing to the discussion of disruptive group members in this chapter, the term *challenging* will be used in place of *difficult*. Here again, defining what is challenging for a group leader encounters subjective interpretation; however, in general, the challenges referred to in this chapter presume disruption to overall form and/or function of group dynamics.

IDENTIFYING GROUP MEMBERS WHO ARE CHALLENGING

The phrase *challenging group members* typically evokes the worst-case scenarios in group dynamics that require immediate heroic interventions from group leaders. Examples of those extremely difficult group members are likely what come to the mind of a novice group leader in the anxious moments anticipating the first meeting of group. Those imagined members are typically aggressively confrontational, hyper-resistant, perhaps violent, and always disruptive to the point of leaving the group leader in stunned inaction. Exciting as it might be to lead a group like that with such high-energy investment for change, the reality is that those members are exceedingly rare, especially in groups in which any amount of prescreening is done (Gladding, 2015; Jacobs, Masson & Harvill, 2016). The more typical situations in which members might need immediate response from the leaders are those in which a member is not aware of or not adhering to group norms. Situations in which norms are directly disregarded present a unique threat to safety in the group and can disrupt group dynamics to a degree that the members shut down completely. The direct response for that type of situation is to reinforce the group norms and enact consequences for those who may not adhere to them. Those consequences are best established by the group members in developing norms and should include exclusion from the group if a member continues to disregard group norms.

Moving past the initial notion of group members who require immediate intervention, there emerge infinite ways that group facilitators can experience challenge from group members. Some of that challenge can be anticipated based on group member characteristics. Chapter 3 of this text provided an excellent introduction to many member behaviors that can cause difficulty for leaders, so readers are encouraged to refer to that discussion for review. This chapter will add to that discussion by providing guidelines for group leaders to identify and respond to challenging group members in an ongoing and responsive manner. Moving forward, the term *diagnose* will be used to refer to the process of identifying what is happening in the group so that an appropriate and effective intervention can be recommended. In this chapter, the term *diagnosis* will also be used to characterize the result of assessing a particular group process or set of behaviors, but it does not refer to the process of clinical diagnosis using the *Diagnostic and Statistical Manual of Mental Disorders*.

DIAGNOSING CHALLENGING GROUP MEMBERS

The practice of diagnosing a challenging group member can have both immediate and long-term consequences for the overall dynamics of a group. Likewise, the challenging behaviors and/or dispositions of group members manifest in varying ways across the life of the group (Berg, Landreth & Fall, 2013; Gans, 2010). This discussion of diagnosing challenging group members will focus on behaviors and/or dispositions that emerge gradually rather than those behaviors and/or dispositions that require more immediate intervention. Focusing the discussion this way reflects the frequency in which challenge is presented in group dynamics; gradually emerging challenges occur with greater likelihood than immediate or spontaneous challenges in groups.

Accepting the position that most challenging group members are created through group process, the primary informant for diagnosing a challenging group member is group process dynamics. Group process dynamics here are defined as

- how individual members are interacting with one another,
- how individual members are interacting with the leader,
- how the group as a whole is interacting with individual members,
- how the group as a whole is interacting with the leader, and
- how work is getting done in the group.

The ecological context in which the group is functioning must also be considered when defining process dynamics. Group location, institutional support, and sociopolitical issues are just a few of the considerations for ecological influences on group process. In summary, diagnosing challenging group members created through group process is a multistep process that involves assessing each of the following questions:

- What is happening?
- Who is involved?
- Where is the group?

In the following subsections, we will look at each step of diagnosing challenging group members in more detail.

Step 1: What Is Happening?

The first step in assessing this question is to clearly identify any critical incidents in the group's functioning. A *critical incident* can be defined simply as a shift in the group's energy or progress. That shift in energy can be further defined as *facilitative* (e.g., members begin supporting each other and providing encouragement), *disrupting* (e.g., members avoid confronting each other), *retroflex* (e.g., members return to an attitude of mistrust and protection after a period of safety and risk taking), or some combination of the three. The hallmark of a critical incident is that the group process changes, and it is most easily recognized in hindsight via guided critical reflection (Donigian & Hulse-Killacky, 1999). It is also important to note that the critical incident can occur at the individual level, the member-to-member level, the group-as-a-whole level, or the group-in-context level. The *group-in-context* level refers to how ecological factors impact group process dynamics and will be further described later in this chapter.

Once a critical incident is identified, the next step is assessing the nature of the incident. What impact the incident is having on the group as a whole is of the utmost consideration because group members who are considered challenging invariably affect overall group dynamics. Readers are directed to Chapter 3 of this text for a discussion of challenging member behavior, but three areas of particular importance to consider for challenging group members are potential member fears, types of group process, and nonparticipating behavior. Fear can be an equally strong motivator and inhibitor in many situations, and in group work fear can be heightened due to the public nature of disclosure. Typical member fears include the fear of self-disclosure, the fear of rejection, the fear of being vulnerable, and the fear of being judged or misunderstood (Corey, Corey, & Corey, 2014). A common factor all those fears share is a perceived or actual loss of control. Stated directly, members cannot control what happens to the information that they share in group, regardless of any assurances from the facilitator and/or the members. That lack of control can lead to many challenging behaviors from members, including acting out to exert control over others as well as turning inward and resisting connection from others.

Member fears are just one source for potential critical incidents within a group. Donigian and Malnati (1997) identified different types of group process that also can

---

SIDEBAR 10.1

Guided Critical Reflection

1. This group session focused on the following issues or themes:
2. My goals for this session were . . .
3. In these ways, the group went as expected:
4. In these ways, the group surprised me:
5. My most successful intervention/leadership skill was . . .

    And I chose it because . . .

    And the intervention resulted in . . .

6. If I could do this session again, I would/wouldn't . . .
7. Overall, the group is currently in the stage of development, and the evidence we have for group development stage includes . . .
8. I noticed the group dynamic shifted at this point in the group:

    a. My reaction to the shift was . . .
    b. The group members' reactions to the shift were . . .

contribute to a critical incident. Contagion, conflict, anxiety, consensual validation, universality, family reenactment, and instillation of hope can be both the cause of and a contributor to critical incidents. Unlike member fears, these group process dynamics involve more than one member and often include the group as a whole. Taken from a facilitative perspective, process types such as consensual validation, installation of hope, and universality can be indicative of overall group cohesion and connection between members. Viewed from a disruptive perspective, those same process types can slow down and block group dynamics.

Take, for example, contagion, which is generally considered a positive process dynamic in groups. Contagion can facilitate group dynamics in that it provides feedback to the leader that members are connected in the group to the extent that they are sharing a mutual experience and emotion in the group. As a disruptive process in groups, contagion can also provide feedback to the leader that the group has become enmeshed to the extent that there is little to no individuation among members who may dissent from the dominant perspective of an experience or emotion shared in group. The same dualistic perspective applies to a process dynamic that is often seen as disruptive to the group, such as conflict. Adversarial conflict can provide feedback to the leader that the group and/or members are experiencing disconnection and an overabundance of fear. Alternatively, creative conflict can provide the leader with feedback that the group has a supportive balance between group and individual identity and that it is ready for the working/action phase.

Moving back to the individual member experience in assessing what is happening in the group, Corey (2017) presents several types of nonparticipating member behaviors. These behaviors were covered individually in Chapter 3 along with brief examples of how to intervene when they are present, but these behaviors are highlighted here for the role that they play in encouraging a particular facilitative, disrupting, or retroflex critical incident. For example, consider the nonparticipating behavior of protection against oppression. In assessing the nature of a critical incident that is facilitative, that behavior can indicate members' willingness to acknowledge systemic and structural oppression and exemplify their ability to take steps to protect themselves against it. For group members with marginalized and oppressed identities, this can be a critical step in their group development. In groups where members perceived safety and took a risk and then perceived rejection after taking that risk, members can withdraw to protect themselves from perceived oppression. This retroflex critical incident might require the group to revisit building safety and trust within the group. A disrupting critical incident

---

SIDEBAR 10.2
Examining Group Process

Consider the following types of process described by Donigian and Malnati (1997) and identify the ways in which they might both facilitate and disrupt group dynamics:

Contagion

Conflict

Anxiety

Consensual validation

Universality

Family reenactment

Instillation of hope

could result from protection against oppression if members are accustomed to having their needs met by enacting victimized or persecuted roles in their lives. Such members find comfort and a sense of control in casting others in the role of oppressor in their lives and can take offense easily at what is happening in groups at any given moment.

This last example can be exemplified by a member who actively seeks to be in the minority opinion/experience in the group and consistently takes the dissenting perspective in the group despite previously endorsing an alternate view or experience. For example, Sasha identifies that she prefers everyone to share one thing that they are nervous about in group when most others would prefer to maintain the right to pass. She complains that the group is trying to bully her into their way of thinking, and she threatens to leave the group if everyone does not endorse her preferred norm. In a show of support for Sasha the group elects to establish the norm of not passing except in occasional and extreme circumstances. Later in the life of the group, Sasha often passes in conversations rather than following her own norm to share. When the group confronts her on this she again complains that she is in the minority opinion in the group and that the group is trying to bully her by not supporting her decision to pass.

Step 2: Who Is Involved?

After the initial step of identifying a critical incident and assessing it based on what is happening in the group at the individual, member, and group levels, the next step is to further determine who is involved in the critical incident. The previous step involved assessing some of the behaviors of the members involved; this step expands that perspective to include characteristics and traits of those participants in the critical incident. In any assessment, it is a critical first step to examine who is doing the assessment. For critical incidents in group sessions, the leader is the primary evaluator, so it is important to begin by examining the leader characteristics (Brown, 2006). Chapter 3 can once again provide depth to this examination by referring to its discussion of leader characteristics.

Leader characteristics define expectations for the group purpose, for member participation, and for outcomes in the group. Simply stated, the leader is the primary prism through which the group is focused. For example, leaders who might characterize themselves as more opaque, prefer a high degree of structure, and stay more detached from the group process might interpret as disruptive members who inquire directly about the leader's opinion or about interpersonal feedback. Conversely, leaders who identify their style near the other end of those spectra as more transparent, laissez faire, and participant would likely see that same member behavior as facilitative to group process. This example highlights the important role that leader perspective plays in the group and highlights that leaders must take the time to nurture their own self-awareness and learn about their own leadership style preferences.

Developing a regular and consistent practice of critical reflection as a group leader is essential to nurturing self-awareness for leaders and assists with the next dimension of assessing who the actors are in the critical incident. This time, the reflection is directed at members' general roles in the group. As covered in previous chapters, members tend to settle into predictable roles in group dynamics, and Gladding (2015) organizes the major roles as generally facilitative/building, maintaining, and/or blocking. Members express their affiliation to these roles in a wide variety of ways. *Facilitative* members are most often connected to growing the process and moving the group momentum forward. They tend to lead conversations, take interpersonal risks, and in general actively participate in the group process. Taken to the extreme, members in the facilitative role can be characterized as moving the group too quickly through various stages or pushing the edge of intensity in the group to a point that others withdraw; they can seem to have an agenda that is pulling the group process forward differently than the leader intends.

Members acting out the *maintaining* role tend to present as slowing the group down compared to the facilitative/building members. If facilitative/building members have a forward-reaching agenda for group process, then maintaining members prefer that the status quo of the group be maintained. They may present as cautious or hesitant to take risks in the group, preferring to ease into group process. They are reliable stewards for cohesion and member-to-member interpersonal connections in the group. Maintaining members also tend to be protective of other group members and work to make sure that all members experience comfort before the group moves forward. This last tendency can directly challenge a group leader who is trying to move the group process forward. A maintaining member can seem obstinate and alarmist about new progress in the group.

The *blocking* role is characterized by group members who actively work against the group leader and subvert the group process. They tend to disrupt connections in the group and resist the group process. Like members in the facilitating/building role, blocking members seem to have their own agendas; however, the agenda for the blocking member moves directly against the leader and the benefit of the group as a whole. They also differ from maintaining members in that blocking is more of an active (and often aggressive) disruption of group process. Sometimes, a visual representation can be useful to conceptualize these member roles in groups, so picture three children standing next to a pool on a hot summer day. The pool is a metaphor for the group process. The facilitating member runs full force, cannonballs into the pool, and immediately begins splashing and playing about. The maintaining member dips a toe in and then slowly eases into the water, hands held high, careful to not get wet too fast. The blocking member sits outside of the pool, arms folded tightly, looking frustrated that no one is getting out of the pool to play. Characterizing who these members are in terms of the critical incident can contextualize why the incident has occurred and potentially provide insight about how to react.

The final area to assess in determining who is involved in the critical incident includes factors related to power, privilege, and oppression and is perhaps the most self-evident and potentially the most critical (DeLucia-Waack & Donigian, 2004). It is also the area that most directly involves individual characteristics of group members. Those factors are based on individual member identity status and the intersection of multiple identities. Specifically, how members define their identity related to gender, sexual orientation, ethnicity, affectional orientation, age, ability, education, socioeconomic status, and culture impacts, both singularly and collectively, members' participation in group. Furthermore, the stages in which group members find themselves in identity development on any of those dimensions also have significant bearing on member participation in the group process. It is beyond the scope of this chapter to fully delineate the impact that diverse intersecting identities can have on group process dynamics; however, it is clear that power and empowerment are essential components

SIDEBAR 10.3
Who Has the Power?

In most groups, the leader possesses most of the power over process, structure, content, and interactions in the group. Possessing and acting from that power can be complicated for group leaders who also have identities that are typically oppressed outside of groups. Take a moment to consider the identities listed to the right and place a checkmark next to any of the identities that are privileged outside of a group that you might lead. After you have completed the list, consider any other identities salient to you that were not listed and indicate which of those might be privileged outside of a group that you are leading. How might your privilege status outside of group influence your work with members who have more privilege than you? How might your privilege status influence your work with members who have less privilege than you?

Gender identity

Sexual orientation

Affectional orientation

Ethnicity

Racial identity

Cultural identity

Socioeconomic status

Education level

Age

Ability status

Citizenship status

Religious/spiritual affiliation

Employment status

in any group (Bemak & Chung, 2004b). Within the group, who does/does not have access to power, how power is earned or endowed, and what acceptable uses are for power are some of the critical considerations for all group leaders. When diagnosing a critical incident, answering these questions of power, privilege, and oppression based on member identities benefits the leader and can provide insight into motivation for member behavior.

Step 3: Where Is the Group?

The final question to consider in diagnosing challenging group members relates to assessing the stage of the group and evaluating ecological variables that interact with the group. Determining the stage of the group can account for many behaviors in a group. In early stages, it is natural for members to experience and express anxiety related to the group. Managing their own risk and safety is of paramount importance for group members in the forming or warm-up stage of group development. Members often approach that initial vulnerability by attempting to control and master the situation presented in group, and their control is expressed either passively or assertively. Unaware or inexperienced group leaders might misdiagnose that initial member assertion as a challenge and respond to it as if it were a threat to their leadership. They could then further embed conflict in the group by seeking to exert more control or structure over members. In this way, group leaders who are not adept at identifying the group stage risk creating more challenge for themselves and their group members.

More effective group leaders can identify group stages accurately and have knowledge about typical group behavior in those stages. The skill of accurately characterizing member behavior in the context of the group stage is also particularly useful in identifying challenging group members. For example, consider a group that has progressed to a performing or working stage in which members are comfortably balancing their own senses of risk and safety. Despite the stage development, one member continues to express aggressive anxiety about sharing personal feedback in the group. That behavior can signal the leader that the anxious member needs additional intervention. Accurately recognizing unexpected or atypical member behavior based on group stage is a crucial skill for diagnosing challenging group members.

Assessing the question of where the group is also involves consideration of ecological variables related to group work. *Ecological variables* can include the influence that systems exert on individual members, on member-to-member connections, and on the group as a whole. These considerations are like the identity variables discussed in the previous section but are differentiated by the perspective from which they are asserted. In the second step, group leaders were asked to consider how members experienced their individual identities and whether they were oppressed or privileged in those identities. Now in this step, group leaders are expected to shift focus to understand how a system might experience (i.e., oppress or privilege) those same member identities. Take, for example, a marginalized identity such as transgender identity. In the previous step, the leader seeks to understand the transgender identity from an individual perspective and how it shapes the member's involvement in group dynamics. In this subsequent step, the leader is expected to understand more globally how transgender identity status either privileges or oppresses the member. In this sense, the focus is shifted to understand how a system might experience (and oppress) a trans-identified member. The shift in perception might be slight, but the impact can be significant and present a challenge for the member.

Consider a group being held at a community agency that primarily serves economically under-resourced clients. Imagine that the most direct route to the agency requires a car for access. Some members can use a rideshare to arrive at the group on time, but one member is consistently late due to unreliable public transportation. The late arrival of that member invariably results in disruption to the group process at every group meeting. The late-arriving member can be arbitrarily labeled as *difficult* by the leader who does not take into account the member's transportation issues. Negligence on the part of group leaders in considering ecological factors of group members results in members being misdiagnosed as challenging or difficult.

Ecological factors can also have an impact on the overall group as well (Conyne & Mazza, 2006; McMahon, Mason, Daluga-Guenther, & Ruiz, 2014). The location of the group, frequency, thematic content, promotion of the group, and so on can all have direct impact on the group as a whole. Take, for example, a gender-non conforming support group being held in a school. Well-intending group facilitators promote this group in the school and the community as a show of advocacy and solidarity for students who identify as gender nonconforming. In so doing, they create a situation in which members must "out" themselves to participate in group; this leads to low participation and reticence among group members. In answering from an ecological perspective the question of where the group is, group leaders can isolate factors that might cause group members to behave in ways that are perceived as challenging and difficult.

SIDEBAR 10.4
Putting Together a Group Diagnosis

Now that you have had a chance to explore the various steps in diagnosing a critical incident with a challenging group member individually, it is time to bring those steps together into one process. For this activity, you will need to choose a group to observe. You can use video examples or live groups, and any type of group can work. It is helpful to first choose a group that you are not responsible for leading so that you can practice this process without the added accountability of group leadership. Once you have some familiarity and/or comfort with this process, you can move toward utilizing this process in all the groups you lead.

While observing the group, watch for a critical incident, then record your observations using the following guided reflection. It can be helpful to have a colleague participate in this activity along with you so that you can compare and discuss your individual reflections.

What is happening?

   Describe the critical incident and include details of what was happening immediately before and after the event.

   What is the impact of the critical incident in the group?

   Describe any of the following that you observe:

      Type of group process

      Member fears

      Nonparticipating behavior

Who is involved?

   Did this critical incident happen at the group level, the member-to-member level, the member-to-leader level, or the individual level?

   Identify the members/leaders participating in the critical incident, both those who are initiating it and those who might be impacted by it.

Describe what you know about those participants in terms of their

      role in group,

      leader characteristics (if leader is involved), and

      identity characteristics (including leader's).

Reflect on the identity characteristics and mark those that might be privileged in the group. Repeat the process for those that might be marginalized in the group.

Where is the group?

   What is the purpose of this group? How is that purpose communicated and reinforced for group members?

   Describe the group stage and, using a group-development model, provide some typical characteristics of that stage as it relates to the group you are observing.

   List ecological characteristics of the group and describe how they might influence group dynamics. Some examples include the following:

Physical condition of room (lighting, space, furniture, etc.)	How many members
	Member-to-leader ratio
Time	Process to join/leave group
Setting	
Duration	Positioning (how the seats are arranged and who sits where)
Location	
Group rules	
Group norms	

RESPONDING TO CHALLENGING GROUP MEMBERS

Now that we have discussed the process to identify challenging group members, it is time to switch focus to creating a planned response to those members. It seems important to reiterate here that some challenging members require immediate attention from group leaders, and, in those situations, the leader's best response is one that adheres to the group's established norms. As mentioned earlier, establishing effective norms in the group should also include setting guidelines for consequences when members violate those norms. Conditions or characteristics for continued group membership are important norms for groups to establish, as are the consequences for members who do not adhere to those conditions of membership. This implies that one of the best ways to respond to a challenging member is to create group dynamics that prevent extreme behavior. Prescreening, consensus building, and norm setting are just a few of the ways in which leaders can work to foster supportive group members and minimize the likelihood of extreme member behaviors. That type of preplanning for conflict in the group provides leaders with greater flexibility for responding to disruptive group members.

Expanding beyond the situations that require immediate response from a leader, most interventions to address a challenging member are built in response to the diagnosis of the challenging group member. Like the process of diagnosing the challenge, group leaders follow a process to construct a response. Before moving into that process, it is important to first set the intention for change with some critical guiding questions. The primary questions that leaders need to ask themselves when they have identified a challenging group member include (a) What do I want to have happen here? and (b) What would I consider to be a successful outcome for this situation?

After answering those guiding questions, the process follows three different steps and focuses on (a) the intended level (or target) of intervention, (b) the level of risk, and (c) the level of intensity. The process to construct a response may seem somewhat cumbersome initially for novice group leaders; however, the process is fairly intuitive and with practice becomes almost automatic. The additional benefit of learning how to construct a response is that it virtually eliminates reliance on others to prescribe an activity or intervention for your group. To use a metaphor of creating clothing, learning the process to construct a response to challenging group members is like learning to design and sew your own garments. Once you learn the skill, you can tailor a perfect fit for any situation.

In the following subsections, we will look at each step of constructing a response to challenging group members in more detail.

Step 1: Level of Intervention

The first consideration in responding to a challenging group member is the level at which the intervention will be delivered. Donigian and Malnati (1997) identify several types of interventions that involve members and leaders, and those have been adapted here to create three primary categories of group levels: group, interpersonal, and individual. Group-level interventions are ones that account for group dynamics as a whole. That accounting may include viewing the group as one organism that expresses a common emotion or perspective. Likewise, the group may encounter the impact of ecological factors such as systemic oppression or marginalization. Group-level interventions are intended to have an impact on the overall functioning of group dynamics and shift any of the shared experiences, values, or perspectives of the members that constitute it.

Interpersonal-level interventions address the dynamics between and among group members, and the focus of such interventions is the relationship between the two. This might include member-to-member, leader-to-member, or even (in groups with multiple facilitators) leader-to-leader dynamics. The interpersonal-level interventions can also address various subgroup interactions in situations in which group members affiliate more strongly with some members than others. Finally, individual-level interventions are directed at specific members with the intention of addressing their particular behavior, affect, or perspective in the group.

In deciding which level of intervention to choose, it is important to first reflect on the initial diagnosis of the challenging group member, with careful attention to the intersectionality of identity characteristics. Without carefully considering these factors first, leaders risk oppressing and/or marginalizing their members and can further exacerbate the challenging behavior in the group. A similar note of caution applies to considering the ecological factors in play that might be negatively impacted by a certain level of intervention. A third area for reflection is the group stage because there are particular expectations for group dynamics based on the stage of the group. For example, a subgroup that has formed at the beginning stages of the group may be an attempt to create safety and connection and therefore may be viewed as an expression of early group cohesion. This same subgrouping behavior expressed in the working stages of a group could signal something quite different, such as a split or disconnection among members, and may require a different response from the leader.

Once leaders have reflected on the diagnostic dimensions of the challenging member, they are encouraged to look forward to potential outcomes. Important questions to consider might include these: What do I expect to happen as a result of this intervention? If this intervention is successful, what might happen? If this intervention is not successful, what might happen? Each level of potential intervention also generates questions for consideration. For example, if the leader chooses the individual level for intervention, what impact might that have on the other members witnessing the intervention? Ultimately, arriving at a choice for intervention level will involve balancing costs with benefits and will generate new directions for growing group dynamics.

Step 2: Level of Risk

The next two steps are closely connected in that they involve sliding the scale between risk and safety in a group. Balancing risk and safety for group members is one of the primary tasks for all group leaders. Too much risk in a group can shut people off and create a resistive group dynamic. On the other side of the scale, too much safety can similarly slow the group process and create complacency and resistance. Both risk and safety are integral to the change process, with risk being the precursor to change and safety being the opportunity to integrate that change into action.

Choosing a level of risk involves developing awareness of group members and applying self-awareness. Here again, the first step is to review all the diagnostic information gathered for the challenging group member. Group development is important to consider because risk and safety tend to vary across stages, with risk being generally heightened near transition times in the group. This means that leaders could expect heighted risk for members during the warm-up/forming stages, during conflict/storming stages, and again near the end during closure/termination (Berg et al., 2013). By contrast, working stages for groups tend to be characterized by a greater sense of overall safety, even though risk taking might be heightened; it is from a sense of secure safety that risk seems like a viable option. Continuing with a review of the diagnostic information, critical attention is required when considering the intersecting identities of the group member because the potential risk can vary greatly based on those characteristics. Similar care is needed to consider the risk of other members involved in the intervention, whether directly or indirectly included in the intervention. Both contemporary and historic conditions of power, privilege, and oppression dynamics are well worth considering because they can directly shape perceptions of risk and safety.

Moving from awareness of others to awareness of self represents an additional dimension of this step. The ability for the leader to empathize with group members can be essential to moderating risk and safety. An easy way to develop that sense of empathy is for group leaders to participate in groups as members. Being able to draw on experiences of taking risks as members of groups provides insight into how their own group members might respond to a challenge to safety. The general gauge of group leaders self-reflecting on how they might react to a challenge in group may not be completely accurate, but it at least approximates the potential for what could happen.

Step 3: Level of Intensity

This final step is linked to member safety because it addresses power in the group. This power may be actual, as in groups in which the leader is acting as an authority figure or gatekeeper, or it may be perceived. Regardless of perceived or actual power, the person who holds the most power in a group is typically the leader. Exercising that power will create an impact on the group, and that impact can reverberate through the group dynamic.

Responding to a challenging group member most often involves some form of confrontation, and confrontation involves expressions of power. These expressions of power may not necessarily be overt, but they invariably shift the group dynamic. In choosing a level of intensity, group leaders may use their power to directly confront a challenging member. This typically is considered high intensity and would involve directly addressing the challenging behavior and the member who is acting out. Lower on the continuum of intensity would be a leader who chooses to transfer the power to members and empowers them to have a voice in addressing the challenging member. An intervention that would be toward the bottom end of the intensity continuum is a comment from the leader to the group level about challenging behavior observed in the group. In this example, the leader is empowering the whole group, including the challenging member, to make a change.

It likely appears self-evident that when the intensity level of an intervention is high, so rises the risk level. That is most often accurate; however, the converse of that is not consistently predictable, because an intervention that is intended to spread power among the entire group can precipitate a lack of safety in a group. When leaders diagnose a challenging member in a group, they can be confident that their group members have similarly recognized the challenge and are expecting some response. In groups structured with a more directive and leader-focused dynamic, members are likely to expect direct action from the leader to address challenging members. An intervention less than that is likely to highlight some ambiguity for members and may generate subsequent anxiety and lower senses of safety.

Sidebar 10.5 provides an opportunity to apply the concepts and suggestions in this section to the world of the practitioner, building on the exercises presented in Sidebars 10.1 through 10.4.

SIDEBAR 10.5

Constructing a Response to Challenging Members

Now that you have reviewed the steps for constructing a response to a challenging group member, it is time to apply this process in a succinct way to an actual group example. Return to the group diagnosis that you put together in Sidebar 10.4 and use the following steps to construct a response.

Guiding questions:

What do I want to have happen here?

What would I consider to be a successful outcome for this situation?

Level of intervention:

At what level is the challenge happening: group, interpersonal, or individual?

At what level would I like group dynamics to shift: group, interpersonal, or individual?

What potential impact might this intervention have on the group, interpersonal relations, and the individual?

Level of risk:

How are risk and safety balanced at this stage of the group?

How might this intervention impact risk and/or safety at the group, interpersonal, and individual levels?

Level of intensity:

How is power expressed in this group by the leader(s)?

How is power expressed in this group by the member(s)?

What is the potential impact of expressing my power at the group, interpersonal, and individual levels?

Summary

This chapter focused on reframing what some facilitators may consider to be difficult member behaviors so that these behaviors are linked to a transient state that members often find themselves in, rather than to their character. Identifying members who are challenging, the steps for diagnosing challenging behaviors, and the steps for responding to challenging group members were all addressed.

11 Group Work with Children: Applications for School and Other Settings

Tamara E. Davis

Research has shown that 13 percent to 20 percent of children living in the United States experience a mental disorder each year (Centers for Disease Control and Prevention [CDC], 2013). According to the Child Mind Institute (CMI, 2015), half of all psychiatric illnesses occur prior to age 15. Further, the median age of onset of anxiety orders for children is age 6 and the median age of onset for attention-deficit/hyperactivity disorder (ADHD) and behavior disorders is age 11 (CMI, 2017). Many parents may wait to get help to address these concerns. The CMI's (2017) *National Center's Mental Health Report Card* indicated that "43% of parents say they waited more than one year during which children exhibited symptoms before seeking help and nearly one quarter (22%) waited more than 2 years" (p. 1). Ocasio, Van Alst, Koivunen, Huang, & Allegra (2015) suggested early intervention to address mental health issues, including internalizing and externalizing behaviors. The need for counseling interventions with children is evident, and early intervention may include small-group counseling. For the purposes of this chapter, references to a child or children will include youth from preschool to age 12.

Group work with children differs from group work with other age groups because it requires specific planning and preparation due to the unique cognitive, social, and emotional levels of children. Small-group counseling with children should provide simple, concrete information to help organize children's thinking, but information may need to be reinforced because young children tend to view the world from their own perspective (Piaget & Inhelder, 1969), and group work often requires considering the perspective of others. At the same time, children are developing social/emotional interests and moving through Erikson's (1950) psychosocial stages. It is during childhood that the focus on self begins to transition to an interest in peers; movement from free play or playing independently becomes more structured and may include teamwork as a natural progression of competence (Child Development Institute, n.d.). Although these important areas of development are occurring in children, physical, social, or emotional conditions as well as life circumstances and family situations have an impact on how children relate to the world. Group counseling offers a forum in which children can explore those issues and find support to successfully proceed in their growth and development and learn coping and cooperative strategies at an early age that may help them throughout their lives.

Dr. Davis would like to acknowledge the contributions of Shannon Kamenick, school counseling graduate student at Marymount University, to the revision of this chapter.

SIDEBAR 11.1
Self-Awareness: Are They Different?

Think about children receiving counseling in a variety of settings—schools, hospitals, outside clinical mental health facilities: What do you think might be unique to working with children in each setting? What are the internal characteristics of children and the external factors of different environments that might have an impact on group counseling with children in that setting? Which environment do you feel might be the most attractive to you should you become a counselor who does group work?

According to the American School Counselor Association (ASCA, 2014b) position statement, "Group counseling is an efficient and effective way to meet students' academic, career, social/emotional developmental and situational needs" (p. 1, para. 2). Because belonging and being a part of a group seems to be a normative developmental process for children, group counseling may be an effective counseling approach to address a child's circumstances or emotions. "Some children may feel pressurized and isolated in a one-to-one counseling context but thrive in a group setting where they can remain in the background until they build the confidence to participate fully" (Head, 2006, p. 43).

In this chapter, group counseling will be discussed in terms of group work with children in schools and group work with children in other settings. According to Shechtman (2002), as much as 80 percent of group work with children occurs in the school setting. However, ASCA (2014) has indicated that school counselors "do not provide therapy or long-term [group] counseling in schools to address psychological disorders . . . when students require long-term counseling or therapy, school counselors make referrals to appropriate community resources" (p. 1, para. 5). Often, school counselors will refer students to outside mental health counselors or counseling facilities due to the intensity or nature of the student's issues that cannot be addressed due to the time constraints and structure of schools. Although the setting may vary, many of the considerations and applications for group work with children are similar, regardless of environment. This chapter will both differentiate and integrate information specific to group work with children across settings.

GROUP COUNSELING WITH CHILDREN: A COMPARISON OF SCHOOLS AND OTHER SETTINGS

Group counseling is a direct counseling service provided by school counselors. Paisley and Milsom (2007) stated, "If professional school counselors intend to promote academic, career, and personal/social development for all students, then acknowledging the potential benefits of group work and identifying opportunities to implement groups will be critical" (p. 16). ASCA (2012) has recommended that school counselors spend between 15 and 45 percent of their time in direct services to students, which includes group counseling.

Research has indicated that most school counselors are conducting small-group counseling in schools. After surveying 80 school counselors, Burnham and Jackson (2000) found that 90 percent of the counselors conducted small-group counseling and those counselors spent 10 percent to 23 percent of their entire counseling time conducting small groups. More recently, Steen, Bauman, and Smith (2007) found that 87 percent of the 802 counselors surveyed indicated they conducted groups in their schools; however, participants also noted that group counseling in schools may not be supported due to time and scheduling constraints that are inherent to the school day. The structure of a school day and the emphasis of student time on task is a challenge for conducting group counseling in schools.

Although the overall goal of helping group members achieve healthy psychological functioning is still primary, the school setting requires that group work also focus on helping students become effective learners despite the issues that bring them to group counseling. For example, when a student is mourning the death of a close family member, he or she understandably may have difficulty concentrating on schoolwork. The purpose of this child participating in small-group counseling on grief/loss is two-fold: (1) to help the student work through the grieving process in a healthy manner and (2) to provide support within the school setting so that the child can concentrate on academic performance. The dual obligation to the participant—first as a person but also as a student—differentiates group counseling in schools from group counseling in other settings.

On the other hand, if a grieving child is in a small group in a mental-health agency or clinical counseling setting, the focus of the group can focus solely on the emotions around the loss without regard to the impact on academics, unless that arises as an issue presented by a group member or members. In most situations, counselors working in settings outside of schools seem to have more freedom and flexibility to explore social/emotional issues in greater depth due to the length of time children may stay in counseling sessions (typically 50 minutes) as opposed to the short amount of time children may spend participating in groups in schools (typically 30–45 minutes, sometimes during the student's lunch time). Further, the school counselor should be cognizant of the fact that she or he is sending group members back to join with their classmates and the regular schedule of the school day, even if emotional material has been discussed. Children participating in small-group settings outside of the school may have more flexibility and opportunity to debrief with group members and check-in to make sure members are ready to close the group session.

An advantage for school counselors who conduct group work in schools is that there is a readily accessible population because of compulsory school-attendance laws; if the student attends school, he or she is also present for group sessions. In other counseling settings, it may be a challenge to get group members to attend the scheduled group sessions because the children rely on the transportation of their parents or others.

SIDEBAR 11.2
Case Study: Group Member Attendance

You are conducting a small group for children of alcoholics at your local mental health counseling facility. You have five group members, ages 6 to 9, and in the first 3 weeks attendance was 100 percent. In the following 2 weeks, at least two members have been missing the sessions each week, and one member has missed 2 weeks in a row. How might you address the attendance issue? What might be some strategies for improving attendance at this point in the group?

In addition to the availability of students to participate in small groups, school counselors also have access to sources for group referrals from teachers, parents, or student self-referrals. This differs for counselors conducting groups for children in other settings. Referral sources may vary and come from family therapy or situations in which the counselor has been working with the child in individual counseling and decides to develop a small group for several children. Another difference in settings is that, though there is an available population of students to participate in groups in schools, participation in schools is not mandatory; group counseling in other settings may be mandated or required for participants, such as court-mandated group or family counseling.

A final difference between group work in schools and group work in other settings is that schools are highly focused on outcome-based data-driven programming that supports academic instruction. Due to the nature of schools and high-stakes testing, the academic focus in schools has an impact on the delivery of group-counseling services. Auger (2004) recommended that group leaders in school use a variety of approaches for evaluating school-based counseling groups: pre- and post-test surveys, self-report questionnaires, parent and/or teacher ratings, single-subject research designs, and observer (leader) ratings. Evidence of effective group work assists in gaining support for group counseling in the school setting, and group counseling that focuses on closing the achievement gap among students is regarded positively in the school setting (Campbell & Brigman, 2005). Quantitative evidence of success may not be the focus of group work with children in other settings, although progress may need to be documented for insurance purposes or for internal support for continuation of group-counseling services.

BENEFITS OF GROUP WORK WITH CHILDREN

Group counseling with children can be an effective way to provide counseling services for several reasons: (a) the ability for children to connect to each other and discuss their feelings in a safe and structured environment in which inappropriate interactions are not condoned (Sweeney, 2011), (b) the opportunity to recognize that there are shared feelings and issues that are not unique to just one child, and (c) the use of peer interaction and group reflections to discuss feelings and issues that may not be as easily discussed with an adult. Barratt and Kerman (2001) noted that, in their experience, children's issues came "alive" (p. 316) more quickly during group counseling because the counseling process may be slower in individual therapy. An obvious benefit of group work with children is that a greater number of children may participate in counseling in a group than in individual counseling; in schools, group counseling is an effective way to meet with more students because there is often limited time to meet with students individually due to concerns about missed instructional time. In other settings (e.g., private practice, agencies, hospitals), group counseling may be a beneficial way to work with children and families who share similar concerns or who may not be interested in individual counseling for their children.

A unique factor when working with children is that group counseling may involve counseling or collaborating with significant adults in the child's environment. In schools, this may be teachers or parents. In clinical or mental health settings, counseling may involve the parents or family. In schools, parents must be informed of a student's participation in group counseling (ASCA, 2016). The nature of the school setting may not allow for immediate feedback or consultation with parents to follow up on behaviors being worked on in the group. In other settings, parents and families may be more immediately involved due to the reality that the parents/guardians are often transporting the child to counseling.

Research has supported that working with parents/guardians or families simultaneously can be effective. Barratt and Kerman (2001) conducted drama and art therapy in small groups with children and, concurrently, offered a meeting with parents. By having the parents engaged in their own counseling activities, the group leaders felt there was more of a shared sense of the counseling experience between the children and their parents. In addition, should there be a serious breach of group rules during the children's small-group session, a child could be removed from the group and interact with the parent immediately (Barratt & Kerman, 2001). This is not the case in schools because the parent usually is not present when children are participating in group work; if there is going to be parent/guardian interaction, it usually happens sometime after the group has occurred via a phone call or email. Regardless of setting, follow-up with parents/guardians of children participating in a group is critical in terms of determining effective outcomes and reinforcing key concepts or behaviors that may need practice outside of the group counseling environment. Involving parents may also help them be in a better position to support their child should any difficulties or negative feelings arise between group-counseling sessions (Head, 2006).

TYPES OF GROUPS FOR CHILDREN

Group work with children may occur around several topics and issues. School groups typically are formed to address a specific need or issue that emerges within the school setting. Chapter 10 discussed types of groups and their applicability to a variety of settings. Of the four types of groups (task, psychoeducational, counseling, and psychological), task groups and psychoeducational groups lend themselves most readily to the school environment (Gerrity & Delucia-Waack, 2007; Paisley & Milsom, 2007). Schechtman (2002) indicated that appropriate group work with children outside the school setting would more likely be in the form of counseling groups focused on developmental difficulties that might not be addressed in the school setting or therapy groups, which should be small and conducted by experts based on specific therapeutic conditions.

In general, groups in schools tend to be task or psychoeducational groups based on common issues that occur at certain stages of development, and external group counseling with children may be more counseling or therapeutic. However, because children do not exist in a vacuum, it is reasonable to assume that some of these topics may be addressed across all settings in which group counseling may occur. Therefore, it is not unusual for a school counselor to lead a "changing families" counseling group in the school setting because some of the family changes could impact academic performance. Further, it is not unusual for counselors in other settings to also provide group counseling for children whose families are going through divorce to address the impact on the child and family. It is possible, and often helpful, for group leaders in each setting to confer with each other if consent is given to share information.

Table 11.1 gives examples of types of groups that might be appropriate in schools, in other settings, or in both.

TABLE 11.1 Possible Topics of Groups for Children in Schools or Other Settings

Task/Psychoeducational	Counseling/Therapy
Study skills	Changing families
Social skills/friendships	Grief/loss
Assertiveness skills	Gender-specific issues
New students/transitions	Family relationships
Bullying (victims/bystanders)	Body image/self-concept
Attentional issues	Stress management
ADHD	Diversity/multicultural issues
Test-taking skills	Stress management
Anger management	Substance use or abuse
College/career topics	Children of incarcerated parents
Behavior management	Siblings of children with special needs
Homework groups	Adoptive or foster children

Although the listing of possible group-counseling topics in Table 11.1 is not exhaustive, it represents a range of issues that may be appropriate for group work with children in schools and other settings.

UNIQUE CONSIDERATIONS FOR GROUP WORK WITH CHILDREN

Other chapters in this book have discussed the intricacies and unique considerations that are inherent to group work and group counseling. This section will explore specific aspects to consider when conducting group work with children.

Developmental Level

Perhaps the greatest challenge and opportunity of working with children through group counseling is the varied stages of development that group participants may exhibit. Because of their cognitive and developmental levels, children typically adapt rapidly to the group environment and may jump quickly into the working stage of group development (Schechtman, 2002). In addition, because of the openness of students and the natural tendency to want to connect with others, children in groups are more likely to self-disclose right from the beginning of the group. This may differ depending on the composition of the group or the group topic, but group cohesion may not be as necessary for children as group members to be ready to share and interact with others. This will be true especially if the group leader has developed a small-group counseling environment in which participants can feel safe and valued and if group rules and expectations are understood by group members.

Group Leadership

The Council for the Accreditation of Counseling and Related Educational Programs (CACREP) requires coursework in group work and group counseling as part of counselor preparation in graduate counseling programs (CACREP, 2015). Group leaders will benefit from having the awareness, knowledge, and skills to be successful when facilitating groups with children. One of the tasks of the group leader is to be acquainted with methods to encourage each child's individual self-expression while managing the group experience (Schechtman, 2002). Monitoring groups of children, particularly younger children, may require more structure than is ordinarily required for group work with other populations. There should be a balance of group member engagement, interaction, and processing, and the group leader is the catalyst for ensuring the group is making progress. This may include addressing disruptive behaviors of group members because young children are often easily distracted by other children or may act out for attention. For this reason, including coleaders or cofacilitators for the group may be beneficial.

Researchers have recommended the use of coleaders for work with children and emphasized the need for coleaders or cofacilitators to be appropriately qualified to guide the group process (Head, 2006). Canham and Emanuel (2000) conducted a year-long psychoanalytic group for 4- to 8-year-olds and found that coleadership was an effective way to monitor individual group members and develop group cohesion; however, they also warned that having two adults as leaders may overwhelm the children and that there could be attempts by individual group participants to divide the group leaders. Also, Barratt and Kerman (2001) noted that competitiveness could occur among children in small-group counseling, especially if there are siblings in the group. A child's natural tendency to want to win or be the center of attention could bring about conflict in the group; having coleaders may reduce the likelihood of negative interactions among group members. Group coleaders need to have clear expectations and boundaries for group-counseling sessions and open communication and feedback in terms of process and outcome. Consider the situation in Sidebar 11.3.

Member Screening and Parental Consent

Regardless of the setting, it is important and ethical to meet with each child who is being considered as a potential member for the group. The screening of participants for group counseling is ethically required by the American Counseling Association (ACA, 2014, Standard A.9), as well as by ASCA (2016, Standard A.7.c). This is especially critical when the group topic may be emotionally charged, such as grief or divorce. Although parental consent is sought for the child's participation in the group, having the student/client assent to counseling is important as well.

SIDEBAR 11.3

Case Study: A Group Out of Control

You are the group leader for seven boys between the ages of 6 and 8 who are participating in group counseling due to issues of impulse control, which has led to misbehavior in school and other settings. The group meets for 45 minutes weekly. You try to engage the students in activities that are meaningful, and you reward appropriate behavior. After the second session, you realize that you have lost control of the group: members are constantly distracted, and little productive work is being accomplished in the group. What might be the benefit of adding another group facilitator? Would there be other steps you might take to gain control so that progress could be made in the group?

Dear Parent/Guardian:

As part of a comprehensive school counseling program, students are often invited to participate in small-group counseling sessions. Your child has been invited to join a Study Skills group that is starting this month. The group offers an opportunity for your child to recognize his/her own learning style, to set personal goals, to improve study habits, and to learn time-management skills. The goal of the group is to improve work habits and grades in the next grading period.

This group will meet weekly for eight sessions for half an hour each session. The time that the Study Skills group will meet will be coordinated with the teacher so your child will not miss valuable class time. I will follow up with you after the group has concluded.

Please indicate your permission by signing the form below, and return the form to the Counseling Office as soon as possible. Your signed permission is necessary before your child can participate in the group. If you have questions, please contact me at 123-456-7890. I look forward to working with you and your child.

Sincerely, [Name]
Group Leader

Student _____   Teacher _____

- -

_____ Yes, I give permission for my child, _____, to participate in the group.

_____ No, I do not give permission for my child, _____, to participate in the group.

_____
(Parent/Guardian signature & date)

FIGURE 11.1 Sample Parent/Guardian Consent for Group Counseling in Schools

Because children are under the age of 18, it is ethical practice to secure permission for students to participate in small-group counseling (ASCA, 2016, Standard A.7.b). See Figure 11.1 for an example of a parent/guardian consent form that might be used with school children to request approval for their participation in small-group counseling.

In counseling settings outside of schools, group participants and their parents typically complete an intake form that would include the opportunity for a parent/guardian to give permission for the child to participate in small-group counseling. Again, including the child in the decision-making process in any setting is a helpful way to indicate to the child that her or his thoughts and decisions matter and may also help the child invest more quickly in the group-counseling process.

Composition of the Group

Many factors go into planning and implementing a group for children. One factor that influences who is in the group and how many group members to have is the group topic. Table 11.1 indicated a variety of topics that may be covered through small-group counseling. The nature of the topics may dictate whether groups should be smaller (four to six members) or larger (seven to ten members). Typically, small-group counseling with children works ideally with six to eight members, depending on the age and the topic. For example, a first-grade group of students with attentional issues may present different group counseling needs than a fifth-grade girls group on self-image, so the number of group members may vary accordingly.

Another decision is whether the group should be homogeneous or heterogenous. These groupings could be based on gender, age, topic, developmental level, or level of dealing with the issue. Some groups may be more successful and have greater cohesion with members who are closer in age, and other groups may be more effective with members who share a certain issue or experience regardless of age difference. Also, depending on the topic, some groups may be more cohesive if they only include members of one gender, whereas other groups may benefit from having both male and female children. Many factors should be considered prior to the selection of the group, which is why prescreening is a critical and ethical part of the process (ACA, 2014; ASCA, 2016).

Group Structure and Process

Because of the developmental level of children and the cognitive capacity for more concrete activities in group, structured groups tend to be most appropriate for this age group. In my experience, groups that are successful have combined enough structure and activity to keep the group members engaged but also allowed time to process and assess if the group has been successful for students. There have been several stage models for the group-counseling process, but because of the developmental level of the group participants, movement through stages in a specific order may not always occur the same way for children's groups as for other groups. It is important for the group leader to be flexible and meet the group participants wherever they are in the group process.

Lowenstein and Sprunk (2010) formalized a process that has proven to be effective with small-group counseling with students. The first step is assessment, to make sure the group addresses the needs of individual style and to secure parent/guardian commitment to the process. Second, Lowenstein and Sprunk recommended using initial session(s) to build rapport by providing engagement activities that are creative and play based so that children can begin to feel comfortable in the group. Another recommendation is to not overwhelm the child with too much talk or too much activity. Controlling the pace of the sessions and maintaining a balance of activity and discussion seem to be natural ways to build rapport and reinforce the group leader's need to be flexible during group work with children.

Group Closure and Follow-Up

Evidence-based practice has suggested that there should be formative and summative evaluation to determine if results warrant the continuation of the group or if group outcomes have been achieved so that the group can terminate. Group leaders should have an evaluation component in place so that group outcomes can be assessed. One of the biggest differences between groups with children in schools and groups with children in other settings is that closure/follow-up must be different. A school-counseling small-group leader may conclude a small group one day, but she will see those children in the hallway, in the cafeteria, or at recess that day, and in the days to follow, as a natural part of being in a school with the students. There is a natural process for follow-up with group members that occurs at schools simply because of access to students.

For group work with children in external agencies and facilities, group closure and follow-up may be more like a medical follow-up, with the scheduling of an appointment and a specific time for checking in to see how the child is doing. Regardless, follow-up with children in the group and the adults that interact with them is an ethical responsibility (ASCA, 2016) as well as best practice for those who facilitate groups with children.

ETHICAL CONSIDERATIONS FOR GROUP WORK WITH CHILDREN

The ASCA (2016) ethical standards (Standard A.7.c) emphasize the necessity of screening group participants prior to beginning group work and protecting group participants from harm. Another critical area addressed is consent for a student's participation in group counseling. Protocol for acquiring consent may vary from school to school, but most would agree that parental consent for a minor child to participate in counseling services is imperative. Parental support is necessary for group participation in schools because children are being taken out of class. For counseling children outside of the school setting and when dealing with minor children, parental consent also is necessary.

Although ACA's (2014) ethical standards related to group work do not specifically identify children as group participants, the standards are general enough to apply to children in small-group counseling, including those related to member screening and confidentiality.

Confidentiality

An ethical concern for group work with children in schools is confidentiality. Because the group membership involves children and adolescents, it is difficult to be sure that confidentiality will be maintained. Breaching confidentiality seems to be more of a threat in the school setting than in other counseling settings. ASCA's (2016) ethical standards require that, as group leaders, school counselors should "communicate the aspiration of confidentiality as a group norm, while recognizing and working from the protective posture that confidentiality for minors in schools cannot be guaranteed" (Standard A.7.e, p. 4). All precautions and safeguards to protect the confidentiality of group participants should be followed, but there is no certainty of confidentiality. The structure of the school day gives students opportunities for free time in which to interact—such as during lunch, recess, between classes, and at bus stops. The open nature of counseling in schools can lead to the accidental breaching of confidentiality. Consider Sidebar 11.4.

In a more general sense and more applicable to group work outside the school setting, Ware and Taylor (2014) suggested a proactive approach from the group leader to manage potential issues, particularly those related to confidentiality, by having both

SIDEBAR 11.4
Case Study: Breach of Group Confidentiality

An elementary school counselor has been conducting a social skills small group of fifth-grade students and learns that one of the group members shared information with a non–group member about another group member's disclosure during group. She said she "forgot" the rules about confidentiality. As a group leader, how would you address this breach of confidentiality? If you find the group process is interrupted by the breach, what steps might you take to restore group cohesion?

children and their parents included in this approach. Discussing confidentiality issues with children begins during the screening process, in which the counselor's focus is to establish a sense of trust and to gain an understanding of the children in the group and their developmental level; this discussion helps provide insight into their ability to understand and to maintain confidentiality (Ware & Taylor, 2014). In schools, a way to address the possible breach of confidentiality is to address the issue with potential group members and, because the group members are children, inform parents about the limitations of confidentiality, possibly by including a disclaimer on the parental consent form. Similarly, Ware and Taylor emphasize establishing guidelines for confidentiality with the parents prior to the initial session. Issues to be discussed with parents include the differentiation between legal and ethical confidentiality, the ability to discuss issues related to their own child, and concerns regarding revealing information about other children in the group (Ware & Taylor, 2014).

School counselors and other group-work leaders must emphasize the importance of confidentiality and provide concrete examples of when and how a breach might occur. Within the group, the leader should introduce the topic of how a breach of confidentiality might be handled in the group and the consequences for breaches. Should ethical issues arise despite this proactive approach, Seymour and Rubin (2006) suggested the incorporation of the *principles, principals, and process* (P^3) model to manage the ethical decision-making process; this model addresses the ethical and legal principles involved, the key people (principals) involved, and a process that emphasizes critical thinking and consultation when making ethical decisions. In Section F of the ASCA ethical standards, ASCA (2016) also offers ethical decision-making steps to assist when there are ethical problems in schools.

Other Ethical Issues in Group Work with Children

Several ethical issues arise in group work in general, and group work with children may present other ethical dilemmas as well. Crespi (2009) explored several issues to be considered when working with children in group counseling across all settings: breaching confidentiality, selecting group members, selecting topics, how to proceed if a concern arises regarding danger to self or others, how much to disclose to parents, and ethical and legal works. If counselors are abiding by the ethical codes of their counseling association, following an ethical decision-making model, and consulting with colleagues and professional organizations regarding ethical dilemmas, it seems that counselors across settings can feel confident in their ability to be ethical practitioners as they conduct small groups with children.

CULTURAL CONSIDERATIONS FOR GROUP WORK WITH CHILDREN

Just as changing demographics indicate a huge influx of diverse ethnic groups into communities, counseling—including small-group counseling—must support the cultural needs of a diverse group of children. Chapter 6 explored the considerations for cross-cultural group counseling, but special consideration for small group work with children from various cultures is warranted.

The research on culturally homogeneous or heterogenous group work is mixed. Stroh and Sink (2002) support a mixed composition of students in group counseling to promote understanding of cultural differences. Diversity is integral to the group counseling process: heterogeneous group membership not only reflects more accurately the diversity of persons in the school, community, and world, but it also expands opportunities for learning through varied interpersonal interactions (Stroh & Sink, 2002). On the other hand, Perrone and Sedlacek (2000) advocated for homogeneous groups of children from similar cultural backgrounds, although there is some concern that a homogeneous group does not foster divergent and creative thinking. Group work with children who share common concerns and cultural experiences is a catalyst for identifying sources of support within the school setting, and group leaders must be culturally responsive to the needs of all students. Although this is true of group work in other counseling settings, schools are a setting in which the interaction of cultural groups should be encouraged and the uniqueness of cultures should be celebrated.

One group-counseling approach that seems to be responsive to a diverse range of cultural needs of children is group play therapy (GPT). Culturally competent GPT uses a variety of items to addresses a wide range of needs—from the simple, such as supplies and materials, to the complex, such as cultural beliefs (Bratton et al., 2013; Misurell & Springer, 2013; Shen, 2016). In terms of materials, dolls of different skin colors and ethnic play food and utensils should be incorporated into GPT for group members from different ethnic backgrounds, and sensory tool kits and crutches or wheelchairs for dolls could be beneficial for children with special needs (Shen, 2016).

From a broader perspective, Misurell and Springer (2013) highlighted several characteristics innate to GPT that worked well with the children in their group, most of whom were African-American and Latinx: an emphasis on collectivism, a strengths-based approach, a focus on the present, an active style, and a sense of warmth and genuineness. Even in group counseling that dealt with highly emotional material, play therapy helped children process their thoughts and feelings concerning death, helped in resolving symptoms, developed resiliency, and assisted members to resume the typical development process (Gil, 2006).

Baggerly and Abugideiri (2010) described a group grief-counseling program for Muslim preschool and elementary school children after the loss of a preschool classmate. In addition to the rituals that were part of the religious observances for the children during this loss, counselors provided religiously respectful interventions to Muslim children through teacher and parent consultation, group grief counseling, play therapy, and community outreach and advocacy (Baggerly & Abugideiri, 2010). They recommended that counselors should inform school personnel or any counselors working with children about "(a) unique religious and cultural beliefs and practices, (b) typical and atypical symptoms of children, (c) the range of available counseling interventions and resources (both inside and outside of school), and (d) basic stabilization interventions for upset children" (Baggerly & Abugideiri, 2010, p. 117).

In addition to culture as it relates to ethnic diversity, there is also support for effective group work with children with special needs. Small-group counseling with students with special needs is not unusual in the school setting; often, heterogenous grouping occurs with students with special needs and students who are not diagnosed with special needs. This natural melding of children helps to promote greater tolerance and understanding for the exceptionalities of others. Group counseling with children outside of the school setting with students with specific diagnoses has also showed success. Epp (2008) found that social skills could be taught through art therapy in

SIDEBAR 11.5

Self-Awareness: Cultural Awareness

Consider the ethnic diversity of children who might be present in a small group. What would you do to promote acceptance and tolerance for cultural differences among the group members? How would you keep your own cultural worldview in check?

therapeutic group settings that sufficiently met the needs of children on the autism spectrum: "Group therapy and art therapy very likely lend themselves well to this kind of intervention" (p. 34). Art therapy has also been used in group work with siblings of children with hearing loss (Raghuraman, 2002). The group occurred during a summer session and siblings (ages 5–11) of children with hearing loss were given the opportunity to explore their identities as individuals and as members of their families. The bonding experience of the siblings combined with the art techniques used to draw members out to communicate and share their emotions resulted in a positive experience for all participants (Raghuraman, 2002).

When considering the culturally competent approaches that might be most effective with children in group counseling, it makes sense to consider their cognitive and social/emotional level, as well as activities or techniques that will facilitate a positive outcome. Group leaders must also keep their multicultural perspectives in check so that they help and do not hinder culturally competent group progress with children. The next section discusses a variety of approaches that seem appropriate for group work with children.

THEORIES/TECHNIQUES FOR GROUP WORK WITH CHILDREN

Although there is research that several counseling approaches may be beneficial for children in small-group counseling, GPT is prevalent in the literature with substantiated evidence of positive outcomes for group members who are children. Emerging as a primary intervention for children, *play therapy* enables children to use toys and games to explore and to express themselves naturally, spontaneously, and metaphorically (Allen & Barber, 2015; Winburn, Gilstrap, & Perryman, 2017). According to Bratton, Ray, Rhine, and Jones (2005), "play allows children to bridge the chasm between their experiences and understanding, thereby providing the means for insight, learning, problem solving, coping, and mastery" (pp. 376–377). The Association for Play Therapy (2016) stated the following goal and benefit of play therapy for children: "Children between the ages of 3 to 12 years old should participate in play therapy as an intervention to alleviate symptoms related to behavioral and emotional problems, as well as contribute to overall wellness and healthy development" (p. 2). Group play allows children to explore, experiment, and learn about themselves and others, ultimately linking the experiences in group with reality (Cheung & Ray, 2016).

GPT with children serves a broad spectrum of needs, ages, modes, and settings; more important, GPT can be a powerful and transformative experience. Stone and Stark (2013) reflected on the many ways in which the GPT counselor's role can be dichotomous. Group leadership can be directive and/or nondirective, structured or free-form, challenging or supportive, and limit setting or permissive; further, the counselor "encourages both conformity to group norms and freedom of self-expression" (Stone & Stark, 2013, p. 26). Also, play and art therapy activities can be used to diffuse children's anxiety about talking about their thoughts and feelings, which provides an important medium for self-expression (Gil, 2006).

Although the role of the counselor as group leader in GPT can vary, even within a single session, some traits remain consistent. Garza, Kinsworthy, and Bennett (2014) compiled a checklist of skills a competent GPT counselor should incorporate. Establishing and fostering a safe, cooperative, trusting, and accepting environment in which the children interact is imperative (Allen & Barber, 2015; Cheung & Ray, 2016; Misurell & Springer, 2013; Perryman, Moss, & Cochran, 2015; Swank & Cheung, 2017; Webb, 2011; Winburn et al., 2017). The ultimate responsibility of the GPT counselor is to understand the combined interactions, nuances, intricacies, and process of events and experiences that occur in the group (Garza et al., 2014) and to respond within these contexts (Webb, 2011). Because of the activity involved in play and the child's natural tendency to explore and seek to be engaged, the group leader must be present in the here and now. This also reinforces the idea of coleadership of groups with children for observations and interactions to be captured in a meaningful way (Canham & Emanuel, 2000; Head, 2006).

The range of issues addressed in the application of GPT is extensive and can be preventive or remedial in nature. Researchers have recognized the strong correlation between social and emotional development and academic achievement, and they implement a variety of GPT programs to create and enhance social and emotional competencies at the school-age level (Allen & Barber, 2015; Blanco & Ray, 2011; Cheung & Ray, 2016; Stone & Stark, 2013). Additional education-based research supports the use of GPT for children with developmental delays and specific learning disabilities (Reddy, 2016). Behavioral problems—such as hyperactivity, aggression, attention issues, impulsivity, and conduct problems—and disruptive behaviors are also frequently addressed using GPT (Bratton et al., 2013; Reddy, 2016; Swank & Cheung, 2017; Winburn et al., 2017). GPT is effective at treating situational issues as well, such as grief, trauma, and abuse (Misurell & Springer, 2013; Webb, 2011). It is evident that play as a medium for working with children in small-group counseling seems well supported by research and is a viable option for counselors who engage in group work with children.

Group Play Therapy and Other Theories/Techniques

GPT is frequently integrated with a wide spectrum of counseling theories. One commonly used approach to GPT is child-centered group play therapy (CCGPT), which is based upon the tenets of Carl Rogers's person-centered theory (Blanco & Ray, 2011; Bratton et al., 2013; Perryman et al., 2015; Swank & Cheung, 2017). Adlerian theory has been used with GPT with a focus on empowering the child (Garza et al., 2014; Kottman & Meany-Walen, 2016). In addition, Misurell and Springer (2013) worked with a group of children who had been sexually abused using a game-based cognitive behavioral therapy (GB-CBT), which incorporates trauma-focused CBT (TF-CBT) with GPT to reduce both internalizing and externalizing behavioral problems and enhance social skills, emotional regulation, and coping skills. Also, Reddy (2016) utilized cognitive-behavioral group play interventions with a group of children with ADHD to target similar skills. Obviously, GPT combines effectively with other therapies and theories.

Adventure-based therapy seems to be a natural extension of play therapy, as they can both represent alternatives to verbal expression. Swank and Cheung (2017) explored new possibilities in integration by taking GPT outdoors with nature-based child-centered group play therapy (NBCCGPT). This intervention sought to increase social skills and peer interactions for a child experiencing behavior difficulties using natural play materials—for example, "dirt, sand, water, leaves, [and] sticks, although a few materials such as buckets and shovels are used to facilitate interactions with nature" (2017, p. 48). Fortunately, GPT offers the flexibility to function well autonomously and to simultaneously accommodate innovation.

Group Play Therapy: Evidence-Based Outcomes Across Settings

In addition to being multifaceted in its theoretical approach, GPT can be applied effectively in a variety of settings. Winburn et al. (2017) indicated that play therapy aligns well with the ASCA National Model (ASCA, 2012) because GPT is a direct counseling service used when delivering group work with children in schools. Research has supported the use of GPT to improve social and emotional development, which removes barriers to learning and leads to academic success (Allen & Barber, 2015; Blanco & Ray, 2011). In addition, using GPT enhanced a student's problem-solving skills, heightened social interaction and cooperation, increased self-confidence (resulting in improved learning skills and participation), and diminished both internalizing and externalizing behavioral problems (Blanco & Ray, 2011; Ocasio et al., 2015).

Although there is limited research on group counseling with children younger than school age, some studies have addressed the use of GPT as an effective intervention before a child even begins school. The academic and social/emotional needs of preschool-age children will vary based on development, experience, and exposure to information and relationships. Early interventions that serve the needs of younger children in preventive or remedial capacities may take place in preschools and through agencies, such as Head Start (Bratton et al., 2013; Cheung & Ray, 2016; Ocasio et al., 2015). Mental health providers often partner with service and community organizations such as the American Red Cross and Save the Children to aid in crisis situations, including natural disasters such as Hurricane Katrina; terrorist attacks such as the events of September 11, 2001; and school shootings such as the event that occurred at Sandy Hook Elementary School (Webb, 2011). In these unique scenarios, the materials required for GPT must be modified to serve as a "psychological first aid" kit and can include items such as rescue vehicles and medical kits, along with standard supplies like dolls, puppets, and blocks (Webb, 2011, pp. 136–138). It appears that GPT can be used in many situations in group work with children, including trauma.

SIDEBAR 11.6

Is It Counseling or Is It Playing?

Play therapy has sometimes been considered more play than true counseling. How do you think you might utilize some of the GPT techniques mentioned here as a way of conducting counseling? Describe how you might use a play therapy technique to facilitate a counseling dialogue or emphasize a concept with children in your small group.

Art Therapy

Although art therapy is often considered in the realm of play therapy, there is evidence that art, drawing, painting, and other artistic techniques are effective ways to work with children in small-group counseling. For children who are not expressive verbally, drawing or producing art may be a way to express things vividly (Barratt & Kerman, 2001). Epp (2008) effectively used art therapy in small-group counseling with school-age children on the autism spectrum to improve social skills. Art therapy was combined with cognitive behavioral therapy to encourage positive self-talk when group partici-pants might typically be negative or self-derogatory. One specific technique used was the *comic strip technique* (Epp, 2008), in which a comic strip was drawn by the group leader and the children then continued the comic strip with discussion and anal-ysis of portrayed events. Epp found that using drawing to resolve conflict or address issues seemed less threatening than other techniques, such as role-playing. Drama ther-apy also has been used successfully in children's groups at a child and family consulta-tion center; it allowed children to have the opportunity for self-expression through a medium other than oral communication (Barratt & Kerman, 2001, p. 318). It is evident that different mediums can be effective when working with children in small groups due to the active and interactive nature of the techniques in these approaches and the appropriate matching to the developmental level of child participants.

GROUP COUNSELING WITH CHILDREN: DOES IT WORK?

In addition to the research already cited in this chapter that provides support for GPT and other theoretical approaches as effective counseling practices for group work with chil-dren, other researchers have provided evidence that group counseling with children is an effective way to address children's needs around a variety of issues. Webb and Myrick (2003) conducted a 6-week group intervention program with elementary school students with ADHD. Survey results from the students and teachers supported the need and usefulness of the program, and a longer intervention (12 weeks) resulted in significant improvement in how students and teachers rated its success.

Similarly, group-counseling interventions have been used with students who have behavioral-adjustment problems. Nelson and Dykeman (1996) used solution-focused group counseling to help a group of elementary school students identify social problems, initiate goal setting, generate solutions, analyze consequences of the solu-tions, and evaluate the success of the solutions. Teachers of students who participated in the group noted marked improvement in the behaviors of the group participants. More recently, DeRosier (2004) found that a social-skills group-counseling intervention with 187 third-grade students increased peer liking, enhanced self-esteem and self-efficacy, and decreased social anxiety related to bullying.

Small-group counseling with children may also be an opportunity for children to work through normative emotions, such as worry or anxiety. Anxiety is an issue for children as early as age 6 (CMI, 2015), and it seems that children are not immune from the circumstances or situations that may result in extreme anxiety. Rose, Miller, and Martinez (2009) conducted small-group counseling with students who had demon-strated signs of anxiety in school. The small-group curriculum aimed at "providing opportunities for the children to model positive behaviors, have their own fears and worries normalize, and be positively reinforced for desired behaviors" (Rose et al., 2009, p. 402). Results indicated that anxiety scores on pre- and post-test measures were significantly reduced, and 86 percent of the participants liked the program and could differentiate between helpful and unhelpful thoughts to calm themselves down when they felt anxious (Rose et al., 2009). Most people think that counseling is only useful for crises or negative circumstances, but there is evidence that children may benefit from group work to deal with emotions or experiences and thus respond to life events in healthy and productive ways.

Life circumstances and family situations may be effectively addressed through small groups in schools and in other settings. In a meta-analysis of effective group-counseling sessions with children, Whiston and Sexton (1998) found support for the use of groups to develop social skills and positively address family problems such as experiencing parental divorce (Delucia-Waack & Gerrity, 2001; Richardson & Rosen 1999). Riddle, Bergin, and Douzenis (1997) found that a group-counseling intervention was effective in raising the self-concept of children of alcoholics: group participants demonstrated significant improvements in self-perception of their academic and personal lives. Several group-counseling studies report successful group intervention with students as they experience life circumstances such as parental incarceration (Lopez & Bhat, 2007) and parental deployment (Rush & Akos, 2007). Although most of these groups occurred in the school setting, others were conducted outside of the educational environment. The common goal of group counseling across settings is the successful intervention with children who are experiencing stress or difficulty in their young lives. Research has supported that working through these issues within the context of a safe group in which emotions can be expressed and shared under the leadership of a trained counselor can be an effective way to support children.

Summary

Group work with children requires a unique awareness and knowledge of skills in the school setting and in other counseling settings. This chapter has explored the benefits of group work with children as well as the special opportunities and challenges that are inherent to group counseling with children from preschool to age 12. The types of groups conducted in schools and in other counseling settings were compared, and similarities as well as differences were identified. Special consideration was given to the distinctive aspects of group work with children, given their developmental level and the types of issues that might be present in their lives. Ethical and cultural aspects were discussed in terms of counseling diverse groups of children, and the effective cultural competence of group leaders to meet diverse student needs was emphasized.

Theoretical approaches and techniques that have proven to be effective in group work with children, particularly group play therapy (GPT), were presented, as well as evidence-based research that supports that group work with children in schools and in other settings has been effective. Early counseling intervention through group work with children is recommended to address the increase and early onset of mental health needs in children and the normative developmental issues and life circumstances that may occur for children. Counseling through group work with children is supported by research and should be encouraged across counseling settings.

12 Groups for Adolescents

Janice DeLucia

"Adolescents face enormous developmental challenges. . . . At no time in the country's history have young people been confronted simultaneously by such a wide array of positive and negative influences and opportunities" (Laser & Nicotera, 2011, p. xiii). Between 17 percent and 22 percent of children and adolescents have serious developmental, emotional, or social problems (Shechtman, 2014). Malekoff (2004) delineated four developmental tasks of adolescence: (a) separation from family, (b) forging a healthy sexual identity, (c) preparing for the future, and (d) developing a moral value system. "The group format is a logical choice . . . given the amount of time children and adolescents spend in groups with their peers . . . it provides the context within which children and adolescents will receive preventative interventions and will practice and utilize them in their 'real lives'" (Kulic, Horne, & Dagley, 2004, p. 139). Beyond the benefits of time- and cost-efficiency, groups provide qualitatively different experiences to promote change. Many normative developmental issues that adolescents typically struggle with are interpersonal and best addressed in groups, such as self-awareness and peer and romantic relationships (Davies, 2011).

Psychoeducational and counseling groups are the treatment of choice for adolescents (Falco & Bauman, 2014; Shechtman, 2014) and the most common groups in schools (Gerrity & DeLucia-Waack, 2007). "They are a natural way for adolescents to relate to each other; they emphasize the learning of life skills, they focus on generalizing behaviors practiced in the group to real life situations, and they provide multiple feedback and increase self-esteem that comes from helping others" (Shechtman, Bar-El, & Hadar, 1997, pp. 203–204). See Chapter 8 for a detailed discussion of the four types of group work.

Much of what we know is based on research on adult groups. Thus, it is essential that group design, leadership, and interventions address the unique needs of adolescents. The revised *Best Practice Guidelines* from the Association for Specialists in Group Work (ASGW; Thomas & Pender, 2008), in line with and expansive of the American Counseling Association's *Code of Ethics* (Berg, Landreth, & Fall, 2013), suggest three major emphases: planning, performing, and processing. This chapter will be organized around these three ASGW emphases.

RATIONALE FOR GROUPS FOR ADOLESCENTS

The therapeutic factors inherent in groups offer experiences and growth opportunities not readily available in individual counseling. The relational nature of groups is beneficial for adolescents dealing with stressors or problems that result in feelings of rejection, anger, alienation, and isolation. Belonging is particularly important for adolescents as a protective factor (Laser & Nicotera, 2011). Peer-group support and acceptance are integral as self-awareness and empathy develop. For some adolescents, the feelings of having contributed to and helped others in group may be the only way in which they receive praise and feelings of accomplishment. Groups provide a place to share personal concerns and problems openly, give and receive feedback, let members interact and learn about themselves and others, and let members learn and practice new interpersonal skills.

When planning groups for adolescents, it is important to consider that therapeutic factors in effective psychoeducational groups differ from those in counseling groups (Kivlighan & Holmes, 2004). Kivlighan and Holmes's cluster analysis reported four group types based on ranking of importance of therapeutic factors. *Cognitive support* (vicarious learning, guidance, and self-understanding) and *cognitive insight* (interpersonal learning, self-understanding, and vicarious learning) resembled factors in psychoeducational groups. In contrast, *affective support* (acceptance, catharsis, interpersonal learning, and self-understanding) and *affective insight* (acceptance, instillation of hope, and universality) resembled factors in counseling groups.

Groups are an excellent fit for the developmental transitions of adolescence due to the importance of peer relationships and the interpersonal nature of adolescents' struggles. Developmentally, this exchange of thoughts and feelings with peers (much more so than with adults) increases interpersonal awareness, perspective taking, and reasoning. Carrell (2000) makes several strong points that resonate with me each time I lead a group for adolescents:

1. *Groups challenge the myth of uniqueness by emphasizing shared emotions and experiences.* Many adolescents think that no one else feels the way they do or has had the same experiences. Often in group, they are surprised by how similar they feel (universality) and/or how someone else has survived something even worse (instillation of hope).
2. *Groups provide adult leadership that adolescents want but with avenues to assert power and independence.* Adolescents want to learn how to interact with adults but learn best from vicarious learning, instruction, and practice.
3. *Groups reduce the discomfort of adult-child dynamics that occur in individual counseling, particularly with adolescents with bad experiences with adults.*
4. *Groups confront adolescent self-absorption because members need to take turns talking and helping each other.* I joke that all adolescents are self-absorbed because of their developmental stage. Groups help adolescents develop empathy and notice that the world does not revolve around them, that they can receive help from others, and, most important, that they can help others and how good it feels to do so (altruism).
5. *Groups may be the first place that an adolescent truly experiences peer acceptance.* This is true especially for those with limited social skills or those who appear different.

In addition, feedback from peers is much more meaningful and often more accepted than feedback from a counselor. Group members also learn empathy, communication, and leadership skills by vicarious learning of group leaders and then practice as they take more ownership of the group. In addition, multiple perspectives are a reality. It is helpful to know group members view the same situation differently. In addition, members learn that their viewpoints can be different and still be valid and useful to other group members; in fact, differing viewpoints are helpful to group members as they try to problem solve new ways of thinking, feeling, and behaving.

GROUP LEADER PLANNING FOR GROUPS

The ASGW *Best Practices Guidelines* (Thomas & Pender, 2008) suggest that planning should focus on pregroup decision making and on selection and preparation of members and leaders. Good planning ensures that group members are carefully selected and prepared for group, that group goals match group interventions and individual goals, and that coleaders have a good working relationship and an agreed-on plan for the group.

Group Type

Psychoeducational groups focus on problem solving, decision making, communication skills, and role-playing and are most commonly used in schools for both prevention and the first intervention for students at risk (Gerrity & DeLucia-Waack, 2007). Counseling groups focus on remediation, providing structure for adolescents to give and receive feedback from peers, practice new skills in a safe place, and identify and express feelings to work on interpersonal problems and promote positive behavior and emotional development (Falco & Bauman, 2014).

DeLucia-Waack and Kalodner (2005) suggest the following guiding questions:

- Who will be the members?
- What is the reason for forming the group?
- Are symptoms being treated? If so, what are they? What are the severity levels?
- Is this prevention or treatment?
- What is the intended outcome?
- How long is the group intervention?
- Are the goals realistic for the length of the group?

Group Goals

Groups allow group members to discuss feelings, connect with others, and identify potential solutions for their concerns, with the inherent goals of teaching identification and expression of emotions, problem solving, decision making, effective communication, empathy, assertiveness, self-awareness, and awareness of others. Goals for psychoeducational groups are behavioral and specific, focusing on positive skills, cognitive styles, and coping strategies.

Group Specifications

Effective planning for groups includes decision making about group size, gender mix, session length and structure, and choice and use of activities.

GROUP SIZE   For counseling groups, the ideal group size is eight to maximize group dynamics; psychoeducational groups should contain no more than 12 members (Falco & Bauman, 2014). A high rate of absenteeism may suggest adding two to four members to ensure a critical mass.

GENDER MIX Diversity in emotions and reactions in mixed groups provides opportunities to learn to communicate openly and honestly with all peers (Falco & Bauman, 2014). Carrell (2000) suggested mixed-sex groups for older teens because so much of their focus and concern is on relationships. Same-sex groups in middle school may lessen the self-consciousness and decreased self-disclosure that may result from boys and girls being in the same group.

LENGTH AND NUMBER OF SESSIONS In schools, 40- to 75-minute sessions for 6 to 10 weeks is typical. Agencies may be able to sustain longer groups, ideally 12 to 16 sessions (1 hour to 1.5 hours), allowing time to deal with more complex issues and for behavior change to occur (it takes 10 weeks to acquire a new habit or behavior). Psychoeducational groups tend to be shorter in duration (typically 6 to 20 sessions, vs. 3 months to ongoing; Kulic et al., 2004) and shorter in minutes (30 to 45 minutes, especially in schools, vs. 90 minutes).

Structure

The structure of the group (format, content, and stage of group) and the structure of individual sessions are important to consider.

GROUP STAGE STRUCTURE Initial stage sessions are devoted to establishment of ground rules and goals and introduction of members to each other and to how groups work. This is especially important for adolescents as they may not have chosen to be in a group; even if they did, they may not be familiar with how groups work, and positive social interactions are not within their group norms or skills (Shechtman, 2014). Malekoff (2004) noted that the rules of both these groups are different than others (don't raise your hand, if swearing is allowed, cross-talk) and suggested that group leaders might allow group members to behave in somewhat inappropriate ways for them to feel accepted as individuals and begin to figure out how to relate to each other in authentic and helpful ways. Adolescents need to "get hooked" in the first session, which is difficult sometimes when so much of what happens may be less interactive than future group sessions. Group leaders must involve group members in creating the group rules, articulating how groups work, and getting to know each other. Malekoff (2004) also identified the effect of the group coming up with its own name as moving from stigma to valued identity: how true! These tasks help adolescents take ownership and begin to express their thoughts and feelings, negotiate, make decisions, and come to consensus. It is important for group leaders to guide adolescents in their interactions: provide structure to form relationships, develop a language of emotions, reduce anxiety, and increase the language of support (Shechtman, 2014). Initially, activities should be used in both psychoeducational and counseling groups to teach names and how groups work and to begin and moderate self-disclosure.

Working stage activities for psychoeducational groups focus on teaching effective cognitive, behavioral, and affective skills. In counseling groups, group members experience cognitive and affective exploration, self-expressiveness, cathartic experiences, and insight so that change occurs.

SIDEBAR 12.1
Swimming Pool Rules as a Metaphor for Group Ground Rules

1. [Say:] Just as there are rules posted to inform swimmers of acceptable/unacceptable behaviors to create a safe place to swim, a group also needs rules to inform participants of their responsibilities and to provide a safe and comfortable environment for sharing. Let's take some time and create the rules for our group so that we begin to feel comfortable taking risks, trying out new behaviors and skills, and giving and receiving feedback. Let's start with naming some typical pool rules and then decide how they might translate to guidelines for our group. Can someone write two columns on the board:

   a. Pool rules
   b. What the pool rules mean for our group

Possible Rules and Translations

- One person on a diving board at a time: One person talking at a time.
- Stay in the pool area (fence): Confidentiality.
- Don't go too deep: Choose something to work on that you can accomplish in the time we have.
- Getting out of the shallow end: Opening up, taking risks, trying out new behaviors.
- Lifeguards: Group leaders are responsible to teach and instruct.
- Take a shower before entering the pool: Be prepared with something to talk about when you come to group.
- No peeing in the pool: No creating messes in group.
- No running on deck: Be slow and deliberate in what you say, especially when giving feedback.

SIDEBAR 12.2
Why Do Groups Work? Web of Cohesion Activity

[Say:] It is important to talk about how groups work and why they are a good place for adolescents to learn and change and grow. We are also going to remind each other of our names. The first round, we will each say our name and one reason that groups are helpful. Then, throw the ball of yarn (still holding onto the string) to the person you would like to go next. As we continue, we will create a web. For the next round, say another reason groups work and then who you will throw the ball to. For the third round, say how you can uniquely help the group and then the name of the person you will throw the ball to.

Possible Reasons Why Groups Work

- We can learn from each other.
- It is nice to be supported.
- We don't have to be on the hot seat all the time.
- We can help others.
- We can practice in here and then do it in our "real life."

- We get lots of feedback.
- I don't feel like I am the only one with the problem.
- It is our group, not a class.
- We can feel accepted.

After everyone has taken a turn, the result is a web between all group members. Discuss how our choices and behaviors not only impact ourselves but also the group as a whole. Describe how each student can make positive and negative choices.

Next, lead a discussion about group cohesion, how each member has the potential to impact others in a positive way, and that when we are all respectful, we can form a tight-knit group.

Finally, ask several members to drop their end of the yarn, resulting in a weakened web. Assist group members in identifying what type of behaviors, comments, attitudes, and assumptions may weaken cohesion.

SIDEBAR 12.3
Writing Ending Activity

Group members can complete this letter prior to the last session to help them identify what has been helpful in group, what they learned, and what they will continue to practice.

Dear Future Group Member,

I am writing to tell you about how to get the most out of being in a group.

These are some of the things that we talked about and did in group that were most helpful for me:

Topic/activity   What I learned from it

_____

_____

_____

_____

I am different in how I feel. For example, I _____.
I am different in how I think. For example, I _____.
I am different in how I act. For example, I _____.
About myself, I learned _____.
About others, I learned _____.
About group, I learned _____.
The best way to get something out of group is to _____.
I wish I had done more of _____ and less of _____.

Good luck in group!

Sincerely,
A Fellow Group Member

Ending-stage sessions focus on helping group members summarize what they have learned, express their feelings about group and group members, and discuss how they will use what they have learned outside of group. For psychoeducational groups, a general guideline is to use one to two sessions for introduction, one to two sessions for termination, and one to two sessions for each goal to be addressed. For open, ongoing counseling groups, each time new members join, the session must focus on introductions; each time a group member leaves, the session must focus on ending.

GROUP SESSION STRUCTURE Structure within a group session is essential to provide safety and continuity, manage time efficiently, and focus on relevant issues. Psychoeducational groups are more structured with activities, whereas topics in counseling groups are determined by the needs of the group members in each session with occasional activities. It is recommended that psychoeducational group sessions typically include four parts. See Box 12.1 for a list of processing questions. The *opening* reviews material from a previous session, discusses homework efforts, and/or introduces topics. *Working* focuses on group goals to learn and/or on practicing skills. *Processing* focuses on making sense of activities and applying them to life outside of group. *Closing* activities help group members prepare to leave group and plan for future sessions.

BOX 12.1 Format of a Psychoeducational Group Session

Opening. Questions to open group include the following:

- What did you do this week with what you learned in the last session?
- Could we have a report on how you did with your homework assignments?
- What would you like to practice this week that you learned last week?

Processing and Ending. Processing questions help members reflect on an activity, discussion, or group session; learn about themselves and others; and transfer learning to their real lives. Guiding questions and sentence stems include the following:

- What I learned from group today. . . .
- You had some different feelings during this session. What did you learn about yourself from this?
- If you were to summarize the key themes we discussed today, what would they be?
- What was it like for you to be here today?
- One thing that I will take from group today is . . .
- One thing I need to practice outside of group is. . . .
- One new skill I will try out during the week is. . . .
- What is one thing you are willing to do outside of the group this week to move toward your goal?
- What are you willing to do with the tension (or any other feeling) you feel?
- What will help you to remember what you want to do differently?
- What can you do between now and the next session to practice what you've just learned?
- A homework assignment I'd like you to consider is. . . .

Helping group members to become a cohesive group and see the value in participating and learning from other members is essential. To emphasize instillation of hope, altruism, vicarious learning, and interpersonal learning, it is helpful to ask questions such as the following:

- What did you hear yourself or anyone else say that seemed especially significant to you?
- Who did you most connect with today and why?
- Who was most helpful to you today and why?
- Who did you learn the most from today, and what did you learn?
- Could we have everyone say what he or she is feeling right now?
- I like it when you. . . .

Questions that help emphasize the influence of the group and identify how they helped others in group include the following:

- How did we work together today as a group?
- What did someone say or do today that was most helpful for you? What did you learn from it?
- What did we do as a group to generate new ideas? Try a new behavior? Learn something?
- What did you do today to help you learn something new?
- What did you do differently today in group?
- What did you do today to help someone else learn something?
- Does anyone want to give anyone else any feedback?
- Are there any changes you'd like to make in the group?
- What is each of you willing to say about each other's work?
- How is the group going for you so far?

Counseling groups for adolescents have a similar structure: *opening* reflects on what was helpful from last session, changes attempted between sessions, and what group members would like to focus on; *working* focuses on group members working on goals; and *ending* focuses on what was helpful and how members will work on their goals. Some structure in early sessions is helpful, such as a short activity, to generate some insight into personal issues or introduce a framework to work on personal issues. Completing a brief checklist of strengths or reading a poem related to the group topic helps focus group members. Adolescents may take ownership by bringing a poem, song, activity, or inspirational quote to open group.

CREATIVE INTERVENTIONS   Dingle, Gleadhill, and Baker (2008) suggested that music helps adolescents with emotional expression. Bibliotherapy is strongly encouraged for adolescents, particularly stories, poems, and films, as well as phototherapy (sharing personal and family photos; Shechtman, 2014). Popular movies and TV shows can be useful. I often use the movie *The Breakfast Club* to talk about how each character acted out poor self-esteem differently and what they learned about themselves and others by being in that Saturday detention group. Typical discussions often focus on how each character felt alone despite very different family situations and groups of friends and how each experienced difficulty in different areas: sometimes personal, sometimes academic. See Chapter 9 for a detailed discussion of creative arts in groups.

Group Leader Preparation

Group leaders must prepare themselves personally and professionally for each group they lead.

PROFESSIONAL LEADER PREPARATION   ASGW provides three essential documents to review prior to leading a group. *Professional Standards for Training of Group Workers* (Wilson, Rapin, & Haley-Banez, 2000b) defines and suggests training for four group types. *Best Practices Guidelines* (Thomas & Pender, 2008) outlines best practice guidelines. *Multicultural and Social Justice Competence Principles for Group Workers* (Singh, Merchant, Skuryzk, & Ingene, 2012) suggests group leaders "understand the extent to which general group leadership skills and functions may be appropriate or inappropriate for group work facilitation with multicultural group members" (p. 4) and "model relationship skills essential for connecting with and creating connections between multicultural group members while planning, performing, and processing groups" (p. 5). Hage and Romano (2013) also provide best practices for prevention groups.

Once group type, goals, and population are decided, a review of the literature identifies effective theoretical approaches, interventions, activities, and special considerations. Many resources are available for adolescent groups (see Box 12.2). A literature search will identify current research on effectiveness, group protocols, individual group sessions, and specific activities.

SIDEBAR 12.4
Cultural Self-Awareness Exercise

1. Describe who you are in terms of age, race, any physical disability, sexual orientation, ethnicity and culture, family patterns, gender, socioeconomic status, and intellectual ability (educational background).
2. How do you see yourself as a unique individual based on your ethnic, cultural, and family background?
3. How does your background contribute to your view of how groups work?

4. What strengths do you bring to this group based on your cultural background and beliefs? What limitations do you bring?
5. How does who you are as described at the beginning of this exercise differ from your group members? How might those differences impact group process, trust, disclosure, and sharing?
6. How might your answers to question #3 differ from those of your group members? How will you reconcile these differences?

BOX 12.2 Resources for Groups for Adolescents

Resources for Planning and Leadership of Groups for Adolescents

Bauman and Steen DVDs (2011, 2012)	Bieling, McCabe, & Antony (2006)	Brigman & Goodman (2008)		
Carrell (2000)	Conyne (2014)	Davis (2007)	DeLucia-Waack (2006)	
DeLucia-Waack, Bridbord, Kleiner, & Nitza (2006)	DeLucia-Waack, Kalodner, & Riva (2014)	DeLucia-Waack, Segrist, & Horne, (2006)	DeMarco (2001)	Erford (2010)
Falco & Bauman (2014)	Fineran, Houltberg, Nitza, McCoy, & Roberts (2014)	Fitch & Marshall (2011)	Foss, Green, Wolfe-Stiltner, & DeLucia-Waack (2008)	
Guerra (2009)	Minardi (2008)	Salazar (2009)	Shechtman (2014)	Smead (1995)
Spargo & Blasko DVD (2017)	Springer & Moss (2017) www.blueprintsprograms.com			

Resources for Specific Types of Groups

Anxiety

Bieling et al. (2006)   Fitch & Marshall (2011)

Bullying Prevention

Committee for Children (2014)	Davis (2007)	Guerra (2009)	Horne, Nitza, Dobias, Joliff, & Raczynski, (2012)
Limber (2000)	Newman, Horne, & Bartolomucci (2000)	Raczynski & Horne (2014)	Swearer, Espelage, & Napolitano (2009)

Career Exploration/Decision Making

Bailey & Bradbury-Bailey (2010)	Burger & Sandy (2000)	DeLucia-Waack, Kalodner, et al. (2014)
Fitch & Marshall (2011)	Malott & Magnusom (2004)	Rowan-Kenyone, Swan, & Creager (2012)

Communication, Social, and Relationship Skills

Bieling et al. (2006)	Brigman & Goodman (2008)	Committee for Children (2014)
Delucia-Waack, Korta et al. (2014)	Guerra (2009)	Nestler & Goldbeck (2011)
Spoth et al. (2007)	Steen (2009)	Vernon (2012, 2013)

Cognitive Coping Skills

Bieling et al. (2006)	Committee for Children (2014)	Guerra (2009)
DeLucia-Waack, Athalye, Floyd, Howard, & Kuszczak (2011)	Smead (1990, 2000)	Vernon (2012, 2013)

(continued)

BOX 12.2   *(continued)*

Resources for Planning and Leadership of Groups for Adolescents

Depression/Suicide

Bieling et al. (2006)	Fitch & Marshall (2011)	Young, Mufson, & Schueler (2016)	

Diversity

Committee for Children (2014)	Fitch & Marshall (2011)	Salazar (2009)	Smead (2000)

Eating Disorders

Bieling et al. (2006)	Fitch & Marshall (2011)	Johnston, O'Gara, Koman, Baker, & Anderson (2015)	Kalodner et al. (2014)

Family Changes/Transitions

Brigman & Campbell (2008)	DeLucia-Waack (2011)	Fitch & Marshall (2011)	Smead (1990)

Grief

Brigman & Campbell (2008)	Smead (1990)

Managing Emotions

Brigman & Campbell (2008)	Committee for Children (2014)	Fitch & Marshall (2011)	
Guerra (2009)	Smead (2000)	Spoth et al. (2007)	Vernon (2012, 2013)

School Success

Brigman & Campbell (2008)	DeLucia-Waack et al. (2014)	Fitch & Marshall (2011)	
Steen (2009)	Smead (1990, 2000)		

Sexual Orientation/Gender Identity

Fitch & Marshall (2011)	Horne et al. (2014)

Stress Management

Brigman & Campbell (2008)	Committee for Children (2014)	Guerra (2009)
Fitch & Marshall (2011)	Smead (1990)	Vernon (2012, 2013)

Substance Abuse Prevention/Treatment

Bieling et al. (2006)	Bhat, Pillay, & Selvaraj (2015)	Committee for Children (2014)
Fitch & Marshall (2011)	Spoth et al. (2007)	

Violence Prevention

Center for the Study and Prevention of Violence (2012)	Committee for Children (2014)	Smead (1990)

From the first group session, every discussion should be directed toward group goals and norms. If time is spent on a topic not related to group or group members do not understand how it relates to group goals even once, then a precedent has been set that it is okay to get off track; it is then much harder to keep group members on topic later. One common mistake is selecting an activity because it is fun or because group members will like it (not that fun and humor are not key pieces of creating cohesion and community in adolescent groups). Instead, fun activities should have a clear relationship to the tasks at hand. For example, Glass's (2008) "Group Juggling" encourages levity, humor, and laughter and asks group members to identify how they work effectively together. Crowell's (2008) "Out with the Trash" uses humor to help group members vent about their issues/problems.

The choice of an activity should be based on its *intensity* (Jones & Robinson, 2000), defined as "the extent to which the group topic, structured exercises, and group techniques do the following: (a) evoke anxiety among group participants, (b) challenge group participants to self-disclose, (c) increase awareness, (d) focus on feelings, (e) concentrate on the here-and-now, and (f) focus on threatening issues" (p. 358). For adolescents, it is important that they have an emotional connection to the discussion and understand how it applies to their "real" lives.

PERSONAL GROUP LEADER PREPARATION   Group leaders must prepare for each group through assessment of leadership skills and identification of areas of strengths and improvement. In addition, group leaders must reflect on the type of group and their assumptions about group participants related to individual characteristics, potential biases related to group members or problem areas, expected behaviors, how problems or situations occur and/or impact group members, and how group might benefit the group members.

Coleadership

The benefits of coleadership include providing role models for appropriate interactions for resolving disagreements, cooperating, working together, decision making, compromising, and giving and receiving feedback. Also, two leaders can jointly observe the content and process of the group. Male–female coleadership for adolescent groups is preferred to model collaboration between, and provide contact with, supportive and caring adults of both sexes. Malekoff (2004) stressed the importance of coleaders in adolescent groups having a strong partnership and being able to communicate effectively in group; otherwise, they risk recreating dysfunctional family dynamics and evoking confusion, fear, and anger among group members.

Screening and Selection of Group Members

As noted in Chapter 3, effective screening and selection of group members are essential to the continuation and success of groups. If adolescents are not selected and prepared carefully, they may drop out and/or sabotage the group (DeLucia-Waack, 2006). Screening interviews help *group members and leaders* decide if this group is a good fit. Voluntary participation is critical for adolescents (Geroski & Kraus, 2010), so it is helpful to ask directly whether they are willing to participate, share, and try out new behaviors. Two measures have been shown to be effective in highlighting potential misperceptions that can be addressed prior to entering the group: the group counseling

---

SIDEBAR 12.5

Personal and Coleader Planning Before Group

- What are my strengths as a group leader?
- In what areas do I need to improve?
- Why do I believe groups are effective? What do I see as my role in making them effective? What drawbacks or hesitancies about group do I have? How will I deal with them before and during group?
- What are my beliefs about the nature of the problem, the symptoms, the possible causes, the interventions, and how a group can best help these group members?
- How can I see my group members as individuals and not just problems or symptoms?

- How will I draw out their strengths and make connections among them? Support and encourage them when they are doing things I view as unhelpful? Or they are attacking me?
- What interventions do I think work best for this type of group? What does the literature say? How comfortable am I in leading those interventions?
- How comfortable am I with confrontation? Blocking? Cutting off? Redirecting? Being attacked? Silence? Being ignored?

Failures in Group Work (Conyne, 1999) and *Critical Incidents in Group Counseling* (Tyson, Perusse, & Whitledge, 2004) provide specific situations that may occur in group as a stimulus for reflection and discussion with your coleader.

---

survey (Sodano, Guyker, Amos, & DeLucia-Waack, 2017) and the group readiness questionnaire (Burlingame et al., 2012).

It is recommended to choose adolescents with similar problems and focal areas to create cohesion and accelerate interactions (Conyne, 2014). Select group members with similar cognitive styles and emotional development—usually within one grade, two at most (Falco & Bauman, 2014). A wider range of group members may be necessary when there are fewer eligible students, such as those who are experiencing grief or who have type 1 diabetes. To avoid having a group member be scapegoated or isolated as different, a balance of diversity is ideal (e.g., different cultures, races/ethnicities, sexual orientations, genders). If an adolescent is a good candidate for a group but would be the only one of a particular status, it is helpful to discuss it with that person before the first group meeting and to focus on commonalities with others.

In school settings, it is helpful to inquire about relationships to avoid putting best friends together (possible unhealthy alliance) and avoid bringing past negative interactions into group. Group members may still be able to be in group together if they agree to work with others when working in pairs and that if disagreements come up in group, they will be resolved in group. Siblings should not be in the same group due to the impossibility of validating the multiple realities of siblings and the near impossibility of maintaining confidentiality. In addition, I intentionally ask myself with whom (and how) each group member would initially connect. For whom could they be a role model? I want to link adolescents and note commonalities in the first session, even if they are as simple as "You both have a cat." I also want to instill hope by noting someone who can help them and create altruism by identifying someone they can help (Malekoff, 2004). Adolescents often report that they will come to group "when they don't need to" because they know that the group and/or a specific person is counting on them.

GROUP LEADER PERFORMING

Performing (Thomas & Pender, 2008) focuses on group leadership skills, provision of effective interventions, and assessment of effectiveness.

Group Leadership Skills

As described in Chapter 3, effective leaders are "positive, supportive, provide sufficient structure, attend to developing group cohesion, allow group members to take ownership of their group, and provide a meaningful context for what occurs in the group" (Riva, Wachtel, & Lasky, 2004, p. 35). The framework identified by Lieberman, Yalom, and Miles (1973) is useful to conceptualize effective group leadership behaviors: caring, emotional stimulation, meaning attribution, and executive functioning. See DeLucia-Waack (2006) for a more detailed discussion of the four categories, group stage, and specific leadership behaviors.

CARING   Caring interventions help group members feel cared about and accepted so that they can make the most of their group experience. Warmth, empathy, support, positive regard, acceptance, genuineness, and concern can be displayed *by both group leaders and members.* In addition, active listening, reflecting thoughts and feelings, summarizing, and clarifying are helpful. It is important to note this does not mean that members should never be challenged but that they should be challenged with constructive feedback. It is also important to note the definition of caring from Lieberman et al. (1973) includes leader protection.

EMOTIONAL STIMULATION   A moderate level of emotional stimulation helps group members make a personal connection to what is happening in the group, identify and explore feelings, and connect feelings to behaviors.

MEANING ATTRIBUTION   Meaning attribution helps members make meaning of what happens during the group experience, learn from it, and apply this learning to their lives. *Processing* involves "capitalizing on significant happenings in the here-and-now interactions of the group to help members reflect on the meaning of their experience, better understand their own thoughts and feelings and actions, and generalize what is learned to their life outside of the group" (Stockton, Morran, & Nitza, 2000, p. 345).

One of the most common mistakes group leaders make is not processing activities or events sufficiently. Sufficient time for processing must be allotted; sometimes it takes as long to process an activity as to perform the activity itself. Due to adolescents sometimes resisting "homework" and/or being told to do something, it is helpful to invite them to try out something new (rather than assign or require) and ask each member to set her or his own goal. It also helps to explain the purpose of any activity or homework so that adolescents understand how it will benefit them. It is hard to say no to something that clearly will help you.

EXECUTIVE FUNCTIONS   Executive functions create structure and promote safety. Group leaders should provide more structure in the initial and termination stage; less structure is needed in middle sessions as adolescents take more responsibility for the group.

GROUP INTERVENTIONS

The theoretical orientation of a group determines its goals, emphasis, foci, interventions, and leadership style.

Cognitive Behavioral Groups

Cognitive behavioral therapy (CBT) interventions have been shown to be moderately to very effective in adolescent groups (Hoag & Burlingame, 1997; Laser & Nicotera, 2011; Prout & Prout, 1998). Key elements of CBT groups are education, skill development (e.g., problem solving, decision making, communication, assertiveness, managing stress, identification and disputing of irrational beliefs, asking for help, and identification/expressing feelings), and role-playing.

Mindfulness

Mindful group interventions have also been shown to be effective with adolescents (Tan & Martin, 2014; Windle, Newsome, Waldo, & Adams, 2014), with goals of increased emotional awareness, self-regulation, and enhanced relationships.

Dialectical Behavior Therapy

Dialectical behavior therapy (DBT) groups have also been shown to be helpful with adolescents (Laser & Nicotera, 2011; Windle et al., 2014). DBT was developed to complement cognitive behavioral interventions when group members feel invalidated or misunderstood when changing maladaptive thoughts and behaviors; DBT emphasizes acceptance and validation of pain and encourages acceptance of self. DBT consists of mindfulness, emotional regulation—recognizing that primary emotions are adaptive and understandable responses to stressors and secondary emotions (shame, rage, misery) are judgements about one's experience and more often the source of distress—interpersonal effectiveness (social skills training), and distress tolerance. Mindfulness has been noted by group members as the most helpful and most practiced emphasis in DBT (Windle et al., 2014).

Specific Types of Groups

What follows are suggestions for best practices for adolescent groups based on current literature and research. See Box 12.2 for specific references. Supervised practice is highly recommended when working with new groups and interventions (Thomas & Pender, 2008).

CAREER EXPLORATION   Structured career exploration groups have shown efficacy (Dagley & Calhoun, 2014). Career exploration groups for females that foster gender equity in STEM (Rowan-Kenyone, 2012) and career groups for African-American boys (Bailey & Bradbury-Bailey, 2010) has shown efficacy. Dagley and Calhoun (2014) identified critical ingredients of career groups: affective, behavioral, and cognitive components; occupational information; written activities (e.g., an autobiography of work experiences; a family vocational genogram) to begin self-exploration and disclosure in group; individualized test interpretations; discussion of case studies and career dilemmas (Santos, 2004); and observation of role models. Incorporating fictional characters as positive and negative models is a creative way to engage adolescents (e.g., characters from the TV show *The Office*).

COMMUNICATION AND SOCIAL SKILLS   CBT has been shown to be moderately effective for adolescents in general and highly effective for those at risk (Brigman & Campbell, 2003; Falco & Bauman, 2014; Gerrity & DeLucia-Waack, 2007; Steen, 2009). Specific skills include social skills, empathy development, assertiveness, interpersonal problem-solving skills, communication, and listening skills.

EATING DISORDERS   Effectiveness has been shown for CBT psychoeducational and counseling groups (Kalodner, Coughlin, & Seide, 2014) and DBT counseling groups (Johnston et al., 2015; Keel, Mitchell, Davis, & Crow, 2002). Psychoeducational groups may include peer-group critiques of media messages about body image (Laser & Nicotera, 2011), peer-helper programs (Valente & Pumpuang, 2007), and mindfulness and CBT interventions. Groups help to reduce shame and isolation and focus on self-understanding, vicarious learning, universality, and instillation of hope.

Sometimes group members may compete with each other about the best ways to continue their eating disorders (e.g., how little they have eaten, how to throw up, how to burn the most calories, how long they exercised). Such conversations must be stopped quickly and processed: Why are we having this conversation? What is it like to hear someone else telling you how little they ate? How is this helpful to you changing your behavior (e.g., finding other ways to manage stress or hang out with your friends)? It sounds like we're having a competition about who can tell the most extreme story. Why would we be doing that?

EMPATHIZING WITH OTHERS (BULLYING PREVENTION AND INTERVENTION)   Bullying prevention is essential, with 30 percent to 40 percent of students in the United States reporting being bullied (Due, Holstein, & Soc, 2008). Raczynski and Horne (2014) noted verbal and relational bullying as the most common and advocated prevention over intervention, with psychoeducational groups to disseminate info and develop skills. They also noted, less optimistically but realistically, that these interventions are less useful for adolescents than for younger children, and the efficacy of group counseling alone is limited, suggesting the need for multiple interventions, including with parents and teachers. Horne et al. (2012) delineated a model in which high school students serve as peer-group leaders of psychoeducational groups for freshmen, focusing on life skills and skill building and resulting in connectedness and altruism among those who would not normally be connected.

Counseling groups are useful for both bullies and victims of bullying but never in the same group. Peer conflict is not the same as bullying, and though peer conflict might be mediated face-to-face, bullying should not be due to the power differential. Leaders must have a keen awareness of etiology and characteristics of bullying (Raczynski & Horne, 2014); be very active in helping group members identify goals, commit to group, and engage in self-awareness and change (Shechtman, 2014); be authoritative and asser-tive (e.g., total openness to caring but zero tolerance of acceptance of continuation of behaviors); and focus on growth of group members as opposed to "straightening kids out" (Raczynski & Horne, 2014). Raczynski and Horne also cautioned that putting "bullies" all in one group sometimes may reinforce aggressive behaviors; it may be best to include students with prosocial behaviors in the group.

DEPRESSION/SUICIDE   CBT groups (Rohde, Stice, Shaw, & Gau, 2015), DBT groups (Miller, Wyman, & Huppert, Glassman, & Rathus, 2000), mindfulness groups (Broderick, & Metz, 2009; Burke, 2010; Raes, Griffith, Van der Gucht, & Williams, 2014), and interpersonal psychotherapy (Young, et al., 2016) have all been shown to be effective with adolescents. A culturally adapted group CBT has been found to decrease depression in Latinx youth (Bernard & Rossello, 2008) and depressed youth in Nigeria (Bella-Awusah, Ani, Ajuwon, & Omigbodun, 2015).

FAMILY SHIFTS/TRANSITIONS/ISSUES   CBT groups have been shown to be effective (DeLucia-Waack, 2011; DeLucia-Waack & Gellman, 2007; Falco & Bauman, 2014) for teaching skills: expressing feelings, problem solving, thinking positively, managing emotions, and coping with current and future situations. Irrational beliefs, particularly about divorce or other family situations, have been shown to be mediators of depression (e.g., "I caused the divorce; my parents will reunite"), so cognitive interventions are particularly useful. Trust is an issue for adolescents with family shifts/disruptions, so Malekoff (2004) recommends structure, predictability, flexible handling, clarity, and consistency. Tronsden and Tjori (2014) reported that an online support group for adolescents with a mentally ill parent provided universality, normalization, cohesion, and vicarious learning.

GRIEF   Grief groups support adolescents who have lost someone important, whether a family member, friend, or pet (Falco & Bauman, 2014). LeGrand's (2006) *Kid's Grief Kit* and the *Grief Box* (Malekoff, 2004) are helpful to process grief. Malekoff suggested that younger adolescents benefit from structured group activities to identify and fully express feelings, whereas older adolescents may be able to process more intense emotions in an unstructured environment.

MANAGING EMOTIONS (ANGER MANAGEMENT)   Group interventions are more effective than individual counseling (Gerrity & DeLucia-Waack, 2007; Shechtman, 2004; Shechtman & Ifaragran, 2009). Stories, poems, and films are particularly useful for aggressive adolescents who may be reluctant to examine their own behaviors (Shechtman, 2004) from a distance. One suggested activity is for group members to identify and create a lifelong time line for a literary or historical figure, then create a parallel time line for themselves, reflecting on what is happening in each at specific times and how they handled events, particularly adversity. This activity is useful with students of color to help them discuss the impact of racism, prejudice, and discrimination on their lives and perhaps suggest alternative ways of thinking and behaving. For White students, it may provide valuable insight into their "White privilege" when they choose a person socially or culturally different from them and examine their significant milestones and events. Burt (2015) also suggested using Brazilian martial arts in culturally diverse adolescent groups aimed at anger management.

SCHOOL SUCCESS   CBT groups to teach study skills (e.g., organization, time management, note taking, study strategies, transition, anxiety reduction) are effective for middle and high school students (Brigman & Campbell, 2003; Falco & Bauman, 2014; Steen, 2009). When students transition to a new school, it is helpful for them to be in a group initially to increase feelings of hope and success, rather than waiting until they are struggling.

SEXUAL ORIENTATION/GENDER IDENTITY   Groups for gay, lesbian, bisexual, transgender, queer, and questioning (GLBTQQ) adolescents are helpful (Horne, Levitt, Reeves, & Wheeler, 2014). Adolescents who are questioning their sexual orientation and/or gender identity are at heightened risk for depression, suicide, and substance abuse (Laser & Nicotera, 2011) as well as rejection by family members, homelessness, and HIV-positive status (Horne et al., 2014). Counseling groups can combat isolation, provide acceptance and hope, and provide opportunities to observe and learn from other members' skills and strategies. Psychoeducational groups include peer support or gay–straight alliance groups focused on support and increasing visibility and safety within schools (www.glsen.org; Horne et al., 2014). Mixed-gender groups for adolescents highlight the universal concerns of the GLBTQQ experience and increase needed support networks. Horne et al. (2014) also noted that it is more difficult for persons of color to disclose sexual or gender identity due to multiple sources of oppression; thus, group leaders may acknowledge this to give members permission to discuss concerns and share experiences.

STUDENTS WITH DISABILITIES   CBT group interventions are most helpful (Ellis, Simpson, Rose, & Plotner, 2014), including modeling and practice of social skills (Stephens, Jain, & Kim, 2010), cognitive restructuring, and relaxation. Groups should focus on identity development (acceptance of the disability and debunking of self-stigma), autonomy, and compliance with health-related interventions. Cohesion, instillation of hope, and imparting of information are important therapeutic factors for groups. DBT also may be useful with some adolescents with disabilities (Sakdalan, Shaw, & Collier, 2010). Ellis et al. (2014) recommended that group leaders focus on the person (not the disability), view disability as a cultural dimension, accommodate and destigmatize, then cultivate belongingness and modify for level of ability. Bonete, Calero, and Fernandez-Parra (2015) identified three interventions as particularly helpful: increasing positive behaviors in social situations, cognitive restructuring for social skills, and improving interpersonal (cognitive) problem-solving skills.

SUBSTANCE ABUSE   For adolescents, I prefer the term *substance misuse* because much of their behavior is associated with risk taking and experimentation (Laser, Leibowitz, & Nicotera, 2011). Psychoeducational groups focused on managing emotions, communication and relationship skills, as well as stress and anxiety management, are helpful. CBT groups have been shown to be effective; newer culturally adapted CBT groups have also been shown to be effective with Hispanic adolescents (Burrows-Sanchez, Minami, & Hops, 2015). Mindfulness interventions have been shown to decrease willingness to smoke and increase emotional self-control (Butzer, LoRusso, Shin, & Khalsa, 2016).

It is important for group leaders to note that, for some, being a member of a drug subculture may be their place of acceptance/social connection, so helping group members feel connected may help change their peer-support system. I like using the *Board of Directors* activity (Jacobs, 2006) to help adolescents reflect on who supports them and their messages. Adolescents are usually good at identifying who is a negative influence and take joy in symbolically "firing" them. As with eating disorders, group members may brag about their usage and share ways to use. Such conversations must be stopped quickly and processed.

GROUP LEADER PROCESSING OF GROUPS

Processing (Thomas & Pender, 2008) focuses on assessment of effectiveness and ongoing supervision. "Processing group work is much more complicated . . . because of all of the potential topics and interactions . . . case conceptualizations of both individual and group goals and the current stage of the group, assessment of interventions on individual group members and the group as a whole, and transference and countertransference" (DeLucia-Waack & Kalodner, 2005, p. 77).

Evaluation

Is the group effective in meeting the intended goals? What makes the group effective for each group member and the group as a whole? Continual assessment is needed to tailor groups specifically to the needs of group members. See Sodano et al. (2014) for a comprehensive review of group process and outcome measures.

PROCESS MEASURES   It is useful to assess group process often—sometimes each session—to clarify if and how group is helpful. The *Critical Incident Questionnaire* (Kivlighan & Goldfine, 1991, p. 152) asks group members to respond in writing to the following: "Of the events which occurred in this group session today, which one do you feel was the most important to/for you personally? Describe the event: what actually took place, the group members involved, and their reactions. Why was this important to you? What did you learn from this event?" I routinely end group sessions similarly by asking these questions: What was helpful today? Why? What have you learned? How did you learn it? Who said or did something that was helpful to you? Such questions clarify what group members learned, identify learning styles, and create cohesion, altruism, and belongingness.

The *Short Group Climate Questionnaire* (MacKenzie, 1993) can be completed by group leaders and members. It is helpful to compare leader and group member perceptions and to look for outliers among the group members. Those group members who view the group as more conflictual, less engaged, and more avoidant may need to be engaged and connected quickly.

OUTCOME MEASURES   Smead (1990, 2000) includes multiple pre- and post-tests. Other measures that are useful include the following: Revised children's anxiety manifest scale (Reynolds & Richmond, 1985), Children's depression inventory (Kovacs, 1992), Resiliency scales for children and adolescents (Prince-Embury, 2006), Children's acceptance and mindfulness measure (Greco, Smith, & Baer, 2011), Response styles questionnaire (Davis & Nolan-Hoeksema, 2000), Reynolds' Bully victimization scales (Reynolds, 2004), Perfectionism (www.bb.co.uk/science.humanbody.mind/surveys/), Perceived stress scale (Cohen, Kamarck, & Mermelstein, 1983; http://www.mindgarden.com/products/pss.htm), Brief COPE (coping styles; Carver, 1997; http://www.psy.miami.edu/faculty/ccarver/sciBrCOPE.html), Inventory of Interpersonal

Problems-circumplex-item response theory (Sodano & Tracy, 2011), and the Outcome questionnaire-45 (Wells, Burlingame, Lampert, Hoag, & Hope, 1996).

Supervision

"Self-knowledge has been identified as critical to effective group leadership and focuses on the continual evaluation of the group leader's impact on the individual group members and the group as a whole" (DeLucia-Waack & Kalodner, 2005, pp. 76–77). Without supervision, group leaders may not identify mistakes or generate new plans of action; instead, they become stuck in a cycle of repeated, ineffective interventions. Two recent books are particularly helpful: *Group Work Experts Share Their Favorite Supervision Activities* (Volumes 1 and 2; Luke & Goodrich, 2015a, 2015b). Group leaders must continually discuss the content and process of their groups and their reactions with their coleader, a supervisor, or in supervision groups.

For a list of additional factors to consider when leading groups with adolescents, see Box 12.3.

BOX 12.3 Special Considerations for Leading Groups with Adolescents

What follows are suggestions for best practices in leading groups for adolescents:

1. Humor and a playful spirit are essential (Malekoff, 2004); see humor and/or absurdity in a situation and do not take yourself too seriously. Adolescents are critical of adults in general, watching for when they make a mistake. Do not fall into the trap of replicating the negativity the adolescents may experience with other adults; teens love to tease and criticize but appreciate the modeling of how to take it in stride.

2. Think of adolescents as a different cultural group. Help them to help you understand their unique identity and perspective within the backdrop of being an adolescent.

3. Do not assume the parent role.

4. If you are a younger group leader, it is important not to identify too much with them, want to be their friend, or gain their approval.

5. They do not want to hear your stories of adolescence. Malekoff (2004) recommends accessing your feelings and experiences to better understand, but do not share them.

6. Address diversity as a normative adolescent issue; help group members tune into ethnically and racially charged events affecting youth; confront prejudice, stereotyping, and oppression consistently; model effective cross-cultural communication and cultural self-awareness; promote understanding and respect for different worldviews; and tune in to the differential experiences of group members (Malekoff, 2004).

7. Assume a stance of uncertainty (Malekoff, 2004) to help them develop a relationship with you that goes beyond the group leader as the expert. Find your balance between tolerance and overcontrol.

8. Co-create a real relationship with them that is different than with teachers by asking them to call you by your first name in group and/or allowing certain language or topics of discussion not typically condoned. Because of the value of autonomy and being heard, group members should determine the content of the group related to group goals. To help adolescents determine what is important, I will sometimes ask "Can we have this conversation with the door open? How will this conversation help you to change? If not, what can we talk about that would be helpful to you?" Provide structure to alleviate the anxiety of talking about their issues and trying out new ways of thinking and behaving, but allow them freedom in determining the situations they need help with.

(continued)

BOX 12.3 *(continued)*

9. Invite the whole person to participate (Malekoff, 2004), not just the troubled, broken, or hurt parts.
10. Balance information, activities, and skill development with group-member interaction and group process (Conyne, 2014). Adolescents need to learn skills, but it is best to teach them when they bring it up. These are the teachable moments that group members will learn the most from when emotional stimulation results in meaning attribution.
11. Risk taking and experimentation are typical for adolescents, so it is important not to overdiagnose or overreact. However, listen carefully as group members discuss their experiences. Peers may often express concern for others before the individual in question does. Such concern and/or feedback from other group members is valuable. Also note that risk taking is a way to combat stress (Laser & Nicotera, 2011), so it may be useful to explore when and why these behaviors are occurring.
12. Adolescents feel their emotions intensely, so emotional regulation and self-regulation are important to teach and practice.
13. Reframe resistance as reluctance. Adolescents, like the rest of us, are unsure about change, trying out new behaviors, and taking risks. They may also not have the necessary skills to be different. Begin with teaching skills; then, if they can perform the skill in group but don't apply it in their lives outside of group, ask why. Encourage members with support, ask if they want help from others, who would they like help from, would they like to see someone role-play for them, and so on. If reluctance results in limited participation, use structure to help all participate easily, with check-ins at the beginning and end of each session. During activities, I will ask for feedback and comments. Once I have heard from a few people, I will ask "Anyone else want to comment?" If an adolescent has been silent for more than 15 minutes, looks like she or he is reacting in group, or appears disconnected, I will invite her or him to respond. All such comments are made with kindness and caring, with the intent to encourage participation.

Summary

"Am I ever gonna fit in?" and "Am I ever gonna be good at something?" are two major issues that adolescents struggle with (Malekoff, 2004). Groups have been shown to be effective and the treatment of choice. CBT interventions are particularly useful, including skill development in problem solving, decision making, communication, assertiveness, empathy, self-regulation of emotions, and identification and expression of feelings. Psychoeducational and counseling groups are useful, depending on the goals of the group and the needs of the group members.

13 Groups with Individuals, Couples, and Families in Mental Health Settings

Cynthia A. Briggs, Linda H. Foster, and Martina Moore

Group work in mental health settings includes work with couples and families, as well as individuals focused on family and developmental life-span issues—for example, intimate partner violence, parenting, and divorce. Some of the first to benefit from multiple-family groups were families with a member diagnosed with schizophrenia (Lurie & Harold, 1967). Although family therapy is, in essence, group work, multiple-family groups have come to be regarded as a viable form of group counseling (Schafer, 2008; Thorngren & Kleist, 2002). These groups tackle a variety of issues, such as parenting, substance-abusing teens, family enrichment, and adjustment after divorce. Couples groups are valuable and are an effective way to focus on a host of partner and family issues. They often focus on relationship enrichment, marital discord, divorce adjustment, and parenting in blended families.

The desirability of group counseling has increased because groups are less expensive and thus offer greater access to counseling. Some couples, for example, may be better able to pay $40 for a couples psychoeducation group than $125 for a couples therapy session. Considering the limited resources of clients, the last several decades have witnessed a movement toward implementing "evidence-based" mental health practices with the notion that these are more effective and cost-controlling (Barrett & Greene, 2004; Geddes, Reynolds, Streiner, & Szatmari, 1997). For example, the Centers for Disease Control and Prevention (CDC) website lists a series of "best-evidence" group-level interventions (2007). By lowering the costs involved in counseling, greater access is created and can help clients make the choice to commit to the work of counseling. Without counseling, there can be significant costs; for example, consider the cost of successful counseling compared to the financial, psychological, health, and social costs of dealing with a litigious divorce. Group counseling for couples and families is valuable because it can alter the life course of vital relationships that are stuck in long-term unhealthy patterns.

Group therapist Irvin Yalom offered these words:

> The kinds of issues that we deal with are issues that people are struggling with for 10 or 20 years and change happens slowly. *Psychotherapy* is a form of education and education is not something that can be crammed into a course. I think the idea that you have to do therapy in some mechanistic way following some sort of manual is exactly the opposite of what you actually want to do—which is to form an authentic relationship, let the relationship unfold, and as the patient begins to develop trust in this relationship, change will occur simultaneously to that. There are certain things that can't be rushed. (Duffrene, 2004, p. 9)

This chapter offers a foundational introduction to the vast scope of groups as they are applied to couples, families, and individuals with family-focused concerns. We present examples of three groups: (1) women's groups composed of members working on issues such as depression, anxiety, post-traumatic stress disorder, and other mental health issues, (2) couples-oriented groups for building healthy relationships, and (3) groups for women and their families dealing with bulimia nervosa (BN).

GROUPS FOR WOMEN IN CRISIS

A group of women sat waiting for the first session of group counseling to begin.

Angie looked at her fingers guiltily. Despite her best efforts, she had bitten down to the quick of her exposed and raw nail beds. She did feel good, though, about keeping her appointment for what she called the "class to help me with my nerves."

Across the waiting room, Susan leaned against a wall, restless and fidgeting nervously. Thoughts raced through her mind as she wondered, "How has life come to this?"

As Kat hunched in a chair near the exit, she was fearful that people would notice her bruised face. She was completely covered with clothing so that only her face and her hands were exposed. Kat did not want to interact with anyone for fear they would learn her secret.

Tricia sat in a corner chair wracked with guilt, believing she was failing her struggling family. "This is a waste of time and money," she thought while considering her family needs. Yet she lacked the energy to move. She felt exhausted all the time.

Keely sat in a corner opposite Tricia with reddened eyes, trying to hold back her tears. She cried easily and too often. Life overwhelmed her. She no longer felt connected to friends and family. Although her involvement in her church had been substantial and important to her, more recently she felt isolated and detached from everyone and everything.

Each of these women enters counseling sharing a feeling of instability resulting from many reasons, including social, economic, political, or cultural conditions. Women in crisis enter group counseling with a variety of lived experiences and backgrounds and share unique counseling concerns ranging from anxiety and depression to stress and grief. Issues impacting women's mental health include intimate partner violence, post-traumatic stress disorder, substance abuse, and family life cycle issues such as pregnancy, parenting, and elder care. The World Health Organization (WHO, 2017) provides insight into the mental health issues experienced by women. Specific gender risk factors that disproportionately impact women include gender-based violence, low income and income inequality, lower social status, and primary responsibility as caregivers for others. Overwhelmingly, women are affected to a greater extent than men with symptoms of depression, anxiety, psychological distress, sexual violence, and substance abuse. In addition, the WHO states that the increase in mental health issues for women is directly correlated with the increased pressure of societal and cultural factors impacting women. The common thread connecting these women is the social, cultural, and political aspects of their life experiences, including oppression stemming from racism, sexism, and classism. This connection creates a unique opportunity to utilize group counseling to create

---

SIDEBAR 13.1
Self-Awareness: Gender Differences in Mental Health

Did you know that gender roles impact mental health? Did you know that societal and economic factors also are determinants of a woman's mental health? Have you considered that violence against women increases vulnerability to depression? For women, the commonality of these factors creates a propensity toward significant mental health concerns. The impact of societal, cultural, environmental, and legal factors creates inequality for women, resulting in higher rates of depression, anxiety, intimate partner violence, PTSD, and other mental health issues. Distress for women creates a unique opportunity for counselors to create group counseling as a safe environment for exploring and resolving some of these stressors. As future counselors, please consider how you can create a safe environment for group counseling so that women in distress will make connections, share experiences, and discover new ways of relating to the outside world.

---

a safe environment to share experiences so that these women in crisis can discover new ways of relating to the outside world. Through group counseling, connections are made, insight is gained, and healing begins.

Conceptual Framework

Group counseling is one of several treatment options available for women in crisis. Using group counseling for women in crisis is a viable option because of its efficiency and effectiveness, but more important is the sense of belonging and commonality that group counseling provides. Group counseling also offers a safe environment for sharing experiences and results in women feeling supported and validated (McLeod, Hays, & Chang, 2010). Women reported they gained confidence, giving them a voice to speak out freely and find acceptance (Molina, Lawrence, Azhar-Miller, & Rivera, 2009). Group counseling also offers a safe environment for sharing experiences, giving and receiving feedback, and learning new ways of behaving and coping (Jacobs, Schimmel, Masson, & Harvill, 2016).

Mental health agencies promote group counseling as a way of working through issues such as depression, anxiety, post-traumatic stress disorder, and other mental health issues impacting women (National Institute of Mental Health [NIMH], 2016). Women communicate, deal with stress, react to therapy, and have ways of being and knowing that differ from the ways of men. Consequently, women in crisis describe the value of realizing other women also have similar experiences; this helps them feel more visible, connected, and congruent (Phillips and Daniluk, 2004). Women may be able to speak more freely without the mixed-gender group dynamics that can perpetuate entrenched and oppressive behaviors (Ivey, Pedersen, & Ivey, 2001). In short, common bonds lend support to healing and learning.

Clinicians who work with women in crisis should be well informed about women's issues, especially as these relate to clients' culture, family, and profession. Statistics on women's mental health issues indicate that women are particularly vulnerable to depression and anxiety and nonthreatening suicidal behavior (Mental Health America [MHA], 2017; National Alliance on Mental Illness [NAMI], 2008a; NIMH, 2016; WHO, 2017). Worldwide estimates of physical and/or sexual intimate partner violence or sexual violence to women range from 35 percent to 70 percent over a woman's lifetime

(UN Women, 2016). Life cycle issues also impact women: one in eight women will experience postpartum depression (CDC, 2016; NAMI, 2008b). The WHO (2017) estimates that 1 in 12 women will develop alcohol dependence over their lives. The statistics for women who have been affected by these issues is staggering.

A safe, supportive environment is essential for group members to process experiences and to develop effective coping strategies (Yalom, 2005). Moreover, Yalom suggests that the group process enhances the transfer of new behavior to real life by providing a microcosm for becoming and transforming oneself. Clients' issues differ because of their varying backgrounds and can be a source of strength, but commonalities, too, may be explored in group. *Mutuality* is one word used to describe the shared experiences that provide the impetus for women in crisis to relate to, empathize with, and understand each other (Fearday & Cape, 2004). Further, this connection creates the safe environment needed to begin healing and long-term change.

Purpose of the Group

Group counseling for women in crisis requires a master treatment plan outlining specific goals, objectives, and measurable outcome criteria. Groups can be designed to help clients

- reduce negative symptoms and live successfully;
- cope with specific symptoms related to anxiety, depression, PTSD, and other symptoms impacting their daily lives;
- identify and develop support systems and processes;
- make behavioral, cognitive, and emotional adjustments that decrease the intensity of symptoms; and
- feel supported by healthy communication among people who share common but also unique lived experiences.

Finally, the group creates a therapeutic opportunity in the form of a supportive environment for sharing concerns, information, support, and behavioral interventions.

Group Goals

Goals for dealing with trauma, stress, depression, and anxiety revolve around symptom prevention, management, and improvement. The following goals can be met by providing psychoeducation and supportive learning experiences within the context of a group:

1. *Self-monitoring:* Clients can learn to self-monitor signs and symptoms of trauma, stress, depression, and anxiety and can learn and reinforce new ways of behaving.
2. *Decreasing negative thinking:* Critical to the process is to replace catastrophic and nonproductive thinking and emotions with positive and realistic thoughts.
3. *Self-care:* Clients learn and practice relaxation techniques, anxiety-reduction practices, how to recognize oppressive environments, and how to manage stress.
4. *Support:* Through the group process, these women get a chance to be heard in a way that might not have occurred in their lives and within their social environments promoting trust.
5. *Emotional catharsis:* In the group, clients can express deep and complex emotions in a safe environment.

6. *Normalization:* Hearing stories of trauma, stress, depression, and anxiety from others has a normalizing and leveling effect. Group members begin to see that they are not alone and that many others are dealing with similar issues.
7. *Communication:* The group offers an opportunity for clients to practice positive and assertive communication, helping clients to have their needs met and goals achieved.

Pregroup Screening and Orientation

Although clients at first may appear to have the same diagnosis and presenting symptoms, many confounding variables and cultural influences can impact the group process and cohesion. Clinicians screen clients to discover what is not apparent in case paperwork. The evaluation and screening of clients for possible inclusion in the group should be systematic. This is particularly relevant when the group is time limited and topic specific.

Screening for women's groups has important implications for treatment planning, selecting interventions, and evaluation. For example, an important clinical issue that often surfaces in a prescreening interview is a client's earlier traumatic experience, such as physical or sexual abuse. This is especially relevant when dealing with women in therapeutic settings because symptoms such as depression and anxiety often develop in the aftermath of abusive and other traumatic experiences (NAMI, 2008a).

Screening for a group of this nature should evaluate the client's willingness to engage in self-discovery, trust building, and ability to share with others. Participants should demonstrate a commitment to the process and agree to respect the confidentiality of group members. Clients must be functional enough to participate as active members who are willing to support, communicate, and cooperate with group members to meet goals of the group.

Although diagnostic, behavioral, and therapeutic issues occur on a continuum, these issues should not impede the clients' ability to establish a connection with one another. Depending on the quantity and complexity of the group goals, individual screenings should evaluate historical, medical, social/cultural, and individual goals and readiness for the group. The screening should include an orientation to the group process, therapeutic expectations, commitments, and risks and benefits of participation. Group membership varies, but generally a group composite should total between five and eight members. Sessions should last 90 to 120 minutes and be held weekly for 8 to 12 weeks to allow for development, growth, and synthesis of new information and behaviors.

Potential Challenges, Barriers, and Other Considerations

Women who are in treatment for depression and anxiety, intimate partner violence, or even family life cycle concerns may be reluctant to seek group counseling for fear of escalation of symptoms, continued victimization, or societal stigma. The group process can be stressful for some, with the associated potential for dysfunctional behavior. Group leaders should have systems in place to reduce these challenges for women in crisis.

BARRIERS TO PARTICIPATING IN GROUP COUNSELING Group leaders should be mindful of the barriers that can restrict successful group participation, including the client's ability to be financially, emotionally, and physically present for the group. Scheduling conflicts

SIDEBAR 13.2
Self-Awareness: Barriers to Success

There are barriers to creating successful group counseling for women in distress because of societal, cultural, economic, environmental, and legal parameters. Two other important barriers could be related to being emotionally and physical present. As a future group leader, it will be important to consider how you will address some of these barriers to successful groups when working with women in distress. First and foremost, how will you work to ensure that your group members can be present physically for group sessions? Next, and certainly important as well, is the emotional aspect: What steps can you take to ensure your group members can be emotionally or psychologically present in each session? As you think about other barriers, such as societal or cultural ones, what steps can you take to help eliminate any possible stigma attached to counseling? Environmental and legal impediments should also be considered as you try to eliminate barriers that prevent women in distress from seeking group-counseling experiences.

with work, family responsibilities, and transportation can be significant barriers impeding active and consistent participation. There may also be social and psychological barriers for some women (Fearday & Cape, 2004). Leaders can assist clients in addressing these issues and scheduling group sessions to accommodate members whenever possible.

CONSIDERATIONS FOR A SUCCESSFUL GROUP EXPERIENCE   Along with the expected best practices of screening group members, providing informed consent, and orientation to the group experience, group leaders should consider the unique needs of women. Women's cultural and lived experiences may require a safe environment in which they can feel supported, connected, and empowered to begin the healing process through group work. Through connections with other women, members learn new ways of coping, relating to the outside world, and, most important, increasing their self-worth.

Group Sessions by Stages

Group counseling consists of stages as any group evolves. Group topics for women can range from depression and anxiety to trauma and PTSD to parenting and family life cycle issues. However, the stages for the group process remain constant. The usual progression follows the definitive, personal involvement, group involvement, and enhancement and closure stages of group work proposed by Capuzzi and Gross in Chapter 2.

DEFINITIVE STAGE   In the beginning stage of group therapy, members often have questions about what is going to happen in the group and how they will fit in. This is the stage when the "getting to know you" dynamics take place and the parameters of the process are outlined. Establishing basic and solid trust, clarifying, and engaging with self and others is essential at this early stage. Members begin to accept their responsibility in the group process, and self-awareness begins to emerge. Members start to lose the sense of loneliness and isolation that often accompanies depression and anxiety. This is the stage in which group members discuss and agree upon the goals of the group.

This stage is particularly challenging due to the ambiguity and mistrust that may exist for women in crisis. Establishing clear guidelines and distributing informational packets can ease the anxiety of these clients when they are exposed to new and often threatening situations. Group counselors should be particularly mindful that these women may be experiencing enormous stress and vulnerability in entering a group-counseling process and that these symptoms may intensify. The leader may also want to allow for follow-up phone calls and contacts because the client's ability to fully participate may be impeded.

PERSONAL INVOLVEMENT STAGE   At the personal involvement stage, group processes are mobilized at a more in-depth level. The initial trust and sharing become richer as the group members get to know one another in a way they may not have experienced before in their lives. Women in particular need a safe environment to share experiences so that they can discover new ways of relating to the outside world. The group begins to model and provide feedback, and the direction moves away from the leader, who assumes more of a facilitative role. During the stage of sharing of common experiences, women can begin to see the powerful impact on their lives. Through connections with other women, insight is gained and healing begins (Fearday & Cape, 2004).

GROUP INVOLVEMENT STAGE   Once alliance and trust have been established and the group members feel valued and heard, they begin to mobilize resources and look toward solutions. They become unstuck as they engage and learn from one another. The group members pull each other forward. They, along with the leader, examine the patterns of behavior and dysfunction that impede healthy living. They challenge one another in respectful ways.

This stage is uncomfortable for some but not too threatening in a safe and supportive environment. Family, cultural, career, and social systems are explored in regard to their influence on a condition and its symptoms. The group members also examine these factors in terms of the support they can bring to bear. They address grief, loss, hope, and the reality and conditions of their lives.

ENHANCEMENT AND CLOSURE STAGE   During the enhancement and closure stage, group members ready themselves for saying good-bye. Bargaining to continue the group is an issue that frequently emerges during the latter stages of group work. In preparing for termination, the group and the therapist deal with issues of closure, continuance of support, referral, and development of other resources. The group manages the anxiety that often is present when the group nears its end. Moreover, termination is an issue that does not begin in the late stages of therapy. Prepared therapists deal with these issues early on, instituting them in the screening process by disclosing the risks and expectations of the group process.

Relationships end, but the leader's modeling of healthy termination and closure strategies can have a lifelong impact on members' functioning, setting boundaries, and engaging in healthy relationships. It is essential for the leader to assist members in fostering healthy connections, developing resources, and gaining support practices that will give them balance and avoid additional stress.

Strategies to Evaluate the Group

The evaluation is determined by the nature and goals of the group. Depression and anxiety groups in an outpatient setting are diagnosis specific, well defined, time limited, short term, and goal focused. Evaluation of the group should include issues such as clients' satisfaction, the minimizing of dysfunctional symptomology, and the learning of positive behaviors and coping strategies. This information can be gathered in several ways: from clinical data indicating therapeutic improvement, clinician and client surveys, self-reports, and pre- and post-treatment questionnaires and evaluations. These measures yield information about the integration of client gains in lifestyle.

Follow-Up and Referral

Because women have unique issues and deal with life in complex ways, prevention and ongoing support related to their issues and concerns must be woven into termination plans. Therapists must have a working knowledge of community issues, and wise group leaders will cultivate women's resources and community contacts and referrals to help clients deal with the pressures of society specifically as these pressures relate to gender. Access to resources is critical to clients' sustained recovery.

In addition, the therapist must understand the individual needs of clients from social, cultural, and familial perspectives. No two women are the same, though some overlying issues have an impact on all women. Women who have been in a period of instability will experience the complexities of life in varying ways and should be supported as they move toward wellness.

Medical and wellness referrals should be part of the follow-up because women have a biological and physical propensity for recurring bouts of depression. Support groups and possible career development and education are other possible components to be woven into the referral process.

It is useful for group leaders to incorporate follow-up timetables with clients in planning long-term strategies for their wellness. In addition, the group counselor should examine with these women cyclical trends and issues such as employment, reproduction, menopausal issues, and care of elderly family members.

HEALTHY RELATIONSHIPS GROUPS

As with individual counseling, couples often seek professional help when problems occur rather than when circumstances are favorable. At some point—maybe after the hundredth verbal battle or another day living under the same roof without talking or some indefinable barrier stifling intimacy—couples look to counseling for solutions. Group counselors work under the assumption that couples can learn to cultivate healthier relationships. In this section, we provide a model for relationship-enhancement groups for couples.

Conceptual Framework

A desired outcome of group participation is increased intimacy and relational satisfaction. Participation is expected to increase couples' awareness of the essential components of the relationship and to increase the skill base that is vital to maintaining healthy relationships. Allowing couples to share and connect with other couples in a group-work format provides unique opportunities that may not be found in couples' therapy with just the one couple present. This format allows clients to see the work that it takes to make any relationship work, not just their own. The aim is to improve the quality of this primary relationship with the idea that it is the quality, rather than quantity, of

---

SIDEBAR 13.3

Conceptual Framework: Benefits of Couples in Group Counseling

---

The framework of group counseling for couples is an excellent resource to provide couples with access to other couples much like themselves who may be experiencing problems with intimacy, communication, trust, and other issues. The group process allows for role modeling to take place from one couple to another. The microcosm of group counseling for couples can provide a framework that teaches couples how to improve their relationship by watching and hearing from other couples. The group process also provides the opportunity for couples to see that their problems are common with many others and can be improved. What are some of the advantages of group couples counseling that you would describe to couples who may be considering couples counseling? What types of relational issues do you believe would be appropriate for group couples counseling? Which relational issues, if any, would not be appropriate, and why?

---

relationships that matters most, and to encourage well-being and satisfaction (Schofield et al., 2015). Our model is intended to enhance the quality of relationships by examining adaptive processes and, to a lesser extent, life events and social/cultural influences.

Many relational problems are environmental and arise because the client's past or current social environment has lacked opportunities for creating close, supportive, and healthy relationships. The environment affects the systems that support healthy relationships. For example, poverty and the lack of associated community resources that are vital to mental health (e.g., other families, churches, community agencies) often affect couples and families negatively (Browning, 2002; Dodge, Pettit, & Bates, 1994; McLeod & Shanahan, 1993).

Relationship groups have been carried out under a wide range of theoretical modalities and have been shown to improve relationships. In a literature review of research on relationship-enrichment-education groups, Fagan, Patterson, and Rector (2002) asserted that relationship education produces significant outcomes. The following factors are emphasized by this group model:

- Self-regulation
- Awareness of intimacy and other vital relationship components
- Conflict resolution
- Problem solving
- Improving communication skills
- Increasing positive-to-negative ratios of interaction
- Engaging in pleasant activities
- Exploring family context through genograms

FIRST- AND SECOND-ORDER CHANGE   *First-order change* occurs when a specific problem is settled (e.g., making up after a specific verbal confrontation), but it does little to change the cycles of thought and behavior that led to the problem. *Second-order change* occurs when the system changes the way it operates (Fraser & Solovey, 2007). For example, the fighting couple adopts and integrates a new way to communicate. Two second-order change goals for this group are self-regulation and intimacy.

SELF-REGULATION   Even when working on skill development, the goal is to produce second-order change, and conducting a relationship-enrichment group within a framework of self-regulation may produce the most lasting results (Halford, Wilson, Lizzio, & Moore, 2002). For example, teaching self-regulation along with communication techniques can help participants learn to self-regulate around issues of communication in the future. *Self-regulation* is a self-directed process of guiding behaviors, cognitions, and emotions toward goal attainment (Knapp, Norton, & Sandberg, 2015). Through self-regulation, members are helped to learn independently so that they are better able to personally manage problems in the future.

Halford, Sanders, and Behrens (1994) proposed that self-regulation of a relationship has four phases:

1. Self-appraisal
2. Self-directed goal setting
3. Self-implementation of change
4. Self-evaluation

As with the therapeutic alliance, goals play a vital part in self-regulation. Effective goal setting requires that people set a long-term goal; break it into short-term, attainable subgoals; monitor progress and assess capabilities; adjust the strategy and goal as needed; and set a new goal when the present one is attained (Schunk, 2001).

INTIMACY   Another important concept emphasized in this type of group is intimacy, a multidimensional aspect of relationship. Enhancing intimacy in romantic and platonic relationships has a positive effect on physical and mental well-being and on overall satisfaction with the relationship (Mehta, Walls, Scherer, Feldman, & Shrier, 2016). Various components of intimacy have been discussed in the research literature (Dorian & Cordova, 2004; Hatfield & Rapson, 1993; Hook, Gerstein, Detterich, & Gridley, 2003), including the following:

• Closeness
• Ability to self-disclose without punishment
• Connectedness
• Self-validation and other validation
• Physical affection
• Bonding

Individuals experience intimacy differently. Further, some studies suggest gender differences in the way intimacy is experienced (Mehta et al., 2016). The group outlined in Sidebar 13.4 builds on strengths found in different experiences of intimacy and allows participants to assess, explore, share, and learn from others.

With many relationships, fighting and distressful behaviors are the impetus for involvement in counseling because discord and distress have many negative consequences. Research by Gottman and Levenson (2000) suggested that the presence of negative reciprocity and negative affect during conflict correlates with early divorce.

TIME-OUTS AND REPAIR ATTEMPTS   Time-outs and repair attempts are used in teaching, personalizing, and having members practice how to disrupt negative interaction. Even though *time-outs* are best known as a behavioral technique used with children, adults can learn to stop unwanted behavior by self-imposing a break, self-soothing, and returning with an attitude conducive to teamwork. This technique should be used in a highly structured manner and is best when developed by participants for personal fit.

SIDEBAR 13.4

Intimacy: Addressing Sexual Issues in Counseling

Many couples entering counseling define the presenting problem as lack of intimacy. What is often discovered in counseling is that intimacy for one person in the relationship looks different from what the other person has described. It is important in couples counseling to help the couple define individually what intimacy means to each person and how they prefer to express intimacy.

This can begin the path to addressing many other issues, such as communication, trust, and security.

Imagine you are working with a couple, and the husband has mentioned several times that his wife refuses to please him sexually. The wife insists that no matter what she does in the bedroom, he is not pleased. Take a moment and think about how you would feel about addressing intimate details about a couple's sexual encounters on a deeper level. Does this make you uncomfortable? Where do you feel the line should be drawn when discussing these topics in counseling?

---

1. *Repair Attempts:* (Gottman, 1999; Taberas, Driver, & Gottman, 2004) are communication efforts to stop negative reciprocity by emphasizing teamwork, compromise, and personal responsibility in the middle of an argument. For example, one partner may attempt repair by saying "I see that I'm responsible for some of the problem" or "We've worked through problems like this before, so let's start over and tackle this together." As a resource, Gottman (1999) created a repair checklist that is useful for a group exercise.

COMMUNICATION AND PROBLEM SOLVING   Couples intuitively believe that communication and problem solving are central to a good relationship (Boerner, Jopp, Carr, Sosinsky, & Kim, 2014). In accord with these intuitions, research suggests that effective communication is a marker of a healthy relationship (Gottman, 1994; Weiss & Heyman, 1997). Yelsma and Marrow (2003) studied emotional expressiveness in couples and discovered that if either spouse had problems communicating his or her emotions, then both spouses experienced impaired marital satisfaction. Lavner, Karney, and Bradbury (2016) found that decreasing negative communication and increasing positive communication were associated with decreased risk of marital distress. Communication exercises teach active listening and dialogue that emphasizes reflection, empathy, warmth, and other skills, including summarization and concreteness.

Problem solving is most effective when the communication is constructive rather than defense provoking (Whiting & Cravens, 2016). Effective problem solving occurs in the presence of hearing and understanding, teamwork, brainstorming, opening possibilities, and collaboration.

ACCENTUATING THE POSITIVE   Even though decreasing negative affect and reciprocity is one change agent, many counselor interventions focus on the negative aspects of relationships (Rugel, 1997) at the expense of more strength-based interventions. Increasing positive affect outside of conflictual contexts is just as important as stopping harmful behaviors in making lasting changes for partners (Gottman, 1999; Driver & Gottman, 2004).

Assessing and implementing strategies for positive connection is part of the group process. Learning and acting on ways people feel loved and engaging partners in planning pleasant activities are two fundamental ways to achieve this. For example, one woman took this principle to heart and had a favorite meal delivered to her husband during his lunch break. It was the talk of his crew, and he felt special—which resulted in some associated and unexpected shifts in the counseling group. For other couples, just committing to time together is enough to set up and boost connections. Shifting the emphasis from problems to positive interactions and intimate encounters fosters revitalized relationships and educates participants on the importance of proactive relationship building (Whisman & Li, 2015).

Group Goals

The goals of this couples group are

- to practice and integrate communications skills, including reflective listening and empathy;
- to learn more about the building blocks of relationships, the reality of relationships, and intimacy as an ongoing process requiring effort;
- to practice setting aside time weekly for pleasant and rewarding activities;
- to increase self-confidence and efficacy in relationships; and
- to practice and integrate useful skills, such as time-outs and problem-solving techniques.

Pregroup Screening and Orientation to the Group

During the orientation with participants prior to group participation, issues of professional disclosure, confidentiality, expectations, client rights and responsibilities, counselor responsibilities, and agency concerns related to the group are discussed (Association for Specialists in Group Work [ASGW], 2007). These issues from the initial orientation are repeated at the first session of the group.

A relationship-enrichment group is designed for adults of diverse backgrounds, skills, and abilities. Referrals might come from an agency that is already providing counseling services to couples. In these cases, the group leader should obtain a release of information and contact these service providers to make sure that group participation is in the clients' best interests. The costs to the couple in time and money to participate in both group and couples counseling should be considered.

If domestic violence is a concern, the group leader should consider deselection and referral. The prescreening should probe for legal issues involved in a couple's efforts to find counseling because couples group work may be effective only after counseling and group work dealing specifically with domestic violence has been seriously engaged. Also, the group leader should consider deselection and referral for couples who have moderate to severe problems related to substance disorders if concurrent treatment is not in progress.

Couples groups can range from 10 to 20 participants. Groups of this size will be effective so long as assistants are added as needed to help with break-off groups and activities.

Possible Challenges, Limitations, and Ethical Considerations

A basic challenge of the group leader is to promote an idea of *relationship* that addresses the needs and realities of all group members so that they can relate to the various lived experiences within the group. This may require the consistent use of reframing.

This educational component validates the many differences in the range of possible relationships.

Therapeutic leverage and participants' motivation may be additional considerations in a larger group, in which less time is spent on an individual and dyad level. One study (Simons & Harris, 1997) elicited some of the reasons that 640 respondents chose not to attend premarital education:

- Marital privacy
- Lack of interest
- Lack of relationship problems
- No need for counseling
- Did not want to discuss personal issues

These same items may be present as challenges in the couples group.

In a psychoeducational couples group, the level of personal and intimate sharing is monitored for levels of self-disclosure because the size and context of the group may not be as supportive as therapeutic groups are. Sometimes this creates an environment in which couples can remain on the surface of current problems. Also, the larger groups may not afford as much attention to couples and individuals as smaller groups or couples therapy could. The amount of time given to this group (8 to 10 weeks) is only a booster to the longer process of relationship enrichment.

Breakups sometimes occur during the course of the group, and this challenges the individuals who are breaking up to be brave and the group to be supportive of these members whether they choose to stay or to leave. In a breakup situation, the group leader should consider the ramifications of both partners' staying. The leader would be wise, going into the group, to have a clearly stated policy related to relationship endings.

In addition, in an effort to maintain a confidential space, group participants should be asked not to get together outside of the group and discuss the group but, instead, to wait until after the last session. The leader must inform members about the limitations of confidentiality in groups and especially must note that a counselor cannot enforce confidential communication by group members.

Group Sessions by Stages

The sample course of a couples group is presented here. The progression follows the definitive, personal involvement, group involvement, and enhancement and closure stages of group work proposed by Capuzzi and Gross in Chapter 2.

DEFINITIVE STAGE   The purpose of the definitive stage is to make introductions and set the ground rules for the group, including a review of clients' rights and responsibilities. The leader discusses safe sharing, which may take the form of icebreakers related to healthy relationships. The leader presents an overview of some of the most important information so that group members can set goals jointly with the group leader.

During this stage, the leader encourages participants' sharing what they believe are the qualities and components of a healthy relationship. The leader comments on societal myths about relationships (e.g., heterosexual marriage is the most important type of relationship, or happy relationships are always exciting).

PERSONAL INVOLVEMENT STAGE   The purpose of the personal involvement stage is to begin the assessment of current relationships and start to formulate goals. It also is important to expand and reframe the meanings of *relationship*, discuss barriers to relationships, and enhance member rapport through sharing. This is the time to begin creating personalized homework.

A primary goal at this stage is to expand the notion and meaning of *relationship*, to create leverage for personal motivation. Highlights might include the following:

1. *Reframing a relationship as teamwork* is essential, to redirect the propensity of individuals to point to their partners as the source of relationship problems.
2. *Phases of a relationship* must be understood so that participants know there are ebbs and flows and what to expect and gain from different phases of intimacy.
3. The leader can *expand the meaning of relationship* to encompass spiritual, physical, emotional, relational, and other aspects of one's self.
4. Emphasizing that *little things count* in a relationship helps create space for incorporating strategies to meet newly forming goals.
5. *Personal responsibility* is highlighted, followed by a discussion of how individuals may look with magical eyes at relationships to solve personal problems, to fill a sense of emptiness, to provide care that one should give to oneself, to obtain a sense of self-worth, or to gain external validation.
6. The importance of *self-regulation* is discussed as an important learning tool. This includes self-appraisal, self-directed goal setting, self-implementation of change, and self-evaluation (Halford et al., 1994).

GROUP INVOLVEMENT STAGE   The purpose of the group involvement stage is to teach, over several sessions, the concept of self-efficacy in relationships. The group involvement stage also should continue to build on skills and enhance participants' motivation and understanding through involvement. This should advance a supportive effect.

At the beginning of each group, the group leader facilitates a discussion of the successes and roadblocks to integrating the material and skills learned in the group, introduces new skill-building techniques, and reviews those techniques covered previously. The leader incorporates assessment tools and examines personal strategies and their implementation. As participants practice the time-outs, repair attempts, communication exercises, and other self-created enrichment techniques, the leader provides a framework for different ways to evaluate their attempts to improve relationship.

ENHANCEMENT AND CLOSURE STAGE   The purpose of the enhancement and closure stage is to provide an overview and initiate closure by emphasizing the important gains the group has made and real steps that the participants have made in improving their relationships. The leader builds in time to discuss other resources and future possibilities for continued work in the realm of relationships.

During this stage, participants evaluate the usefulness of techniques and goals they have implemented over the duration of the group. Their individual sharing about what they have gotten out of the group is followed by eliciting some of their ideas for postgroup growth and continued pursuit of relationship enrichment. Finally, a sharing of sentiments for and about the group precedes the leader awarding a certificate of accomplishment to each participant for completing this group.

Strategies to Evaluate the Group

Self-evaluation is a component of this type of group. A simple evaluation measure can be handed out for members to gauge their changes in relationships. Each week, group participants fill out a brief relationship-satisfaction questionnaire. The participants keep track of their scores, and the group leader retains the scores of all members as a basis for discussion about their findings toward the end of group.

Follow-Up and Referral

The group leader may want to encourage couples to take a further step toward healthy relationships by enrolling in a therapeutic group for couples. The leader may see a need to refer others to individual and couples counseling. The group leader can present options for continual growth by providing a variety of resources, including books for continued study and practice on issues covered in the group.

SPECIALIZED GROUPS FOR YOUNG WOMEN WITH BULIMIA NERVOSA

Overall, 10 percent of young women meet the criteria for an eating disorder, including the following diagnoses: bulimia nervosa (BN), anorexia nervosa (AN), binge-eating disorder (BED), and eating disorder not otherwise specified (EDNOS). A typical age of onset is 20 years. Eating disorders are further complicated by chronicity and high rates of relapse, along with other mental health impairment, including depression, anxiety, suicidality, and substance abuse (Stice, Marti, & Rohde, 2013).

AN is often perceived as the most severe of the eating disorder categories, due to clients' dramatic weight loss and physical transformation and because of the risk of death as a direct result of the diagnosis. However, according to Choate (2010), "BN is considered one of the leading causes of psychological impairment among women" (p. 1). Young women with BN are more likely to attempt suicide than other eating-disordered clients (standardized mortality ratios of 6.5 for BN, 4.7 for AN, and 3.9 for EDNOS; Stice et al., 2013). BN often begins in adolescence and persists over the lifespan, a chronic condition with high rates of relapse. Lifetime prevalence is found in 1 percent to 3 percent of women, but subthreshold diagnoses (those that don't exactly meet *Diagnostic and Statistical Manual of Mental Disorders (DSM-V)* criteria) are higher and can be just as debilitating (Choate, 2010). The *DSM-5* includes the following diagnostic criteria for BN:

1. Recurring episodes of binge eating.
2. Recurring inappropriate compensatory behaviors (such as self-induced vomiting, misuse of laxatives, fasting, or excessive exercise) to prevent weight gain.
3. Binge eating and inappropriate compensatory behaviors both occur, on average, at least once per week for 3 months.
4. Self-evaluation is unduly influenced by body shape and weight.
5. The disturbance does not occur exclusively during episodes of AN (American Psychiatric Association, 2013).

Although the prevalence of AN and BED appears consistent across cultural groups in the United States (Latinx, Asian-Americans, African-Americans, and non-Latinx Whites), BN appears more prevalent among Latinx and African-Americans than non-Latinx Whites (Marques et al., 2011). Because the overall long-term mortality rate for

SIDEBAR 13.5
Self-Reflection: Perceptions of Eating Disorders

Like addictions, eating disorders are often hidden from view and create feelings of shame and guilt for clients. Because these disorders are relatively rare and are often kept secret, many counselors have little personal experience with them. Thus, biases, misperceptions, and confusion may exist. Take a moment to self-reflect on what you understand about eating disorders. What perceptions do you carry about women who struggle with BN? Is this an area of group counseling you feel interested in, curious about, or anxious about? What steps can you take to raise your expertise and clinical awareness of this population?

women with BN sits at 10 percent (Sonnenberg & Chen, 2003) and BN treatment has a 50 percent failure rate (Wnuk, Greenberg, & Dolhanty, 2015), group counselors must increase their knowledge of culturally sensitive, effective treatment options.

Research literature fails to provide a clear picture of what kind of therapy is most helpful to young women struggling with BN. Group counseling is a popular option; however, there is a dearth of research literature demonstrating greater effectiveness than individual counseling (Downey, 2014). Regardless, group counseling is preferred for several reasons (Gerlinghoff, Gross, & Backmund, 2003; Lenihan & Sanders, 1984):

- In this age of managed care, long-term inpatient treatment for eating disorders has been shortened by as much as 85 percent (Wiseman, Sunday, Klapper, Klein, & Halmi, 2002). Long the preferred treatment modality, inpatient care is no longer a financially viable option for many clients with BN.
- The demand for resources addressing treatment for BN is high, and group treatment is one way to meet the needs of many clients at once without taxing clinical resources excessively (McKisack & Waller, 1997).
- Feminist theorists assert that BN results from a relational disconnect, and group therapy is an effective means for women to reconnect with one another in an authentic way (Tantillo, 2000).

In addition to group counseling for clients with BN, inclusion of family interventions is recommended. Although research demonstrates that family systems are not the cause of BN, the family process can maintain the eating disorder once it is established. When a member of a family develops an eating disorder, the whole family may be affected. Feelings of powerlessness and shame develop, and conflicts arise as the family attempts to manage the disordered eating. Social activities and bonding around food (such as family dinners) may become stressful, may decrease, or may cease altogether. The eating disorder may become the central organizing principle of the family (Downs & Blow, 2013). Family-based therapy (FBT) is an intensive outpatient treatment model that relies on the family as the primary support for renourishment during clients' recovery, and including it in a comprehensive treatment plan increases treatment efficacy over the long term (Couturier, Kimber, & Szatmari, 2013). Ahead, we present a conceptual framework for treating young women with BN, incorporating culturally sensitive group counseling with FBT.

Conceptual Framework

Group treatment for clients with BN has been approached from nearly every possible theoretical framework, including psychoanalytic, supportive, feminist, cognitive behavioral, and eclectic. Traditionally, it was assumed that treatment had to be long term and intensive to maximize positive results. Although longer-term treatment has been tied to higher success rates for women with BN (Matthias, 2005), time-limited treatment is more clinically and financially viable. Cognitive behavioral group therapy (CBGT) is the most researched modality for treating BN and currently is the treatment of choice in both the United States (Lundgren, Danoff-Burg, & Anderson, 2004; McKisack & Waller, 1997) and abroad (Murphy, Russell, & Waller, 2005). CBGT treatment is relatively short term—averaging 14 weeks and meeting approximately 2.5 hours per week.

In contrast, feminist theorists assert that the use of CBGT, a separation-individuation approach, may not be the most effective treatment for women with BN. Feminist theorists perceive the presence of BN to be a result of broader societal norms, including individuation, competition, and autonomy over community and intimacy (Black, 2003). In addition, eating disorders tend to evolve in affluent Western cultures in which beauty and thinness are perceived as commodities and status symbols. Thus, a refusal to eat may be the ultimate symbol of rebellion from cultural control (Russell-Mayhew, Stewart, & MacKenzie, 2008), and therefore counselors who focus solely on eating behaviors and not on the larger cultural constructs in which the disorder evolved will not assist clients in creating lasting change. Feminist counselors focus on relationship building and collective empowerment within the group setting. In this way, clients can heal their perceived disconnect from others (Tantillo, 2000) and reclaim their role in community. The goal is to create a curative culture rather than merely to reduce the symptoms of BN (Black, 2003).

An eclectic approach incorporates elements of both CBGT and feminist-theory techniques. Preliminary studies have determined that combining psychodynamic factors (including building rapport and working alliance) with CBGT techniques is as effective as CBGT alone (Murphy et al., 2005). This supports the feminist notion that relatedness and connection are indeed important to women recovering from BN.

Group Goals

The initial goal is to reduce symptoms and thereby improve physical and mental health. Because much of BN and the binge/purge cycle exists in secrecy, participants can use the group to increase accountability for their behaviors. More broadly, participants can use the group experience to enhance authenticity, reconnect with their feelings, and learn self-care (Tantillo, 2000). Once symptoms are reduced, group members will deconstruct negative and reconstruct positive perceptions of self in context as they raise awareness of cultural influences on their eating behaviors and self-perceptions (Weber, Davis, & McPhie, 2006). Finally, personal and collective empowerment can be achieved by assisting women in identifying ways they might themselves advocate on behalf of others suffering from voluntary or involuntary starvation (Russell-Mayhew et al., 2008). Over the course of treatment, clients will learn the following skills (Tantillo, 2000; Weber et al., 2006; Wiseman et al., 2002):

- Building awareness of patterns of food consumption
- Identifying interpersonal patterns
- Fostering intimacy
- Increasing self-awareness
- Evaluating strengths and maladaptive behaviors

- Problem solving
- Assertiveness
- Reworking cognitive distortions
- Identifying cultural influences on disordered eating
- Mapping effects of BN on all areas of life

Pregroup Screening and Orientation to the Group

Each prospective group member must meet individually with the group leader prior to beginning treatment—perhaps for one or more additional sessions if warranted (Lenihan & Sanders, 1984). These pregroup sessions are necessary for several reasons:

- The group leader should determine whether the prospective client will benefit from treatment and will not hinder the treatment of others.
- The prospective group member may have a concurrent diagnosis (e.g., personality disorder, addiction, suicidality) that requires more intense immediate care.
- Motivation for change can be assessed, and additional individual sessions can be used to build and enhance motivation if the potential member is in the precontemplation or contemplation stage of change (Gerlinghoff et al., 2003).
- Prospective members can be acclimated to group norms, including confidentiality, commitment to attendance, and commitment to personal change (Lenihan & Sanders, 1984).

Possible Challenges, Limitations, and Ethical Considerations

Despite the clear benefits that can result from group treatment for women with BN, it is important to keep the following caveats in mind:

- Clients with BN are more likely to drop out of group treatment than individual treatment (Chen et al., 2003). In general, clients with eating disorders have created an interpersonal culture of silence, avoidance, and secrecy and, as a result, struggle to achieve intimacy in the group setting. Women from minority cultures or who have immigrated to the United States are less likely to seek or complete treatment for BN (Franko, 2007).
- The overall failure rate for BN treatment is about 50 percent (Wnuk et al., 2015).
- Clients with concurrent diagnoses, especially personality disorders, may be disruptive to the group process, may require more intensive treatment, or may drop out of treatment prematurely. All of these effects can be minimized by thorough pregroup screening, assessment, and referral.

Group Sessions by Stages

The progression of group counseling for young women with BN follows the definitive, personal involvement, group involvement, and enhancement and closure stages of group work proposed by Capuzzi and Gross in Chapter 2.

DEFINITIVE STAGE   This initial stage in the BN treatment group involves establishing and maintaining task focus and group cohesion (Tantillo, 2000). The group leader facilitates this process by validating the group members' strengths and abilities, modeling empathy, positively reinforcing risk taking, and encouraging open dialogue among group members (Tantillo, 2000). Lenihan and Sanders (1984) also emphasize the importance of appropriate confrontation and direct communication with clients early on. Empathy alone may generate disrespect from group members.

The primary activity during this stage is for each member to establish a food diary, in which they are to monitor their intake and relationship with food throughout each day (Lenihan & Sanders, 1984; Tantillo, 2000). The diary will be a group tool throughout treatment. As a note of caution, group leaders should not overemphasize food as the primary focus of conversation. Group members will benefit more from a balanced discussion, including relational issues.

PERSONAL INVOLVEMENT STAGE   During this stage, group members begin to evaluate their own internal processes in relation both to food and to other group members. A primary goal of this stage is to stabilize self-concept (Gerlinghoff et al., 2003). This is accomplished as the participants experience and process the inevitable disconnect they will feel from other group members and the group leader. Throughout this process, members are encouraged to practice self-empathy rather than resorting to internal shaming (Tantillo, 2000).

The group leader and group members practice providing feedback to one another regarding observed relational patterns (Tantillo, 2000). The emphasis is on accuracy in expression of emotions and acknowledgement of personal responsibility. Clients also are given time to openly acknowledge their accomplishments to the group. Additional skill development might include relaxation and assertiveness training (Lenihan & Sanders, 1984).

GROUP INVOLVEMENT STAGE   Central to this stage is the extension of personal skills into the group process (Gerlinghoff et al., 2003). Now that a safe and validating environment has been established, the group members are more ready to examine interpersonal differences, to address the tension that might exist between leader and group-member expectations, and to attend to perception differences between members (Tantillo, 2000).

At this point, clients are encouraged to compare their interactions within the group with their familial, peer, and professional relationships and note similarities in maladjusted patterns (Tantillo, 2000). As intimacy grows, leaders might consider engaging group members in creative therapies, such as art, music, or dance therapy (Gerlinghoff et al., 2003). Furthermore, family patterns of behavior may be analyzed by creating a genogram (Lenihan & Sanders, 1984). In addition to self-examination, clients begin examining self in context, coming to understand how cultural norms and attitudes around gender identity, beauty, and sexuality may have contributed to disordered-eating behaviors (Russell-Mayhew et al., 2008).

ENHANCEMENT AND CLOSURE STAGE   The focus of this final stage is on reviewing personal accomplishments, celebrating achievements, and processing the impending loss of the group. The group has become a laboratory for exploring the disconnect/connect cycle of relationships, and detachment from the group can be a powerful learning tool for group members (Tantillo, 2000). The group members review their food diaries, noting progress and change in their binge/purge behaviors and in their relationship to food as a whole.

Collectively, group members can consolidate what they've learned about societal and cultural norms related to body image and disordered eating. Counselors may want to encourage clients to determine concrete ways of incorporating social justice and advocacy efforts into future plans. As clients learn that *everything is connected to everything*, they become empowered to act as agents for change in their own lives and in the lives of others (Russell-Mayhew et al., 2008).

Family-Based Therapy

Although the family unit is not the cause of BN, the family can offer support during the healing process. Eliciting family support in the recovery process rather than "blaming" the family for the disease can result in increased family engagement and counseling efficacy (Downs & Blow, 2013). FBT is an intensive outpatient-treatment model that relies on the family as the primary support for renourishment during clients' recovery. It typically takes place over a 9- to 12-month period and involves a counselor and physician working as a team. Research studies demonstrate that significant differences were found in 6- to 12-month follow-ups, indicating that FBT has better long-term efficacy than individual therapy alone (Couturier et al., 2013).

FBT involves three main tasks: (1) eliciting family involvement, (2) analyzing family systems, and (3) establishing interventions. These tasks occur over three phases. In the first phase, the family is empowered to address the eating disorder with the client, helping her realize the severity of the problem. Anxiety is intentionally raised during this phase to promote action. In the second phase, the counselor observes a typical family meal. In this phase, the parents/caregivers are "in charge" of the client's eating. In the third phase, as the client develops healthier eating patterns, control over eating is transferred back to the client, along with skill development for continued positive eating patterns (Downs & Blow, 2013). In addition to these interventions, FBT might include psychoeducational components such as lectures, manuals, posters, group activities, and professional coaching in an online community (Bai, Wang, Yang, & Niu, 2015).

Strategies to Evaluate the Group

Studies have found that mean post-treatment binge abstinence rates range from 50 percent to 70 percent, and purge abstinence rates average 35 percent to 50 percent. Overall, reduction in binging ranges from 70 percent to 94 percent, and reduction in purging

---

SIDEBAR 13.6

Case Study: Who Is the Client?

When working with families, shame and guilt often emerge. These emotions can manifest as blame, anger, resistance, or distancing and may be used as a coping mechanism for a family that fears they have "failed" the identified client. Imagine you are a group counselor engaged in FBT. The client is doing well in counseling and overcoming her disordered eating behaviors. FBT is entering the final phase, but the client's parents absolutely refuse to give up control over her eating. "She'll just start throwing up again," her father insists. The client's mother agrees. "No. We're in charge now, and it's best that it stays that way. She just can't be trusted." What might you do to help this family move forward with FBT, supporting your client's self-efficacy and overcoming the family's resistance to her autonomy?

ranges from 75 percent to 94 percent (Lundgren et al., 2004). Clearly, although the results are far from perfect, quantitative evidence indicates substantial benefits from treatment.

To monitor ongoing client status, follow-up contact at 3, 6, and 12 months will yield useful information for evaluation. Surveys evaluating what components of treatment were most helpful or effective are particularly informative (McKisack & Waller, 1997).

Referral and Follow-up

Once group treatment is over, some clients may find it necessary to continue with therapy at a less intense level than in individual counseling. In these instances, Lenihan and Sanders (1984) encourage individual group members to continue with group treatment. As stated, some research shows that longer treatment may increase the overall efficacy of group therapy. In addition to follow-up group work, clients may be encouraged to seek ongoing individual counseling and medication management, particularly to address depressive or anxious symptoms (McKisack & Waller, 1997).

Summary

Group therapy in mental health settings is a cost-effective and interpersonally impactful intervention that can be conducted with individuals, couples, or families. Many clients come to group counseling due to familial or relationship issues. Thus, approaching those concerns from the perspective of the nuclear family or family of origin can help create lasting benefits. This chapter presented three examples of groups in mental health settings, including a group for women in crisis, a healthy relationships group, and a group for young women struggling with bulimia nervosa.

For women in crisis, group counselors move beyond the presenting diagnosis and include political, socioeconomic, gender, and relationship dimensions in the group process. Trust, community, and vulnerability are themes throughout the group process. Group leaders remain attuned to the relationships in the clients' lives, including liabilities and supports.

In a healthy relationships group, couples come together in the group setting to discuss and address their unhealthy relationship patterns. Counselors aspire to move beyond merely settling the initial conflict, supporting group members in creating self-reflection and self-regulation practices within their primary relationship. Intimacy, communication, and problem solving all serve as foci for the group process.

Young women struggling with BN benefit from group counseling enhanced by family involvement, psychoeducation, and support. Family-based therapy is an intensive outpatient-treatment model that relies on the family as the primary support for renourishment during clients' recovery and has been demonstrated as more effective than group counseling alone for clients.

Incorporating groups into mental health settings benefits clients and the community and allows agencies to better serve more clients. Furthermore, incorporating those in intimate relationships with clients, including partners and family members, can enhance therapeutic outcomes.

14 Groups in Rehabilitation Settings

Debra A. Harley and Byung Jin Kim

Rehabilitation counselors are professional counselors who specialize in providing counseling and related services to persons with mental, physical, sensory, and emotional disabilities. They assist individuals with disabilities with psychosocial adjustment and coping, environmental and societal discrimination and barriers, psychological conflict or distress, crisis, and loss or alteration of physical, sensory, or cognitive functional ability. The goal of rehabilitation counseling is to improve the quality of life and increase autonomy and self-sufficiency for people with disabilities (Rubin, 2016) by helping people reach their personal, career, and independent-living goals.

Research has identified seven job functions of rehabilitation counselors: vocational counseling and consultation, counseling intervention, community-based rehabilitation service activities, case management, applied research, assessment, and professional advocacy. In addition, rehabilitation counselors are required to demonstrate knowledge across six domains: career counseling, assessment, and consultation; counseling theories, techniques, and applications; rehabilitation services and resources; case and case-load management; health care and disability systems; and medical, functional, and environmental implications of disability (Leahy, 2012). In a survey to examine the perceived importance of knowledge areas for credentialing in rehabilitation counseling, Leahy, Chan, Sung, and Kim (2013) identified four essential domains: (a) job placement, consultation, and assessment, (b) case management and community resources, (c) individual, group, and family counseling and evidence-based practice, and (d) medical, functional, and psychosocial aspects of disability.

Rehabilitation counselors work in independent living centers, public vocational rehabilitation agencies, private and nonprofit community-based rehabilitation settings, hospitals and clinics, mental health organizations, employee-assistance programs (EAPs), school-transition programs, forensic settings, employer-based disability prevention and management programs, geriatric rehabilitation settings, substance-abuse treatment facilities, and correctional facilities (Leahy, 2012). Across all these settings, group counseling has become an important and prevalent modality in rehabilitation counseling. Moreover, group work has made significant strides in rehabilitation-counseling settings toward achieving the stature of long-respected individual treatment modes of delivering mental health services, vocational counseling, and counseling toward psychosocial adaptation to chronic illnesses and disabilities (Ramaprasad & Kalyanasundaram, 2015). Group counseling for people with disabilities can be offered in hospital or treatment settings (outpatient and inpatient) and community rehabilitation centers. Group counseling in hospital settings is more concerned with assisting individuals with adjusting to immediate medical diagnoses and prognoses and reaction to the onset of disability. Community-based groups tend to focus on external concerns such as attitudinal barriers, potential of employment, and long-term functional limitations that can affect people with disabilities (Grizzell, 2015).

ADVANTAGES AND DISADVANTAGES OF GROUPS IN REHABILITATION

Group counseling in rehabilitation counseling settings offers several advantages over individual counseling. Some of these advantages reflect economic benefits in terms of both time or shared workload and expenses. At times, group-based activities are a preferred method for completing a task or delivering a service. Moreover, when operating effectively, groups can support the completion of a task in a manner that is more efficient or effective than can individuals dealing with it on their own (de Raaf, Hui, & Sims, 2011). Clearly, if counselors can see more clients in less time by utilizing the group approach, they can make more efficient use of their own time and the clients' economic resources. More important, however, are the significant therapeutic benefits that accrue when the group-counseling approach is applied in the context of rehabilitation settings. For example, application of group counseling has been effective in use with persons with traumatic brain injury (Bertisch, Rathe, Langenbahn, Sherr, & Diller, 2011), physical disability (Pulvino & Bentin, 2011), substance abusers (Scheffler, 2014), individuals living with HIV/AIDS, and persons with chronic mental illness (Ramaprasad & Kalyanasundaram, 2015) and managing emotions.

The group approach offers individuals who have disability-related barriers the opportunity to learn that their questions and concerns, problems, impediments, and hopes and fears are not unique, and this normalizing perspective can be highly therapeutic. Group settings afford clients many therapeutic opportunities, ranging from learning to practice new and healthier ways of relating to others to realizing they are not alone to benefiting from a safety net. In addition, group counseling gives counselors the opportunity to provide information efficiently; to teach vocational, functional, social, and coping skills; and to observe and provide feedback on social interactions (Gidron, 2013).

The group-counseling approach has some disadvantages as well. First, the counselor's role is one of facilitator, in which he or she encourages communication and interaction. Typically, each group member decides the extent to which he or she wants to participate in the group. When members are not dedicated to contributing to group, it is highly unlikely the group process will be productive and effective. The type of disability or diagnosis of clients can also impact group effectiveness. For example, clients with a diagnosis of social phobia are less likely to benefit from group counseling. Another disadvantage of groups is that absolute confidentiality is difficult and often unrealistic. Although the counselor is obligated by ethical principles (e.g., autonomy, beneficence, fidelity, justice, nonmaleficence, and veracity) to maintain confidentiality, the counselor has no way of ensuring members will observe such a practice beyond stressing the importance of confidentiality to group members. Other disadvantages include less opportunity for personal attention, that issues brought up in groups may not be relevant to other group members, that the therapeutic alliance between the counselor and individual member is not as strong as it is in individual counseling, that groups rarely divide the total time equally between all members of the group, and that the size of the group can affect effectiveness, especially if too large.

With both advantages and disadvantages, the application of group counseling to people with disabilities offers enough benefits to outweigh the disadvantages. The ability of counselors to use the power of the group to harness the resources within members to be constructive (Gladding, 2015) is one possible explanation for the advantageousness of group work with people with disabilities.

Counselors must be mindful of issues and concerns related to group work when engaging and working with culturally diverse populations (see Chapter 6). It is critical that counselors have awareness and understanding of any biases that may exist in the group-counseling process, as well as of the resistance and suspicion of culturally diverse clients toward self-disclosure and showing trust in the group leader or members. Counselors will need to exhibit cultural competence (i.e., awareness, knowledge, skills) in using group approaches to not only address counseling concerns but also to remedy stereotypes and generalizations that may dramatically influence a client's decision making and response to treatment. In addition, the counselor must be competent in the application of ethical principles with culturally diverse populations. Clearly, the advantages and disadvantages of group processes should be examined through a cultural lens. Gaffney (2006) emphasizes the need for awareness in many disciplines of "the inappropriateness of applying concepts undiluted from one culture to another" (p. 206) in the context of groups and group work.

SIDEBAR 14.1

Self-Awareness: Ethical Dilemma of Individual Confidentiality in Groups

Confidentiality is one of the keystone conditions of group work. The group leader is ethically obligated to keep the confidences of group members and to encourage group members to keep one another's confidences. However, there is the expectation that information and experiences are shared in group and that whatever is discussed in group is not necessarily protected by legal privilege. What can a rehabilitation counselor do as a group leader to promote the intent of confidentiality within group? Consider these practices:

- At the onset, discuss the limits of confidentiality and inform members of reporting procedures required of them.
- Emphasize the importance of maintaining confidentiality and consider having members sign contracts agreeing to it.
- Clearly state the penalty or consequences for violation of confidentiality.
- Model the importance of maintaining confidentiality.
- Be aware of ways in which members may test the leader to see if he or she will keep this promise (fidelity).
- Know when disclosure is in the best interest of members (beneficence) and welfare of others (nonmaleficence).

The rehabilitation counselor can do little to guarantee that members maintain confidentiality. It is crucial, however, for the counselor to repeatedly remind members to respect confidentiality. When it is evident or even suspected that members have violated group confidentiality, the counselor has the responsibility of confronting the matter as early as possible.

TYPES OF GROUPS TYPICALLY USED IN REHABILITATION

Group work in rehabilitation settings takes many forms (e.g., psychoeducational, psychotherapy, self-help, support groups), occurs across numerous settings (e.g., vocational, correctional, medical), and involves working with people who have different disabilities across age, gender, and culturally diverse groups. Of the various group formats, four are most frequently used in rehabilitation counseling: psychoeducational or educational groups, social support groups, psychotherapeutic groups, and coping and skill-training groups.

Psychoeducational groups, sometimes referred to as *educational* or *guidance groups*, "focus on developing members' cognitive, affective, and behavioral skills through structured set[s] of procedures within and across group meetings" (Corey, Corey, & Corey, 2014, p. 8). The focus of psychoeducational groups in rehabilitation settings is on imparting facts about disability or illness to participants. Examples include groups in which participants with diabetes learn to monitor and control their condition and groups in which people who have incurred a recent spinal cord injury learn self-care and mobility skills. *Social support groups* allow participants with disabilities to receive support from peers in a forum designed to foster the sharing of ideas, information, concerns, and problem-solving methods. Among the many possible support groups are those for people with cancer, multiple sclerosis, and traumatic brain injury. *Psychotherapeutic groups* emphasize the affective domain. These groups promote increased self-understanding by directly addressing emotional issues such as anxiety, depression, anger, and changes in identity. Finally, *coping and skill-training groups* tend to have a cognitive behavioral orientation. In these groups, participants learn skills and coping mechanisms for dealing with the personal, social, and environmental impacts of disability or chronic illness (Berven, Thomas, & Chan, 2015).

In this chapter, we discuss three specific types of groups in which rehabilitation counselors in various settings are likely to be engaged: job clubs, offender and mandated-population groups, and groups in hospital/medical settings. Specific advantages, limitations, associated research, challenges, and ethical considerations are described in the context of each group modality. This selection of groups represents different foci and different skill and knowledge requirements, and it reflects the increasing diversity found in rehabilitation counseling.

JOB CLUB AND GROUP-BASED EMPLOYMENT COUNSELING

The primary focus of rehabilitation counselors frequently is to help individuals with disabilities achieve successful employment outcomes, especially because a disability or chronic illness influences an individual's ability to attain and maintain employment in several ways. The world of work has taken on a new dimension known as the *new normal of employment* (i.e., the changing configuration of employment expectations between employers and employees, including the movement from long-term employment to short tenure, from jobs with benefits to contract employment, and from permanent to temporary work; Jelski & George, 2015).

The *job club* is an efficient and frequently successful approach to job seeking for people with disabilities. Job clubs offer members support, as well as opportunities to observe and learn from the experiences of others and "to gain confidence in using the

SIDEBAR 14.2
Self-Awareness: Job Placement Challenges for People with Disabilities

People with disabilities are disproportionately unemployed and underemployed. Many employers are seeking to hire part-time, temporary, or contingency workers, a practice known as the *new normal.* The new normal reduces the opportunity for people with disabilities that get hired under this approach to access to insurance as part of employment. Often, for those receiving Medicare, the new normal is a disincentive. What job-seeking strategies might help a person participating in a job club who is facing such a challenge?

information and resources they are receiving to conduct a successful job search" (de Raaf et al., 2011, p. 8). Globally, significant research supports the efficacy of the job-club model and suggests that job-club participants with a wide range of disabilities and employment barriers are more likely to find employment—more quickly and at a higher rate of pay—than those involved in traditional, individual-placement approaches (Moore, Kapur, Hawton, & Richards, 2016).

Conceptual Framework

A job club is an intensive, highly structured, short-term behavioral group approach to vocational counseling. This group-based job-search strategy was developed by Azrin and associates (Azrin & Besalel, 1980; Azrin, Flores, & Kaplan, 1975) in the 1970s and has been used continuously since then with demonstrated efficacy. Emphasis is placed on the development of interpersonal skills, job-seeking skills, and personal responsibility, in the context of a highly structured and supportive group process. The job club is essentially an open group, into which new members can be enrolled continually.

The job club represents a behavioral approach to group employment-seeking skills training. When applied to job-search skills, the behavioral approach focuses on observable behavior rather than the mental processes that accompany the behavior. The group is outcome oriented rather than process oriented. The primary objective is to help the group members find jobs. The job-club structure should be flexible to accommodate the needs of a particular group, program, or agency, and the planning process of the core structure should pay attention to the frequency, duration, and format of club meetings. Although the job-club approach has been modified for use in different settings and agencies, a typical job club includes common basic components (see Azrin & Besalel, 1980; Grant, 2008).

Group Goals

The stated goal of the job club is to help individual members "obtain a job of the highest feasible quality within the shortest feasible time period" (Azrin & Besalel, 1980). Job seekers have an opportunity to share job leads and experiences and to receive direction and additional leads from the facilitating agency. The job-club approach involves coordinating the activities of each individual in the context of a group of job seekers working together to promote the success of the participants under the supervision, instruction, and encouragement of a skilled leader. The job-club approach is unique both in the specific way each procedure is used and in the standardized, consistent, intensive application of every procedure to all job seekers (Russ & Parish, 2016). Every job seeker is considered employable, regardless of disability, educational background, or employment outlook. The group leader assumes that employment is possible—that a job exists for everyone—and views his or her task as helping the job seeker to find that job.

Pregroup Screening and Orientation to the Group

Each prospective participant in the job club must attend an orientation meeting prior to participating. Azrin and Besalel (1980) suggested that this may be accomplished in either a group or an individual format, depending on the time available to the counselor. Regardless of format, in this session the counselor orients the potential participants to the details of the program, addressing issues such as cost of the program, the group leader's commitment to finding each member a job, expectations of the participants, benefits of the group approach, potential impact of employment on any benefits the participant is currently receiving, and transportation or scheduling issues. The job-club approach represents an intensive commitment, and typically the group meets daily for several hours per day. Members must understand and be able to commit to the various requirements in terms of time and effort. However, such frequency can become repetitious and may not yield updated information of significant value to warrant a daily club.

Possible Challenges, Limitations, and Ethical Considerations

Even though the job club is an effective, economical, and efficient approach to job seeking, group leaders must be aware of the potential limitations and challenges associated with this approach. When the group member's goal is to attain employment, the participant and the group leader must decide which of the various forms and levels of employment counseling are most appropriate. Because vocational rehabilitation counselors work with people who have a wide range of disabilities and differing levels of severity and psychosocial impact, no single method of employment counseling is appropriate for everyone.

An important consideration is the level of support and information the participant will require. If a person can complete most of the work of locating, applying for, and interviewing for jobs, the counselor generally plays a supportive role and offers information and other assistance when required. In other cases, when the client has more limited awareness of or experience with work and the job-seeking process, the counselor must take significantly more responsibility in the job-finding tasks and work more intensively with the client on developing work skills. The counselor should consider asking a series of questions (e.g., Do you want to work alone or in a team? In what type of environment do you want to work?), which in turn will help the counselor work with the client to promote autonomy and informed choice.

In deciding whether the job club is the most appropriate approach to employment counseling for an individual client, the counselor should assess the client's level of understanding of work and job seeking. Although it is beneficial to have a range of experience within the job club, extreme differences between members may affect the progress and coherence of the group and its membership. The counselor also should assess the client's comfort with a group approach because a group is not appropriate for everyone. Therefore, group leaders should describe the experience, expectations, and makeup of the group and then assess the client's concerns. Although entering a group situation may engender responses ranging from uncomfortable to frightening, and some level of concern is to be expected, counselors must assess whether the client's concerns,

---

SIDEBAR 14.3

Case Study: Planning Job Club with James

James is a 21-year-old Korean male with a diagnosis of autism spectrum disorder (ASD). James currently lives with his parents. He completed high school and earned a certificate of attendance. While in school, James attended vocational classes and career-planning training sessions. He has never had a full-time job in competitive employment. His work experience is limited to supervised training in school, in which he worked with the custodial staff to empty trashcans, dust, mop, and perform other general-cleaning duties.

James's parents would like him to obtain employment to increase his sense of self-worth. James has moderate functional limitations. James needs comprehensive services but will benefit from some type of employment. He is working with a vocational-rehabilitation counselor who believes James will benefit from a job club. He has an established individual plan of employment.

Determine answers to the following questions as the vocational-rehabilitation counselor:

1. What steps do you need to determine before moving further in the planning process? What process would you employ to determine James's work preferences?
2. What functional limitation could impact James's participation in a job club?
3. What goal will you identify for James in a job club? Is he in need of competitive employment, a network of mutual support, or other services?
4. What challenges and concerns must be addressed with James in the job application and interview processes (e.g., dealing with disclosure about his disability, workplace accommodations, etc.)?
5. What cultural considerations do you need to address?

---

fears, or expectations are such that they may have negative consequences for the client or the group as a whole. Let's look at the case of James in Sidebar 14.3 and consider these challenges and limitations, along with other questions.

Group Sessions by Stages

The definitive, personal involvement, group involvement, and enhancement and closure stages of group work proposed by Capuzzi and Gross in Chapter 2 are reviewed ahead with respect to the job club.

DEFINITIVE STAGE   The job club, even in this initial stage, involves intensive activity at a relatively fast pace. Azrin and Besalel (1980) have developed a highly structured format for the job club and its progress, including what the first session should include. Essentially, the members receive information about the group and take part in several orienting activities. These activities include completing a written agreement of responsibilities between the group leader and each member of the group, followed by member introductions. The activities consist of information provided by the counselor, alternating with individual, partner, and group exercises.

PERSONAL INVOLVEMENT STAGE   One of the most important elements of the job club is the opportunity for members to learn from and with each other, to cooperate and assist each other in the job-seeking process. These benefits begin to emerge in the personal involvement stage, as the participants begin to engage in member-to-member interactions through the cooperative activities. The group leader promotes personal involvement by allowing and encouraging this interaction, observing members' interactions as they grow more comfortable with the group and become more committed.

Because much of the work after the initial meeting is done independently (e.g., searching for job leads), the group leader must alternate group activities with individual activities. Further, because of the intensive and relatively directive nature of the job club, the leader must remain vigilant in maintaining the rules and promoting members' progress. Activities at this stage include role-play and rehearsal and the continued use of group education alternating with individual or partnered job-seeking activities.

GROUP INVOLVEMENT STAGE   Although the purpose of the job club is for individual members to achieve success in the workplace, the effectiveness of the group depends on the cooperative efforts of the members. As members' personal comfort and confidence with the group and their own roles increase, they will realize the benefits of cooperation and shared efforts. At this stage, the group members increasingly take on responsibility for the group's progress. As new members join, more experienced members welcome and assist them. The leader, though always actively involved, particularly seeks to facilitate and encourage these leadership behaviors of the members.

ENHANCEMENT AND CLOSURE STAGE   Given the open nature of the typical job club, closure generally is an individual rather than a group effort. In the case of the job club, though, closure typically means employment and the realization of the exiting member's vocational goals. The importance of formally recognizing this success is vital to the job club because it encourages the members that they can reach their goals, it recognizes and rewards the successful efforts and hard work of the member and marks the member's achievement in leaving the group, and the member who leaves to begin employment becomes a potential resource for employment for the other members. Thus, a formal method for maintaining contact with members of the group who are successful in finding employment is part of this stage.

Strategies to Evaluate the Group

Obviously, with the job-club approach, the primary measure of success is the members' attaining employment. As described previously, research evaluating the effectiveness of this approach has been very positive in general. Although employment is the primary goal of the job club, other potential benefits to participation may guide additional approaches to evaluation. In today's labor market, it is unusual for anyone to remain in the same job for the course of a career. It is far more likely that a person will change jobs several times in a career. The job club plays such an appropriate and important role in rehabilitation counseling in part not only because members get a job but also because they *learn how* to get a job. If the job club is successful in this goal, the benefits to the members are significant and last over time.

Follow-up and Referral

As noted, the job club might not be appropriate for some job seekers, and this may not become apparent until after a person has started to participate in the group. If a group leader determines that a member is inappropriate for the job club, the reasons should be discussed with the member to reach a decision on a different approach.

Following up with previous members is crucial. Azrin and Besalel (1980) suggested keeping a list of successful members and contacting them at regular intervals, if for no other reason than because they represent potential resources for current job-seeking members.

Further, former members are encouraged to return as needed. The job club is described as a resource continually available to its members. In addition, follow-up offers the benefit of allowing members to celebrate success. Inviting members to return and share their story provides positive reinforcement for other members and helps motivate those who are searching for employment. Successful members should be encouraged to "pay it forward" by helping others to develop their networks or by serving as mentors. In addition, even if job seekers must return to the job club, they usually require less assistance and remain for a shorter time than new members (Azrin & Besalel, 1980).

GROUPS WITH OFFENDER AND MANDATED POPULATIONS

Offender populations include both incarcerated (i.e., housed in a secure correctional environment) and nonincarcerated (on parole, probation, etc.) individuals and mandated clients who are required to attend treatment services by a governing agency (e.g., a department of corrections, the judicial system, parole/probation officers). Many offenders have disabilities, are in need of rehabilitation services, and are being overlooked (Harley, 2014). Overwhelmingly, incarcerated offenders have a low level of educational attainment, lack vocational skills, have higher than average rates of unemployment, have mild mental retardation or learning disabilities, are alcohol and/or drug dependent, and have some form of serious emotional disturbance (Cronin, 2011; Peters, Wexler, & Lurigio, 2015). Yet offender clients frequently resist the therapeutic process and may actively avoid engaging in treatment or rehabilitation. Reasons for their resistance and avoidance can be explained by certain characteristics exhibited commonly by offender populations (see Box 14.1). In efforts to involve offenders in treatment or rehabilitation groups, counselors should take into consideration the unique nature of this population because its members present problems that are not typical of therapy groups in other settings (Baillargeon, Hoge, & Penn, 2010). Typically, offenders are a disenfranchised group, represent a captive audience (involuntary), exhibit chronic/repetitive behaviors (offenses), and have a host of psychosocial adjustment issues (especially adult offenders). Among the specific types of adult offenders targeted for treatment in groups are those serving time for sex offenses or substance abuse, as well as individuals found guilty of driving under the influence, shoplifting, and domestic violence (Gladding, 2015; Substance Abuse and Mental Health Services Administration [SAMHSA], 2005).

BOX 14.1 Cognitive Characteristics of Offenders Populations

Offenders often exhibit one or more of the following characteristics:

- Immature or developmentally delayed thought patterns
- Limited problem-solving and decision-making skills
- Inability to consider the effects of behavior
- Egocentric views and negative beliefs or lack of trust in other people

- Distorted thoughts that impede their ability to reason and accept blame for inappropriate behavior or wrongdoing
- Sense of entitlement, making it difficult for them to delay gratification and easy for them to confuse wants and needs and disrespect others
- Lack of self-control and empathy
- Use of force and violence to achieve their goals

Source: Clark (2011).

Relevant Research

Research examining the success of group work with offender populations in general has been mixed, but group work and counseling services have been an important component of rehabilitation for offender populations in correctional settings, resulting in positive treatment gains across a range of outcome variables (Van Voorhis & Salisbury, 2016). Research indicates a wide range of benefits of group counseling with offender populations, including providing socially and therapeutically appropriate outlets for them to talk out their thoughts and feelings about their past criminal activity; providing the opportunity to learn healthier attitudes and behaviors and new ways of thinking, feeling, and behaving; aiding understanding that their actions have consequences for others; and offering offenders a forum for developing strategies on how to resolve conflicts and transfer this knowledge into their daily lives. Generalizability of responsibility to society can be a secondary benefit (Frisch & Emery, 2016).

Conceptual Framework

Of the primary types of groups, three are highly applicable to work with offender and mandated clients: psychoeducational groups, counseling groups, and psychotherapy groups (Morgan, 2014). The belief among correctional mental health professionals is that if psychotherapy can be facilitated in prisons, it can be facilitated anywhere. This belief is predicated on the idea that the environment of incarceration is not conducive to change and that offenders are suspicious of and resistant to insight and growth (Morgan, Kroner, & Mills, 2006). The following subsections describes the application of each type of group for offender and mandated clients.

Psychoeducational Groups

The aim of psychoeducational groups with offender and mandated clients is to foster cognitive changes that may reduce the likelihood of criminal behaviors in the future. Psychoeducational groups offer concrete functional outcomes such as decreased defensiveness; less of a need to test the group, therapeutic boundaries, or the therapist; and heightened direction and focus in early group sessions. In psychoeducational groups with offenders, out-of-group homework exercises tend to yield the greatest improved outcomes, but offenders often resist completing work outside of group sessions. Thus, counselors/therapists will have to provide a clear and logical rationale for this intervention and promptly address any lack of client compliance with assigned homework (Morgan, 2014).

Group Counseling

Group counseling is basically preventive, with an educational, vocational, social, or personal focus aimed at promoting growth (Gladding, 2015). Examples of counseling groups with offenders and mandated clients include institutional-adjustment groups, support groups, interpersonal communication/relationship-building groups, and vocational groups. According to Morgan (2014), an institutional-adjustment group is aimed specifically at assisting offenders to function at the highest possible level within the correctional environment, rather than at remediation. Many offenders have made poor life decisions, and group counseling can help these clients achieve an optimal level of functioning within the penitentiary setting and after release into society. The goals of group counseling with offender populations are to increase self-awareness; prompt identification of attitudes, choices, and behaviors that led to problematic behavior; and promote prosocial decision making and behaviors. The group focuses on strategies for reducing recidivism, fostering prosocial integration back into society, cognitive restructuring, addressing criminogenic needs, and supplementing other rehabilitative programs such as substance-abuse, vocational, educational, and leisure programs (Morgan, 2014).

Group Psychotherapy

Group psychotherapy with offenders and mandated clients is directed to the remediation of problematic behaviors and personality restructuring (Clark, 2010). Group psychotherapy examines conscious and hidden patterns of thought and behavior that are relatively pervasive in the individual's life. The goal of psychotherapy groups for offender or mandated populations is to reduce their harmful behaviors and antisocial acts in the future. The focus of group psychotherapy is on the here and now of dysfunctional interactions as they occur within the group, with the aim of using these interactions to facilitate greater self-awareness and behavioral change. The aim of group psychotherapy is to assist the offender in reducing dysfunctional symptoms and developing adaptive coping skills. It is important to understand that the application of psychotherapy with offenders presents challenges not encountered with other groups.

Group Goals

The focus on development of a healthier lifestyle seems essential to rehabilitation. The ultimate outcome of an intervention is to either stop or alter a behavior (Morgan, 2014). Group goals for incarcerated offenders focus on self-exploration and learning within a supportive group environment and group relationship building, as well as the importance of reducing addictive behaviors, learning healthier attitudes and behaviors, conformity, prosocial behavior, lifestyle, and institutional adjustment. Each of these goals is applicable to general group work; however, specific factors (e.g., prosocial behavior modification, conformity issues, and institutional-adjustment issues) are unique to group work with offender and mandated populations (Morgan, 2014). Morgan stressed that these group goals are consistent with the criminogenic needs of offenders as found by researchers, and each of these goals is reported to be critical to the effectiveness of treatment programming with offenders.

Pregroup Screening and Orientation to the Group

Pregroup screening interviews are recommended to counter the manipulation and resistance associated with offender and mandated clients and to facilitate the client's development of therapeutic goals. Offender clients tend to be resistant to group participation. In addition, some group members enter treatment without identified therapeutic goals (Morgan, 2014). Thus, prescreening identifies the appropriateness of individuals for placement in a group while also addressing group cohesion. Morgan (2014) outlined three steps of orientation to the group for offender populations: orient members to the group's focus, review members' valued therapeutic factors, and establish a therapeutic environment.

Possible Challenges, Limitations, and Ethical Considerations

Many adult offenders have a low level of trust and high level of anger, frustration, and sense of deprivation, which is potentially problematic for group leaders. The group leader must take care to consider the unique ethical implications of working with offender populations because conducting groups in this context creates many potentially problematic dynamics. For one thing, when members feel pressured or forced to participate in counseling without their acquiescence, it is likely to affect their relationship with the group leader. Also, group leaders should examine their own feelings about why group members have been incarcerated or treatment in the group has been mandated, and they should be cognizant of the impact of these feelings on the development of the counseling relationship. Often, additional information is disclosed by members in groups, which may have other legal implications and can affect the therapeutic process (Morgan, 2014).

Group leaders further must be aware of the potential power that group members may perceive them as having—and indeed that they have when their assessments, reports, or perceptions of progress may have a direct bearing on the participant's situation (Bersot & Arrifo, 2011).

Group Sessions by Stages for Offender Populations

In outlining the developmental stages of groups for offender and mandated populations, we will follow the sequence presented in Chapter 2: (a) definitive stage, (b) personal involvement stage, (c) group involvement stage, and (d) enhancement and closure stage. Although the development of each offender and mandated group is unique, each progresses in approximately the same manner as described in the group-counseling literature.

DEFINITIVE STAGE   If the appropriate foundational steps (described in Chapter 2) have been taken in establishing the group, the role of the leader in this stage is to explain the rules and the consequences of breaking the rules. Given the mandated or otherwise not-entirely-voluntary nature of participation, the leader must be very clear about both the rules and the consequences of breaking them. The leader then engages members in activities aimed at acquainting them with each other and attempts to draw from the participants their goals and expectations for the group. The leader attempts to model behaviors expected of the group members.

Group members typically are involved with evaluating the leader in terms of skills, ability, and capacity to understand and trust offender members, as well as evaluating the other members in terms of their commitment, safety, confidentiality, observation of rules, and any use of intimidation to control or manipulate participants. Members define the group experience in terms of their life experiences while living on the outside and while incarcerated. A major goal is to build trust.

PERSONAL INVOLVEMENT STAGE   At this stage, the leader's role is to foster interpersonal interactions, openness and sharing of information, and working through power struggles in an environment in which power is considered the definitive representation of status. Members may openly challenge other members, the leader, and the organizational structure of the prison environment and those in authority as they strive to find their place in the group. Members may resist integrating the feedback they receive when they perceive the suggested changes making them too weak to survive in the prison environment. Over time, however, group members generally become more willing to share themselves with others and take a more active role in the group process.

The leader demonstrates awareness of the emotional makeup of the group and encourages affective expression. He or she works to provide an environment conducive to privacy and safety within the regulations of the prison or environment and is aware of and may seek to highlight the impact of the prison environment on the offenders' behaviors. The leader allows members to move through this stage at their own pace.

GROUP INVOLVEMENT STAGE   During the group involvement stage, offender populations move toward more cooperation and cohesion while decreasing conflict and confrontation. With the leader's encouragement, members become more confident in themselves and their ability to relate effectively in the group environment. The members focus more on developing self-adjustment skills that will help them avoid recidivism. Finally, members increasingly are observed to support other members and work within the organizational structure to effect change. The leader functions more in a helping capacity to enhance the development of individual members and the group as a whole in improving the quality of life in prisons.

ENHANCEMENT AND CLOSURE STAGE   In this final stage, the group members must evaluate their success and prepare for the group to come to an end. The members evaluate the amount of progress they have made during the life of the group. This is a period during which members share their concerns about what will happen when they make the transition to life outside of prison. Leaders can use this period of evaluation to assist members in evaluating their growth and development. Leaders may explore with members the various options facing individual members, explore previous and ineffective responses, and reinforce new learning and the capacity to make more effective choices.

As members start to deal with the loss that group closure will bring, the leader should encourage consideration of alternatives outside the group that members might engage in to gain the positive support the group provided. The leader facilitates closure by initiating structured ways of saying good-bye for those who will leave not only the group but also prison. Finally, the leader explains and encourages members to take advantage of follow-up procedures and transition services that will assist them when they leave prison.

Strategies to Evaluate the Group

Many important questions remain with regard to evaluating the efficacy of groups for offenders and mandated clients. Evaluating the success of these groups is a complex endeavor, partly because members, leaders, and facilities may have different goals for the group and different ideas about "success" and partly because of the mandated nature of the members' participation. See Morgan (2014) for strategies that should be considered and implemented in evaluating groups for offender populations.

Follow-up and Referral

Follow-up with offender populations is guided by logistics (e.g., members who are incarcerated, are on probation, or who have been paroled). Following up with offender populations

SIDEBAR 14.4
Case Study: Female Offenders with Disabilities

Reintegration of offenders with disabilities into the community requires a multistage and multipronged process because they face employment, housing, family, and other obstacles as they transition back into the community. Many of the stressors encountered by offenders cause psychosocial-adjustment concerns. In addition, challenges experienced by offenders differ based on gender, with a large percentage of female offenders having histories of mental illness, domestic violence, and sexual abuse.

Review Box 14.1 for cognitive characteristics of offender populations. As a rehabilitation counselor, what behaviors might you observe in a female offender with diagnoses of bipolar disorder and substance abuse? How would you address these behaviors, and what goals would you set for her in group?

is much easier if they are incarcerated. Once they are paroled or on probation, it becomes more difficult to locate them and track their progress. The type of facility (minimum versus maximum security) also may influence follow-up with offender populations. For example, incarcerated inmates in minimum-security correctional environments may have opportunities to make a transition back to society slowly by spending some time between full incarceration and freedom (e.g., work-and-study-release status; James, 2015). Probation and parole officers can play an important role in the follow-up when group participation is a condition of the offenders' probation or parole requirements.

The procedure for referral of offender populations to groups depends in part upon the type of offender (e.g., violent, nonviolent, juvenile), severity of the offense, and logistics. For example, drug offenders may be required to attend groups as part of their sentencing in drug court, whereas other offenders are prohibited from group activities and placed in solitary confinement because of their offense. In addition, the referral process should be sensitive to gender and cultural needs and perceptions regarding various components of and the interaction of offenders with the correctional system.

GROUPS IN HOSPITALS AND MEDICAL SETTINGS

Groups in hospitals and inpatient facilities are common, although inpatient groups have their own theoretical framework (Karademas, 2009). Group counseling in hospital/medical settings may involve working with individuals who have recent-onset disabilities, chronic illnesses such as diabetes, mental illness and psychiatric disorders, terminal diagnoses, and life-threatening disorders including cancer, AIDS, and others. Group approaches are used in medical and health care settings because they are time- and cost-efficient (Blount et al., 2007). Social adjustment is an area of particular vulnerability for individuals diagnosed with chronic or terminal illnesses. Patients with chronic or terminal illnesses find group counseling beneficial in adjusting to psychosocial problems that can exacerbate their medical conditions.

The flexibility of group formats can be applied to a wide array of issues specific to a medical condition or unique to a given population. Specific group formats used in medical and health care settings include social support, educational, psychoeducational, counseling, and task groups. See the *Journal of Clinical Psychology in Medical Settings* for articles on the therapeutic properties of groups in addressing the many issues accompanying various health-related problems.

Purpose

Groups with patients in medical and health care settings may serve many separate or conjoint purposes. In general, these groups are designed to assist patients with coping and psychosocial adjustment to illness; to provide education about effective medical and functional management of the chronic illness, condition, or disability with which the members are living; to develop an atmosphere of support and communication among those who share the experience of living with a disability or illness and its psychosocial effects; to increase communication among the patient, family members, and medical providers; and to reduce or eliminate physical symptoms through behavior change.

Relevant Research

Research concerning the benefits and efficacy of group counseling in hospitals and medical settings has been very supportive in general. The limitations of space and the significant body of literature associated with relevant research does not allow for in-depth discussion of findings here. Among the benefits reported, group counseling of different types in hospital and medical settings has been shown to improve psychosocial adaptation, reduce psychological distress, improve illness self-management and self-efficacy, promote improved compliance with treatment, encourage the development of supportive relationships between and among members, and counter social isolation and provide solidarity for group members. Although psychoeducational groups in hospital and medical settings have improved attitudes toward medical service and adherence to regimen, they do not appear to be effective in improving symptoms.

Many inpatient and outpatient substance-abuse treatment programs use groups and are considered indispensable. Groups in substance-abuse treatment enable people to witness the recovery process (SAMHSA, 2015). Although the success of group members varies depending on individual characteristics and motivation, groups have been a core aspect of substance-abuse treatment for decades and have proven to be very effective (Southern & Thornton, 2013).

Conceptual Framework

Patients with chronic or terminal illness, especially upon receiving a serious medical diagnosis, experience psychological, emotional, and spiritual distress from the impact of the news. The effects can be pervasive, impinging on all aspects of their life. Common reactions include anxiety about pain and discomfort, fear and uncertainty about the future, and depression. Although individuals dealing with an illness or medical

---

SIDEBAR 14.5
Self-Awareness: Psychosocial Adjustment to Late-Onset Disability or Chronic Illness

Late-onset disability or chronic illness produces many adjustment issues for individuals, especially when they occur at prime working age. Although medical treatment is a direct intervention for a physical diagnosis, the psychological response or lack of adequate coping skills often presents as much of a reason for concern as the physical condition. Imagine yourself receiving a late-onset disability. As your own rehabilitation counselor, what group-counseling goals would you set for yourself?

crisis may not fully regain their previous level of functioning, group counseling is an effective approach to utilize coping strategies to improve their quality of life, and it often negates the social isolation clients experience and allows them to gain positive affirmation.

The *educational group* is the most commonly used modality of group counseling in the medical/hospital setting. The purpose of an educational group in this setting is to disseminate specific information to participants. Educational groups often are part of interdisciplinary treatment programs (e.g., pain management) that may include counselors, nurses, psychologists, nutritionists, pharmacists, and physical and occupational therapists. Educational groups can effectively augment interdisciplinary treatment programs and, over time, participants show significant improvements in various domains (Karademas, 2009). Groups may be open or closed (to limit the number of participants or when dealing with sensitive materials and subject matter [e.g., HIV/AIDS, cancer]). Self-disclosure is voluntary; as self-disclosure increases, concern for confidentiality increases as well. Refer to the *Patient Education and Counseling* journal for additional research studies.

Group Goals

The goals of groups for patients with medical illnesses depend on the type of group (e.g., support) and its purpose or theme (e.g., acceptance of an illness, preparing to die). Nevertheless, several general goals in medical settings are applicable across various types of groups, including social support, expression of emotion, anxiety reduction and fears associated with death and dying, reordering life priorities, family support, effective communication with physicians and medical staff, and symptom management (Hwee, Cauch-Dudek, Victor, Ng, & Shah, 2014). These group goals in hospital/medical settings are effective in helping patients with medical crises reduce their anxiety related to psychosocial adjustment to illness, death, and dying; strengthen interpersonal relationships; and improve their quality of life. For patients who endure the necessary traditional medical interventions for illness, it is important to note the evidence indicating that group psychotherapy is an effective adjunct to treatment (Hwee et al., 2014).

Pregroup Screening and Orientation to the Group

Because of the considerable variance in the nature, size, focus, and form of group counseling in medical and hospital settings, conducting pregroup screening and orientation will vary considerably as well. The general considerations are discussed here. See Ditchman, Lee, and Huebner (2015) for fundamental guidelines for group formation.

Prior to consenting to participate, members should be made aware of the nature and purpose of the group. Group leaders should identify whether the purpose will be primarily educational, to develop social support, to foster coping strategies, and so on. The potential members should be made aware of the expectations and potential risks involved in participation. To the extent possible, based on variables such as time since diagnosis and response to diagnosis, age of the potential participant, and type of illness or disability, group leaders should attempt to select members whose needs and goals are compatible with the goals of the group, who will not impede the group process, and whose well-being will not be jeopardized by the group experience (Commission on Rehabilitation Counselor Certification, 2017).

Possible Challenges, Limitations, and Ethical Considerations

The most appropriate type of group in terms of format, theoretical approach, and specific methods applied in hospital-based groups will be determined to some extent by the constraints of the environment and the needs of the members (Ditchman et al., 2015). Based on the population, the availability to patients of alternative counseling modalities (e.g., individual counseling), and the financial and physical constraints of the hospital or other facility, group leaders may be involved with groups characterized by rapid turnover of members and significant variation in terms of the interests and needs, ages, and level and type of illness or disability of the members. Group leaders may be faced with decisions concerning the format, open or closed nature of the group, and content, or these decisions may be made for them by the hospital or agency hosting the group. Group leaders must consider the barriers and limitations to full participation of the members based on illness- or disability-related variables. Factors such as cognitive and physical limitations, communication barriers, limitations in mobility, and the potential effects of treatment on attention and energy level must be considered when planning interventions, activities, and the group's time and space parameters.

Group Sessions by Stages

The stages of groups for clients in hospital/medical settings are outlined ahead, following the sequence presented in Chapter 2: the (a) definitive stage, (b) personal involvement stage, (c) group involvement stage, and (d) enhancement and closure stage.

DEFINITIVE STAGE   Initially, group members are likely to have questions and concerns about the nature and purpose of the group and their participation in it. Depending on the group's purpose, members may be encouraged to discuss their own experiences with illness or disability, significant disability-related problems, or questions they may have about their experience. Group leaders use methods such as reflection, role-playing, clarification, self-disclosure, and positive reinforcement to encourage development of trust, involvement, and personal commitment.

PERSONAL INVOLVEMENT STAGE   The typical personal involvement stage is characterized by a deeper level of personal sharing and exploration; an awareness, through this sharing, of the similarities and commonalities of the current experience; and increased willingness to express oneself. Leadership at this stage begins to take a less directive form and involves providing encouragement, linking shared experiences, and proposing and maintaining themes or topics for the meetings.

GROUP INVOLVEMENT STAGE   As the group members become increasingly comfortable with the process and the experience of sharing and working together with the other members, their attention is likely to shift from sharing problems and issues to discussing solutions and resources. At this stage, the leader plays a critical role in providing information and resources about methods of coping, problem solving about and planning for the future, and, in some cases, community, social, and/or family reintegration. Specific topics that leaders may encourage members to consider include the impact of disability- or illness-related changes on familial, social, and work roles; the realization of increased dependence on others or on accommodations; and coping with the emotional impact of living with a chronic or permanent condition.

SIDEBAR 14.6
Case Study: Goal Setting for Megan

A critical aspect of effective treatment planning is goal setting. When goals are set, both interventions and outcomes result from them. Treatment for cancer can be classified as multistage, with initial, intermediate, and final stages. Each of these stages reflects a symptom-based treatment goal that is sequential. While the treatment of symptoms is occurring, Megan needs psychosocial adjustment at each stage as well. Determine which psychosocial and support interventions are appropriate for Megan at each stage. Then identify an appropriate group approach for her. Next, develop group-counseling goals, interventions, and outcomes that might assist in the necessary self-management, illness monitoring, and behavior change for the goals.

ENHANCEMENT AND CLOSURE STAGE   The presence or absence of, and extent of, a sense of loss of the group's support—whether that support comes primarily in the form of education or social support—depends largely on the purpose and nature of the group. In the case of psychoeducational groups, which are highly structured and in which group cohesion is typically lower than in more support-based groups, members may experience little or no sense of loss. The same may be true to some extent for groups conducted in acute rehabilitation settings over a short period of time. In other cases, however, the loss of support may be significant. This may be particularly true for group members experiencing the simultaneous loss of function and for those engaged in significant life changes due to illness or the onset of disability.

As the group nears closure, grieving a loss of function may produce more anger or dependency than might be typical (Ditchman et al., 2015). Counselors should evaluate the members in this regard well before the group ends and assess the need for ongoing services and the development of longer-term supports.

Strategies to Evaluate the Group

Evaluation of groups in hospital/medical settings depends on the nature of the group. In psychoeducational groups, evaluation is likely to be based on the development of new skills, such as self-management, illness monitoring, improved mobility, or behavior change such as increased awareness of lifestyle on disease management and subsequent adaptive changes. In support groups or groups aimed at helping people cope with the emotional and psychosocial impact of illness or disability, evaluation of the group's effectiveness may be based on reduction of depression or anxiety, enhanced feelings of self-efficacy or confidence, or more concrete goal attainment, such as the member's return to work or other pre-illness activities.

Follow-up and Referral

Given the significant changes that are likely to occur simultaneously with group participation, careful attention must be paid to both follow-up and referral. Counselors should make clear to members the availability of returning to the group, participating in new groups, or other means of continued access to support. Ethically, rehabilitation counselors are bound to be knowledgeable about referral resources and to suggest appropriate alternatives. Members must be informed that further support, even if not currently required, will be available in the future. Supplemental sessions may be necessary to help participants who live with a chronic health condition and those who have difficulty maintaining health-promoting behaviors.

Summary

As the profession of rehabilitation counseling continues to experience growth and expansion into new and different areas of focus and professional practice, skill in conducting group counseling will become even more critical. Opportunities to conduct group counseling in rehabilitation settings will occur increasingly across the range of professional settings (e.g., vocational, educational, correctional, medical) and involve working with people from diverse backgrounds with respect to cultural, disability, age, and gender characteristics. Outside of the traditional vocational-rehabilitation settings, rehabilitation counselors are increasingly likely to be engaged in group counseling with the populations discussed in this chapter. Across the range of professional settings in which rehabilitation counselors are employed, they will be responsible increasingly for conducting psychoeducational groups, counseling groups, and psychotherapy groups aimed at assisting persons with disabilities to achieve their goals and fulfill their potential.

15 Groups with Older Adults: Loss, Transitions, and End-of-Life Issues

Ann Vernon

Loss is a universal phenomenon that we typically equate with death. However, it is considered more accurately within the broader context of losing someone or something close to us (Doka, 2016; Ellis, 2006). As Fiorini and Mullen (2006) suggested, loss can be the result of a change or disruption in someone's life, which implies that even happy events that may be life changing can result in some degree of loss. Parkes (2001) noted that loss is inescapable, and it is tied intricately to change and growth, loss and gain. A major loss entails "something in a person's life in which the person was emotionally invested" (Harvey, 2002, p. 5), which Harvey differentiated from minor losses that occur daily and are not associated with emotional attachment.

Loss is multifaceted. It is associated with homelessness (Harvey, 2002), mental illness (Morse, 2000), terminal illness (Ellis, 2000), dementia (James & Friedman, 2009), aging (Harvey, 2002), chronic illness (Thompson & Kyle, 2000), infertility (Humphrey, 2009), miscarriage (Bray, 2015), death (Kübler-Ross & Kessler 2005; Malkinson, 2007), violence and war (Harvey, 2002), relationship infidelity (Boekhout, Hendrick, & Hendrick, 2000), and loss of close interpersonal relationships (Murphy, 2012). Losses also can include loss of expectations, dreams, abilities, power, and freedom.

Rando (2000) distinguished between *physical loss,* which is the loss of something tangible, and *psychosocial* or *symbolic loss,* which is the loss of something intangible, such as the loss of health resulting from a chronic illness. James and Friedman (2009) discussed loss associated with nonevents—the dreams that are never realized or the events that are reasonable to expect but never happen. Kluger-Bell (2000) described the concept of silent loss, such as in the case of abortion, which is something that is often shrouded in secrecy. Doka (2016) noted that there are various types of loss associated with different stages of life, citing the example of elderly people losing their independence when they can no longer drive. Although this type of loss is not secret, it is usually not openly acknowledged or perhaps not generally recognized as a type of loss. Loss can also be associated with shame, self-doubt, and uncertainty, as in the case of losing a job (Christensen, 2009). Fiorini and Mullen (2006) suggested that there are intangible losses that correspond with larger loss experiences, such as the loss of innocence or trust that occurs in conjunction with a relationship infidelity.

Boss (2006) identified another type of loss, *ambiguous loss,* as when a family member is either physically or psychologically absent. Boss maintained that of all the losses experienced in personal relationships, ambiguous loss is the perhaps the most difficult

Think of an example of a personal loss associated with a nonevent, an ambiguous loss, a silent loss, or an intangible loss. What feelings and issues are/were associated with this type of loss, and how has it impacted you? Based on your own experience, what wisdom could you share with others dealing with a similar type of loss?

because there is no closure; the loss is unclear and can be immobilizing. According to Boss, child abduction, incarceration, and adoption are examples of ambiguous loss in which an individual is physically absent but psychologically present, and Alzheimer's disease, addictions, and chronic mental illnesses are examples of losses in which a person is physically present but psychologically absent. Boss noted that ambiguous losses are not ritualized or officially documented.

Harvey (2000) maintained that "life is full of losses, small and large, sustainable and sometimes insuperable and incalculable in their impacts" (p. 1). According to Harvey and Miller (2000), positive outcomes such as changes in self-perceptions, social relationships, and life perspective are frequent results of a loss. Losses are necessary, according to Viorst (1986), because "we grow by losing and leaving and letting go" (p. 16).

Thus, whether the loss involves a dream, an ideal, a job, a home or possessions, an absent family member, an ability, a friendship, or one's health, looks, status, or self-esteem, losses are inevitable. As Harvey (2000) noted, we are affected by a sense of personal loss from youth to death. Harvey concluded that "loss is such a fundamental part of our lives that it beckons us to begin negotiating it early in life" (p. 297).

Loss is transformational; as a result of loss, one's attitudes, values, beliefs, and perceptions are altered (Humphrey, 2009). Adapting to loss and using it as a vehicle for change and growth requires an adjustment to new patterns, relationships, roles, and events (Kübler-Ross & Kessler, 2005). The impact of a loss depends on whether the loss is temporary or permanent, the nature of the loss and how it occurred, previous history of significant losses, the individual's psychological makeup, other life stressors, whether the loss is disenfranchised (e.g., unrecognized by others or not socially sanctioned), and whether it occurred in isolation or as part of a series of losses (Doka, 2016). From another viewpoint, the extent of a social support system, current lifestyle and circumstances, and philosophical and spiritual beliefs determine the impact of the loss (Roos, 2002).

Another factor in understanding the impact of loss relates to the nature of primary loss and secondary loss (Humphrey, 2009). A *secondary loss* is a physical or psychosocial loss that coincides with or develops as a result of the initial loss. Secondary losses are

Think about a loss you have experienced at some point during your life and how it impacted you. What factors influenced the impact of this loss? As a result, how were your attitudes, beliefs, values, or perceptions altered?

like ripple effects. For example, immigration as a primary loss may result in secondary losses such as those associated with cultural identity, safety, and connectedness (Humphrey, 2009). Humphrey noted that primary losses generally are recognized, whereas secondary losses are often overlooked, at least initially.

Before we can fully comprehend the impact of a loss, we must understand the relationship between attachment and loss and recognize that all losses are legitimate (Harvey, 2000; Worden, 2009). Humphrey (as cited in Shallcross, 2009) stated, "If it's meaningful for me and I lose it, then it's a loss" (p. 29). Walter (2003), Harvey (2002), and Malkinson (2007) all cited John Bowlby's pioneering research on attachment and loss, which proposed that the goal of attachment is to maintain an affectional bond. When this bond is threatened, grief like behavior ensues. According to this theory, the greater the attachment or dependency, the greater the sense of loss.

Although grieving a loss is a natural and necessary process, Harvey (2000) noted that some people have difficulty transforming losses into something positive and growing from them. Harvey and Miller (2000) cited several factors that can influence growth and vulnerability, including the following: an individual's coping style, an optimistic versus a pessimistic outlook on life, a strong sense of self, perceptions of control, and the existence of preexisting vulnerability. Malkinson (2007) also stressed the important role that cognitions play in response to grief, emphasizing that how people think about the loss impacts the way in which they deal with it.

Given that people experience a plethora of types of loss and react in a multitude of ways, counselors can play a key role in offering support and intervention. It is imperative that counseling professionals take into account cultural and religious factors and understand that there are no universal templates for helping people work through loss. Furthermore, it behooves counselors to identify the most effective methods of helping people deal with loss. Group work has been shown to be one of the most efficacious approaches because groups can be a significant source of social and emotional support (Lubas & De Leo, 2014; Rice, 2015), and the personal connections with and sharing by group members who have had similar experiences with loss provide a sense of hope and universality (Corey, 2012a).

The topics of this chapter include loss associated with transitions among older adults, the bereavement process, feelings associated with loss, end-of-life issues, the purpose and format of loss groups, and considerations in conducting these groups. A specific example of a loss group is offered.

LOSS ASSOCIATED WITH TRANSITIONS

As previously noted, although we often equate loss with death or other such negative events, loss is also associated with transitions: from dependence to independence, from childhood to adulthood, from being single to being married, from work to retirement, from life to death. Whereas loss due to death is acknowledged and ritualized, loss that can accompany life transitions may not be recognized.

A *transition* is the time between two periods of stability, the changes—gains as well as losses—that affect everyone and necessitate adjustment. Anderson, Goodman, and Schlossberg (2012) described a transition as "any event or nonevent that results in changed relationships, routines, assumptions, and roles" (p. 39). Bridges (2001) defined transition as "the process of letting go of the way things used to be and then taking hold of the way they subsequently become" (p. 2). According to Bridges, transitions may be reactive, triggered by an external event such as death, or they may be developmental in nature, such as transitions between periods of life—living independently, then moving to assisted living, for example.

Transitions include expected events, such as retiring or getting remarried after losing a spouse. These transitions are typically associated with social milestones or personal choice. In contrast, other transitions may be unanticipated or surprise events typically associated with some type of crisis or disruption, such as getting fired or being demoted, divorce and separation, and illness of a spouse of child. Or they may be *nonevents*, which are events that we expect to happen but never do, such as never getting married or not being promoted after years of hard work (Anderson et al., 2012). Regardless of whether they are the result of a crisis, expected or unexpected, or more developmental in nature, the consensus is that transitions provide opportunities for growth and transformation (Anderson et al., 2012; Bridges, 2001).

Although the onset of a transition often can be connected with an identifiable event or nonevent, a transition is a process that takes place over time (Anderson et al., 2012). The impact of the transition relates to whether it was gradual or sudden, reversible or irreversible, major or minor, anticipated or unexpected, and voluntary or involuntary, as well as how the transition influences an individual's roles, relationships, routines, and assumptions (Anderson et al., 2012).

Regardless of the type of transition, it involves a three-phase process: (1) an ending, characterized by preoccupation with the change and how to let go of the old before picking up the new; (2) a disruption, which may seem chaotic as the old roles and routines are replaced with new ones, with the potential for creativity; and (3) completion of the transition, when the individual has accommodated to the new way of life (Bridges, 2001). As Schlossberg (2004) pointed out, even though we face transitions regularly, we do not receive any training or preparation for dealing with them. We may assume that some transitions, such as retirement or getting remarried, are easy, but in reality people frequently approach transitions of this nature feeling anxious, upset, or overwhelmed.

The Tasks of Transitions

In order to deal successfully with transition, Golan (1986) proposed that people need to accomplish material (instrumental) tasks and psychosocial (affective) tasks. The material tasks include recognizing the need to do something about the old situation; exploring solutions, looking at options, and weighing alternatives; making a choice and taking on the new role; and functioning under the new circumstances. The psychosocial tasks involve dealing with the loss and the lack of security; coping with anxiety, frustration, pressure, and ambivalence; handling the stress of taking on the new role or adjusting to the new situation; adapting to shifts in status or position, which may result in feelings of inferiority, lack of satisfaction, or lack of appreciation from others; and learning to live with the different reality, which may involve adjusting to new standards and levels of satisfaction. Anderson et al. (2012) stressed the importance of determining how the transition will change a person's life and the potential resources for coping with it. They referred to the four S's—situation, self, support, and strategies—as critical aspects in adjusting to the transition, along with taking charge and strengthening resources.

SIDEBAR 15.3

Case Study: Transitioning to Retirement

After 36 years of teaching, Suzanne is retiring, primarily because the incentive package for early retirement was too good to pass up. Suzanne loved teaching and has no idea what she will do in retirement, but her colleagues are envious, reminding her how lucky she is and how great the next chapter of her life will be. Identify four specific strategies you would use as a counselor to help Suzanne work through this transition.

The Transition to Late Adulthood

Although the span from ages 60 to 65 is generally considered the transition period to late adulthood, this transition may start before age 60 as individuals realize they now have lived longer than they will likely live in the future (Vernon & Davis-Gage, 2016). At this point, people begin to think more about what their life includes and its meaning (Broderick & Blewitt, 2006).

Although the transition to late-adult years is part of normal life cycle changes, this stage differs from earlier life cycle changes because it involves continuously adapting to decreasing abilities and increasing dependence. The multiple physical and emotional adjustments that accompany this period present a challenge to which individuals respond in different ways, depending on their life experiences and personalities (Vernon & Davis-Gage, 2016).

The following areas are among those that may be of concern in late adulthood: adjusting to retirement, role shifts/identity issues, changes in living conditions/arrangements, changes in looks/physical appearance, financial security after employment, finding a new balance with society and self, establishing new relationships, declining health and limited physical stamina, emotional well-being, dementia, terminal illness, and end-of-life issues (Vernon & Davis-Gage, 2016). It is beyond the scope of this chapter to address these topics in depth, but readers might want to consult Vernon and Davis-Gage (2016) on emotional and social development during late adulthood and Flamez, Ordway, Vela, and Hicks (2016) on generativity, death, dying, and bereavement for further information.

During late adulthood, *ego integrity versus despair* is of central concern to a person's development. Shortly before his death at age 91, Erik Erikson, a renowned psychologist, and his wife, Joan, examined their own grappling with ego integrity and the potential for despair in late life (Gusky, 2012). In this last of Erikson's eight-stage comprehensive theory of life-span development, people over 65 look back on their lives

SIDEBAR 15.4

Case Study: Transitioning to Late Adulthood

Edna just turned 90. She still lives independently in her own home, and up until recently she remained quite active, playing golf, walking her dog, and socializing with friends. However, she fell and broke her hip and has been in rehabilitation for several weeks. Her family is pressuring her to move to an assisted-living facility, and Edna is resisting. Identify six types of loss Edna is facing at this stage of her life and how you might help her deal with this transition.

and feel despair if life was not as productive or meaningful as they had hoped. This despair relates to the past as well as to the future as adults in this stage of development realize that they are nearing the end of the life cycle and death will be inevitable at some point in time. Joan felt strongly that this stage needed to be reconceptualized because when you actually confront issues at this last stage of development it is difficult to do so with integrity and wisdom, although it is easy to theorize about something. Consequently, she developed a ninth step a year after her husband's death, describing it as the *woven cycle of life.* Just like thread is woven to complete a piece of fabric, so are our lives. When we are strong, the colors are more vibrant, and when we are weak, the colors are not as bright. According to Gusky (2012), Joan Erikson believed that personality and identity continue to evolve past age 65, but in the ninth stage individuals look at life differently, placing less importance on material things and superficial relationships. As they continue to search for meaning and a new understanding of existential factors, they perceive life and death differently and have less fear of death.

End-of-Life Transition

As you have read, transitions are associated with an ending, a period of disruption, and a new beginning. Although there is loss associated with transitions, there are also gains. End-of-life transitions, however, are the exception. These transitions typically are not elected ones, although that is changing as some states now allow dying individuals to terminate their lives under certain conditions. Regardless, all individuals need to come to terms with their own mortality; the challenge is how people can do so with dignity and grace (Shallcross, 2012). Clearly, there are physical and psychological issues, as well as interpersonal and spiritual factors, to consider. For the most part, this is not a subject that is readily talked about because it is a difficult one to deal with for a multitude of reasons.

The reality is that "death is a part of life" (Flamez et al., 2016, p. 575), whether we like it or not. It is the final stage of the life cycle. Premature deaths rob people of living through each stage of the life cycle, but regardless of when the end of life occurs, this is perhaps the biggest challenge people ultimately are forced to confront. *Death anxiety,* which refers to discomfort about death (Cavanaugh & Blanchard-Fields, 2011), is a factor to consider when dealing with end-of-life issues. Counselors can provide death education that includes factual information to help older adults reduce their anxiety.

According to Niemiec and Schulenberg (2011), there are also some positive psychological factors that can impact attitudes about the end of life. Specifically, focusing on strategies that promote happiness and well-being, helping individuals come to terms with the past and recognize their strengths, and finding meaning can be helpful in coping with end-of-life issues. Spirituality or religiosity also can help individuals reframe their thoughts about death and work through the grieving process.

BEREAVEMENT, GRIEF, AND MOURNING

The terms *bereavement, grief,* and *mourning* have been used interchangeably in the literature (Humphrey, 2009; Malkinson, 2007), although some experts offer distinctions. Stroebe, Hansson, Stroebe, and Schut (2001) described bereavement as "the objective situation of having lost someone significant" (p. 6), noting that the usual reaction to bereavement is grief. Rando (2000) explained grief as the "process of experiencing the psychological, behavioral, social, and physical reactions to the perception of loss" (p. 60) and mourning as the conscious and unconscious processes and courses of action that help an individual break ties with a loved one or object, adapt to the loss, and learn to adapt to the new reality. According to Rando, grief is the beginning of mourning, but because it relates only to the reactions and perceptions of loss, the mourning process is what helps the individual read-just, adapt, and integrate. A culturally sensitive approach to grief counseling is essential because the mourning process is influenced by culture, traditions, and customs (Churn, 2003). As Rubin, Malkinson, and Witztum (2005) pointed out, "there are diverse ways to define what is normal and complicated within a specific cultural context" (p. 3).

It is very important to understand the meaning that people attribute to their loss because how we experience loss is very individualized. Despite the variability, every loss involves (a) accepting the reality of the loss; (b) letting go of the loss and working through the pain for both primary and secondary losses; (c) transitioning, adapting, and adjusting to the new reality without forgetting the old; and (d) reinvesting in a new beginning (Murphy, 2012; Worden, 2002). Worden described this last stage as withdrawing from the lost relationship and investing emotional energy elsewhere. Later, he revised this fourth task, so that rather than withdrawing from the relationship, the mourner remains con-nected but in a way that will not prevent him or her from getting on with life (Worden, 2009). This task is similar to the acceptance stage of grief as described by Kübler-Ross and Kessler (2005), in which the mourner must learn to live with the loss and readjust. In so doing, a new relationship with the lost loved one begins.

Although many experts contend that there is a general progression from one task to the next, many grief experts maintain that the stage theory originally proposed by Kübler-Ross is no longer relevant because in reality mourning is a fluid process that varies from person to person. The phases or tasks overlap, and individuals pass back and forth through them (Horn, as cited in Shallcross, 2012; Humphrey, 2009; James & Friedman, 2009). Mourning must be looked at in context, taking into account the individual's beliefs and coping skills and noting that the process might have no fixed endpoint because some people are so overwhelmed by a key loss that there may never be complete closure. Horn suggested that rather than "getting over" their loss and returning to normal, individuals adapt and adjust to the changes but may never resolve or complete their grief (Shallcross, 2012, p. 9).

Accepting the Reality of a Loss

Whether the loss involves control, self-esteem, ability to function, relocation, or per-sonal autonomy, the first task of mourning is to accept the reality of the loss (Doka, 2016; Murphy, 2012). This is often difficult, and denial is common—denying the facts of the loss, denying the meaning of the loss by making it seem less significant than it really is, selectively forgetting by blocking out the reality of a person or an event, or denying that the loss is irreversible (Worden, 2009). As Kübler-Ross and Kessler (2005) noted, being in denial is like being "paralyzed with shock or blanketed with numbness" (p. 8). Although the denial functions as a buffer by allowing the mourner to absorb the reality of the loss over time and not become overwhelmed, working through it is essential before a person can experience the pain of grief. Although periods of disbelief are com-mon, the reality of the loss ultimately must be acknowledged.

Experiencing the Pain of Grief

"Your grief is like no other. It is as unique as your fingerprints" (Doka, 2016, p. 51), and there is no one predictable pathway to grieving because it can be expressed in many different ways. Regardless, it is a profound experience related to the pain of detachment (Neimeyer, 2005). Although not everyone experiences the same intensity of pain or feels it in the same way, no one can lose someone or something without some pain. Pain that is not acknowledged and worked through impacts physical and mental well-being (Worden, 2009).

As Neimeyer (2005) emphasized, grief is an idiosyncratic process that is influenced by a multitude of variables, including age and culture (Malkinson, 2007). According to experts (Doka, 2016; Humphrey, 2009), there is little agreement regarding the time period for normal grief. It is not uncommon that in the case of loss involving death, many people maintain an emotional involvement with the deceased that does not necessarily imply an unhealthy adaptation. In reality, some aspects of grief will continue for several years after the loss or never will be totally resolved.

Although grieving is a normal, healthy process that is a necessary part of healing, society is often uncomfortable with grieving and may send the subtle message that people just need to get over it and stop feeling sorry for themselves. The pressure for people to "get over" grief also may be based on an oversimplified view of what loss is. Loss is not a simple event, and everything that is lost is not relegated to one period of time. Instead, a sequence of secondary losses that occur as a result of the primary loss can span many years or a lifetime (Malkinson, 2007).

Loss almost always entails a mixture of intense feelings that must be acknowledged and resolved before grief can be resolved (Ellis, 2006; Meyers, 2016). This crucial step is difficult for many adults who find it difficult to recognize and express their own negative feelings (Kübler-Ross & Kessler, 2005). Nevertheless, helping mourners identify, accept, and achieve a realistic balance between positive and negative feelings is necessary before they can let go and move to the next task: adjusting to a new environment.

Transitioning, Adapting, and Adjusting to a New Environment

Depending on the extent of attachment to the person or object of loss, transitioning and adjusting to a new environment means different things and may be multifaceted. Death of a spouse, for example, may mean loss of a companion, a sexual partner, a financial provider, a helpmate—depending on the roles this person played (Doka, 2016). In the case of diagnosis of a terminal illness, critical adjustments have to be made to accommodate new medications, limited physical stamina, probable loss of employment at some point, and reactions of family and friends.

The process of developing new skills and assuming new roles is often accompanied by feelings of resentment or anxiety. Depending on the nature of the loss, many people are faced with the challenge of forming a new identity or finding a new direction in life. Loss can threaten fundamental life values and beliefs (Worden, 2009).

Adjusting to a new environment implies accommodation to the reality. The primary task is to break old habits and adjust to the new reality with new patterns and interactions, which Attig (2002) described as involving emotional, behavioral, physical, social, and intellectual change. This task is not an easy, and when people are unable to adapt to a loss, they may promote their own helplessness, withdraw, or be unable to develop coping skills for the new environment. These nonadaptations make the outcome of mourning more difficult.

Reinvesting in a New Beginning

The task of reinvesting in a new beginning requires withdrawing from the person or object of loss and moving on to another relationship or situation. For many people, particularly after loss from death or divorce, this is associated with a fear of reinvesting their emotions in another relationship and risking another loss (Worden, 2009). To move on, it may be necessary to memorialize the loved one and maintain some connection but still get on with life. With other types of loss as well, a person has to successfully work through the withdrawal stage to live fully in the here and now. As Straub (2001) noted, "Your life may never be the same again, but it doesn't have to be. If you have hope, then love, peace, and happiness will return" (p. 81).

The prospect of moving on may create ambivalence, and people often are tempted to hold onto the past attachment rather than work through the feelings associated with the new reality (Worden, 2009). It is easy to get stuck at this point because it is so painful to give up the past reality.

FEELINGS ASSOCIATED WITH LOSS

Following many types of loss, people experience a sense of unreality and numbness that helps them temporarily disregard the loss (James & Friedman, 2009; Worden, 2009). However, accepting the loss is important, and people must be encouraged to talk about it and to identify and express their feelings. The feelings commonly associated with loss are anger, guilt, sadness, anxiety, loneliness, helplessness, hopelessness, frustration, and depression (Cavanaugh & Blanchard-Fields, 2011; Ellis, 2006; Meyers, 2016). Meyers (2016) also pointed out that a person may feel emancipated and relieved, particularly if the loss was associated with the deceased's long illness or a negative situation.

Although the feelings mentioned above are typical, all people do not express their feelings in the same way. The expressions of loss are somewhat dependent on cultural and religious beliefs, as well as on gender (Jacobs, Masson, Harvill, & Schimmel, 2012). For example, men in Western cultures are expected to be strong and not to openly express their feelings. They may be more reluctant to seek help and support, instead feeling responsible for resolving their own grief (Fiorini & Mullen, 2006). The reality remains, however, that they probably have the common feelings associated with loss even though they might not express their feelings in the same way.

It is important for grievers to understand that their feelings are normal in this circumstance. This point is extremely important because many people believe that they shouldn't feel the way they do or that they shouldn't express their feelings—that they should "be strong" for others.

Anger

"Anger is the shadow of grief" (Straub, 2001, p. 83), and it is linked to a loss of power and control. Although feeling angry over a loss is natural and understandable, many people have trouble admitting this anger because they feel ashamed or are frightened by it. Kübler-Ross and Kessler (2005) stressed that anger manifests itself in various ways and does not have to be logical, but it also is a necessary part of the healing process. James and Friedman (2009) disagreed, maintaining that it is wrong to assume that anger is an automatic part of grief: some people may experience anger, but others may not.

Guilt

Guilt plays a major role in most types of loss and can take various forms—survivor guilt ("Why not me?"), guilt over betrayal, and guilt related to feeling responsible for the loss. Doka (2016) called this *causation guilt,* in which the survivor's belief is that the death was somehow his or her fault. He also described *role guilt,* in which the survivor feels guilty about not having been a better spouse or son, for example. Harvey (2000), however, pointed out that people need to realize they cannot always prevent bad things from happening. Guilt slows recovery, and those who are convinced that the loss was their fault must work on forgiveness. They also may have to reconcile the reality that they cannot change the situation.

Sadness and Depression

"Sadness is the most common feeling found in the bereaved" (Worden, 2002, p. 11) and is associated with all types of loss. The sadness may be accompanied by tears and an awareness of how much someone or something is missed, and generally it is in direct proportion to the strength of attachment and the meaning attributed to the person or situation (James & Friedman, 2009).

Depression is another significant feeling in the grief process (Rando, 2000) and is one of the necessary steps in the healing process, according to Kübler-Ross and Kessler (2005). Often, depression is connected to what is lost from the past, what one misses in the present, and the losses one anticipates for the future (Doka, 2016).

Anxiety and Helplessness

Anxiety often develops after a loss, stemming from fear of the unknown, having to learn new skills, and being unable to perceive how one will manage without the support of a partner or the security of a familiar situation or way of being (Doka, 2016). Anxiety also is related to a heightened sense of one's own vulnerability. Individuals may need help in identifying the uncertainties they feel and the sources of their anxiety, as well as to recognize ways they managed situations prior to the loss and how, with some adjustment, they will be able to do so again.

Counseling professionals can support people who have experienced losses by encouraging them to express their feelings, legitimizing and normalizing these feelings, and helping them understand the meaning of the loss. Respecting cultural and gender differences and recognizing that different grieving styles exist are critical. Specifically, some grievers are more affective and others are more cognitive, so it is important to help clients grieve in the way that is most natural to them (Shallcross, 2012). Counselors should also convey the expectation that even though the present situation is difficult, they will be able to tolerate it and at some future time will have less pain and more pleasure.

SIDEBAR 15.5

Case Study: Alberto

===

Alberto's wife was on her way to the pharmacy to pick up a prescription for him when a car ran a stop sign and broadsided her car. She was killed instantly. Alberto feels guilty because he was out drinking with his buddies who were visiting from his hometown in Mexico, which is why he asked his wife to run the errand. He is also angry at God for taking his wife and leaving him alone. How would you help this client deal with his guilt and anger, taking into account his religious beliefs and his cultural background?

Loss Groups

Group work for various types of loss has expanded considerably over the past several years (Hutchinson, 2017; Rice, 2015), and online grief support groups are also becoming more common (Lubas & De Leo, 2014). The group format can be very effective because it encourages catharsis, creates community, puts the locus of control on the individual, and emphasizes interaction and growth—all essential ingredients in bereavement. Rice (2015) stressed the importance of group work in providing opportunities for social support and attachment. Further, group participation helps individuals cope with pain and maintain attention to the reality of the loss, which prevents them from delaying or distorting the mourning process.

Yalom and Leszcz (1985, as cited in Anderson et al., 2012) identified the following therapeutic benefits of groups: (a) instillation of hope, (b) universality, (c) imparting information, (d) altruism, (e) interpersonal learning, (f) catharsis, (g) group cohesiveness, (h) development of socializing techniques, (i) imitative behavior, (j) existential factors, and (k) corrective recapitulation of the family of origin. It is beyond the scope of this chapter to provide further detail on each of these factors, but several will be highlighted as follows.

UNIVERSALITY   Perhaps the most important function of groups is to provide the support that comes from meeting with others who share a similar experience (Cox, Bendiksen, & Stevenson, 2002). Following a loss, people frequently feel a sense of isolation because they are reluctant to divulge their feelings to people in their usual support system. They may feel a need to protect others from the pain or may think others won't understand because they haven't had the same experience. Meeting with people who have had a similar experience helps them feel less alone and can create a bonding as group members share reactions they all readily understand (Anderson et al., 2012).

IMPARTING INFORMATION AND EDUCATION   Again, depending on the type of loss, group members may have to be assured about the normalcy of their reactions and feelings (Anderson et al., 2012), as well as issues connected with the loss, such as how to get help with finances following the death of a spouse, how to cope with the loss of physical function following injuries incurred in an accident, or what to do with one's time following retirement.

The leader(s), as well as group members, can facilitate discussions about coping with loss. Because the coping skills needed are so varied, each group member likely will have some of the skills but not others. Group members who have dealt successfully with at least one of the problems can relate their experiences and offer suggestions. Hearing that others have dealt successfully with a similar concern restores a sense of control and instills a more positive outlook. The group leader also may be a good source of information because he or she can be more objective and draw from experiences in previous leadership roles.

EXISTENTIAL CONSIDERATIONS   Whether the loss involves death, dismemberment, serious illness, or change in status, loss often leads to the realization that the present is temporary. People begin to see that, ultimately, they have the responsibility for their own lives and happiness, looking at their priorities and what they value most. This realization brings several results: recognizing the importance of living each day to the fullest, clarifying what is important and meaningful in life, and learning the importance of not leaving things unsaid (Doka, 2016).

A group leader can facilitate discussion about the nature of loss, the meaning of the loss, and how it affects one's future. Dealing with these existential issues can help members grapple with their present losses and with their future impacts. Understanding these issues can lead to positive growth and change.

Loss Group Formats

Loss groups can be conducted in several different formats (Anderson et al., 2012; Corey, Corey, & Corey, 2010):

- *Self-help support groups, which usually center on a common theme, such as death of a family member or losing a loved one by suicide.* Members gain support from each other, validate reactions, and provide reassurance that they will ultimately resolve their grief and gain control over their lives. This type of group may not have a group leader, but if there is one, he or she may be a volunteer or a trained layperson. Many different dynamics can occur in loss groups; if there is no group leader to resolve these dynamics, the group may not be as productive (Jacobs et al., 2012).
- *Support groups run by a leader whose goal is to create a safe environment in which members can discuss their issues.* In this type of group, the leader invites members to share concerns and ideas and works to establish trust, commitment, and caring among members (Jacobs et al., 2012).
- *Counseling groups that have a designated leader with a counseling degree and are more structured than self-help or support groups* (Corey et al., 2010). The purpose of this type of group is to help members resolve specific issues related to the loss or transition.

As Anderson et al. (2012) noted, all three of these groups can be beneficial for people working through loss and transition. They stressed that there should be a good fit between the needs of the individual and the purpose and format of the group. Regardless of the type of group, all loss groups allow people to share common problems, fears, sorrows, and coping strategies and thereby help people develop new social support systems (Corey et al., 2010). In addition to helping members learn more about different styles of grieving and validating their experience, groups provide emotional and educational support, which has a direct relationship to problem solving. In addition to receiving encouragement and relief, learning about resources, and mastering burdens, group members benefit from the opportunity to help others gain strength (Anderson et al., 2012).

Unless it is a self-help support group, a loss group typically meets 8 to 10 times for 2-hour sessions (Corey et al., 2010). A group has between 8 and 12 members, who may be referred or who may join voluntarily. They likely will be in varying stages of the grief process. Sessions may be facilitated by either a coleader team or by one leader, though the coleadership model is encouraged.

Leadership and Membership Considerations

Members of all loss groups share the common experience of some sort of loss for which they are seeking emotional relief and a supportive atmosphere in which they can discuss problems and seek solutions. Because group members most likely are at different points in grieving their loss, modeling is an important learning tool as participants share their feelings and describe how they are coping. Modeling is just one of the considerations in conducting loss groups. Additional leadership and membership issues also must be addressed.

LEADERSHIP Facilitating a loss group is an intense process, and leaders may experience their own unresolved grief issues or overidentify with group members' situations because group leaders bring their own values and life experiences to a group (Corey, 2012a). Group leadership may be facilitative or instructional. In groups that are basically informational, the leader tends to be more instructional. He or she will have expertise or experience in a specific area of loss and can dispense appropriate information, as well as structure discussion or activities around predetermined topics. The goal of facilitative leaders is to encourage people to share their feelings and skills that enable them to cope more effectively with the loss, and they are less likely to provide information. These groups typically do not have as much structure, and they do not have a predetermined agenda. Topics for discussion emerge from the group members, and the leader facilitates the exchange.

Because people who are experiencing loss need information and support, both styles of leadership are often found in groups, with the dual focus of helping participants take control of their lives through problem solving and emotional support. Regardless of style, the leader must actively set the tone for mutually sharing and exploring feelings.

Leaders should model respect, acceptance, nonjudgmental attitudes, and encouragement (Corey, 2012a). Group leaders also must work actively to remain open to the members' losses, avoiding the tendency to placate or protect. They must be skilled in dealing with communication barriers and problematic behaviors such as monopolizing. Also essential to good leaders are flexibility and sensitivity.

Empathy is another essential leadership trait. Corey et al. (2010) described empathy as "the ability to tune into what others are subjectively experiencing and to see the world through their eyes" (p. 144). When people experience empathy, they feel as if others understand and accept them, and they are much more likely to share their deeper concerns. Conveying empathy encourages further disclosure, exploration, and release of feelings. It is important for leaders to model empathy and to point out to group members how certain behaviors, such as inappropriate questioning and defensiveness, block empathic understanding.

The group leader also can encourage mourners to reminisce. Reminiscing is vital to the grieving process and can be facilitated through photos, scrapbooks, and other mementos. Telling the story of a loss helps to relieve pain and provides necessary catharsis. Group members often feel uplifted and relieved after shedding this emotional burden (Humphrey, 2009).

Group leaders should continue to help members acknowledge the truth of their loss. Avoiding the reality will prolong the grief process, and grief could be incomplete (Worden, 2002).

MEMBERSHIP   Membership in loss groups may be open or closed. In a closed group, the same members attend for a series of sessions, which usually results in more cohesiveness. Open groups continue indefinitely, with members rotating in and out depending on their needs (Jacobs et al., 2012). Open membership may offer more opportunities for modeling and sharing because of the wide range in the stages of grief represented as new members join and others leave.

Individuals may be recommended for a loss group by a physician, a religious leader, a hospice organization, or a mental health clinic. Other members are self-referred. It is advisable to screen potential group members individually to explain the purpose of the group, ascertain the individual's type of loss and expectations for the group, and determine whether group or individual counseling or therapy would be most appropriate (Corey et al., 2010; Hutchinson, 2017).

Participants in loss groups are motivated to attend the group because they want human contact. Nolen-Hoeksema and Larson (1999) noted that people who have experienced loss tend to be open from the beginning and that this sense of openness frequently results in spontaneous sharing, which has implications for the amount of structure imposed on the group. According to Nolen-Hoeksema and Larson, participants in a loss group should have the opportunity to share what bothers them instead of holding it in and trying to "be strong," gain insight into their experience by asking questions and listening to others relate similar circumstances, receive support for the way they are handling their lives, and receive advice and help with decision making on a variety of issues that emerge as a result of a major loss.

A LOSS GROUP DEALING WITH DEATH OF A PARTNER

Although all loss involves similar feelings and stages, group members gain the most benefit from a group that addresses their specific kind of loss. The following example is designed for those who have lost a partner to death.

Of all losses, the death of a partner is the number-one stressor (Holmes & Rahe, 1967). The actual experience of losing a spouse varies depending on the circumstances under which the spouse died, the age and gender of the people involved, and the stage in the family's life cycle during which the death occurred (Becvar, 2001). The closeness of the bond contributes to the depth and extent of the grieving process (Harvey, 2002).

In fact, the death of a spouse results in numerous losses, as the couple may have shared confidences, shared parenting and household responsibilities, advised one another in financial matters and career issues, and serves as links to each other's extended family (Becvar, 2001). Because of the numerous roles that spouses fill for each other, the survivor experiences an increasing sense of loss that is "intensified because the grief is not only for the person who has died, but for the connection to the spouse, as well as for the bereaved person's plans, hopes, and dreams for a future with the spouse" (Walter, 2003, p. 13).

Following the loss of a spouse, relationships with friends, family, and social networks change considerably. Widows and widowers are particularly vulnerable, and loss groups represent an excellent approach with this population because this format can lessen the intense social isolation, provide emotional support and coping skills to help them accept the reality of the death, and help participants move forward as they share their pain with others who have experienced a similar loss (Walter, 2003). This format also provides instrumental support, such as helping with the funeral and household tasks, and validational support—helping mourners know what to expect during this period of grief and reassuring them that what they are experiencing is normal (Corey et al., 2010).

The group format encourages members to cope with their pain in an atmosphere in which they are understood by others, combating the social isolation and supporting members as they face the many changes that the death of a spouse brings (Walter, 2003). In a group format, members "can struggle together with the common feelings related to being cheated out of a long and happy marriage" (Harvey, 2002, p. 269).

Specific Issues

In addition to providing a place for catharsis and for normalizing and dealing with the feelings associated with the loss, groups can address several specific issues.

LONELINESS AND ALONENESS   After the death of a partner, the mourner loses the daily intimacies of having someone special with whom to share significant events and the sense of being the most important person in someone else's life (Walter, 2003). The struggle with loneliness includes a shift in identity from "we" to "I" (p. 14) and taking responsibility for oneself. Even though the intensity of a relationship with the deceased usually diminishes over time, the relationship does not disappear entirely. Facing the reality of being single rather than part of a couple is also a difficult transition, as is the realization that part of the mourner's "history" died with the partner (Doka, 2016).

SENSE OF DEPRIVATION   The sense of deprivation following the death of a partner is particularly acute. Widowers and widows may feel deprived financially, socially, sexually, physically, and emotionally, in any combination. Redefining one's roles becomes a major task that is frequently painful, overwhelming, and frustrating.

FREEDOM AND GROWTH   Despite the negative impact of loss, mourners find an awareness of freedom and the potential for change. Losses are linked to gains; loss can result in "creative transformations" (Viorst, 1986, p. 326). Helping group members recognize the strength that comes from facing and surviving loss and coping effectively with adversity is an important step in recovery. Encouraging participants to look at the potentials of independence and freedom is also essential. Frequently, participants come to appreciate the freedom of not having to adhere to a schedule or do things to please a partner. Creating and choosing new and different ways to meet one's needs results in greater awareness of who one is and what one enjoys, resulting in a positive change in self-esteem.

IDENTITY AND CHANGE   A spouse often represents the other's main source of identity (Becvar, 2001), so following his or her death, the survivor may engage in major introspection and struggle with his or her identity. In addition, the survivor often has to learn new behaviors that result in personal change—learning to cook and care for a house, handling repairs and financial responsibilities, and making decisions alone (Walter, 2003). A major lifestyle change, such as relocating or starting a job, also may accompany loss. Even though these changes can be positive, stress and readjustment are to be expected. The occasion of death can be used as a turning point in one's life (Harvey, 2000).

NEW RELATIONSHIPS   Forming a new relationship may signify readiness to put aside the past and move ahead, but this change is often difficult (Becvar, 2001). Widows and widowers often feel as if they would betray their marriage or diminish their love for the deceased mate if they were to enter into a new relationship due to the fact that they consider their spouse irreplaceable and think they would be betraying their ties with the deceased partner or partner's extended family if they were to become involved with someone else (Becvar, 2001).

Group leaders should be sensitive to these issues but at the same time encourage participants to address the fallacy of the "perfect marriage" or the notion that they would be discounting the significance of the previous relationship if they were to form a new one. At the same time, the leader should point out the importance of completing the necessary tasks of grieving before forming another relationship.

The Sessions

The following is a sample progression for a loss-of-partner closed group that meets once a week (2-hour sessions) for 8 weeks. This outline is only one of several group approaches that could be used to deal with loss of this nature.

SESSION 1   The group members introduce themselves, and the leader (or coleaders) facilitates a discussion on the group's purpose, soliciting participants' hopes and expectations and emphasizing confidentiality. The leader reassures the participants that the group will provide a safe atmosphere for them to talk about painful issues and that a goal will be to help members move ahead despite the pain. During this first session, the members each are invited to describe their situation involving the loss of their partner.

Because the participants usually are eager to relate their story to others who have gone through a similar experience, the leader typically does not have to introduce any more structure during this initial session. The sharing of experiences most likely will evoke a good deal of emotion, so the group leader will want to monitor the process closely and intervene if a member becomes too emotional, checking to see if the speaker should stop talking and receive other support or referral. At the end of the first session, and depending on the group's openness, the leader may want to ask the participants to bring photos or similar mementos to the next session.

SESSION 2   The leader begins Session 2 with a brief go-around in which members are invited to express their reactions to the first group session and thoughts they have had during the past week related to this experience or to their loss in general. If group members brought mementos to the session, these can be used to stimulate further discussion. Whether the discussion is more open ended or is introduced by sharing the mementos, the focus may be on memories, on what participants miss most (and least) about the deceased partner. The group leader encourages expression of feelings and helps members recognize the commonality of their experiences.

SESSION 3   To introduce the third session, the leader invites group members to talk about how they are dealing with the changes that have occurred due to their losses. If the group is cohesive and the sharing is spontaneous and open, a simple invitation may be sufficient to start participants talking about ways in which their lives have changed. If this is not the case, a structured activity such as the following could be introduced.

Activity: Give each group member a large index card and ask them to divide their cards into four squares labeled as follows: roles, relationships, routines, and responsibilities (adapted from Anderson et al., 2012). Invite group members to reflect on each of these areas and to write words in each square describing how these factors have changed as a result of the loss of their spouse. Depending on the group's cohesiveness, participants can share some of the ideas on their cards with a partner or with the entire group. Debriefing should center on the participants' feelings and challenges relative to these factors, how they are dealing with these changes, and if any of these changes and challenges have been growth enhancing.

SESSION 4   The first three sessions were directed largely toward the past, offering the group members an opportunity to share common feelings, concerns, and experiences. Likewise, looking to the future and entering the healing and renewal phase are important. As a transition, the leader might introduce the topic of freedom and growth.

In general, by this session little structure is needed because the participants have developed trust and rapport based on their common experiences with loss. If necessary to stimulate discussion, the leader might introduce the following activity:

Activity: On separate sheets of poster paper, write the following:

"What I can do or am learning to do now that I didn't or couldn't do before" and "Freedoms or new experiences I have now that I didn't have before." Then invite group members to randomly share their thoughts on these two topics and write their responses on the appropriate poster. After all responses have been recorded, invite discussion about what it has been like to learn new things or experience new freedoms. In debriefing this activity, help the participants realize that growth comes through pain and that loss can offer each of them an opportunity to become a more fully developed person.

SESSION 5   The theme of the fifth session is also change and growth but with more emphasis on the pragmatics of change. Because a partner assumes so many roles and responsibilities, the survivor may have to learn new behaviors to carry out these functions. By this stage, group cohesiveness probably will allow the participants to share information and advice openly on their new roles and responsibilities, such as finances, household responsibilities, settling an estate, or disposing of personal effects. The group leader may want to provide information on community resources relative to these concerns.

SESSION 6   As widows and widowers work through the stages of grief, their perspectives on life changes and new relationships may be a good topic to explore. If group sharing is spontaneous and open, the leader may simply invite participants to share their reactions, feelings, and experiences about this topic. Or, the leader could introduce the subject through the following activity.

Activity: Give each group member an index card and ask them to select one of three future periods—1 month from now, 6 months from now, or 12 months from now. After identifying the time period, ask participants to project what their life might be like in relation to (a) where they might be living, (b) how they might be spending their time, (c) who they might be spending their time with, and (d) what kinds of feelings they might have about these changes.

Have each participant write the time period and responses on the card. Then invite them to share their responses, focusing on their feelings concerning change and new relationships. Specific issues might include guilt about getting involved with another person, how to enter the single world, how society views new relationships, how new relationships may be a way of avoiding grief, and anxiety about change in general.

SESSION 7   The leader may use this session to encourage the group participants to continue exploring issues and feelings carried over from the previous session. Because members enter the group at different places in the grieving process, they are ready to make changes and enter into new relationships at different points. Encouraging discussion about anxieties and concerns may offer members the opportunity to clarify issues and support one another in these transitions.

During this session, the group might wish to discuss the meaning of life in general. Marriage may have provided some members a basic sense of purpose. The loss in these cases may necessitate an examination of their personal identity and life purpose. Straub (2001) suggested a structured exercise in which participants are asked first to think about how they would like to be remembered, then to write an obituary and share it with the group as a good way to think about their own lives. Prior to completing this exercise, it might be helpful for group members to talk with a partner or the entire group about dreams or desires they might have set aside during their marriage and whether those dreams still have a place in their present life.

SESSION 8   In this last session, the leader encourages group members to deal with what they have left unsaid or unasked and what regrets they expect to have after the group is over. This process could be loosely structured by inviting members to express an appreciation and a regret about what the group has meant to them. An activity such as this evokes powerful feelings and reinforces the idea that support from others is vital. The leader may want to encourage post-termination meetings for periodic support.

SIDEBAR 15.6

Self-Awareness: Personal Reflection

After reading this chapter, do you agree with Viorst that we grow by giving up? Cite several examples from your past or present to support her theory.

Summary

Throughout the life cycle, we are faced with losses that Viorst (1986) described as necessary and having "subsequent gains" (p. 366). If we fail to mourn, we will express grief in a delayed or distorted way. Mourning involves accepting the reality of the loss, experiencing the pain of grief, acknowledging and resolving conflicting feelings, adjusting to a new environment, and reinvesting in a new beginning. In dealing with loss, people need support on some level, and group counseling is an effective way to help mourners of all ages in the adjustment and grieving process (Anderson et al., 2012; Cox et al., 2002).

Another form of loss results from life transitions signified by developmental passages or marker events. To adjust to these losses, individuals must accomplish material (or instrumental) tasks and psychosocial (or affective) tasks. The transition to the late adult years involves potentially difficult losses because people are faced with adapting to diminishing abilities, relinquishing social roles, and grappling with the reality that at this stage in life they inevitably will be dealing with their own deaths and the deaths of loved ones.

Viorst (1986) maintained that "even though loss involves a great deal of pain, throughout our life we grow by giving up. We give up some of our deepest attachments to others. We give up certain cherished parts of ourselves. . . . Passionate investment leaves us vulnerable to loss"(p. 16). Looking at loss as it relates to growth and change can facilitate the healing process.

16 Support Along the Journey: Groups Focused on Addiction and Recovery

Mita M. Johnson

Group therapy and individual therapy are effective tools in treatment and recovery for addictions; clients ideally are placed in the settings that will most benefit their specific circumstances. Evidence-based data support that therapeutic, experiential, and relational value found in group therapy is not always experienced by a client in individual therapy. Therapeutic objectives of group therapy may include fostering of healthy attachments, identification and development of appropriate emotional expression, and treating a co-occurring mental health disorder (COD; i.e., depression, anxiety, isolation, guilt, and shame). Experiential factors necessary for effective group therapy include safety, support, and therapeutic engagement. Relational experiences that are capitalized upon in a group setting include affiliation, validation, connection, positive peer reinforcement, learning new social skills, and healthy boundary setting.

People are relational beings by nature. Group therapy provides a safe place for a member to explore his or her addiction with his or her peers and to begin or continue the journey toward abstinence and healing. Group therapy can cost-effectively deliver a diverse range of therapeutic services, comparable in efficacy to those delivered in individual therapy. People struggling with substance-use disorders (SUDs), addictive-behavior disorders (ABDs), and CODs are more likely to stay sober and committed to abstinence when treatment is provided in groups (Substance Abuse and Mental Health Services Administration [SAMHSA], 2014).

Substance-related and addictive behavior disorders are a significant behavioral health care concern. The United States is in the midst of a prescription-drug abuse epidemic, mainly for opioid painkillers and benzodiazepines (Inaba & Cohen, 2014). To understand the level of concern, consider the following data from the 2015 National Survey on Drug Use and Health (SAMHSA, 2016a) regarding the prevalence of substance use and co-occurring mental health disorders in the United States:

- Approximately 20.8 million people age 12 or older had an SUD related to their use of alcohol or illicit drugs in the past year.
- About 7.7 million people ages 12 to 20 reported drinking alcohol in the past month, including 5.1 million who reported binge alcohol use and 1.3 million who reported heavy alcohol use. About two out of five young adults ages 18 to 25 were current binge alcohol users, and 1 out of every 10 young adults were heavy alcohol users.
- An estimated 8.1 million adults (3.3 percent of all adults) had at least one COD and at least one SUD in the past year.

DEFINING ADDICTION

The definition of addiction from the American Society of Addiction Medicine (ASAM, 2011) is widely accepted:

> Addiction is a primary, chronic disease of brain reward, motivation, memory and related circuitry. Dysfunction in these circuits leads to characteristic biological, psychological, social and spiritual manifestations. This is reflected in an individual pathologically pursuing reward and/or relief by substance use and other behaviors. Addiction is characterized by inability to consistently abstain, impairment in behavioral control, craving, diminished recognition of significant problems with one's behaviors and interpersonal relationships, and a dysfunctional emotional response. Like other chronic diseases, addiction often involves cycles of relapse and remission. Without treatment or engagement in recovery activities, addiction is progressive and can result in disability or premature death.

DIAGNOSING A SUBSTANCE-USE DISORDER

Psychoactive substances are substances that directly affect the central nervous system, including physiology, neurology, cognition, and emotion. The number of individuals living with an SUD is rising for many reasons, including heightened exposure to psychoactive substances, decriminalization of marijuana, exponential rise in the misuse of opiate and other prescription medications, increased incidents of trauma, and improved quality, availability, and pricing of heroin, methamphetamine, and cocaine. The rise in SUDs and ABDs (gambling, pornography, gaming, Internet, social media, eating disorders, hoarding, etc.) has amplified the need for evidence-based, outcome-driven treatments along the entire continuum of care, using group and individual modalities.

The *Diagnostic and Statistical Manual of Mental Disorders*, Fifth Edition (*DSM-5*; American Psychiatric Association [APA], 2013), provides diagnostic criteria for 10 substances (alcohol, caffeine, cannabis, hallucinogens, inhalants, opioids, sedative-hypnotics and anxiolytics, stimulants, tobacco, and other substances not previously categorized) and gambling in the Substance-Related and Addictive Disorders section. The criteria are based on patterns of behavior related to the substance or activity. The *DSM-5* (APA, 2013) diagnostic criteria for diagnosing an SUD or ABD include problematic patterns of behavior leading to clinically significant impairment or distress, which have to be met over a minimum of 12 months.

The *DSM-5* (APA, 2013) makes a distinction between SUDs and *substance-induced disorders*, which include intoxication, withdrawal, and substance/medication-induced mental disorders. The *DSM-5* no longer promotes distinct categories of substance abuse versus addiction/dependence. SUDs are diagnosed along a continuum, based on current degree of severity: (a) mild current severity = the presence of two or three symptom criteria, (b) moderate current severity = the presence of four or five symptom criteria, and (c) severe current severity = six or more symptom criteria (what we would define as addiction or dependence). Available specifiers include early remission of the SUD, sustained remission, and being in a controlled environment in which access is restricted.

Gambling is the first addictive behavior to be recognized in the *DSM-5* (APA, 2013). Eating disorders, behaviors associated with obsessive-compulsive disorder, and hoarding are in other sections of the *DSM-5*. Nine diagnostic criteria are related to persistent and recurrent problematic gambling, of which four would need to have been met, at a minimum, in a 12-month period. A differential assessment is needed to diagnose the gambling behavior as operating independently of a manic episode. Specifiers for a gambling disorder include episodic versus persistent symptoms, early versus sustained remission, and mild, moderate, or severe current severity.

IN BRIEF: KEY CONCEPTS RELATED TO ADDICTION

Engaging in addictive substance use or behavior can progress along a continuum ranging from abstinence to experimentation to social/recreational use to habitual use, abuse, and dependence. Many factors influence how long it takes for an individual to progress from initial use to dependence. Although the initial decision to use a substance or engage in a specific addictive behavior was a choice made by the individual in most cases, dependence steals the client's ability to make a choice. Substance and behavioral dependence, also referred to as addiction, is a neurobiological disorder of the brain, resulting in significant alterations to the areas responsible for reward, motivation, and memory. Dependence on a substance or behavior can be physiological, psychological, or both. Psychoactive substances and addictive behaviors dysregulate key neurotransmitters in the brain, affecting the normal neurotransmission of dopamine, serotonin, GABA, norepinephrine, epinephrine, glutamate, acetylcholine, and endorphins.

Psychoactive substances and addictive behaviors change a person's motivational hierarchies and override self-care and health-related behaviors (ASAM, 2011). Substances and addictive behaviors hijack the prefrontal cortex of the brain and the underlying white-matter connections between the frontal cortex and circuits of reward, motivation, and memory (ASAM, 2011). Once hijacked, symptoms include altered impulse control, impaired judgment, dysfunctional pursuit of rewards, heightened emotional lability, and inability to defer gratification. Adolescents and young adults are particularly vulnerable to the effects of psychoactive substances because their brains are undergoing a radical reconstruction/maturation phase between the ages of 12 and 24. The adolescent/young adult brain is more susceptible to addiction, trauma, and arrested brain development than an adult brain.

Many theories and models attempt to explain addiction. The biopsychosocial (including emotional and spiritual) model integrates elements of several other models, including the medical, sociocultural, and psychological models, to help explain the etiology of addiction. The biopsychosocial model explains addiction as the result of a combination of factors, including genetic predisposition, exposure to addicting substances, reaction to the substances consumed, social factors, learning, and environmental influences (Engel, 1977). According to this model, these factors are reciprocally interactive and may function to promote or inhibit the development of an addiction (Anthenelli & Schuckit, 1992). For example, a genetic predisposition may team up with the social influence of a college binge-drinking culture, accompanied by the psychological desire to feel more relaxed in social settings, resulting in alcohol abuse. From the perspective of this model, no single factor is responsible for the addiction; instead, it is a cumulative interactive effect (Erickson, 2005).

Psychoactive substances gain entrance into our bodies through various means (i.e., orally; by injecting, snorting, or smoking; mucosally; or topically), cross the blood–brain barrier, and cause chemical changes in the brain. These substances are used to relieve pain, stimulate the mind and body, relax the mind and body, give pleasure, cause hallucinations, offer escape, and achieve intoxication (Porter, 2005). All substances that have the potential to be addicting are classified according to their effect on the central nervous system. The major categories of substances that can precipitate an SUD are stimulants, depressants, psychedelics, and other (i.e., inhalants, performance-enhancing drugs, psychiatric medications, and some designer drugs).

Stimulants constrict blood vessels, increase heart rate, raise blood pressure, and may increase respiration. Stimulants include cocaine, methamphetamine and other amphetamines, designer stimulants (bath salts), diet pills, plant stimulants (betel nuts, khat, caffeine, nicotine), and psychostimulants (attention-deficit/hyperactivity disorder [ADHD] medications, medications for narcolepsy). Clients who use stimulants want to feel more confident, energetic, and engaged. Psychostimulants (dexamphetamine, methylphenidate, modafinil) and other stimulants like cocaine and meth reduce fatigue and increase alertness and wakefulness; prolonged exposure to/use of stimulants eventually depletes the body's energy reserves, disrupts brain chemistry, and induces exhaustion, depression, paranoia, anger, violence, and intense cravings (Inaba & Cohen, 2014).

Depressants lower heart rate, blood pressure, and respiration. Major depressants include alcohol, opioids/opiates (including heroin), barbiturates, benzodiazepines (anxiolytics), and sedative-hypnotics. Minor depressants include over-the-counter depressants, antihistamines, and skeletal-muscle relaxants (Inaba & Cohen, 2014). Depressants work by depressing systemic functioning to control pain, reduce anxiety, promote sleep, and lower inhibitions. They are capable of inducing euphoria (Inaba & Cohen, 2014). Clients who use depressants often want to feel less emotional/psychological/physiological pain, trauma, and social anxiety. Most opiates/opioids control physical and emotional pain, can induce euphoria, and help with suppressing cough spasms and diarrhea.

Psychedelics, also known as *hallucinogens,* have qualities that make them behave like amplified stimulants or depressants. What is unique about this class of drugs is its ability to significantly alter a person's perceptions so they are intensified to the level of illusions, delusions, and hallucinations. Psychedelics alter one's perception of reality—often outside of her or his conscious awareness. The most commonly used hallucinogens are LSD, psilocybin mushrooms, mescaline and/or peyote, ecstasy and/or MDMA, ketamine, PCP, DMT, cannabis, and synthetic cannabinoids (Spice, K2).

Marijuana (from the *Cannabis sativa* and *Cannabis indica* plants) is the most popular psychoactive substance used worldwide, followed by alcohol. Marijuana is primarily classified as a hallucinogen with depressant and stimulant qualities. Marijuana can induce relaxation, sedation, increased appetite, heightened sense of novelty, giddiness, bloodshot eyes, short-term memory impairment, impaired tracking ability, respiratory impairment, mental confusion, hyperemesis, problems with learning, and psychoses.

Inhalants are a widely abused substance type that includes volatile solvents (i.e., gasoline, glue, spray paint, aerosol paint, lacquer thinner, correction fluid), volatile nitrites (i.e., amyl, isopropyl, isobutyl, cyclohexyl), and anesthetics (i.e., nitrous oxide, chloroform, ether; Inaba & Cohen, 2014). Inhalants are used for their intoxicating and psychedelic effects.

Performance-enhancing drugs are widely abused among athletes and those who exercise excessively. *Steroids,* hormones that we naturally manufacture as testosterone, build muscle and increase weight but also potentially cause aggression, physiological problems, abuse, and addiction (Inaba & Cohen, 2014).

Addictive behaviors, also referred to as *process addictions* or *behavioral addictions,* are compulsive behaviors that incur all the same negative consequences in a person's life as an SUD, without the physical issues specific to substances. Process addictions cause a person to compulsively and continually engage in an activity or behavior despite a negative impact on the person's ability to remain mentally and/or physically healthy and functional—at home, at work, and in the community. The most common behavioral addictions include video gaming, gambling, food, sex, pornography, love, shopping, hoarding, risky behavior, and exercise. It is not uncommon for a person to cross-addict: a person might give up a substance addiction but substitute a behavioral addiction, or vice versa.

Group therapy is a powerful therapeutic tool for helping individuals struggling with SUDs or ABDs. Advantages of group therapy for addictions include providing helpful and timely information to people new to recovery, efficiency in delivery of services (one facilitator working with 3–12 clients simultaneously), positive peer support, peer pressure to maintain abstinence and stay on track, a safe place to learn new coping strategies and life skills, a safe space to receive feedback from others, appropriate modeling of healthy relationships and relational styles, encouragement, coaching, support, reinforcement, structure, and hope. Groups are not necessarily comprised of members all using the same substance; it is common to have members with diverse drug experiences and life struggles. Groups that are individually tailored to specific substances tend to be 12-step recovery-support groups like Alcoholics Anonymous (AA), Adult Children of Alcoholics, Narcotics Anonymous, and Gamblers Anonymous. It is important to know which SUDs, ABDs, and CODs a client has been struggling or living with. Information about current and past addictions will inform the clinician's choice of group to recommend to the client and will inform the group-treatment plan.

TREATMENT MODALITIES: GROUP THERAPY

Group therapy is the most widely used treatment modality for SUDs and ABDs (Weiss, Jaffee, de Menil, & Cogley, 2004). According to the National Institute on Drug Abuse (NIDA, 2003), research has shown that positive outcomes are achieved when group therapy either is offered in conjunction with individualized drug counseling or is formatted to reflect the principles of cognitive behavioral therapy or client-centered care. Groups offer a number of advantages, including cost-effectiveness, opportunities to learn and practice social skills and self-care, and support and encouragement along the journey of recovery. Research generally indicates that group therapy is as effective as individual therapy for treating SUDs (Weiss et al., 2004). Groups provide positive peer pressure that helps members stay on track with their goals. Members can identify with each other and come from a place of understanding and experience when they confront and challenge one another about SUDs and ABDs. Participation in group therapy reduces their anxiety in social situations. Clients in recovery are admonished to stop associating with anyone they previously used with and to make new friends who practice abstinence. A safe, engaged group becomes a "system" of like-minded journeyers, all of whom are taking advantage of this opportunity to heal from the guilt, shame, stigma, and isolation associated with SUDs and ABDs.

There are seven group dynamics/variables that promote an active therapeutic environment (Yalom & Leszcz, 2005): instilling hope, recognizing the universality of problems, gaining information, caring for each other, creating a healthy family environment, improving social skills, and modeling healthy behaviors. Being an active group member can increase self-understanding, psychological growth, emotional healing, and true intimacy (SAMHSA, 2014).

Assessment

Clients fall somewhere along the continuum of care for SUDs: prevention (precontemplation, contemplation), treatment (preparation, action), or recovery-support services (maintenance, relapse prevention). For clients struggling with an SUD or ABD, treatment includes screening and assessment, diagnosis and treatment planning, delivery of treatment and case-management services, and referral to recovery-support services. Treatment modalities include individual, family, couples, and group therapy; clients may be in more than one modality of service at any given time during their recovery journey. Group therapy can be provided in hospital/inpatient, residential, and outpatient community and private settings. Assessment is multidimensional, with a biopsychosocial-spiritual-emotional focus. Because CODs and trauma are the norm among clients struggling with SUDs, a clinician will assess for polysubstance use (most clients use more than one substance concurrently—i.e., alcohol plus cocaine plus marijuana) and concurrent CODs (depression, anxiety, bipolar disorder, psychoses, ADHD, post-traumatic stress disorder [PTSD], anger-management issues, relational issues, etc.). A thorough and accurate assessment and diagnosis are necessary to place a person in the appropriate group. At times the therapist will need to refer the client to a psychiatrist or psychologist to get a psychiatric evaluation due to the nature of the symptoms. Once a working diagnosis and environmental/social picture have been mapped out, the client is recommended to specific group options for actual treatment and support.

Primary Modalities

Within addictions work, counselors will be exposed to various types of groups, including psychoeducational, skills-development, cognitive behavioral/problem solving, interpersonal process, and support groups (SAMHSA, 2014). In addition to these primary modalities, numerous specialty subgroups are utilized frequently for the treatment of addictions. These subgroups are often determined by funding sources, licensing requirements, needs of the group participants, location of the group meetings, and so on. Examples of specialty groups include culturally specific, abstinence-oriented, harm-reduction-oriented, anger-management, creative/expressive, fixed-membership, heterogeneous, homogeneous, problem-focused, court-mandated, relapse-prevention, and revolving-membership groups. Each modality has specific tools that support members in their recovery journeys.

COGNITIVE BEHAVIORAL GROUPS Cognitive behavioral therapy groups have a long history in the world of addiction treatment and recovery. Cognitive behavioral therapy looks at the connections among a person's cognitions, feelings, and behaviors; all three are intimately linked. Cognitive behavioral therapy groups (CBTGs) are focused on changing learned behaviors by changing thinking patterns, beliefs, perceptions, attitudes, and emotions. CBTGs are typically highly structured in their format (they may be curriculum driven), utilize teaching and role-playing activities, and include out-of-session homework such as thought logs or specific relational activities. The goal is to examine and correct and/or replace behaviors, thoughts, and beliefs that are maladaptive. The group facilitator(s) will determine if the group is going to focus on healthy versus self-destructive behaviors, internalized core beliefs, development of critical-thinking and problem-solving capabilities, or other areas. One area of focus specific to CBTGs is on common thinking errors that clients have, with the intent to dispute and replace faulty thinking. Examples of erroneous beliefs a client might hold that are in need of disputation include the following: "I am a failure," "I am different," "I am not strong enough to quit," "I am unlovable," "I am a loser," "I am worthless," and "I am a bad person."

CBTGs are an important source of social support and can help group participants learn about their addiction and the recovery process. Topics might include education about CODs, identifying and learning tools to manage overwhelming emotions, identifying and learning life skills that are needed to live safely in their community, and developing coping strategies for cravings and triggers that promote relapse prevention. CBTGs can reach a large number of clients as a cost-effective, low-cost treatment modality. The techniques used in group are largely determined by the leaders, their expertise, the needs of a referral source such as the court system, and the specific needs of the individual members of the group. The typical leadership style of CBTGs is that of active engagement by the facilitators and a consistent and directive presence.

INTERPERSONAL PROCESS GROUPS Interpersonal process groups (IPPGs) promote abstinence, harm reduction, recovery, and healing using the psychodynamic theory of how people function psychologically. The group facilitators continually monitor three dynamics: (a) *intrapsychic dynamics,* the psychological functioning of each group member; (b) *interpersonal dynamics,* the manner in which the people in the group are relating to one another; and (c) *group-as-a-whole dynamics,* how the group is functioning as a unit. IPPG facilitators illuminate and focus on those developmental issues within each member that are contributing to the person's addiction and may be interfering with the person's treatment and recovery.

Facilitators of IPPGs focus on the interactions between members and experiences within individual members, rather than the content of the session. The facilitators are studying the interpersonal dynamics for signs of transference and countertransference. The leaders can choose to concentrate on the internal cognitive and emotional processes of individual members, monitor and direct the way members are relating to one another, or focus on the group as a dynamic system of its own.

PSYCHOEDUCATIONAL GROUPS Psychoeducational groups (PEGs) are meant to educate clients about their substance use, co-occurring disorders, relapse prevention, and connections between behaviors and consequences. PEGs typically are structured and content driven. The facilitators may use a lecture format and a curriculum to guide the group experience and show videos or bring in speakers to teach key points. Facilitators determine how the information will be presented and work with members to help each one incorporate what they are learning into their own lives. PEGs are a great option to learn how psychoactive substances with addiction potential work on the brain and in the body, learn coping strategies for stress, learn conflict resolution skills, discuss attachment and healthy emotions, discover self-care tools that help with recovery, explore family dynamics, and more.

PEGs are particularly useful for people who are contemplative about the impact of substance use on their lives. PEGs provide a setting to challenge people to look at their options, think about meaningful changes that they can make in their lives, and develop realistic short-term and long-term life goals. Clients early in their sobriety and recovery benefit from educational discussions about triggers and cravings, relapse, roadblocks to recovery, and the impact of anniversaries/specific dates on recovery. This is a safe place to learn about family and social dynamics that either keep them trapped in their use or encourage their efforts to change. Participants learn a lot about who they are and what they like and want, and PEGs are a great way to learn what they need to support change. Group members are exposed to resources while in PEGs. Most clients need a variety of supports that promote healthy recovery: focused self-care, relaxation training, meditation, exercise, yoga, nutrition, anger management, and spiritual development. Groups like PEGs are a safe way to learn about the influence of culture and familial history on one's own parenting skills. The goal of most PEGs is to help prompt productive behavior, clarity of thinking, and emotional growth and development.

SKILL-DEVELOPMENT GROUPS Skill-development groups (SDGs), much like PEGs, teach clients how to maintain their recovery, whether through abstinence or harm reduction. SDGs are highly structured and focused. Topics typically include all facets of relapse prevention: refusal skills, social skills, communication skills, anger-management and conflict-resolution skills, specific parenting skills, and money-management skills. Facilitators of SDGs assess all members carefully to determine what each member's skill-development needs are. The assessment will determine what the client's current level of skill is and what skills need to be taught. Facilitators of SDGs have basic group-therapy knowledge and skills, understand how people relate to one another in groups, know how to foster engagement and connections among members, and are adept at managing conflict within a group.

SUPPORT GROUPS Support groups are a powerful part of the recovery process. Although treatment is highly targeted in its scope, support groups allow the members' efforts to be developed and strengthened through social interaction and relational connection. Members support one another as they learn to manage their thoughts, emotions, and behaviors; support groups develop interpersonal skills vital to a successful recovery journey. Support groups range from problem-focused groups to interpersonally focused groups. The idea is to learn how to make it through early recovery, achieve abstinence, and manage the business of day-to-day living.

Group facilitators can initiate and manage group discussions. The facilitators encourage members to share their experiences and how they overcome difficult challenges. The group is a safe place for validation, honesty, and experimentation with new life skills. The group is respectful, nonjudgmental, caring, and encouraging—fostering open and honest communication among all members. Support groups are less directive and agenda driven than the other groups. Facilitators are more interpretive and observational, facilitating the growth of support among group members. There is a distinction between therapy groups and support groups. Therapy groups are facilitated by behavioral health professionals, whereas community-support groups are peer driven and peer led. Group-counseling groups include those support groups that are led by a therapist or other professional.

Many people appear unable to recover from dependency without a community-driven support group, such as AA, other 12-step groups, Rational Recovery, Celebrate Recovery, SMART Recovery, and so on. Most effective treatment programs make attendance at AA or another similar program a mandatory part of the treatment process because they are a complementary component of the recovery journey (SAMHSA, 2014). The first effective community intervention for those seeking to maintain sobriety from an SUD consisted of peer-led support groups (Fisher & Harrison, 2000). In 1935, the self-help organization known as Alcoholics Anonymous was born. The AA organization was founded by alcoholics, for alcoholics. Bill W., one of the founders of AA, credited his recovery to an encounter of a spiritual nature and the power of conversation between alcoholics. While out of town, Bill W. met another alcoholic, Dr. Bob. Bill W. spoke with Dr. Bob face to face about his addiction and recovery. When Dr. Bob subsequently became sober, the two men decided to share the word and thereby strengthen their own recovery. From these encounters, the essential components of AA were formed, which include sharing personal experiences, recognizing alcoholism as a disease, requesting spiritual intervention, and engaging in conversation to help other alcoholics achieve sobriety. The goal of 12-step groups (such as AA) and other community-led support groups is to abstain from alcohol and other addicting substances entirely (Nace, 1992). These community support groups are autonomous and may be very different from each other (Doweiko, 2006), but commonalities (Rootes & Aanes, 2006) include peer leadership; members sharing their experiences; the format is educational, not psychotherapeutic; each member is encouraged to take responsibility for his or her actions; the purpose is to help the member achieve and maintain sobriety; membership is anonymous and voluntary; and the goal is a change in lifestyle.

SPECIALIZED GROUPS   Specialty subgroups have a specific, specialized focus, including relapse prevention, culturally specific, and expressive/creative. These specialty groups also include "focus" groups that address a specific behavior or concern, such as smoking, eating, substance use, grief and loss, trauma, shyness, anxiety management, and so on.

Relapse-prevention groups are focused on helping members abstain from using a substance or behavior. Members of this group are in a state of sobriety, having attained abstinence. The purpose of these groups is to help clients maintain their sobriety by providing them with skills and knowledge to anticipate, identify, and manage high-risk situations that can lead to relapse while working on life balance, self-care, and future goals. Psychoeducation, skill building, problem solving, and interpersonal process are all components of these groups. Leaders of relapse-prevention groups are familiar with the skills needed for relapse prevention and are able to navigate group-process issues and concerns. Facilitators are continually assessing members for risks of relapse, including those that the member may not be cognizant of and including internal and external risk factors and risky behaviors. Facilitators know how to intervene when necessary and are able to process relapse events without judgment or punitive demeanor.

The relapse-prevention group provides a safe place to learn about triggers; cravings; risky people, places, and things; and how to respond to temptations to relapse or an actual relapse event. Facilitators often teach their members functional-analysis tools so they can determine what led or could potentially lead to a relapsing event. Relapse is an event; members are taught that they did not lose all their work toward their recovery.

Culturally specific groups include groups that are gender specific (all male, all female), ethnically specific (Hispanic, Asian, Native American/Native Peoples, African American/Black, etc.), or community specific (LGBTQ, assault victims, veterans, first responders, professionals, persons with developmental disabilities, etc.). SUDs and ABDs are experienced differently by different cultures; recovery is directly and indirectly influenced by cultural variables. Members can relate to one another on a deep level that is both validating and counter to the isolation that many members experience when looking at their recovery journey. These groups adjust therapy to meet highly specific cultural values. They tend to be strengths focused. Groups focus on recovery and wellness, using a cultural lens. Facilitators are aware of the specific cultural attitudes and areas of resistance within the cultural group. The facilitators have to be culturally sensitive, patient, and creative about how they make the group meaningful to its participants. The group facilitators are sensitive to differences in communication, substance use, social constraints, past and current oppression, and the dominant culture's views and areas of discrimination and microaggression. Each culture has specific activities that can be used in treatment groups. Examples of culturally specific activities include rituals, celebrations, retreats, storytelling, and rites-of-passage activities. Weaving cultural elements into these groups has been helpful for group members; a person in recovery performs recovery work within the fabric of cultural identifications and psychosocial context.

Expressive groups are an amazing tool for helping clients express their conscious and subconscious thoughts and emotions when they are having difficulty expressing them using oral communication alone. Expressive therapy groups use a specific tool or multiple tools, such as art, music, poetry, drama, psychodrama, bioenergetics, psychomotor, Gestalt, games, and dance or free movement. Groups centered on creativity foster social engagement among their members. Facilitators are very engaged in these groups and use a highly interactive leadership style. Leaders have to juggle the focus on creative activities with the focus on group-process issues related to SUDs, ABDs, and recovery. Effective expressive-therapy groups have high client participation.

Specialty focus groups address a specific behavior or concern, such as smoking, eating, substance use, grief and loss, trauma, shyness, anxiety management, and so on. These groups are typically cognitive behavioral–style groups that are working to eliminate or modify a specific problem or behavior. The groups are short term, highly structured, and focused on symptom reduction or behavioral rehearsal. Within specialty focus groups, some groups have shown positive results using horses, dogs, and cats as part of therapy.

Group Structure

The structure of a group is determined prior to clients being accepted (Yalom & Leszcz, 2005). The success of a group-therapy experience for a member is dependent upon appropriate placement. Facilitators take the following into consideration when placing

SIDEBAR 16.1
Premature Termination

Yalom and Leszcz (2005) note that it is a common practice for the group facilitators to attempt to interrupt premature termination by persuading the member to attend one more sessions. The hope is that the other members of the group will persuade the member not to leave the group. Research has not found this to be an overly effective technique (SAMHSA, 2015). A more effective tactic is to discuss the pros and cons of premature termination during the introduction and group-agreements phase. This policy regarding "one more session" can be part of the initial group agreement. The group agreement/contract must be presented as a "genuine and informed commitment" to the group, not just as a formality or administrative process.

a person into a particular group: particular SUD and/or ABD, legal engagement, client characteristics, specialized needs, cultural affiliations, preferences, stage of treatment and recovery, and types of groups available. Facilitators must assess the client's readiness to be in a group; not everyone is appropriate for group therapy. People who may not be suitable for a group experience include those who refuse to participate, cannot honor group agreements, are in the middle of a life crisis or life-altering event, cannot control impulses, have defenses that interfere with group work, and experience severe internal discomfort in groups (SAMHSA, 2014). The typical SUD and ABD group size is 8 to 12 members, preferably with two cofacilitators. Yalom & Leszcz (2005) advocate for groups that include between 5 and 10 members. Groups may be organized to include members with diverse characteristics, or they may be homogeneous with members who are like each other along a certain dimension. In open and closed groups, members can encourage attendance through peer pressure. In open groups, new members benefit from the experiences of others who are further along in the recovery process. These more seasoned members act as role models for members who are less familiar with the recovery process (Golden, Khantzian, & McAuliffe, 1994).

AGREEMENTS   There are two types of groups typically used for treating SUDs and ABDs: open membership (revolving enrollment, with people dropping out or graduating and being added on an ongoing basis; the group may not have a specified termination date for its members) and closed groups (fixed membership for a fixed duration). Establishing firm boundaries and educating the participants about the ground rules increases the likelihood that their goals will be met. A group agreement is used to establish the expectations that group members have of each other, the leaders, and the group itself (SAMHSA, 2014). Group contracts/agreements/rules have been found to be the single most important factor contributing to the success of outpatient therapy groups and include policies pertaining to attendance, substance use, confidentiality, physical contact, contact outside of the group, participation, financial responsibilities, appropriate communication styles, acceptable conduct during sessions, and termination (SAMHSA, 2014). When new members enter a group, they are oriented to know what to expect, which promotes safety and participation. It is recommended that facilitators include members in the process of creating group rules; group ownership and engagement are strengthened when the members help to create the rules. Facilitators create the group rules for open groups and inform new members of the rules prior to their first date of attendance.

SIDEBAR 16.2
To Touch or Not to Touch

Touch in a group is never neutral. People have different personal histories, cultural backgrounds, and trauma experiences that lead to different interpretations of what touch means. Consequently, the leader should evaluate carefully any circumstance in which physical contact occurs, even when it is intended to be positive.

In most groups, touch (including hugs and hand-holding) is not recommended—unless it is an expressive group, dance group, or so on. In expressive and creativity groups, touch may be acceptable and normative. Group agreements/contracts always discuss touch and prohibit physical violence (SAMHSA, 2015).

COFACILITATION Cofacilitation is generally advisable when running SUD and ABD therapy groups. The group benefits from multiple perspectives, and facilitators can share the stress of leading the group. The leaders can be positive role models for what it looks like to collaborate and work together. Effective coleadership has the same requirements as a good marriage. The coleaders must agree on fundamental principles, theoretical orientation, and the group process, have mutual respect, be compatible and cooperative, and share program coordination. Their skills must complement each other. The group leaders should coordinate their efforts by meeting regularly outside of the session to discuss the group members, their progress or lack of progress, and possible interventions (Washton, 1992). Cofacilitators are encouraged to engage in regular and open communication among themselves and to remain vigilant to signs that members are playing one leader against the other. Leaders must confront these issues as they come up. There is a school of thought that groups dealing with gender-sensitive issues should have leaders of the same gender as the group participants. Although historically the belief has been that women should lead groups designed for women who were subjected to sexual abuse, there is not a lot of evidence to support this claim. In one study, women were randomly assigned to either a male–female counselor dyad or a female co-counselor-led group, and there were no significant differences in the outcome (Nesmith, Wilcoxon, & Satcher, 2000).

SIDEBAR 16.3
Showing Up High or Intoxicated

Periodically, a group member will show up for a group session high and/or intoxicated. The member cannot participate in the group process if he or she is functionally, physiologically, and/or intellectually impaired. Members cannot leave the group location and drive themselves home in this state of intoxication; if the member were to be in an accident, the facility could be liable for damages because the facility knew the member left high and/or intoxicated. Several options are available to handle this tricky situation:

(a) members can sit in the lobby or a different room and be monitored until they are no longer intoxicated, using a breathalyzer to test the level of intoxication; (b) the facility or a facilitator can call a taxi to give the member a ride home; (c) the facility or a facilitator can call a significant other or identified adult to give the member a ride home; or (d) the facility can call law enforcement to take the person to detox, if there are no other reasonable solutions available.

GROUP DEVELOPMENT   We advise that group leaders meet with each prospective group member prior to convening the group to make sure the person would be appropriate for the group and to begin forming a therapeutic alliance, reach consensus on what will be accomplished in the group, educate the client about group therapy, allay anxiety, and explain the basics of a group agreement (SAMHSA, 2014). The tasks in the initial sessions of the group include introductions, creating and/or reviewing a group agreement, establishing an emotionally safe environment and positive group norms, and focusing the group on its purpose (SAMHSA, 2014). The sessions begin with get-acquainted activities, with the goal of increasing a sense of community and honest interactions. In the middle phase, the members interact, work on specific issues and concerns, and make changes that assist their recovery. Sessions may emphasize self-disclosure, drug refusal strategies, social skills, and leisure activities (Johnson, 2003). Some groups address coexisting psychiatric disorders (Rose, 1998). The end phase introduces and works toward termination or closure of the group. Through the initial group-therapy sessions, members are particularly vulnerable to relapse and discontinuation of treatment (SAMHSA, 2014). Retention rates are enhanced by member preparation, maximum member involvement, feedback, prompts to encourage attendance, provision of wraparound services, and timing and duration of the group (SAMHSA, 2014).

SIDEBAR 16.4
Diversity and Group Cohesion

To promote group cohesion, the group leader should (a) inform potential group members that the group will include diverse ethnicities and backgrounds, (b) discuss sensitive topics in a timely, safe, and nonjudgmental manner, (c) set the tone for the group experience by having an open discussion about how to handle differences in beliefs and feelings, (d) help clients address microaggressions and member bias in a way that supports healthy self-esteem, and (e) integrate new clients into a group slowly, allowing them to set their own pace initially while encouraging their eventual participation (SAMHSA, 2015).

SIDEBAR 16.5
Nothing Leaves This Room

A surefire way for a group to implode is to violate confidentiality. Groups are most effective when they are safe, nonjudgmental, and confidential. Members expect that what they say in group stays in group. It is the facilitator's responsibility to share with outside sources mandating reports (i.e., parole or probation) only pertinent information and nothing beyond that. Clinical supervision and consultation are not for gossip; only pertinent information is shared in supervision and is kept confidential by all members of the supervision/consultation team. Members also share and gossip outside of groups; we cannot control what members say and do. One way to address this is to remind all members about the confidentiality needs of the group at the beginning and end of every session, thereby setting the tone for what is shared and hopefully discouraging outside breaches of confidentiality. Gossip is never good. All members have a right to hear what other members are saying about them. If a member is not present for a session, she or he will not be discussed or gossiped about in that session. Even after a person is no longer a member of the group, facilitators must make sure that there are no discussions about that member in group.

STAGES OF GROUP THERAPY   Recovery occurs in stages, and there are corresponding stages of treatment. In the early phase of treatment, clients are ambivalent about the problems they are facing and their need to be in recovery. Their brains may be detoxing and entering the initial stages of healing. Cognitive functioning may be lower than expected. Early phases of group treatment are focused on cracking the ambivalence so that clients can realistically see the issues of and concerns about their use and behaviors.

The brain is working actively toward greater biochemical stability during the middle phase of recovery. Cognitive capacity is increasing. Clients during this middle phase are helping one another to acculturate into a culture of recovery. Facilitators are discussing relapse prevention more specifically, while also highlighting positive changes in each member and working on immediate concerns clients may have about their present and future.

In the late phase of treatment, clients are more stable as their brains achieve greater biochemical stability and cognitive capacity. Clients in the late phase of treatment are better able to face situations that involve conflict and emotion. They are having to confront painful realities about their lives, repair and build healthy relationships, and work on communication and conflict-resolution skills. Clients need tools to help them heal and grow. Effective group facilitators can juggle the many nuances of the group experience (phases of recovery, relationships, emotions, conflicts, etc.).

EXAMPLE OF CONVENING A GROUP: PREVENTING RELAPSE AND RECIDIVISM   *Recidivism* occurs when clients return to their former SUD or ABD activities; *relapse* is a singular event without completely recidivating. Because the risk of relapse is high for clients struggling with SUDs and/or ABDs, preventing relapse is a logical topic in most recovery groups (Doweiko, 2006). Many variables might cause relapse, including lack of social support, mood disorders, impulsivity, poor social skills, high levels of anxiety and stress, familial issues, co-occurring mental health issues, trauma, and lack of needed wraparound services. Chiauzzi (1990) identified four factors that contribute to relapse:

1. *Personality traits.* These include compulsive behavior, difficulty adapting to change, passive-aggressive behavior, a tendency to blame others, antisocial personality traits, impulsivity, and refusing to ask for help.
2. *Tendency to substitute addictions.* Often, clients will cross-addict from one substance or behavior to another substance or behavior.
3. *Restricted view of the recovery process.* Instead of changing their personal perspectives and lifestyles, individuals focus on changing a single characteristic while keeping other aspects of their lives intact. These people follow treatment in a superficial manner, avoiding insight and self-awareness. People in recovery refer to "talking the talk" but not "walking the walk." True recovery requires changing recreational and other activities as part of the lifestyle change needed to leave the world of SUDs and ABDs.
4. *Failure to attend to warning signs.* Many people early in recovery and even some later in their recovery don't recognize the "seemingly meaningless" decisions that put them on the slippery slope of relapse.

SIDEBAR 16.6
Check In

Groups for members struggling with SUDs and ABDs are an ideal place to process what has transpired since the last group session. Typically, during the initial group start and check-in, the facilitators will ask each member to share the following information about what has happened since last session: cravings, triggers, relapses, occurrence of a life-altering event like the death of a family member or friend, difficulties the person is struggling with in the daily business of living, court appearances, and if they have something urgent for the group to discuss. Check-in is an important time for recognizing successes and positives for the members; this is a way for members to reconnect with one another and with the facilitators. The facilitators make note of the concerns that may need to be addressed later in the session or a later session. This is an important time for the members to get feedback and encouragement from their peers. This check-in gives structure to what is shared so the group does not go off on numerous and unrelated tangents.

The same factors that created the addiction can be powerful forces that trigger a relapse. For example, a deficit in social support may take the form of a spouse who continues to drink alcohol and is actively sabotaging the other's abstinence. People have reported that their spouses say things such as "I liked you better when you were drinking"—and peer pressure is one of the primary causes for starting drug use in the first place. Group members might be asked to complete checklists to help them identify the risk factors associated with relapse. To maintain recovery, clients must learn to manage their cravings while also learning to deflect the social pressure to use. People in recovery often discover that it is difficult to get away from their drug dealers. To the dealers, recovery is bad for business; they will go to great lengths to keep their customers using. Therapy groups are the ideal place to learn and practice refusal skills and assertive communication. Role-plays and discussions regarding hypothetical or real scenarios are appropriate activities during group sessions. Videos are useful for sparking conversation about SUDs and ABDs.

A six-session group for people in recovery, with an emphasis on preventing relapse, might be organized as follows:

- *Session 1:* introductions and getting to know each other
- *Session 2:* education regarding dependence, withdrawal, and causes of relapse
- *Session 3:* relationship development and maintenance
- *Session 4:* environmental supports
- *Session 5:* self-development—who am I?
- *Session 6:* summarizing time together, looking forward and termination

ADDICTIONS WORK: HOW PEOPLE CHANGE IN GROUPS

Society has made *change* such a dirty word that many people take the stance consciously or subconsciously that no one can make them change. Yet the business of living is about change: everything is continually in motion, and everything, including people, is continually changing. Change is about growth, doing something different, looking at a situation or a person with a new lens. To change is not easy and has the potential for invoking strong emotions laced with legitimate apprehensions. The words we use matter when it comes to change and our motivation to change. We are continually communicating with the intent to motivate and influence one another in simple and very complex ways.

Motivational Interviewing

Motivational interviewing (MI) is a way of communicating with clients that involves attention to natural language about change such that people talk themselves into change based on their own values and interests (Miller & Rollnick, 2012). Rather than directing or following a conversation, MI guides a conversation designed to find a way through the challenges that often arise when a provider seeks to elicit and engage the client's motivation for change. A guiding style of communication includes arousing, assisting, collaborating, encouraging, eliciting, motivating, inspiring, and supporting.

Our intention as providers working with people struggling with addictions is to collaboratively guide clients to unpack and explore their internal ambivalence toward change, which is an area in which most clients find themselves stuck. Ambivalence is that pivotal feeling between wanting change and not wanting change, in which the status quo does not seem so painful as the prospect of doing something different. MI-style conversations are designed to understand clients' ambivalence while helping them arrive at a way to argue for the changes that they need and want. There is no hidden agenda, no intent to coerce or manipulate. The client has the right to autonomy and self-direction; as providers, we can elicit from within clients their motivation to not use substances illicitly or not engage in harmful addictive behaviors. MI is a collaborative conversation style used to strengthen a client's own motivation and commitment to change.

There are many MI tools that a facilitator can use in a group-counseling setting. Group facilitators express genuine empathy, develop discrepancies, de emphasize labels, emphasize personal choice and responsibility, accurately reflect thoughts and emotions, and meet the clients in their ambivalence using approaches that are collaborative, evocative, and affirming of a client's right to autonomy. MI is most effective when a strong therapeutic alliance has been established between the client and the provider. The facilitator engages clients through acceptance (absolute worth, accurate empathy, autonomy, and affirmation), compassion, a desire to create a collaborative partnership, and the ability to evoke from clients what they need and what they are willing to do to meet those needs (Miller & Rollnick, 2012). These collaborative conversations about motivation and change occur within the group, using engagement, focusing, evoking, and planning activities (Miller & Rollnick, 2012).

Therapeutic conversations about motivation to change occur when a facilitator uses open-ended questions, affirmations, reflections, and summarizations (OARS; Miller & Rollnick, 2013). Change-talk occurs when the client is talking about the disadvantages of the status quo, advantages of change, intention to change, and optimism about change (Miller & Rollnick, 2013). The client is most open to making changes in his or her life when he or she is able to articulate, with the help of the facilitator, his or her

DARN—that is, *desire* (what she or he wants to be different), *ability* (what the client believes he or she can change), *reasons* (why this change is necessary), and *needs* (what changes have urgency now; Miller & Rollnick, 2013). Mobilizing commitment talk (CT) that precipitates change requires not only the tools of MI (i.e., OARS, DARN, and CT) but also that the facilitator/provider understands what stage of change the client is currently in.

Stages of Change

Lasting change takes time and effort and can be internally or externally motivated. Research by Prochaska and DiClemente (1983) demonstrated that there are five stages of change that most people progress through as they seek solutions to their problems. The five phases are precontemplation (not seeing the problem as a problem), contemplation (seeing the problem and considering action versus inaction), preparation (making plans to act), action (actively making changes), and maintenance (maintaining the changes made).

It is important to look at how MI and stages of change are a natural adjunct to group therapy. By knowing what stage the client is in, the clinician can place the client in the group with the best fit. Figure 16.1 illustrates group-placement recommendations based on stage of recovery. Figure 16.2 illustrates group-placement recommendations based on stage of or readiness for change.

It is important to note that the journey through the stages is rarely linear. Most journeys through the stages of change have as many steps backward as they do forward, and for some struggling with SUDs and ABDs, the journey through the stages looks and feels more like a roller coaster with unanticipated twists and turns. Prochaska and

Client Placement by Stage of Recovery								
	Psycho-education	Skill Building	Cognitive–Behavioral	Support	Interpersonal Process	Relapse Prevention	Expressive	Culture-Specific
Early	+++	++	+	+++	+		+	*
Middle	+	++	++	++	+++	+++	+	*
Late and Maintenance			++	+	+++			*

Key:

Blank Generally not appropriate
+   Sometimes necessary
++   Usually necessary
+++   Necessary and most important
*   Depends on the culture and the context of treatment

FIGURE 16.1 Client Placement by Stage of Recovery

Source: SAMHSA, 2016a. Results from the 2015 National Survey on Drug Use and Health: Detailed tables. Retrieved from https://www.samhsa.gov/data/sites/default/files/NSDUH-DetTabs-2015/NSDUH-DetTabs-2015/NSDUH-DetTabs-2015.htm#fn1.

Client Placement Based on Readiness for Change								
	Psycho-education	Skill Building	Cognitive–Behavioral	Support	Interpersonal Process	Relapse Prevention	Expressive	Culture
Precontemplation	+		+		+			+
Contemplation	+	+	+	+	+		+	+
Preparation	+	+	+	+	+		+	+
Action	+	+	+	+	+	+	+	+
Maintenance		+	+	+	+	+	+	+
Recurrence		+	+	+	+	+	+	+

FIGURE 16.2   Client Placement Based on Readiness for Change

Source: SAMHSA, 2014. Substance abuse treatment: Group therapy. Retrieved from https://store.samhsa.gov/shin/content/SMA12-3991/SMA12-3991.pdf.

DiClemente (1983) identified 10 processes of change (5 are experiential and 5 are behavioral) that support a person as he or she moves from one stage to the next and that are very applicable to group work.

EXPERIENTIAL PROCESSES   The five experiential processes are as follows.

Consciousness Raising.   Group facilitators offer information to the client about their SUDs and ABDs. To make informed decisions that lead to meaningful changes, clients learn about themselves and the negative physiological, psychological, emotional, and spiritual effects of SUDs and ABDs.

Dramatic Relief.   Group facilitators understand that people change because they have an emotionally compelling reason to change. Few people change due to logic and inductive reasoning. Groups are a safe way to explore the emotions linked to the problems and concerns.

Self-Re evaluation.   There are noteworthy moments in our lives when we need to assess our personal values and life goals and determine how current thoughts, beliefs, emotions, and behaviors are a barrier to pursuing those values and goals. Group facilitators are able to help clients learn about themselves (many clients do not know who they are because their identities have been tied to their SUD or ABD): what they value, what their purpose is, and what the possibilities are for the next chapters of their life.

Environmental Re evaluation.   Most clients do not realize how their SUDs and/or ABDs are impacting those in their environment. Facilitators raise awareness that SUDs and ABDs impact not only the clients but also their families and friends and their communities.

Social Liberation.   Facilitators recognize that clients need a healthy social environment that is conducive to behavioral change. This group process explores supports available to the client, in the community, that assist with creating and maintaining behavioral changes.

BEHAVIORAL PROCESSES   The five behavioral processes are as follows.

Stimulus Control.   Collective wisdom within groups can help a member recognize and avoid cues that trigger behaviors associated with SUDs and ABDs.

Counterconditioning.   Groups provide a safe way for a member to explore unhealthy behaviors and responses that are triggers and to replace unhealthy with healthy behaviors and responses. Members also benefit from learning how to alter their responses to the cues by substituting healthy alternative responses when the cues cannot be avoided.

Reinforcement Management.   Also known as *contingency management,* this tool rewards a member for positive behavior changes with incentives (e.g., candy, haircuts, manicures, toys, and certificates) or positive consequences (e.g., one less urinalysis this week or one group-attendance requirement taken off the total). Rewarding positive behaviors has been shown to engage the client more deeply in the recovery process and can extend the length of sobriety time (SAMHSA, 2014).

Self-Liberation, Including Self-Efficacy.   Self-efficacy is the internal belief and confidence that a person has that he or she can be successful at a given task, behavior, or change. When clients have high self-efficacy, they are more able to alter their behaviors and have a deeper commitment to their SUD or ABD change goals.

Helping Relationships.   People do not change in isolation; people change within relationships. Relationships that are supportive, caring, accepting, and nonjudgmental strengthen a person's resolve in recovery. Healthy relationships formed with group members and facilitators validate the member's value, worth, and resolve while reducing feelings of shame, alienation, and isolation. People need people in recovery; a person does not have to be in recovery to have a positive impact on a person who is in recovery.

ENHANCING CLIENT RETENTION   Groups are most effective and have a better chance for positive outcomes when members attend regularly. Retention rates are influenced by client preparation, client connection and engagement during early stages of treatment, use of feedback, prompts that encourage attendance, provision of necessary wraparound services (e.g., bus passes, transportation, child care) so a client can attend, and the timing and length of group. Group induction relates to those activities pregroup and early in the group experience that reduce incidences of dropout. Early on, watching videos and hearing interviews or presentations on group therapy and member experiences can increase retention because the client experiences what the process will be as therapy. Helping each member (new or veteran) engage in the process and connect with the other members and the facilitators will go a long way toward retention and participation.

Summary

Group therapy is an effective option for treating SUDs and ABDs. Rewarding aspects of group therapy include reducing isolation while promoting recovery and healing. The group becomes a microcosm that reflects a culture of growth and recovery. There are numerous advantages to using group therapy for treating addictions. Groups provide a roadmap of information for clients new to their recovery journey. One educated, trained, and supervised group facilitator can work with multiple clients concurrently, which is an efficient model of service delivery. A cohesive group provides positive peer support that promotes harm reduction and abstinence. Group members learn positive values; they learn that they have value and worth. Members encourage, coach, support, and reinforce one another through their time together. Members identify which social skills they have been using that are detrimental and learn new social skills that they can use in their recovery. Peers hold each other accountable for their thoughts, feelings, and actions and confront concerns from a place of knowing and understanding. Well-led groups instill hope in each of their members—hope that they can make it in their recovery and that they are not alone. Groups create and develop relationships that are healthy and supportive and that have the potential to continue long after the group has dissolved.

17 Group Work: Gay, Lesbian, Bisexual, and Transgender Clients

Stephanie F. Hall, Jessica R. Burkholder, and David U. Burkholder

Mental health professionals have been slow to respond to the mental health needs of lesbian, gay, bisexual, and transgender (LGBT) clients. As evidence of this slow response, the American Psychiatric Association labeled homosexuality as a form of mental illness until 1973, and the American Psychological Association did the same until 1975; although homosexuality was removed from the *Diagnostic Statistical Manual* (DSM), it was replaced with "sexual orientation disturbance." Homosexuality was not completely removed from the DSM until 1987. The status of LGBT clients within the mental health professions has evolved over time, and today the official position of the counseling profession is to train counselors to affirm clients' gender identity, gender expression, and sexual orientation. This position was recently codified in the American Counseling Association's (ACA) 2014 revision to its *Code of Ethics*, which included Standard A.11.b, requiring counselors to refrain from referrals based on personally held values or beliefs and respect diversity of clients. In addition, Standard C.5 of the ACA's *Code of Ethics* specifically prohibits discrimination based on gender identity and sexual orientation. Counseling theory and practice have paralleled the profession's affirming stance toward the LGBT population, including group work with these populations.

It is important to begin this chapter with some foundational concepts. Counseling LGBT clients is similar to counseling other culturally different populations in that practitioners require culture-specific preparation. One element of culture-specific knowledge of the LGBT population is defining the important distinction between sexual orientation and gender identity because of the implications that exist for group work. *Sexual orientation* refers to emotional, romantic, and sexual attraction,

---

SIDEBAR 17.1

Case Study: What Is Kasey's Responsibility?

Kasey is a mental health counselor working in a community agency that serves clients of all ages, backgrounds, and presenting concerns. Kasey's coworker, Natalie, discloses that she has been assigned a transgender client and intends to refer the person because she is uncomfortable counseling people who are "gay or transgender." She states that it will not be a problem because she has not met the client yet. Does Kasey have a responsibility in this situation? If so, what course of action should she pursue? According to the ACA *Code of Ethics*, what is Natalie's responsibility?

whereas *gender identity* refers to a person's concept of self as male, female, both, or neither. A person's gender identity does not dictate sexual orientation, and gender identity can be the same as or different from the sex assigned at birth.

This chapter deals with language and terminology issues related to gay, lesbian, bisexual, and transgender communities, including the cultures of sexual minorities in U.S. society, heterosexism, homophobia, LGBT-affirmative counseling, general group approaches with these populations, and specific groups for clients who identify as LGBT. In addition, though there is often overlap in the experiences of LGBT persons, there can also be profound differences. As a demonstration of this, the ACA has adopted separate competencies for working with transgender clients (Burnes et al., 2010) to serve that population's needs that are unique from the needs of lesbian, gay, and bisexual clients. Consequently, in this chapter some concepts will be discussed in regard to the entirety of the LGBT population, whereas others will be addressed specifically as they pertain to transgender persons.

The authors would like to emphasize that this chapter should serve as an introduction to group work with LGBT persons and is in no way a comprehensive description. Although some basic concepts are clarified (e.g., sexual orientation versus gender identity), counselors should make a commitment to continued growth, awareness, and skills regarding sexual orientation and gender identity. We recommend that students/counselors take a course on human sexuality when possible. A first step for counselors is to examine their own belief systems to ascertain whether they can offer empathic and effective counseling that affirms LGBT clients. Many counselor-training programs struggle to provide trainees with the skills necessary for working with diverse populations. In the emerging gay-affirmative atmosphere in the counseling profession, it is becoming easier for counselors to access resources needed to develop skills and sensitivity. Given that multicultural competency is a lifelong endeavor, counselors must continue to seek out opportunities for growth.

A WORD ABOUT WORDS

LGBT persons experience biased and oppressive language throughout their lives. Experiencing this kind of language or antigay hate speech can lead to "negative psychological, emotional, and cognitive affects as well as feelings of vulnerability, stress and fear" (Dickter, 2012, p. 1113). It is important for counselors to possess awareness and understanding of such biased and oppressive language to effectively empathize and communicate with LGBT clients, including *homosexual, sexual preference,* and the global use of the term *gay.*

Many individuals reject the term *homosexual* because it is a word often used by dominant and oppressive groups. Although professional literature, media, and popular fiction frequently use the word *homosexual,* the term reflects an inaccurately narrow, clinical focus on sexual conduct. Thus, many regard this term as archaic, imprecise, and misleading (Krajeski, 1986). The word *homosexual* is typically used with a pejorative connotation; those who support or affirm LGBT persons seldom use the term. Another phrase commonly encountered within society is *sexual preference.* The term *sexual preference* is not embraced by the LGBT community and should be avoided in favor of *sexual orientation.* The word *preference* implies that individuals choose to be gay, lesbian, or bisexual, whereas *orientation* suggests that sexual predisposition is innate.

SIDEBAR 17.2

Case Study: A Group Member Discloses She Is Questioning

Alisha is coleading an adolescent self-esteem group with LGBT clients. During the third session, one of the group members, Ally, reports that she has previously identified as a lesbian but now believes that she is bisexual because she is attracted to a boy in her class. Other group members begin questioning Ally, and one person states that she is probably just confused. Alisha notices that Ally is looking at the floor and seems uncomfortable. How might you guide the group toward being more affirming of Ally?

Another topic of debate involves using *gay* as an umbrella term to describe gay men, lesbians, and bisexuals, as in *Gay Rights Parade, gay marriage,* and *gay-affirmative counseling.* Although this use of the term is meant to encompass gays, lesbians, and bisexuals, it is not always perceived as inclusive. This usage also obscures the unique identities and issues of lesbians, gay men, and bisexual individuals. Of particular importance is the special consideration and care that must be taken to include the term *bisexual* in our language. As first noted by Wolf (1992), "bisexuality has been continually attacked as a nonentity, a transitional stage from heterosexuality to homosexuality or vice-versa, and as a denial of one's homosexuality" (p. 175). Because the term *bisexual* describes a unique identity, that word should be used.

Beyond awareness and understanding of biased and oppressive language, group leaders must recognize their position of power and model appropriate language for other members. Consequently, group leaders should be aware of their own language use and directly address the question of terminology with members. It is appropriate to ask these questions: "How do you prefer to have your sexual orientation described?" "What terms would you like the group to use?" "How do you describe yourself?" Counselors should also be aware of the importance of using the correct name and appropriate pronoun when working with transgender clients. Leaders' sensitivity surrounding biased and oppressive language, their own language usage, and transgender-specific language issues indicate openness in discussing sexual orientation and gender identity with group members.

CULTURAL TRENDS AND ISSUES

It is difficult to determine exactly how many LGBT people are living in the United States, mainly because the U.S. Census does not currently include information about transgender persons or those who identify as lesbian, gay, or bisexual. However, some data and projections do exist. It is estimated that 1.4 million adults in the United States identify as transgender (Flores, Herman, Gates & Brown, 2016). In addition, the U.S. Census compiles information on persons who report living with a same-sex partner. According to the U.S. Census Bureau (2017), approximately 646,464 people were living in same-sex partnerships in the United States in 2010. This figure, however, should be considered within the larger cultural context of the United States. Many individuals do not report same-gender activity because of the continued stigma attached to being non-heterosexual in American society. Whatever the exact number of gays, lesbians, bisexuals, and transgender persons in the United States, this group has become increasingly visible and active in the pursuit of equal rights.

Prior to the 1970s, LGBT persons were a largely invisible part of the American population. Remaining invisible was, to a large extent, a survival tactic. Most LGBT people chose to avoid the stigma and consequences associated with disclosing their sexual orientation or gender identity. Over the past 45 years, LGBT people have developed a community identity to counteract the negative reactions from society. As evidence of this community, in 1969 there were 50 gay and lesbian organizations in the United States; in 1996, there were an estimated 3,000 lesbian, gay, bisexual, and transgender organizations active in North America (Brelin, 1996). That number continues to grow: An Internet search yields thousands of organizations available to the LGBT community. Other cultural and political events provide evidence for the increased support of the LGBT community. On June 26, 2015, in the case of *Obergefell vs. Hodges*, the Supreme Court of the United States found bans on marriage equality to be unconstitutional. This finding guaranteed same-sex couples the right to marry and have their marriages legally recognized. Public opinion also is shifting slowly to a more tolerant attitude, and research affirms this (Baunach, 2012).

Regardless of the political and cultural shifts toward equality for LGBT persons, oppression and challenges to equality persist today. For example, in only 20 states, the District of Columbia, Guam, and Puerto Rico do individuals perceived to be gay, lesbian, bisexual, and transgender have legal protection against discrimination in public and private employment (American Civil Liberties Union [ACLU], 2017). Also, in legislatures across the United States, religious freedom bills are being advanced and, in some states, have been signed into law. LGBT persons and supporters of LGBT equality have long identified such bills as discriminatory and anti-LGBT. It is apparent that despite the significant cultural and political shifts that have occurred, great challenges for the LGBT community persist.

Heterosexism or Homophobia?

Heterosexism refers to a set of political assumptions that empowers heterosexual persons, especially heterosexual white males, and excludes people who are openly transgender, gay, lesbian, or bisexual from social, religious, and political power. This system demands heterosexuality in return for first-class citizenship and forces LGBT persons into silence. Heterosexism also is seen when dominant groups pity LGBT persons who "can't help their situations."

Because heterosexism is the societal norm in the United States, the assumption is that people will marry someone of the opposite sex. The media largely portray only heterosexual relationships as positive and satisfying. Teachers talk in class as though all students are heterosexual. These examples illustrate subtle and indirect ways by which heterosexuality is reinforced in the United States as the only viable, acceptable life option.

Homophobia, first defined by Weinberg in 1973, is an attitude of fear and loathing toward individuals perceived to be gay, lesbian, or bisexual. This belief system supports negative attitudes and stereotypes toward LGB persons and is used to justify discrimination based on sexual orientation. Homophobic people downgrade, deny, stereotype, or ignore the existence of lesbian, gay, and bisexual persons. Their responses range from telling or laughing at "queer" jokes to condoning, supporting, or participating in violent hate crimes. These reactions create a devalued minority amid a hostile society.

SIDEBAR 17.3

Self-Awareness: Heterosexism in the Workplace

Heterosexism often leaves LGB persons feeling invisible in the workplace. As a lesbian, having your boss say to you "You're welcome to bring your boyfriend or husband to the holiday party" is uncomfortable and feels like a microaggression. This comment assumes that being heterosexual is the norm and leaves the employee with a decision to either (a) come out to her boss or (b) withhold a response, which can feel shameful. Using inclusive language like *spouse* or *partner* (regardless of sexual orientation) is a more valid approach. Ways to challenge heterosexism include (a) not assuming everyone you meet is heterosexual, (b) instead of asking "Do you have a boyfriend/girlfriend?", try "Are you seeing anyone?" and (c) speak up when you see heterosexist behavior (remember that silence is complicity). Can you think of a recent time when you noticed heterosexist language? How did you feel? Consider possible responses for pointing out the use of heterosexist language and alternative wording that is more inclusive. We have provided one example of a microaggression that might be experienced—can you identify others? Many include statements (e.g., "That's so gay!" referring to something undesirable), and others include nonverbal behaviors.

Smith, Oades, and McCarthy (2012) argue for using the term *heterosexism* rather than *homophobia* to describe the marginalization of LGBT persons because the construct is "more inclusive, as it includes the mental and physical health problems resulting from invalidating social environments created by the stigma, prejudice and discrimination carried out by the majority group" (p. 41). The word *homophobia* is less useful because the term is narrow and doesn't include reference to problems such as social injustice. Heterosexism can be seen in both societal customs/institutions and in individual attitudes and behaviors. In addition, the term heterosexism centers on "the normalizing and privileging of heterosexuality rather than merely a fear of homosexuality" (p. 41).

Internalized Homonegativity

As an alternative to the word *homophobia,* Dermer, Smith, and Barto (2010) suggest the term *homonegativity* due to its multidimensional nature. LGB individuals often internalize the negative assumptions, attitudes, and prejudice common in the dominant culture. Internalized homonegativity manifests itself in a variety of ways, including total denial of one's sexual orientation; contempt for or mistrust of openly gay, lesbian, or bisexual people; attempts to "pass" as heterosexual; increased fear; and withdrawal from friends and families. Individuals who internalize values of otherwise credible sources (such as friends, family, religious organizations, schools, and mass media) that differ from their own experience personal dissonance and low self-esteem, which become a major source of distress. Frequent symptoms of internalized homonegativity are acute anxiety attacks, self-destructive use of alcohol and drugs, and missed work or therapy sessions. This internalization can lead to self-hatred, depression, despair, or suicide (Kasl, 2002). Even those who are self-accepting may have lingering societal messages of inferiority; this can be referred to as *covert internalized homonegativity* (Dermer et al., 2010).

Counselor Bias

Mental health professionals also may be uninformed and/or hold discriminatory assumptions. Some counselors assume that all their clients are heterosexual and cisgender.

SIDEBAR 17.4

Case Study: Is This Internalized Homonegativity?

You are a group leader, and one of your clients, Brian, is gay. He is the only person in the group who has disclosed his sexual orientation and seems confident in this part of his identity. He discusses his relationship openly and reports that being gay has nothing to do with his choice to come to therapy. During one group session, Brian reports that he has had two jarring experiences during the week. First, he came outside after a hockey game to notice that his truck was vandalized. He says to the group, "My first thought was that if I weren't gay this wouldn't have happened." Next, he reports a fight with his partner because he did not want to be affectionate in public. A group member asks for more details about the story, and Brian states that he felt like people were watching and judging them. As the group leader, you are wondering about the possibility of internalized homonegativity. Is it appropriate to bring up the discussion in this group setting? If so, how might you approach the topic?

Other counselors are tolerant of LGBT persons but lack adequate information, exposure, and skills to provide counseling. Although the counseling profession officially supports an LGBT-affirmative position, counselors do not receive enough information in their counselor-preparation programs to provide proper, adequate, and helpful services (Alderson, 2004; Burkholder & Hall, 2014; Lynne, 2001; Newman, Dannenfelser, & Benishek, 2002). Therefore, practicing counselors must continue to educate themselves about the specific issues and needs of their LGBT clients. As previously noted, the ACA's *Code of Ethics* prohibits values-based referrals, necessitating that clinicians whose values interfere with practicing LGBT-affirmative counseling seek training and exposure to increase effectiveness in working with this population.

Counselor educators must ensure that counselor-preparation programs include information about and exposure to LGBT populations. Trainees and educators alike will have to confront and overcome their own heterosexist beliefs and behaviors. It is important for counselors to understand that biases outside of their awareness can often cause harm, even without intent. The questions in Figure 17.1 can help counselors, supervisors, and counselor educators identify their own biases about sexual orientation and gender identity.

LGBT-Affirmative Counseling

Counselors who have examined and challenged their own heterosexist and homonegative attitudes are in a powerful position to help LGBT clients recognize and accept themselves, improve their interpersonal and social functioning, and value themselves while living in a predominantly heterosexual society. LGBT-affirmative counseling goes beyond addressing bias and involves embracing a positive view of the population and addressing negative environmental influences. The affirmative counselor is not only committed to avoiding discrimination but also engages in a continual examination of ways to strengthen commitment to LGBT persons both professionally and personally.

GROUPS AND ORGANIZATIONS IN THE LGBT COMMUNITY

As LGBT persons have become more visible, organized groups have become more common. LGBT persons have taken the initiative and created organizations and groups to provide social support for members of their community. Groups offer support to offset

1. Do you stop yourself from certain behaviors because someone might think you are gay, lesbian, or bisexual? If yes, what kinds of behavior?
2. Do you ever intentionally do or say things so that people will think you are not gay, lesbian, or bisexual? If yes, what kinds of things?
3. If you are a parent, how would you (or do you) feel about having a lesbian daughter or a gay son?
4. How would you feel if you were to discover that one of your parents or parent figures, or a brother or sister, is gay, lesbian, or bisexual?
5. Are there any jobs, positions, or professions that you think lesbians, gays, or bisexuals should be barred from holding or entering? If yes, why so?
6. Would you go to a physician you knew to be or believed to be gay or lesbian if that person were of a different gender from you? If that person were of the same gender as you? If not, why not?
7. If someone you care about were to say to you "I think I'm gay," would you suggest that the person see a therapist?
8. Would you wear a button that says "Don't assume I'm heterosexual"? If not, why not?
9. Can you think of three positive aspects of being gay, bisexual, or lesbian? Can you think of three negative aspects?
10. Have you ever laughed at a "queer" joke?

The following questions apply particularly to counseling in groups and suggest how easily values and assumptions can affect group leaders.

11. Do you assume that all members of your groups are heterosexual?
12. If a group member uses the term *partner*, do you assume he or she is speaking of someone of the opposite sex?
13. If a group member uses a derogatory term for a gay or lesbian, do you let the comment pass unchallenged? What do you do when a group member uses a derogatory term for a racial minority?
14. If a group member is gay, lesbian, or bisexual, do you assume that all of his or her issues are somehow related to sexual orientation? Would you make the same assumption about heterosexual group members?
15. Do you assume that all of the past partners of members of your groups have been the same gender as the current partners?

FIGURE 17.1 Personal Values Assessment

Source: Lesbian and Gay Issues: A Resource Manual for Social Workers, edited by H. Hidalgo, T. Peterson, & N. J. Woodman. Washington, DC: National Association of Social Worker, 1985. Adapted by permission.

the isolation, oppression, and alienation of being gay, lesbian, bisexual, and transgender in U.S. society. There are groups for women, men, racial and ethnic minorities, youth, and older individuals. There are groups that address coming out, gender transition, relationships, career and life planning, spirituality, and parenting. There are groups for parents of gay, bisexual, lesbian, and transgender children, their own children, and their spouses. In addition, there are groups addressing issues that are not necessarily related to sexual orientation or gender identity, such as substance abuse, personal growth, and specific mental health concerns. All these diverse groups in the LGBT community can be divided into three primary categories: common interest, self-help, and counseling (or therapy) groups.

Common-Interest Groups

The ultimate reward from developing a sense of community with other gay [or lesbian or bisexual] people is that you are no longer alone. . . . There are people who share your values. There are people to learn from and models to emulate. . . . There is the assurance of people who care and understand—people who can share familiar feelings and offer mutual support. (Clark, 2005)

Multitudes of common-interest groups are available to LGBT persons. Examples include professional-support groups for lawyers, social workers, teachers, health care providers, scientists, business owners, and artists. Organizations on many university and college campuses offer several group activities for LGBT students. An increasing number of religious denominations have groups that offer a way to participate in religious activities without discriminatory overtones. Other interest groups are organized around recreational activities. Political action committees (PACs) are another form of common-interest groups. PACs help empower the LGBT community and give members political strength and influence. All these groups provide an opportunity for social support while sharing common concerns and interests.

Support Groups

Support groups vary in focus and dynamics. They are member governed and emphasize self-advocacy (Markowitz, 2015). They provide an environment for the development of universality and a place for empowerment.

Support groups are effective for people who are stigmatized by the dominant culture. These groups break down the sense of personal isolation caused by an unhealthy condition or habit and help disenfranchised individuals cope and change (Bringaze & White, 2001). Support groups are common in LGBT communities and address a variety of issues, including alcoholism, drug addiction, trauma, and eating disorders. Mainstream recovery groups such as Narcotics Anonymous, Cocaine Anonymous, Alcoholics Anonymous, Overeaters Anonymous, and Al-Anon often have groups specifically for gay and lesbian members. Some support groups address issues that are unique to the LGBT experience, including coming-out groups, groups for persons experiencing gender transition, groups for children of gay or lesbian parents, and groups for parents of gay or lesbian children.

Counseling (Therapy) Groups

A therapy group can be a place of refuge, a place to share the most private aspects of oneself, a place to practice social skills, to get support for changing behavior. People go to groups for a variety of reasons and that provides the diversity that makes groups so productive (Hall, 1985).

The distinction between counseling groups and self-help groups is sometimes confusing. One important difference is that credentialed counselors almost always lead counseling groups. LGBT persons become participants in counseling groups to address the same issues that heterosexual and cisgender persons seek to address, including depression, anxiety disorders, panic attacks, self-esteem, sexual dysfunction, and personality disorders. Others join groups with themes of personal growth or relationship issues. Regardless of the specialty, group counseling is particularly effective with the LGBT population because groups offer a balance to the indifference and hostility of the general culture. A therapeutic group environment fosters the development of a positive identity (Bringaze & White, 2001). In counseling groups, LGBT clients can share their experiences and feelings and can find out how others cope with similar situations.

When seeking group counseling, LGBT clients will decide whether to attend a group organized specifically for LGBT individuals or a group in which sexual orientation/gender identity is not the basis for selection. Even in groups that do not specifically address sexual orientation or gender identity, being LGBT is likely to be discussed in the group. LGBT persons who attend a group that is not organized around those aspects of identity might be faced with the decision of whether and how to come out in the group. Coming out always involves risks. In counseling groups, many members will be accepting, but it is common for at least one person in the group to reject an LGBT member. It is the group leader's responsibility to ensure a safe and welcoming environment for all members. Because counselors are powerful facilitators, they must be sensitive to the group's attitudes and behaviors toward LGBT persons. Leaders have a responsibility to recognize and confront heterosexism among the group's members.

SPECIFIC LGBT COUNSELING NEEDS

Groups help LGBT clients navigate developmental tasks. They often are structured to help participants address and successfully accomplish the age-related and sexual-identity developmental tasks that all people face: sexuality, career, relationships, spirituality, parenting, and aging. Although these tasks are not unique to LGBT clients, the lack of societal support systems often exacerbates these issues. Counseling groups create an environment in which the prejudice, oppression, and heterosexism that the general society directs toward LGBT persons are countered by support, acceptance, and universality.

Through an interactive process between the individual and his or her environment, people develop and define their identities and sense of self-worth. As LGBT persons ask "Who am I in this world?" and "How do I relate with others?", they face challenges and controversies directly related to sexual orientation and/or gender identity. Specific groups, such as those discussed in the following subsections, can help members begin to arrive at answers to these questions.

Coming Out

The process of voluntarily identifying as gay, lesbian, bisexual, or transgender is called *coming out.* There is a distinct difference between people's understanding of their identity and sharing that identity with others, such as parents, friends, children, employers, and coworkers. Coming out is a process that spans the entire life of an LGBT person, and the person may incur social losses on many levels. Counselors should be careful not to underestimate the consequences of coming out and should assist clients with acquiring additional social support. A group can provide meaningful support during this process. The group can provide invaluable support during these times but should never pressure a client to disclose before they are ready to do so.

Those who choose not to disclose sexual orientation or gender identity are said to be "living in the closet." Maintaining such an existence supports internalized bias, shame, and guilt and reinforces a negative self-image by implying that certain feelings and aspects of being gay, lesbian, bisexual, or transgender are too shameful to disclose to anyone (Stone, 2003). Closeted persons lead constricted lives, constantly monitoring their thoughts, emotions, and responses. Being closeted can harm a person's sense of

---

SIDEBAR 17.5

Self-Awareness: What Is My Role in Helping a Client Who Is Contemplating the Coming-Out Process?

Coming out is a lifelong process for LGBT persons. The process involves first coming out to oneself and can happen at any age or stage of life. When were you first aware of your sexual orientation/gender identity? How did those identities develop and what influenced their development? If you have a client in group counseling who says "I think I might be gay," what is your role as leader? What is the role of the group? If a client reports questioning gender identity, what is the role of the leader? What is the role of the group?

---

integrity and leaves the person in a dissonant position that detracts from mental health and well-being. Stress, depression, and substance abuse are all related clinically to maintaining a secret existence (Bringaze & White, 2001).

Individuals may decide to come out at any age. Some have indicated that they knew as early as age 6 or 7. Coming out as a teenager can be particularly difficult because adolescents are most often financially and emotionally dependent on their parents, who may not be supportive. In addition, parental and peer acceptance and approval are important to young people, and adolescents risk being disowned by parents or harassed by peers if they identify themselves as LGBT.

Many individuals do not come out until their later years. Coming out can be an identity crisis, and whenever it occurs most people will benefit from assistance with coming-out issues and developing a positive sense of self. LGBT individuals are under constant, conflicting pressure both to stay in and to come out of the closet. Every day, they face decisions about whether to come out.

No matter what the stage of development, groups provide an environment for members to address daily issues of being gay, lesbian, bisexual, or transgender. For example, a 45-year-old woman who has lived an active and "out" life as a lesbian may find that attending a group with people in different stages is invaluable in assessing her current issues.

Group leaders will find it useful to familiarize themselves with various coming-out models. Several models provide a framework for understanding identity development for gays and lesbians. Regardless of their sexual orientation, leaders must confront their own bias, face the coming-out issues in their own lives when applicable, and be comfortable discussing sexual issues, including their own sexual orientation or gender identity, in the group. Otherwise, they may find themselves impeding rather than helping the group process.

Groups for LGBT Youths

Peer groups are important for all adolescents, and many organizations provide teenagers with opportunities to participate in groups. Most school, religious, and community groups, however, do not serve the specific needs of LGBT youth. Many gay, lesbian, bisexual, and transgender teens have experienced rejection by and discrimination from friends, family, church, and teachers; many also have experienced violence from their families, peers, or the community (Huebner, Rebchook, & Kegeles, 2004; Salzburg, 2004). The approval and inclusion that groups provide can be particularly important in helping youth accomplish basic developmental tasks and in serving as an antidote to family difficulties, violence, hopelessness, and isolation.

Groups give LGBT youth an opportunity to address their identities and provide opportunities to learn from and with other gay, lesbian, bisexual, and transgender teens. The chance to compare experiences with other group members who are wrestling with similar identity issues enhances self-esteem and promotes emotional growth in all the participants (Hansen, 2007).

Suicide

Gay, lesbian, and bisexual teens are at high risk for self-destructive behavior, including suicide (Frankowski, 2003). One of the reasons for a higher suicide rate in this population is an increase in risk factors, such as higher rates of substance abuse (Grossman and D'Augelli, 2007) and depression, and rejection by both parents and peers (Ryan, Huebner, Diaz and Sanchez, 2009). Oswalt and Wyatt (2011) reported that LGB persons were more at risk for mental health concerns due to environmental responses to their sexual orientation/gender identity. In a study about transgender youth, Grossman and D'Augelli (2007) found that almost 50 percent of the participants had considered suicide, while approximately one quarter made an attempt. Leaders of gay, lesbian, and bisexual teen groups must be prepared to address the issue of suicide in their groups. In some cases, the leader may initiate the discussion to reassure members that the topic is not off limits.

Leaders

Leaders serve many functions in counseling groups for LGBT teens:

- They offer a stable hub, which is particularly important in a group in which the membership is likely to fluctuate.
- They reinforce and model the norms of confidentiality and safety within the group. These norms must be discussed explicitly whenever new people attend the group.
- They facilitate the group's process during discussions by modeling and reinforcing behaviors such as active listening and nonjudgmental acceptance of each group member.
- They can encourage linking between group members and can draw connections between what the members discuss.
- Leaders who are comfortable discussing their own sexual orientation and/or gender identity in the group make a powerful statement and serve as positive role models for group members.

Group leaders may find that advocating in the community is inevitable (Frankowski, 2003; Stone, 2003). This can mean many things, from networking with school counselors about LGBT students to advocating at school board meetings. Group leaders and group members alike often find themselves working as activists to promote change on a community level.

Couples Groups

Most often, the concerns that LGBT couples bring to group counseling are no different from the issues in heterosexual relationships: differences in socioeconomic and family backgrounds; differences in education, religion, or values; communication problems;

previous relationships; illness; financial issues; individual emotional problems; sexual dysfunction; and jealousy. LGBT couples, however, face additional relationship challenges related to sexual orientation.

Group counseling provides an opportunity to explore these unique relationship issues in a safe, supportive environment. Groups can help these couples look at what happens in a relationship when one member of the couple is more open about discussing sexual orientation or gender identity than the other. Groups also can help members realize that despite a lack of modeling for LGBT couples, which creates uncertainty about how to behave as a couple, the absence of strict, societal guidelines allows for creativity in establishing ground rules for the relationship. The group leader and other group participants provide couples with mirrors of their relationship. The various group members offer each couple a variety of role models to consider. The group leader and group members can suggest books to read, videos to view, and lectures and other community events to attend to help couples explore alternative models of behavior.

LGBT couples face the effects of societal sex- and gender-role stereotypes in their relationships. Group leaders who work with male couples should know about the developmental model created by McWhirter and Mattison (1984). Their six-stage model describes and identifies the tasks that male couples encounter as they progress through predictable developmental stages in their relationship. Group facilitators working with lesbian couples might find the developmental model proposed by Clunis and Green (2004) helpful. Leaders may use these models in group counseling to assess whether the partners are moving at the same pace or are on different developmental tracks.

Domestic Violence

As a related issue, group leaders working with LGBT couples may have to address the serious problem of violence and battering (Peterman, 2003). Domestic violence is as frequent in gay and lesbian couples as it is in the society at large, but it has been grossly ignored and underreported (Peterman, 2003). Most victims tell no one, and authorities often fail to ask. Domestic violence is a taboo topic in U.S. society, especially in gay, lesbian, and bisexual communities (Peterman, 2003). Data on the rates of transgender persons experiencing domestic violence are extremely limited, but according to Messinger (2017), lifetime prevalence rates are as high as 57 percent experiencing psychological violence in a relationship and somewhere between 43 percent and 46 percent experiencing physical violence in a relationship.

Battering has a profound impact on the victim. Closeness and equality in the relationship disappear, and fear, mistrust, and disillusionment take over. Counseling the victim and perpetrator of domestic violence in separate counseling groups is the ethical and effective way for group counselors to work with these couples. Although group couples counseling works effectively with most of the problems LGBT face, domestic violence is an exception. As in all issues of violence, the victim's safety takes precedence over supporting the relationship or taking care of the batterer's current emotional needs.

Insisting on separate groups sends the clear message that the violence is not the victim's fault or responsibility. It also underscores the seriousness of the issue: Domestic violence is a crime, and the victim has the right, as with all crimes, to be protected from the perpetrator. Even if the couple requests to continue in the same group after disclosing an incident of domestic violence, the leader must refuse this request to provide safety and security for the victim.

Parenting Groups

Increasingly, LGBT couples are choosing to become parents and are bringing up their children in redefined families. Between 6 million and 9 million children in the United States have one or two gay or lesbian parents (Stein, Perrin, & Potter, 2004).

Many of the difficulties of LGBT parenting are the same stressors that all parents feel—jealousy, time spent with children, privacy, and communication. Stein et al. (2004) found that a parent's sexual orientation had little or no effect on a younger child's development and functioning.

Other stressors are unique to LGBT parents. Same-sex couples face difficulty if they wish to adopt children. Further, many states discriminate against LGBT persons in awarding child custody and visitation rights; in some states, these parents are considered unfit. Concerns about coming out also affect the children of LGBT parents. Some children choose to hide their parents' sexuality or gender identity from friends.

Parents of LGBT Children

Parents of gay, lesbian, and bisexual children may have difficulty accepting the sexual orientation of their children. A national organization, Parents and Friends of Lesbians and Gays (PFLAG), is a support and information network for these parents and coordinates local meetings at which parents can share the guilt, shock, and pain they may feel (Salzburg, 2004). These groups help parents overcome the cultural messages of rejection and hatred and move toward acceptance and peace. The positive effects of these groups often exceed the original intention. Field and Mattson (2016) pointed out that although parents of transgender children attending PFLAG were convinced that their experiences were "unique, much more difficult than parents of LGB kids, and even impossible for outsiders to understand, they do share much with other parents" (p. 427).

Children with LGBT Parents

Children whose parents are lesbian, gay, bisexual, or transgender may have many issues of their own. Younger children may be confused about why their parent or parents are not like those they see in books or on television or at their friends' homes. Older children may feel embarrassed about being different or may be uncertain about inviting friends to their homes for fear of teasing or repercussions. Teenagers may try to make their parent(s) "pass." Sometimes, other parents restrict their children's friendships with children who live in same-sex households or have transgender parents.

SIDEBAR 17.6

Self-Awareness: How Do My Values Affect My Beliefs About LGBT Persons Adopting Children/Having Families?

Families are socially, not biologically, constructed and are influenced by the economic, political, and cultural context in which they exist (Mezey, 2015). When you think of the word *family*, what comes to mind? Who should be able to get married? Who should be able to raise children? How do families benefit society? What family structures are you most comfortable with and why?

All these issues can be dealt with effectively in children's groups. Some counselors may wish to consider running concurrent groups for children and their LGBT parents. These groups can meet simultaneously with facilitators who help the children and parents process their own feelings. The two groups can merge at the beginning or end of each or some of the sessions.

Drug- and Alcohol-Abuse Recovery Groups

Many mental health professionals assume that drug and alcohol abuse is higher in the LGBT community than society as a whole. The evidence seems to suggest that sexual-minority individuals do experience higher rates of alcohol- and substance-use disorders (Cochran, Acherman, Mays, & Ross, 2004). Intake and assessment procedures with all clients should include questions about drinking and using drugs.

Internalized homophobia may explain the etiology and high incidence of alcoholism in gay men and lesbians (Chang, 2003; Herek and Garnets, 2007). According to Pettinato (2005), LGB individuals tend to misuse alcohol or drugs to ameliorate their feelings related to societal rejection, alienation, and stress. Although the substance abuse may originate with internalized homophobia, counselors cannot work on a client's self-image while the client is drinking or using drugs. Accepting oneself does not typically happen during periods of abuse. Leaders can work with individuals in groups only after they have successfully treated the substance-abuse problem—an approach consistent with that of other substance-abusing populations.

LGBT persons who come to treatment groups that are not specifically targeted for sexual minorities may experience heightened shame and guilt as they start this new experience. Therefore, leaders should ask questions about the group members' identities in a routine and nonjudgmental manner. By asking these questions, leaders give group members a choice about whether to reveal their sexual orientation and/or gender identity. As noted by Finnegan and McNally (2002), if the question of sexual orientation is not posed, gay or lesbian clients might feel as if heterosexuality is assumed and homosexuality possibly is unacceptable. Addressing sexual orientation and gender identity in groups as a part of the treatment plan demonstrates sensitivity.

Group leaders focusing on substance-abuse issues should be familiar with local self-help groups and resources and be able to make appropriate referrals because many LGBT individuals will need to be in both counseling and self-help groups to stay clean and sober.

Groups for Older Adults

The assumption that aging is synonymous with decline becomes particularly negative when generalized to older LGBT persons who have been incorrectly portrayed as lonely and pathetically miserable. The LGBT community and mental health professionals alike have tended to overlook the needs of elderly individuals. As we learn more about these individuals, the stereotypes and myths of persons living isolated and lonely lives are giving way to greater understanding. Older LGBT adults are not inevitably alone and unhappy. Many have created alternative families that provide friendship and support (Shippy, Cantor, & Brennan, 2004).

Older gays and lesbians face issues of aging like those faced by all older adults (Shippy et al., 2004), including the aging process and physical changes of aging, sensible nutrition, sex as an older adult, issues of ageism, managing finances, bereavement overload, and, in some cases, isolation and loneliness. Other issues are related more specifically to aging as a sexual minority, such as heterosexism/homophobia in terms of housing, job discrimination, social/human services, and institutional support. Groups for LGBT persons have emerged to address issues of aging. These groups provide opportunities for peer sharing, socialization, and social activities. Bearing in mind that identities are fluid, multidimensional, and intersectional, group leaders should expect diversity among older LGBT adults.

Personal-Growth Groups

Personal-growth groups can be a resource and refuge for LGBT individuals who receive limited support from friends, parents, siblings, or family members. In personal-growth groups, members address their feelings of guilt and internalized oppression. They learn to take responsibility for themselves rather than blaming society and the people in their lives for the awful state of "my world." Growth groups help members address the anger they feel toward society. Group members who learn to express their anger in positive ways are more apt to avoid the inward expressions of anger often associated with loneliness, substance abuse, and suicidal ideation.

The group can encourage self-affirmative statements that allow members to embrace being gay, lesbian, bisexual, and transgender. Honest discussion in groups is liberating and lays the foundation for honest and direct interaction with other people. The ultimate reward for developing this sense of community within personal-growth groups is learning that one does not have to fight these issues alone.

Transgender-Specific Groups

It is important to note that transgender people have long been pathologized by mental health professions and that much counseling history focuses on "curing" and oppressing trans people (Fouad, Gerstein, & Toporek, 2006). Dickey & Loewy (2010) underscored this when outlining the history of group therapy with transgender clients. Beginning in the 1970s, therapy was centered on "repairing" people and returning them to their genders assigned at birth. During that same time, transgender persons began their own support groups to address their needs through strengths-based perspectives (Dickey & Loewy, 2010).

It is imperative for group leaders to maintain a trans-positive environment that addresses issues of power and oppression within and outside the group. Collazo, Austin, and Craig (2013) assert that clinicians should focus on depathologizing the needs and experiences of transgender persons and engage in advocacy associated with the medical, legal, and social aspects of transitioning. Bockting, Knudson, and Goldberg (2006) identify several areas for assessment when gender concerns arise: gender identity, gender expression, and the role of others' perceptions of the client's gender. In addition to maintaining a trans-positive environment, Dickey and Lowey (2010) highlighted that group leaders should be knowledgeable about transition-related issues such as locating trans-affirming counselors, physicians, and surgeons, as well as legal issues such as name changes and birth certificates.

Although clients may choose to explore issues related to gender identity, clinicians should not label the gender identity as the problem. Instead, clinicians should be mindful to focus on the distress and environmental challenges faced by the transgender person. This shift in focus is reflected in the *DSM-5* label change from *gender identity disorder* to *gender dysphoria,* as well as the same being removed from the Paraphilic Disorders chapter. This revised diagnosis emphasizes the distress associated with gender incongruence. However, because the diagnosis of gender dysphoria focuses on the transgender individual rather than societal oppression, concerns exist that gender dysphoria remains in the DSM.

Two distinct group types are noted in the literature for transgender persons: (a) coming-out groups and (b) transitioning groups. When considering group membership, it is important to note that significant variation may exist among transgender persons concerning transition issues. Namely, some transgender persons may pursue gender-reassignment surgery, whereas others may not. Such differences require consideration when selecting clients for transgender groups. Clinicians should bear in mind that trans-affirmative clinical practice always involves depathologizing gender variance, recognizing the broad range of transgender identities, and supporting individual client needs (Collazo et al., 2013).

Summary

Professional groups have been slow to respond to gay, lesbian, bisexual, and transgender individuals and their unique concerns. This mirrors the attitudes of the American public, which continues to favor heterosexism. As a product of homonegativity, some gay, lesbian, and bisexual persons have internalized society's negative attitudes and deny their own sexual orientation. Some counseling professionals have adopted heterosexist and homonegative attitudes, and many do not possess adequate knowledge to be culturally competent with the LGBT population.

What is needed is LGBT-affirmative counseling, in which leaders create an atmosphere of acceptance and advocacy. Effective group leaders are sensitive to LGBT concerns, openly address sexual orientation and gender identity, and create and model norms of nonjudgmental acceptance of all group members.

Types of groups in which LGBT persons can find support include common-interest groups, self-help groups, and counseling groups. Specific LGBT groups include coming-out groups, transition groups, youth groups, couples' groups, parenting groups, drug- and alcohol-abuse recovery groups, and groups for older LGBT adults.

For additional resources, see Box 17.1.

BOX 17.1 Additional Reading

If you would like to read more about this topic, consider the following resources:

Goodrich, K. M., & Luke, M. (2015). *Group counseling with LGBTQI persons.* Alexandria, VA: American Counseling Association.

Nadal, K. L. (2013). Intersectional microaggressions: Experiences of lesbian, gay, bisexual, and transgender people with multiple oppressed identities. In *That's so gay! Microaggressions and the lesbian, gay, bisexual, and transgender community* (pp. 108–151). Washington, DC: American Psychological Association. doi:10.1037/14093-006

Sue, D. W. (2010). *Microaggressions in everyday life: Race, gender and sexual orientation.* Hoboken, NJ: John Wiley and Sons, Inc.

REFERENCES

Aasheim, L., & Niemann, S. (2006). Guidance/psychoeducational groups. In D. Capuzzi, D. Gross, & M. Stauffer (Eds.), *Introduction to group work* (pp. 269–293). Denver, CO: Love Publishing.

Abramowitz, C. V., Roback, H. B., Abramowitz, S. I., & Jackson, C. (1974). Differential effectiveness of directive and nondirective group therapies as a function of client internal–external control. *Journal of Consulting and Clinical Psychology, 42,* 849–853. http://dx.doi.org/10.1037/h0037572

Adams, J. K. (1998). Court-mandated treatment and required admission of guilt in cases of alleged sexual abuse: Professional, ethical and legal issues. *Issues in Child Abuse Accusations, 99*(3–4), 96–107.

Adler, A. (1938). *Social interest.* London, UK: Faber & Faber.

Adler, M. (2013). Hunger and longing: A developmental regulation model for exploring core relational needs. In S. P. Gantt, B. Badenoch, S. P. Gantt, & B. Badenoch (Eds.), *The interpersonal neurobiology of group psychotherapy and group process* (pp. 147–170). London, UK: Karnac Books.

Agazarian, Y. M. (2012). Systems-centered group psychotherapy: Putting theory into practice. *International Journal of Group Psychotherapy, 62*(2), 171.

Aichinger, A., & Holl, W. (2017). *Group therapy with children: Psychodrama with children.* New York, NY: Springer.

Alderson, K. G. (2004). A different kind of outing: Training counselors to work with sexual minority clients. *Canadian Journal of Counseling, 38,* 193–210.

Allen, K. B., & Barber, C. R. (2015). Examining the use of play activities to increase appropriate classroom behaviors. *International Journal of Play Therapy, 24*(10), 1–12. doi:10.1037/a0038466

American Civil Liberties Union. (2017, January 19). *The rights of lesbian, gay, bisexual and transgendered people.* Retrieved from https://www.aclu.org/other/rights-lesbian-gay-bisexual-and-transgendered-people

American Counseling Association. (2014). *ACA code of ethics.* Alexandria, VA: Author. Retrieved from http://www.counseling.org/Resources/aca-code-of-ethics.pdf

American Group Psychotherapy Association. (2007a). *Selection of clients.* Retrieved from http://www.agpa.org/home/practice-resources/practice-guidelines-for-group-psychotherapy

American Group Psychotherapy Association. (2007b). *Therapist interventions.* Retrieved from http://www.agpa.org/home/practice-resources/practice-guidelines-for-group-psychotherapy

American Group Psychotherapy Association and National Registry of Certified Group Psychotherapists. (2002). *Guidelines for ethics.* Washington, DC: Author.

American Mental Health Foundation. (2017). *The foundations of psychodynamic group therapy: Part one.* Retrieved from http://americanmentalhealthfoundation.org/books/the-foundations-of-psychodynamic-group-therapy-part-1/

American Psychiatric Association. (2013). *Diagnostic and statistical manual of mental disorders* (5th ed.). Washington, DC: Author.

American Psychological Association. (2017a). *Ethical principles of psychologists and code of conduct.* Washington, DC: Author. Retrieved from http://www.apa.org/ethics/code

American Psychological Association. (2017b). *Psychotherapy: Understanding group therapy.* Retrieved from http://www.apa.org/helpcenter/group-therapy.aspx

American School Counselor Association. (2012). *The ASCA national model: A framework for school counseling programs* (3rd ed.) Alexandria, VA: Author.

American School Counselor Association. (2014a). *The professional school counselor and group counseling.* Alexandria, VA: Author. Retrieved from https://www.schoolcounselor.org/asca/media/asca/PositionStatements/PS_Group-Counseling.pdf

American School Counselor Association. (2014b). *The school counselor and group counseling.* Alexandria, VA: Author. Retrieved from https://www.schoolcounselor.org/asca/media/asca/PositionStatements/PS_Group-Counseling.pdf

American School Counselor Association. (2016). *Ethical standards for school counselors.* Alexandria, VA: Author. Retrieved from https://www.schoolcounselor.org/asca/media/asca/Ethics/EthicalStandards2016.pdf

American Society of Addiction Medicine. (2011). *Quality & practice: Definition of addiction.* Retrieved from http://www.asam.org/quality-practice/definition-of-addiction

Anchor, K. N. (1979). High- and low-risk self-disclosure in group psychotherapy. *Small Group Behavior, 10,* 279–283.

Anderson, D. (2002). Multicultural group counseling: Cross-cultural considerations. In D. Capuzzi & D. Gross (Eds.), *Introduction to group counseling* (3rd ed., pp. 205–235). Denver, CO: Love Publishing.

Anderson, D. (2007). Multicultural group work: A force for developing healing. *The Journal for Specialists in Group Work, (32)*3, 224–244.

Anderson, J. D. (1979). Social work with groups in the generic base of social work practice. *Social Work with Groups, 2,* 281–293.

Anderson, J. D. (1985). Working with groups: Little-known facts that challenge well-known myths. *Small Group Behavior, 16,* 267–283.

Anderson, M. L., Goodman, J., & Schlossberg, N. K. (2012). *Counseling adults in transition: Linking Schlossberg's theory with practice in a diverse world.* New York, NY: Springer.

Anthenelli, R. M., & Schuckit, M. (1992). Genetics. In J. H. Lowinson, P. Ruiz, R. B. Millman, & J. G. Langrod (Eds.), *Substance abuse: A comprehensive textbook* (2nd ed., pp. 39–50). Baltimore, MD: Williams & Wilkins.

Antonsen, B. T., Kvarstein, E. H., Urnes, Ø., Hummelen, B., Karterud, S., & Wilberg, T. (2017). Favourable outcome of long-term combined psychotherapy for patients with borderline personality disorder: Six-year follow-up of a randomized study. *Psychotherapy Research, 27*(1), 51–63. doi:10.1080/10503307.2015.1072283

Anwar, K. (2016). Working with group-tasks and group cohesiveness. *International Education Studies, 9*(8), 105–111.

Arbuckle, D. (1975). *Counseling and psychotherapy: An existential-humanistic view*. Boston, MA: Allyn & Bacon.

Arch, J. J., Wolitzky-Taylor, K. B., Eifert, G. H., & Craske, M. G. (2012). Longitudinal treatment mediation of traditional cognitive behavior therapy and acceptance and commitment therapy for anxiety disorders. *Behaviour Research and Therapy, 50*, 469–478. doi:10.1016/j.brat.2012.04.007

Arnold, K. A., Connelly, C. E., Walsh, M. M., & Martin Ginis, K. A. (2015). Leadership styles, emotion regulation, and burnout. *Journal of Occupational Health Psychology, 20*(4), 481–490. https://doi.org/10.1037/a0039045

Arora, P. G., Connors, E. H., Blizzard, A., Coble, K., Gloff, N., & Pruitt, D. (2017). Dissemination and implementation science in program evaluation: A telemental health clinical consultation case example. *Evaluation and Program Planning, 60*, 56–63. http://dx.doi.org/10.1016/j.evalprogplan.2016.09.003

Arredondo, P., Toporek, R., Brown, S. P., Jones, J., Locke, D., Sanchez, J., & Stadler, H. (1996). Operationalization of the multicultural counseling competencies. *Journal of Multicultural Counseling and Development, 24*, 42–78.

Ashkenas, R., & Tandon, R. (1979). Eclectic approach to small group facilitation. *Small Group Behavior, 10*, 224–241.

Association for Play Therapy. (2016). *Evidence-based practice statement: Play therapy*. Retrieved from http://www.a4pt.org/?page=EvidenceBased

Association for Specialists in Group Work. (1989). *Ethical guidelines for group counselors*. Alexandria, VA: Author.

Association for Specialists in Group Work. (1991). *Professional standards for the training of group workers* (Rev. ed.). Alexandria, VA: Author.

Association for Specialists in Group Work. (1995). *Group work rainbow*. Retrieved from http://www.psyctc.org/mirrors/asgw/std_task.html

Association for Specialists in Group Work. (1999). Principles for diversity-competent group workers. *Journal for Specialists in Group Work, 24*, 7–14.

Association for Specialists in Group Work. (2000). *Professional standards for the training of group workers* (Rev. ed.). Alexandria, VA: Author. Retrieved from https://static1.squarespace.com/static/55cea634e4b083e448c3dd50/t/55d3f615e4b0d900e228c831/1439954453323/ASGW_training_standards.pdf

Association for Specialists in Group Work. (2007). *Best practices guidelines for group counselors*. Alexandria, VA: Author. Retrieved from http://www.asgw.org/best_practices.pdf

Association for Specialists in Group Work. (2008). *Best practice guidelines, 2007 revisions. Journal for Specialists in Group Work, 33*, 111–171.

Attig, T. (2002). Relearning the world: Always complicated, sometimes more than others. In G. R. Cox, R. A. Bendiksen & R. G. Stevenson (Eds.), *Complicated grieving and bereavement: Understanding and treating people experiencing loss* (pp. 7–19). Amityville, NY: Baywood Publishing.

Auger, R. W. (2004). Evaluating school-based counseling groups. *School Social Work Journal, 29*, 55–69.

Averett, P., Crowe, A., & Hall, C. (2015). The youth public arts program: Interpersonal and intrapersonal outcomes for at-risk youth. *Journal of Creativity in Mental Health, 10*(3), 306–323. doi:10.1080/15401383.2015.1027840

Azrin, N. H., & Besalel, V. A. (1980). *Job club counselors manual: A behavioral approach to vocational counseling*. Baltimore, MD: University Park Press.

Azrin, N. H., Flores, T., & Kaplan, S. (1975). Job finding club: A group assisted program for obtaining employment. *Behavior Research and Therapy, 17*, 17–22.

Baggerly, J., & Abugideiri, S. E. (2010) Grief counseling for Muslim preschool and elementary school children. *Journal of Multicultural Counseling Development, 308*, 112–124.

Bai, G., Wang, Y., Yang, L., & Niu, W. (2015). Effectiveness of a focused, brief psychoeducation program for parents of ADHD children: Improvement of medication adherence and symptoms. *Neuropsychiatric Disease and Treatment, 11*, 2721–2735.

Baider, L., & De Nour, A. K. (1989). Group therapy with adolescent counselor patients. *Journal of Adolescent Health Care, 10*, 35–38. http://dx.doi.org/10.1016/0197-0070(89)90044-2

Bailey, D., & Bradbury-Bailey, M. (2010). Empowered youth programs: Partnerships for enhancing postsecondary outcomes of African American adolescents. *Professional School Counseling, 14*, 64–74. doi:10.5330/prsc.14.1.0vk554458027081n

Baillargeon, J., Hoge, S. K., & Penn, J. (2010). Addressing the challenge of community reentry among released inmates with serious mental illness. *American Journal of Community Psychology, 46*, 361–375.

Baker, S. B. (2011). The state of primary prevention in the American school counseling profession: Past, present, and future. *Turkish Psychological Counseling and Guidance Journal, 4*(36), 105–113.

Bales, R. F. (1950). *Interaction process analysis: A method for the study of small groups*. Cambridge, MA: Addison-Wesley.

Bales, R. F. (1953). The equilibrium problem in small groups. In T. Parson, R. F. Bales, & E. A. Shils (Eds.), *Working papers in the theory of action* (pp. 111–161). Glencoe, IL: Free Press.

Barker, R. L. (1995). *The social work dictionary*. Washington, DC: NASW Press.

Barlow, S. H. (2013). Ethics, legalities, and other issues in group specialty practice. In *Specialty competencies in group psychology* (pp. 195–207). New York, NY: Oxford University Press.

Barlow, S. H., Burlingame, G. M., & Fuhriman, A. (2000). Therapeutic applications of groups: From Pratt's "thought control classes" to modern group psychotherapy. *Group Dynamics: Theory, Research, and Practice, 4*(1), 115–134. doi:10.1037/1089-2699.4.1.115

Barratt, G., & Kerman, M. (2001). Holding in mind: Theory and practice of seeing children in groups. *Psychodynamic Counseling, 7*(3), 315–328. doi:10.1080/13533330110062360

Barrett, K., & Greene, R. (2004, February). A case of neglect: Why health care is getting worse, even though medicine is getting better. *Governing*. Retrieved from http://www.governing.com/topics/health-human-services/Case-Neglect.html

Barry, K. L., & Panel, C. (1999). *Brief interventions and brief therapies for substance abuse*. Treatment improvement protocol (TIP) series 34. Rockwell, MD: Substance Abuse and Mental Health Services Administration. Retrieved from https://www.ncbi.nlm.nih.gov/books/NBK64936/

Bauman, S., & Steen, S. (Producers). (2011). *Group counseling with children: A multicultural approach* (DVD). Alexandria, VA: ASGW.

Bauman, S., & Steen, S. (Producers). (2012). *Group counseling with adolescents: A multicultural approach* (DVD). Alexandria, VA: ASGW.

Baunach, D. M. (2012). Changing same-sex marriage attitudes in America from 1988–2010. *Public Opinion Quarterly, 76*(2), 364–378. doi:10.1093/poq/nfs022

Bean, B. W., & Houston, B. K. (1978). Self-concept and self-disclosure in encounter groups. *Small Group Behavior, 9,* 549–554.

Beck, A. T. (1976). *Cognitive therapy and the emotional disorders.* New York, NY: New American Library.

Beck, J. S. (2011). *Cognitive behavior therapy: Basics and beyond.* New York, NY: Guilford Press.

Becvar, D. S. (2001). *In the presence of grief: Helping family members resolve death, dying, and bereavement issues.* New York, NY: Guilford.

Bell, L. (2007). Theoretical foundations for social justice education. In M. Adams, L. Bell, & P. Griffin (Eds.), *Teaching for diversity and social justice* (2nd ed., pp. 1–14). New York, NY: Routledge.

Bell, R. N., Claydes, C. S., Brown, G. M., Taylor, J. T., Mickens, R. S., Toon, E., . . . Dedato, E. (1980). Celebration [Recorded by Kool & the Gang]. On *Morning star* [Vinyl record]. Santa Monica, CA: De-Lite Records.

Bella-Awusah, T., Ani, C., Ajuwon, A., & Omigbodun, O. (2015). Effectiveness of brief school-based, group cognitive-behavioural therapy for depressed adolescents in south west Nigeria. *Child and Adolescent Mental Health, 21,* 44–50. doi:10.1111. camh.12104

Belmont, J. (2016). *150 more group therapy activities and tips.* Eau Claire, WI: PESI Publishing and Media.

Bemak, F., & Chi Yi Chung, R. (2004). Teaching multicultural group counseling: Perspectives for a new era. *The Journal for Specialists in Group Work, 29,* 31–41.

Bemak, F., & Chung, R. (2004a). Teaching multicultural group counseling: Perspectives for a new era. *Journal for Specialists in Group Work, 29,* 31–41.

Bemak, F., & Chung, R. C. (2004b). Teaching multicultural group counseling: Perspectives for a new era. *Journal for Specialists in Group Work, 29*(1), 31–41.

Bemak, F., & Chung, R. C.-Y. (2015). Critical issues in international group counseling. *Journal for Specialists in Group Work, 40*(1), 6–21. doi:10.1080/01933922.2014.992507

Benchmark Institute. (2010). *Working with task groups: Working efficiently with committees and teams.* Retrieved from http://www.benchmarkinstitute.org/t_by_t/free_stuff/ working_with_task_groups.pdf

Benjamin, A. (1981). *The helping interview* (3rd ed.). Boston, MA: Houghton Mifflin.

Bennis, W. G., & Shepard, H. A. (1956). A theory of group development. *Human Relations, 9,* 415–437.

Berg, R. C., Landreth, G. L., & Fall, K. A. (2006). *Group counseling: Concepts and procedures* (4th ed.). New York, NY: Routledge.

Berg, R. C., Landreth, G. L., & Fall, K. A. (2013). *Group counseling: Concepts and procedures* (5th ed.). New York, NY: Routledge/ Taylor & Francis Group.

Bergin, A. E. (1963). The effects of psychotherapy: Negative results revisited. *Journal of Counseling Psychology, 10,* 244–250. http://dx.doi.org/10.1037/h0043353

Bergin, A. E. (1966). Some implications of psychotherapy research for therapeutic practice. *Journal of Abnormal Psychology, 71,* 235–246. http://dx.doi.org/10.1037/h0023577

Bernard, G., & Rossello, J. (2008). Depression in Latino children and adolescents: Prevalence, prevention, and treatment. In S. Aguilar-Gaxiola & T. Gullotta (Eds.), *Depression in Latinos: Assessment, treatment, and prevention* (pp. 263–275). New York, NY: Springer.

Berne, E. (1961). *Transactional Analysis in Psychotherapy.* New York, NY: Grove Press.

Berne, E. (1964). *Games people play.* New York, NY: Grove Press.

Berne, E. (1966). *Principles of group treatment.* New York, NY: Oxford University Press.

Bernstein, N. (1996). *Treating the unmanageable adolescent: A guide to oppositional defiant and conduct disorders.* Northvale, NJ: Aronson.

Bersot, H. Y., & Arrifo, B. A. (2011). Ethical issues in prisoner treatment, offender therapy, and community reentry: International perspectives and policy considerations. *Journal of Forensic Psychology Practice, 11*(2–3), 99–102.

Bertcher, H. J., & Maple, F. F. (1979). *Creating groups.* Beverly Hills, CA: Sage Publications.

Bertisch, H., Rathe, J. F., Langenbahn, D. M., Sherr, R. L., & Diller, L. (2011). Group treatment in acquired brain injury. *The Journal for Specialists in Group Work, 36*(4), 264–277.

Berven, N. L., Thomas, K. R., & Chan, F. (2015). An introduction to counseling for rehabilitation and mental health professionals. In F. Chan, N. L. Berven, & K. R. Thomas (Eds.), *Counseling theories and techniques for rehabilitation and mental health professionals* (2nd ed., pp. 1–13). New York, NY: Springer Publishing Company.

Berzon, B., Pious, C., & Farson, R. (1963). The therapeutic event in group psychotherapy: A study of subjective reports by group members. *Journal of Individual Psychology, 19,* 204–212.

Beutler, L. E., Jobe, A. M., & Elkins, D. (1974). Outcomes in group psychotherapy: Using persuasion therapy to increase treatment efficacy. *Journal of Consulting and Clinical Psychology, 42,* 547–553. http://dx.doi.org/10.1037/h0036720

Bhat, C., Pillay, Y., & Selvaraj, P. (Eds.). (2015). *Group work experts share their favorite activities for the prevention and treatment of substance use disorders.* Alexandria, VA: ASGW.

Bieling, P., McCabe, R., & Antony, M. (2006). *Cognitive-behavioral therapy in groups.* New York, NY: Guilford.

Billow, R. M. (2016). Psychic nodules and therapeutic impasses: Three case studies. *International Journal of Group Psychotherapy, 66,* 1–19. http://dx.doi.org/10.1080/00207284.2015.1089682

Billow, R. M. (2017). Relational group psychotherapy: An overview. Part I: Foundational principles and practices. *Group Analysis, 50*(1), 6–22. doi:10.1177/0533316416689657

Bion, R. W. (1961). *Experiences in groups.* New York, NY: Basic Books.

Bitter, J., & Main, F. (2011). Adlerian family therapy: An introduction. *The Journal of Individual Psychology, 67*(3), 175–185.

Black, C. (2003). Creating curative communities: Feminist group work with women with eating issues. *Australian Social Work, 56,* 127–140.

Blanco, P. J., & Ray, D. C. (2011). Play therapy in elementary schools: A best practice for improving academic achievement. *Journal of Counseling and Development, 89*(2), 235–243. doi:10.1002/j.1556-6678.2011.tb00083.x

Blatner, A. (2007). Psychodrama, sociodrama, and role playing. In A. Blatner (Ed.), *Interactive and improvisational drama: Varieties of applied theatre and performance* (pp. 153–163). Lincoln, NE: iUniverse.

Bloch, S. (1986). Therapeutic factors in group psychotherapy. In A. J. Frances & R. E. Hales (Eds.), *Annual review* (Vol. 5, pp. 678–698). Washington, DC: American Psychiatric Press.

Blount, A., Schoenbaum, M., Kathol, R., Rollman, B. L., Thomas, M., O'Donohue, W., & Peek, C. J. (2007). The economics of behavioral health services in medical settings: A summary of the evidence. *Professional Psychology: Research and Practice, 38*(3), 290–297.

Blumenfeld, W., & Raymond, D. (2000). Prejudice and discrimination. In M. Adams, W. Blumenfeld, R. Castaneda, H. Hackman, M. Peters, & X. Zuniga (Eds.), *Readings for diversity and social justice: An anthology on racism, anti-semitism, sexism, heterosexism, ableism, and classism* (pp. 21–30). New York, NY: Routledge.

Bockting, W., Knudson, G., & Goldberg, J. M. (2006). *Counselling and mental health care of transgender adults and loved ones.* Vancouver, Canada: Vancouver Coastal Health, Transcend Transgender Support & Education Society, and the Canadian Rainbow Health Coalition. Retrieved from http://lgbtqpn.ca/wp-content/uploads/woocommerce_uploads/2014/08/Guidelines-mentalhealth.pdf

Boekhout, B., Hendrick, S. S., & Hendrick, C. (2000). The loss of loved ones: The impact of relationship infidelity. In J. H. Harvey & E. D. Miller (Eds.), *Loss and trauma: General and close relationship perspectives* (pp. 358–372). Philadelphia, PA: Taylor & Francis.

Boerner, K., Jopp, D., Carr, D., Sosinsky, L., & Kim, S. (2014). "His" and "her" marriage? The role of positive and negative marital characteristics in global marital satisfaction among older adults. *Journals of Gerontology Series B-Psychological Sciences and Social Sciences, 69*(4), 579–589.

Boland-Prom, K. W. (2009). Results from a national study of social workers sanctioned by state licensing boards. *Social Work, 54*, 351–360.

Bonete, S., Calero, M., & Fernandez-Parra, A. (2015). Group training in interpersonal problem-solving skills for workplace adaptation of adolescents and adults with Asperger syndrome: A preliminary study. *Autism, 19*, 409–420. doi:10.1177/1362361314522354

Bordin, E. S. (1994). Theory and research on the therapeutic working alliance: New directions. In A. O. Horvath & L. S. Greenberg (Eds.), *The working alliance* (pp. 13–37). New York, NY: Wiley.

Boss, P. (2006). *Loss, trauma, and resilience.* New York, NY: Norton.

Bowen, D. J., Neill, J. T., & Crisp, S. J. R. (2016). Wilderness adventure therapy effects on the mental health of youth participants. *Evaluation and Program Planning, 58*, 49–59. doi:10.1016/j.evalprogplan.2016.05.005

Boyle, P. J., Hanlon, D., & Russo, J. E. (2012). The value of task conflict to group decisions. *Journal of Behavioral Decision Making, 25*, 217–222. doi:10.1002/bdm.725

Bradford, L. P., Gibb, J. R., & Benne, K. D. (Eds.). (1964). *T-group theory and laboratory method: Innovation in re-education.* New York, NY: Wiley.

Bradshaw, S., Shumway, S. T., Wang, E. W., Harris, K. S., Smith, D. B., & Austin-Robillard, H. (2015). Hope, readiness, and coping in family recovery from addiction. *Journal of Groups in Addiction & Recovery, 10*(4), 313–336. doi:10.1080/1556035X.2015.1099125

Brandes, N. S. (1977). Group therapy is not for every adolescent: Two case illustrations. *International Journal of Group Psychotherapy, 27*, 507–510. doi:10.1080/00207284.1977.11491331

Bratton, S. C., Ceballos, P. L., Sheely-Moore, A. I., Meany-Walen, K., Pronchenko, Y., & Jones, L. D. (2013). Head start early mental health intervention: Effects of child-centered play therapy on disruptive behaviors. *International Journal of Play Therapy, 22*(1), 28–42. doi:10.1037/a0030318

Bratton, S. C., Ray, D., Rhine, T., & Jones, L. (2005). The efficacy of play therapy with children: A meta-analytic review of treatment outcomes. *Professional Psychology: Research and Practice, 36*(4), 376–390. doi:10.1037/0735-7028.36.4.376

Bray, B. (2015). Empty crib, broken heart. *Counseling Today, 58*(4), 27–35.

Brehm, J. W. (1966). *A theory of psychological reactance.* New York, NY: Academic Press.

Brelin, C. (1996). *Strength in numbers: A lesbian, gay, and bisexual resource.* Detroit, MI: Visible Ink Press.

Breshears, E., & Volker, D. (2013). *Facilitative leadership in social work practice.* New York, NY: Springer Publishing.

Bridbord, K., DeLucia-Waack, J. L., Jones, E., & Gerrity, D. A. (2004). The nonsignificant impact of an agenda setting treatment for groups: Implications for future research and practice. *Journal for Specialists in Group Work, 29*, 301–315.

Bridges, W. (2001). *The way of transition: Embracing life's most difficult moments.* Cambridge, MA: Perseus Publishing.

Brigman, G., & Campbell, C. (2003). Helping students improve academic achievement and student success behavior. *Professional School Counseling, 2*, 91–98.

Brigman, G., & Goodman, B. (2008). *Group counseling for school counselors* (2nd ed.). Portland, ME: J. Weston Walsh.

Bringaze, T. B., & White, L. J. (2001). Living out proud: Factors contributing to healthy identity development in lesbian leaders. *Journal of Mental Health Counseling, 23*(2), 162–173.

Brinson, J., & Lee, C. (1997). Culturally responsive group leadership: An integrative model for experienced practitioners. In H. Forrester-Miller & J. Kottler (Eds.), *Issues and challenges for group practitioners* (pp. 43–56). Denver, CO: Love Publishing.

Broderick, P. C., & Blewitt, P. (2006). *The life span: Human development for helping professionals* (2nd ed.). Upper Saddle River, NJ: Pearson Education.

Broderick, P. C., & Metz, S. (2009). Learning to BREATHE: A pilot trial of mindfulness curriculum for adolescents. *Advances in School Mental Health Promotion, 2*, 35–46. doi:10.1080/1754730X.2009.9715696

Brooks, D., Gordon, C., & Meadow, H. (1998). Ethnicity, culture, and group psychotherapy. *Group, 22*, 53–80.

Brouzos, A., Vassilopoulos, S. P., & Baourda, V. C. (2015). Therapeutic factors and members' perception of co-leaders' attitudes in a psychoeducational group for Greek children with social anxiety. *The Journal of Specialists in Group Work, 40*(2), 204–224.

Brown, A., & Mistry, T. (1994). Group work with "mixed membership" groups: Issues of race and gender. *Social Work with Groups, 17*, 5–21.

Brown, N. W. (2006). Reconceptualizing difficult groups and difficult members. *Journal of Contemporary Psychotherapy, 36*(3), 145. doi:10.1007/s10879-006-9018-9

Brown, N. W. (2011). *Psychoeducational groups: Process and practice* (3rd ed). New York, NY: Taylor & Francis Group.

Brown, N. W. (2014). *Facilitating challenging groups: Leaderless, open, and single session groups.* New York, NY: Routledge/Taylor & Francis Group.

Browning, C. R. (2002). The span of collective efficacy: Extending social disorganization theory to partner violence. *Journal of Marriage & Family, 64,* 4.

Budman, S., Demby, A., & Randall, M. (1980). Short-term group psychotherapy: Who succeeds, who fails? *Group, 4,* 3–16. doi:10.1007/BF01456623

Budman, S. H., Demby, A., Feldstein, M., & Gold, M. (1984). The effects of time-limited group psychotherapy: A controlled study. *International Journal of Group Psychotherapy, 34,* 587–603. doi:10.1080/00207284.1984.11732562

Burger, C., & Sandy, M. (2000). *A guide to gender-fair counseling for science, technology, engineering, and math.* Hampton, VA: Virginia Space Grant Consortium.

Burke, C. A. (2010). Mindfulness-based approaches with children and adolescents: A preliminary review of current research in an emergent field. *Journal of Child and Family Studies, 19,* 133–144. doi:10.1007/s10826-009-9282-x

Burkholder, D., & Hall, S. F. (2014). *Ward v. Wilbanks:* Students respond. *Journal of Counseling and Development, 92*(2), 232–240.

Burlingame, G., Davies, D., Cox, D., Baker, E., Pearson, M., Beecher, M., & Gleave, R. (2012). *The Group Readiness Questionnaire Manual.* Salt Lake City, UT: OQ Measures.

Burlingame, G. M., Gleave, R., Erekson, D., Nelson, P. L., Olsen, S., Thayer, S., & Beecher, M. (2015). Differential effectiveness of group, individual, and conjoint treatments: An archival analysis of OQ-45 change trajectories. *Psychotherapy, 26*(5), 556–572. doi:http://dx.doi.org/10.1080/10503307.2015.1044583

Burnes, T. R. (2014). Psychological services with consumers living with HIV: Changing contexts and intersecting, thematic understandings. *National Register of Psychologists Report, 40,* 34–38.

Burnes, T. R., & Hovanesian, P. N. T. (2017). Psychoeducational groups in LGBTQ psychology. In T. R. Burnes and J. L. Stanley (Eds.), *Teaching LGBTQ psychology: Queering innovative pedagogy and practice* (pp. 117–138). Washington, DC: American Psychological Association. doi:10.1037/0000015-007

Burnes, T. R., Singh, A. A., Harper, A. J., Harper, B., Maxon-Kann, W., Pickering, D. L., . . . Hosea, J. (2010). American Counseling Association competencies for counseling with transgender clients. *Journal of LGBT Issues in Counseling, 4,* 135–159.

Burnham, J. J., & Jackson, C. M. (2000). School counselor roles: Discrepancies between actual practice and existing models. *Professional School Counseling, 4,* 41–49.

Burns, S. T. (2008). Utilizing fictional stories when counseling adults. *Journal of Creativity in Mental Health, 3*(4), 441–454. doi:10.1080/15401380802530609

Burrows-Sanchez, J., Minami, T., & Hops, H. (2015). Cultural accommodations of group substance abuse treatment for Latino adolescents: Results of an RCT. *Cultural Diversity and Ethnic Minority Psychology, 21,* 571–583. doi:10.1037/cdp0000023

Burt, I. (2015). Transcending traditional group work: Using the Brazilian martial art of Capoeira as a clinical therapeutic group for culturally diverse adolescents. *Journal for Specialists in Group Work, 40,* 187–203. doi:10.1080/01933922.2015.1017068

Butler, T., & Fuhriman, A. (1980). Patient perspective on the curative process: A comparison of day treatment and outpatient psychotherapy groups. *Small Group Behavior, 11,* 371–388.

Butler, T., & Fuhriman, A. (1983). Curative factors in group therapy: A review of recent literature. *Small Group Behavior, 14,* 131–142. https://doi.org/10.1177/104649648301400201

Butzer, B., LoRusso, A., Shin, S., & Khalsa, S. (2016). Evaluation of yoga for preventing adolescent substance abuse risk factors in a middle school setting: A preliminary group-randomized controlled trial. *Journal of Youth Adolescence, 46,* 603–632. doi:10.1007.s10964-016-0513-3

Cady, E. T., Harris, R. J., & Knappenberger, J. B. (2008). Using music to cue autobiographical memories of different lifetime periods. *Psychology of Music, 36*(2), 157–177. doi:10.1177/0305735607085010

Camacho, S. (2001). Addressing conflict rooted in diversity: The role of the facilitator. *Social Work with Groups, 24,* 135–153.

Campbell, C. A., & Brigman, G. (2005). Closing the achievement gap: A structured approach to group counseling. *The Journal for Specialists in Group Work, 30,* 67–82.

Canham, H., & Emanuel, L. (2000). "Tied together feelings": Group psychotherapy with latency children: The process of forming a cohesive group. *Journal of Child Psychotherapy, 26*(2), 281–302.

Capuzzi, D., & Gross, D. (2006). *Introduction to group counseling* (4th ed.). Denver, CO: Love Publishing.

Capuzzi, D., & Gross, D. (2009). *Introduction to the counseling profession* (5th ed.). Upper Saddle River, NJ: Pearson Education.

Capuzzi, D., & Gross, D. R. (2013a). Group counseling. In D. Capuzzi & D. R. Gross (Eds.), *Introduction to the counseling profession* (6th ed, pp. 228–255). New York, NY: Routledge.

Capuzzi, D., & Gross, D. R. (2013b). *Introduction to the counseling profession* (6th ed.). New York, NY: Routledge/Taylor & Francis Group.

Capuzzi, D., & Gross, D. R. (2017). *Introduction to the counseling profession* (7th ed.). New York, NY: Routledge.

Capuzzi, D., & Stauffer, M. (2016). *Counseling and psychotherapy: Theories and interventions* (6th ed.). Alexandria, VA: ACA.

Carkhuff, R. R. (1969). *Helping and human relations: A primer for lay and professional helpers: Vol. 2. Practice and research.* New York, NY: Holt, Rinehart & Winston.

Carkhuff, R. R., & Berenson, B. G. (1977). *Beyond counseling and therapy* (2nd ed.). New York, NY: Holt, Rinehart & Winston.

Carrell, S. (2000). *Group exercises for adolescents: A manual for therapists* (2nd ed.). Thousand Oaks, CA: Sage.

Carroll, M., Bates, M., & Johnson, C. (1997). *Group leadership: Strategies for group counseling leaders* (3rd ed.). Denver, CO: Love Publishing.

Carroll, M. R., & Wiggins, J. (1997). *Elements of group counseling: Back to the basics* (2nd ed.). Denver: Love Publishing.

Carver, C. (1997). You want to measure coping but your protocol's too long: Consider the Brief COPE. *International Journal of Behavioral Medicine, 4,* 92–100. doi:10.1207/s15327558ijbm0401_6

Case, C. R., & Maner, J. K. (2014). Divide and conquer: When and why leaders undermine the cohesive fabric of their group. *Journal of Personality and Social Psychology, 107*(6), 1033–1050. doi:10.1037/a0038201

Cavanaugh, J. C., & Blanchard-Fields, F. (2011). *Adult development and aging* (6th ed.). Belmont, CA: Wadsworth.

Celinska, K. (2015). Effectiveness of functional family therapy for mandated versus non-mandated youth. *Juvenile and Family Court Journal, 66*(4), 17–27. doi:10.1111/jfcj.12049

Center for the Study and Prevention of Violence. (2012). *Blueprints for violence prevention.* Boulder, CO: University of Colorado. Retrieved from http://www.colorado.edu/cspv/blueprints/modelprograms.html

Centers for Disease Control and Prevention. (2007). *Subset of best-evidence interventions, by characteristic.* Retrieved from http://www.cdc.gov/hiv/topics/research/prs/subset-best-evidence-interventions.htm

Centers for Disease Control and Prevention. (2013). *Mental health surveillance among children—United States, 2005–2011.* Retrieved from https://www.cdc.gov/mmwr/preview/mmwrhtml/su6202a1.htm?s_cid=su6202a1_w

Centers for Disease Control and Prevention. (2016). *Depression among women.* Retrieved from https://www.cdc.gov/reproductivehealth/depression/index.htm

Chang, Z. (2003). Issues and standards for counseling lesbians and gay men with substance abuse concerns. *Journal of Mental Health Counseling, 25*(4), 323–326.

Chapman, C. L., Burlingame, G. M., Gleave, R., Rees, F., Beecher, M., & Porter, G. S. (2012). Clinical prediction in group psychotherapy. *Psychotherapy Research, 22*(6), 673–681. doi:10.1080/10503307.2012.702512

Chen, E., Touyz, S. W., Beumont, P. J. V., Fairburn, C. G., Griffiths, R., Butow, P., . . . Basten, C. (2003). Comparison of group and individual cognitive–behavioral therapy for patients with bulimia nervosa. *International Journal of Eating Disorders, 33,* 241–254.

Chen, M., & Rybak, C. J. (2004) *Group leadership skills: Interpersonal process in group counseling and therapy.* Belmont, CA: Brooks/Cole.

Cheng, J., Craske, M. G., & Niles, A. N. (2017). Exposure reduces negative bias in self-rated performance in public speaking fearful participants. *Journal of Behavior Therapy and Experimental Psychiatry, 54,* 101–107. doi:10.1016/j.jbtep.2016.07.006

Cheng, M., Hasche, L., Huang, H., & Su, X. S. (2015). The effectiveness of a meaning-centered psychoeducational group intervention for Chinese college students. *Social Behavior and Personality, 43*(5), 741–756. doi:10.2224/sbp.2015.43.5.741

Cheung, Y., & Ray, D. C. (2016). Child-centered group play therapy: Impact on social-emotional assets of kindergarten children. *The Journal for Specialists in Group Work, 41*(3), 209–237. doi:10.1080/01933922.2016.1197350

Chi Yin Chung, R. (2004). Group counseling with Asians. In J. L. DeLucia-Waack, D. A. Gerrity, C. R. Kalodner, & M. T. Riva (Eds.), *Handbook of group counseling and psychotherapy* (pp. 200–212). Thousand Oaks, CA: Sage.

Chiauzzi, E. (1990). Breaking the pattern that leads to relapse. *Psychology Today, 23*(12), 18–19.

Child Development Institute (n.d.). *Erik Erikson's stages of social-emotional development.* Retrieved from https://childdevelopmentinfo.com/ages-stages/#.WM961fnyuUk

Child Mind Institute (2015). *Children's mental health report: Introduction.* Retrieved from https://childmind.org/our-impact/childrens-mental-health-report

Child Mind Institute (2017). *National children's mental health report card.* Retrieved from https://childmind.org/article/national-childrens-mental-health-report-card

Choate, L. (2010). Interpersonal group therapy for women experiencing bulimia. *The Journal for Specialists in Group Work, 35*(4), 349–364. doi:10.1080/01933922.2010.514977

Choate, L. H., & Manton, J. (2014). Teen court counseling groups: Facilitating positive change for adolescents who are first-time juvenile offenders. *Journal for Specialists in Group Work, 39*(4), 345–365. doi:10.1080/01933922.2014.948236

Chou, C. L., Promes, S. B., Souza, K. H., Topp, K. S., & O'Sullivan, P. S. (2012). Twelve tips for facilitating successful teleconferences. *Medical Teacher, 34*(6), 445–449. doi:10.3109/0142159X.2012.668241

Christensen, J. (2009). Finding hope after losing a job. *Counseling Today, 51*(8), 38–41.

Chung, S. F. (2013). A review of psychodrama and group process. *International Journal of Social Work and Human Services Practice, 1*(2), 105–114.

Churn, A. (2003). *The end is just the beginning: Lessons in grieving for African Americans.* New York, NY: Broadway Books.

Clark, A. A. (2015). Disability awareness and etiquette: Transforming perceptions through a series of experiential exercises. *Journal of Creativity in Mental Health, 10*(4), 456–470. doi:10.1080/15401383.2015.1022679

Clark, D. H. (2005). *Loving someone gay* (4th ed.). Berkeley, CA: Celestial Arts.

Clark, P. (2010). Preventing future crime with cognitive behavioral therapy. *National Institute of Justice Journal, 265,* 22–25.

Clark, P. M. (2011, February/March). An evidence-based intervention for offenders. *Corrections Today.* Retrieved from https://www.ncjrs.gov/pdffiles1/nij/239776.pdf

Clunis, D. M., & Green, G. D. (2004). *Lesbian couples: A guide to creating healthy relationships* (4th ed). Seattle, WA: Seal Press.

Cochran, S. D., Ackerman, D., Mays, V. M., & Ross, M. W. (2004). Prevalence of non-medical drugs use and dependence among homosexually active men and women in the U.S. population. *Addiction, 99,* 989–998.

Coco, G. L., Gullo, S., Fratello, C. D., Giordano, C., & Kivlighan, D. M. (2016). Group relationships in early and late sessions and improvement in interpersonal problems. *Journal of Counseling Psychology, 63*(4), 419–428. doi:10.1037/cou0000153

Cohen, A. M., & Smith, D. R. (1976). *The critical incident in growth groups: Theory and techniques.* La Jolla, CA: University Associates.

Cohen, M. B. (2011). Using student task groups to teach group process and development. *Social Work with Groups, 34,* 51–60. doi:10.1080/01609513.2010.503384

Cohen, S., Kamarck, T., & Mermelstein, R. (1983). A global measure of perceived stress. *Journal of Health and Social Behavior, 24,* 385–396. doi:10.2307/2136404

Colbert, K., & Erickson-Klein, R. (2015). *Engage the group, engage the brain: 100 experiential activities for addiction treatment.* Las Vegas, NV: Central Recovery Press.

Colby, S. L., & Ortman, J. M. (2015). Projections of the size and composition of the U.S. population: 2014 to 2060. *Current Population Reports* (P25-1143). Washington, DC: U.S. Census Bureau.

Collazo, A., Austin, A., & Craig, S. L. (2013). Facilitating gender transition among transgender clients: Components of effective clinical practice. *Clinical Social Work, 41,* 228–237.

Combs, A. W., Avila, D. L., & Purkey, W. W. (1978). *Helping relationships: Basic concepts for the helping professions.* Boston, MA: Allyn & Bacon.

Commission on Rehabilitation Counselor Certification. (2017). *Code of professional ethics for rehabilitation counselors.* Schaumburg, IL: Author. Retrieved from https://www.crccertification. com/filebin/pdf/Final_CRCC_Code_Eff_20170101.pdf

Committee for Children. (2014). *Second step: Grades 6, 7, and 8.* Seattle, WA: Author.

Compare, A., Tasca, G. A., Lo Coco, G., & Kivlighan, D. M., Jr. (2016). Congruence of group therapist and group member alliance judgments in emotionally focused group therapy for binge eating disorder. *Psychotherapy, 53,* 163–173. doi:10.1037/pst0000042

Conyne, R. (1999). *Failures in group work.* Thousand Oaks, CA: Sage.

Conyne, R. (2014). Prevention groups. In J. DeLucia-Waack, C. Kalodner, & M. Riva (Eds.), *Handbook of group counseling and psychotherapy* (2nd ed., pp. 531–543). Thousand Oaks, CA: Sage.

Conyne, R. K. (2014). *Group work leadership: An introduction for helpers.* Los Angeles, CA: Sage.

Conyne, R. K., & Mazza, J. (2006). Ecological group work applied to schools. *Journal for Specialists in Group Work, 32*(1), 19–29.

Conyne, R. K., Harvill, R. L., Morganett, R. S., Morran, D. K., & Hulse-Killacky, D. (1990). Effective group leadership: Continuing the search for greater clarity and understanding. *Journal for Specialists in Group Work, 15,* 30–36. doi:10.1080/01933929008411909

Conyne, R. K., Rapin, L. S., & Rand, J. M. (1997). A model for leading task groups. In H. Forester-Miller & J. A. Kottler (Eds.), *Issues and challenges for group practitioners* (pp. 117–132). Denver, CO: Love Publishing.

Corey, G. (2008). *Theory and practice of group counseling* (7th ed.). Belmont, CA: Thomson Brooks/Cole.

Corey, G. (2012a). *Theory and practice of counseling and psychotherapy* (8th ed.). Belmont, CA: Thomas Brooks/Cole.

Corey, G. (2012b). *Theory and practice of group counseling* (8th ed.). Pacific Grove, CA: Brooks/Cole.

Corey, G. (2015). *Theory and practice of group counseling* (9th ed.). Belmont, CA: Thomson Brooks/Cole.

Corey, G. (2017). *Theory and practice of group counseling* (10th ed.). Belmont, CA: Cengage.

Corey, G., Corey, M. S., Callanan, P., & Russell, J. M. (2014). *Group techniques.* Boston, MA: Cengage Learning.

Corey, G., Corey, M. S., Corey, C., & Callanan, P. (2015). *Issues and ethics in the helping professions* (9th ed.). Pacific Grove, CA: Brooks/Cole.

Corey, M. S., Corey, G., & Corey, C. (2010). *Groups: Process and practice.* Belmont, CA: Brooks/Cole.

Corey, M. S., Corey, G., & Corey, C. (2014). *Groups: Process and practice* (9th ed.). Belmont, CA: Brooks/Cole.

Corey, M. S., Corey, G., & Corey, C. (2017). *Groups: Process and practice* (10th ed.). Pacific Grove, CA: Brooks/Cole.

Cornell, W. F. (2013). Relational group process: A discussion of Richard Erskine's model of group psychotherapy from the perspective of Eric Berne's theories of group treatment. *Transactional Analysis Journal, 43*(4), 276–283. doi:10.1177/0362153713515180

Corsini, R., & Rosenberg, B. (1955). Mechanisms of group psychotherapy: Processes and dynamics. *Journal of Abnormal & Social Psychology, 51,* 406–411.

Cottone, R. R., & Tarvydas, V. M. (2007). *Ethical and professional issues in counseling* (3rd ed.). Upper Saddle River, NJ: Merrill/Prentice Hall.

Couch, R. D., & Childers, J. H. (1987). Leadership strategies for instilling and maintaining hope in group counseling. *Journal for Specialists in Group Work, 12,* 138–143. doi:10.1080/01933928708411763

Council for the Accreditation of Counseling and Related Educational Programs. (1994). *Accreditation procedures manual and application.* Alexandria, VA: Author.

Council for the Accreditation of Counseling and Related Educational Programs. (2001, 2016). *CACREP accreditation procedures manual and application.* Alexandria, VA: Author.

Council for the Accreditation of Counseling and Related Educational Programs (2015). *2016 CACREP standards.* Retrieved from http://www.cacrep.org/wp-content/uploads/2016/06/2016-Standards-with-Glossary-rev-2.2016.pdf

Council for the Accreditation of Counseling and Related Educational Programs. (2016). *2016 standards.* Alexandria, VA: Author. Retrieved from http://www.cacrep.org/for-programs/2016-cacrep-standards

Council on Rehabilitation Education. (2014). *Accreditation manual for rehabilitation counselor education programs.* Schaumburg, IL: Author. Retrieved from http://www.core-rehab.org

Counselman, E. F. (2017). First put your chairs in a circle: Becoming a group therapist. *International Journal of Group Psychotherapy, 67,* 124–133. doi:10.1080/00207284.2016, 1203588

Couturier, J., Kimber, M., & Szatmari, P. (2013). Efficacy of family-based treatment for adolescents with eating disorders: A systematic review and meta-analysis. *International Journal of Eating Disorders, 46*(1), 3–11.

Cox, G. R., Bendiksen, R. A., & Stevenson, R. G. (Eds.). (2002). *Complicated grieving and bereavement: Understanding and treating people experiencing loss.* Amityville, NY: Baywood Publishing.

Craig, S. L. (2013). Affirmative supportive safe and empowering talk (ASSET): Leveraging the strengths and resiliencies of sexual minority youth in school-based groups. *Journal of LGBT Issues in Counseling, 7,* 372–386. doi:10.1080/15538605.2013.839342

Craig, S. L., Austin, A., & McInroy, L. B. (2014). School-based groups to support multiethnic sexual minority youth resiliency: Preliminary effectiveness. *Child and Adolescent Social Work Journal, 31,* 87–106. doi:10.1007/s10560-013-0311-7

Crane, J. M., & Baggerly, J. N., (2014). Integrating play and expressive art therapy into educational settings: A pedagogy for optimistic therapists. In E. J. Green & A. A. Drewes (Eds.), *Integrating expressive arts and play therapy with children and adolescents* (pp. 231–249). Hoboken, NJ: Wiley.

Crespi, T. D. (2009). Group counseling in the schools: Legal, ethical, and treatment issues in school practice. *Psychology in the Schools, 46*(3), 273–280.

Crichton, H., & Templeton, B. (2013). Collaboration or confrontation? An investigation into the role of prior experiences in the completion of collaborative group tasks by student teachers. *European Journal of Teacher Education, 36*(1), 84–96. doi:10.1080/02619768.2012.678487

Cronin, J. (2011, September). *The path to successful reentry: The relationship between correctional education, employment and recidivism.* Columbia, MO: University of Missouri Institute of Public Policy.

Crowell, J. (2008). Out with the trash. In L. Foss, J. Green, K. Wolfe-Stiltner, & J. L. DeLucia-Waack (Eds.), *School counselors share their favorite activities* (pp. 201–202). Alexandria, VA: ASGW.

Crown, S. (1983). Contraindications and dangers in psychotherapy. *British Journal of Psychiatry, 143,* 436–441. doi:10.1192/bjp.143.5.436

Dagley, J., & Calhoun, G. (2014). Career and transition counseling in groups. In J. DeLucia-Waack, C. Kalodner, & M. Riva (Eds.), *Handbook of group counseling and psychotherapy* (2nd ed., pp. 544–559). Thousand Oaks, CA: Sage.

Dai, G., & DeMeuse, K. P. (2013). Types of leaders across the organizational hierarchy: A person-centered approach. *Human Performance, 26*(2), 150–170. doi:10.1080/08959285.2013.765879

Davies, D. (2011). The family environment. In J. Laser & N. Nicotera, *Working with adolescents* (pp. 71–93). New York, NY: Guilford.

Davies, D., Burlingame, G., Johnson, J., Gleave, R., & Barlow, S. (2008). The effects of a feedback intervention on group process and outcome. *Group Dynamics: Theory, Research, and Practice, 12,* 141–154. doi:10.1037/1089-2699.12.2.141

Davis, R., & Nolan-Hoeksema, S. (2000). Cognitive inflexibility among ruminators and nonruminators. *Cognitive Therapy and Research, 24,* 699–711. doi:10.1023/A:1005591412406

Davis, S. (2007). *Schools where everyone belongs: Practical strategies for reducing bullying.* Champaign, IL: Research Press.

de Raaf, S., Hui, S. T., & Sims, K. (2011). *Group-based employment assistance benefits: Final report.* Ottawa, Canada: Social Research and Demonstration Corporation. Retrieved from http://www.srdc.org/uploads/group_based_en.pdf

de Shazer, S. (1985). *Keys to solution in brief therapy.* New York, NY: Norton.

de Shazer, S., Dolan, Y., Korman, H., Trepper, T., McCollum, E., & Berg, I. K. (2007). *More than miracles: The state of the art of solution-focused brief therapy.* Binghamton, NY: Haworth Press.

DeJong, P., & Berg, I. K. (2001). Co-constructing cooperation with mandated clients. *Social Work, 46,* 4.

Delgado-Romero, E., Barfield, J., Fairley, B., & Martinez, R. (2005). Using the multicultural guidelines in individual and group counseling situations. In M. Constantine & D. Wing Sue (Eds.), *Strategies for building multicultural competence* (pp. 39–55). Hoboken, NJ: John Wiley & Sons.

Delgadillo, J., Kellett, S., Ali, S., McMillian, D., Barkham, M., Saxon, D., . . . Lucock, M. (2016). A multi-service practice research network study of large group psychoeducational cognitive behavioural therapy. *Behaviour Research and Therapy, 87,* 155–161.

Delsignore, A., Carraro, G., Mathier, F., Znoj, H., & Schnyder, U. (2008). Perceived responsibility for change as an outcome predictor in cognitive-behavioural group therapy. *British Journal of Clinical Psychology, 47,* 281–293. doi:10.1348/014466508X279486

DeLucia-Waack, J., Colvin, F., Korta, S., Maertin, K. Martin, E., & Zawadski, L. (Eds.). (2014). *School counselors share their favorite classroom guidance activities.* Alexandria, VA: ASGW.

DeLucia-Waack, J., & Gerrity, D. (2001). Effective group work for elementary school age children whose parents are divorcing. *Family Journal: Counseling and Therapy for Couples and Families, 9,* 273–284.

DeLucia-Waack, J., & Kalodner, C. (2005). Contemporary issues in group practice. In S. Wheelan (Ed.), *The handbook of group research and practice* (pp. 65–84). Thousand Oaks, CA: Sage.

DeLucia-Waack, J., Segrist, A., & Horne, A. (Producers). (2006). *Leading groups with adolescents* (DVD). Alexandria, VA: ASGW.

DeLucia-Waack, J. L. (2006). *Leading psychoeducational groups for children and adolescents.* Thousand Oaks, CA: Sage.

DeLucia-Waack, J. L. (2011). Children of divorce groups. In G. Greif & P. Ephross (Eds.), *Group work with at-risk populations* (3rd ed., pp. 93–114). New York, NY: Oxford University.

DeLucia-Waack, J. L., Athalye, D., Floyd, K., Howard, M., & Kuszczak, S. (2011). Outreach for college students related to mood and anxiety management. In T. Fitch & J. Marshall (Eds.), *Group work and outreach guide for college counselors* (pp. 273–287). Alexandria, VA: ACA.

DeLucia-Waack, J. L., Bridbord, K. H., Kleiner, J. S., & Nitza, A. (Eds.). (2006). *Group work experts share their favorite activities* (Vol. 1). Alexandria, VA: ASGW.

DeLucia-Waack, J. L., & Donigian, J. (2004) *The practice of multicultural group work: Visions and perspectives from the field.* Belmont, CA: Brooks/Cole.

DeLucia-Waack, J. L., & Gellman, R. (2007). The efficacy of using music in children of divorce groups: Impact on anxiety, depression, and irrational beliefs about divorce. *Group Dynamics, 11,* 272–282. doi:10.1037/1089-2699.11.4.272

DeLucia-Waack, J. L., Kalodner, C., & Riva, M. (Eds.). (2014). *Handbook of group counseling and psychotherapy* (2nd ed.). Thousand Oaks, CA: Sage.

DeMarco, J. (2001). *Adolescent group facilitator's guide: Dynamic discussion starters.* Center City, MN: Hazelden.

Dermer, S. B., Smith, S. D., & Barto, K. K. (2010). Identifying and correctly labeling sexual prejudice, discrimination and oppression. *Journal of Counseling and Development, 88,* 325–331.

DeRosier, M. E. (2004). Building relationships and combating bullying: Effectiveness of school-based social skills group intervention. *Journal of Clinical Child and Adolescent Psychology, 33,* 196–201.

Desmond, K. J., Kindsvatter, A., Stahl, S., & Smith, H. (2015). Using creative techniques with children who have experienced trauma. *Journal of Creativity in Mental Health, 10*(4), 439–455. doi:10.1080/15401383.2015.1040938

Dickey, L. M., & Loewy, M. I. (2010). Group work with transgender clients. *The Journal for Specialists in Group Work, 35*(3), 236–245.

Dickter, C. L. (2012). Confronting hate: Heterosexuals' responses to anti-gay comments. *Journal of Homosexuality, 59*(8), 1113–1130. doi:10.1080/00918369.2012.712817

Dierick, P., & Lietaer, G. (2008). Client perception of therapeutic factors in group psychotherapy and growth groups: An empirically-based hierarchical model. *International Journal of Group Psychotherapy, 58*(2), 203–230.

Dies, R. R. (1973). Group therapist self-disclosure: An evaluation by clients. *Journal of Counseling Psychology, 20,* 344–348.

Dingle, G., Gleadhill, & Baker, F. (2008). Can music therapy engage patients in group cognitive behavior therapy for substance abuse treatment? *Drug and Alcohol Review, 27,* 190–196. doi:10.1080/09595230701829371

Dinkmeyer, D. C., & Muro, J. J. (1979). *Group counseling: Theory and practice* (2nd ed.). Itasca, IL: Peacock.

Ditchman, N., Lee, E. J., & Huebner, R. A. (2015). Group procedures. In F. Chan, N. L. Berven, & K. R. Thomas (Eds.), *Counseling theories and techniques for rehabilitation health professionals* (2nd ed., pp. 279–298). New York, NY: Springer.

Dodge, K. A., Pettit, G. S., & Bates, J. E. (1994). Socialization mediators of the relation between socioeconomic status and child conduct problems. *Child Development, 65,* 649–665.

Doka, K. J. (2016). *Grief is a journey: Finding your path through loss.* New York, NY: Atria Books.

Donigian, J., & Hulse-Killacky, D. (1999). *Critical incidents in group therapy.* Belmont, CA: Wadsworth.

Donigian, J., & Malnati, R. (1997). Systemic group therapy: A triadic model. Pacific Grove, CA: Brooks/Cole.

Dorian, M., & Cordova, J. V. (2004). Coding intimacy in couple's interactions. In P. K. Kerig & D. H. Baucom (Eds.), *Couple observational coding systems* (pp. 243–256). Mahwah, NJ: Lawrence Erlbaum.

Doweiko, H. E. (2006). *Concepts of chemical dependency* (6th ed.) Pacific Grove, CA: Thompson Brooks/Cole.

Downey, J. (2014). Group therapy for adolescents living with an eating disorder. *SAGE Open, 4*(3), 1–11. doi:10.1177/2158244014550618

Downs, K. J., & Blow, A. J. (2013). A substantive and methodological review of family-based treatment for eating disorders: The last 25 years of research. *Journal of Family Therapy, 35*(1), 3–28.

Dreikurs, R. (1932). Early experiments with group psychotherapy. *American Journal of Psychotherapy, 13,* 882–891.

Driver, J. L., & Gottman, J. M. (2004). Turning toward versus turning away: A coding system of daily interactions. In P. K. Kerig & D. H. Baucom (Eds.), *Couple observational coding systems* (pp. 209–225). Mahwah, NJ: Lawrence Erlbaum.

Due, P., Holstein, B., & Soc, M. (2005). Bullying victimization among 13- to 15-year-old school children: Results from two comparative studies in 66 countries and regions. *International Journal of Adolescent Medicine and Health, 20,* 115–127. doi:10.1093/eurpub/cki105

Duffey, T. (2005). A musical chronology and the emerging life song. *Journal of Creativity in Mental Health, 1,* 141–147. doi:10.1300/J456v01n01_09

Duffey, T. (2015). *Therapist series workshop: Creativity in counseling.* Presented at Rollins College Master Therapist Series, Winter Park, FL.

Duffey, T. (2016). *Therapist series workshop: Creativity in counseling.* Presented at Rollins College Master Therapist Series, Winter Park, FL.

Duffey, T. (2017). *Therapist series workshop: Creativity in counseling.* Presented at Rollins College Master Therapist Series, Winter Park, FL.

Duffey, T., & Haberstroh, S. (2012). Using developmental relational counseling as a spectrum for self-understanding in relation to others. *Journal of Creativity in Mental Health, 7,* 263–271.

Duffey, T., & Haberstroh, S. (2013). Deepening empathy in men using a musical chronology and the emerging life song. *Journal of Counseling & Development, 91*(4), 442–450. doi:10.1002/j.1556-6676.2013.00116x

Duffey, T., & Haberstroh, S. (2014). Developmental relational counseling with men. *The Journal of Counseling and Development, 92,* 104–113.

Duffey, T., & Haberstroh, S. (2016). Relational cultural theory and supervision: Evaluating developmental relational counseling. *The Journal of Counseling and Development, 94*(4), 405–414.

Duffey, T., Haberstroh, S., & Trepal, H. (2009). A grounded theory of relational competencies and creativity in counseling: Beginning the dialogue. *The Journal of Creativity in Mental Health, 4*(2), 89–112.

Duffey, T., Haberstroh, S., & Trepal, H. (2016). Creative approaches in counseling and psychotherapy. In D. Capuzzi & M. Stauffer (Eds.), *Counseling and psychotherapy: Theories and interventions* (pp. 445–468). Alexandria, VA: American Counseling Association Press.

Duffey, T., Somody, C., & Clifford, S. (2006/2007). Conversations with my father: Adapting a musical chronology and the emerging life song with older adults. *Journal of Creativity in Mental Health, 2*(4), 45–64. doi:10.1300/J456v02n04_05

Duffrene, A. (2004, July). Dr. Irvin Yalom. *Counselling & Psychotherapy Journal, 15*(6), 8–11.

Dufrene, R. L., Henderson, K. L., & Eckart, E. C. (2016). Adlerian theory. In D. Capuzzi & M. D. Stauffer (Eds.), *Counseling and psychotherapy: Theories and interventions* (6th ed., pp. 121–146). Alexandria, VA: American Counseling Association.

Duyan, V., Şahin-Kara, G., Camur Duyan, G., Özdemir, B., & Megahead, H. A. (2016). The effects of group work with institutionalized elderly persons. *Research on Social Work Practice, 27*(3), 366–374. doi:1049731516654572

Dyer, W. W., & Vriend, J. (1973). Effective group counseling process interventions. *Educational Technology, 13*(1), 61–67.

Dykeman, C., & Appleton, V. E. (2006). Group counseling: The efficacy of group work. In D. Capuzzi & D. R. Gross (Eds.), *Introduction to group counseling* (4th ed., pp. 123–159). Denver, CO: Love Publishing.

Edwards, B., & Rodgers, N. (1979). We are family [Recorded by Sister Sledge]. On *We are family* [Vinyl record]. New York, NY: Cotillion Records.

Ellis, C. (2000). Negotiating terminal illness: Communication, collusion, and coalition in caregiving. In J. H. Harvey & E. D. Miller (Eds.), *Loss and trauma: General and close relationship perspectives* (pp. 286–304). Philadelphia, PA: Taylor & Francis.

Ellis, S. K., Simpson, C. G., Rose, C. A., & Plotner, A. J. (2014). Group counseling services for persons with disabilities. In J. DeLucia-Waack, C. Kalodner, & M. Riva (Eds.), *Handbook of group counseling and psychotherapy* (2nd ed., pp. 264–287). Thousand Oaks, CA: Sage.

Ellis, T. M. (2006). *This thing called grief: New understandings of loss.* Minneapolis, MN: Syren.

Engel, G. L. (1977). The need for a new medical model: A challenge for biomedicine. *Science, 196*(4286), 129–136. doi:10.1126/science.847460

Epp, K. M. (2008). Outcome-based evaluation of a social skills program using art therapy and group therapy for children on the Autism Spectrum. *Children & Schools, 30*(1), 27–36.

Erford, B. (2010). *Group work in the schools.* Boston, MA: Pearson.

Erickson, S. (2005). Etiological theories of substance abuse. In P. Stevens & R. Smith (Eds.), *Substance abuse counseling: Theory and practice* (3rd ed., pp. 87–122). Upper Saddle River, NJ: Pearson.

Erikson, E. H. (1950). *Childhood and society.* New York, NY: Norton.

Eusden, S., & Pierini, A. (2015). Exploring contemporary views on therapeutic relating in Transactional Analysis game theory. *Transactional Analysis Journal, 45*(2), 128–140.

Evensen, E. P., & Bednar, R. L. (1978). Effects of specific cognitive and behavioral structure on early group behavior and atmosphere. *Journal of Counseling Psychology, 25*, 66–75. doi:10.1037/0022-0167.25.1.66

Ezell, M. (2001). *Advocacy in the human services.* Belmont, CA: Brooks/Cole.

Fagan, P. F., Patterson, R. W., & Rector, R. E. (2002). *Marriage and welfare reform: The overwhelming evidence that marriage evidence works.* Washington, DC: The Heritage Foundation.

Falco, L. D., & Bauman, S. (2014). Group work in schools. In J. DeLucia-Waack, C. Kalodner, & M. Riva (Eds.) *Handbook of group counseling and psychotherapy* (2nd ed., pp. 318–328). Thousand Oaks, CA: Sage.

Fazal, Z. (2015). Behavior skills training in 4 steps. Retrieved from http://www.bsci21.org/behavior-skills-training-in-4-steps

Fearday, F. L., & Cape, A. L. (2004). A voice for traumatized women: Inclusion and mutual support. *Psychiatric Rehabilitation Journal, 27*(3), 258–265.

Federici, A., Rowa, K., & Antony, M. M. (2010). Adjusting treatment for partial- or nonresponse to contemporary cognitive-behavioral therapy. In D. McKay, J. S. Ambramowitz, S. Taylor, D. McKay, J. S. Abramowitz, & S. Taylor (Eds.), *Cognitive-behavioral therapy for refractory cases: Turning failure into success* (pp. 11–37). Washington, DC: American Psychological Association. doi:10.1037/12070-002

Fenster, A., & Fenster, J. (1998). Diagnosing deficits in "basic trust" in multiracial and multicultural groups: Individual or social psychopathology? *Group, 22*, 81–93.

Field, T. L., & Mattson, G. (2016). Parenting transgender children in PFLAG. *Journal of LGBT Family Studies, 12*(5), 412–429.

Fineran, K., Houltberg, B., Nitza, A., McCoy, J., & Roberts, S. (2014). *Group work experts share their favorite activities* (Vol. 2). Alexandria, VA: ASGW.

Finlay, L. D., Abernethy, A. D., & Garrels, S. R. (2016). Scapegoating in group therapy: Insights from Girard's mimetic theory. *International Journal of Group Psychotherapy, 66*, 188–204. doi:10.1080/00207284.2015.1106174

Finnegan, D. G., & McNally, E. B. (2002). *Counseling gay, lesbian, bisexual and transgendered substance abusers: Dual identities.* New York, NY: Routledge.

Fiorini, J. J., & Mullen, J. A. (2006). *Counseling children and adolescents through grief and loss.* Champaign, IL: Research Press.

Fisher, G. L., & Harrison, T. C. (2000). *Substance abuse: Information for school counselors, social workers, therapists, and counselors* (5th ed.). Upper Saddle River, NJ: Pearson.

Fitch, T., & Marshall, J. (Eds.). (2011). *Group work and outreach plans for college counselors.* Alexandria, VA: ACA.

Flamez, B. N., Ordway, A. M., Vela, J. C., & Hicks, J. F. (2016). Generativity, death, dying, and bereavement. In D. Capuzzi & M. D. Stauffer (Eds.), *Human growth and development across the lifespan: Applications for counselors* (pp. 575–608). Hoboken, NJ: Wiley.

Flores, A. R., Herman, J. L., Gates, G. J., & Brown, T. N. T. (2016). *How many adults identify as transgender in the United States?* Los Angeles, CA: The Williams Institute.

Flowers, J. V. (1979). The differential outcome effects of simple advice, alternatives and instructions in group psychotherapy. *International Journal of Group Psychotherapy, 29*, 305–316. doi:10.1080/00207284.1979.11491997

Fonagy, P., Campbell, C., & Bateman, A. (2017). Mentalizing, attachment, and epistemic trust in group therapy. *International Journal of Group Psychotherapy, 67*, 176–201. doi:10.1080/00207284.2016.1263156

Forester-Miller, H. (1998). History of the Association for Specialists in Group Work: Timeline of significant events. *Journal for Specialists in Group Work, 23*(4), 335–337.

Foss, L., Green, J., Wolfe-Stiltner, K., & DeLucia-Waack, J. (Eds.) (2008). *School counselors share their favorite group activities.* Alexandria, VA: ASGW.

Fouad, N. A., Gerstein, L. H., & Toporek, R. L. (2006). Social justice and counseling psychology in context. In R. L. Toporek, L. H. Gerstein, N. A. Fouad, G. Roysicar, & T. Isreal (Eds.), *Handbook for social justice in counseling psychology: Leadership, vision and action* (pp 1–16). Thousand Oaks, CA: Sage.

Foxx, S. P., Baker, S. B., & Gerler, E. R. (2017). *School counseling in the 21st century* (6th ed.). New York, NY: Routledge.

Frank, J. (1957). Some determinants, manifestations, and efforts of cohesiveness in therapy groups. *International Journal of Group Psychotherapy, 7*, 53–63.

Frank, J., & Ascher, E. (1951). The corrective emotional experience in group therapy. *American Journal of Psychiatry, 108*, 126–131.

Franko, D. L. (2007). Race, ethnicity, and eating disorders: Considerations for DSM-V. *International Journal of Eating Disorders, 40*, S31–S34.

Frankowski, B. L. (2003). Sexual orientation and adolescents. *Pediatrics, 113*(6), 1827–1832.

Fraser, J., & Solovey, A. (2007). *Second-order change in psychotherapy: The golden thread that unifies effective treatments.* Washington, DC: American Psychological Association.

Frew, J. (2016). Gestalt therapy: Creatively adjusting in an increasingly diverse world. *Gestalt Review, 20*(2), 106.

Frew, J. E. (2013). Gestalt therapy. In J. Frew & M. Spiegler (Eds.), *Contemporary psychotherapies for a diverse world* (pp. 215–257). New York, NY: Routledge.

Frisch, P., & Emery, A. (2016). *Inmate counseling & therapy: Eight years inside San Quentin.* Retrieved from https://orgonomictherapy.com/inmaye-counseling-therapy

Frykedal, K. F., & Rosander, M. (2015). The role as moderator and mediator in parent education groups: A leadership and teaching approach model from a parent perspective. *Journal of Clinical Nursing, 24*(13–14), 1966–1974. doi:10.1111/jocn.12856

Gaffney, A. (2006). Gestalt with groups: A cross-cultural perspective. *Gestalt Review, 10*(3), 205–219.

Gans, J. S. (2010). *Difficult topics in group psychotherapy.* London, UK: Karnac Books.

Garrett, M. T. (2001). Inner circle/outer circle: A group technique based on Native American healing circles. *Journal for Specialists in Group Work, 26,* 17–30.

Garza, Y., Kinsworthy, S., & Bennett, M. M. (2014). Supervision in group play therapy: A skills checklist. *The Journal of Individual Psychology, 70*(1), 31–44.

Gates, G. J. (2011). *How many people are lesbian, gay, bisexual, and transgender?* The Williams Institute, UCLA School of Law. Retrieved from https://williamsinstitute.law.ucla.edu/wp-content/uploads/Gates-How-Many-People-LGBT-Apr-2011.pdf

Gazda, G. (1971). *Group counseling: A developmental approach.* Boston, MA: Allyn & Bacon.

Gazda, G. M. (1985). Group counseling and therapy: A perspective on the future. *Journal for Specialists in Group Work, 10*(2), 74–76.

Gazda, G. M. (1986). Discussion of "When to recommend group treatment: A review of the clinical and research literature." *International Journal of Group Psychotherapy, 36,* 202–206. doi:10.1080/00207284.1986.11491447

Gazda, G. M. (1989). *Group counseling: A developmental approach* (4th ed.). Boston, MA: Allyn & Bacon.

Gazda, G. M., Horne, A., & Ginter, E. (2000). *Group counseling and group psychotherapy.* Boston, MA: Allyn & Bacon.

Gazda, G., Ginter, E., & Horne, A. (2001). *Group counseling and group psychotherapy: Theory and application.* Boston, MA: Allyn & Bacon.

Gazda, G. M., & Peters, R. W. (1975). An analysis of research in group psychotherapy, group counseling and human relations training. In G. M. Gazda (Ed.), *Basic approaches to group psychotherapy and group counseling* (pp. 38–54). Springfield, IL: Charles C Thomas.

Geddes, J., Reynolds, S., Streiner, D., & Szatmari, P. (1997). Evidence based practice in mental health. *British Medical Journal, 315,* 1483–1484.

Geller, J. J. (1950). Proposed plan for institutionalized group psychotherapy. *Psychiatric Quarterly Supplement, 24,* 270–277.

Gelso, C. J., & Carter, J. A. (1994). Components of the psychotherapy relationship: Their interaction and unfolding during treatment. *Journal of Counseling Psychology, 41,* 296–306. doi:10.1037/0022-0167.41.3.296

George, R. L., & Dustin, D. (1988). *Group counseling: Theory and practice.* Englewood Cliffs, NJ: Prentice-Hall.

Gerlinghoff, M., Gross, G., & Backmund, H. (2003). Eating disorder therapy concepts with a preventive goal. *European Child & Adolescent Psychiatry, 12,* 72–77.

Geroski, A., & Kraus, K. (2010). *Groups in schools: Preparing. leading, and responding.* Upper Saddle River, NJ: Pearson.

Gerrity, D. A., & Delucia-Waack, J. L. (2007). Effectiveness of groups in schools. *The Journal for Specialists in Group Work, 32,* 97–106.

Gholamreza, L., Aziz, R., & Maryam, J. (2016, February). Positive and negative motivational self-talk affect learning of soccer kick in novice players, mediated by anxiety. *International Journal of Humanities and Cultural Studies* [Special issue], 1945–1952.

Gibb, J. E. (1964). Climate for trust formation. In L. P. Bradford, J. R. Gibb, & K. D. Benne (Eds.), *T-group theory and laboratory method: Innovation in re-education* (pp. 279–300). New York, NY: Wiley.

Gibson, R. L., & Mitchell, M. M. (1995). *Introduction to counseling and guidance* (4th ed.). Columbus, OH: Merrill.

Gidron, Y. (2013). Group therapy/intervention. *Encyclopedia of behavioral medicine* (pp. 880–881). New York, NY: Springer Science+Business Media.

Gil, E. (2006). *Helping abused and traumatized children: Integrating directive and nondirective approaches.* New York, NY: Guilford Press.

Gladding, S. T. (1997). *Community and agency counseling.* Columbus, OH: Merrill.

Gladding, S. T. (2008). The impact of creativity in counseling. *Journal of Creativity in Mental Health, 3*(2), 97–104. doi:10.1080/15401380802226679

Gladding, S. T. (2011). *Groups: A counseling specialty* (6th ed.). New York, NY: Merrill.

Gladding, S. T. (2012). *Groups: A counseling specialty.* Boston, MA: Pearson.

Gladding, S. T. (2015). *Group work: A counseling specialty* (7th ed.). Columbus, OH: Pearson.

Glass, J. (2008). Group juggling. In L. Foss, J. Green, K. Wolfe-Stiltner, & J. L. DeLucia-Waack (Eds.), *School counselors share their favorite activities* (pp. 9–22). Alexandria, VA: ASGW.

Glatzer, H. T. (1978). The working alliance in analytic group psychotherapy. *International Journal of Group Psychotherapy, 28,* 147–161. doi:10.1080/00207284.1978.11491603

Glosoff, H. L., Herlihy, B., & Spence, E. B. (2000). Privileged communication in the counselor-client relationship. *Journal of Counseling and Development, 78,* 454–462.

Golan, N. (1986). *The perilous bridge: Helping clients through mid-life transitions.* New York, NY: Free Press.

Golden, S., Khantzian, E., & McAuliffe, W. (1994). Group therapy. In M. Galanter & H. Kleber (Eds.), *Textbook of substance abuse treatment* (pp. 303–314). Washington, DC: American Psychiatric Press.

Goodman, J. A., Alexander, M. G., Chizhik, A. W., Chizhik, E. W., & Eidelman, S. (2010). Indirect influence and divergent thinking as a function of member status and task structure in small groups. *European Journal of Social Psychology, 40,* 1184–1199. doi:10.1002/ejsp.713

Goodrich, K. M., & Luke, M. (2015). Group counseling with LGBTQI persons. Alexandria, VA: American Counseling Association.

Gottman, J. M. (1994). *What predicts divorce? The relationship between marital processes and marital outcomes.* Hillsdale, NJ: Erlbaum.

Gottman, J. M. (1999). *The marriage clinic: A scientifically based marital therapy.* New York, NY: Norton.

Gottman, J. M., & Levenson, R. W. (2000). The timing of divorce: Predicting when a couple will divorce over a 14-year period. *Journal of Marriage and the Family, 62,* 737–745.

Goulding, M., & Goulding, R. (1979). *Changing lives through redecision therapy.* New York, NY: Brunner/Mazel.

Grabo, A., & van Vugt, M. (2016). Charismatic leadership and the evolution of cooperation. *Evolution and Human Behavior, 37*(5), 399–406. doi:10.1016/j.evolhumbehav.2016.03.005

Grant, M. (2008, October). *Job club at work: Manual for job seekers. Helping job seekers help one another find jobs.* USAID, Social Protection Systems Strengthening Project. Retrieved from http://pdf.usaid.gov/pdf_docs/Pnads642.pdf

Greco, L., Smith, R., & Baer, G. (2011). Assessing mindfulness in children and adolescents: Development and validation of the child and adolescent mindfulness measure (CAMM). *Psychological Assessment, 23.* doi:10.1037/a0022819

Green, Z., & Stiers, M. (2002). Multiculturalism and group therapy in the United States: A social constructionist perspective. *Group, 26,* 233–246.

Greenberg, K. R. (2003). *Group counseling in K–12 schools: A handbook for school counselors.* Boston, MA: Allyn & Bacon.

Greenfield, S. F., Sugarman, D. E., Freid, C. M., Bailey, G. L., Crisafulli, M. A., Kaufman, J. S., & Fitzmaurice, G. M. (2014). Group therapy for women with substance use disorders: Results from the Women's Recovery Group study. *Drug and Alcohol Dependence, 142,* 245–253. doi:10.1016/j.drugalcdep.2014.06.035

Griffin, P., & Ouellett, M. L. (2007). Facilitating social justice education courses. In M. Adams, L. Bell, & P. Griffin (Eds.), *Teaching for diversity and social justice* (2nd ed., pp. 89–116). New York, NY: Routledge.

Grizzell, S. (2015). *The use of feedback in group counseling in a state vocational rehabilitation setting: A pilot study* (Doctoral dissertation). Retrieved from Utah State University DigitalCommons. (Paper 4252)

Gross, D., & Capuzzi, D. (2002). Group counseling: Stages and issues. In D. Capuzzi & D. Gross (Eds.), *Introduction to group counseling* (3rd ed., pp. 37–55). Denver, CO: Love Publishing.

Grossman, A. H., & D'Augelli, A. R. (2007). Transgender youth and life-threatening behaviors. *Suicide and Life Threatening Behavior, 37*(5), 527–537.

Grow, A., Flache, A., & Wittek, R. (2015). An agent-based model of status construction in task focused groups. *Journal of Artificial Societies and Social Simulation, 18*(2). doi:10.18564/jasss.2740

Gruner, L. (1984). Membership composition of open and closed groups. *Small Group Behavior, 15,* 222–232.

Guerra, N. (2009). *Positive life changes: A cognitive behavioral intervention for adolescents and young adults: Leaders' guide.* Champaign, IL: Research Press.

Gusella, J., Butler, G., Nichols, L., & Bird, D. (2003). A brief questionnaire to assess readiness to change in adolescents with eating disorders: Its applications to group therapy. *European Eating Disorders Review, 11,* 58–72. doi:10.1002/erv.481

Gusky, J. (2012). Why aren't they screaming? A counselor's reflection on aging. *Counseling Today, 55,* 60–61.

Gutheil, T. G., & Gabbard, G. O. (1993). The concept of boundaries in clinical practice: Theoretical and risk-management dimensions. *American Journal of Psychiatry, 150,* 188–196.

Haberstroh, S. (2005). Facing the music: Creative and experiential group strategies for working with addiction related grief and loss. *The Journal of Creativity in Mental Health, 1*(3/4), 41–55.

Hadley, S. W., & Strupp, H. H. (1976). Contemporary views of negative effects in psychotherapy. *Archives of General Psychiatry, 33,* 1291–1302. doi:10.1001/archpsyc.1976.01770110019001

Haen, C., & Aronson, S. (2016). *Handbook of child and adolescent group therapy: A practitioner's reference.* New York, NY: Taylor & Francis.

Hage, S., & Romano, J. (2013). Best practices in prevention. In R. Conyne & A. Horne (Eds.), *Prevention practice kit: Action guides for mental health practitioners* (pp. 1–59). Thousand Oaks, CA: Sage.

Hage, S. M., & Romano, J. L. (2010). History of prevention and prevention groups: Legacy for the 21st century. *Group Dynamics: Theory, Research, and Practice, 14*(3), 199–210. doi:10.1037/a0020736

Haley-Bañez, L., Brown, S., & Molina, B. (1999). Association for specialists in group work principles for diversity-competent group workers. *Journal For Specialists In Group Work, 24*(1), 7–14. doi:10.1080/01933929908411415

Haley, M., Golden, S. H., & Nate, R. D. (2016). Gestalt theory. In D. Capuzzi & M. Stauffer (Eds.), *Counseling and psychotherapy theories and interventions* (6th ed., pp. 195–226). Alexandria, VA: ACA.

Halford, W. K., Sanders, M. R., & Behrens, B. C. (1994). Self-regulation in behavioral couples therapy. *Behavior Therapy, 25*(3), 431–452.

Halford, W. K., Wilson K. L., Lizzio, A., & Moore, E. (2002). Does working at a relationship work? Relationship self-regulation and relationship outcomes. In P. Noller & J. A. Feeney (Eds.), *Understanding marriage: Developments in the study of couple interaction* (pp. 493–517). Cambridge, UK: Cambridge University Press.

Hall, E. T. (1989). *Beyond culture.* New York, NY: Random House.

Hall, K. R. (2006). Solving problems together: A psychoeducational group model for victims of bullies. *The Journal for Specialists in Group Work, 31*(3), 201–217. doi:10.1080/01933920600777790

Hall, M. (1985). *The lavender couch: A consumer's guide to psychotherapy for lesbians and gay men.* Boston, MA: Alyson Publications.

Hamm, J. S., Carlson, J., & Erguner-Tekinalp, B. (2016). Adlerian-based positive group counseling interventions with emotionally troubled youth. *The Journal of Individual Psychology, 72*(4), 255–272.

Han, A., & Vasquez, M. (2000). Group intervention and treatment with ethnic minorities. In J. Aponte & J. Wold (Eds.), *Psychological intervention and cultural diversity* (2nd ed., pp. 110–130). Boston, MA: Allyn & Bacon.

Hanna, F., Hanna, C., & Keys, S. (1999). Fifty strategies for counseling defiant, aggressive adolescents: Reaching, acceptance, and relating. *Journal of Counseling and Development, 77,* 395–404.

Hansen, A. L. (2007). School-based support for GBLT students: A review of three levels of research. *Psychology in the Schools, 44,* 839–848.

Hardiman, R., Jackson, B., & Griffin, P. (2007). Conceptual foundations for social justice courses. In M. Adams, L. Bell, & P. Griffin (Eds.), *Teaching for diversity and social justice* (2nd ed., pp. 35–66). New York, NY: Routledge.

Harley, D. A. (2014). Adult ex-offender population and employment: A synthesis of the literature on recommendations and best practices. *Journal of Applied Rehabilitation Counseling, 45*(3), 10–21.

Harro, B. (2000). The cycle of socialization. In M. Adams, W. Blumenfeld, R. Castaneda, H. Hackman, M. Peters, & X. Zuniga (Eds.), *Readings for diversity and social justice: An anthology on racism, anti-semitism, sexism, heterosexism, ableism, and classism* (pp. 15–20). New York, NY: Routledge.

Hartley, D., Roback, H. B., & Abramowitz, S. I. (1976). Deterioration effects in encounter groups. *American Psychologist, 31,* 247–255. doi:10.1037/0003-066X.31.3.247

Harvey, J. H. (2000). *Give sorrow words: Perspectives on loss and trauma.* Philadelphia, PA: Brunner/Mazel.

Harvey, J. H. (2002). *Perspectives on loss and trauma: Assaults on the self.* Thousand Oaks, CA: Sage.

Harvey, J. H., & Miller, E. D. (2000). *Loss and trauma.* Philadelphia, PA: Brunner-Routledge.

Hatfield, E., & Rapson, R. L. (1993). *Love, sex, and intimacy: Their psychology, biology, and history.* New York, NY: HarperCollins.

Haug, I. E. (1999). Boundaries and the use and misuse of power and authority: Ethical complexities for clergy psychotherapists. *Journal of Counseling and Development, 77,* 411–417.

Head, C. (2006). Ready, steady, check it out. *Therapy Today, 17*(8), 43–46.

Headley, J. A., Kautzman-East, M., Pusateri, C. G., & Kress, V. E. (2015). Making the intangible tangible: Using expressive art during termination to co-construct meaning. *Journal of Creativity in Mental Health, 10*(1), 89–99. doi:10.1080/15401383.2014.938185

Helms, J. (1995). An update of Helms's white and people of color racial identity models. In J. Ponterotto, J. Casas, L. Suzuki, & C. Alexander (Eds.), *Handbook of multicultural counseling* (pp. 181–198). Thousand Oaks, CA: Sage Publications.

Helms, J., & Cook, D. (1999). *Using race and culture in counseling and psychotherapy: Theory and process.* Boston, MA: Allyn & Bacon.

Henretty, J. R., Currier, J. M., Berman, J. S., & Levitt, H. M. (2014). The impact of counselor self-disclosure on clients: A meta-analytic review of experimental and quasi-experimental research. *Journal of Counseling Psychology, 61*(2), 191–207. doi:10.1037/a0036189

Herek, G. M., & Garnets, L. D. (2007). Sexual orientation and mental health. *Annual Review of Clinical Psychology, 3,* 353–375.

Herlihy, B., & Corey, G. (2014). *Boundary issues in counseling* (3rd ed.). Alexandria, VA: American Counseling Association.

Hershenson, D., Power, P. L., & Waldo, M. (1996). *Community counseling: Contemporary theory and practice.* Boston, MA: Allyn & Bacon.

Hoag, M. J., & Burlingame, G. M. (1997). Evaluating the effectiveness of child and adolescent group treatment: A meta-analytic review. *Journal of Clinical Child Psychology, 26,* 234–246. doi:10.1207/s15374424jccp2603_2

Hoffman, A. (2013). Bridging the divide: Using culture-infused counseling to enhance therapeutic work with digital youth. *Journal of Infant, Child, and Adolescent Psychotherapy, 12,* 118–133. doi:10.1080/15289168.2013.791195

Hogan-Garcia, M. (2003). *The four skills of cultural diversity competence: A process for understanding and practice* (2nd ed.). Pacific Grove, CA: Brooks/Cole.

Holmes, T. H., & Rahe, R. H. (1967). Social readjustment rating scale. *Journal of Psychosomatic Research, 11,* 213–218.

Hook, M. K., Gerstein, L. H., Detterich, L., & Gridley, B. (2003). How close are we? Measuring intimacy and examining gender differences. *Journal of Counseling & Development, 1*(4), 462–472.

Horne, A., Nitza, A., Dobias, B., Joliff, D., & Raczynski, C. (2012). *Empowering teen peers to prevent bullying: The Bully Busters approach.* Champaign, IL: Research Press.

Horne, S. G., Levitt, H. M., Reeves, T., & Wheeler, E. E. (2013). Group work with gay, lesbian, bisexual, transgender, queer, and questioning clients. In J. DeLucia-Waack, C. Kalodner, & M. Riva (Eds.), *Handbook of group counseling and psychotherapy* (2nd ed., pp. 253–263). Thousand Oaks, CA: Sage.

Horvath, A. O. (2000). The therapeutic relationship: From transference to alliance. *Journal of Clinical Psychology, 56,* 163–173. doi:10.1002/(SICI)1097-4679(200002)56:2<163::AID-JCLP3>3.0.CO;2-D

Horwitz, L. (1976). Indications and contraindications for group psychotherapy. *Bulletin of the Menninger Clinic, 40,* 505–507.

Huang, Y. M., Liu, C. J., Shadiev, R., Shen, M. H., & Hwang, W. Y. (2015). Investigating an application of speech-to-text recognition: A study on visual attention and learning behavior. *Journal of Computer Assisted Learning, 31,* 529–545. doi:10.1111/jcal.12093

Huebner, D. M., Rebchook, G. M., & Kegeles, S. M. (2004). Experiences of harassment, discrimination, and physical violence among young gay and bisexual men. *American Journal of Public Health, 94*(7), 1200–1204.

Hulse-Killacky, D., Killacky, J., & Donigian, J. (2001). *Making task groups work in your world.* Upper Saddle River, NJ: Prentice-Hall.

Hulse-Killacky, D., Kraus, K. L., & Schumacher, R. A. (1999). Visual conceptualizations of meetings: A group work design. *Journal for Specialists in Group Work, 24,* 113–124.

Hummelen, B., Wilberg, T., & Karterud, S. (2007). Interviews of female patients with borderline personality disorder who dropped out of group psychotherapy. *International Journal of Group Psychotherapy, 57,* 67–91. doi:10.1521/ijgp.2007.57.1.67

Humphrey, K. M. (2009). *Counseling strategies for loss and grief.* Alexandria, VA: American Counseling Association.

Hutchinson, D. R. (2017). *Great groups: Creating and leading effective groups.* Thousand Oaks, CA: Sage.

Hwee, J., Cauch-Dudek, K., Victor, J. C., Ng, R., & Shah, B. R. (2014). Diabetes education through group classes leads to better care and outcomes than individual counseling in adults: A population-based cohort study. *Canadian Journal of Public Health, 105*(3), e192–e197.

Ibrahim, F. A. (2015). International consultation and training on group work in South Asia. *Journal for Specialists in Group Work, 40*(1), 55–73.

Inaba, D. S., & Cohen, W. (2014). *Uppers, downers, all arounders* (8th ed.). Medford, OR: CNS Productions.

Ivey, A., Ivey, M., & Zalaquett, C. (2013). *Intentional interviewing and counseling: Facilitating client development in a multicultural society.* Belmont, CA: Brooks/Cole.

Ivey, A. E., Pedersen P. B., & Ivey, M. B. (2001). *Intentional group counseling: A microskills approach.* Belmont, CA: Wadsworth.

Jackson, M. (1995). Multicultural counseling: Historical perspectives. In J. Ponterotto, J. Casas, L. Suzuki, & C. Alexander (Eds.), *Handbook of multicultural counseling* (pp. 3–16). Thousand Oaks, CA: Sage Publications.

Jacobs, E. (2006). Your personal board of directors. In J. DeLucia-Waack, K. Bridbord, J. Kleiner, & A. Nitza (Eds.), *Group work experts share their favorite activities* (Vol. 1, pp. 131–132). Alexandria, VA: ASGW.

Jacobs, E., Masson, R. L., Harvill, R. L., & Schimmel, C. J. (2012). *Group counseling: Strategies and skills* (7th ed.). Pacific Grove, CA: Brooks/Cole.

Jacobs, E., & Schimmel, C. J., (2013). *Impact therapy: The courage to counsel.* Morgantown, WV: Impact Therapy Associates.

Jacobs, E., Schimmel, C. J., Masson, R. L., & Harvill, R. L. (2015). *Group counseling: Strategies and skills* (8th ed.). Pacific Grove, CA: Brooks/Cole.

Jacobs, E. E., Masson, R. L., & Harvill, R. L. (2009). *Group counseling: Strategies and skills* (6th ed.). Belmont, CA: Thomson Brooks/Cole.

Jacobs, E. E., Masson, R. L., & Harvill, R. L. (2016). *Group counseling: Strategies and skills* (8th ed.). Belmont, CA: Brooks/Cole.

Jacobs, E. E., Masson, R. L., Harvill, R. L., & Schimmel, C. J. (2012). *Group counseling: Strategies and skills* (7th ed.). Boston, MA: Cengage Learning.

Jacobs, E. E., Schimmel, C. J., Masson, R. L., & Harvill, R. L. (2016). *Group counseling: Strategies and skills* (8th ed.). Independence, KY: Cengage Publishing.

Jagger, M., & Richards, K. (1978). Miss you [Recorded by The Rolling Stones]. On *Some girls* [Vinyl record]. New York, NY: Rolling Stones Records.

James, J. W., & Friedman, R. (2009). *The grief recovery handbook: The action program for moving beyond death, divorce, and other losses.* New York, NY: Harper Perennial.

James, N. (2015). *Offender reentry: Correctional statistics, reintegration into the community, and recidivism.* Washington, DC: Congressional Research Service. Retrieved from https://fas.org/sgp/crs/misc/RL34287.pdf

Janis, I. L. (1972). *Victims of group think: A psychological study of foreign-policy decisions and fiascos.* Boston, MA: Houghton Mifflin.

Jelski, D., & George, T. F. (2015). *Your future job: Building a career in the new normal.* Modena, NY: Plattekill Press.

Jensen, D. R., Abbott, M. K., Beecher, M. E., Griner, D., Golightly, T. R., & Cannon, J. N. (2012). Taking the pulse of the group: The utilization of practice-based evidence in group psychotherapy. *Professional Psychology: Research and Practice, 43*(4), 388–394. doi:10.1037/a0029033

Johnson, D. W., & Johnson, F. P. (2017). *Joining together: Group theory and group skills* (12th ed.). Columbus, OH: Pearson.

Johnson, J. E. (2013). Beware of storming: Research implications for interpreting group climate questionnaire scores over time. *International Journal of Group Psychotherapy, 63*(3), 433–446. doi:10.1521/ijgp.2013.63.3.433

Johnson, S. (2003). *Therapist's guide to substance abuse intervention.* Boston, MA: Academic Press.

Johnston, J., O'Gara, J., Koman, S., Baker, C., & Anderson, D. (2015). A pilot study of Maudsley family therapy group dialectical behavioral therapy skills training in an intensive outpatient program for adolescent eating disorders. *Journal of Clinical Psychology, 71,* 527–543. doi:10.1002/jclp.22176

Joines, V. S. (2010). Combining one-to-one and group-as-a-whole work in redecision group therapy. *Transactional Analysis Journal, 40*(2), 144–148.

Joines, V. S. (2016). Understanding second order structure and functioning: Ego state structures, relational units, and the divided psyche. *Transactional Analysis Journal, 46*(1), 39–49.

Jones, K., & Robinson, E. (2000). Psychoeducational groups: A model for choosing topics and exercises appropriate for group stage. *Journal for Specialists in Group Work, 35,* 343–355. doi:10.1080/01933920008411679

Jordan, J. V. (2010). *Relational-cultural therapy.* Washington, DC: American Psychological Association.

Joseph, T. (2015). Stressed out [Recorded by 21 Pilots]. On *Blurryface* [CD]. New York, NY: Fueled by Ramen.

Jourard, S. (1971). *The transparent self* (Rev. ed.). New York, NY: Van Nostrand Reinhold.

Kalodner, C., Coughlin, J., & Seide, M. (2014). In J. DeLucia-Waack, C. Kalodner, & M. Riva (Eds.), *Handbook of group counseling and psychotherapy* (2nd ed., pp. 484–494). Thousand Oaks, CA: Sage.

Kaplan, R. E. (1982). The dynamics of injury in encounter groups: Power, splitting, and the mismanagement of resistance. *International Journal of Group Psychotherapy, 32,* 163–187. doi:10.1080/00207284.1982.11492344

Kaplan, S. R., & Roman, M. (1963). Phases of development in an adult therapy group. *International Journal of Group Psychotherapy, 13,* 10–26.

Karademas, E. C. (2009). Counselling psychology in medical settings: The promising role of counselling health psychology. *European Journal of Counselling Psychology, 1*(1), 18–37.

Karatas, Z. (2014). Effects of psychodrama practice on university students' subjective well-being and hopelessness. *Egitim Ve Bilim, 39*(173), 117–128.

Kasl, C. S. (2002). Special issues in counseling lesbian women for sexual addiction, compulsivity, and sexual codependency. *Sexual Addiction & Compulsivity, 9,* 191–208.

Keck School of Medicine of USC. (2016). *Psychoeducation.* Retrieved from http://keck.usc.edu/adolescent-trauma-training-center/chapter-6-psychoeducation/

Keel, P., Mitchell, J., Davis, T., & Crow, S. (2002). Long-term impact of treatment of women diagnosed with bulimia nervosa. *International Journal of Eating Disorders, 31,* 151–158. doi:10.1002/eat.10017

Kennair, N., Mellor, D., & Brann, P. (2016). Curative factors in adolescent day programs: Participant, therapist, and parent perspectives. *International Journal of Group Psychotherapy, 66*(3), 382–400.

Kim, J. S., & Franklin, C. (2015). Understanding emotional change in solution-focused brief therapy: Facilitating positive emotions. *Best Practices in Mental Health, 11*(1), 25–41.

Kit, P. L., & Teo, L. (2012). Quit now! A psychoeducational expressive therapy group work approach for at-risk and delinquent adolescent smokers in Singapore. *The Journal for Specialists in Group Work, 37*(1), 2–28. doi:10.1080/01933922.2011.606557

Kivlighan, D. M., & Holmes, S. E. (2004). The importance of therapeutic factors in counseling groups: A typology of therapeutic factors studies? In J. DeLucia-Waack, D. Gerrity, C. Kalodner, & M. Riva (Eds.), *Handbook of group counseling and psychotherapy* (pp. 23–36). Thousand Oaks, CA: Sage Publications.

Kivlighan, D. M., & Kivlighan, D. M. (2016). Examining between-leader and within-leader processes in group therapy. *Group Dynamics: Theory, Research, and Practice, 20*(3), 144–164. doi:http://dx.doi.org/10.1037/gdn0000050

Kivlighan, D. M., Jr., & Goldfine, D. C. (1991). Endorsement of therapeutic factors as a function of stage of group development and participant interpersonal attitudes. *Journal of Counseling Psychology, 38*, 150–158. doi:10.1037/0022-0167.38.2.150

Klein, E. B. (1985). Group work: 1985 and 2001. *Journal for Specialists in Group Work, 10*(2), 108–111.

Kline, W. (2003). *Interactive group counseling and therapy.* Upper Saddle River, NJ: Merrill/Prentice Hall.

Kluger-Bell, K. (2000). *Unspeakable losses: Healing from miscarriage, abortion, and other pregnancy loss.* New York, NY: Harper Collins.

Knapp, D., Norton, A., & Sandberg, J. (2015). Family-of-origin, relationship self-regulation, and attachment in marital relationships. *Contemporary Family Therapy: An International Journal, 37*(2), 130–141. doi:10.1007/s10591-015-9332-z

Knapp, S., & VandeCreek, L. (2003). *A guide to the 2002 revision of the American Psychological Association's Ethics Code.* Sarasota, FL: Professional Resource Press.

Koocher, G. P. (2003). Ethical issues in psychotherapy with adolescents. *Journal of Clinical Psychology, 59*, 1247–1256.

Kottler, J., & Shepard, D. S. (2014). *Introduction to therapeutic counseling: Voices from the field* (8th ed.). Stamford, CT: Cengage Learning.

Kottler, J. A. (1983). *Pragmatic group leadership.* Pacific Grove, CA: Brooks/Cole.

Kottler, J. A. (1994a). *Advanced group leadership.* Pacific Grove, CA: Brooks/Cole.

Kottler, J. A. (1994b). Working with difficult group members. *Journal for Specialists in Group Work, 19*, 3–10.

Kottler, J. A. (2001). *Learning group leadership: An experimental approach.* Boston, MA: Allyn & Bacon.

Kottler, J. A., & Brown, R. W. (2000). *Introduction to therapeutic counseling: Voices from the field* (4th ed.). Belmont, CA: Brooks/Cole.

Kottman, T., & Meany-Walen, K. (2016). *Partners in play: An Adlerian approach to play therapy.* Hoboken, NJ: Wiley.

Kovacs, M. (1992). *The Children's Depression Inventory Manual.* North Tonawanda, NY: MultiHealth Systems.

Krajeski, J. P. (1986). Psychotherapy with gay men and lesbians: A history of controversy. In T. S. Stein & C. J. Cohen (Eds.), *Contemporary perspectives on psychotherapy with lesbians and gay men* (pp. 9–25). New York, NY: Plenum.

Kübler-Ross, E., & Kessler, D. (2005). *On grief and grieving: Finding the meaning of grief through the five stages of loss.* New York, NY: Schribner.

Kulic, K., Horne, A., & Dagley, J. (2004). A comprehensive review of prevention groups for children and adolescents. *Group Dynamics, 8*, 139–151. doi:10.1037/1089-2699.8.2.139

Lacoursiere, R. (1980). *The life-cycle of groups: Group development stage theory.* New York, NY: Human Sciences.

Lambert, M. J., Shapiro, D. A., & Bergin, A. E. (1986). The effectiveness of psychotherapy. In S. L. Garfield & A. E. Bergin (Eds.), *Handbook of psychotherapy and behavior change* (pp. 157–212). New York, NY: Wiley.

Laser, J., Leibowitz, G., & Nicotera, N. (2011). Substance abuse. In J. Laser & N. Nicotera, *Working with adolescents* (pp. 163–179). New York, NY: Guilford Press.

Laser, J., & Nicotera, N. (2011). *Working with adolescents.* New York, NY: Guilford Press.

Lasky, G. B., & Riva, M. T. (2006). Confidentiality and privileged communication in group psychotherapy. *International Journal of Group Psychotherapy, 54*, 455–476.

Lavner, J. A., Karney, B. R., & Bradbury, T. N. (2016). Does couples' communication predict marital satisfaction, or does marital satisfaction predict communication? *Journal of Marriage & Family, 78*(3), 680. doi:10.1111/jomf.12301

Leahy, M. J. (2012). Qualified providers of rehabilitation counseling services. In D. R. Maki & V. M. Tarvydas (Eds.), *The professional practice of rehabilitation counseling* (pp. 193–211). New York, NY: Springer

Leahy, M. J., Chan, F., Sung, C., & Kim, M. (2013). Empirically derived test specifications for the certified rehabilitation counselor examination. *Rehabilitation Counseling Bulletin, 56*, 199–214.

Lee, F., & Bednar, R. L. (1977). Effects of group structure and risk taking deposition on group behavior, attitudes, and atmosphere. *Journal of Counseling Psychology, 24*, 191–199. doi:10.1037/0022-0167.24.3.191

Lee, M. W., Hunter, M., Goss, R., Bock, R. C., Almanzan, R., Christensen, D., . . . Vasquez, H. (1994). *The color of fear: A film* [Motion picture]. Berkeley, CA: Stir-Fry Productions.

Lefley, H. P. (2009). A psychoeducational support group for serious mental illness. *The Journal for Specialists in Group Work, 34*(4), 369–381. doi:10.1080/01933920903219094

LeGrand, K. (2006). The kid's grief kit. In J. DeLucia-Waack, K. Bridbord, J. Kleiner, & A. Nitza (Eds.), *Group work experts share their favorite activities* (Vol.1, pp. 123–124). Alexandria, VA: ASGW.

Lemma, A., & Fonagy, P. (2013). Feasibility study of a psychodynamic online group intervention for depression. *Psychoanalytic Psychology, 30*(3), 367–380. doi:10.1037/a0033239

Lenihan, G. O., & Sanders, C. D. (1984). Guidelines for group therapy with eating disorder victims. *Journal of Counseling & Development, 63*, 252–254.

Lennon, J., & McCartney, P. (1967). With a little help from my friends [Recorded by The Beatles]. On *Sgt. Pepper's Lonely Hearts Club Band* [Vinyl record]. London, UK: EMI Studios.

Levine, N. (1971). Emotional factors in group development. *Human Relations, 24,* 65–89.

Lewin, K. (1944). The dynamics of group action. *Educational Leadership, 1,* 195–200.

Li, X., Kivlighan, D. M. J., & Gold, P. B. (2015). Errors of commission and omission in novice group counseling trainees' knowledge structures of group counseling situations. *Journal of Counseling Psychology, 62*(2), 159–172. doi:10.1037/cou0000070

Lieberman, M. A., Yalom, I. D., & Miles, M. B. (1973). *Encounter groups: First facts.* New York, NY: Basic Books.

Limber, S. (2000). Implementation of the Olweus bullying prevention program in American schools: Lessons learned from the field. In D. Espelage & S. Swearer (Eds.), *Bullying in American schools* (pp. 351–363). New York, NY: Guilford Press.

Lipchik, E., Derks, J., LaCourt, M., & Nunnally, E. (2012). The evolution of solution-focused brief therapy. In C. Franklin, T. Tepper, W. Gingerich, & E. McCollum (Eds.), *Solution-focused brief therapy: A handbook of evidence-based practice* (pp. 3–19). New York, NY: Oxford University Press.

Long, L. D., & Cope, C. S. (1980). Curative factors in a male felony offender group. *Small Group Behavior, 11,* 389–398.

Lopez, C., & Bhat, C. S. (2007). Supporting students with incarcerated parents in schools: A group intervention. *The Journal for Specialists in Group Work, 32,* 139–153.

Lowe, M., Willan, V. J., Kelly, S., Hartwell, B., & Canuti, E. (2017). CORE assessment of adult survivors abused as children: A NAPAC group therapy evaluation. *Counselling & Psychotherapy Research, 17*(1), 71–79. doi:10.1002/capr.12095

Lowenstein, L., & Sprunk, T. P. (2010). *Creative interventions to assess children and families.* Retrieved from http://www.lianalowenstein.com/assessmentArticle.pdf

Lubas, M., & De Leo, G. (2014). Online grief support groups: Facilitators' attitudes. *Death Studies, 38,* 517–521.

Luft, J., & Ingham, H. (1961). The Johari window. *Human Relations Training News, 5*(1), 6–7.

Luke, M., & Goodrich, K. (2015a). *Group work experts share their favorite supervision activities* (Vol.1). Alexandria, VA: ASGW.

Luke, M., & Goodrich, K. (2015b). *Group work experts share their favorite supervision activities* (Vol. 2). Alexandria, VA: ASGW.

Lundgren, J. D., Danoff-Burg, S., & Anderson, D. A. (2004). Cognitive–behavioral therapy for bulimia nervosa: An empirical analysis of clinical significance. *International Journal of Eating Disorders, 35,* 262–274.

Lurie, A., & Harold, R. (1967). Multiple group counseling with discharged schizophrenic adolescents and their parents. Laurel, MD. (ERIC Document Reproduction Service No. ED 027550).

Lynne, C. (2001). Teaching outside the box: Incorporating queer theory in counselor education. *Journal of Humanistic Counseling, 40*(1), 49–58.

Lyons, T. (2016). Groups in addiction and recovery: Signs of a paradigm shift. *Journal of Groups in Addiction & Recovery, 11*(1), 1–2. doi:10.1080/1556035X.2016.1136150

Maarif, S. (2016). Improving junior high school students' mathematical analogical ability using discovery learning method. *International Journal of Research in Education and Science, 2*(1), 114–124.

MacKenzie, K. R. (1993). The clinical application of a group climate measure. In R. Dies & K. R. MacKenzie (Eds.), *Advances in group psychotherapy.* New York, NY: International Universities Press.

MacKenzie, K. R., & Grabovac, A. D. (2001). Interpersonal psychotherapy group (IPT-G) for depression. *The Journal of Psychotherapy Practice and Research, 10,* 46–51.

Malat, J., & Leszcz, M. (2015). Group psychotherapy. In A. Tasman, J. Kay, J. A. Liberman, M. B. First, & M. Riba (Eds.), *Psychiatry* (4th ed., pp. 1923–1942). Hoboken, NJ: John Wiley.

Malekoff, A. (2004). *Group work with adolescents* (2nd ed.). New York, NY: Guilford.

Malkinson, R. (2007). *Cognitive grief therapy: Constructing a rational meaning to life following loss.* New York, NY: W. W. Norton.

Malott, K., & Magnusom, S. (2004). Using genograms to facilitate undergraduate students' career development: A group model. *The Career Development Quarterly, 53,* 178–186. doi:10.1002/j.2161-0045.2004.tb00988.x

Maples, M. (1988). Group development: Extending Tuckman's theory. *Journal for Specialists in Group Work, 13,* 17–23. doi:10.1080/01933928808411771

Markowitz, F. E. (2015). Involvement in mental health self-help groups and recovery. *Health Sociology Review, 24*(2), 199–212.

Marques, L., Alegria, M., Becker, A. E., Chen, C.-n., Fang, A., Chosak, A., & Diniz, J. B. (2011). Comparative prevalence, correlates of impairment, and service utilization for eating disorders across US ethnic groups: Implications for reducing ethnic disparities in health care access for eating disorders. *International Journal of Eating Disorders, 44*(5), 412–420. doi:10.1002/eat.20787

Marshall, A. (2000). *Oops, you're stepping on my boundaries.* Paper presented at the Annual National Consultation on Career Development, Ottawa, Ontario.

Martin, L., & Jacobs, M. (1980). Structured feedback delivered in small groups. *Small Group Behavior, 1,* 88–107.

Matsukawa, L. (2001). Group therapy with multiethnic members. In W. Tseng & J. Streltzer (Eds.), *Culture and psychotherapy: A guide to clinical practice* (pp. 243–264). Washington, DC: American Psychiatric Press.

Matthias, R. (2005). Effective treatment of eating disorders in Europe: Treatment outcome and its predictors. *European Eating Disorders Review, 13,* 169–179.

McConnell, K. J., Guzman, O. E., Pherwani, N., Spencer, D. D., Van Cura, J. D., & Shea, K. M. (2017). Operational and clinical strategies to address drug cost containment in the acute care setting. *Pharmacotherapy: The Journal of Human Pharmacology and Drug Therapy, 37*(1), 25–35. doi:10.1002/phar.1858

McKisack, C., & Waller, G. (1997). Factors influencing the outcome of group psychotherapy for bulimia nervosa. *International Journal of Eating Disorders, 22,* 1–13.

McLaughlin, J. E. (2013). Post-structuralism in group theory and practice. *Journal of Systemic Therapies, 32*(2), 1–16

McLeod, A. L., Hays, D. G., & Chang, C. Y. (2010). Female intimate partner violence survivors' experiences with accessing resources. *Journal of Counseling and Development, 88*(3), 303–310.

McLeod, J. D., & Shanahan, M. J. (1993). Poverty, parenting, and children's mental health. *American Sociological Review, 58,* 351–366.

McMahon, H. G., Mason, E., Daluga-Guenther, N., & Ruiz, A. (2014). An ecological model of professional school counseling. *Journal of Counseling & Development, 92*(4), 459–471.

McWhirter, D. P., & Mattison, A. M. (1984). *The male couple: How relationships develop.* Englewood Cliffs, NJ: Prentice-Hall.

Mehta, C., Walls, C., Scherer, E., Feldman, H., & Shrier, L. (2016). Daily affect and intimacy in emerging adult couples. *Journal of Adult Development, 23*(2), 101–110. doi:10.1007/s10804-016-9226-9

Mental Health America. (2017). *Depression in women.* Retrieved from http://www.mentalhealthamerica.net/conditions/depression-women

Merta, R. (1995). Group work: Multicultural perspectives. In J. Ponterotto, J. M. Casas, L. Suzuki, & C. Alexander (Eds.), *Handbook of multicultural counseling* (pp. 567–585). Thousand Oaks, CA: Sage Publications.

Messinger, A. M. (2017). *LGBTQ Intimate partner violence: Lessons for policy, practice and research.* Oakland, CA: University of California Press.

Metta Institute. (2011). *Metta meditation.* Retrieved from http://www.mettainstitute.org/mettameditation.html

Meyers, L. (2016). Grief: Going beyond death and stages. *Counseling Today, 59*(5), 27–32.

Mezey, N. J. (2015). *LGBT families.* Thousand Oaks, CA: Sage Publishing.

Miles, M. B. (1953). Human relations training: How a group grows. *Teachers College Record, 55,* 90–96.

Milgram, D., & Rubin, J. S. (1992). Resisting resistance: Involuntary substance abuse group therapy. *Social Work with Groups, 15,* 95–110.

Miller, A., Wyman, S., & Huppert, J., Glassman, S., & Rathus, J. (2000). Analysis of behavioral skills used by suicidal adolescents researching dialectical behavior therapy. *Cognitive and Behavioral Practice, 7,* 183–187. doi:10.1016/S1077-7229(00)80029-2

Miller, W. R., & Rollnick, S. (2009). Ten things that motivational interviewing is not. *Behavioural and Cognitive Psychotherapy, 37,* 129–140.

Miller, W. R., & Rollnick, S. (2012). *Motivational interviewing: Helping people change* (3rd ed.). New York, NY: Guilford Press.

Mills, T. M. (1964). *Group transformation.* Englewood Cliffs, NJ: Prentice-Hall.

Minardi, N. G. (2008). *Fifty steps closer: Group counseling guide in reflections of school-aged boys and girls.* Mustang, OK: Tate Publishing.

Misurell, J. R., & Springer, C. (2013). Developing culturally responsive evidence-based practice: A game-based group therapy program for child sexual abuse (CSA). *Journal of Child and Family Studies, 22,* 137–149. doi:10.1007/s10826-011-9560-2

Molina, O., Lawrence, S. A., Azhar-Miller, A., & Rivera, M. (2009). Divorcing abused Latina immigrant women's experiences with domestic violence support groups. *Journal of Divorce & Remarriage, 50,* 459–471. doi:10.1080/10502550902970561

Moore, T. H. M., Kapur, N., Hawton, K., & Richards, A. (2016). Interventions to reduce the impact of unemployment and economic hardship on mental health in the general population: A systematic review. *Psychological Medicine, 47*(6), 1062–1084. doi:10.1017/S0033291716002944

Moreno, Z. T. (1987). Psychodrama, role theory, and the concept of the social atom. In J. K. Zeig (Ed.), *The evolution of psychotherapy* (pp. 341–366). New York, NY: Brunner/Mazel.

Morgan, R. D. (2014). Groups with offenders and mandated clients. In J. L. DeLucia-Waak, D. A. Kalodner, & M. T. Riva (Eds.), *Handbook of group counseling and psychotherapy* (2nd ed., pp. 388–400). Thousand Oaks, CA: Sage.

Morgan, R. D., Kroner, D. G., & Mills, J. E. (2006). Group psychotherapy in prison: Facilitating change inside the walls. *Journal of Contemporary Psychotherapy, 36,* 137–144.

Morse, G. A. (2000). On being homeless and mentally ill: A multitude of losses and the possibility of recovery. In J. H. Harvey & E. D. Miller (Eds.), *Loss and trauma: General and close relationship perspectives* (pp. 249–262). Philadelphia, PA: Taylor & Francis.

Murphy, S., Russell, L., & Waller, G. (2005). Integrated psychodynamic therapy for bulimia nervosa and binge eating disorder: Theory, practice and preliminary findings. *European Eating Disorders Review, 13,* 383–391.

Murphy, S. N. (2012). Space to grieve everyday losses. *Counseling Today, 54*(9), 58–61.

Nace, E. (1992). Alcoholics Anonymous. In J. Lowinson, P. Ruiz, R. Millman, & J. Langrod (Eds.), *Substance abuse: A comprehensive textbook* (2nd ed., pp. 486–495). Baltimore, MD: Williams & Wilkins.

Naranjo, C. (1993/2007). Psychological judo. In *Gestalt therapy: The attitude and practice of an atheoretical experientialism* (pp. 131–133). Williston, VT: Crown House Publishing. Retrieved from https://www.crownhouse.co.uk/assets/look-inside/9781899836543a.pdf

National Alliance on Mental Illness. (2008a). *Women & depression: 1 in 8; twice the rate of men.* Retrieved from http://www.nami.org/Press-Media/Press-Releases/2008/Women-Depression-1-in-8;-twice-the-rate-of-men

National Alliance on Mental Illness. (2008b). *Postpartum depression affects 1 in 7 mothers: Bipolar rate strikingly high, study finds.* Retrieved from http://www.nami.org/About-NAMI/NAMI-News/Postpartum-Depression-Affects-1-in-7-Mothers;-Bipo

National Institute of Mental Health. (2016). *Women and mental health.* Retrieved from https://www.nimh.nih.gov/health/topics/women-and-mental-health/index.shtml

National Institute on Drug Abuse. (2003). *Group therapy research.* Retrieved from https://archives.drugabuse.gov/meetings/grouptherapy.html

Neff, K. D. (2012). The science of self-compassion. In C. Germer & R. Siegel (Eds.), *Compassion and wisdom in psychotherapy* (pp. 79–92). New York, NY: Guilford Press.

Neimeyer, R. A. (2005). Re-storying loss: Fostering growth in posttraumatic narrative. In L. Calhoun & R. T. Tedeschi (Eds.), *Handbook of posttraumatic growth: Research and practice.* Mahwah, NJ: Erlbaum.

Nelson, J. R., & Dykeman, C. (1996). The effects of a group counseling intervention on students with behavioral adjustment problems. *Elementary School Guidance & Counseling, 31,* 21–33.

Nelson, M. L., & Neufeldt, S. (1996). Building on an empirical foundation: Strategies to enhance good practice. *Journal of Counseling and Development, 74,* 609–615.

Nesmith, C. L., Wilcoxon, S. A., & Satcher, J. F. (2000). Male leadership in an addicted women's group: An empirical approach. *Journal of Addictions & Offender Counseling, 20*(2), 75–83.

Nestler, J., & Goldbeck, L. (2011). A pilot study of social competence group training for adolescents with borderline intellectual functioning and emotional and behavioural problems (SCT-ABJ). *Journal of Intellectual Disability Research, 55*, 231–241. doi:10.1111/j.1365-2788.2010.01369.x

Neukrug, E. (1998). *The world of the counselor.* Pacific Grove, CA: Brooks/Cole.

Newman, B., Dannenfelser, P., & Benishek, L. (2002). Assessing beginning social work and counseling students' acceptance of lesbians and gay men. *Journal of Social Work Education, 38*(2), 273–288.

Newman, D., Horne, A., & Bartolomucci, C. (2000). *Bully Busters: A teacher's manual for helping bullies, victims, and bystanders (grades 6 to 8).* Champaign, IL: Research Press.

Nielsen, M. (2015). CBT group treatment for depression. *The Cognitive Behaviour Therapist, 8,* 1–11. doi:10.1017/S1754470X15000173

Nielsen, M. B. (2013). Personality and social psychology bullying in work groups: The impact of leadership. *Scandinavian Journal of Psychology, 54,* 127–136. doi:10.1111/sjop.12011

Niemiec, R. M., & Schulenberg, S. E. (2011). Understanding death attitudes: The integration of movies, positive psychology, and meaning management. *Death Studies, 35,* 387–407.

Nolen-Hoeksema, S., & Larson, J. (1999). *Coping with loss.* Mahwah, NJ: Lawrence Erlbaum Associates.

Northeastern Society for Group Psychotherapy Foundation. (2015). *Facts about group therapy: The history of group therapy.* Retrieved from http://www.nsgpf.org/facts.aspx

O'Hanlon, W. H., & Weiner-Davis, M. (2003). *In search of solutions: A new direction in psychotherapy* (Rev. ed.). New York, NY: Norton.

Ocasio, K., Van Alst, D., Koivunen, J., Huang, C., & Allegra, C. (2015). Promoting preschool mental health: Results of a 3 year primary prevention strategy. *Journal of Child and Family Studies, 24,* 1800–1808. doi:10.1007/s10826-014-9983-7

Ohlsen, M. M. (1970). *Group counseling.* New York, NY: Holt, Rinehart & Winston.

Ohlsen, M. M., Horne, A. M., & Lawe, C. F. (1988). *Group counseling* (3rd ed.). New York, NY: Holt, Rinehart & Winston.

Ohrt, J. H. (2014). An exploration of group and member development in experiential groups. *Journal for Specialists in Group Work, 39*(3), 212–235.

Ohrt, J. H., Ener, E., Porter, J., & Young, T. L. (2014). Group leader reflections on their training and experience: Implications for group counselor educators and supervisors. *Journal for Specialists in Group Work, 39*(2), 95–124. doi:10.1080/01933922.2014.883004

Okech, J. E. A., Pimpleton, A., Vannata, R., & Champe, J. (2015). Intercultural communication: An application to group work. *Journal for Specialists in Group Work, 40,* 268–293. doi:10.1080/01933922.2015.1056568

Okech, J. E. A., Pimpleton-Gray, A., Vannata, R., & Champe, J. (2016). Intercultural conflict in groups. *Journal for Specialists in Group Work, 41*(4), 350–369. doi:10.1080/01933922.2016.1232769

Okech, J. E. A., & Rubel, D. (2007). Diversity competent group work supervision: An application of the supervision of

group work model (SGW). *Journal for Specialists in Group Work, 32*(3), 245–266.

Önemli, M., & Yöndem, Z. D. (2012). The effect of psychoeducational group training depending on self-regulation on students' motivational strategies and academic achievement. *Educational Sciences: Theory and Practice, 12*(1), 67–73.

Oswalt, S. B., & Wyatt, T. J. (2011). Sexual orientation and differences in mental health stress and academic performance in a national sample of U.S. college students. *Journal of Homosexuality, 58*(9), 1255–1280.

Pack-Brown, S. P., Whittington-Clark, L. E., & Parker, W. M. (1998). *Images of me: A guide to group work with African-American women.* Needham, MA: Allyn & Bacon.

Paisley, P. O., & Milsom, A. (2007). Group work as an essential contribution to transforming school counseling. *The Journal for Specialists in Group Work, 32,* 9–17.

Paolini, S., Harris, N. C., & Griffin, A. S. (2015). Learning anxiety in interactions with the outgroup: Towards a learning model of anxiety and stress in intergroup contact. *Group Processes and Intergroup Relations, 19*(3), 275–313. doi:10.1177/1368430215572265

Paradise, L. V., & Kirby, P. C. (1990). Some perspectives on the legal liability of group counseling in private practice. *Journal for Specialists in Group Work, 15,* 114–118.

Parker, R. I., & Vannest, K. (2009). An improved effect size for single-case research: Nonoverlap of all pairs. *Behavior Therapy, 40,* 357–367. doi:10.1016/j.beth.2008.10.006

Parkes, C. M. (2001). *Bereavement: Studies of grief in adult life.* Philadelphia, PA: Taylor & Francis.

Parloff, M. B., & Dies, R. R. (1978). Group therapy outcome instrument: Guidelines for conducting research. *Small Group Behavior, 9,* 243–286.

Patterson, R. J. (2000). *The assertiveness workbook.* Oakland, CA: New Harbinger Publications.

Pender, D. A. (2009). Group work evaluation. In the American Counseling Association (Ed.), *The American Counseling Association Encyclopedia of Counseling* (pp. 230–231). Alexandria, VA: American Counseling Association.

Perls, F. S. (1969). *Gestalt therapy verbatim.* Moab, UT: Real People Press.

Perrone, K. M., & Sedlacek, W. E. (2000). A comparison of group cohesiveness and client satisfaction in homogeneous and heterogeneous groups. *Journal for Specialists in Group Work, 25,* 243–251.

Perryman, K. L., Moss, R., & Cochran, K. (2015). Child-centered expressive arts and play therapy: School groups for at-risk adolescent girls. *International Journal of Play Therapy, 24*(4), 205–220. doi:10.1037/a0039764

Peterman, L. (2003). Domestic violence between same sex partners: Implications for counseling. *Journal of Counseling and Development, 81*(1), 40–47.

Peters, R. H., Wexler, H. K., & Lurigio, A. J. (2015). Co-occurring substance use and mental disorders in the criminal justice system: A new frontier of clinical practice and research. *Psychiatric Rehabilitation Journal, 38*(1), 1–6.

Pettinato, M. (2005). Practicing, understanding, and changing: Three research paradigms regarding alcohol use among lesbians. *Journal of Lesbian Studies, 9,* 91–101.

Phillips, A., and Daniluk, J. C. (2004). Beyond "survivor": How childhood sexual abuse informs the identity of adult women at the end of the therapeutic process. *Journal of Counseling and Development, 82*(2), 177–184.

Phillips Sheesley, A., Pfeffer, M., & Barish, B. (2016). Comedic improv therapy for the treatment of social anxiety disorder. *Journal of Creativity in Mental Health, 11*(2), 157–169. doi:10.10 80/15401383.2016.1182880

Piaget, J., & Inhelder, B. (1969). *The psychology of the child* (H. Weaver, Trans.). New York, NY: Basic Books

Platow, M. J., Haslam, S. A., Reicher, S. D., & Steffens, N. K. (2015). There is no leadership if no-one follows: Why leadership is necessarily a group process. *International Coaching Psychology Review, 10*(1), 20–37.

Polster, E., & Polster, M. (1973). *Gestalt therapy integrated*. New York, NY: Brunner/Mazel.

Pomeroy, H., & Clark, A. J. (2015). Self-efficacy and early recollections in the context of Adlerian and wellness theory. *The Journal of Individual Psychology, 71*(1), 24–33.

Pope, K. S., & Keith-Spiegel, P. (2008). A practical approach to boundaries in psychotherapy: Making decisions, bypassing blunders, and mending fences. *Journal of Clinical Psychology, 64*, 638–652.

Porter, J. (2005). Major substances of abuse and the body. In P. Stevens & R. Smith (Eds.), *Substance abuse counseling* (3rd ed., pp. 36–86). Upper Saddle River, NJ: Pearson.

Posthuma, B. W. (1999). *Small groups in counseling and therapy* (3rd ed.). Boston, MA: Allyn & Bacon.

Powers, Y. O., & Kalodner, C. R. (2016). Cognitive behavior theories. In D. Capuzzi & M. Stauffer (Eds.), *Counseling and psychotherapy theories and interventions* (6th ed., pp. 227–252). Alexandria, VA: ACA.

Pratt, J. H. (1907). The organization of tuberculosis classes. *Medical Communications of the Massachusetts Medical Society, 20*, 475–492.

Pratt, J. H. (1945). Group method in the treatment of psychosomatic disorders. *Sociometry, 8*, 323–331.

Prince-Embury, S. (2006). *Resiliency scales for adolescents: A profile of personal strengths*. San Antonio, TX: Harcourt Assessment.

Prochaska, J. O., & DiClemente, C. C. (1983). Stages and processes of self-change of smoking: Toward an integrative model of change. *Journal of Consulting and Clinical Psychology, 51*, 390–395.

Proctor, S. L., & Simpson, C. (2016). Improving service delivery to ethic and racial minority students through multicultural program training. In S. L. Graves & J. Blake (Eds.), *Psychoeducational assessment and intervention for ethnic minority children: Evidence-based approaches* (pp. 251–265). Washington, DC: American Psychological Association.

Proudlock, S., & Wellman, N. (2011). Solution focused groups: The results look promising. *Counselling Psychology Review, 26*(3), 45–54.

Prout, S., & Prout, H. (1998). A meta-analysis of school-based studies of counseling and psychotherapy: An update. *Journal of School Psychology, 36*, 121–136. doi:10.10.1016/j.bbr.2011. 03.031

Pulvino, C. J., & Bentin, S. (2011). Counseling the physically disabled student: Accepting the challenge. *Journal of Humanistic Education and Development, 24*(3), 116–134.

Raczynski, K., & Horne, A. (2014). Psychoeducational and counseling groups for bullying. In J. DeLucia-Waack, C. Kalodner, & M. Riva (Eds.), *Handbook of counseling and psychotherapy* (2nd ed., pp. 495–505). Thousand Oaks, CA: Sage.

Raes, F., Griffith, J., Van der Gucht, K., & Williams, J. (2014). School-based prevention and reduction in depression in adolescents: A cluster-randomized controlled trial of a mindfulness group program. *Mindfulness, 5*, 477–486. doi:10.1007/s12671-013-0202-1

Raghuraman, R. S. (2002). Art as a cathartic tool for siblings of children with a hearing loss. *American Journal of Art Therapy (40)*, 203–209.

Ramaprasad, D., & Kalyanasundaram, S. (2015). Group intervention in a therapeutic community for persons with chronic mental illness. *The International Journal of Psychosocial Rehabilitation, 19*(2), 12–20.

Rando, T. A. (2000). *Clinical dimensions of anticipatory mourning: Theory and practice in working with the dying, their loved ones, and their caregivers*. Champaign, IL: Research Press.

Rast, D. E. I., Hogg, M. A., & Giessner, S. R. (2016). Who trusts charismatic leaders who champion change? The role of group identification, membership centrality, and self-uncertainty. *Group Dynamics: Theory, Research, and Practice, 20*(4), 259–275. doi:10.1037/gdn0000053

Ratts, M. J., Singh, A. A., Nassar-McMillan, S., Butler, S. K., & McCullough, J. R. (2015). *Multicultural and social justice counseling competencies*. Retrieved from http://www.counseling. org/docs/default-source/competencies/multicultural-and-social-justice-counseling-competencies.pdf?sfvrsn=20

Reddy, L. A. (2016). Child ADHD multimodal program: Use of cognitive-behavioral group play interventions. In L. A. Reddy, T. M. Files-Hall, & C. E., Schaefer (Eds.), *Empirically based play interventions for children* (2nd ed., pp. 181–201). Washington, DC: American Psychological Association.

Reid, C. (1965). The authority cycle in small group development. *Adult Leadership, 13*(10), 308–331.

Remley, T. P., & Herlihy, B. (2016). *Ethical, legal, and professional issues in counseling* (5th ed.). Upper Saddle River, NJ: Merrill/Prentice Hall.

Resnik, S. (2015). "Transferring" and transference. *International Forum of Psychoanalysis, 24*(3), 135–142. doi:10.1080/08037 06X.2012.712218

Reyes-García, V., Pyhälä, A., Díaz-Reviriego, I., Duda, R., Fernández-Llamazares, Á., Gallois, S., . . . Napitupulu, L. (2016). Schooling, local knowledge and working memory: A study among three contemporary hunter-gatherer societies. *PLOS ONE 11*(1), e0145265. doi:10.1371/journal.pone.0145265

Reynolds, R., & Richmond, B. (1985). *Revised children's manifest anxiety scale*. Los Angeles, CA: Western Psychological Services.

Reynolds, W. (2004). *Reynolds bully victimization scale*. San Antonio, TX: Harcourt Assessment.

Ribner, N. G. (1974). Effects of explicit group contract on self-disclosure and group cohesiveness. *Journal of Counseling Psychology, 21*, 116–120. doi:10.1037/h0036195

Rice, A. (2015). Common therapeutic factors in bereavement groups. *Death Studies, 39*, 165–172.

Richardson, B. G., Surmitis, K. A., & Hyldahl, R. S. (2012). Minimizing social contagion in adolescents who self-injure: Considerations for group work, residential treatment, and the Internet. *Journal of Mental Health Counseling, 34*(2), 121–132. doi:10.17744/mehc.34.2.206j243468882617

Richardson, C. D., & Rosen, L. A. (1999). School-based interventions for children of divorce. *Professional School Counseling, 3,* 21–26.

Riddle, J., Bergin, J. J., & Douzenis, C. (1997). Effects of group counseling on the self-concept of children of alcoholics. *Elementary School Guidance and Counseling, 31,* 192–203.

Ritchie, M. H., & Huss, S. N. (2000). Recruitment and screening of minors for group counseling. *Journal for Specialists in Group Work, 25,* 146–156.

Riva, M., Wachtel, M., & Lasky, G. (2004). Effective leadership in group counseling and psychotherapy. In J. DeLucia-Waack, D. Gerrity, C. Kalodner, & M. Riva (Eds.), *Handbook of group counseling and psychotherapy* (pp. 37–48). Thousand Oaks, CA: Sage.

Roback, H. B. (2000). Adverse outcomes in group psychotherapy. *Journal of Psychotherapy Practice & Research, 9,* 113–122.

Rohde, P., Stice, E., Shaw, H., & Gau, J. (2015). Effectiveness trial of an indicated cognitive-behavioral group adolescent depression program versus bibliotherapy and brochure control at 2-year follow-up. *Journal of Consulting and Clinical Psychology, 83,* 736–747.doi:10.1037/ccp0000022

Rohde, R. I., & Stockton, R. (1994). Group structure: A review. *Journal of Group Psychotherapy, Psychodrama, and Sociometry, 46,* 151–158.

Roos, S. (2002). *Chronic sorrow: A living loss.* New York, NY: Brunner-Routledge.

Rootes, L. E., & Aanes, D. L. (2006). A conceptual framework for understanding self-help groups. *Hospital and Community Psychiatry, 43*(4), 379–381. doi:10.1176/ps.43.4.379

Rose, H., Miller, L., & Martinez, Y. (2009). "Friends for Life": The results of a resilience-building, anxiety prevention program in a Canadian Elementary School. *Professional School Counseling, 12*(6), 400–407.

Rose, S. (1998). Mental health and substance abuse. In *Group work with children and adolescents: Prevention and intervention in school and community systems* (pp. 124–140). Thousand Oaks, CA: Sage Publications.

Rotter, J. B. (1966). Generalized expectancies for internal versus external locus of control reinforcement. *Psychological Monographs, 80,* 1–28. doi:10.1037/h0092976

Rowan-Kenyone, H., Swan, A., & Creager, M. (2012). Social cognitive factors, support, and engagement: Early adolescents' math interests and precursors to choice of career. *The Career Development Quarterly, 60,* 2–15. doi:10.1002/j.2161-0045. 2012.000001.x

Rowe, W., & Winborn, B. B. (1973). What people fear about group work: An analysis of 36 selected critical articles. *Educational Technology, 13*(1), 53–57.

Royal College of Nursing. (2010). *Memory boxes.* Retrieved from http://mentalhealthpractice.rcnpublishing.co.uk/

Rubel, D., & Pepperell, J. (2010). Applying the ACA advocacy competencies to group work. In M. J. Ratts, J. Lewis, & R. Toporek (Eds.), *The ACA advocacy competencies: An advocacy framework for counselors* (pp. 195–207). Alexandria, VA: ACA.

Rubin, S. E. (2016). *Foundations of the vocational rehabilitation process* (7th ed.). Austin, TX: Pro-Ed.

Rubin, S. S., Malkinson, R., & Witztum, E. (2005). The sacred and the secular: The changing face of death, loss, and bereavement in Israel. In J. D. Morgan & P. Lainngani (Eds.), *Death and Bereavement Around the World: Vol. 4. Asia, Australia, and New Zealand* (pp. 65–80). New York, NY: Baywood.

Rugel, R. P. (1997). *Husband-focused marital therapy: An approach to dealing with marital distress.* Springfield, IL: Thompson.

Rush, C. M., & Akos, P. (2007). Supporting children and adolescents with deployed caregivers: A structured group approach for group counselors. *The Journal for Specialists in Group Work, 32,* 113–125.

Russ, D. P., & Parish, D. (2016, June 23). *Reviving the job club: Results from the first year.* Retrieved from http://apse.org/wp-content/uploads/2016/07/Reviving-the-Job-Club-Results-from-the-First-Year.pdf

Russell-Mayhew, S., Stewart, M., & MacKenzie, S. (2008). Eating disorders as social justice issues: Results from a focus group on content experts vigorously flapping our wings. *Canadian Journal of Counselling, 42,* 131–146.

Rutan, J. S., & Rice, C. A. (1981). The charismatic leader: Asset or liability? *Psychotherapy: Theory, Research and Practice, 18,* 487–492.

Rutan, J. S., Stone, W. N., & Shay, J. J. (2014). *Psychodynamic group psychotherapy* (5th ed.). New York, NY: The Guilford Press.

Ruzek, J. I., Eftekhari, A., Rosen, C. S., Crowley, J. J., Huhn, E., Foa, E. B., . . . Karlin, B. E. (2016). Effects of a comprehensive training program on clinician belief about and intention to use prolonged exposure therapy for PTSD. *Psychological Trauma: Theory, Research, Practice, and Policy, 8*(3), 348–355. doi:10.1037/tra0000004

Ryan, C., Huebner, D., Diaz, R. M., & Sanchez, J. (2009). Family rejection as a predictor of negative health outcomes in White and Latino lesbian, gay and bisexual young adults. *Pediatrics, 123,* 346–352.

Sack, R. T. (1985). On giving advice. *AMHCA Journal, 7,* 127–132.

Safran, J. D., & Muran, J. C. (2000). *Negotiating the therapeutic alliance: A relational treatment guide.* New York, NY: Guilford Press.

Sakdalan, J., Shaw, J., & Collier, V. (2010). Staying in the here-and-now: A pilot study on the use of dialectical behavior therapy group skills training for forensic clients with intellectual disability. *Journal of Intellectual Disability Research, 54,* 568–572. doi:10.1111/j.1365-2788.2010.01274.x

Salazar, C. (2009). *Group work experts share their favorite multicultural activities.* Alexandria, VA: ASGW.

Salzburg, S. (2004). Learning that an adolescent child is gay or lesbian: The parent experience. *Social Work, 49*(1), 109–118.

Santos, P. (2004). Career dilemmas in career counseling groups: Theoretical and practical issues. *Journal of Career Development, 31,* 31–44. doi:10.1177.0894530403100103

Sauer-Zavala, S., Gutner, C. A., Farchione, T. J., Boettcher, H. T., Bullis, J. R., & Barlow, D. H. (2017). Current definitions of "transdiagnostic" in treatment development: A search for consensus. *Behavior Therapy, 48,* 128–138.

Sayin, A., Karslioglu, E., Sürgit, A., Sahin, S., Arslan, T., & Candansayar, S. (2008). Perceptions of Turkish psychiatric inpatients about therapeutic factors of group psychotherapy.

International Journal of Group Psychotherapy, 58, 253–263. doi:10.1521/ijgp.2008.58.2.253

Schaefer, G. (2008). Multiple family group therapy in drug and alcohol rehabilitation centre: Residents' experiences. *The Australian and New Zealand Journal of Family Therapy, 29*(2), 86–96.

Scheffler, S. (2014). Assessment and treatment of clients with co-occurring psychiatric and substance use disorder. In S. L. A. Straussner (Ed.), *Clinical work with substance abusing clients* (3rd ed., pp. 371–394). New York, NY: Guilford Press.

Scheidlinger, S. (1994). An overview of nine decades of group psychotherapy. *Hospital and Community Psychiatry, 45*(3), 217–225.

Schermer, V. L. (2015). Psychodrama in perspective: An interview with Jonathan Moreno on his father, Jacob Moreno, and the lasting impact of his ideas. *Group Analysis, 48*(2), 187–201. doi:10.1177/0533316415580539

Schlossberg, N. K. (2004). *Retire smart, retire happy: Finding your true path in life.* Washington, DC: American Psychological Association.

Schmit, E. L., Schmit, M. K., & Lenz, A. S. (2016). Meta-analysis of solution-focused brief therapy for treating symptoms of internalizing disorders. *Counseling Outcome Research and Evaluation, 7*(1) 21–39.

Schmuck, R. A., & Schmuck, P. A. (1997). *Group process in the classroom* (7th ed.). Madison, WI: Brown & Benchmark.

Schofield, M. J., Mumford, N., Jurkovic, I., Jurkovic, D., Chan, S. P., & Bickerdike, A. (2015). Understanding profiles of couples attending community-based couple counseling and relationship education services. *Journal of Couple & Relationship Therapy, 14*(1), 64–90. doi:10.1080/15332691.2014.953654

Schuh, S. C., Zhang, X., & Tian, P. (2013). For the good or the bad? Interactive effects of transformational leadership with moral and authoritarian leadership behaviors. *Journal of Business Ethics, 116*(3), 629–640. doi:10.1007/s10551-012-1486-0

Schunk, D. H. (2001). Self-regulation through goal setting. *ERIC/ CASS Digest.* Greensboro, NC: ERIC Clearinghouse on Counseling and Student Services. (ED 462 671).

Schutz, W. D. (1958). *FIRO: Three-dimensional theory of interpersonal behavior.* New York, NY: Rinehart.

Schwartz, D. C., Nickow, M. S., Arseneau, R., & Gisslow, M. T. (2015). A substance called food: Long-term psychodynamic group treatment for compulsive overeating. *International Journal of Group Psychotherapy, 65*(3), 386–409. doi:10.1521/ ijgp.2015.65.3.386

Seymour, J. W., & Rubin, L. (2006). Principles, principals, and process (P³): A model for play therapy ethics problem solving. *International Journal of Play Therapy, 15*(2), 101–123.

Shallcross, L. (2009). Rewriting the "rules" of grief. *Counseling Today, 52*(3), 28–36.

Shallcross, L. (2012). A loss like no other. *Counseling Today, 54*(12), 26–31.

Shapiro, J. L. (1978). *Methods of group psychotherapy and encounter: A tradition of innovation.* Itasca, IL: Peacock.

Shapiro, J. L., & Bernadett-Shapiro, S. (1985). Group work to 2001: Hal or haven (from isolation)? *Journal for Specialists in Group Work, 10*(2), 83–87.

Shaughnessy, P., & Kivlighan, D. M. (1995). Using group participants' perceptions of therapeutic factors to form client typologies. *Small Group Research, 26,* 250–268. doi:10.1177/1046496495262005

Shechtman, Z. (2002). Child group psychotherapy in the school at the threshold of a new millennium. *Journal of Counseling and Development, 80,* 293–299.

Shechtman, Z. (2004). Group counseling and therapy with children and adolescents: Current practice and research. In J. DeLucia-Waack, D. Gerrity, C. Kalodner, & M. Riva (Eds.), *Handbook of group counseling and psychotherapy* (pp. 429–444). Thousand Oaks, CA: Sage.

Shechtman, Z. (2014). Counseling and therapy groups with children and adolescents. In J. DeLucia-Waack, C. Kalodner, & M. Riva (Eds.), *Handbook of group counseling and psychotherapy* (2nd ed., pp. 585–596). Thousand Oaks, CA: Sage.

Shechtman, Z., Bar-El, O., & Hadar, E. (1997). Therapeutic factors in counseling and psychoeducational groups for adolescents: A comparison. *Journal for Specialists in Group Work, 22,* 203–214. doi:10.1080/01933929708414381

Shechtman, Z., Hiradin, A., & Zina, S. (2003). The impact of culture on group behavior: A comparison of three ethnic groups. *Journal of Counseling & Development, 81,* 208–216.

Shechtman, Z., & Ifaragan, M. (2009). School-based integrated and segregated interventions to reduce aggression. *Aggressive Behavior, 35,* 342–356.

Shechtman, Z., & Perl-Dekel, O. (2000). A comparison of therapeutic factors in two group treatment modalities: Verbal and art therapy. *Journal for Specialists in Group Work, 25*(3), 288–304.

Shechtman, Z., & Toren, Z. (2009). The effect of leader behavior on processes and outcomes in group counseling. *Group Dynamics: Theory, Research, and Practice, 13*(3), 218–233. doi:10.1037/a0015718

Shen, Y. (2016). A descriptive study of school counselors' play therapy experiences with the culturally diverse. *International Journal of Play Therapy, 25*(2), 54–63. doi:10.1037/ pla0000017

Shepherd, D. A., Patzelt, H., Williams, T. A., & Warnecke, D. (2014). How does project termination impact project team members? Rapid termination, "creeping death," and learning from failure. *Journal of Management Studies, 51*(4), 513–546. doi:10.1111/joms.12068

Shippy, R. A., Cantor, M., & Brennan, M. (2004). Social networks of aging gay men. *Journal of Men's Studies, 13*(1), 107–120.

Short, E. L., & Williams, W. S. (2014). From the inside out: Group work with women of color. *Journal for Specialists in Group Work, 39*(1), 71–91. doi:10.1080/01933922.2013.859191

Sierra Hernandez, C. A., Piper, W. E., Ogrodniczuk, J. S., Joyce, A. S., & Weideman, R. (2016). Use of referential language in short-term group psychotherapy for complicated grief. *Group Dynamics: Theory, Research, and Practice, 20*(1), 1–15. doi:10.1037/gdn0000038

Simons, M., & Harris, R. (1997). Non-participation in adult education: A case study of pre-marriage education programmes. *New Zealand Journal of Adult Learning, 25*(2), 31–52.

Singh, A. A., Merchant, N., Skudrzyk, B., & Ingene, D. (2012a). Association for specialists in group work: Multicultural and social justice competence principles for group workers. *Journal for Specialists in Group Work, 37*(4), 312–325. doi:10.1080/ 01933922.2012.721482

Singh, A. A., Merchant, N., Skudryzk, B., & Ingene, D. (2012b). Group worker principles for seeking multicultural and social justice competences. *Journal for Specialists in Group Work, 37,* 312–325. doi:10.1080/01933922.2012.721482

Singh, A. A., Merchant, N., Skudrzyk, B., & Ingene, D. (2012c). *Multicultural and social justice competence principles for group workers.* Alexandria, VA: ASGW. Retrieved from http://www.asgw.org/knowledge/

Slavson, S. R., & Schiffer, M. (1975). *Group psychotherapy for children: A textbook.* New York, NY: International Universities Press.

Smead, R. (1990). *Skills for living: Group counseling activities for young adolescents.* Champaign, IL: Research Press.

Smead, R. (1995). *Skills and techniques for group work with children and adolescents.* Champaign, IL: Research Press.

Smead, R. (2000). *Skills for living: Group counseling activities for young adolescents* (Vol. 2). Champaign, IL: Research Press.

Smith, I. P., Oades, L., & McCarthy, G. (2012). Homophobia to heterosexism: Constructs in need or revisitation. *Gay & Lesbian Issues and Psychology Review, 8*(1), 34–44.

Smith, J. A., & Smith, A. H. (2001). Dual relationships and professional integrity: An ethical dilemma case of a family counselor as clergy. *Family Journal, 9,* 438–443.

Smith, T., & Kehe, J. (2004). Glossary. In T. Smith (Ed.), *Practicing multiculturalism: Affirming diversity in counseling and psychology* (pp. 325–337). Boston, MA: Pearson Education.

Smokowski, P., Rose, S., & Bacallao, M. (2001). Damaging experiences in therapeutic groups: How vulnerable consumers become group casualties. *Small Group Research, 32,* 223–251. doi:10.1177/104649640103200205

Snortum, J. R., & Myers, H. F. (1971). Intensity of T-group relations as function of interaction. *International Journal of Group Psychotherapy, 21,* 190–201.

Sodano, S., Guyker, W., Amos, B., & DeLucia-Waack, J. (2017). *Group counseling expectations in undergraduate students and graduate counselor trainees.* Submitted for publication.

Sodano, S., Guyker, W., DeLucia-Waack, J., Cosgrove, H., Altabef, D., & Amos, B. (2014). Measures of group process, dynamics, climate, behavior, and outcome: A review. In J. DeLucia Waack, D. Gerrity, C. Kalodner, & M. Riva (Eds.), *Handbook of group counseling and psychotherapy* (pp. 159–177). Thousand Oaks, CA: Sage.

Sodano, S., & Tracy, T. (2011). A brief Inventory of Interpersonal Problems-Circumplex Using Nonparametric Item Response Theory: Introducing the IIP-C-IRT. *Journal of Personality Assessment, 93,* 62–75. doi:10.1080/00223891.2010.528482

Somody, C. (2010). Meaning and connections in older populations: A phenomenological study of reminiscence using a musical chronology and the emerging life song (Doctoral dissertation). Retrieved from ProQuest. (3433230)

Song, H., Kim, J., & Luo, W. (2016). Teacher-student relationship in online classes: A role of teacher self-disclosure. *Computers in Human Behavior, 54,* 436–443.

Sonnenberg, S. L., & Chen, C. P. (2003). Using career development theories in the treatment of clients with eating disorders. *Counselling Psychology Quarterly, 16,* 173–185.

Sonstegard, M. A., & Bitter, J. R., with Pelonis, P. (2004). *Adlerian group counseling and therapy: Step-by-step.* New York, NY: Brunner-Routledge.

Southern, S., & Thornton, B. (2013). Group treatment in the continuum of care. In P. Stevens & R. L. Smith (Eds.), *Substance abuse counseling theory and practice* (pp. 203–239). Boston, MA: Merrill.

Spargo, A., & Blasko, S. (Producers). (2017). *Mindfulness groups: A demonstration.* Alexandria, VA: ASGW.

Spoth, R., Redmond, C., Shin, C., Greenberg, M., Clair, S., & Feinberg, M. (2007). Substance abuse outcomes at 18 months past baseline: The PROSPER community-university partnership trial. *American Journal of Preventative Medicine, 34,* 43–57. doi:10.1016/j.amepre.2007.01.014

Springer, S., & Moss, L. (2017). *A school counselor's guide to small groups: Coordination, leadership, and assessment.* Alexandria, VA: ASGW.

Springer, S. I. (2016). Examining predictors of group leader self-efficacy for preservice school counselors. *Journal for Specialists in Group Work, 41*(4), 286–311. doi:10.1080/01933922.2016.1228723

Stava, L. J., & Bednar, R. L. (1979). Process and outcome in encounter groups: The effect of group composition. *Small Group Behavior, 10,* 200–213.

Steen, S. (2009). Achieving success everyday: A group counseling model for school counselors. *The Group Worker, 38,* 7–10. Retrieved from http://www.asgw.org/PracticeIdeas-Spring2009.pdf

Steen, S., Bauman, S., & Smith, J. (2007). Professional school counselors and the practice of group work. *Professional School Counseling, 11,* 72–80.

Stein, M., Perrin, E., & Potter, J. (2004). A difficult adjustment to school: The importance of family constellation. *Pediatrics, 114,* 1464–1467.

Stephens, D., Jain, S., & Kim, K. (2010). Group counseling techniques for teaching social skills to students with special needs. *Education, 130,* 509–513.

Stice, E., Marti, C. N., & Rohde, P. (2013). Prevalence, incidence, impairment, and course of the proposed DSM-5 eating disorder diagnoses in an 8-year prospective community study of young women. *Journal of Abnormal Psychology, 122*(2), 445–457. doi:10.1037/a0030679

Stockton, R., & Morran, D. K. (1982). Review and perspective of critical dimensions in therapeutic small group research. In G. Gazda (Ed.), *Basic approaches to group psychotherapy and group counseling* (pp. 37–83). Springfield, IL: Charles C Thomas.

Stockton, R., Morran, D. K., & Nitza, A. (2000). Processing group events: A conceptual map for leaders. *Journal for Specialists in Group Work, 25,* 343–355. doi:10.1080/01933920008411678

Stockton, R., Morran, D. K., & Velboff, P. (1987). Leadership of therapeutic small groups. *Journal of Group Psychotherapy, Psychodrama, & Sociometry, 39,* 157–165.

Stogdill, R. M. (1974). *Handbook of leadership.* New York, NY: Free Press.

Stone, C. B. (2003). Counselors as advocates for gay, lesbian and bisexual youth: A call for equity and action. *Journal of Multicultural Counseling and Development, 3,* 143–155.

Stone, S., & Stark, M. (2013). Structured play therapy groups for preschoolers: Facilitating the emergence of social competence. *International Journal of Group Psychotherapy, 63*(1), 25–50. doi:10.1521/ijgp.2013.63.1.25

Straub, S. H. (2001). *Death without notice*. Amityville, NY: Baywood.

Stroebe, M. S., Hansson, R. O., Stroebe, W., & Schut, H. (Eds.). (2001). *Handbook of bereavement research: Consequences, coping, and care*. Washington, DC: American Psychological Association.

Stroh, H. R., & Sink, C. A. (2002). Applying APA's learner-centered principles to school-based group counseling. *Professional School Counseling, 6*(1), 71–78.

Substance Abuse and Mental Health Services Administration. (2005). *Treatment Improvement Protocol (TIP) Series, No. 44. Substance abuse treatment for adults in the criminal justice system*. Rockville, MD: Center for Substance Abuse Treatment.

Substance Abuse and Mental Health Services Administration. (2014). *Treatment Improvement Protocol (TIP) Series, No. 41. Substance abuse treatment: Group therapy* (HHS Publication No. SMA 15-3991). Rockville, MD: Author.

Substance Abuse and Mental Health Services Administration. (2015). *Treatment Improvement Protocol (TIP) Series, No. 41. Substance abuse treatment: Group therapy—a treatment improvement protocol*. Rockville, MD: Author. Retrieved from http://store.samhsa.gov/shin/content/SMA15-3991/SMA15-3991.pdf

Substance Abuse and Mental Health Services Administration. (2016a). *Key substance use and mental health indicators in the United States: Results from the 2015 National Survey on Drug Use and Health* (HHS Publication No. SMA 16-4984, NSDUH Series H-51). Retrieved from http://www.samhsa.gov/data

Substance Abuse and Mental Health Services Administration. (2016b). *Treatment for substance use disorders*. Retrieved from https://www.samhsa.gov/treatment/substance-use-disorders

Sue, D., & Sue, D. (2003). *Counseling the culturally diverse: Theory and practice* (4th ed.). New York, NY: John Wiley and Sons.

Sugar, M. (1993). Research in child and adolescent group psychotherapy. *Journal of Child and Adolescent Group Therapy, 3,* 207–226. doi:10.1007/BF00995396

Suitt, K. G., Franklin, C., & Kim, J. (2016). Solution-focused brief therapy with Latinos: A systematic review. *Journal of Ethnic & Cultural Diversity in Social Work, 25*(1), 50–67. doi:10.1080/15313204.2015.1131651

Sullivan, K. R., & Mahalik, J. R. (2000). Increasing career self-efficacy for women: Evaluating a group intervention. *Journal of Counseling & Development, 78,* 54–62. doi:10.1002/j.1556-6676.2000.tb02560.x

Swank, J. M., & Cheung, C. (2017). Nature-based child-centered group play therapy and behavioral concerns: A single-case design. *International Journal of Play Therapy, 26*(1), 47–57. doi:10.1037/pla0000031

Swearer, S., Espelage, D., & Napolitano, S. (2009). *Bullying prevention and intervention: Realistic strategies for schools*. New York, NY: Guilford Press.

Sweeney, D. S. (2011). Group play therapy. In C. E. Schaefer (Ed.), *Foundations of play therapy* (2nd ed., pp. 227–252). Hoboken, NJ: Wiley.

Swenson, L. C. (1997). *Psychology and the law for the helping professions* (2nd ed.). Pacific Grove, CA: Brooks/Cole.

Taberas, A. A., Driver, J. L., & Gottman, J. M. (2004). Repair attempts observational coding system: Measuring de-escalation of negative affect during marital conflict. In P. K. Kerig & D. H. Baucom (Eds.), *Couple observational coding systems* (pp. 227–243). Mahwah, NJ: Lawrence Erlbaum.

Tan, L., & Martin, G. (2014). Taming the adolescent mind: A randomised controlled examining clinical efficacy of an adolescent mindfulness-based group programme. *Children and Adolescent Mental Health, 20,* 49–55. doi:10.1111/camh.12057

Tantillo, M. (2000). Short-term relational group therapy for women with bulimia nervosa. *Eating Disorders, 8,* 99–121.

Tatham, M., Athanasia, E., Dodd, J., & Waller, G. (2016). The effect of pre-treatment psychoeducation on eating disorder pathology among patients with anorexia nervosa and bulimia nervosa. *Advances in Eating Disorders: Theory, Research, and Practice, 4*(2), 167–175. doi:10.1080/21662630.2016.1172975

Tatum, B. (2000). The complexity of identity: Who am I? In M. Adams, W. Blumenfeld, R. Castaneda, H. Hackman, M. Peters, & X. Zuniga (Eds.), *Readings for diversity and social justice: An anthology on racism, anti-Semitism, sexism, heterosexism, ableism, and classism* (pp. 9–14). New York, NY: Routledge.

Tchanturia, K., Doris, E., & Fleming, C. (2014). Effectiveness of cognitive remediation and emotion skills training (CREST) for anorexia nervosa in group format: A naturalistic pilot study. *European Eating Disorders Review, 22*(3), 200–205. doi:10.1002/erv.2287

Thelen, H., & Dickerman, W. (1949). Stereotypes and the growth of groups. *Educational Leadership, 6,* 309–316.

Thomas, V., & Pender, D. (2008). Association for Specialists in Group Work Best Practice Guidelines, 2007 revisions. *Journal for Specialists in Group Work, 33,* 111–117. doi:10.1080/019339920801971184

Thompson, S. C., & Kyle, D. J. (2000). The role of perceived control in coping with the losses associated with chronic illness. In J. H. Harvey & E. D. Miller (Eds.), *Loss and trauma: General and close relationship perspectives* (pp. 131–142). Philadelphia, PA: Taylor & Francis.

Thorngren, J. M., & Kleist, D. M. (2002). Multiple family group therapy: An interpersonal/postmodern approach. *Family Journal: Counseling and Therapy for Couples and Families, 10*(2), 167–176.

Tidikis, V. (2015). The effects of leadership and gender on dyad creativity. *Psichologija, 52,* 7–21. doi:10.15388/Psichol.2015.52.9329

Torres-Rivera, E., Wilbur, M. P., Roberts-Wilbur, J., & Phan, L. (1999). Group work with Latino clients. *Journal for Specialists on Group Work, 24,* 383–404.

Toseland, R. W., & Siporin, M. (1986). When to recommend group treatment: A review of the clinical and the research literature. *International Journal of Group Psychotherapy, 36,* 171–201. doi:10.1080/00207284.1986.11491446

Tronsden, M., & Tjori, A. (2014). Communal normalization in an online self-help group for adolescents with a mentally ill parent. *Qualitative Health Research, 24,* 1407–1418.

Trotzer, J. P. (2006). *The counselor and the group: Integrating theory, training and practice* (4th ed.). New York, NY: Taylor & Francis.

Trotzer, J. P. (2013). *The counselor and the group: Integrating theory, training, and practice* (4th ed.). New York, NY: Routledge.

Truax, C. B., & Carkhuff, R. R. (1967). *Toward effective counseling and psychotherapy: Training and practice.* Chicago, IL: Aldine.

Tuckman, B. W. (1965). Developmental sequence in small groups. *Psychological Bulletin, 63,* 384–399. doi:10.1037/h0022100

Tuckman, B. W., & Jensen, M. A. (1977). Stages of small group development revisited. *Groups & Organizational Studies, 2,* 419–427.

Tuckman, B. W., & Jensen, M. A. (2010). Stages of small-group development revisited. *Group Facilitation, 10,* 43.

Turri, M. G. (2015). Transference and catharsis, Freud to Aristotle. *The International Journal of Psychoanalysis, 96,* 369–387. doi:10.1111/1745-8315.12243

Tyson, L., Perusse, R., & Whitledge, J. (2004). *Critical incidents in group counseling.* Alexandria, VA: ACA.

Tziner, A., & Chernyak-Hai, L. (2012). Perspectives on groups and work teams in the workplace. *Revista de Psicología del Trabajo y de las Organizaciones, 28*(1), 51–66.

UN Women. (2016). *Facts and figures: Ending violence against women.* Retrieved from http://www.unwomen.org/en/what-we-do/ending-violence-against-women/facts-and-figures

U.S. Census Bureau. (2017, January 15). *Households and families.* Retrieved from https://www.census.gov/2010census

Valente, T., & Pumpuang, P. (2007). Identifying opinion leaders to promote behavior change. *Health Education and Behavior, 34,* 881–896. doi:10.1177/1090198106297855

van Tilburg, W. A. P., Sedikides, C., & Wildschut, T. (2015). The mnemonic muse: Nostalgia fosters creativity through openness to experience. *Journal of Experimental Social Psychology, 59,* 1–7. doi:10.1016/j.jesp.2015.02.002

Van Voorhis, P., & Salisbury, E. J. (2016). *Correctional counseling and rehabilitation* (9th ed.). New York, NY: Routledge.

Vander Kolk, C. J. (1985). *Introduction to group counseling and psychotherapy.* Columbus, OH: Merrill.

Vannest, K. J., Parker, R. I., Gonen, O., & Adiguzel, T. (2016). *Single case research: Web based calculators for SCR analysis* (Version 2.0) [Web-based application]. College Station, TX: Texas A&M University. Retrieved from http://www.singlecaseresearch.org/calculators/nap

Vasquez, M. J. (2007). Cultural difference and the therapeutic alliance: An evidence-based analysis. *American Psychologist, 62*(8), 878–885.

Vernon, A. (2012). *The Passport Program: A journal through emotional, social, cognitive, and self-development (grades 9 to 12).* Champaign, IL: Research Press.

Vernon, A. (2013). *The Passport Program: A journal through emotional, social, cognitive, and self-development (grades 6 to 8).* Champaign, IL: Research Press.

Vernon, A., & Davis-Gage, D. (2016). Late adulthood: Emotional and social development. In D. Capuzzi & M. D. Stauffer (Eds.), *Human growth and development across the lifespan: Applications for counselors* (pp. 543–572). Hoboken, NJ: Wiley.

Villalba, J., Gonzalez, L. M., Hines, E. M., & Borders, L. D. (2014). The Latino Parents-Learning About College (LaP-LAC) program: Empowerment of Latino families throughout psychoeducational group work. *Journal for Specialists in Group Work, 39,* 47–70. doi:10.1080/01933922.2013.859192

Viorst, J. (1986). *Necessary losses.* New York, NY: Simon & Schuster.

Walter, C. A. (2003). *The loss of a life partner: Narratives of the bereaved.* New York, NY: Columbia University Press.

Walther, B. (2015). Bylaw governance. *Journal of Corporate and Financial Law, 20*(2), 399–459.

Wanlass, J., Moreno, J. K., & Thomson, H. M. (2005). Group therapy for eating disorders: A retrospective case study. *The Journal for Specialists in Group Work, 30,* 47–66. doi:10.1080/01933920590908697

Ward, B. W., Dahlhamer, J. M., Galinsky, A. M., & Joestl, S. S. (2014). Sexual orientation and health among US adults: National health interview survey, 2013. *National Health Statistics Reports, 77,* 1–10.

Ward, D. E. (1985). Levels of group activity: A model for improving the effectiveness of group work. *Journal of Counseling and Development, 64*(1), 59–64.

Ware, J. N., & Taylor, D. (2014). Concerns about confidentiality: The application of ethical decision-making within group play therapy. *International Journal of Play Therapy, 23*(3), 173–186. doi:10.1037/a0036667

Washton, A. M. (1992). Structured outpatient group therapy with alcohol and substance abusers. In J. Lowinson, P. Ruiz, R. Millman, & J. Langrod (Eds.), *Substance abuse: A comprehensive textbook* (2nd ed., pp. 39–50). Baltimore, MD: Williams & Wilkins.

Watson, J. C., & Bedard, D. L. (2006). Clients' emotional processing in psychotherapy: A comparison between cognitive-behavioral and process-experiential therapies. *Journal of Consulting and Clinical Psychology, 74*(1), 152–159.

Watson, P. J., & Workman, E. A. (1981). The non-concurrent multiple baseline across-individuals design: An extension of the traditional multiple baseline design. *Journal of Behavior Therapy and Experimental Psychiatry, 12,* 257–259. doi:10.1016/0005-7916(81)90055-0

Webb, L. D., & Myrick, R. D. (2003). A group counseling intervention for children with attention deficit hyperactivity disorder. *Professional School Counseling, 7,* 108–115.

Webb, N. B. (2011). Play therapy for bereaved children: Adapting strategies to community, school, and home settings. *School Psychology International, 32*(2), 132–143. doi:10.1177/0143034311400832

Weber, M., Davis, K., & McPhie, L. (2006). Narrative therapy, eating disorders and groups: Enhancing outcomes in rural NSW. *Australian Social Work, 59,* 391–405.

Wegerer, J. (2014, February 6). *Five reasons to make a memory box for Alzheimer's patients* [Blog post]. Retrieved from http://www.alzheimers.net/2014-02-06/memory-boxes-for-patients/

Weinberg, G. (1973). *Society and the healthy homosexual.* Garden City, NJ: Anchor Books.

Weiss R. D., Jaffee W. B., de Menil V. P., & Cogley, C. B. (2004). Group therapy for substance use disorders: What do we know? *Harvard Review of Psychiatry, 12*(6), 339–350. doi:10.1080/10673220490905723

Weiss, R. L., & Heyman, R. E. (1997). Couple interaction. In W. K. Halford & H. J. Markman (Eds.), *Clinical handbook of marriage and couples intervention* (pp. 13–41). New York, NY: Wiley.

Welfel, E. R. (2016). *Ethics in counseling and psychotherapy: Standards, research, and emerging issues* (6th ed.). Pacific Grove, CA: Brooks/Cole.

Wells, M., Burlingame, G., Lampert, M., Hoag, M., & Hope, C. (1996). Conceptualization and measurement of patient change during psychotherapy: Development of the outcome questionnaire and youth outcome questionnaire. *Psychotherapy: Theory, Research, Practice, Training, 33,* 249–258. doi:10.1037/0033-3204.33.2.275

West-Olatunji, C. A., & Rush-Ossenbeck, M. (2016). Constructionist theories: Solution-focused and narrative therapies. In D. Capuzzi & M. Stauffer (Eds.), *Counseling and psychotherapy theories and interventions* (6th ed., pp. 195–226). Alexandria, VA: ACA.

Whisman, M., & Li, A. (2015). Assessment of positive and negative relationship adjustment in marriage. *Personal Relationships, 22*(4), 679–691. doi:10.1111/pere.12103

Whiston, S. C., & Sexton, T. L. (1998). A review of school counseling outcome research: Implications for practice. *Journal of Counseling and Development, 76,* 412–426.

White, M., & Epston, D. (1990). *Narrative means to therapeutic ends.* New York, NY: Norton.

Whiting, J., & Cravens, J. (2016). Escalating, accusing, and rationalizing: A model of distortion and interaction in couple conflict. *Journal of Couple and Relationship Therapy, 15*(4), 251–273. doi:10.1080/15332691.2015.1055417

Whitten, K. M., & Burt, I. (2015). Utilizing creative expressive techniques and group counseling to improve adolescents of divorce social-relational capabilities. *Journal of Creativity in Mental Health, 10*(3), 363–375. doi:10.1080/15401383.2014.986594

Wilson, F. R., Rapin, L. S., & Haley-Banez, L. (2000a). *Professional standards for the training of group workers.* Alexandria, VA: Association for Specialists in Group Work. Retrieved from http://www.asgw.org/knowledge

Wilson, R., Rapin, L. S., & Haley-Banez, L. (2000b). Association for Specialists in Group Work professional standards for the training of group workers. *Journal for Specialists in Group Work, 25,* 327–342. doi:10.1080/01933920008411677

Winburn, A., Gilstrap, D., & Perryman, M. (2017). Treating the tiers: Play therapy responds to intervention in the schools. *International Journal of Play Therapy, 26*(1), 1–11. doi:10.1037/pla000004

Windle, C., Newsome, S., Waldo, M., & Adams, E. (2014). Mindfulness and group. In J. DeLucia-Waack, C. Kalodner, & M. Riva (Eds.), *Handbook of group counseling and psychotherapy* (2nd ed., pp. 474–483). Thousand Oaks, CA: Sage.

Winton, S. L., & Kane, T. D. (2016). Effects of group goal content on group processes, collective efficacy, and satisfaction. *Journal of Applied Social Psychology, 46*(2), 129–139. doi:10.1111/jasp.12336

Wiseman, C. V., Sunday, S. R., Klapper, F., Klein, M., & Halmi, K. A. (2002). Short-term group CBT versus psycho-education on an inpatient eating disorder unit. *Eating Disorders, 10,* 313–320.

Wnuk, S. M., Greenberg, L., & Dolhanty, J. (2015). Emotion-focused group therapy for women with symptoms of bulimia nervosa. *Eating Disorders, 23,* 253–261. doi:10.1080/10640266.2014.964612

Wolf, T. J. (1992). Bisexuality: A counseling perspective. In S. Dworkin & F. Gutierrez (Eds.), *Counseling gay men and lesbians: Journey to the end of the rainbow* (pp. 175–187). Alexandria, VA: American Counseling Association.

Worden, J. W. (2002). *Grief counseling and grief therapy: A handbook for the mental health practitioner* (3rd ed.). New York, NY: Springer.

Worden, J. W. (2009). *Grief counseling and grief therapy: A handbook for the mental health practitioner* (4th ed.). New York, NY: Springer.

World Health Organization. (2017). *Gender and women's health.* Retrieved from http://www.who.int/mental_health/prevention/genderwomen/en/

Wright, F. (2014). Being seen, moved, disrupted, and reconfigured: Group leadership from a relational perspective. In R. Grossmark & F. Wright (Eds.), *The one and the many: Relational approaches to group psychotherapy* (pp. 27–37). New York, NY: Routledge.

Wu, C., & Wang, Z. (2015). How transformational leadership shapes team proactivity: The mediating role of positive affective tone and the moderating role of team task variety. *Group Dynamics: Theory, Research, and Practice, 19,* 137–151. doi:10.1037/gdn0000027

Yalom, I. D. (1970). *The theory and practice of group psychotherapy.* New York, NY: Basic Books.

Yalom, I. D. (1975). *The theory and practice of group psychotherapy* (2nd ed.). New York, NY: Basic Books.

Yalom, I. D. (1985). *The theory and practice of group psychotherapy* (3rd ed.). New York, NY: Basic Books.

Yalom, I. D. (1995). *The theory and practice of group psychotherapy* (4th ed.). New York, NY: Basic Books.

Yalom, I. D. (2005). *The theory and practice of group psychotherapy* (5th ed.). New York, NY: Basic Books.

Yalom, I. D., & Leszcz, M. (2005). *The theory and practice of group psychotherapy* (5th ed.). New York, NY: Basic Books.

Yelsma, P., & Marrow, S. (2003). An examination of couples' difficulties with emotional expressiveness and their marital satisfaction. *Journal of Family Communication, 3,* 41–62.

Yontef, G., & Jacobs, L. (2014). Gestalt therapy. In D. Wedding & R. Corsini (Eds.), *Current psychotherapies* (10th ed., pp. 299–338). Belmont, CA: Brooks/Cole.

Young, H., & Garrard, B. (2016). Bereavement and loss: Developing a memory box to support a young woman with profound learning disabilities. *British Journal of Learning Disabilities, 44*(1), 78–84. doi:10.1111/bld.12129

Young, J., Benas, J., Schueler, C., Gallop, R., Gillham, J., & Mufson, L. (2016). A randomized depression prevention trial comparing interpersonal psychotherapy—adolescent skills training to group counseling in schools. *Prevention Science, 17,* 314–324. doi:10.1007/s11121-015-0620-5

Young, J., Mufson, L., & Schueler, C. (2016). *Preventing adolescent depression: Interpersonal psychotherapy-adolescent skills training.* New York, NY: Oxford.

Young, T. L. (2013). Using motivational interviewing within the early stages of group development. *Journal for Specialists in Group Work, 38*(2), 169–181. doi:10.1080/01933922.2013.764369

Zhuang, Y., Feng, W., & Liao, Y. (2017). Want more? Learn less: Motivation affects adolescents learning from negative feedback. *Frontiers in Psychology, 8,* 1–10. doi:10.3389/fpsyg.2017. 00076

Ziff, K., Ivers, N. N., & Shaw, E. G. (2016). ArtBreak group counseling for children: Framework, practice points, and results. *The Journal for Specialists in Group Work, 41*(1), 71–92. doi:10. 1080/01933922.2015.1111487

Ziff, K., Pierce, L., Johanson, S., & King, M. (2012). ArtBreak: A creative group counseling program for children. *Journal of Creativity in Mental Health, 7*(1), 107–121. doi:10.1080/ 15401383.2012.657597

Zimpfer, D. G. (1967). Expression of feelings in group counseling. *Personnel & Guidance Journal, 45,* 703–708.

Zimpfer, D. G. (1984). Patterns and trends in group work. *Journal for Specialists in Group Work, 9,* 204–208. doi:10.1080/ 01933928408412529.

NAME INDEX

SUBJECT INDEX

Group Psychotherapy journal, 4
Group Readiness Questionnaire, 18
group stages
    adolescent groups, 222–225
    creativity and, 169–171
    difficult group members and, 194–195
    eating disorders groups, 256–257
    efficacy and evaluation assessment and, 135
    facilitation, 52–59
    healthy relationships groups, 251–252
    in hospitals and medical settings, 277–278
    issues and, 23–40
    job clubs and employment counseling, 267–268
    multicultural counseling, 122–128
    offender population groups, 272–273
    psychodrama, 73–74
    substance abuse groups, 314–315
    transitions in, 24–30
    women-in-crisis groups, 244–245
group therapy
    addiction and recovery, 305–314
    defined, 10
Group Therapy Questionnaire, 18
group work
    composite conceptualizations of, 30–37
    current trends in, 6–7
    defined, 131–132
    efficacy and evaluation of, 131–146
    goals, 7–10
    history of, 2–6
    leaders belief in, 15
    models for, 10–11
    myths connected with, 17–21
    overview, 1–22
    training and specialization in, 5
group workers, ethical guidelines, 88
Group Work Experts Share Their Favorite Supervision Activities
        (Luke & Goodrich), 237
growth, loss and, 295–296
guidance groups, rehabilitation settings, 264
guided imagery process, 177–179
guilt, loss and, 290

H
harmful interventions, 139–140
Health Insurance Portability and Accountability Act
        (HIPAA), 99
healthy relationships groups, 246–253
    ethics, challenges and limitations, 250–251
helplessness, grief and, 290–291
heterogeneous groups, 12
    diversity and, 125
heterosexuality, 324–325
holism, 74
homework, in psychoeducational groups, 157
homogeneous groups, 12
    diversity and, 125
    psychotherapy groups, 161–162
homonegativity, internalization of, 325
homophobia, 324–325

hope, instillation of, multicultural counseling and, 119
hospitals, group work in, 274–279
humor, in group leaders, 16

I
icebreaker activities, 170
identity
    development models, 112–114
    diversity and, 112
    loss and, 296
imitative behavior, multicultural counseling, 120
impact therapy groups, 11
individual group members
    goals of, 9–10
    intervention with, 197
individual identity, 112
information sharing
    loss groups, 291–292
    in multicultural counseling, 120
informed consent, 93–94
inhalants, 304
insider status, group involvement stage, 35–36
inspirational group lectures, 2
institutional discrimination, 114
instruction
    in group counseling, 134
    in psychoeducational groups, 157
integrative task/work group model, 151
intellectualization, 63–64
intensity, level of, difficult group members and, 199–200
internalized homonegativity, 325–326
internalized oppression, 114
International Journal of Group Psychotherapy, 4
interpersonal dynamics, 307
interpersonal leadership style, 44, 163–164
    difficult group members, 196–197
interpersonal learning, multicultural counseling, 120
interpersonal process groups (IPPGs), addiction treatment, 307
interventions
    adolescent groups, 232–236
    in adolescent groups, 225
    difficult group members, 196–200
    harmful interventions, 139–140
    leadership skills for, 166
intimacy, healthy relationships and, 248–249
intrapersonal leadership style, 44
intrapsychic dynamics, 307
intratherapeutic self-disclosure, 38
inventiveness, of group leaders, 15
involuntary groups, ethics of working with, 95, 99

J
job club counseling, 264–269
Johari Window 144
Journal for Specialists in Group Work, 7
Journal of Creativity in Mental Health, 173
The Journal for Specialists in Group Work, 5
Jungian psychology, group work and, 2